Oxford Studies in Epistemology

OXFORD STUDIES IN EPISTEMOLOGY

Oxford Studies in Epistemology

Volume 7

Edited by
TAMAR SZABÓ GENDLER
and
JOHN HAWTHORNE

Associate Editor
JULIANNE CHUNG

OXFORD
UNIVERSITY PRESS

OXFORD
UNIVERSITY PRESS

Great Clarendon Street, Oxford, OX2 6DP,
United Kingdom

Oxford University Press is a department of the University of Oxford.
It furthers the University's objective of excellence in research, scholarship,
and education by publishing worldwide. Oxford is a registered trade mark of
Oxford University Press in the UK and in certain other countries

First Edition published in 2023
Impression: 1

Published in the United States of America by Oxford University Press
198 Madison Avenue, New York, NY 10016, United States of America

British Library Cataloguing in Publication Data
Data available

Library of Congress Control Number: 2006234438

ISBN 978–0–19–286897–8

DOI: 10.1093/oso/9780192868978.001.0001

Printed and bound in the UK by
TJ Books Limited

Contents

Editors' Preface vi
Contributors ix

1. Selfless Receptivity: Attention as an Epistemic Virtue 1
Nicolas Bommarito and Jonardon Ganeri

2. Knowledge and Independent Checks in Mīmāṃsā 15
Nilanjan Das

3. Content-Focused Epistemic Injustice 48
Robin Dembroff and Dennis Whitcomb

4. The Art of Learning 71
Jason Konek

5. Conceptions of Genuine Knowledge in Wang Yangming 134
Harvey Lederman

6. Knowledge and Legal Proof 176
Sarah Moss

7. Trust as an Unquestioning Attitude 214
C. Thi Nguyen

8. There's More to Transparency than Windows 245
Catherine Prueitt and Kateryna Samoilova

9. Me-Knowledge and Effective Agency 261
Hagop Sarkissian

10. Meditations on Beliefs Formed Arbitrarily 278
Miriam Schoenfield

11. "Getting It Oneself" as an Alternative to Testimonial Knowledge and Deference to Tradition 306
Justin Tiwald

12. Elements of Knowledge-First Epistemology in Gaṅgeśa and Nyāya 336
Anand Vaidya

13. Vaidya on Nyāya and Knowledge-First Epistemology 365
Timothy Williamson

Editors' Preface

Published bi-annually under the guidance of a distinguished editorial board, each volume of *Oxford Studies in Epistemology* seeks to publish not only traditional work in epistemology, but also work that brings new perspectives to traditional epistemological questions, and that opens new avenues of investigation. We are therefore particularly excited about this seventh volume of *OSE*, which, like others before it, provides a showcase for some of the most exciting new work in the field of epistemology from throughout the English-speaking world. However, this issue will, for the first time, feature a selection of papers that bring elements of Asian philosophies into dialogue with contemporary issues in Anglo-analytic epistemology. Among the topics discussed are: the nature of epistemic virtue, how knowledge and action are related, conceptions of "genuine knowledge," trust, transparency, self-knowledge, moral deference, and connections between knowledge-first and Nyāya epistemology. As ever, we hope that readers will be stimulated by the insights and ideas that these articles will inspire.

In addition, this volume includes the winners of the third and fourth bi-annual Sanders Prize in Epistemology competitions, supported by the Marc Sanders Foundation and open to any scholar within 15 years of receiving their PhD. They are: Miriam Schoenfield's "Meditations on Beliefs Formed Arbitrarily" (winner of the 2017 prize) and Sarah Moss's "Knowledge and Legal Proof" (winner of the 2019 prize). Schoenfield takes an accuracy-centered first-personal approach to the question of how to respond to the arbitrary way in which many of our beliefs are formed, explaining how considerations of accuracy motivate different responses to this sort of information depending on the type of attitude we take towards the belief in question upon subjecting the belief to doubt. Moss defends an account of legal proof that addresses several classic questions in the legal scholarship on evidence, including why merely statistical evidence is often insufficient to meet the burden of proof. Moss develops a unified answer to these questions, arguing for the thesis that legal proof requires knowledge. We are also delighted to present the runners-up for each of the two aforementioned prize competitions: Jason Konek's "The Art of Learning" (2017), in which he argues that confirmational holism is at odds with Jeffrey conditioning and outlines and defends a new updating policy that in his view does better; and, C. Thi Nguyen's "Trust as an Unquestioning Attitude" (2019), in which he argues that while accounts of trust tend to presume that trust can only be directed towards agents, there is another, distinctive form of trust: the unquestioning attitude. Finally, we are pleased to present a paper that received an honourable mention in 2019's competition: Robin Dembroff and Dennis Whitcomb's "Content-Focused Epistemic Injustice," in which they describe several cases of what they call *content-focused injustice*, and theoretically interrogate those cases by building up a general framework through which to understand them as a genuine form of epistemic injustice that stands in intertwined relationships to other forms of epistemic injustice.

The cross-cultural papers selected for this volume also shed light on a variety of issues in contemporary epistemology. In "Selfless Receptivity: Attention as an Epistemic Virtue," drawing on the work of sixth-century CE Indian Buddhist Buddhaghosa and Simone Weil, Nicolas Bommarito and Jonardon Ganeri highlight aspects of epistemic virtue that do not fit a standard model, particularly ways in which epistemic virtues can be non-voluntary and not goal-directed. In "Knowledge and Independent Checks in Mīmāṃsā," Nilanjan Das, following the Nyāya philosopher Jayanta Bhaṭṭa (ninth century CE), reconstructs the Bhāṭṭa Mīmāṃsakas' arguments against the Independent Check Thesis, explaining how these arguments reveal a tension between this thesis and a plausible principle that connects knowledge and action. In "Conceptions of Genuine Knowledge in Wang Yangming," Harvey Lederman develops and compares four different interpretations of the notion of "genuine knowledge": the perceptual, practical, normative, and introspective, arguing that the introspective model is to be preferred over the alternatives. In "There's More to Transparency than Windows," Catherine Prueitt and Kateryna Samoilova introduce a new scaffold for thinking about the transparency datum, developed through cross-cultural engagement with classical South Asian epistemology. In "Me-Knowledge and Effective Agency," drawing on classical Chinese sources Hagop Sarkissian explains why knowing the 'me' as seen from the perspective of a particular other is crucial to enhance one's efficacy in the world. In, "'Getting It Oneself' as an Alternative to Testimonial Knowledge and Deference to Tradition," Justin Tiwald offers the first sustained philosophical account of 'getting it oneself' as it occurs in the writings of eleventh–twelfth century CE Neo-Confucians Cheng Hao, Cheng Yi, and Zhu Xi, also pointing to some of the broader implications of his reading for both the history of philosophy and current debates about moral deference. In "Elements of Knowledge-First Epistemology in Gaṅgeśa," Anand Vaidya explores epistemological connections between the fourteenth century CE father of Navya-Nyāya, Gaṅgeśa, and Timothy Williamson's knowledge-first program in contemporary epistemology. And, in "Vaidya on Nyāya and Knowledge-First Epistemology," Timothy Williamson replies to Vaidya, questioning Vaidya's classification of classical Indian theories of perception as specifically disjunctivist, clarifying the role of prime conditions in his own externalism and explaining that comparative work on classical Indian and contemporary analytic epistemology affords a rich field for future study.

We would like to extend thanks to our referees Alexander Guerrero, Daniel Greco, Karyn Lai, Amy Kind, Jennifer Nagel, Malcolm Keating, Susanna Siegel, Elisa Freschi, Jeremy Fantl, Ram Neta, P.J. Ivanhoe, David Wong, Evan Thompson, and six anonymous reviewers, as well as to our editorial board members Keith DeRose (Yale University), Richard Fumerton (University of Iowa), Alvin Goldman (Rutgers University), Alan Hájek (Australian National University), Frank Jackson (Australian National University), Jim Joyce (University of Michigan), Jennifer Lackey (Northwestern University), Jennifer Nagel (University of Toronto), Jonathan Vogel (Amherst College), and Timothy Williamson (Oxford University). We are also most grateful, as always, to Peter Momtchiloff for his much-appreciated ongoing support of this series.

Tamar Szabó Gendler, Yale University
John Hawthorne, University of Southern California
Editors
Julianne Chung, York University
Associate Editor

Contributors

Nicolas Bommarito Simon Fraser University

Nilanjan Das University of Toronto

Robin Dembroff Yale University

Jonardon Ganeri University of Toronto

Jason Konek University of Bristol

Harvey Lederman Princeton University

Sarah Moss University of Michigan

C. Thi Nguyen University of Utah

Catherine Prueitt University of British Columbia

Kateryna Samoilova California State University, Chico

Hagop Sarkissian City University of New York

Miriam Schoenfield University of Texas at Austin

Justin Tiwald University of Hong Kong

Anand Vaidya San Jose State University

Dennis Whitcomb Western Washington University

Timothy Williamson University of Oxford

1

Selfless Receptivity

Attention as an Epistemic Virtue

Nicolas Bommarito and Jonardon Ganeri

1. The Limits of Archery

On a common way of thinking about epistemology, it's about when a belief counts as knowledge or what the rational response to certain kinds of evidence is and why. Recent trends in virtue epistemology, however, have approached epistemology in a different way and in doing so have raised new questions about what it means to be a good knower and what kinds of skills are important for getting it right about the world.

A central analogy that has emerged in examining these new questions is that of the archer. A skilled archer is one who hits her target not just by accident, but because she has developed a skill and uses it well. Her skill has a variety of aspects: she is strong enough to pull the string back, focused enough to avoid distraction, and calm enough to avoid getting flustered by the task. In the same way, a good knower is one who does "hit the truth" but doesn't get things right just by accident, but by examining evidence carefully, double checking for errors, being open-minded, and so on.[1]

But skill, especially in difficult tasks, rarely means perfection. Even when an unpredictable gust of wind blows the arrow off course, the archer is still a good one. Someone might be quite skilled at responding to the evidence they have, but still get it wrong about how the world really is. Being a good archer doesn't mean hitting the bullseye every single time and being a good knower doesn't require *always* getting at the truth. The philosopher Bimal Matilal, for example, uses the analogy on behalf of the Nyāya epistemologists of classical India, to draw a distinction between epistemic skill and infallibility: "a cognitive episode... is a knowledge-episode when it hits the truth. Knowledgeness consists in its truth-hitting character, and not in its indubitability... Even an archer cannot always hit

[1] Sosa (2015: 96) talks of competence, meaning that one is disposed to succeed when one tries. Though Sosa focuses on attempts and trying rather than success, he still sees epistemic life as centered on goal-directed voluntary activity.

Nicolas Bommarito and Jonardon Ganeri, *Selfless Receptivity: Attention as an Epistemic Virtue* In: *Oxford Studies in Epistemology, Volume 7.* Edited by: Tamar Szabó Gendler, John Hawthorne, and Julianne Chung, Oxford University Press.
 DOI: 10.1093/oso/9780192868978.003.0001

the bull's-eye. Nyāya fallibilism says that if it is possible for him to hit it, it is also possible for him to miss it."[2]

Our aim is not to object to virtue epistemology as an approach, but rather to highlight particular ways in which the archer analogy can be misleading within this framework. The archer analogy has two features in particular that we will put pressure on: it presumes epistemic virtue to be both goal-directed and voluntary. When an archer shoots an arrow, she is aiming at a target, she has a goal in mind. She also deliberately, willfully acts not only by shooting that particular arrow, but over time by cultivating the necessary skills. But there are types of epistemic virtue that do not fit this model; they are non-voluntary and do not aim at any particular goal. This suggests a radically different form of virtue epistemology, one that places less emphasis on effortful acts of the will, instead emphasizing virtues that are not linked to the idea of the achievement of a particular goal. Our view, stated in brief, is that unguided attention can be an epistemic virtue. In elaborating this view, we will draw on the work of an unlikely pair of philosophers. Though neither holds exactly this view themselves, both provide important insights into this kind of virtue epistemology.

2. An Unlikely Pair

The sixth-century Indian Buddhist Buddhaghosa and the twentieth-century French philosopher Simone Weil, vastly distanced in place, time and culture as they are, nevertheless share a profound philosophical sympathy, for they are two philosophers who emphasize the role of attention in epistemology and ethics.

Simone Weil was a brilliant French philosopher whose short life ended in 1943. Her most famous work is *Gravity and Grace* (*La Pesanteur et la grâce*), which collected fragments from the many notebooks she wrote that were only posthumously published. Though Weil wrote widely on subjects from religion to politics to metaphysics, here we will focus on her work on attention and its importance.

Half the world away and hundreds of years earlier, another brilliant philosopher also had insights about attention and its importance. Buddhaghosa is also a hugely important figure in the history of philosophy, though too often under-appreciated in English-language philosophy. Living in fifth-century Sri Lanka and writing in Pāli, he is most famous for his *Path of Purification* (*Visuddhimagga*), an

[2] Matilal (1986: 141). See Sosa (2007, 2015) for a more recent appeal to this metaphor. Some criticisms of virtue epistemology have centered on how grounding an account of knowledge on epistemic virtues can fail to count something as knowledge even when produced via skills (see Pritchard 2009 and Lackey 2007). These often focus on those well-known fake barn-type cases where a competent knower forms a true belief partly via their skills, but also partly via luck. Śrīharṣa, indeed, in the classical tradition criticized Nyāya epistemology on just such grounds (see Ganeri 2020). We are not offering a criticism of virtue epistemology here, merely of some misleading features of the archer analogy.

impressive work that systematizes Theravāda Buddhist thought, though we will also draw on less famous works such as his *Dispeller of Delusion* (*Sammoha-vinodanī*).

In drawing on Weil and Buddhaghosa our primary aim is not one of historical interpretation. Though our interpretation aims to be both charitable and historically responsible, our primary aim is not to illuminate the one true reading of any of the texts we will discuss. As with many philosophical classics, they are texts that admit of a wide range of fruitful and plausible interpretations. Our aim here is to draw out the insights these thinkers had that are relevant to the role of attention in epistemic and moral life.

In addition to highlighting the central place of attention for both of these thinkers, we will discuss their arguments that attention is both morally and epistemically relevant and how there are associated virtues that do not fit well with the archer model, the model of an agent performing voluntary, goal-directed actions.

We'll begin with Buddhaghosa's argument for the epistemic relevance of attention and how norms of attention contribute to knowledge. Then we turn to Weil's insight that attention, especially of an epistemically and morally relevant kind, is often neither voluntary nor involuntary. In particular, her notion of receptivity or waiting which has both active and inactive aspects. Finally we will turn to the role of the self in this kind of attention, giving it both moral and epistemic significance.

3. Buddhaghosa: Attention as Epistemic

It's a common assumption in Analytical philosophy that epistemology is about belief and knowledge and that its norms govern cognitive attitudes we hold towards propositions. It concerns claims like "it is raining outside" and when certain attitudes towards those claims are justified and when they count instances of knowledge. But if we think of epistemology in the more general sense of getting it right about the world, we can see that other kinds of mental activity are relevant. Expertise, for example, isn't merely about having the right intellectual attitude to certain propositions, but also involves a skill in perceptual judgment.

For many Buddhists, attention is intrinsically epistemic. A classic example can be found in *The Question of King Milinda* (*Milinda-pañha*), a dialogue between a Greek king and a Buddhist monk written around the first century CE. The following passages introduces the normative concept of "proper" (*yoniso*) attention:

> What is the distinguishing mark of proper attention (*yoniso manasikāro*), what is the distinguishing mark of insight, revered sir? Hitting upon (*ūhana*) is the

> distinguishing mark of proper attention, sire, cutting off is the distinguishing mark of insight . . . Make a simile . . . As, sire, a barley-reaper grasps a handful of barley in the left hand and a sickle in the right hand and cuts it off with the sickle, even so, sire, does the earnest student of yoga, taking hold of the mind with attention, cut of the defilements with insight.[3]

Here proper attention is an essential tool for the task of getting it right about the world. Just as it's important to hold on to something in order to cut it properly, attention is necessary to allow other epistemic processes, like insight, to operate effectively and accurately.

It's important to note here that attention isn't just an unrelated necessary condition for getting it right. There can be necessary conditions for knowledge that involve norms that are not epistemic. For example, I need to be alive to know anything, so norms of proper diet might be necessary for knowing anything. But the relationship between attention and knowledge is closer than that; norms of attention are epistemic because they are part of the activity of getting it right about the world. As the passage points out, cutting norms, the way to cut things well, involve holding norms, a proper way to hold things. Holding things the right way is part of being able to cut them in the right way. So too attentional norms are part of epistemic norms because they play a central role in the activity of knowing.[4]

Buddhaghosa gives an argument that attention is responsive to an epistemic norm.[5] His claim is that when attention is appropriately trained, the attentive person achieves knowledge. For such a person, "attention works as incisively and sharply as a lightning flash, like a red-hot spear plunged into a basket of leaves" (*Path* 636 [xx. 121]).[6] Insight is expert knowledge: it is "skillfully completed" (*kosalla-sambhūta*) and a "practice to be cultivated" (*paribrūhetabba*) (Sasaki 1986: 92–3, 96). It "has the characteristic of penetrating the individual essences of states. Its function is to abolish the darkness of delusion, which conceals the individual essences of states. It is manifested as non-delusion. Because of the words 'One who is attends absorbedly knows and sees correctly' (A v.3) its proximate cause is absorbed attention" (*Path* 438 [xiv.7]). That attention is an immediate cause for "knowing and seeing correctly" is also affirmed in S.ii. 30: "And what is the proximate cause for knowledge, for seeing things as they really are? It should be said: attention."

[3] *Milinda-pañha* 32–3.

[4] For recent work on this theme see Watzl (2017) and Siegel (2017: 157 ff..). For other recent work on Buddhaghosa, see Heim (2017a and 2017b).

[5] For a more detailed discussion of this argument, see Ganeri (2017: 130–58).

[6] We use the following abbreviations when referring to Buddhaghosa's works: *Path* for his *Path of Purification* (*Visuddhimagga*) Buddhaghosa (1991), *Dispeller* for his *The Dispeller of Delusion (Sammoha-vinodanī)* Buddhaghosa (1996), and *Fount* for his *The Fount of Meaning* (*Atthasālinī*) Buddhaghosa (2005 [1942]).

Consider, for example, a standard case of expertise-influenced fixation:

> You and moth expert X take a walk in the forest, looking for moths on tree bark. You look at the same piece of bark. X sees moths where you see none. That's because her familiarity with the exact shapes of moths lets her fixate more easily on moth-shaped pieces of bark.[7]

Expertise is not simply a matter of knowing a lot more facts about moths than the average person, but the result of practice and training in the processes of distractor-exclusion and attractor-amplification. Churchland makes an analogous point in connection with perceptual expertise:

> A physics student does not come to see the motions of common objects in a new way simply by memorizing Newton's three laws... [but] by having practiced the skills of applying those laws in a wide variety of circumstances. They do come to perceive a common pattern in the behaviour of moving bodies that was hitherto invisible to them, but memorizing the laws was only the first step in a fairly lengthy process... The process of reshaping one's perception takes time, and it requires more than the mere adoption of a belief or three.[8]

So the basic claim is that when suitably educated the exercise of attention is an instrument in the acquisition of knowledge. Perhaps Buddhaghosa's clearest example is the case he gives of the money-changer:

> Suppose there were three people, a child without discretion, a villager, and a money-changer, who saw a heap of coins lying on a money-changer's counter. The child without discretion knows merely that the coins are figured and ornamented, long, square or round; he does not know that they are reckoned as valuable for human use and enjoyment. And the villager knows that they are figured and ornamented, etc., and that they are reckoned as valuable for human use and enjoyment; but does not know such distinctions as 'This one is genuine, this is false; this is half-value'. The money-changer knows all those kinds.[9]

Here three people with varying levels of expertise all fixate on the same object, an object with a certain shape lying on a counter. The villager, unlike the child, is expert in discriminating between coins and other pieces of metal, and the money-changer is expert in discriminating between genuine and fake coins. Buddhaghosa continues:

> Recognition is like the child without discretion seeing the coin, because it apprehends the mere mode of appearance (*upaṭṭhānākāra-matta*) of the object

[7] Siegel (2012: 205). [8] Churchland (1988: 176). [9] *Path* 437 [xiv.4].

> as blue and so on. Cognition is like the villager seeing the coin, because it apprehends the mode of the object as blue, etc., and because it extends further, reaching the penetration of its characteristics. Insight is like the money-changer seeing the coin, because, after apprehending the mode of the object as blue, etc., and extending to the penetration of the characteristics, it extends still further, reaching the manifestation of the path.[10]

The child sees the coin as blue, accessing the property blue from a region selected by shape. With ordinary expertise in money, the villager sees the coin as a coin, as something bearing monetary value. The money-changer, with expertise in handling genuine and fake coins, sees the coin as real. This is a very nice example of a situation in which cognitive penetration does not undermine justification, and indeed, to the contrary, enhances it. The "top-down" effect is the result not of an additional belief or a need or whim, but of cultivated skill in attending to things. The object is rightly "hit on" and the result is a dispelling of delusion. So when attention is expert, there is not merely a boost in justification, but a crossing of the threshold of knowledge. It follows from the account of attention developed above that expertise in fixing and identifying just is what the cultivation of attention consists in. So the norm to which attention is accountable in Buddhaghosa appears to be: cultivate your attention in such a way that you can see things as they truly are.

4. Weil: Receptivity and Attention

It might seem that this cultivation of proper attention will work straightforwardly on the model of the archer: like shooting an arrow at a target, it can seem like a voluntary, goal-directed activity. We aim to have certain attentional patterns and then take deliberate steps to bring about that end; and in our practices of attention we deliberately focus on particular targets. Weil, however, offers a challenge to this assumption. So we find her saying, for example, when discussing moral endeavor: "I must try to cure my faults through the attention and not through the will" (N265; GG 116).[11] Though it might seem as though trying involves the will, for Weil eliminating faults involves a very special kind of effort that is distinct from willful action.[12]

[10] Ibid.

[11] We use the following abbreviations for Weil's works: N for her *Notebooks* (Weil 2004) and GG for *Gravity and Grace* (Weil 2002). *BhG* for passages from the *Bhagavad-gītā* discussed by Weil.

[12] So, for example, when we find a reference to the archer in Weil's notebooks (30n1) she explicitly emphasizes Daoist techniques, such as lying down under a loom, that retrain involuntary perception. See also Zhuangzi (19:4) on the archer's lack of conscious goals.

The reason that exercises of will are the wrong sort of effort is that willful effort is self-defeating (GG 118); it is self-defeating because it is always mediated by the desires of the one controlling it, so that its object ends up being *the ego of the willer* rather than interventions in the world itself. Moral endeavor is "effort without desire" (GG 116), she says, effort only with consent, and that is what attention is for Weil:

> We liberate energy in ourselves, but it constantly reattaches itself. How are we to liberate it entirely? We have to desire that it should be done in us—to desire it truly—simply to desire it, not to try to accomplish it. For every attempt in that direction is vain and has to be dearly paid for. In such a work all that I call "I" has to be passive. Attention alone—that attention which is so full that the "I" disappears—is required of me. I have to deprive all that I call "I" of the light of my attention and turn it on to that which cannot be conceived.[13]

For Weil, willful action is an obstacle to both moral and epistemic ideals because of the way it inserts and reinforces our self-centeredness. In trying to act in this deliberate and goal-directed way, we get in our own way. Trying to get past ourselves is the only action that can help, and even that is an intermediate state. So we find Weil writing, "The destruction of the 'I' is the one and only free act that lies open to us" (N 337); "I must suppress the 'I'" (N 265). As David Cockburn points out, this is both a moral and epistemic ideal: to see things as they really are is to see them "in a way which involves a cancelling of those concerns which involve a reference to the object's relation to myself."[14]

In much contemporary literature on the psychology of attention a distinction is drawn between what is referred to as "endogenous" and "exogenous" attention, between *goal-directed* and *stimulus-driven* determinants of attentional control (searching for someone in a room vs having one's attention drawn to someone by a slap on the back). Endogenous attention is described as "a voluntary system that corresponds to our ability to *willfully* monitor information at a given location," while exogenous attention is "an involuntary system that corresponds to an *automatic* orienting response to a location where sudden stimulation has occurred . . . [and] . . . when the cue is uninformative regarding the target location" (Carrasco 2011: 1488). Again, "in many cases, shifts of spatial attention are under the control of the observer, directing attention *at will* from one location to the next. In other circumstances, events in the environment (such as the sudden appearance of an object) may pull your attention towards the event, as if attention were automatically and reflexively controlled by the environment" (Theeuwes 2014: 232).

[13] Weil (2002: 118). [14] Cockburn (1997: 327).

With this distinction at hand, we can say, to a first approximation, that the sort of attention which for Weil is associated with ethical endeavor is exogenous and not endogenous. "The wrong way of seeking: The attention fixed on a problem" (GG 117, cf. N 286). This is so, however, only because Weil has a highly distinctive understanding of endogenous and exogenous attention. For her, attention is endogenous when it is not simply goal-directed but rather when one attends to oneself in attending to the object: "When one pays attention to attention, one is not attentive at all. When one is attentive to the object, one doesn't pay attention to oneself," she says, with two uses of the term "attention" clearly in play (1988: 392).

The passivity of exogenous attention, on the other hand, is not best understood as the psychologists do, as consisting in an automatic response, but rather in a sort of receptivity that is accurately expressed as "waiting" (rendering the French term *attendre*). As Mark Shiffman describes it, for Weil attention is "the 'negative effort' of clearing oneself out of the path of receiving the true perception of reality."[15] Or as Ann Pirruccello puts it, "attention is the activity of waiting, of expecting in a way that embodies self-diminishment."[16]

Weil's description of this kind of receptive attention is explicit when she discusses the value of scholarly activity:

> In every school exercise there is a special way of waiting upon truth, setting our hearts upon it, yet not allowing ourselves to go out in search of it. There is a way of giving our attention to the data of a problem in geometry without trying to find the solution, or to the words of a Latin or Greek text without trying to arrive at it the meaning, a way of waiting, when we are writing, for the right word to come of itself at the end of our pen, while we merely reject all inadequate words.[17]

The basic idea is that our mental lives are constantly influenced by our sense of self, by our interests, goals, and desires. This affects what we think, remember, and doubt. It changes not only what we attend to but how we attend to it. This happens in both obvious and subtle ways: when conversing with someone we notice a tone of praise or dismissal in what the other person says, we latch on to phrases that resonate with our own experience, we ignore what is irrelevant to what we're interested in. The problem, as Weil highlights, is that the more we try to get past this the more we form a new goal and re-insert ourselves into what is happening, blocking our sensitivity to what is really going on.

[15] This is from Shiffman's 2013 review of Robert Chenavier's *Simone Weil: Attention to the Real* (Chenavier 2012). An explicit description of attention as a negative effort can be found in Weil's 1942 essay "Reflections on the Right Uses of School Studies with a View to the Love of God" where she distinguishes attention from "muscular effort." See Weil (2021: 65).

[16] Pirruccello (1995: 61).

[17] Weil (2021: 68).

The solution, then, is to solve the problem with a kind of attention that is neither fully voluntary nor involuntary. Think of the kind of attention associated with really, truly *listening* to someone. This kind of state has both active and passive aspects. It's active in the sense that it's something you're doing, you're not just sitting there letting their words wash over you, you're involved in the task of interpreting and reflecting on what they're saying. But it's passive in the sense that you're not driving the conversation, bending it to your will. You are in an open and receptive state, ready to go with the speaker.

In the same way, attention for Weil is not under the control of the will but neither is it an entirely passive reaction to a stimulus. In carving out space for this special notion of attention Weil draws on another classical Indian text, the *Bhagavad-gītā*.[18] In particular she draws on the idea of "inactive action," which she adopts or adapts from *Gītā*: "He is wise who perceives inaction in action and action in inaction" (*BhG* 4.18), and "even when performing action, in effect does nothing at all" (*BhG* 4.20).

Gavin Flood says that in Weil's employment of the notion of 'inactive action' that it signifies that "action becomes not goal-directed, but is a response to the demands of a situation" (49), to "necessity" in Weil's phrase. This is exactly to reiterate the point about Weil's interest being in a notion of the exogenous as implying a response, and so as being both active (responsive, receptive) at the same time as being inactive (not goal-directed, not under the direction of the will). It is unlike the archer who simply willfully acts on a static and inanimate target. It is instead a more complex response that does not fall cleanly into the categories of active or passive. This is important because for Weil, willful actions, like that of the archer, work to reinforce one of the main blocks to idea epistemic and moral engagement: ourselves.

5. Selfless Receptivity

Although Weil's principal Indian influence seems to have been the *Gītā*, there are important commonalities (as well as significant differences) with Buddhaghosa's view of attention. Both identify the self with will, and so think it needs to be negated. Buddhaghosa makes this clear when he remarks that "there is no agent (*kattā*) or author (*kāretā*), saying "You be default state, you be orienting, you be seeing, you be receiving, you be investigating, you be determining, you be running" (*Fount* 272), and "There is no inner self (*abbhantare attā*) which does the

[18] Weil often turns to the *Bhagavad-gītā* in her *Notebooks*. She was indeed deeply immersed in Indian thinking, teaching herself Sanskrit for example, and engaging in careful study of a wide range of Indian philosophical texts. Linda Woodhead (1987) has written extensively on what she terms Weil's "conversation" with the *Bhagavad-gītā*, a very appropriate term because Weil's relationship with the text was highly creative and not at all appropriative.

looking towards or looking away" (*Dispeller* 356). When Weil says "the education of the attention—that is the chief thing" (N545), she might have been channeling Buddhaghosa, for the "education of attention" is the fundamental organizing principle of Buddhaghosa's magnum opus, *The Path of Purification*, which deals with attention and its cultivation in Part II (chapters iii to xii) and with insightful knowledge in Part III (chapters xiv to xxiii). That leaves only two chapters out of twenty three, one of which describes virtue and the other ascetic practices.

Tellingly, Buddhaghosa provides this select quotation from the historical Buddha: "Cultivate attention, bhikkhus; a bhikkhu who attends knows things as they are."[19] What is put forward here is an application of a general epistemic principle: that attention is, in certain circumstances, sufficient for knowledge. The application in question speaks of a particular sort of attention, expert absorbed attention (*samādhi*), and a particular sort of knowledge, insight (*paññā*) into fundamental moral truths.

It is evident from this quotation, however, that the cultivation of attention is regarded not as an intrinsic good, a good in itself, but rather as valuable because instrumental in the achievement of another good, knowledge of things as they really are. Though both Weil and Buddhaghosa complicate the division between the ethical and epistemic domains in many ways, here it is the achievement of knowledge which is held up as the non-instrumental good.[20]

Though epistemology is often thought of in terms of belief, justification, and knowledge, both Weil and Buddhaghosa demonstrate how attention plays an important epistemic function. Both see patterns of attention that are colored by the self as a barrier to seeing how the world really is. However, it's not necessary to accept that the self is always a barrier to seeing the world, merely that it *can* be.

It's common to think about the aim of a belief in virtue ethical terms, of an epistemic agent aiming at truth. But as Weil highlights, it's not always the object or aim of attention that is important, but the *way* in which we attend. To make this clear it is helpful to refer to Sebastian Watzl's useful classification of the norms on attention (Watzl 2022). Watzl classifies attentional norms along two dimensions. He distinguishes between content-based and manner-based attention norms. Content-based norms concern the objects of attention: to what should one attend? It seems evident that there is something morally reprehensible about simply failing even to notice a person's distress, never mind the more obvious vice of noticing

19 *Samādhiṃ, bhikkhave, bhāvetha; samāhito, bhikkhave, bhikkhu yathābhūtaṃ pajānāti*, S iii.13.

20 Weil's writings on the importance of receptive attention in education is telling here; "The solution of a geometry problem does not in itself constitute a precious gift, but the same law applies to it because it is an image of something precious" (2021: 67). For more recent work questioning the division between ethical and epistemic norms see Dalmiya (2016) and McRae (2022).

but not caring. Manner-based norms concern the way one attends: *how* should one attend?

Many commentators on Weil have assumed that attention, particularly ethical attention, is directed at persons. Gavin Flood, for example, says that Weil's attentiveness is fundamentally ethical when it consists in a response to another: "Inactive action is a response to external demands: 'I see the beggar's hunger and I give him food.'"[21] This reading of Weil in fact has its origin in Iris Murdoch. Murdoch says that "I have used the word 'attention', which I borrow from Simone Weil, to express the idea of a just and loving gaze directed upon an individual reality."[22] There is no doubt that Weil is extremely concerned with empathy, which she understands as a way of attending to others:

> Beneficence—feeding, clothing, etc. others—has no value in itself, but only as a sign. There is a natural inclination, weak certainly, but which exists, to relieve distress, and when what acts as a barrier to this inclination is removed, it is exercised. A right form of attention directed towards others' misery is precisely what breaks down such a barrier. (Inattention is generally the reason why this inclination is not exercised.)[23]

But there is more than that to Weil's conception of attention. Murdoch's reading of Weil is in danger of conflating two different strands in Weil's thought. The first is that love expresses itself in the way one attends to the plight of another, a theme one certainly finds in Weil's writing. The other strand, though, equally prominent, is that attention placed receptively on the world is what keeps one in touch with reality. It is this second thought which is the real reason Weil regards patterns of attention as a matter of moral and epistemic concern.

If attention is "the 'negative effort' of clearing oneself out of the path of receiving the true perception of reality," then that is both a moral and epistemic good in itself. Though it is important that we attend to others in a way that recognizes and validates them, it is of equal importance that we attend in a way that removes the distorting and corrupting influence the self from our experience of the world.[24] All of this is cannot simply be captured as a willful act aiming at a particular goal, but is instead a receptive mode of our mental lives.

The image of the archer can seem like an apt one if we focus on cases of deliberate investigation. It conjures up the Enlightenment ideal of an impartial investigator, deliberately inquiring into a subject, aiming at truth. This character seems very much like an archer aiming at a target. There is much that is attractive

[21] Flood (2004: 50). [22] Murdoch (1970: 33). [23] N 289.

[24] As Weil notes in her "decreative prayer" to decreate oneself is to live "without the possibility of bringing about any act of my will." The import seems clearly to be that to live decreatively is to live in receptive consent with what is real, and that just is to live attentively.

in this image: aiming at the wrong target (fame, novelty, or what feels comforting) is an epistemic vice. Like archery, hitting the target means practice and the development of particular skills.

But the kind of receptivity or negative effort that Weil emphasizes is also an important part of coming to see the world as it really is. It highlights how deliberate effort and goal-directed activity can reinforce blind spots. Our sense of self colors much of our experience in shades that obscure and getting past them is often trickier than simply training for other skills. Sometimes coming to see the world accurately is less like shooting an arrow and more like listening. The more you focus on listening well, the less you actually hear the other person. You might decide to do it and work at it, but when it works you disappear into a state of open receptivity.

The claim is not that epistemic virtue *never* works on the model of the archer, but that it does not always do so. Some aims are best achieved through deliberate, goal-directed effort. Other aims, however, recede farther the more they are pursued. The harder we try to fall asleep, the more we lie awake in bed. The more you try to force yourself to be an engaged and present conversational partner, the more you ignore the person you're supposed to conversing with. What's needed is a negative effort; to get out of your own way so you can be completely focused and receptive to what is happening around you.

So, then, our thesis is that this kind of attention is both an epistemic and moral matter. Getting past the limits imposed by our sense of self makes you not just a better knower, but a better person. But it's not necessary to take on this idea in order to see the point that many important ways of attending have epistemic value and do not fit well into a model that assumes a framework of deliberate, goal-directed activity. By focusing on attention we challenge the common assumption that epistemology is just about belief and knowledge and the idea that we can cleanly divide states into voluntary and involuntary. And perhaps most fundamentally, we highlight the ways in which the very self that experiences the world can get in the way of experiencing it accurately.

References

Buddhaghosa. 1991. *Path (Visuddhimagga)*: Ñāṇamoli, Bhikkhu, transl. *The Path of Purification: Visuddhimagga by Bhadantācariya Buddhaghosa* (Kandy: Buddhist Publication Society, 5th ed.).

Buddhaghosa. 1996. *Dispeller (Sammoha-vinodanī)*: Ñāṇamoli, Bhikkhu, transl. *The Dispeller of Delusion (Sammohavinodanī)*, Revised for publication by L. S. Cousins, Nyanaponika Mahāthera, and C. M. M. Shaw (Oxford: Pāli Text Society, 2 vols.).

Buddhaghosa. *Fount (Attha-sālinī)*: (1) Nyānaponika, Bhikkhu (2005 [1942]), transl. *Darlegung der Bedeutung (Atthasālinī)*, Edited for publication by Sven Bretfeld and

Rainer Knopf (Oxford: Pāli Text Society). (2) Tin, Pe Maung (1920), transl. *The Expositor (Atthasālinī): Buddhaghosa's Commentary on the Dhammasangaṇī, the First Book of the Abhidhamma Piṭaka* (Oxford: Pāli Text Society, 2 vols.).

Carrasco, Marisa. 2011. Visual Attention: The Past 25 Years. *Vision Research*, 51(3): 1484–525.

Chevanier, Robert. 2012. *Simone Weil: Attention to the Real*, translated by Bernard Doering. Notre Dame: University of Notre Dame Press.

Churchland, P. 1988. Perceptual Plasticity and Theoretical Neutrality: A Reply to Fodor. *Philosophy of Science*, 55: 167–87.

Cockburn, David. 1997. *Other Times*. Cambridge: Cambridge University Press.

Dalmiya, Vrinda. 2016. Caring to Know. New Delhi: Oxford University Press.

Flood, Gavin. 2004. *The Ascetic Self: Subjectivity, Memory and Tradition*. Cambridge: Cambridge University Press.

Ganeri, Jonardon. 2017. *Attention, Not Self*. New York: Oxford University Press.

Ganeri, Jonardon. 2020. Śrīharsa's Dissident Epistemology: Knowledge as Assurance. In Jonardon Ganeri (Ed.), *The Oxford Handbook of Indian Philosophy* (pp. 522–39). New York: Oxford University Press.

Heim, Maria. 2017a. *The Forerunner of All Things*. New York: Oxford University Press.

Heim, Maria. 2017b. Buddhaghosa on the Phenomenology of Love and Compassion. In Jonardon Ganeri (Ed.), *The Oxford Handbook of Indian Philosophy* (pp. 171–89). New York: Oxford University Press.

Lackey, Jennifer. 2007. Why We Don't Deserve Credit for Everything We Know. *Synthese*, 158(3): 345–61.

Matilal, Bimal Krishna. 1986. *Perception: An Essay on Classical Indian Theories of Knowledge*. Oxford: Oxford University Press.

McRae, Emily. forthcoming. Equanimity and the Loving Eye: A Buddhist-Feminist Account of Loving Attention. In Jennifer McWeeny and Keya Maitra (Eds.), *Feminist Philosophy of Mind*. New York: Oxford University Press.

Milinda-pañha. 1963. *Milinda's Questions*, translated by I. B. Horner. Oxford: Pali Text Society, 2 vols.

Murdoch, Iris. 1970. *The Sovereignty of Good*. London: Routledge.

Pirruccello, Ann. 1995. Interpreting Simone Weil: Presence and Absence in Attention. *Philosophy East and West*, 45: 61–72.

Pritchard, Duncan. 2009. Apt Performance and Epistemic Value. *Philosophical Studies*, 143(3): 407–16.

Sasaki, H. 1986. *Linguistic Approach to Buddhist Thought*. Delhi: Motilal Banarsidass.

Shiffman, Mark. 2013. Review of *Robert Chevanier, Simone Weil: Attention to the Real*, in *Notre Dame Philosophical Reviews*, March 31.

Siegel, Susanna. 2012. Cognitive Penetrability and Perceptual Justification. *Noûs*, 46(2): 201–22.

Siegel, Susanna. 2017. *The Rationality of Perception*. New York: Oxford University Press.

Sosa, Ernest. 2007. *Apt Belief and Reflective Knowledge, Volume 1: A Virtue Epistemology*. Oxford: Oxford University Press.

Sosa, Ernest. 2015. *Judgment and Agency*. Oxford: Oxford University Press.

Theeuwes, Jan. 2014. Spatial Orienting and Attentional Capture. In Anna Nobre and Sabine Kastner (Eds.), *The Oxford Handbook of Attention* (pp. 231–52). Oxford: Oxford University Press.

Watzl, Sebastian. 2022. The Ethics of Attention: A Framework. In Sophie Alice Archer (Ed.), *Salience: A Philosophical Inquiry*. London: Routledge.

Watzl, Sebastian. 2017. *Structuring Mind: The Nature of Attention and How it Shapes Consciousness*. Oxford: Oxford University Press.

Weil, Simone. 1988. Premiers écrits philosophiques. In André A. Devaux and Florence de Lussy (Eds.), *Oevres complètes de Simone Weil (Tome I)*. Paris: Gallimard.

Weil, Simone. 2002. *Gravity and Grace*, translated by Emma Crawford and Mario von Der Ruhr. London: Routledge.

Weil, Simone. 2004. *The Notebooks of Simone Weil*, translated from the French by Arthur Wills. London: Routledge.

Weil, Simone. 2021. Reflections on the Right Use of School Studies with a View to the Love of God. In *Waiting for God*. London: Routledge.

Westerhoff, Jan. 2018. *The Golden Age of Buddhist Philosophy*. New York: Oxford University Press.

Woodhead, Linda. 1987. Simone Weil's Conversation with the *Bhagavad Gītā*. *Theology*, 90: 24–32.

2

Knowledge and Independent Checks in Mīmāṃsā

Nilanjan Das

Suppose I look at the wall before me, and come to believe that it is red. As a result, I know that it is red. But how can I rationally believe that I know this? My initial perceptual belief is about the wall and its colour, but my higher-order belief is about whether I know. It's natural to think that, to form a belief about this epistemological matter, I cannot simply rely on my perceptual belief (or my introspective knowledge that I have that belief). I need some further source of information, e.g., the recent track record of my colour vision, or a recent test report from the ophthalmologist's lab, which provides evidence for the truth or reliability of my original perceptual belief. More generally, to rationally believe that I know that the wall is red, I need to run an *independent check*. This supports:

> *The Independent Check Thesis.* If an agent is to rationally believe (or judge) that she knows that *p*, she must rely on some source of information that provides evidence for the truth or reliability of the relevant belief (or judgement) independently of that belief (or judgement).

The *Independent Check Thesis* is significant: if it is right, then we must reject the KK principle, i.e., the principle that, if an agent knows that *p*, then she is in a position to know that she knows that *p*.[1] The *Independent Check Thesis* says that, in scenarios where an agent isn't in a position to run an independent check on a belief (or judgement), she won't be able to rationally believe (or judge) that she knows. So, if I know that the wall is red but don't have enough information about the track record of my colour vision or easy access to an ophthalmologist's lab, I won't be able to rationally believe that I know that the wall is red. If knowledge

[1] Even though the KK principle has been traditionally popular (see Hintikka 1962), Alston (1980), Feldman (1981), and Williamson (2000) have recently raised powerful objections against it. In response, there has been a resurgence of KK defenders, such as Greco (2014), Stalnaker (2015), Das and Salow (2018), and Dorst (2019).

Nilanjan Das, *Knowledge and Independent Checks in Mīmāṃsā* In: *Oxford Studies in Epistemology, Volume 7.*
Edited by: Tamar Szabó Gendler, John Hawthorne, and Julianne Chung, Oxford University Press.
DOI: 10.1093/oso/9780192868978.003.0002

requires rational belief, an agent who finds herself in such a situation won't be in a position to know that she knows.[2]

The aim of this chapter is to examine a classical Indian debate about the *Independent Check Thesis.*[3] Some Buddhists and Nyāya philosophers (henceforth, the Naiyāyikas) wanted to preserve a version of the *Independent Check Thesis.* They subscribed to the *theory of extrinsic knowledgehood* (*parataḥprāmāṇyavāda*): roughly, the theory that we can rationally ascribe knowledge to ourselves only by running an independent check. The Mīmāṃsā philosophers (henceforth the Mīmāṃsakas) rejected the *Independent Check Thesis.* They defended the *theory of intrinsic knowledgehood* (*svataḥprāmāṇyavāda*): roughly, the view that we don't need to run an independent check in order to rationally ascribe knowledge to ourselves.

Here, I will take a careful look at this debate. I will consider a cluster of arguments against the *Independent Check Thesis,* given by a group of Mīmāṃsakas who were followers of Kumārila Bhaṭṭa (seventh century CE) and therefore were called the Bhāṭṭa Mīmāṃsakas. In doing so, I won't be drawing directly on the works of Kumārila himself or his commentators. Rather, I will be focusing on a text called *The Raceme of Reasoning* (*Nyāyamañjarī*) written by a Nyāya philosopher, Jayanta Bhaṭṭa (ninth century CE), who engaged closely with Kumārila. Jayanta's reconstruction of the Mīmāṃsā position highlights an aspect of that view which is not obvious from the work of Kumārila or his followers: namely, that the *Independent Check Thesis* is in tension with an attractive principle that connects knowledge and action.

Here is my plan. After taking care of some conceptual housekeeping in section 1, I will set up the debate about knowledgehood in section 2. Then, I will explain the Bhāṭṭa Mīmāṃsakas' arguments (as presented by Jayanta) against the *Independent Check Thesis* in sections 3–5. In section 6, I will consider a Buddhist response. In section 7, I will sketch the positive view that Jayanta ascribes to the Mīmāṃsakas: the *Default Knowledgehood Thesis.* In section 8, I will close the paper by highlighting some aspects of the Bhāṭṭa Mīmāṃsakas' view.

1. Conceptual Housekeeping

Indian epistemologists often theorize in terms of the notion of *pramā.* Here, I will show that the notion is intimately connected to our concept of knowledge:

[2] The tension between the independent check thesis and the KK principle has been discussed by Greco (2014) and Das and Salow (2018).

[3] For discussion, see Taber (1992), Arnold (2008), Freschi and Graheli (2005), and McCrea (2015). Matilal (1986, ch. 5) and Immerman (2018) have argued that the Mīmāṃsā position could be understood as a defence of the KK principle. Keating (forthcoming) disagrees. I respond to Keating in footnote 19.

an episode of *pramā* is an awareness-event (*jñāna*)[4]—i.e., an experience or thought—whereby one learns or comes to know something; it is an *event of knowledge-acquisition*.

In *The Raceme of Reasoning*, Jayanta doesn't explicitly define the notion of *pramā*. Rather, he gives us a characterization of a *pramāṇa*, a means or instrument by which episodes of *pramā* arise. He says: 'A *pramāṇa* is a collection of causes (*sāmagrī*), which give rise to non-erroneous and doubt-free apprehension of an object, and which may or may not have the nature of awareness.'[5] Let's unpack this. As Jayanta explains, the defining characteristic of a *pramāṇa* is that, if an awareness arises from a *pramāṇa*, then the relevant subject couldn't be mistaken or in doubt about the relevant object. Moreover, insofar as a *pramāṇa* is the means (or the collection of causes) by means of which such an awareness arises, it may or may not include awareness-events. For example, in the case of veridical perception, the causes of the relevant awareness include a sense-faculty, which isn't an awareness itself. In contrast, a correct inferential judgement invariably arises from other awareness-events: when I infer the presence of fire on the hill after observing smoke coming out of it, my inferential judgement is caused by my initial observation of smoke and my recollection of the fact that fire always accompanies smoke.[6]

Given the kind of infallibility that Jayanta associates with the notion of *pramā*, it is tempting to think that the notion of *pramā* is nothing but our notion of knowledge. There is some plausibility to this idea: there are two important similarities between the concept of knowledge and the concept of *pramā*. First, like any belief that has the status of knowledge, any awareness that has the status of *pramā* must be *accurate* or *true* (*yathārtha*). If I perceive the mother-of-pearl before me as a piece of silver, my perceptual awareness—insofar as it is inaccurate—isn't an episode of *pramā*. Call this the *accuracy condition* on *pramā*.

[4] I am translating the expression '*jñāna*' everywhere as 'awareness' or 'awareness-event' instead of resorting to the usual translation 'cognition'. This is because, in contemporary philosophy of mind and cognitive science, the term 'cognition' is typically reserved for mental states, such as judgements or beliefs, whose contents are accessible for the purposes of verbal reports, practical reasoning, etc. However, according to some Indian philosophers, non-conceptual perceptual experiences aren't of this sort but count as *jñāna*. So, it's better to use the more neutral term 'awareness' or 'awareness-event' for the more general category of *jñāna*. My use of the term 'awareness' has two features: first, awareness-events are non-factive (i.e., they can be false), and second, an agent needn't necessarily be conscious of all her awareness-events.

[5] NM I.31.6–7: *avyabhicāriṇīm asandigdhām arthopalabdhiṃ vidadhatī bodhābodhasvabhāvā sāmagrī pramāṇam* |

[6] Even though Jayanta is a Naiyāyika, his conception of a *pramāṇa* is unorthodox by Nyāya standards: for him, the means or instrument (*karaṇa*) by which an episode of *pramā* arises isn't merely one amongst the many causes of that awareness, but rather is the entire collection of causes (*sāmagrī*) (NM I.31.10–38.11). This is incompatible with earlier Nyāya views, e.g., Uddyotakara's theory of *pramāṇa*s in his sub-commentary *Detailed Commentary on Nyāya* (*Nyāyavārttika*) on the *Nyāyasūtra* (NV 6.7–22).

Naiyāyikas such as Jayanta and (at least some) Bhāṭṭa Mīmāṃsakas accept the accuracy condition.[7] Second, like any belief that has the status of knowledge, any awareness that has the status of *pramā* must be produced by a set of causes that couldn't (easily) have led to an error. In other words, an episode of *pramā* must have good causal pedigree. Call this the *pedigree condition*. Once again, some Bhāṭṭa Mīmāṃsakas and Naiyāyikas such as Jayanta endorse a version of this condition. For the Bhāṭṭa Mīmāṃsakas, if a set of causes is to produce an episode of *pramā*, those causes must be free from epistemic defects (*doṣa*) that lead to error. For some Naiyāyikas like Jayanta, the mere absence of epistemic defects isn't sufficient; the causes underlying an episode of *pramā* must also include certain positive factors—called epistemic virtues (*guṇa*)—that guarantee the truth or accuracy of the relevant awareness.[8]

Despite these similarities between the concept of *pramā* and the concept of knowledge, it would be wrong to treat them as the same. There are two salient differences. Here is the first one. States of knowing can be dispositional: an implicitly held belief that doesn't manifest itself through any occurrent experience or judgement could still have the status of knowledge. By contrast, for Jayanta and other Indian philosophers, mental states that have the status of *pramā* are not dispositional states; they are occurrent states—experiences and thoughts—which we have been calling awareness-events (*jñāna*). The second disanalogy is this.

[7] Jayanta's definition of *pramāṇa* entails the accuracy condition. Other Naiyāyikas concur: Uddyotakara says that a *pramāṇa*, i.e., the means by which episodes of *pramā* arise, is what discriminates an object (*arthaparicchedaka*) (NV 2.21–3.2), and Vācaspati Miśra says that the distinguishing feature of a *pramāṇa* is its property of not erring from its object (*arthāvyabhicāritā*) (NVTṬ 4.1–4, 4.19–20). Some Bhāṭṭa Mīmāṃsakas also agree with this. Kumārila's earliest commentator, Umbeka, says that Kumārila's definition of *pramāṇa* (here, to be understood as *pramā*) rules out error (ŚVTṬ 66.16–17), and elsewhere defines the property of being *pramā* as a property of not erring from the relevant object (*arthāvyabhicāritva*) (ŚVTṬ 56.11–14). Another commentator, Pārthasārathi Miśra, defines the property of being *pramā* as the relevant intentional objects' property of being the way the awareness represents them to be (*viṣayatathātva* or *arthatathātva*) (NRK 53.18–19; NRM 30.8–9). As McCrea (2015) notes, Kumārila's only other major commentator, Sucarita Miśra, is an exception to this trend: he doesn't impose an accuracy condition on episodes of *pramā*.

[8] Kumārila endorses the Bhāṭṭa version of the pedigree condition in his lost work *Great Commentary* (*Bṛhaṭṭīkā*) (RNA 106.9–11): 'Among those [awareness-events], a *pramāṇa* [which is here equivalent to *pramā*] is accepted by ordinary people to be an awareness of a new object, which is certain, unrebutted and produced from non-defective causes' (*tatrāpūrvārthārthavijñānaṃ niścitaṃ bādhavarjitam | aduṣṭakāraṇārabdhaṃ pramāṇaṃ lokasammatam ||*) In verse 47 of his *Detailed Commentary on Verse* (*Ślokavārttika*) on *Mīmāṃsāsūtra* 1.1.2, he says that the status of every *pramāṇa* (here, to be understood as *pramā*) as a *pramāṇa* is intrinsic (*svataḥ*), because it is impossible for something else to produce a capacity in something when that capacity is intrinsically absent (*svato 'satī*). In his commentary, Umbeka takes Kumārila to mean that the status of a *pramāṇa* as a *pramāṇa* doesn't depend on any positive factor like an epistemic virtue, but merely on the absence of defects (ŚVTṬ 54.1–21). Jayanta defends the Nyāya version of the pedigree condition at NM_P 4.2.2.2. For a later defence, see Udayana's *The Flower-Offering of Reason* (*Nyāyakusumāñjali*), especially his commentary on verse II.1 (NK, pp. 210–33).

Many of these Indian philosophers, including Jayanta, also accept the idea that awareness-events generated by memory—recollective awareness-events (*smṛti*)—cannot be *pramā*.[9] If episodes of *pramā* were states of knowing, this would make no sense. States of remembering do count as states of knowing.

These differences lend support to another hypothesis: episodes of *pramā* aren't states of knowing, but rather are events of *learning* or *knowledge-acquisition*, i.e., thoughts or experiences in undergoing which we learn or come to know something.[10] This explains both the similarities and dissimilarities between the concept of *pramā* and the concept of knowledge. First, it explains why episodes of *pramā* are subject to both an accuracy condition and a pedigree condition: if a piece of information isn't true or isn't acquired from a sufficiently reliable source, one couldn't possibly learn or come to know it. Second, it explains why episodes of *pramā* must be occurrent rather than dispositional states, and why recollective awareness-events can't have the status of *pramā*. Since episodes of *pramā* are *events* of learning or knowledge-acquisition, they have to be occurrent (and not dispositional) states. And, typically, when one remembers something, one is merely retrieving information that one had acquired from another source; one isn't learning anything new or acquiring knowledge independently of what one already had learnt.

This is how I shall understand the notion of *pramā* for the rest of our discussion. In what follows, I translate the term '*pramā*' as 'knowledge-event' to capture the thought that these are events of knowledge-acquisition or learning. I use the term 'method of knowing' to refer to the means by which knowledge-events arise (*pramāṇa*). Finally, I use the word 'knowledgehood' to talk about the property of being a knowledge-event (*prāmāṇya*).

[9] The Bhāṭṭas justify this by appealing to a novelty requirement on *pramā*: namely, that an episode of *pramā* shouldn't apprehend something that has already been apprehended; it must be a source of new information. This is explicit in the passage from the *Great Commentary* quoted in footnote 8; see Kataoka (2003) for discussion. Prābhākara Mīmāṃsakas and Naiyāyikas reject this novelty requirement. They point out that, in a case where an agent undergoes a series of perceptual awareness-events that have the same content, each of the perceptual awareness-events could have the status of *pramā*. For alternative ways of ruling out recollective awareness from the scope of knowledge-events, see Śālikanātha Miśra's *Topical Elaborations* (*Prakaraṇapañcikā*) (PP 124.9–125.5), Jayanta's *Raceme of Reasoning* (NM I.59.7–10 and NM I.60.50–6), and Vācaspatimiśra's and Udayana's sub-commentaries on the *Nyāyasūtra* (NVTṬ 17.21–18.4, NVTP 52.12–53.9).

[10] We might wonder if there is a conceptual analogue of knowledge on this picture. I think there is. Typically, when an agent undergoes an episode of *pramā*, the relevant awareness produces a memory impression (*saṃskāra*) which is nothing but a dispositional state that manifests itself through later recollective awareness-events with the same content. Since this dispositional state produced by the episode of *pramā* carries the information that the agent has learnt and can be retrieved for the purposes of making verbal reports and engaging theoretical and practical reasoning, it can be treated as a state of knowing.

2. The Debate

In the third chapter (*āhnika*) of *The Raceme of Reasoning*, Jayanta frames the debate about the intrinsicness of knowledgehood in the voice of his Bhāṭṭa opponent:

> It has been said that something is a knowledge-event (*pramāṇa*) just in case it reveals how things are. The knowledgehood of that [awareness] simply consists in its not erring from the object to be known by it (*svaprameyāvyabhicāritva*). Moreover, that [knowledgehood] should be described as extrinsic only when it is dependent on other factors. But this is not dependent on other factors anywhere. For that dependence—if it were to exist—would pertain either to its production, or to bringing about its own effect, or to the ascertainment of knowledgehood.[11]

The Bhāṭṭa opponent here makes two important claims. Let's flesh them out.

First, the Bhāṭṭa claims that the status of an awareness as a knowledge-event boils down to the property of not erring from the object to be known by it (*svaprameyāvyabhicāritva*), which is roughly the same as accuracy. This might seem questionable: we've already seen knowledge-events are subject not only to an accuracy condition but also to a pedigree condition.

Here's a possible explanation. At least some of these Nyāya and Mīmāṃsā authors think that there is an important connection between the accuracy condition and the pedigree condition: in cases where one arrives at an awareness on the basis of epistemically defective causal conditions, one comes to inaccurately represent the world.[12] For example, suppose I see what appears to be smoke coming out of a hill. I take it to be smoke, but it is only vapour. Since I take it to be smoke and I know from previous investigations that fire invariably accompanies smoke, I infer that there is fire on the hill. But suppose there is in fact fire on the hill. This is a Gettier case: we would typically say that my judgement is true but only as a matter of luck. However, Indian philosophers like Kumārila tend to deny this: they would claim that my inferential judgement is inaccurate insofar as the fire that I infer doesn't really exist on the hill. Why? The fire that I ascribe to the hill is something I believe to be the source of (or, more generally, connected to)

[11] NMP §3.3: *arthatathātvaprakāśakaṃ hi pramāṇam ity uktam |tasya svaprameyāvyabhicāritvaṃ nāma prāmāṇyam | ataś ca parāpekṣāyāṃ satyāṃ hi parata iti kathayitum ucitam|na cāsya parāpekṣā kvacid vidyate || sā hi bhavantī utpattau vā syāt svakāryakaraṇe vā prāmāṇyaniścaye vā |*

[12] A good expression of this thought occurs in verses 156–64 of the section called 'On Objectlessness' (*Nirālambanavāda*) in *The Detailed Commentary on Verse*, where Kumārila argues that an inferential mark (*hetu*) which doesn't exist—the misperceived smoke in one of our examples—cannot give rise to an accurate or true awareness. For the verses with Umbeka's, Pārthasārathi Miśra's and Sucarita Miśra's commentaries on them, see ŚVTṬ 229–231, ŚVK II.78–81, and NRK 182–4. For discussion, see Ganeri (2007, ch. 5).

the smoke that I take myself to have perceived on the hill. Since there is no such smoke, there is also no such fire on the hill. So, my judgement is false. The explanation generalizes to other Gettier cases. This, in turn, might suggest that awareness-events which are brought about by epistemically defective causes (e.g., by defective evidence in this case) are inevitably inaccurate: they involve an element of misrepresentation. So, on a simplified version of this view, the property of being a knowledge-event—what I am calling knowledgehood—simply boils down to the property of *accuracy* (*yāthārthya*) (when restricted to non-recollective awareness-events).

Second, the Bhāṭṭa claims that knowledgehood cannot be *extrinsic*, i.e., dependent on other factors. While Jayanta's text identifies three distinct senses of extrinsicness, what matters for our purposes is the extrinsicness of knowledgehood *with respect to ascertainment*.[13] For Naiyāyikas like Jayanta and some Buddhists like Dharmakīrti (seventh century CE) and his followers, knowledgehood is extrinsic with respect to ascertainment: in order to rationally ascertain (i.e., to judge) that an awareness is a knowledge-event, we have to rely on some awareness that is distinct from both the original awareness and an introspective awareness about it.[14,15] Let's unpack this.

[13] Knowledgehood can be extrinsic (1) with respect to its production, (2) with respect to bringing about its own effect, or (3) with respect to the ascertainment of knowledgehood. If knowledgehood is extrinsic with respect to production, then the status of an awareness as a knowledge-event will causally depend on positive factors, e.g., epistemic virtues, distinct from the ordinary causal conditions that normally give rise to awareness-events of the relevant type. If knowledgehood is extrinsic with respect to bringing about its own effect, then a knowledge-event will depend on other factors, e.g., an awareness of itself, in order to produce its proprietary effects, e.g., the manifestation of an object. If knowledgehood is extrinsic with respect to ascertainment, then it can be rationally ascertained only by relying on an awareness distinct from the original awareness and any introspective awareness about the original awareness. Kataoka (2003, Part 2, pp. 84–5) points out that Kumārila himself talks about intrinsicness or extrinsicness with respect to production (*utpatti*), operation (*pravṛtti*), and awareness (*jñapti*), but uses these notions interchangeably (ibid., n. 208). Umbeka distinguishes the production- and operation-related senses of intrinsicness/exrinsicness (ŚVTṬ 55.22–3), while another commentator, Pārthasārathi, distinguishes the production- and awareness-based senses (NRK 45.7–20). For differences between these commentators, see Taber (1992) and Arnold (2008).

[14] Here, 'introspection' means a method of learning about one's own present, or recently past, mental states or processes. I have characterized the theory of extrinsic knowledgehood following the Nyāya opponents of the Bhāṭṭa Mīmāṃsakas characterize their own view: for example, see Jayanta's *Raceme of Reasoning* (NM_P §4.2.1) as well as Vācaspati's and Udayana's sub-commentaries on the *Nyāyasūtra* (NVTṬ 4.3–13 and 9.14–12.3 and NVTP 14.1–18 and 33.10–40.7).

[15] Throughout this discussion, I will assume that Jayanta and his Bhāṭṭa opponents are discussing the question of how a *rational* agent comes to judge that an awareness is a knowledge-event. This is suggested by a number of passages where the Bhāṭṭa says that an agent who inquires into the epistemic status of an awareness after he has already acted on the basis of it would be 'someone who inspects auspicious occasions after he is done with his wedding' (NM_P §3.3.3.3.4) and that this investigation would be like 'an examination of the stars by someone who has already shaved his head' (NM_P §3.3.3.3.3.2). The idea everywhere is the same: it makes sense to find auspicious occasions before one's wedding or to check the stars before shaving one's head, because scheduling a wedding or a shave at the wrong time can lead to disaster (a terrible marriage or a short life). But engaging in such investigation after the deed is done is practically futile and therefore irrational.

All these philosophers agree that we can learn about our own awareness-events by some method of introspection. This could be either epistemically direct or indirect. For the Naiyāyikas and Buddhists, the method is epistemically direct (i.e., non-inferential). The Buddhists who follow Dharmakīrti think that every awareness is reflexively aware of itself. By contrast, the Naiyāyikas think that there is an inner sense (the *manas*) that gives us perceptual access to our own present, or recently past, awareness-events. By contrast, for the Bhāṭṭa Mīmāṃsakas, the method of introspection is (broadly speaking) inferential. On their view, whenever we undergo an awareness, the awareness makes its intentional objects manifest (*prakaṭa* or *prakāśamāna*) to us in a certain way; for example, a knowledge-event will typically do this by determining things in the world to be a certain way. Since these objects wouldn't be manifest to us in that way unless we were aware of them, the relevant manifestness—which we are aware of as a result of our original awareness—is inexplicable (*anupapanna*) without the existence of the original awareness. So, on the basis of that manifestness, we can infer that we are aware of those objects. On this view, we can learn about our own present or recently past mental states not by gazing inward but rather by looking outwards at the world and then making an inference. In this respect, it is similar to (but not the same as) certain transparency-based accounts of self-knowledge, which say that we can gain knowledge of mental states like belief simply by reflecting on the contents of those mental states.[16]

The disagreement amongst these philosophers consists in this. The Naiyāyikas and Buddhists think that, in order to rationally ascertain that an awareness is a knowledge-event, we have to resort to a method of knowing, which is distinct from the method that yields the original awareness or the introspective awareness of the relevant awareness. This is because they subscribe to a version of the *Independent Check Thesis*. They think that, in order to rationally ascertain that an awareness is a knowledge-event, we need evidence for the truth or accuracy of that awareness *independently of it*. But neither the original awareness nor an introspective awareness about it can provide such evidence. For example, when I enter a room and judge that the wall before me is red, I may become aware of my judgement by introspection. But neither my judgement nor my introspective awareness of it can give me independent evidence for thinking that I've learnt that the wall is red. I can only rationally make this further judgement if there is a distinct

[16] The relevant piece of reasoning is an instance of postulation (*arthāpatti*), i.e., a method of knowing where one postulates something to be true because some piece of evidence would be inexplicable without it. The view is introduced by the commentator of the *Mīmāṃsāsūtra*, Śabarasvāmin (ŚBh 32.4), and presented by Kumārila at v. 182 in the section called 'On Emptiness' (*Śūnyavāda*) in his *Detailed Commentary in Verse*; for explanations, see the commentaries of Umbeka, Sucarita, and Pārthasārathi (ŚVTṬ 283.20–22; ŚVK 166.8–12; NRK II.227.17–228.24). Jayanta refutes this view at length in NM I 42.14–56.3. For contemporary transparency-based accounts of self-knowledge, see Evans (1982), Dretske (1994), Gallois (1996), Moran (2001), Byrne (2005, 2018), and Fernandez (2013).

means of knowing that indicates the truth or accuracy of my initial judgement. This is the sense in which knowledgehood is extrinsic with respect to ascertainment.

The Bhāṭṭa Mīmāṃsakas dissent from this. They think knowledgehood is intrinsic with respect to ascertainment: in order to rationally judge that an awareness is a knowledge-event, we don't need anything over and above an introspective awareness about the awareness itself. For our purposes, it will be useful to focus on one Bhāṭṭa account due to Kumārila's first commentator, Umbeka Bhaṭṭa (eighth century CE), with whom Jayanta engages at length. For Umbeka, knowledgehood *qua* accuracy is a property of awareness-events, and, as such, can only be grasped after we have become introspectively aware of the relevant awareness-events. So, whenever we become introspectively aware of an awareness by means of the manifestness-based inference, then (absent defeating evidence) the same inference puts us in a position to rationally judge that the awareness is a knowledge-event.[17] For example, when I see that the wall is red and therefore judge that it is red, I can become introspectively aware of my judgement by using the inference from manifestness. Provided that I have no reason to doubt the accuracy of my judgement, I can also rationally conclude that my judgement about the colour of the wall is a knowledge-event. This view is incompatible with a version of the *Independent Check Thesis*: it implies that no independent evidence for the truth of an awareness is necessary for us to rationally ascertain its knowledgehood.[18]

If we accept one more assumption about self-knowledge, this Bhāṭṭa theory of intrinsic knowledgehood will yield an argument for an analogue of the KK principle. The assumption: whenever an agent undergoes an awareness, she is in a position to rationally judge (by means of the inference from manifestness) that she is undergoing that awareness. Given this assumption, the Bhāṭṭa theory will

[17] In his commentary on v. 84 in Kumārila's *Detailed Commentary in Verse* on *Mīmāṃsāsūtra* 1.1.2, Umbeka says (ŚVTṬ 67.16–18): 'This is the import: when rebutters and so on have been removed, the awareness—which is being inferred because the determination of the object is inexplicable otherwise—is inferred to be a knowledge-event' (*ayam āśayaḥ—bādhakādinivṛttau satyāṃ arthaparicchittyanyathānupattyā jñānam anumīyamānaṃ pramāṇabhūtam anumīyata iti*|)

[18] Other Bhāṭṭas defend stronger claims. Pārthasārathi thinks that introspection isn't necessary for grasping the epistemic status of one's own awareness-events. Unlike Umbeka, Pārthasārathi claims that knowledgehood (qua *accuracy*) is not apprehended as a property of an awareness. Rather, it is a feature of the intentional objects of awareness-events: namely, their property of being a certain way, i.e., the way they are represented (*viṣayatathātva*). For instance, the knowledgehood of my judgement that the wall is red just consists in the wall's being red. So, we don't have to rely on introspection to grasp the knowledgehood of an awareness: an awareness can help us grasp its own knowledgehood insofar as it involves an awareness as of its intentional objects being exactly the way it represents them (NRK 53.18–20; NRM 33.4–14). When (in the absence of defeating evidence) I judge that the wall is red, since the knowledgehood of my judgement just consists in the wall's being red, I thereby apprehend its knowledgehood. Sucarita (who doesn't accept the accuracy-based conception of knowledgehood) also says something similar (ŚVK I.104.24–25 and I.105.5–7). Despite these differences, the views of these other Bhāṭṭas are compatible with (and may even entail) Umbeka's claim that, in order to rationally *explicitly* judge that an awareness is a knowledge-event (in the absence of defeating evidence), we need nothing over and above the introspective awareness of that awareness.

imply that, if an agent undergoes a knowledge-event, then (absent defeating evidence) she is in a position to judge that the relevant awareness is a knowledge-event. But recall: on the view we're considering, knowledgehood consists simply in accuracy (for non-recollective awareness-events). So, this view predicts that, if an agent undergoes a knowledge-event, then (absent defeating evidence) she is in a position to learn or acquire knowledge that the relevant awareness is a knowledge-event. This is an analogue of the KK principle.[19]

Whether these Bhāṭṭas are committed to this version of the KK principle will depend on whether they accept the extra assumption about self-knowledge. I won't try to decide that question here. I will focus solely on their arguments against the *Independent Check Thesis.*

3. Against the Independent Check Thesis: First Pass

Indian defenders of the *Independent Check Thesis* say that we can rationally judge or believe that we've learnt something only if we have access to a method of knowing that provides independent evidence for the truth of the relevant awareness. What is this method of knowing? Jayanta's imagined Bhāṭṭa Mīmāṃsaka considers three possibilities. First, it may be something that indicates that the causes of the awareness possess certain accuracy-conducive epistemic virtues (or are free from inaccuracy-conducive epistemic defects). Second, it may be something that indicates that there is no rebutting awareness (*bādhakapratyaya*) for the relevant awareness. Finally, it may be something that confirms the original awareness. The Bhāṭṭa Mīmāṃsaka argues that these proposals are indefensible. In this, and the next two, sections, I will flesh out the Bhāṭṭa arguments against these three proposals.

Consider the first proposal.

Proposal 1. We rationally judge that an awareness is a knowledge-event only by determining that it was produced by epistemically virtuous causes.

[19] Against Immerman (2018), Keating (forthcoming) argues that Bhāṭṭas like Pārthasārathi are not committed to the KK principle. For Pārthasārathi, even after an agent has undergone a knowledge-event, a further inference is necessary for her to judge that she is undergoing the relevant awareness. From that, Keating concludes that the agent who has undergone a knowledge-event may not be in a position that her awareness is a knowledge-event. But this seems to be based on a misunderstanding of what 'being in a position to know' means (which Keating may have inherited from Immerman). According to our version of the KK principle, if an agent undergoes a knowledge-event, then she is in a position to learn (by inference) that she has undergone a knowledge-event. As Williamson (2000, ch. 4) notes, to be in a position to know or learn that *p*, one doesn't have to know or learn that *p*; it only has to be the case that, if one did all that one is in a position to do in order to decide whether *p*, one would know or learn that *p*. So, when an agent has undergone a knowledge-event, if she is in a position to decide by inference that she has undergone that knowledge-event (absent defeating evidence), she will be in a position to know or learn that she has undergone that knowledge-event.

The Bhāṭṭa Mīmāṃsaka argues that this proposal fails. According to some Bhāṭṭa Mīmāṃsakas, if an awareness is to be a knowledge-event, it has to be produced by a set of non-defective causes; in order to explain its epistemic status, we don't have to posit positive factors, like epistemic virtues, over and above the absence of epistemic defects. So, the first response of such Bhāṭṭas Mīmāṃsakas to *Proposal 1* is predictable: 'First of all, it [the ascertainment of knowledgehood] isn't due to an awareness of the epistemic virtues of its causes. For we have just now repudiated the epistemic virtues, etc.'[20] But note that this response isn't really convincing. While it may be true that we have no reason to posit epistemic virtues to explain how knowledge-events arise, we could still argue that we can rationally determine the epistemic status of an awareness only by determining whether its causes are non-defective. So, we could endorse a modified version of *Proposal 1*:

> *Proposal 1**. We rationally judge or ascertain that an awareness is a knowledge-event only by determining that it was produced by epistemically non-defective causes.

So, the basic intuition that motivates the proposal could still succeed.

Perhaps, that is why the Bhāṭṭa Mīmāṃsaka offers a second argument. Consider the case where I see that the wall is red. Here, the causes of my awareness include my visual sense. Given that I cannot perceive my own visual sense, I cannot discover whether it possesses any epistemic virtue (or is free from epistemic defects) by means of perception. So, I would have to rely on an inference. How can I do this? I could always perform some action which yields evidence in favour of the claim that my awareness is accurate, and, therefore, indicates that its causes possess the epistemic virtues whose absence would make an awareness inaccurate (or are free from epistemic defects whose presence would make an awareness inaccurate). In short, I must perform an evidence-gathering act that yields independent evidence that the relevant awareness is accurate.[21]

In response, the Bhāṭṭa Mīmāṃsaka poses a dilemma: *Proposal 1** either makes any investigation into the epistemic status of an awareness futile, or faces a charge of circularity or regress.[22] The argument depends on:

[20] NMp §3.3.3.1.1: *na tāvat kāraṇaguṇajñānāt kāraṇaguṇānām idānīm eva nirastatvāt* |

[21] NMp §3.3.3.1.2: 'Moreover, an awareness about the epistemic virtues of the causes [of the relevant awareness] doesn't have any sense-faculty as its cause. For the epistemic virtues—insofar as they reside in imperceptible causes [of the awareness]—are imperceptible. Rather, the nature of an epistemic virtue is to be known from the correctness of its result, i.e., the apprehension. Furthermore, for a knower who doesn't undertake an action, there is no [awareness of the] correctness of the result.' (*api ca na kāraṇaguṇajñānam indriyakāraṇakam atīndriyakārakādhikaraṇatvena parokṣatvād guṇānām |api tūpalabdhyākhyakāryapariśuddhisamadhigamyaṃ guṇasvarūpam |apravṛttasya ca pramātur na kāryapariśuddhir bhavati* |).

[22] The basic idea behind the dilemma is already present in Umbeka's commentary on Kumārila's verses 49–51 in the section of his *Detailed Commentary in Verse* on *Mīmāṃsāsūtra* 1.1.2 (ŚVTṬ 56.9–25).

> *The Action-Knowledge Principle.* An agent can rationally undertake an action on the assumption that *p* only if she antecedently rationally judges that she knows (or has learnt) that *p*.

According to the Bhāṭṭa, denying the *Action-Knowledge Principle* is costly: it makes any investigation into the epistemic status of our awareness-events futile. Both the Bhāṭṭas and their opponents agree that it is practically useful for us to determine whether or not our awareness-events are knowledge-events. Recall that, on this view, when it comes to non-recollective awareness-events, knowledgehood is nothing other than accuracy. The whole point of investigating whether an awareness is a knowledge-event is to make sure that it is accurate enough for its content to be relied upon for the purposes of planning future action. But if the *Action-Knowledge Principle* were false, then we could rationally plan and undertake actions on the basis of an awareness without antecedently determining it to be accurate. So, it would be practically useless to determine *later* whether that awareness was accurate. As Jayanta's imagined Bhāṭṭa Mīmāṃsaka puts the point:

> Now, in those cases, the practical undertaking[23] (*pravrtti*) must be caused by the ascertainment of knowledgehood. Or, if that weren't the case, since the practical undertaking would be brought about by an awareness which in fact hasn't been ascertained to be a knowledge-event, what would be the point of ascertaining it later?[24]

So, let's suppose the *Action-Knowledge Principle* is true.

Next, consider two scenarios where I arguably gain independent evidence for the status of an awareness as a knowledge-event.

> *Red Wall 1.* I have no idea how reliable my colour vision is. I go into a room with a red wall in it, and judge that the wall is red. Later, when I am being quizzed about the colour of the wall, I unhestitatingly say that it's red. The answer is right, and I am told this. Given suitable background evidence, this shows that my judgement was produced by epistemically virtuous or non-defective causes.
>
> *Red Wall 2.* I have no idea how reliable my colour vision is. I go into a room with a red wall in it, and judge that the wall is red. After coming out of the room, I wonder if I know that the colour of the wall is red. So, I go to the ophthalmologist's lab, and get my colour vision tested. The results are normal. Given

[23] A practical undertaking (*pravṛtti*) is not an action. As *Nyāyasūtra* 1.1.17 says, it is the commencement of linguistic, mental or intellectual, and physical activity (*vāgbuddhiśarīrārambha*); it's taken to be synonymous with the conscious effort (*prayatna*) that an agent puts into performing an action.

[24] Ibid.: *tatredānīṃ prāmāṇyaniścayapūrvikā pravṛttir bhavet |anyathā vā 'niścitaprāmāṇyād eva jñānāt pravṛttisiddhau kiṃ paścāt tanniścayena prayojanam |*

suitable background evidence, this shows that my judgement was produced by epistemically virtuous or non-defective causes.

In both cases, I perform an action which yields independent evidence that my original judgement was a knowledge-event. The difference is this. In *Red Wall 1*, when I perform that action, I assume that the wall is red. In *Red Wall 2*, I don't make that assumption.

In *Red Wall 1*, the only act I perform is answering the quiz question. This act is based on my assumption that the wall is red. If the *Action-Knowledge Principle* is true, then I can rationally undertake that action only if I antecedently rationally judge that I have learnt that the wall is red. But, according to *Proposal 1**, I can do so only by inferring that my judgement about the colour of the wall was produced by epistemically virtuous or non-defective causes. But this inference must be based on evidence derived from some evidence-gathering act that I perform. Since *ex hypothesi* the only evidence-gathering act here is my act of answering the quiz question, the account will end up being circular. The Bhāṭṭa explains:

> However, if the practical undertaking arises from an awareness that is ascertained to be a knowledge-event, one cannot avoid descending into the hell that is circularity. When a practical undertaking takes place, there is an apprehension of the correctness of the result [i.e., of the fact that the relevant awareness is true]; due to the apprehension of the correctness of the result, there is a knowledge-event regarding the virtues of the causes; due to the knowledge-event regarding the virtues of the causes, knowledgehood is ascertained; due to the ascertainment of knowledgehood, there is a practical undertaking.[25]

The lesson: in cases like *Red Wall 1*, if the *Action-Knowledge Principle* is true, then a problem of circularity will be inescapable.

One might think that this problem only arises in cases like *Red Wall 1*, because the action, e.g., my answering the quiz question, is itself based on the relevant awareness, i.e., my judgement that the wall is red. In *Red Wall 2*, that's not the case. My action of going to the ophthalmologist's lab isn't based on my judgement. But a version of the same problem can be recreated here. When I go to the ophthalmologist's lab to get my eyes tested, I do so on a number of assumptions, e.g., the assumption that I have legs or that there is such a thing as an ophthalmologist's lab. If the *Action-Knowledge Principle* is right, I must rationally take myself to know or have learnt these facts. But, if *Proposal 1** applies to this case, I can only rationally judge that I know or have learnt such facts if I have

[25] Ibid.: *niścitaprāmāṇyāt tu pravṛttau duratikramaḥ cakrakakrakacapātaḥ | pravṛttau satyāṃ kāryapariśuddhigrahaṇam, kāryapariśuddhigrahaṇāt kāraṇaguṇāvagatiḥ, kāraṇaguṇāvagateḥ prāmāṇyaniścayaḥ, prāmāṇyaniścayāt pravṛttir iti |*

undertaken a prior action that yields evidence that the relevant awareness-events are brought about by virtuous or non-defective causes. But, in order to rationally undertake such an action, I must (once again) antecedently take myself to know or learnt certain other facts. Thus, there will be a regress. The lesson: in cases like *Red Wall 2,* if the *Action-Knowledge Principle* is true, then a regress will be unavoidable.

The upshot is clear. If the defender of extrinsic knowledgehood accepts *Proposal 1*,* she will either face a charge of problematic circularity or regress, or will have to reject the *Action-Knowledge Principle.* But, if she rejects this principle, any investigation into the epistemic status of our awareness-events will be practically futile. This is the dilemma.

4. Against the Independent Check Thesis: Second Pass

On the view under discussion, knowledgehood simply boils down to accuracy when it comes to non-recollective awareness-events. The content of an accurate awareness cannot be rebutted (i.e., shown to be false). So, one might be tempted to replace *Proposal 1** with:

> *Proposal 2.* We can rationally judge that an awareness is a knowledge-event only by determining that there is no rebutting awareness (*bādhakapratyaya*) for it.

For example, while travelling through the desert, a traveller may see something that appears to be water on the distant horizon. Suppose she judges it to be water, and starts walking towards the spot where the water appears. If she finds no water there, she will undergo an awareness that will rebut her earlier judgement. But, if after investigation she undergoes no such rebutting awareness, then she may rationally conclude that her earlier judgement was a knowledge-event.

According to Jayanta's Bhāṭṭa Mīmāṃsaka, the success of *Proposal 2* depends on how we interpret 'absence of rebutting awareness'.[26] On one interpretation, in order to rationally judge that an awareness is a knowledge-event, the agent only has to determine that, at that specific time, the awareness is unrebutted. While she can easily determine that, it's insufficient for her to rationally conclude that her awareness is a knowledge-event. On the other interpretation, in order for an agent to rationally treat an awareness as a knowledge-event, she must determine that the

[26] NMP §3.3.3.2: 'The ascertainment of knowledgehood also doesn't take place due to the determination of the absence of rebutters. For, should that absence exist at that time, or should it reside at other times? An absence that exists at that time isn't sufficient for the ascertainment of knowledgehood. For, even though no rebutter may be produced regarding fake gold, etc. for a while, the production of such a rebutter is observed at another time. By contrast, the absence of a rebutter at all times isn't apprehended by a non-omniscient person.' (*nāpi bādhakābhāvaparicchedāt prāmāṇyaniścayaḥ | sa hi tātkāliko vā syāt kālāntarabhāvī vā | tātkāliko na paryāptaḥ prāmāṇyaparinīścaye | kūṭakāñcanādau kiṃcit kālam anutpannabādhake 'pi kālāntare tadutpādadarśanāt | sarvadā tadabhāvas tu nāsarvajñasya gocaraḥ |*)

awareness will remain unrebutted at all other times as well. But that's an impossible task. So, *Proposal 2* fails.

To see the point more clearly, consider the traveller who judges that there is water at a distance on the horizon. Suppose she hasn't reached the spot where the water appears, but is considering whether her judgement is a knowledge-event. If *Proposal 2* is right, then she can rationally treat her judgement as a knowledge-event only by determining that there is no rebutting awareness for her judgement. But this absence of a rebutting awareness could either be an absence of a rebutting awareness at that very time, or an absence of such an awareness at all other times as well. The first option makes things too easy: since the traveller hasn't undergone any rebutting awareness yet, she can easily determine that there is no present rebutting awareness for her judgement. That's not enough for her to rationally treat her judgement to be a knowledge-event. Even in recognized cases of error, we often don't immediately get rebutting evidence against our erroneous judgements: for example, after I've judged fake gold to be real gold, I may only much later discover that my judgement was false. So, in order to rationally treat her judgement as a knowledge-event, the traveller must determine that her judgement will remain unrebutted in the future. This is the second option. But this makes it impossible for non-omniscient agents like us to rationally determine that any of our awareness-events are knowledge-events. For we cannot rationally rule out the possibility that our judgements will be rebutted by some future awareness. So, the traveller—even after she has found water at the spot where water appeared to her earlier—cannot rationally conclude that her judgement won't be rebutted by some future awareness.

The result: *Proposal 2* doesn't work.

5. Against the Independent Check Thesis: Final Pass

The best strategy for the defender of the *Independent Check Thesis* is to appeal to confirmation (*saṃvāda*).

> *Proposal 3.* We can rationally judge that an awareness is a knowledge-event only by undergoing a further awareness that confirms it.

The Bhāṭṭa Mīmāṃsaka begins his attack on this proposal by asking what 'confirmation' in this context means: does it involve undergoing an awareness that has the same content as the earlier awareness, or an awareness with a different content, or an awareness of practical efficacy (*arthakriyā*)?[27] Let's consider each option in turn.

[27] NM$_P$ §3.3.3.3: 'If it is said that the ascertainment of knowledgehood takes place due to confirmation, then it should be stated what this thing called confirmation is. Is it just an awareness that has those [very same] intentional objects [as the original awareness], or an awareness of some other

The first option—the view that an awareness is confirmed by an awareness with the same content—is problematic. If the confirming awareness-event has (roughly) the same content as the original one, we need to say what difference there is between the two, such that the epistemic status of the original awareness can be determined on the basis of the second. Suppose I enter a room and judge on the basis of my perception that there is a red wall before me. Then, I come out, and go into the room once more to make a judgement with roughly the same content. How can the second judgement confirm the original judgement when its own epistemic credentials are equally questionable by my lights? To confirm this second judgement, then, I would need to undergo a further confirming awareness. Thus, this proposal faces a regress worry. This was originally pointed out by Kumārila Bhaṭṭa.

> On the first view, what is the difference between the earlier and the later awareness-events, such that, in virtue of being confirmed by the later awareness, the earlier awareness could attain knowedgehood? Moreover:
>
> > Those who say that earlier awareness-events have knowledgehood in virtue of being confirmed by later awareness-events wouldn't be able to reach the end [of the sequence] even in hundreds of *yuga*s [i.e., the different ages of the world, each spanning hundreds of thousands of years]. By contrast, if one were to ascribe knowledgehood to some awareness just intrinsically even after going quite far, then why should one be averse to doing so with respect to the first?
>
> This is what is said [by Kumārila]:
>
> > On the contrary, if one were to accept the knowledgehood of some awareness just intrinsically, then why should one be averse to the same status with respect to the first?[28]

If the first confirming awareness needs to be confirmed by another awareness, then the latter too needs to be confirmed by another (since, otherwise, its epistemic credentials would be just as questionable as the first one). So, a regress

objects, or an awareness of practical efficacy?' (*atha saṃvādāt prāmāṇyaniścaya ucyate, tarhy ucyatām ko 'yaṃ saṃvādo nāma | kim uttaraṃ tadviṣayaṃ jñānamātram, utārthāntarajñānam, āhosvid arthakriyājñānam iti |*)

[28] NM$_P$ §3.3.3.3.1: *ādye pakṣe kaḥ pūrvottarajñānayor viśeṣaḥ yad uttarajñānasaṃvādāt pūrvaṃ jñānaṃ prāmāṇyam aśnuvīta | api ca—*

> *uttarottarasaṃvādāt pūrvapūrvapramāṇatām |*
> *vadanto nādhigaccheyur antaṃ yugaśatair api ||*
> *sudūram api gatvā tu prāmāṇyaṃ yadi kasyacit |*
> *svata evābhidhīyeta, ko dveṣaḥ prathamaṃ prati ||*

yad āha—

> *kasyacit tu yadīṣyeta svata eva pramāṇatā |*
> *prathamasya tathābhāve vidveṣaḥ kiṃnibandhanaḥ || iti |*

The last verse is verse 76 in Kumārila's *Detailed Commentary in Verse* on *Mīmāṃsāsūtra* 1.1.2.

will be unavoidable. If we try to block the regress by arguing that some of these confirming awareness-events don't require further confirmation, then there's no reason why we shouldn't say that about the first awareness.

The second option—namely, that the confirming awareness should have a different content—also will lead to bad results unless it's properly restricted. An awareness with an arbitrarily different content cannot confirm another one: for example, 'an awareness about a pillar doesn't constitute the confirmation for an awareness about a pitcher'.[29] The third option avoids this problem. It says that an awareness is confirmed by an awareness of practical efficacy. What does that mean? Consider the traveller walking through the desert. When she sees what appears to be water on the distant horizon, she judges that there is water out there. But she might not be sure if this judgement is accurate. She might know that, often, when people make similar judgements under similar circumstances, what they see is a mirage. She could, however, walk towards the spot on the horizon where the water appears. If she finds the water and is able to drink it or bathe in it, then this would show that the original judgement was capable of giving rise to successful actions. This capacity for producing practically successful actions is the practical efficacy (*arthakriyā*) of the judgement. Since this would demonstrate that the original judgement was accurate (and accuracy, in this context, is synonymous with knowledgehood), the traveller could rationally infer that her original judgement was a knowledge-event. In such cases, therefore, the agent's awareness of practical efficacy confirms her original awareness, thereby helping her determine that it was a knowledge-event.

This proposal inherits the problems of the first option. The Bhāṭṭa could again ask whether there is an epistemically significant difference between the original awareness and the awareness of its practical efficacy, which explains why the latter can confirm the former. How can the awareness of practical efficacy help us determine the epistemic status of any awareness when its own epistemic status is equally questionable by our lights? If the opponent responds by appealing to further confirming awareness-events, then there will be another regress. A different response might be that the awareness of practical efficacy is able to confirm the original awareness, simply because it is an awareness of practical efficacy. But this is a bad response. Often, false awareness-events that arise in dreams seem to be confirmed by other false judgements that arise in those very dreams about the practical efficacy of those awareness-events.

[29] NM$_P$, §3.3.3.3.2: *na hi stambhajñānaṃ kumbhajñānasya saṃvādaḥ* |. We might worry that this is too quick: an awareness with a different content can confirm another awareness. For example, if you judge that there's a pitcher carrying water in front of you, your observation that there are glasses filled with water nearby can confirm the original judgement. But note that the regress worry raised earlier will arise here again.

> [The opponent:] But this awareness of practical efficacy arises, having as its intentional object [actions such as] drinking, bathing, etc. of a person who is in the middle of the water. So, since this awareness isn't determined to be erroneous, it gives rise to the ascertainment of knowledgehood.
>
> [Reply:] That too is wrong. For, in the case of dreams, even the drinking and the bathing are found to be erroneous (*vyabhicārin*)... Therefore, since awareness-events about practical efficacy are determined to be erroneous [in some cases], the regress doesn't come to an end given that there is an investigation of their knowledgehood.[30]

So, the regress is unavoidable.

The final response to this third option is the same one that the Bhāṭṭa Mīmāṃsaka gave to *Proposal 1**: it either forces us to reject the *Action-Knowledge Principle* (thereby making it pointless for us to investigate or determine the epistemic status of awareness-events), or paves the way for a problematic sort of circularity or regress. Take, once again, the traveller in the desert. There are two versions of this case. Either the traveller simply starts walking towards the apparent water on the horizon on the assumption that it is water, or she doubts the presence of water but nevertheless performs the same action, because she thinks that the risk of walking towards that place will be worth taking. (These two cases are analogous to *Red Wall 1* and *2*, respectively.)

In the first version of the case, either the traveller performs the relevant action because she takes herself to know (or have learnt) that what she sees is water, or she doesn't. If she takes herself to know (or have learnt) that what she sees is water, then such a judgement (if rational) must arise from an awareness of practical efficacy. But, in this case, the only act that the agent performs is the act of walking towards the water and then bathing in it or drinking it. Since that act is based on her judgement that she knows (or has learnt) that there is water out there, there is a problematic kind of circularity. Alternatively, if the agent performs the action without taking herself to know (or have learnt) that what she sees is water, then the *Action-Knowledge Principle* is false. Thus, the same argument that the Bhāṭṭa gave earlier would apply once more. If we can act on the assumption that *p* without taking ourselves to know or have learnt that *p*, what would be the point of later determining whether we know or have learnt that *p*? If the epistemic status

[30] NM$_P$ §3.3.3.3.3: *idaṃ punar arthakriyāsaṃvedanaṃ ambumadhyavartinaḥ pānāvagāhanādiviṣayam udetīty anavadhāritavyabhicāritayā tatprāmāṇyaniścayāya kalpata iti | tad apy asat | svapne pānāvagāhanasyāpi vyabhicāropalabdheḥ | ...tasmād arthakriyājñānavyabhicārāvadhāraṇāt | tatprāmāṇyaparīkṣāyām anavasthā na śāmyati ||* For a similar point, see Vasubandhu's auto-commentary on verse 2 in *Twenty Verses* (*Viṃśatikā*) at Viṃ 413.13–15.

of our awareness-events were irrelevant to practical decision-making, then investigating the epistemic status of our awareness-events at a later time would be, as Jayanta puts it, 'just as futile as the examination of the stars by someone who has already shaved his head'.[31] The analogy: astrologists advise us to examine the configuration of the stars before shaving our heads, precisely because shaving one's head under unsuitable arrangements of the stars can have inauspicious effects on one's life, so examining the stars after shaving one's head is pointless.

In the second version of the case, the traveller doesn't perform the action on the assumption that what she sees is water. But, arguably, in order to rationally undertake an action, she must assume something about her environment: for instance, she must assume that she has legs, or that there is a spot on the horizon for her to walk towards. If the *Action-Knowledge Principle* is true, then, provided that she rationally undertakes the action on the basis of such assumptions, she must rationally take herself to know (or have learnt) these claims. But, according to *Proposal 3*, that is only possible if she performs some further act that yields a confirming awareness. To undertake that action, she must rationally take herself to know (or have learnt) some other facts. So, there will be a regress. Thus, *Proposal 3* fails.

Let's take stock. There is a single argumentative strategy that the Bhāṭṭa Mīmāṃsaka employs against the defender of the *Independent Check Thesis*. The Mīmāṃsaka assumes that performing an independent check on an awareness must involve either performing an evidence-gathering act that provides independent evidence for the truth of the relevant awareness, or undergoing an awareness that independently confirms the original awareness. If the defender of the *Independent Check Thesis* goes for the first option, she will face a dilemma: either she will have to reject the *Action-Knowledge Principle* (thereby making investigation into the epistemic status of awareness-events redundant) or accept a problematic sort of circularity or regress. If she goes for the second option, she will be forced to countenance a regress. In the next section, we will probe the strength of the Mīmāṃsaka's argumentative strategy, by considering a Buddhist response to the first of these problems.

31 NM$_P$ §3.3.3.3.3.2: 'Moreover, this awareness of practical efficacy doesn't arise for a person who doesn't undertake any action. In that case, if the practical undertaking is caused by a determination of knowledgehood, then—just as in our discussion of ascertaining knowledgehood from the awareness of the epistemic virtues of the causes—the room for a circularity-based objection will indeed remain intact. It has been said that, by contrast, if a person undertakes an action without ascertaining the knowledgehood of his awareness, then a later determination of knowledgehood—even when it arises—is simply futile just like the examination of the stars by someone who has already shaved' (*na cedam arthakriyājñānam apravṭttasya puṃsaḥ samudbhavati* | *tatra prāmāṇyāvadhāraṇapūrvikāyāṃ pravṛttau kāraṇaguṇaniśceyaprāmāṇyacarcāvad cakrakacodyaprasaras tadavastha eva* | *aniścitaprāmāṇyasya tu pravṛttau paścāt tannirṇayo bhavann api kṛtakṣaurasya nakṣatraparīkṣāvad aphala evety uktam* |)

6. A Buddhist Response

In relation to *Red Wall 1*, the Bhāṭṭa Mimamsaka argued that, if I rationally undertake an action in that situation on the assumption that the wall is red, I cannot be doing so without also rationally taking myself to know (or have learnt) that the wall is red. This was supported by the *Action-Knowledge Principle*. The motivation for the principle was just this: it is practically useful for us to investigate or determine whether an awareness is a knowledge-event because that information is relevant to our planning of future actions. If we can rely on a proposition that *p* in the course of planning our actions without taking ourselves to know (or have learnt) that *p*, then what would be the practical use of determining or investigating whether we know (or have learnt) that *p*? So, denying the *Action-Knowledge Principle* makes determining or investigating the epistemic status of our awareness-events practically futile.

However, this principle was partly motivated by the assumption that knowledgehood (when it comes to non-recollective awareness-events) simply boils down to accuracy. Some Buddhists, such as Dharmakīrti (seventh century CE), don't accept any straightforward accuracy condition on knowledge. Dharmakīrti offers a pragmatic conception of knowledge-events: in his *Detailed Commentary on Epistemology* (*Pramāṇavārttika*), he says: 'A *pramāṇa* [which here stands not only for the method of knowing, but also for the knowledge-event] is an awareness that isn't disconfirmed; the lack of disconfirmation is stable practical efficacy (*arthakriyāsthiti*).'[32] If knowledge is simply awareness that reliably leads to practical success, then the natural way to test whether an awareness is a knowledge-event is to check whether it leads to practical success. So, commentators of Dharmakīrti, such as Śākyabuddhi, advocate a version of *Proposal 3:* namely, that we can rationally determine that an awareness is a knowledge-event by checking if it is practically efficacious. These writers deny the *Action-Knowledge Principle*. They think that we can rationally undertake an action on the assumption that *p* without taking ourselves to know (or have learnt) that *p*, but that needn't make subsequent investigation into the epistemic status of the relevant awareness superfluous.

This response crucially depends on the distinction between practical undertakings of two kinds: *initial* (*ādya*) and *familiar* (*abhyasta*).[33] Imagine a farmer who wants to grow rice in his fields and has some rice-seeds. But he isn't in a position to rationally determine whether those seeds, when sown, are capable of giving rise to rice-sprouts. For example, he might worry that they are too dry. But he may

[32] PV II v. 1abc: *pramāṇam avisaṃvādi jñānam arthakriyāsthitiḥ | avisaṃvādanaṃ*...

[33] See, for example, Śākyabuddhi's *Notes on the Detailed Commentary on Epistemology* (*Pramāṇavārttikaṭīkā*) quoted in Steinkellner (1981, p. 290): 'Practical undertakings based on perception are of two kinds – initial and familiar.' (*dvividhā pratyakṣāśrayā pravṛttir ādyā abhyāsavatī ca* |)

take a few of them and sow them in a vessel of water. Once he sees that these seeds give rise to rice-sprouts, he may rationally conclude that the other seeds, in virtue of being of the same kind (*tajjatīya*), also have the same capacity. So, he may go ahead and sow all of them in his fields. The first undertaking is initial, while the latter is familiar. The Buddhist claims that the same is true of our investigations into the epistemic status of awareness-events. Even though an agent may not be in a position to rationally judge that a certain awareness is a knowledge-event, she may still undertake some relatively risk-free action on the basis of it. As a result, she may find out that it is a knowledge-event. But then, later, when an awareness of that kind arises again, she may—on the basis of the fact that it is an awareness *of that kind (tajjatīya)*—infer that it is a knowledge-event, and proceed to perform other (perhaps, more risky) actions on the basis of it. The first undertaking is initial, while the second is familiar. On this picture, determining the epistemic status of an awareness on the basis of the initial undertaking isn't useless: it helps us build up a track record for awareness-events of various kinds (by means of which we later identify awareness-events of the relevant kinds as knowledge-events).[34] This response is simple and powerful, and in fact came to influence Naiyāyikas like Vācaspati Miśra and Udayana.[35]

Jayanta's Bhāṭṭa opponent doesn't find this argument persuasive. Before we see why, it's worth noting that this argument doesn't avoid the regress-based objection that Kumārila raises for *Proposal 3*. The objection was simply that, if an awareness is to be confirmed by a distinct awareness of practical efficacy, it's unclear why we should treat the first awareness as a knowledge-event on the basis of the second, when the epistemic credentials of the latter are just as questionable as the former. Dharmakīrti's commentators, Devendrabuddhi and Śākyabuddhi, bite the bullet here: they point out that some awareness-events, especially the

[34] NM$_P$, §3.3.3.3.3.3: 'In response to that, this may be [said]. Practical undertakings are in fact of two kinds: initial and familiar. Of these, the first takes the form of sowing a few seeds for the sake of examining the capacity of the rice-seeds, etc. in a cup made of smooth clay that has been moistened by the water it contains. Having observed the unimpeded capacity of those [seeds] for producing sprouts in that case, the farmers sow those [seeds] in the fields without any doubt. So, this very practical undertaking is a familiar one. In the same manner, in this case too, some wise person—having initially commenced an activity simply on the basis of an awareness whose knowledgehood hasn't been examined—learns of its knowledgehood by means of his awareness of its results. Later, when an awareness of that kind arises again, he easily performs activities such as practical undertakings without suspecting any fault. So, [the determination of knowledgehood at a later time] is not entirely futile.' *(tatraitat syāt|dvividhā hi pravṛttiḥ—ādyā ca ābhyāsikī ca | tatrādyā yathāvinihitasalilāvasiktamasṛṇamṛdi śarāve śālyādibījaśaktiparīkṣaṇāya katipayabījakaṇāvāparūpā | tatas teṣām aṅkurakaraṇakauśalam avikalam avalokayantaḥ kīnāśā niḥśaṅkaṃ kedāreṣu tāni bījāny āvapantīti seyam ābhyāsikī pravṛttiḥ | evam ihāpi pratham aparīkṣitapramāṇabhāvād eva jñānāt kutaścit kaścid vipaścid api vyavahāraṃ ārabhya phalajñānena tasya prāmāṇyam avagacchan punas tathāvidhe bodhe jāte sati sukham eva pravṛttyādivyavahāram aśaṅkitakāluṣyaḥ kariṣyatīti na sarvātmanā vaiyarthyam iti |)*

[35] See Vācaspatimiśra's *Notes on the Import of the Detailed Commentary on Nyāya* (*Nyāyavārttikatātparyaṭīkā*) at NVTṬ 10.2–16 and Udayana's *Purification of the Import of the Detailed Commentary on Nyāya* (*Nyāyavārttikatātparyapariśuddhi*) at NVTP 34.8–36.7. For discussion of this Nyāya view, see Mohanty (1989), Matilal (1986), and Phillips (2012).

awareness of practical efficacy, are to be ascribed knowledgehood intrinsically, i.e., without any independent check.[36] But, as we have already said, this seems arbitrary without further explanation: if the confirming awareness about practical efficacy can be treated as a knowledge-event without any independent check, then why can't the original awareness also be ascribed the same epistemic status without an independent check?

Let us now return to the farmer example. According to Jayanta's Bhāṭṭa Mīmāṃsaka, there is a disanalogy between the farmer example and the case of determining whether an awareness is a knowledge-event. Why? The farmer infers that the other seeds can give rise to rice-sprouts precisely because they share certain physical features of the seeds that she sowed before and that gave rise to rice-sprouts. These physical features constitute the relevant property of *being-of-that-kind* (*tajjātīyatva*), on the basis of which the farmer infers that the other seeds also have the capacity of giving rise to rice-sprouts. Since these are perceptible features of rice-seeds, the farmer can rationally conclude that the other seeds have the relevant capacity. But the same inference isn't available in the case of awareness-events.[37]

What's the relevant property of *being-of-that-kind* that an awareness shares with other knowledge-events? Surely, it cannot be the mere nature of an awareness (*bodhasvarūpa*) (i.e., the property of being an awareness). Since that is shared by all awareness-events (both knowledge-events and errors), it cannot decisively indicate that an awareness is a knowledge-event. So, it has to be some stronger property that can help us distinguish knowledge-events of the relevant kind from other kinds of awareness. Whatever it might be, this property of being-of-that-kind-ness must be known by means of inference from some fact either (1) about the causes of the relevant awareness (e.g., from the fact that its causes are

[36] For discussion of Devendrabuddhi's and Śākyabuddhi's views, see Inami (1993). For Umbeka's reaction, see ŚVTṬ 65.12ff. For further discussion, see footnote 277 in Kataoka (2011, pt. 2).

[37] NM$_P$ §3.3.3.3.3.5: 'In response to this, the following is said. This example is disanalogous.

> In virtue of being of that kind, a seed of rice and so on comes to be apprehended [as a capable of producing rice-sprouts]. In that case, it is appropriate to undertake an action without doubt, since it is ascertained [to be so capable].
>
> Since the nature of an awareness doesn't vary [across different awareness-events], one should become aware of being-of-that-kind in an awareness-event either on the basis of its effect, or even on the basis of its cause, but not on the basis of its own nature.
>
> Since the causes are imperceptible, it cannot be apprehended by means of them. By contrast, it has been explained that there is no effect in the case of a person who doesn't undertake any action.
>
> Therefore, this isn't a way of refuting the objection about futility. And, if this is so, what sort of ascertainment of knowledgehood can arise from the awareness of practical efficacy?'

(*ucyate | viṣamo 'yaṃ dṛṣṭāntaḥ | tajjātīyatayā bījaṃ brīhyāder yāti veditum | tatra tanniścayād yuktaṃ nirviśaṅkaṃ pravartanam || jñāne tathāvidhatvaṃ tu bodharūpāviśeṣataḥ | kāryād vā kāraṇād vā 'pi jñātavyaṃ na svarūpataḥ || kāraṇānāṃ parokṣatvāt na taddvārā tadāgatiḥ | kāryaṃ tu nāpravṛttasya bhavatīty upavarṇitam || tasmād vaiyarthyacodyasya nāyaṃ parihṛtikramaḥ | evaṃ cārthakriyājñānāt kīdṛk prāmāṇyaniścayaḥ ||*)

non-defective), or (2) about its effects (e.g., from the fact that the awareness reliably leads to practical success).

Option (1) doesn't work. The causes of an awareness, such as the sense-faculties, may not always be perceptible. The only way we can determine that the causes of an awareness are non-defective is by means of an inference from its effects. This takes us to option (2): namely, that an awareness's being of the same kind as other knowledge-events must be inferred from its own effects. This, again, is subject to a regress worry. What are the effects from which we infer that an awareness is of the same kind as other knowledge-events? The most natural answer is that these are simply actions that the agent performs on the basis of the awareness. But, if an agent must perform some action on the basis of the relevant awareness (just as I do in *Red Wall 1*) in order to determine that it is of the same kind as other knowledge-events, then the Buddhist is in trouble. She wanted to argue that it's not pointless to determine the epistemic status of an awareness by means of an initial undertaking, because that puts us in a position to tell whether *other* awareness-events of the relevant kind are knowledge-events. And that is useful because, then, we can rely on that information for the purposes of familiar practical undertakings. However, if we have to perform an action in order to determine the epistemic status of our awareness-events on every occasion, this argument cannot succeed.

So, the Buddhist response fails.

7. The Default Knowledgehood Thesis

So far, the Bhāṭṭa Mīmāṃasakas' strategy has been to show that there is no independent check by running which we can rationally ascribe knowledge-events to ourselves. But the Naiyāyika or the Buddhist might point out that this Bhāṭṭa argument doesn't make the *Independent Check Thesis* any less plausible, since we have extremely good reasons for taking this thesis to be true. Suppose that I perceptually judge that there's a mug on my table. Since the causes of this judgement are non-defective, it is a knowledge-event. Let's say that I am also introspectively aware of my judgement. But, still, I may not be in a position to tell whether my judgement is a knowledge-event. Given that judgements can be both accurate and inaccurate, for all I know (independently of my judgement), my judgement may be inaccurate. So, I may rationally doubt whether my judgement is a knowledge-event. I can only rationally assuage this doubt by running an independent check. This supports the *Independent Check Thesis*.[38]

[38] NM$_P$ §3.4.1: '[The opponent:] But, at the time when an awareness is produced, the distinction between a knowledge-event and what isn't a knowledge-event isn't determined. For that reason, doubt arises by force. Mere determination is the effect of a knowledge-event. Moreover, that is a

The Bhāṭṭa responds as follows:

> It is true that a determination [i.e., a judgement] alone is the effect of a knowledge-event. But when that alone has been produced, it isn't apprehended as suffering from defects such as doubt, etc. Therefore, it attains default (*autsargika*) knowledgehood. The knower, who undertakes an action on the basis of the determination of an object, is caused to undertake that action only by a knowledge-event [from her perspective], not by doubt. Given that default knowledgehood is established in this manner, when in some case there is an exception (*apavāda*) [to that status], there is non-knowledgehood.[39]

The Bhāṭṭa seems to think the following: whenever a rational agent comes to determine the world to be a certain way, her determination or judgement has the default status of being a knowledge-event from her own perspective, unless it suffers from some fault such as doubt, etc. However, in a case where there is an exception to that status, the agent judges that the relevant judgement isn't a knowledge-event.

What constitutes an exception? The Bhāṭṭa explains:

> Moreover, in the case of non-knowledgehood, there must be an exception. Such exceptions are in fact of two kinds: rebutting awareness-events and awareness-events about defects in the causes [of the relevant awareness]. That has been stated by the author of the *Commentary* [i.e., Śabara] as follows: 'An incorrect awareness is simply that which has a defective cause and with respect to which there is an awareness that takes the form, 'This is false,' not anything else.' The author of the *Detailed Commentary* [i.e., Kumārila] has also said:
>
>> Therefore, the knowledgehood of an awareness is attained (*prāpta*) in virtue of its being an awareness. Due to an awareness of things being otherwise or of defects that originate from the causes, this is subject to an exception.

characteristic common to both accurate and inaccurate awareness-events. Furthermore, it is a well-known principle that the apprehension of a common characteristic is the cause of doubt. And, given this, without confirmation or disconfirmation by a distinct knowledge-event, how can there be a determination as to whether [an awareness] is a knowledge-event or something else? Therefore, both [knowledgehood and non-knowledgehood] are extrinsic.' (*nanu cotpattivelāyāṃ na viśeṣo 'vadhāryate | pramāṇetarayos, tena balād bhavati saṃśayaḥ || paricchittimātraṃ pramāṇakāryam|tac ca yathārthetarapramitisādhāraṇaṃ rūpam | sādhāraṇadharmagrahaṇaṃ ca saṃśayakāraṇam iti prasiddhaḥ panthāḥ|evaṃ sthite ca—pramāṇāntarasaṃvādavisaṃvādau vinā | katham pramāṇetaranirṇītir ataś ca parato dvayam ||*)

39 NMP §3.4.2: *satyaṃ paricchittir eva pramāṇakāryam | sā punar upajāyamānaiva na sandehādidūṣitatanur upalabhyate ity autsargikaṃ prāmāṇyam eva sā bhajate | arthaparicchedāc ca pravartamānaḥ pramātā pramāṇenaiva pravartito bhavati na saṃśayāt pravṛttaḥ | sthite caivam autsargike prāmāṇye yatra tasyāpavādaḥ kvacid bhavati tatrāprāmāṇyam ||*

> Amongst these [exceptions], a rebutting awareness arises—by way of refuting the earlier awareness-event—with respect to the same intentional object. So, in virtue of having the same intentional object, it is quite clearly a rebutter. In contrast, even though an awareness of defects in the causes [of the relevant awareness] has a distinct intentional object, it attains the status of a rebutter (*bādhaka*) in virtue of having the same effect [as a rebutting awareness].[40]

Let's unpack this.

When an agent undergoes either an awareness that rebuts her earlier awareness-event, or an awareness that points to a defect in the causal conditions that produced her original awareness, then the default status of her original awareness as a knowledge-event is defeated. Just to illustrate the point, imagine a case where I've been told by Alice that the wall in a room is red. I have no reason to doubt Alice, so I judge that the wall is red. I also immediately judge that I have learnt this on the basis of Alice's testimony. But, when I step into the room, I see that the wall is white. This perceptual awareness ascribes to the wall a colour which is incompatible with the colour ascribed to it by my earlier judgement. Since the two awareness-events ascribe incompatible properties to the same intentional object, the latter rebuts the former. So, I can no longer take myself to know (or have learnt) that the wall is red. Now, consider a different scenario. In this case, I learn on further investigation that Alice is a pathological liar. Here, I discover a defect in one of the causes of my original judgement, but this discovery doesn't straightforwardly rebut my judgement in virtue of ascribing an incompatible property to the same intentional object. However, this too should defeat my earlier attribution of a knowledge-event to myself.

These two kinds of awareness-events, as Jayanta's Bhāṭṭa correctly notes, are different. The content of the first directly conflicts with the content of my original awareness, while the content of the latter doesn't. To use contemporary terminology, the first is a *rebutting* awareness, while the second is an *undercutting* awareness.[41] Both, however, have the same effect, i.e., casting doubt on the

[40] NM$_P$ §3.4.3: *aprāmāṇye cāvaśyaṃbhāvy apavādaḥ | dvividha evāpavādaḥ bādhakapratyayaḥ kāraṇadoṣajñānaṃ ca | tad uktaṃ bhāṣyakṛtā 'yatra ca duṣṭaṃ karaṇam yatra ca mithyeti pratyayaḥ sa evāsamīcīnaḥ pratyayaḥ, nānyaḥ' iti | vārttikakāro 'py āha—*

> *tasmād bodhātmakatvena prāptā buddheḥ pramāṇatā |*
> *arthānyathātvahetūtthadoṣajñānād apodyate || iti |*

tatra bādhakajñānaṃ pūrvajñānopamardadvāreṇaiva tasmin viṣaye jāyata iti samānaviṣayatvāt spaṣṭam eva bādhakam | karaṇadoṣajñānaṃ tu bhinnaviṣayam api kāryaikyād bādhakatāṃ pratipadyate |

The quoted passage from Śabarasvāmin is from his commentary on *Mīmāṃsasūtra* 1.1.5 (ŚBh 34.3–4), while the verse is verse 53 from Kumārila's *Detailed Commentary in Verse* on *Mīmāṃsasūtra* 1.1.2.

[41] A piece of rebutting evidence against the claim that *p* defeats the evidential support for *p* by directly providing evidence for the claim that ~*p*. In contrast, a piece of undercutting evidence against the claim that *p* defeats the evidential support for *p* not by doing so, but rather by undermining the

accuracy of my original awareness-event. While the first kind of awareness directly conveys the falsehood or inaccuracy of my original awareness, the second intimates the presence of an epistemic defect, which makes awareness-events of this sort false or inaccurate. So, even the second kind of awareness-event could be called a *rebutter* in an extended sense of the term.[42]

What happens in a case where neither of these kinds of defeating awareness are present? Jayanta's Bhāṭṭa Mīmāṃsaka defends the following requirement: when an agent undergoes no rebutting or undercutting awareness corresponding to an awareness, she is *required* not to doubt that the awareness is a knowledge-event.

> In a case where neither of these exceptions (*apavāda*) are observed, the default knowledgehood exists without being subject to any exception. So, there is no reason for a doubt about falsehood. This is just as has been said [by Kumārila]:
>
> > When no awareness of any defect has been produced, one should not suspect that [the relevant awareness] is not a knowledge-event.
>
> That is to say:
>
> > When some doubt is produced here, it is simply apprehended by itself (*svasamvedya*): "Is that a tree-stump or person?" Who could deny it?
> >
> > When it is produced by force, it destroys all actions. Even if one were embracing one's wife, one would doubt whether it's one's mother.[43]

This gives us:

> *The Default Knowledgehood Thesis.* If an agent judges that *p*, then, in the absence of any rebutting or undercutting awareness corresponding to her judgement, she is required by rationality not to doubt that she has come to know (or learnt) that *p*.

support that some previous piece of evidence provided to the claim that *p*. In the framework that we are working with, there is no obvious notion of evidence other than the notion of a *pramāṇa*, i.e., a method of knowing. But we can still talk about rebutting or undercutting in terms of the changes in judgements that such rebutting or undercutting awareness-events bring about in minimally rational agents. For example, we can say that a rebutting awareness makes an agent give up her judgement by directly indicating that the content of that judgement is false, while an undercutting awareness makes an agent give up her judgement by directly indicating that the judgement arose from defective cases. For the distinction between rebutting and undercutting defeaters in contemporary epistemology, see Pollock (1986) and Kotzen (2019).

[42] NM_P §3.4.3.2.

[43] NM_P §3.4.3.3.1 *yatra punar idam apavādadvayam api na dṛśyate tatra tad autsargikaṃ prāmāṇyam anapoditam āsta iti na mithyātvāśaṅkāyāṃ nimittaṃ kiñcit | yathāha*

> *doṣajñāne tvanutpanne nāśaṅkyā niṣpramāṇatā iti ||*

tathā hi

> *kaścid utpanna eveha svasaṃvedyo 'sti saṃśayaḥ |*
> *sthāṇur vā puruṣo veti ko nāmāpahnuvīta tam ||*
> *haṭhād utpādyamānas tu hinasti sakalāḥ kriyāḥ |*
> *svabhāryāparirambhe 'pi bhaven mātari saṃśayaḥ ||*

The verse from Kumārila is verse 60cd in *The Detailed Commentary in Verse* on *Mīmāṃsāsūtra* 1.1.2.

Why is this plausible? The argument that Jayanta's Bhāṭṭa opponent sketches proceeds from the destructive nature of doubt. Here's how we can reconstruct it. Suppose the *Default Knowledgehood Thesis* is false. Then, even though an agent may judge that *p* and have no evidence against the claim that *p*, she may be rationally permitted to doubt that she knows that *p*. Given that the *Action-Knowledge Principle* is true, this means that this agent (if rational) cannot undertake any action on the basis of her judgement that *p*. But, given that independent checks cannot help us determine whether any of our awareness-events are knowledge-events, this means that the agent won't be able to rationally undertake any action on the basis of any assumption at all. That is how doubt destroys all actions. But, surely, an agent can rationally undertake actions. So, the *Default Knowledgehood Thesis* must be true.

No obvious problem of regress arises for the *Default Knowledgehood Thesis.* Notice what it doesn't say. It doesn't say that, if an agent judges that *p*, then, in the absence of any rebutting or undercutting awareness corresponding to her judgement, she is required by rationality *to judge* that she knows (or has learnt) that *p*. If it said this, then there would be a regress. For, then, in any scenario where an agent has judged that *p* and has no rebutting or undercutting evidence against the claim that *p*, she would be required to make infinitely many judgements: the judgement that she knows (or has learnt) that *p*, the judgement that she knows (or has learnt) that she knows (or has learnt) that *p*, and so on *ad infinitum.* Surely, agents with finite cognitive resources cannot make infinitely many such judgements. The *Default Knowledgehood Thesis* avoids this problem. Suppose an agent has judged that *p* and has become introspectively aware of her judgement, but has no undercutting or rebutting awareness corresponding to it. Here, the *Default Knowledgehood Thesis* predicts that, if the agent were to consider whether that judgement is a knowledge-event, then she couldn't rationally remain in doubt on that matter; she would be rationally required to judge that it is a knowledge-event. Obviously, she might never become introspectively aware of her judgement at all, and thus might never consider whether that judgement is a knowledge-event. But, then, since she also won't be in doubt about whether her judgment is a knowledge-event, she would be vacuously satisfying the rational requirement laid down by the *Default Knowledgehood Thesis.*

However, we might still wonder if a version of Kumārila's regress worry couldn't be raised against this view. Surely, it's undeniable that in some cases, when we come to rationally doubt whether we have learnt something (in light of some evidence), we do run an independent check to verify if it's true. Consider a variant of the *Red Wall* cases.

> *Red Wall 3.* I have two friends, Alice and Bob. Alice comes out of a room, and tells me that the wall in that room is red. I trust her, so I judge that the wall is red. But, then, Bob tells me that the wall is white but lit up with trick red lighting.

> Since I trust Bob too, I immediately judge that the wall is white but lit up with trick red lighting. But then, I realize that the two judgements conflict with each other. So, I can't take either of these judgements to be a knowledge-event.

How should I resolve the conflict? Suppose I go into the room and check if the wall is white and lit up with red light. There are (at least) two outcomes: either I will discover that the wall was genuinely red, or that it was white but lit up with trick red lighting. So, either my inquiry will yield an awareness that will confirm my first judgement, or an awareness which will confirm my second judgement. In either case, I can rationally judge that the judgement that gets confirmed is a knowledge-event. If, according to the Bhāṭṭas, such independent checks help us determine the epistemic status of our awareness-events, wouldn't the problem of regress also arise here?

The Bhāṭṭa response here is subtle. According to the Bhāṭṭas, knowledgehood is intrinsic, i.e., we can rationally judge an awareness to be a knowledge-event without relying on a method of knowing which is distinct from the method that gives rise to the awareness itself or an introspective awareness about it. However, non-knowledgehood is extrinsic: we cannot rationally judge that an awareness is *not* a knowledge-event without running an independent check. So, even though independent checks needn't (and in fact can't) provide evidence in favour of the status of any awareness as a knowledge-event, they can dispel our doubts about the epistemic status of awareness-events by helping us identify some of them as *not knowledge-events*. The point is explained as follows.

> Moreover, even in some case where a doubt is produced given the presence of some rebutting awareness, there is no regress due to the dependence on a third awareness. Furthermore, this doesn't undermine [the theory of] intrinsic knowledgehood. If a third awareness that confirms the first awareness arises, then the default knowledgehood of the first awareness simply remains intact. However, the third awareness dispels the doubt about the fictitious blemish [i.e., the epistemic defect] ascribed by the second awareness. But the knowledgehood of this first awareness doesn't obtain in virtue of its being confirmed by that third awareness. However, if the third awareness confirms the second awareness, then the first awareness lacks knowledgehood. And that is accepted simply to be extrinsic. But the knowledgehood of the second awareness doesn't obtain in virtue of its being confirmed by the third awareness. Rather, the activity of that third awareness consists in the mere resolution of the bad doubt that was raised. Further, it has been said [by Kumārila]:
>
> > In this way, after three or four awareness-events have arisen, no further awareness is required. And, then, one [of the two conflicting awareness-events] attains intrinsic knowledgehood.[44]

[44] NM$_P$ §3.4.3.3.2: *yatrāpi ca kvacid bādhakapratyaye saṃśayo jāyate tatrāpi tṛtīyajñānāpekṣaṇān nānavasthā | na ca tāvatā svataḥprāmāṇyahāniḥ | yatra prathamavijñānasaṃvādi tṛtīyajñāanam*

The thought is this. If an agent judges that *p*, then, from her perspective, absent defeating evidence, her judgement has the default status of being a knowledge-event. But when the agent undergoes an awareness that indicates that the original judgement was faulty, she can no longer judge that the original judgement was a knowledge-event, or that the second awareness is a knowledge-event. This is exactly what happens to me in *Red Wall 3*. An agent who finds herself in this predicament may run an independent check. Even though the independent check cannot directly show that any of the awareness-events are knowledge-events, it can provide evidence that one of the awareness-events is not a knowledge-event. This can help the agent dispel her doubts about the epistemic credentials of the relevant awareness-events.

As the last part of the passage shows, the regress worry that Kumārila raised against the defender of the *Independent Check Thesis* doesn't arise here. When there are conflicting awareness-events, an agent might run an independent check to determine which of her awareness-events is not a knowledge-event. But this process needn't go beyond three or four levels of higher-order awareness. This is presumably because, typically, the third (or the fourth) awareness will rebut (or undercut) one of the earlier conflicting awareness-events. So, when the agent judges that that conflicting awareness is not a knowledge-event, the default knowledgehood of the other conflicting awareness will be restored. Thus, the regress will stop. This completes the Bhāṭṭa defence of the *Default Knowledgehood Thesis.*

8. Conclusion

Let's sum up. The Bhāṭṭa arguments against the *Independent Check Thesis* reveal a tension between the *Action-Knowledge Principle* and the *Independent Check Thesis.* Suppose an agent judges or believes that *p.* If we accept the *Action-Knowledge Principle,* then it is possible for her to rationally undertake an action on the basis of that belief or judgement only if she antecedently rationally judges that she has come to know (or has learnt) that *p.* But, if the *Independent Check Thesis* is true, she can arrive at such a judgement only by relying on a source of information that provides her independent evidence about the truth or reliability of her belief or judgement that *p.* In order to gain access to such a source, the agent

utpadyate tatra prathamasya prāmāṇyam autsargikaṃ sthitam eva | *dvitīyavijñānāropitālīkakāluṣyaśaṅkānirākaraṇaṃ tv asya tṛtīyena kriyate na tv asya saṃvādāt prāmāṇyam* | *yadi tu dvitīyajñanasaṃvādi tṛtīyaṃ jñānaṃ tadā prathamasyāprāmāṇyam* | *tac ca parata iṣṭam eva* | *dvitīyasya tu jñānasya na tṛtīyasaṃvādakṛtaṃ prāmāṇyam, api tu kalpyamanakuśaṅkāśamanamātre tasya vyāpāraḥ* | *uktaṃ ca*

> *evaṃ tricaturajñānajanmano nādhikā matiḥ* |
> *prārthyate tāvataivaikaṃ svataḥprāmāṇyam aśnute* || *iti* |

The verse from Kumārila is verse 61 in *The Detailed Commentary in Verse* on *Mīmāṃsā sūtra* 1.1.2.

will (at least sometimes) have to perform an evidence-gathering act. Presumably, she will undertake such an act on the basis of some assumption that *q*. But, if the *Action-Knowledge Principle* is true, she can only rationally undertake an action on the assumption that *q* if she antecedently rationally judges that she knows (or has learnt) that *q*. Thus, there will be a regress.

The *Action-Knowledge Principle* also lends support to a positive proposal that Jayanta ascribes to his Bhāṭṭa opponents: namely, the *Default Knowledgehood Thesis*, roughly the thesis that, when an agent believes or judges that *p* and has no defeating evidence against the claim that *p*, she is rationally required not to doubt that she knows (or has learnt) that *p*. If the *Default Knowledgehood Thesis* were false, then—even when an agent has formed the belief or judged that *p* and doesn't have any evidence against the claim that *p*—she could be rationally permitted to be in doubt about whether she knows (or has learnt) that *p*. But, if the *Action-Knowledge Principle* is true, then such doubt would make it impossible for the agent to rationally undertake any action on the assumption that *p*. If the Bhāṭṭas are right in thinking that no independent check can decisively show that we know (or have learnt) something, then such doubt can rationally arise for any of our beliefs or judgements, and can therefore make it impossible for us to rationally undertake any action at all. But, surely, we don't want that. So, the *Default Knowledgehood Thesis* must be true.

Given the background conception of knowledge-events that Jayanta and his Bhāṭṭa opponent are working with, the *Action-Knowledge Principle* does look quite plausible. On this view, a non-recollective awareness is a knowledge-event just in case it's accurate. So, if an agent cannot rationally judge an awareness of hers to be a knowledge-event, she cannot rationally take it to be accurate. But if an agent cannot rationally take an awareness to be accurate, she cannot rationally ignore the possibility that it might be false. So, plausibly, it cannot be rational for her to rely on its content for the purposes of practical reasoning under such circumstances. Thus, the Bhāṭṭas—it seems—have articulated a powerful challenge to the *Independent Check Thesis*.[45]

References

Primary Texts and Abbreviations

NB *Gautamīyanyāyadarśana with the Bhāṣya of Vātsyāyana*. Edited by Anantalal Thakur. New Delhi: Indian Council of Philosophical Research, 1997.

NK *The Nyāyakusumāñjali of Śrī Udayanācārya with Four Commentaries: The Bodhinī, Prakāśa, Prakāśikā (Jalada) and Makaranda by Varadarāja,*

[45] I am grateful to Elisa Freschi and Daniel Greco for helpful comments on earlier versions of this paper.

Varddhamānopādhyāya, Mecha Thakkura and Rucidattopādhyāya and with Notes by Śrī Dharmadatta (Bachchā Jhā). Edited by Padmaprasāda Upādhyāya and Dhundhirāja Śāstri. Benares: Chowkhamba Sanskrit Series, 1957.

NM I *Nyāyamañjarī: Sampādakagrathitanyāyasaurabhākhyaṭippaṇīsamanvitā*. Vol. I. Edited by K.S. Varadacharya. Mysore: Oriental Research Institute, 1969.

NM_P A Critical Edition of the *Prāmāṇya* Section of Bhaṭṭa Jayanta's *Nyāyamañjarī*. Edited by Kei Kataoka. *The Memoirs of Institute for Advanced Studies on* Asia 169 (2016), 562(1)–503(60).

NRK Pārthasārathimiśra's *Nyāyaratnākara* in *Ślokavārttikam Kumārilabhaṭṭapādaviracitaṃ Pārthasārathimiśraviracitayā Nyāyaratnākaravyākhyayā Sanātham*. Edited by Dwarikadas Sastri. Varanasi: Tara Publications, 1978.

NRM *Nyāyaratnamālā of Pārthasārathimiśra: With the Commentary of Rāmānujācārya, Entitled the Nayakaratna*. Critically edited with an introduction and indices, by K.S. Rāmaswami Śāstrī Śiromaṇi. Baroda: Oriental Institute, 1937.

NV *Nyāyabhāṣyavārttika of Bhāravdāja Uddyotakara*. Edited by Anantalal Thakur. New Delhi: Indian Council of Philosophical Research, 1997.

NVTṬ *Nyāyavārttikatātparyaṭīkā of Vācaspatimiśra*. Edited by Anantalal Thakur. New Delhi: Indian Council of Philosophical Research, 1996.

NVTP *Nyāyavārttikatātparyapariśuddhiḥ*. Edited by Anantalal Thakur. New Delhi: Indian Council of Philosophical Research, 1996.

PP *Prakaraṇapañcikā of Śālikanāthamiśra with Nyāyasiddhi of Jaipuri Nārāyaṇabhaṭṭa*. Edited by A. Subrahmaṇya Śāstrī. Varanasi: Banaras Hindu University, 1961.

PV *Pramāṇavārttikakārikā* (Sanskrit and Tibetan). Edited by Y. Miyasaka. *Acta Indologica* 2, (1971/72), 1–206.

RNA *Ratnakīrtinibandhāvaliḥ*. Edited by Anantalal Thakur. Patna: K.P. Jaiswal Research Institute, 1975.

ŚBh Śabarasvāmin's *Bhāṣya* in *Śrīmajjaiminipranīte Mīmāṃsādarśane Āditaḥ Ārabhya Dvitīyādhyāyaprathamapādāntaḥ Prathamo Bhāgaḥ*. Edited by Vināyaka Gaṇeśa Āpate. Pune: Ānandāśramamudraṇālaya, 1929.

ŚVK *The Mīmāṃsāślokavārttika of Kumārilabhaṭṭa: With the Commentary Kāśika of Sucaritamiśra*. Parts I and II. Edited by K. Sāmbaśivaśāstri. Trivandrum: CBH Publications, 1990.

ŚVTṬ *Ślokavārtikavyākhyā (Tātparyaṭīkā) of Bhaṭṭombeka*. Edited by S.K. Ramanatha Sastri. Madras: University of Madras, 1940.

Viṃ *Viṃśikāvṛtti* in *Seven Works of Vasubandhu: The Buddhist Psychological Doctor*. Edited and translated by Stefan Anacker. Delhi: Motilal Banarsidass, 1994.

Translations and Secondary Literature

Alston, William P. 1980. Level-Confusions in Epistemology. *Midwest Studies in Philosophy*, 5(1): 135–50.

Arnold, Daniel. 2008. *Buddhists, Brahmins, and Belief: Epistemology in South Asian Philosophy of Religion*. New York: Columbia University Press.

Byrne, Alex. 2005. Introspection. *Philosophical Topics*, 33(1): 79–104.

Byrne, Alex. 2018. *Transparency and Self-Knowledge.* Oxford: Oxford University Press.

Das, Nilanjan, and Bernhard Salow. 2018. Transparency and the KK Principle. *Noûs,* 52(1): 3–23.

Dorst, Kevin. 2019. Abominable KK Failures. *Mind,* 128 (512): 1227–59.

Dretske, Fred. 1994. Introspection. *Proceedings of the Aristotelian Society,* 94: 263–78.

Evans, Gareth. 1982. *Varieties of Reference.* Oxford: Clarendon Press.

Feldman, Richard. 1981. Fallibilism and knowing that one knows. *Philosophical Review,* 90(2): 266–82.

Fernandez, Jordi. 2013. *Transparent Minds: A Study of Self-Knowledge.* Oxford: Oxford University Press.

Freschi, Elisa, and Alessandro Graheli. 2005. Bhāṭṭamīmāṃsā and Nyāya on Veda and Tradition. In Federico Squarcini (Ed.) *Boundaries, Dynamics and Construction of Traditions in South Asia.* New Delhi: Munshiram Manoharlal.

Gallois, André. 1996. *The World Without, the Mind Within: An Essay on First-Person Authority.* Cambridge: Cambridge University Press.

Ganeri, Jonardon. 2007. *The Concealed Art of the Soul: Theories of Self and Practices of Truth in Indian Ethics and Epistemology.* Oxford: Oxford University Press.

Greco, Daniel. 2014. Could KK Be OK? *Journal of Philosophy,* 111(4): 169–97.

Hintikka, Jaakko. 1962. *Knowledge and Belief: An Introduction to the Logic of the Two Notions.* Ithaca: Cornell University Press.

Immerman, Daniel. 2018. Kumārila and Knows-Knows. *Philosophy East and West,* 68(2): 408–22.

Inami, Masahiro. 1993. Bukkyō ronrigaku no shinriron: Devendrabuddhi to Śākyabuddhi. In Egaku Maeda (Ed.) *Watanabe Fumimaro Hakushi Tsuitō kinen Ronshū. Genshi Bukkyō to Daijō Bukkyō Ge.* Kyoto: Nagata Bunshodo.

Kataoka, Kei. 2003. The Mīmāṃsā Definition of '*Pramāṇa*' as a Source of New Information. *Journal of Indian Philosophy,* 31(1/3): 89–103.

Kataoka, Kei. 2011. *Kumārila on Truth, Omniscience, and Killing. Parts 1 and 2.* Wien: Osterreichischen Akademie der Wissenschaften.

Keating, Malcolm. Forthcoming. Kumārila Bhaṭṭa and Pārthasārathi Miśra on First- and Higher-Order Knowing. *Philosophy East and West.*

Kotzen, Matthew. 2019. A Formal Account of Epistemic Defeat. In Branden Fitelson, Rodrigo Borges, and Cherie Braden (Eds.), *Themes from Klein.* Springer.

Matilal, Bimal Krishna. 1986. *Perception: An Essay on Classical Indian Theories of Knowledge.* Oxford: Clarendon Press.

McCrea, Lawrence. 2015. Justification, Credibility and Truth: Sucaritamiśra on Kumārila's Intrinsic Validity. *Wiener Zeitschrift Für Die Kunde Südasiens/Vienna Journal of South Asian Studies,* 56/57: 99–116.

Mohanty, Jitendra Nath. 1989. *Gaṅgeśa's Theory of Truth: Containing the Text of Gaṅgeśa's Prāmāṇya (jñapti) Vāda with an English Translation, Explanatory Notes, and an Introductory Essay*. Delhi: Motilal Banarsidass.

Moran, Richard A. 2001. *Authority and Estrangement: An Essay on Self-Knowledge*. Princeton, NJ: Princeton University Press.

Phillips, Stephen. 2012. *Epistemology in Classical India*. London: Routledge.

Pollock, John. 1986. *Contemporary Theories of Knowledge*. Savage, MD: Rowman and Littlefield.

Stalnaker, Robert. 2015. Luminosity and the KK thesis. In Sanford Goldberg (Ed.), *Externalism, Self-Knowledge, and Skepticism: New Essays*. Cambridge: Cambridge University Press.

Steinkellner, Ernst. 1981. Philological Remarks on Śākyamati's *Pramānavārttikatikā*. In K. Bruhn and A. Wezler (Eds.) *Studien zum Jinismus und Buddhismus* (pp. 283–95). Wiesbaden 1981.

Taber, John. 1992. What Did Kumārila Bhaṭṭa Mean by *Svataḥ Prāmāṇya*? *Journal of the American Oriental Society*, 112(2): 204–21.

Williamson, Timothy. 2000. *Knowledge and its Limits*. Oxford: Oxford University Press.

3
Content-Focused Epistemic Injustice

Robin Dembroff and Dennis Whitcomb

1. Introduction

HIV posed an enormous threat to public health in the United States in the 1980s and early 1990s, taking tens of thousands of lives. Yet research into its treatment proceeded at a glacially slow pace, and not by accident. The Reagan Administration repeatedly undercut efforts to combat HIV, rejecting clear testimony from numerous public health experts that HIV was an alarming threat that required immediate action. It even flatly refused to approve Congress funding that was eventually allocated for HIV research, brushing off the disease as if "it was measles and it would go away."[1] Commenting on the matter, Don Francis (an official at the Center for Disease Control) testified to Congress in 1987 that:

> Much of the HIV/AIDS epidemic was and continues to be preventable. But because of active obstruction of logical policy, active resistance to essential funding, and active interference with scientifically designed programs, the executive branch of this country has caused untold hardship, misery, and expense to the American public.[2]

While one might wonder why anyone would reject expert testimony about a quickly spreading disease, Reagan's officials did not hide their motivations. Referring to HIV as "the gay disease," they overtly construed support for prevention research as support for the gay community.[3] This construal was the reason, or at least a primary reason, why they rejected expert testimony that HIV research was needed in order to protect public health.

By rejecting this testimony, we think that officials in Reagan's administration committed an epistemic injustice. But this rejection does not fall under either of the two categories of epistemic injustice most commonly discussed: testimonial

[1] Rimmerman (2001: 88). See also Faderman (2015). It took acts of civil disobedience and activism for this research to receive adequate attention and funding.

[2] Rimmerman (2001: 89).

[3] Green (2011). Green notes that during a congressional hearing on HIV, "one Republican, Rep. Bill Dannemeyer of California, delivered a speech on the House floor titled 'What Homosexuals Do' and read graphic descriptions of sexual acts into the Congressional Record."

Robin Dembroff and Dennis Whitcomb, *Content-Focused Epistemic Injustice* In: *Oxford Studies in Epistemology, Volume 7.* Edited by: Tamar Szabó Gendler, John Hawthorne, and Julianne Chung, Oxford University Press. © Robin Dembroff and Dennis Whitcomb 2023. DOI: 10.1093/oso/9780192868978.003.0003

injustice and hermeneutical injustice. In what has become the canonical (though challenged) explication of these notions, Miranda Fricker writes that, "Testimonial injustice occurs when prejudice [regarding a speaker's identity] causes a hearer to give a deflated level of credibility to a speaker's word; hermeneutical injustice occurs at a prior stage, when a gap in collective interpretive resources puts someone at an unfair disadvantage when it comes to making sense of their social experiences."[4] For example, the first occurs when a police officer refuses to believe someone because they are Black, and the second occurs when someone experiences sexual harassment but cannot articulate this experience because they lack a concept of sexual harassment.

The Reagan administration's rejection of expert HIV-related testimony belongs in neither of these categories. The speakers in question were, by and large, heterosexual white men in government and the sciences, making it extremely unlikely that testimonial injustice (in Fricker's sense) was occurring. And these speakers did not lack any concept critical to expressing their testimony, meaning that no hermeneutical injustice was occurring. We think that the administration's rejection of expert testimony is best understood as what we will call content-focused injustice or 'CFI': epistemic injustice focused not on the identity of a given speaker, but rather on the things that speaker communicates.

That, of course, is a preliminary and unspecific way to put it. We'll attempt to add more detail, and thus illuminate the phenomenon at hand. The first step will be to describe several actual cases of the phenomenon in addition to the HIV case. We'll then theorize about these cases by offering up a general model that taxonomizes them (section 2). With that much theorizing on the table, we'll explain why CFI is an epistemic injustice (section 3), and we'll explore its relationships to other forms of epistemic injustice (section 4).

A few clarifying remarks before diving into the details. First, we are by no means the first to discuss the phenomenon we call 'CFI': other scholars, and especially Black feminist and Indigenous scholars, have discussed many instances of CFI (although not under that label), as well as its effects.[5] What we hope to bring to these discussions is a general framework within which to situate these many instantiations of CFI. Second, our framework includes a number of sufficient conditions for CFI, all of which feature prejudice and, in particular, prejudice against structurally oppressed groups—that is, groups that are "systematically and unfairly disadvantaged within a social structure."[6] Prejudice against non-oppressed groups certainly exists. Perhaps it can even yield cases of a non-systematic sort of CFI. But such cases would not fall under the sufficient

[4] Fricker (2007: 1).
[5] See, e.g., The Combahee River Collective (1979), Rich (1980), Lugones (1987, 2006), and Hill Collins (1991).
[6] Haslanger (2004: 98).

conditions we offer. This is because we think it is centrally important to highlight cases that exist within and perpetuate contexts of oppression. This brings us to our third and final clarifying remark: our comments throughout apply only to the central cases of CFI, the cases that—we will argue—collectively control and preempt knowledge about oppressed groups.

2. Varieties of Content-Focused Injustice

This section delineates, illustrates, and offers up sufficient conditions for some of CFI's common manifestations.[7]

2.1 Reactive Content-Focused Injustice

We start with Reactive CFI, which features people's reactions to assertions. Let's consider a few examples. In Oscar Wilde's classic *The Picture of Dorian Gray*, Dorian Gray becomes smitten with a young actress. Speaking about her to his friend, Lord Harry Wotton, the following exchange occurs:

> "Who are you in love with?" asked Lord Henry…
> "Her name is Sibyl Vane."
> "Never heard of her."
> "No one has. People will some day, however. She is a genius."
> "My dear boy, no woman is a genius. Women are a decorative sex. They never have anything to say, but they say it charmingly. Women represent the triumph of matter over mind."[8]

Here, Dorian attempts to communicate some information about Sibyl: she is a genius. Henry prejudicially rejects Dorian's assertion. However—and this distinguishes the case from the sorts of cases Fricker and others have focused on in their discussions of testimonial injustice—he does not reject it because of any prejudice against *the speaker*, Dorian. Rather, he rejects it because of his prejudice involving its content, and more exactly because of his prejudice against a group that Sibyl belongs to—namely, women.[9] Because Henry prejudicially believes women to be

[7] For related work developed contemporaneously with but independently of ours, see Davis (2021), which builds a concept of "Content-based testimonial injustice" and applies it to professional philosophy. While Davis' content-based testimonial injustice is similar to CFI, there are important differences. Our papers are usefully read in tandem.

[8] Wilde (1908: 65).

[9] Though the 'decorative' description reveals that, more specifically, the group in question is white women.

incapable of being geniuses, he rejects Dorian's (a man's) assertion that a woman is a genius.

This form of injustice is not restricted to the fictional worlds of literature. Consider the conservative evangelical response to Alfred Kinsey's pathbreaking 1953 book *Sexual Behavior in the Human Female*. This book revealed that 50% of American females reported having sex before marriage; within this group, 69% of those who were still unmarried reported having no regret about their premarital experiences, and 77% of those who *were* married reported the same.[10] Conservative religious figures reacted to this book far more ferociously than they had reacted to Kinsey's earlier book, *Sexual Behavior in the Human Male*, which had revealed similar data about American males. (Shocking, we know.) In an interpretation we find plausible, historian Marie Griffith writes that:

> [Kinsey's book had] a graphic focus on the sexual activity of women and girls.... the male volume had already proclaimed that men experienced about half their orgasms in situations that most Americans reputedly still reckoned sinful, unlawful, or otherwise objectionable. But when Kinsey claimed to find much the same picture for women, his work threatened to upend... gendered sexual roles and expectations... In short, gender figured deeply in the explosive reactions among religious conservatives to Kinsey's publications.[11]

Such reactions came from (among others) the popular evangelist Billy Graham, who rejected the claim that 'seven out of ten women who had premarital affairs had no regrets.' Calling this claim 'lopsided and unscientific,' he assured his listeners that it did not accurately describe the 'born-again Christian women of this country' who 'thank God... still know how to blush.'[12]

Why did Graham reject Kinsey's claims? One likely answer is that he harbored prejudicial attitudes about women, attitudes construing women as (among other things) sexually passive and so not prone to do the things Kinsey described. Notice, though, that Kinsey was not a member of the group at which the operative prejudices were directed; he was not a woman. If this explanation is correct, it remains true that Kinsey's testimony was *not* rejected due to prejudice about the group he was *a member of*. Rather, it was rejected due to prejudice about the group he was talking about. His treatment therefore amounts to a real-life case of Reactive CFI.

For another case, recall the HIV case. In that case, officials in Reagan's administration rejected speakers' testimony that HIV threatened public health. In this case, the testimony was not about the gay community, or even about particular gay persons; it was about a quickly spreading disease. Nonetheless, the

[10] Griffith (2008: 365). [11] Griffith (2008: 365). [12] Griffith (2008: 366).

association between this disease and the gay community triggered officials' anti-gay prejudice, resulting in their rejection of expert testimony.

These cases of Reactive CFI suggest the following sufficient condition:

> A person or group has committed a reactive content-focused injustice if they reject a speaker's assertion at least in part because of their prejudice involving the assertion's content.

Notice that this condition only concerns rejections of assertions. This is purely for simplicity. We think (but won't argue here) that reactive CFI also occurs in cases of *accepting* or *ignoring* assertions. It also occurs in cases of reacting to speech acts other than assertions (questions for instance), and to items other than speech acts (concepts or physical evidence or as-yet-unasserted theories for instance).[13] As for what 'assertions' are, we think of them as particular (token) speech acts. The contents of assertions are the things people communicate by making those assertions (i.e., propositions).[14]

Also notice that the foregoing condition leaves the word 'involving' open-ended. This is intentional. There are at least two importantly different ways that prejudice can 'involve' the contents of assertions. On the one hand, it can be directed at a group (or a member of a group) the assertion *is about*, as it was in the Kinsey case. On the other hand, it can be directed at a group (or member of a group) the hearer *associates with* the things the assertion is about, as it was in the HIV case.

2.2 Preemptive Content-Focused Injustice

Whereas Reactive CFI features reactions to assertions, Preemptive CFI features preemptions of assertions, as well as other ways of transmitting knowledge about oppressed groups. These preemptions occur when an agent prevents either themself or others from encountering this knowledge, and does so on the basis of prejudice. Let's again begin with concrete examples.

One case of Preemptive CFI occurred when, in the 1950s at Oxford, the influential historian Keith Thomas offered a series of lectures on women's history. Students voted against these lectures with their feet: only about a half dozen showed up to them, whereas several hundred showed up to the lectures Thomas

[13] See Wanderer (2012) on ignoring, Hookway (2010) on questions, Mills (2007) on racist concepts, and Anderson (2017: section 5) on prejudicial reactions to physical evidence.

[14] As we use these terms, the contents of assertions are not *what we explicitly say* by making those assertions. Rather, they are *what we communicate* by making those assertions. Not everything communicated always is explicitly said, and not everything explicitly said always is communicated.

offered shortly afterwards on Aristotle, Hobbes, and Rousseau.[15] We take it as a working hypothesis that, in at least some cases, these students declined to attend Thomas' lectures at least partly because they prejudicially believed that women's history was unimportant. Those students committed an act of preemptive CFI—an act through which they prejudicially prevented *themselves* from encountering knowledge about an oppressed group.

In other cases agents preempt, not *their own*, but a third party's exposure to knowledge about an oppressed group. This preemption can be broad, aimed to prevent the party's exposure in every or nearly every context, or may be narrow, aimed to prevent a party's exposure within a particular context or a small range of contexts. For a broad case consider first the Russian 'gay propaganda' law, which criminalizes

> the distribution of information aimed at forming non-traditional sexual orientations, the attraction of non-traditional sexual relations, distorted conceptions of the social equality of traditional and non-traditional sexual relations among minors, or imposing information on non-traditional sexual relations which evoke interest in these kinds of relations... [including actions] which are committed with the employment of the media and/or information and telecommunications networks (including Internet sites).... [or] by foreign citizens or stateless persons.[16]

In effect, this law is aimed to prevent minors from acquiring any knowledge about LGBTQ persons and relationships in any context. For a contrasting narrower case, consider a South Carolina law regarding sexual health education classes in public schools:

> The program of instruction provided for in this section may not include a discussion of alternate sexual lifestyles from heterosexual relationships including, but not limited to, homosexual relationships except in the context of instruction concerning sexually transmitted diseases.[17]

These laws differ in scope. While the Russian law effectively applies in all contexts, the South Carolina law applies only in the context of the sexual health education classroom.

Preemptive CFI, like Reactive CFI, can feature prejudice that involves content in two importantly different ways. As before, the prejudice at work can be directed

[15] Thomas (1993), and personal communication.

[16] Russian Federal Law #135-FZ. In Decker & Wilson (2013).

[17] S.C. Stat. 59-32-30(5).

at the groups (or group members) the relevant claims are about, or at the groups (or group members) the hearer associates with the things the claims are about.[18]

These cases of Preemptive CFI suggest the following sufficient condition:

> A person or group has committed a preemptive content-focused injustice if they *prevent themself or others from encountering* a speaker's assertion (in a context) at least in part because of theirs prejudice involving the assertion's content.[19, 20]

3. What Makes CFI an Epistemic Injustice?

3.1 CFI and Malignant Misrecognition

Return to our HIV case, where officials rejected scientists' testimony on the basis of anti-gay prejudice. There is room to doubt whether this case features epistemic injustice. After all, the people whose assertions are rejected are not themselves targets of prejudice, and the people who are targets of prejudice (gay men) may not seem to be victims of any particularly *epistemic* harms. Rather, one might think, they only are harmed in more obvious, material ways as a result of lawmakers' rejection of scientific testimony. Where, then, is the epistemic injustice?

The normative terrain here is complex. Close examination of it reveals ways in which, when CFI occurs, the targets of prejudice *are* targets of epistemic harms. Before bringing those harms out, we should note that much of the literature on epistemic injustice has focused on what might be called 'deflationary' and 'hermeneutical' epistemic injustices. Deflationary epistemic injustices occur when a speaker's credibility is deflated due to their social identity or identities, paradigmatically in cases of testimonial injustice. Hermeneutical epistemic injustices, by

[18] While the cases of Keith Thomas and Russia and South Carolina provide examples the former sort, the HIV case provides an example of the latter sort. In that case, not only did the Reagan administration commit Reactive CFI by rejecting scientists' testimony regarding AIDS, they also committed Preemptive CFI. By refusing to direct funding to this research, they effectively prevented persons such as scientists in government-funded labs and public health workers from exposure to new information about AIDS. Moreover, they did this not only because this information was in part gay persons, but also because information about AIDS was, to them, *associated* with gay persons. This cases shows that Preemptive and Reactive CFI are not mutually exclusive: they can occur simultaneously.

[19] Preemptive CFI is similar to what Pohlhaus (2012) calls "willful hermeneutical ignorance." However, there are multiple important differences. For one, willful hermeneutical ignorance, on Pohlhaus's account, is always self-directed, while preemptive CFI includes other-directed cases. In addition, Pohlhaus focuses on cases in which agents refuse to use a marginalized group's epistemic resources, rendering that group's assertions unintelligible or twisted in meaning. This is not a feature of preemptive CFI, which often occurs while the hearer knows full well what the speaker is trying to communicate.

[20] We take it that 'white ignorance' (see e.g. Mills (2007) and Medina (2012)) often features preemptive CFI. See section 3.2.

contrast, occur when someone is—to quote Fricker—put at an "unfair disadvantage" with respect to understanding their social experience.[21]

Acts of CFI often cause or sustain other things that constitute deflationary or hermeneutical injustices. These causal relationships are undeniably important (see section 4). But we do not think acts of CFI *always* cause or sustain those kinds of injustices. Moreover, we think CFI is an epistemic injustice independently of whether it causes or sustains deflationary or hermeneutical injustices.[22] This is because systemic rejection and preemption of knowledge about marginalized groups is a form of *malignant misrecognition* that is itself a form of epistemic injustice.[23]

We take the notion of misrecognition from political philosophy, where it has been discussed in a variety of ways. According to one important tradition, recognition is a positive acknowledgement of one's status as free and equal; and misrecognition—that is, the lack this acknowledgement—is bad due to its *psychological effects*. These effects consist in distorted and devalued relationships to oneself via which, in some cases, one does not even recognize one's own status as a free and equal person. This way of thinking about misrecognition has been used, for instance, to describe psychological harms suffered by enslaved persons as well as by Indigenous persons oppressed under colonial rule.[24]

These psychological harms are real and important, sometimes are properly "epistemic," and sometimes are the result of CFI. However, we locate the key epistemic-injustice-relevant feature of misrecognition a step back, in the distribution and accessibility of relevant, accurate, and sufficient knowledge about social groups and their members. Misrecognition, we think, occurs when knowledge or belief about groups is systematically and unfairly distorted, rejected, or unavailable. This understanding of misrecognition is broad: in this broad sense, all or nearly all social groups—including dominant groups—face some degree of misrecognition. In some cases, in fact, misrecognition of dominant groups functions to *sustain* their social power, as when the history of white supremacy is erased, ignored, or manipulated.

Misrecognition of a group, then, is not enough to show that the group in question suffers an epistemic injustice. But with this broad understanding of

[21] Of course, many authors have complicated Fricker's picture of hermeneutical injustice, e.g. Pohlhaus (2012) and Medina (2012).

[22] In thinking this, we diverge from José Medina (2018), who locates the main injustice of cases that we would consider cases of CFI in their causal contributions to testimonial and hermeneutical injustice. See Medina (2018: 2): "[C]ertain dysfunctional patterns of recognition result in pathologies of public discourse that undermine the intelligibility and credibility of marginalized groups." On our view, CFI is an epistemic injustice even when it doesn't cause or sustain deflationary or hermeneutical injustices.

[23] For other approaches that connect epistemic injustice to misrecognition, see Special Issue Vol 4 No 4 (2018) of *Feminist Philosophy Quarterly*: "Epistemic Injustice and Recognition Theory" (eds Paul Giladi and Nicola McMillan), and the references therein.

[24] Helpful work on this tradition includes Taylor (1994), which traces it from contemporary identity politics back through Fanon to Hegel and in some ways Rousseau; Cudd (2006), which argues that it does not yield an adequate theory of oppression; and Congdon (2018), which focuses on its current standard-bearer Axel Honneth.

misrecognition in place, we follow Nancy Fraser in holding that social justice requires that people and groups have fair access to "parity of participation," or conditions in which they interact as peers on equal footing.[25] Misrecognition, she argues, can undermine this access. It happens to an individual or group when "institutionalized patterns of interpretation and evaluation unjustly deny them . . . equal respect and/or equal opportunity for achieving social esteem."[26]

Misrecognition that has these effects is malignant. Patterns of malignant misrecognition feature numerous phenomena ranging from anti-sodomy laws to demeaning stereotypical depictions of a racial group in the media. Importantly for our purposes, though, the core feature of malignant misrecognition is that it either burdens persons with "excessive ascribed 'difference' from others" or it unfairly fails to "acknowledge their distinctiveness."[27] That is, malignant misrecognition functions to unfairly diminish a group's access to participatory parity through either *error* characterizing them as more different from others than they really are, or *ignorance* rendering their distinctive features not sufficiently characterized (erroneously or otherwise). Malignant misrecognition, then, unfairly diminishes access to participatory parity. It unfairly reduces the access of oppressed groups to interact with others as peers on equal footing. This reduced access is unjust.

We'll now argue that CFI generates malignant misrecognition—or, more carefully, that whenever our sufficient conditions for CFI are met there is also malignant misrecognition. We begin this argument with an illustration, drawn from Marilyn Frye (1983: 10–11). Imagine a bird in a cage. Each wire of the cage, in and of itself, is only a minor inconvenience to the bird; it blocks only one very particular route of escape. And yet, taken together, the wires form a system the parts of which jointly limit the bird in ways that are profound, pervasive, and resilient. The bird's limitations are profound: they diminish its well-being in ways not trivial but enormously important. They also are pervasive: they apply, not in a way that is restricted to just a few parts of its life (however important those parts might be), but instead across a wide range of activities from its eating to its sleeping to its attempts to find other birds in the wild. And they are resilient: they are apt to endure attempts at resistance, because the elements of the cage work to reinforce one another. If you try to push a vertical wire out of place, the horizontal wires (to which it is welded) resist the force you apply. At the same time, those resistant horizontal wires get *their own* reinforcement from each of the vertical wires, welded as they are to each of the horizontals. Many small barriers,

[25] Fraser's works on misrecognition diverge from the tradition (whose members are Honneth and others) discussed above. While those works have been well and widely received, no one (that we know of) has yet connected them to *epistemic* injustice. We think that this is an oversight, and that remedying it illuminates why CFI is an epistemic injustice. We take on many of Fraser's views here, but not all of them; see the footnotes below.

[26] Fraser (1998: 36).

[27] Fraser (1998: 54–5).

each of them but a minor inconvenience on its own, mutually reinforce one another. The net result is a profound, pervasive, and resilient system of barriers.

With Frye's cage analogy in mind, return to our examples of CFI, for instance the examples involving gender and sexual minority groups: the rejection of HIV testimony, the Russian anti-gay propaganda law and the South Carolina sex-education law, and the rejection of Kinsey's work on sex (which, we should add, revealed not only widespread non-passive heterosexual activity by women, but also widespread queer activity). Each of these acts, taken in isolation, is worrisome. But to grasp their injustice, we must view them macroscopically as a whole. Together (along with many other things), they result in widespread ignorance and error about queer and trans persons.

This widespread ignorance and error is not morally inert. Rather, it unfairly diminishes the participatory parity of the queer and trans persons who are its target. For instance, the medical community has been, and continues to be, less knowledgeable about the lives and needs of trans persons than about the lives and needs of non-trans persons. As a result the medical community has treated and continues to treat trans persons using pathologizing, inaccurate understandings of them.[28] Similar treatment occurs in many other contexts as well. To point out just one of them, consider the context of incarceration.[29] Due to widespread error and ignorance about trans persons, trans women and men frequently face mistreatment when incarcerated, mistreatment ranging from being placed in incorrect facilities, to not having access to necessary medical care, to constant misgendering and harassment. The misinformation and ignorances at work here traces back to (among other things) many acts of CFI working in tandem—acts frequently motivated by anti-trans and anti-queer prejudices.

The lesson is that, much like particular wires jointly limit the bird by enclosing it in a small space, particular acts of CFI jointly limit oppressed people by collectively creating misrecognition through which their participatory parity is unfairly diminished—i.e., by collectively creating malignant misrecognition. And the point surely generalizes to other cases of CFI as well, for instance cases involving women or racial minorities. Particular acts of CFI amount to injustices, not in virtue of what they cause individually, but rather in virtue of their networked relationships to other acts taken macroscopically as a whole. Working in concert, the relevant acts unfairly diminish oppressed groups' access to participatory parity. That is why they are injustices.

But why are these injustices *epistemic*, and not merely social or political? The answer is: because they are knowledge-directed; and they are knowledge-directed because to be subjected to CFI is to have knowledge involving oneself (or one's social group) systematically preempted or erased or distorted. It is, in short, to be

[28] See Heyes and Latham (2018). [29] Spade (2015).

harmed as a thing known.[30] When this variety of harm happens, one is harmed in one's capacity as an object of knowledge. This is harmful because, in order to be treated justly, one must not be unfairly blocked off *from being known about* in ways that are required for one to be treated equally as compared to one's peers. It is because CFI features this sort of harm, that it amounts to an epistemic injustice and not merely a social or political one.[31]

To be clear, these points apply only to the central cases of CFI (to which our discussion is restricted), that is to say the cases which perpetuate contexts of oppression. An instance of malignant misrecognition cannot be identified in isolation; it must be a part of larger cultural patterns of interpreting and evaluating information. When it fits into these larger patterns, CFI can be understood as an epistemic injustice.[32]

[30] Here, so far as we know, our view diverges from other extant attempts to explicitly connect epistemic injustice and misrecognition, which take epistemic injustice to involve harming people *as knowers* but don't broach the topic of harming people *as things known*. It also diverges from the literature on epistemic injustice in general, which as far as we know has not broached the idea of harm as a thing known. Consider the following passage from Pohlhaus (2017: 13–14), a passage we think nicely captures the zeitgeist: "Epistemic injustices can therefore be understood as epistemic in at least three senses. First, they harm particular knowers as knowers. Second, they cause epistemic dysfunction, for example by distorting understanding or stymieing inquiry. Third they accomplish the aforementioned two harms from within, and sometimes through the use of, our epistemic practices and institutions, for example, when school curricula and academic disciplines are structured in ways that systematically ignore, distort, and/or discredit particular intellectual traditions... Consequently, an epistemic injustice not only harms a knower as a knower, but also is a harm that a knower perpetrates *as* a knower and that an epistemic institution causes *in its capacity as* an epistemic institution." Harm *as a thing known* does not fit into any of these categories.

[31] None of this is to say that CFI never harms people as knowers. It frequently—but not always—does. These people can be third parties (such as medical doctors treating trans persons) who lack relevant knowledge. They can also be the would-be objects of knowledge themselves (such as queer persons first coming to understand their sexualities, who are in the process hindered by widespread ignorance and misinformation). But they are not *always* the would-be objects of knowledge themselves. In these latter cases, where the harmed-as-knower parties are not personally targeted by the oppression at work, it is not clear that the harms they experience are properly classified as epistemic injustices. (For relevant discussion see Beeby 2011.) This means that CFI doesn't always, or at least doesn't always clearly, count as an epistemic injustice *in virtue of* its involving harm to people or groups as knowers. But it *does* always count as an epistemic injustice. This is because it always generates harm via malignant misrecognition to people or groups as *things known*.

[32] Thus we reject as a false dichotomy the binary between structural bases of injustice such as social norms, and psychological bases of injustice such as identity prejudice. The latter is both psychological (because a mental state) and structural (because, in the ways we argue below, it functions *systematically* to underwrite oppression). In rejecting this binary we part ways with many theorists including Fraser (2008: 86), who writes that "misrecognition is not purveyed primarily through prejudice... Rather, it is relayed through institutions and practices that regulate social interaction according to norms that impede parity." While prejudice may not be the primary purveyor of malignant misrecognition, we think (and will argue below) that it *systematically* underwrites oppression in the same ways institutions, practices, and norms do. This shared systematicity undermines the psychological/structural binary.

3.2 An Application: Epistemic Injustice and White Ignorance

The connections between CFI and malignant misrecognition illuminate the relationships between epistemic injustice and the epistemology of ignorance, including white ignorance.[33] To start showing how, we turn again to José Medina, who in his work on white ignorance has suggested that in cases of white ignorance where epistemic harm is intimately connected to social injustice, the people who are *directly* epistemically harmed are not the victims of injustices. Medina writes:

> The hermeneutical disadvantages inscribed in white ignorance are not only harmful, but wrongful, although the harm is committed against someone else: *interestingly and crucially, the hermeneutical harms are wrongful for others, not for those upon whom the epistemic harms are directly inflicted*... The privileged white subjects' inability to understand... is part of a pattern of injustice not against them, but against those who suffer the consequences of white privilege.[34]

We agree with Medina that what renders white ignorance unjust is not primarily its epistemic harms to its white subjects. Even though the white subjects experience misrecognition (they are "unable to make sense of part of their identity and experience"), this misrecognition is not malignant, and in fact reinforces these subjects' social privilege. We also agree that white ignorance has caused downstream harms to those who suffer the consequences of white privilege. But leaving it at that would suggest that white ignorance is not—or at least is not clearly—an *epistemic* injustice. For its status as unjust would appear to be independent of its direct epistemic harms.

Adding malignant misrecognition to the taxonomy of epistemic injustices allows us to capture why white ignorance *is* an epistemic injustice. It is an epistemic injustice because it features malignant misrecognition of persons of color: misrecognition that unfairly diminishes their access to participatory parity.

With these points laid out we can now describe, in more detail, how CFI relates to the forms of epistemic injustice discussed by Fricker and others.

[33] White ignorance has been characterized in a variety of ways, most influentially by Mills (2007) as a broad range of types of ignorance rooted in systems of white privilege.

[34] Medina (2012: 214); emphasis added. Also see Mason (2011).

4. CFI and Its Cousins: Wires in a Cage

Having illustrated CFI with numerous real-life cases, laid down some sufficient conditions for it, and argued that it constitutes an epistemic injustice, we now move on to explore its relationships to other forms of epistemic injustice. Due to limits of space, we will focus only on a few: those to epistemic oppression of the sort discussed by Dotson, and those to testimonial and hermeneutical injustice of the sort discussed by Fricker and other theorists.

4.1 CFI and Epistemic Oppression

In the large literature on epistemic injustice, many authors occasionally use the term "oppression." As far as we know, though, only one of those authors takes it as their central term of criticism. This author is Kristie Dotson, who has theorized at length about "epistemic oppression," a phenomenon she characterizes in terms of "pervasive, harmful epistemic exclusion":

> Epistemic oppression . . . is primarily characterized by detrimental exclusions from epistemic affairs. Whether concerning hermeneutical resources or discourse on an important matter of social policy, epistemic oppression concerns routine and harmful exclusions from some domain of knowledge production.[35]

Since CFI is (or so we've claimed) an epistemic injustice on account of its role in systems of oppression (through malignant misrecognition), it is important to consider how CFI relates to the phenomena Dotson theorizes. Is CFI a species of Dotsonian epistemic oppression? Are they freestanding phenomena neither of

[35] Dotson (2012: 34). Also see Dotson (2014). Dotson references "species of epistemic oppression" that she calls first order, second order, and third order epistemic oppression. To understand them, start with the notion of "epistemic resources": items we use to produce knowledge, for instance concepts or belief-forming mechanisms. Epistemic oppression counts as *first order* when it can be ameliorated simply by better utilizing the epistemic resources we already possess. For instance, consider the jury's rejection of Tom Robinson's testimony in *To Kill a Mockingbird*. (This case has been widely discussed by Fricker (2007) and others.) This act of rejection counts as first order epistemic oppression because, by better utilizing our epistemic resource *evaluating testimony in unbiased ways*, it could be ameliorated. Epistemic oppression counts as *second order* when its amelioration requires that we construct new epistemic resources. Some second order oppression may have been ameliorated when, for instance, Simone de Beauvoir invented the concept of gender as distinct from the concept of sex. Finally, epistemic oppression counts as *third order* when its amelioration requires that we alter epistemic resources we already possess. Some third-order oppression might have been ameliorated when, for instance, Judith Butler successfully urged many theorists to alter the Beauvoirian concept of sex in such a way that sex is in some sense culturally constructed. See Butler (1999: 9–10): "perhaps this construct called 'sex' is as culturally constructed as gender; indeed, perhaps it was always already gender."

which subsumes the other as a species? Are they intertwined in various non-freestanding (perhaps causal) ways *without* either being a species of the other?

These issues turn on what counts as "exclusion from epistemic affairs." There are two ways in which a person or group might be thus "excluded." First, they might be excluded from being *subjects* of knowledge: from being the producers and spreaders of knowledge. Second, they might be excluded from being *objects* of knowledge: from being involved with the content of the knowledge produced and spread. A wide conception of epistemic exclusion would subsume both of these phenomena. A narrow conception of it would subsume only the first.

We aren't sure whether Dotson's conception of epistemic exclusion is wide or narrow in these senses. But we can say this much: on the wide conception of epistemic exclusion, CFI amounts to a species of Dotsonian epistemic oppression. It excludes the oppressed from being objects of knowledge, because it keeps certain content involving them from playing its proper role in the knowledge economy. On the narrow conception of epistemic exclusion, though, CFI is not a species of Dotsonian epistemic oppression. This is because it does not, at least not in and of itself, block or frustrate the oppressed from producing or spreading knowledge: it frustrates their role, not as knowers, but as things known.

This is not to say that on the narrow conception of epistemic exclusion, Dotsonian epistemic oppression is unrelated to CFI. On the contrary, the two phenomena are (on that conception) related in important ways: the same ways in which CFI, testimonial injustice, and hermeneutical injustice are related. To these relations we now turn.

4.2 CFI and Testimonial Injustice

Is CFI a species of testimonial injustice? Already in Fricker's framework, content plays a role. Recall Tom Robinson. While the jury rejected Tom's testimony that he was innocent, they did not reject *all* of his testimony. For example, when he told them that he often helped his alleged victim with house chores, they believed him without question. We see in this example, then, that prejudicial rejection of testimony, due to the hearer's stereotyping of the speaker, does not typically apply wholesale across contents. Rather, it applies in a more targeted way.[36] Rape testimony is rejected; testimony about chores is not. What happens here is not exactly *that prejudiced hearers don't believe those speakers*. Rather, it is *that prejudiced hearers don't believe those speakers when they say that thing*. Women

[36] Fricker (2007: 131) is explicit on this point. She writes: "Tom Robinson might have been relied on and trusted epistemically on certain matters even by the more thoroughly racist white citizens of Maycomb County—matters relating to his daily work, no doubt, and indeed many everyday matters of practical import, so long as there was... nothing about the subject matter that might be seen to imply that this Negro was getting above himself."

aren't believed when they say they want to prioritize their careers; disabled persons aren't believed when they say they have a high quality of life; Black persons aren't believed when they say they are innocent of crimes.

Indeed, before Fricker, this feature of testimonial injustice was observed by Patricia Hill Collins, who cites South African businesswoman Danisa Baloyi as saying, "As a student doing research in the United States, I was amazed by the [small] amount of information on Black South African women, and shocked that only a minuscule amount was actually written by Black women themselves."[37] Baloyi here observes a result of CFI—a dearth of information about Black South African women—as well as a compounding testimonial injustice: Black South African women's voices were excluded from this body of information. Much of the testimonial injustice was simultaneously CFI: Black South African women were not trusted as experts on their own lives and experiences both because of their identities and because of racist and xenophobic prejudices involving the contents of their would-be contributions.

Although CFI and testimonial injustice often occur simultaneously, we think there are good reasons to distinguish them from one another. First, testimonial injustice—as described by Fricker—has distinct manifestation conditions from CFI. In cases of testimonial injustice, there is always prejudice regarding the speaker. But many cases of CFI don't feature prejudice about the speaker. Prejudice about the speaker is thus essential to testimonial injustice, but inessential to CFI. This difference in manifestation conditions gives rise to a second difference between the CFI and testimonial injustice, namely a difference in kind among the harms associated with the two phenomena. Whenever a hearer commits a testimonial injustice against a speaker, the hearer insults that speaker in particular by impugning that speaker's identity. This personalized insult constitutes a harm and, at least in the cases where the identity at issue is itself subjected to oppression, this personalized insult is an injustice. Such insults need not be made in cases of CFI, where the speaker's identity need not be impugned.

For these reasons, we reserve the phrase "testimonial injustice" for the phenomenon occurring when, due to prejudice regarding a speaker, a hearer rejects that speaker's testimony. CFI is not a species of this phenomenon. Nonetheless, CFI and testimonial injustice do not stand free of one another. Rather, they are importantly related *causally*, in at least two ways.

First, testimonial injustice and content-focused injustice can *overlap*. Suppose a hearer has some prejudice involving the content of some testimony, but not enough to make them reject that testimony. And suppose the same hearer also has some prejudice about the identity of the speaker of that very same testimony, but again not enough to make them reject the testimony. These two vectors of

[37] Hill Collins (1991), 3, citing Baloyi (1995), 41.

prejudice might jointly determine the rejection of an item of testimony even though neither of them is strong enough to do the trick on its own. For example, a Black male speaker might say "women are on average paid less than men for the same work" to a hearer who harbors some (but not very much) anti-Black prejudice and some (but not very much) anti-woman prejudice. Here, the two vectors of prejudice might jointly result in the hearer rejecting the testimony, even though neither of them is strong enough to bring about that result on its own. (And, of course, multiple vectors of prejudice might jointly result in testimony rejection while each of them is strong enough on its own to do the trick, so that they "overdetermine" the outcome.)

Second, content-focused injustice and testimonial injustice *reinforce* one another in the sense that each of them blocks certain paths to the removal of the other. To illustrate this, consider a scenario in which CFI operates and then testimonial injustice subsequently operates as well. Suppose, for instance, that a male worker in an office tells his male boss that women frequently have good ideas. Further suppose that the boss stereotypes women as being incapable of having good ideas, and because of this rejects his worker's assertion, thereby committing an act of CFI. Finally, suppose that at a later point, Susan (another worker in the office) comes to the boss with an idea, and that the boss rejects Susan's idea in an act of testimonial injustice. Now, the following judgement about such a case seems correct: if the boss had believed his male worker, he would have been more likely to believe Susan as well. After all, the male worker's assertion—"Women frequently have good ideas"—challenges the boss's sexist stereotypes. By accepting such an assertion, the boss would begin, if only in a small way, to stop stereotyping women as being incapable of having good ideas. And, should the boss thus begin to stop stereotyping, he would become more likely to accept women's ideas—such as Susan's idea. The key point to notice, though, is that CFI stops this process in its tracks: by prejudicially rejecting his male worker's assertion in an act of CFI, the boss stops a process that would render him less likely to commit future acts of testimonial injustice. The scenario thus illustrates an important (and we think common) causal interaction between CFI and testimonial injustice. In this causal interaction, CFI reinforces testimonial injustice by blocking a path to its removal.[38]

The reinforcement works in the opposite direction as well, with testimonial injustice reinforcing CFI. To illustrate this, suppose that the acts in our scenario happen in a different order. Suppose, in particular, that the first thing to happen is

[38] Young (1990: 65): "The cultural imperialism in which white men make stereotypical assumptions about... Blacks or women, for example, contributes to the marginalization and powerlessness many Blacks and women suffer." The patterns of reinforcement we've broached here begin to fill in the details about how this "contribution" proceeds. As Sonny Kim also pointed out to us, CFI can lead to the creation of certain identities—e.g., sexist men labeling another man as a 'feminist'—that then result in testimonial injustice.

that Susan goes to the boss with an idea which he rejects in an act of testimonial injustice; and that subsequently, the male worker asserts to the boss that women frequently have good ideas—and that the boss rejects this assertion, in an act of CFI. Here, it seems correct to judge that, had the boss believed Susan's assertion in the first place, he would have been more likely to believe his male worker's assertion later as well. After all, believing a woman's assertion renders one more receptive to the thought that women have good ideas (at least if the woman's assertion later bears fruit in practice). In our newly rearranged version of the story, then, the boss would have been more inclined to believe his male worker, had he (earlier on) believed his female worker. The key point to notice, though, is that testimonial injustice stops this process in its tracks: by prejudicially rejecting his female worker's assertion in an act of testimonial injustice, the boss stops a process that would render him less likely to commit future acts of CFI. This version of our scenario illustrates the point that testimonial injustice causally reinforces CFI by blocking paths to its removal.

In sum, CFI and testimonial injustice are mutually reinforcing in the sense that each of them blocks certain paths to the removal of the other. In this way they resemble wires in a cage. Try to push a given wire aside, and the other wires reinforce it; try to push those reinforcing wires aside, and the original wire reinforces *them*. Similarly with testimonial injustice and CFI: try to reduce testimonial injustice by teaching people about oppressed groups, and CFI resists those efforts; try to reduce this resistant CFI, and testimonial injustice resists *those* efforts. In this way testimonial injustice and CFI do not stand free but instead prop one another up. They are not isolated wrongs, but elements of a structure or system which can only be seen macroscopically: a birdcage.

4.3 CFI and Hermeneutical Injustice

Hermeneutical injustice also connects to CFI in important ways. Hermeneutical injustice happens when people can't understand their own experience because, due to unequal social power relations, they lack the necessary tools (e.g., concepts).[39] Such a person, in Fricker's terminology, is "hermeneutically marginalized." This form of injustice both causally reinforces, and is causally reinforced by, CFI; the two forms of injustice also sometimes overlap.

In bringing out these causal connections, we follow Fricker in using the concept of "sexual harassment" as our central example. Before the development and dissemination of this concept, women widely faced a similar set of negative experiences that they found hard to understand or articulately explain. The

[39] See e.g. Fricker (2007: 147–61) and Medina (2013).

concept of sexual harassment served to delineate these particular experiences, giving women the ability to understand them and articulately explain them. The lack of this concept, before its development and dissemination, gave rise to an important instance of hermeneutical injustice.

Using this example of hermeneutical injustice, we can ask about connections between CFI and hermeneutical injustice. We propose that CFI is a causal mechanism that reinforces—or even establishes—hermeneutical injustice. This can occur in at least two ways. The first concerns the development of a concept. The development of a concept like "sexual harassment" typically occurs through persons having a conversation about and realization of their shared experiences. This process is depicted in a first-person account from Susan Brownmiller's memoir of the US women's liberation movement (cited by Fricker):

> We realized that to a person, every one of us . . . had had an experience like this at some point, you know? And none of us had ever told anyone before. It was one of those click, aha! moments, a profound revelation . . . . Eight of us were sitting in an office of Human Affairs . . . brainstorming about what we were going to write on the posters for our speak-out . . . We wanted something that embraced a whole range of subtle and unsubtle persistent behaviors. Somebody came up with "harassment." *Sexual harassment*! Instantly we agreed. That's what it was.[40]

One way CFI can reinforce hermeneutical injustice is by preventing or delaying interactions necessary for developing a particular concept. For example, suppose that male colleagues of women being harassed had gone to administrators to report the mistreatment of their female colleagues, and administrators dismissed their testimony due to prejudicial views about women (for example, as being 'too sensitive'). In such a scenario, CFI would reinforce hermeneutical injustice: by failing to take men's reports of harassment seriously, administrators would not facilitate the discussions necessary for developing a concept of sexual harassment.

A second way that CFI can reinforce hermeneutical injustice concerns access to already-developed concepts. In the previous example, hermeneutical injustice arose because the concept of sexual harassment had not yet been developed. But hermeneutical injustice can occur even when a relevant concept exists. So long as someone does not have access to the needed concept, they will be unable to fully understand or articulate their experience. Lauren Zuniga illustrates hermeneutical injustice in her poem "Confessions of an Uneducated Queer." There, she writes, "This is for the first time I ever heard the term 'heteronormative' and felt like I was handed a corkscrew after years of opening the bottle with my teeth."[41] Zuniga here describes the profound effect of gaining, with a term and concept, the ability to

[40] Fricker (2007: 150). [41] Zuniga (2012).

understand her experience of heteronormativity. Yet the hermeneutical injustice she suffered was due, not to the *non-existence* of a concept of heteronormativity, but rather to Zuniga's *lack of access* to this concept.

CFI can result in someone's being cut off from or delayed from accessing concepts required to understand significant experiences. To see how, it is important to first notice that access to concepts is cut off or delayed when concepts do not have *uptake*: that is, when they are not taken seriously, adopted, or spread within one's community. Failure of uptake is sometimes due to CFI: a concept needed to describe a marginalized group's experience is developed, but those outside of the group reject or ignore testimony deploying that concept due to their prejudice, effectively preventing the spread of this concept.[42] One example of this phenomenon comes from right-wing TV personality Bill O'Reilly. When O'Reilly received reports that many Harvard students were upset by the heteronormative remarks of a visiting speaker, he began a segment on the event as follows:

> Another controversy at Harvard, this one over something called "heteronormative" remarks made by actress Jada Pinkett Smith... We'll define heteronormative in a moment. I can hardly say it. But, apparently Ms. Smith received an award from Harvard and then told the crowd that women in America can have it all, a good career, family, devoted husband, things like that. According to the Harvard "Crimson" newspaper, some gays objected to Ms. Smith's remarks because they were directed at heterosexuals exclusively, thus [motioning scare-quotes] "heteronormative."[43]

In this monologue, O'Reilly mocks the concept of heteronormativity. Moreover, he seemingly does so because he associates this concept with gay persons and harbors prejudice against this group. In mocking the concept, O'Reilly effectively characterizes it as an absurdity that his listeners should not employ or take seriously. Given the predictable result that his listeners then do not deploy this concept, it is more likely that persons in their social circles fail to be exposed to this concept. The ensuing conceptual lacuna creates hermeneutical injustice. O'Reilly's act of CFI blocks a path by which people might gain access to the concept of heteronormativity. In this way, CFI causally reinforces hermeneutical injustice.[44]

[42] This is one of the themes of Pohlhaus (2012) and Medina (2013).

[43] See "Were Jada Pinkett Smith's Recent Comments at Harvard Too 'Heteronormative'?" Fox News, March 9, 2005.

[44] Another case: during a rally for his 2016 presidential campaign, Donald Trump "made thinly veiled jokes about the lack of sexual attractiveness of the female protesters and the lack of heteronormative manliness of the males" (Kurtz 2016). Here again, preemptive CFI occurs when a speaker mocks the concept of heteronormativity.

Plausibly, the reinforcement runs in the other direction too, with hermeneutical injustice causally reinforcing CFI. Rather than illustrate this point, though, we will move on to a new one. In particular, we move on to the point that these two forms of injustice can causally overlap. To see how this might happen, suppose that hermeneutical injustice makes it difficult to articulately describe the experience of interacting with police while being a Black person in contemporary America. Such a supposition would be true if, as is wholly possible, we have not yet zeroed in on concepts adequate to the experience in question, concepts standing to that experience as the concept of heteronormativity stood to Lauren Zuniga's experience. Further suppose that a white person tries to explain to another white person the experience Black persons face when interacting with police. In this case, the speaker may only be able to describe the relevant experience inarticulately. Now suppose that, in a certain case, this inarticulateness is not quite enough on its own to keep the hearer from believing the speaker. In such a case, if the hearer *also* harbors prejudice against Black persons, this prejudice might, in combination with the relevant inarticulateness, bring the hearer to reject the speaker's testimony. In such a case, which seems possible to us, hermeneutical injustice and CFI causally overlap; they jointly determine an unjust rejection of testimony (and, of course, similar cases might feature *over*determination).

Testimonial injustice, hermeneutical injustice, and content-focused injustice form a network of mutually reinforcing injustices. They block paths to the removal of one another and also causally overlap. And so it happens that even when particular acts of the relevant sorts seem like minor inconveniences in and of themselves, those acts jointly constitute a harmful structure which is profound, pervasive, and resilient. They constitute a birdcage.[45]

5. Conclusion

There is a rich and complicated network of epistemic (and social and political) injustices, a network featuring many different phenomena that interact in mutually reinforcing ways. While some of these phenomena feature prejudice against the speaker who makes an assertion, others feature prejudice involving the content of the assertion a speaker makes. Our aim here has been to bring the latter kinds of

[45] To see some of the further wires in the cage, think about cases where someone is taken to be authoritative about a marginalized group precisely because they do *not* belong to it (e.g., heterosexuals about LGBTQ persons, men about women). Such authority often is fragile, and depends in particular on the non-member's claims aligning with dominant, prejudiced beliefs about that group. That is, credibility excess does often attach to people because of their identity, but in many cases, it is contingent on the *content* of their claims matching up with prejudiced views about the groups being reported-on; the credibility excesses at issue can be lost when the reporter contradicts or questions these prejudicial views. In this type of scenario, again, we see that testimonial injustice and CFI work in tandem.

epistemic injustice to light, theorizing about their nature and their relationships to other kinds of epistemic injustice.

For the sake of simplicity we've restricted our analysis to only two kinds of actions: rejections of assertions and preemptions of assertions. We've also restricted speakers and hearers to individuals and groups. Further work on CFI might proceed by removing various aspects of this simplification. For instance, we could consider other sorts of entities as speakers and hearers–institutions, for example. We could also examine further sorts of acts as the bearers of CFI: these might include acts of *ignoring*, *accepting*, *making*, *encouraging*, or *smothering* assertions.[46] In addition, rather than focus on assertions, further work might examine speech acts such as questions. Presumably, instances of CFI can involve any speech act. For that matter, they can presumably involve things other than speech acts. For instance, CFI might concern *concepts* or *physical evidence* or *as-yet-unasserted theories*.[47] Finally, we see no reason to believe that *prejudice* must be involved in every case of CFI. While prejudice does function systematically (in the ways we have tried to illuminate) to lead to malignant misrecognition and (thereby) epistemic injustice, there is no reason to think it is required for this systematic functioning. CFI without prejudice is a live possibility; similarly for CFI without assertion and CFI without speech acts. These further varieties of CFI, far from undermining our analysis, show how that analysis fruitfully suggests new directions for further research. This research might further explore the ways in which the forms of CFI relate to each other, to other forms of epistemic injustice, and to sociopolitical oppression.[48]

References

Anderson, E. 2017 Feminist Epistemology. *Stanford Encyclopedia of Philosophy*. https://plato.stanford.edu/archives/spr2017/entries/feminism-epistemology/

Appiah, A. 1994. Race, Culture, Identity: Misunderstood Connections. *The Tanner Lectures on Human Values*, 17: 51–136.

Baloyi, D.E. 1995. Apartheid and Identity: Black Women in South Africa. In A.O. Pala (Ed.), *Connecting Across Cultures and Continents: Black Women Speak Out on Identity, Race, and Development*. United Nations Development Fund for Women.

[46] On "testimonial smothering," see Dotson (2011).

[47] Examples of people doing these things can be found in Anderson (2017, section 5), Appiah (1994), and Sullivan and Tuana (2007).

[48] For helpful discussion we thank Roxy Barbera, Maren Behrensen, Joanna Blake-Turner, Joe Corabi, Emmalon Davis, Mikkel Gerken, Daniel Greco, Johann Neem, Naomi Scheman, Jason Stanley, Neal Tognazzini, Ryan Wasserman, and audiences at Princeton University, San Francisco State University, Simon Fraser University, and Western Washington University.

Beeby, L. 2011. A Critique of Hermeneutical Injustice. *Proceedings of the Aristotelian Society*, 111/3: 479–86.

Butler, J. 1999. *Gender Trouble*. London: Routledge, 2nd edition.

The Combahee River Collective. 1979. A Black Feminist Statement. *WSQ: Women's Studies Quarterly*, 42(3–4): 271–80.

Congdon, M. 2018. What's Wrong With Epistemic Injustice? In I. Kidd, J. Medina, and G. Pohlhaus (Eds.), *The Routledge Handbook of Epistemic Injustice*. Routledge.

Cudd, A. 2006. *Analyzing Oppression*. Oxford University Press.

Davis, E. 2021. A Tale of Two Injustices: Epistemic Injustice in Philosophy. In Jennifer Lackey (Ed.), *Applied Epistemology* (pp. 215–52). Oxford University Press.

Decker, E., and Wilson, J. 2013. Russia's "Gay Propaganda" Law. *The School of Russian and Asian Studies*. Accessed July 25, 2017.

Dotson, K. 2011. Tracking Epistemic Violence, Tracking Practices of Silencing. *Hypatia*, 26/2: 236–57.

Dotson, K. 2012. A Cautionary Tale: On Limiting Epistemic Oppression. *Frontiers*, 33/1: 24–47.

Dotson. K. 2014. Conceptualizing Epistemic Oppression. *Social Epistemology*, 28(2): 115–38.

Faderman, L. 2015. *The Gay Revolution: The Story of the Struggle*. Simon & Schuster.

Fraser, N. 1998. *Social Justice in the Age of Identity Politics: Redistribution, Recognition, and Participation*. Tanner Lectures On Human Values, vol. 19, ed. G. Peterson, University of Utah Press, pp. 1–67.

Fraser, N. 2008. Why Overcoming Prejudice is Not Enough: A Rejoinder to Richard Rorty. In K. Olson (Ed.), *Adding Insult to Injury: Nancy Fraser Debates Her Critics* (pp. 82–8). Verso.

Fricker, M. 2007 *Epistemic Injustice: Power and the Ethics of Knowing*. Oxford University Press.

Frye, M. 1983. *The Politics of Reality*. Crossing Press.

Green, J. 2011. The Heroic Story of How Congress First Confronted AIDS. *The Atlantic*, https://www.theatlantic.com/politics/archive/2011/06/the-heroic-story-of-how-congress-first-confronted-aids/240131/. Accessed October 11, 2019.

Griffith, M. 2008. The Religious Encounters of Alfred C. Kinsey. *The Journal of American History*, 95/2: 349–77.

Haslanger, S. 2004. Oppressions: Racial and Other. In Michael Levine and Tamas Pataki (Eds.), *Racism in Mind*. Cornell University Press.

Heyes, C., and Latham, J.R. 2018. Trans Surgeries and Cosmetic Surgeries: The Politics of Analogy. *TSQ Transgender Studies Quarterly*, 5(2): 174–89.

Hill Collins, P. 1991. *Black Feminist Thought*. 1st ed. Routledge.

Hookway, C. 2010. Some Varieties of Epistemic Injustice: Reflections on Fricker. *Episteme*, 7/2: 164–78.

Kidd, I., J. Medina, and G. Pohlhaus (Eds.). 2017. *The Routledge Handbook of Epistemic Injustice*. Routledge.

Kinsey, A. et. al. 1953. *Sexual Behavior in the Human Female*. Saunders.

Kurtz, D. 2016. Reader Dispatch From Trump Rally. *TPM Editor's Blog*, March 16. http://talkingpointsmemo.com/edblog/trump-rally-north-carolina.

Lugones, M. 1987. Playfulness, "World"-Travelling, and Loving Perception. *Hypatia*, 2(2): 3–19.

Lugones, M. 2006. On Complex Communication. *Hypatia*, 21(3): 75–85.

Mason, R. 2011. Two Kinds of Unknowing. *Hypatia*, 26/2: 294–307.

Medina, J. 2012. Hermeneutical Injustice and Polyphonic Contextualism: Social Silences and Shared Hermeneutical Responsibilities. *Social Epistemology*, 26(2): 201–20.

Medina, J. 2013. *The Epistemology of Resistance: Gender and Racial Oppression, Epistemic Injustice, and Resistant Imaginations*. Oxford University Press.

Medina, J. 2018. Misrecognition and Epistemic Injustice. *Feminist Philosophical Quarterly*, 4(4): 1–16.

Mills, C. 2007. White Ignorance. In Sullivan and Tuana (2007), pp. 13–38.

Pohlhaus, G. 2012. Relational Knowing and Epistemic Injustice: Towards a Theory of Willful Hermeneutical Ignorance. *Hypatia*, 27: 715–35.

Pohlhaus, G. 2017. Varieties of Epistemic Injustice. In J. Kidd, J. Medina, and G. Pohlhaus (Eds.), *The Routledge Handbook of Epistemic Injustice*. Routledge.

Rich, A. 1980. Compulsory Heterosexuality and Lesbian Existence. *Signs*, 5(4): 631–60.

Rimmerman, C. 2001. *From Identity to Politics: The Lesbian and Gay Movements in the United States*. Temple University Press.

Spade, D. 2015. *Normal Life*. Duke University Press.

Sullivan, S., and N. Tuana (Eds.). 2007. *Race and Epistemologies of Ignorance*. SUNY Press.

Taylor, C. 1994. The Politics of Recognition. In A. Gutmann (Ed.), *Multiculturalism*. Princeton University Press.

Thomas, K. 1993. Shaped by Men and Marzipan. *The Observer*, August 8, 1993, p. 54.

Wanderer, J. 2012. "Addressing Testimonial Injustice: Being Ignored and Being Rejected." *The Philosophical Quarterly*, 62(246): 148–69.

Wilde, O. 1908. *The Picture of Dorian Gray*. Bernhard Tauchnitz.

Young, I. 1990. *Justice and the Politics of Difference*. Princeton University Press.

Zuniga, L. 2012. Confessions of and Uneducated Queer. Vancouver Poetry Slam, November 19, 2012. https://www.youtube.com/watch?v=bGCXJqn6DRg. Accessed October 11, 2019.

4
The Art of Learning

Jason Konek

How confident are you that you will make it through the afternoon without a heart attack? 99%? 99.999%? Whatever your answer, you probably agree on this much: whether you spend an hour reading the news and leaning lazily on your left elbow is *irrelevant* to your prospects. It provides no evidence one way or another about whether you will have a heart attack (unless an oracle told you, "Lean on your elbow and meet your doom!" or something of the sort). Finding out that you have high levels of "bad cholesterol," for example, is bad news. But finding out that you will spend the next hour reading and leaning is neither bad news nor good news. It is *no* news (no *relevant* news anyway). It does not tell you much one way or another about the risk of cardiovascular catastrophe.

But now imagine that you feel your left arm tingling. As a result, your credence that you are about to have a heart attack shoots up. As you start to panic, the kind stranger next to you asks you whether they can help. You explain your situation. They respond calmly, "You do realize that you have been leaning on your left elbow while reading for the last hour, don't you?" Prior to feeling your left arm tingle and spiraling into a panic, you thought this bit of information was no news. It did not, in your view, give you any evidence about whether you will have a heart attack. But now the situation is different. You are well aware that the ulnar nerve runs along the back of your elbow; a nerve that might get pinched if you lean on it for too long and cause your arm to tingle. So *now* the kind stranger's information is *highly relevant news*. Learning that you have been leaning on your left elbow changes your opinion dramatically. It causes you to become pretty sure that you are fine; no heart attack in sight. Irrelevant before, but irrelevant no more!

Your learning experience in this case has multiple effects. It raises your credence that you will have a heart attack. But it also introduces new *undercutting defeaters*. Undercutting defeaters cause you to re-evaluate the evidential import of some prior learning experience. More carefully, if a proposition X undercuts the support that a learning experience $\mathcal{E}$ provides for a hypothesis Y, then learning X makes you think that $\mathcal{E}$ provides *no support whatsoever* for Y.[1] However we cash this out, the following seems true: X undercuts the support that $\mathcal{E}$ provides for Y

[1] Rebutting defeaters, in contrast, undermine your confidence in Y not by undercutting the support for Y provided by some learning experience $\mathcal{E}$, but rather by "telling directly against" the truth of Y.

Jason Konek, *The Art of Learning* In: *Oxford Studies in Epistemology, Volume 7.* Edited by: Tamar Szabó Gendler, John Hawthorne, and Julianne Chung, Oxford University Press.
DOI: 10.1093/oso/9780192868978.003.0004

only to the extent that your post-$\mathcal{E}$ credence for Y conditional on X (immediately after $\mathcal{E}$, before acquiring additional information) is close to your pre-$\mathcal{E}$ credence for Y. The more X undercuts $\mathcal{E}$'s support for Y, the more learning X would push your confidence in Y back near its pre-$\mathcal{E}$ levels. This means that X must be **relevant to** Y to count as an undercutting defeater for Y.

In the case at hand, your learning experience $\mathcal{E}^*$ turns the proposition L *that you lean on your elbow for an hour* into an undercutting defeater for the proposition H *that you will have a heart attack*. Prior to the experience, L is irrelevant to H. And irrelevant propositions do not undercut anything. But *after* the experience you see L as an undercutting defeater for H. Experience $\mathcal{E}^*$ causes you to think that L undercuts the support that $\mathcal{E}^*$ *itself* provides for H. After $\mathcal{E}^*$ you think: Learning L would be good reason to drop my high posterior (post-$\mathcal{E}^*$) credence in H back down to something like its pre-arm-tingling level.

According to Christensen (1992) and Weisberg (2015), cases like this are both utterly ubiquitous, and cause big problems for *Jeffrey conditioning*. Jeffrey conditioning says that you ought to update your credences in light of new learning experiences as follows:

J-Con. If you have prior credences *old* and undergo a learning experience $\mathcal{E}$ that shifts your credences on some partition $\{E_1,..., E_n\}$ to $x_1,..., x_n$, and nothing more, then your new credence for any proposition X ought to be:

$$new(X) = \sum_{i \leq n} x_i \cdot old(X|E_i).$$

According to Weisberg, J-Con bungles the introduction of new undercutting defeaters. A rational agent's confidence in most propositions (maybe all propositions) can be undermined by theoretical considerations. This is one of the basic insights of holist epistemology. Moreover, rational agents change their mind about what undercuts what. Learning experiences introduce *new* undercutting defeaters. In our heart attack case, $\mathcal{E}^*$ causes you to think that L undercuts the support that $\mathcal{E}^*$ *itself* provides for H, despite the fact that you previously thought L was irrelevant to H. But Jeffrey conditioning simply does not allow for this. J-Con is a "rigid" updating rule (§1). And rigid updating rules preserve opinions about irrelevance. So if you thought L was irrelevant to H *before* $\mathcal{E}^*$, then you must think it is irrelevant *after* $\mathcal{E}^*$. But this means that if you update by Jeffrey conditioning in our heart attack case, then $\mathcal{E}^*$ will *not* push you to treat L as an undercutting defeater for H. Hence J-Con makes bad predictions about rational learning.

Christensen's problem is a bit different. Christensen focuses on whether J-Con has the resources to explain how inputs to updating depend on background beliefs. According to Christensen, learning experiences never push your credences up or down *directly*. Rather, the doxastic effects of experience are always mediated by your background beliefs. Whether the tingling in your arm pushes your credence that you are going to have a heart attack up, or down, or leaves it unchanged, ought to depend on your prior opinions on a whole host of matters: your current state of cardiovascular health, what exactly the warning signs of a heart attack are, whether you have been leaning on your left elbow, etc. This is another basic insight of holist epistemology. But Jeffrey conditioning treats the initial effect of experience—a shifting of credences over some partition (sometimes called a "Jeffrey shift")—as an exogenous factor; an output of some "black box" process that serves as an input to Jeffrey conditioning. Hence J-Con fails to explain an important feature of rational learning: how or why the initial effects of experience (the Jeffrey shift) depend on prior opinion.

Jeffrey was comfortable with this. Training the messy network of neurons in your skull to translate perceptive and proprioceptive inputs into sensible Jeffrey shifts is simply not something that formal epistemology *should* speak to. That training happens in one's PhD programme, in the lab, etc. It yields a domain-specific skill; a skill that goes far beyond the skills one might be said to have simply in virtue of being epistemically rational. Christensen, on the other hand, sees Jeffrey's 'concession' as placing "an important cognitive or structural aspect of justification outside the area our theory purports to describe" (Christensen 1992: 547).

My aim in this paper is to describe and defend a new updating policy that answers both Christensen and Weisberg's concerns. Because it shares structural features with J-Con, I call it **J-Kon**. Unlike J-Con, J-Kon makes explicit the way in which inputs to updating depend on background beliefs. J-Kon also naturally accounts for the introduction of new undercutting defeaters. In addition to being more holism-friendly than J-Con, it also has an accuracy-centred justification.

Here is the plan in a bit more detail. In section 1, I will briefly explain why "rigid" updating rules like J-Con have trouble introducing new undercutting defeaters. In section 2, I will describe J-Kon and show how it works in a few simple case. In section 3, I will show that J-Kon is in fact equivalent to what Jeffrey called "super-conditioning" (with a few extra bells and whistles). In section 4, I will extol the epistemic virtues of J-Kon. More carefully, I will provide a *chance-dominance* argument for J-Kon. If you fail to update by J-Kon, then your epistemic life—the sequence of credal states that you adopt in response to your learning experiences—is chance-dominated by some other J-Kon satisfying life. What it means to be chance-dominated is this: *every possible chance function* expects your life to accrue strictly less total epistemic value than the J-Kon satisfying life. If you update by J-Kon, in contrast, your epistemic life is never chance-dominated in this way. This provides a purely alethic (rather than evidential or pragmatic) rationale for updating by J-Kon. In section 5, I will explore the ways in which J-Kon makes inputs to updating depend on background beliefs. I will also run through a few cases that illustrate how J-Kon introduces new undercutting defeaters. In section 6, I will respond to some pressing objections. Finally, in section 7, I will wrap up.

1. Rigidity and Undercutting Defeat

Consider a histopathologist looking at stained cells under a microscope. Careful examination might make her fairly confident that the relevant sample is, *e.g.*, Ductal cell carcinoma. Given her training and expertise, she may well have *good reason* for her confidence. Nevertheless, she might be wholly unaware of what features of the cells she is picking up on. Despite the fact that there *are* definite features that she is tracking, there is no reason to expect that she will have any kind of *privileged access* to information about those features. There is no reason to expect she will store such information as a "passive data structure," or in a more action-guiding fashion (directly in her sensorimotor system), or in any other way that makes that info available as an input to action, decision-making, or reasoning. As Weiskrantz puts it, "a large amount of bodily processing... in sensory channels proceeds quite detached from any awareness... Awareness of an event is a form of privileged access that allows further perceptual and cognitive manipulations to occur; as far as neural processes are concerned, it is probably a minority privilege" (Jeffrey 1992: 197; Weiskrantz 1986: 168–9).

None of this is unique to histopathologists, of course. It is "typical of our most familiar sorts of updating, as when we recognize friends' faces or voices or handwritings pretty surely, and when we recognize familiar foods pretty surely by their look, smell, taste, feel, and heft" (Jeffrey 1992: 79). In these run-of-the-mill learning situations, there are definite features that you are picking up on. And in virtue of your sensitivity to these features, you may well have *good reason* for being fairly confident that the person in the distance is your friend, that Abbi Jacobson is narrating your new favourite podcast, etc. But there typically is no proposition describing those features that you even have an opinion about, let alone become *certain* of. The reason is familiar. For you to count as having an opinion about those features, propositions describing them must be available (in some way or other) as inputs to action, decision-making, or reasoning. But such information typically does *not* enjoy this 'minority privilege'. It is processed and has various downstream effects on your doxastic, affective and conative state, but is not *itself* made available as an input to action, decision-making, or reasoning.

How should you update your credences, then, when you have learning experiences like our histopathologist's? Jeffrey conditioning offers a partial answer. Suppose that you have prior credences $old : \mathcal{F} \to \mathcal{R}$ for propositions in a σ-algebra $\mathcal{F}$ on a set of worlds Ω.[2] Suppose also that you undergo a learning experience $\mathcal{E}$ that (i) does not make you *certain* of anything, but nevertheless (ii) shifts your credences on some partition $\{E_1,..., E_n\}$ of Ω to $x_1,..., x_n$ (and nothing more).

[2] Ω contains the finest-grained possibilities you can distinguish between. Saying that $\mathcal{F}$ is a σ-algebra means that (i) $\mathcal{F}$ contains the tautology Ω, and (ii) $\mathcal{F}$ is closed under complement (negation), countable union (disjunction), and countable intersection (conjunction). We will assume that Ω is finite.

That is, $\mathcal{E}$ induces a "Jeffrey shift" over $\{E_1,\ldots, E_n\}$. Then Jeffrey conditioning (J-Con) says that your new credence for any proposition X ought to be:

$$new(X) = \sum_{i \leq n} x_i \cdot old(X|E_i).$$

When is Jeffrey conditioning appropriate? According to Jeffrey, you ought to update by J-Con just in case two conditions hold.

1. $new(E_i) = x_i$.
2. $new(X|E_i) = old(X|E_i)$.

The first condition says that you take the credences produced directly by $\mathcal{E}$ at face value. For each E_i, you stick with x_i as your new credence (rather than treating this shift in your credences as the aberrant result of momentary mania). The second condition says that you treat $\mathcal{E}$ as the sort of learning experience that provides information about *which* of the E_i is true, but *not* about what else is true *given* that E_i is true. So you hold your credence in X conditional on E_i fixed for each X and each E_i. When this second condition holds, we say that your update is "rigid."

For example, our histopathologist's learning experience (examining stained cells under a microscope) might make her 80% confident that the sample is Ductal cell carcinoma and 20% confident that it is not. And she might take these "direct effects" of experience at face value (stick with them as her new credences). Moreover, she might think that while $\mathcal{E}$ provides information about whether the sample is Ductal cell carcinoma or not, it does *not* provide information about, for example, the patient's survival prospects S *given* that it is (or is not) Ductal cell carcinoma. If the same holds not just for S, but for any proposition X, and she holds her conditional credences fixed as a result (i.e., $new(X|E_i) = old(X|E_i)$), then both conditions (1) and (2) hold.

And in *that* case, J-Con is simply mandated by probabilistic coherence. Given that $new : \mathcal{F} \rightarrow \mathcal{R}$ satisfies the probability axioms, (1) and (2) are jointly equivalent to:

$$new(X) = \sum_{i \leq n} x_i \cdot old(X|E_i).$$

But—and here's the rub—both (1) and (2) are quite strong conditions. Indeed, the rigidity condition (2) is *so* strong that it plausibly *never* holds.

Our heart attack example illustrates the point. Recall, in that example, your learning experience $\mathcal{E}^*$ (tingling arm) raises your credence for the proposition H (that you will have a heart attack).

$$new(H) > old(H).$$

It also turns the proposition L (that you lean on your elbow for an hour) into an undercutting defeater for H. Prior to the experience, L is irrelevant to H.

$$old(H|L) = old(H).$$

But *after* the experience you come to see L as an undercutting defeater for H. After $\mathcal{E}^*$ you think: learning L would be good reason to drop my high posterior (post-$\mathcal{E}^*$) credence in H back down to something like its pre-arm-tingling level.

$$new(H) > new(H|L).$$

The problem is this. Suppose that you accommodate $\mathcal{E}^*$ by Jeffrey conditioning, using your new distribution

$$new(H) = high, new(\neg H) = low$$

over $\{H, \neg H\}$ as an input. Then we must have:

$$new(H) = new(H|L)$$

contra our assumption that $new(H) > new(H|L)$. So J-Con simply fails to introduce L as a new undercutting defeater for H. The proof is dead simple. First, note that $old(H) = old(H|L)$ implies

$$old(L) = old(L|H) = old(L|\neg H).$$

Next, note that since J-Con implies the rigidity condition (2), we have

$$new(L|H) = old(L|H),\ new(L|\neg H) = old(L|\neg H).$$

This straightaway gives us

$$\begin{aligned} new(H|L) &= \frac{new(L|H)new(H)}{new(L|H)new(H) + new(L|\neg H)new(\neg H)} \\ &= \frac{old(L|H)new(H)}{old(L|H)new(H) + old(L|\neg H)new(\neg H)} \\ &= \frac{old(L)new(H)}{old(L)new(H) + old(L)new(\neg H)} \\ &= new(H). \end{aligned}$$

The moral is this. Rigidity forces you to preserve your old opinions about irrelevance. So if your updating rule is rigid with respect to $\{E_1, \ldots, E_n\}$ (it leaves your credences conditional on the E_i unchanged), then that rule cannot take you from thinking that X was irrelevant to E_i before $\mathcal{E}$ to thinking that X is relevant to E_i after $\mathcal{E}$. But turning an irrelevant X into a relevant X is *precisely* what is involved in introducing a new undercutting defeater. So whenever $\mathcal{E}$ *should* introduce a new undercutting defeater for one of the E_i, you should *not* update according to J-Con, or any other rigid updating rule.

This is *really* bad for J-Con. Learning experiences should *almost always* introduce new undercutting defeaters. For any learning experience $\mathcal{E}$ that pushes your credences over some partition $\{E_1,\ldots,E_n\}$ around, there will be *some* proposition X that you previously took to be irrelevant to E_i, but now should take to be relevant; now you should take X to undercut the support that $\mathcal{E}$ provides for E_i. Any X that describes conditions that compromise the reliability of your credence-formation process—the process that pushed your credences for the E_i around—will do the trick. This, again, is one of the basic insights of holist epistemology. And if this insight is right, then according to Jeffrey's own criteria, **it is almost never appropriate to update by Jeffrey conditioning.**

To recap, J-Con bungles the introduction of new undercutting defeaters. Since nearly all learning experiences introduce new undercutting defeaters, J-Con almost never applies. This is Weisberg's main concern. The question now is: Can we do better? The answer: yes.

2. J-Kon

We seem to be back at square one. When our histopathologist examines her cells, she becomes *fairly confident* that the sample is one type of carcinoma rather than another. But she does not become *certain* of anything new. The orthodox Bayesian method for updating in light of such "uncertain learning experiences" is Jeffrey conditioning. But J-Con is almost never appropriate. How then *should* we update in light of uncertain learning experiences?

My aim now is to describe and defend a new updating policy for uncertain learning: **J-Kon**. First, I will describe J-Kon briefly and show how it works in a few cases (sections 2.1–2.2). Then I will show that J-Kon is in fact equivalent to a restricted form of what Jeffrey called *superconditioning*. This will be important for showing that J-Kon has an accuracy-centred justification (section 4). Finally, with this justification for J-Kon in place, I will return to the issues surrounding confirmational holism that we began with. In particular, I will show that J-Kon naturally explains how inputs to updating depend on background beliefs, and naturally accounts for the introduction of new undercutting defeaters (section 5).

2.1 Formal Description

Before outlining J-Kon, we need to introduce one key concept: the *conditional chance estimate.* Estimates are familiar enough. For example, the Met Office's best estimate of the amount of rainfall that London will receive next year might be 597mm. Your best estimate of the number of children that your brother will have might be 2.7. And so on. Estimates are numbers; numbers that fall between the possible values of the quantity that you are estimating; numbers that are evaluated principally on the basis of their *accuracy* (the closer they are to the true value of the quantity, the better).[3] In the Bayesian tradition, rational choice is a matter of choosing the option that you estimate to produce the most utility. And your best estimates of utility (and other quantities) are determined by your best estimates of truth-values, which are captured by your credences, or degrees of belief.

Conditional estimates are also familiar. For example, the Met Office's best estimate of the amount of rainfall that London will receive next year might be 597mm *on the supposition that a catastrophic climate event does not derail the Gulf stream.* Your best estimate of the number of children that your brother will have might be 2.7 *on the supposition that he and his partner work through their issues.* And so on. Like plain old unconditional estimates, conditional estimates are numbers; numbers that fall between the possible values of the quantity that you are estimating. But where unconditional estimates are something like epistemic bets—bets that pay out in an epistemic currency, *viz.*, accuracy—conditional estimates are more like *called-off epistemic bets.* They are evaluable for accuracy only in worlds where their condition holds. In worlds where the condition does not hold, the epistemic bet that they represent is called off.

Conditional *chance* estimates, then, are just conditional estimates of a particular quantity: *chance.* In particular, a conditional chance estimate of the form:

$$est[ch(X|Y)|Y]$$

is an estimate of the conditional chance $ch(X|Y)$ *on the supposition that* Y *is true.* Put differently, it is an estimate of the chance of X when both you and chance take the supposition Y on board.

Following de Finetti, Jeffrey thought of estimation as basic, and credences as capturing a particular type of estimate, *viz.*, an agent's best estimates of truth-values.[4] More carefully, Jeffrey thought of propositions X as "indicator variables" that take the value 1 at worlds where X is true, and 0 where X is false. (In what follows, we will slip between talking of propositions as sets of worlds and indicator

[3] Indeed, one might think that it is *constitutive* of estimates that they are evaluable on the basis of their accuracy. See Konek (2019).

[4] See (Jeffrey 1986: 51).

variables.) Truth-value estimates, then, are simply estimates of the value, 0 or 1, that the proposition takes at the actual world. And an agent's credence for a proposition is just her best estimate of its truth-value.

Treating estimation as basic allows us to see the laws of (finitely) additive probability, *i.e.*,

Normalization. $p(\Omega) = 1$.
Non-negativity. $p(X) \geq 0$.
Finite Additivity. $p(X \cup Y) + p(X \cap Y) = p(X) + p(Y)$.

as straightforward consequences of de Finetti's *laws of estimation* (or what are sometimes called *the axioms of linear previsions*). De Finetti's laws say that your estimates of any two variables, $\mathcal{V}: \Omega \to \mathcal{R}$ and $\mathbb{Q}: \Omega \to \mathcal{R}$, ought to satisfy the following conditions (de Finetti 1974, section 3.1.5):

Boundedness. $inf_{w \in \Omega} \mathcal{V}(w) \leqslant est(\mathcal{V}) \leqslant sup_{w \in \Omega} \mathcal{V}(w)$.
Homogeneity. $est(\lambda \mathcal{V}) = \lambda est(\mathcal{V})$ for $\lambda \in \mathcal{R}$.
Additivity. $est(\mathcal{V} + \mathcal{Q}) = est(\mathcal{V}) + est(\mathcal{Q})$.

The boundedness condition says roughly that your estimate of $\mathcal{V}$ should fall somewhere between the minimum and maximum possible values of $\mathcal{V}$. The homogeneity conditions says that your estimate of $\mathcal{V}$ scaled by λ, *i.e.*, $\lambda \mathcal{V}$, should be the result of scaling your original estimate by λ, *i.e.*, $\lambda est(\mathcal{V})$. The additivity condition says that your estimate of the sum of $\mathcal{V}$ and $\mathcal{Q}$, $\mathcal{V} + \mathcal{Q}$—*i.e.*, the variable whose value at a world is the sum of $\mathcal{V}$'s value and $\mathcal{Q}$'s value, respectively—should equal the sum of your individual estimates for $\mathcal{V}$ and $\mathcal{Q}$. If the unconditional estimates captured by *est* satisfy de Finetti's laws, then we say that *est* is *coherent* (or a *linear prevision*). Similarly, we can see the Rényi-Popper axioms for conditional probability, *i.e.*,

Conditional Probability. $c(\cdot|X)$ is a probability function with $c(X|X) = 1$.
Generalized Ratio Constraint. $c(Y \cap Z|X) = c(Z|X \cap Y)c(Y|X)$ if $X \cap Y \neq \varnothing$.

as straightforward consequences of the *laws of conditional estimation*. The laws of conditional estimation say that your conditional estimates ought to satisfy:

Conditional Boundedness. $inf_{\omega \in X} \mathcal{V}(\omega) \leqslant est(\mathcal{V}|X) \leqslant sup_{\omega \in X} \mathcal{V}(\omega)$.
Conditional Homogeneity. $est(\lambda \mathcal{V}|X) = \lambda est(\mathcal{V})$ for $\lambda \in \mathcal{R}$.
Conditional Additivity. $est(\mathcal{V} + \mathcal{Q}|X) = est(\mathcal{V}|X) + est(\mathcal{Q}|X)$.
Bayes Rule. $est(Y\mathcal{V}|X) = est(\mathcal{V}|X \cap Y)est(Y|X)$ if $X \cap Y \neq \varnothing$ (where $Y\mathcal{V}$ is the product of Y and $\mathcal{V}$, *i.e.* $(Y\mathcal{V})(\omega) = Y(\omega)\mathcal{V}(\omega)$).

If the conditional estimates captured by *est* satisfy the laws of conditional estimation, then we say that *est* is *coherent* (or a *conditional linear prevision*).

With these preliminary remarks in place, we can now outline J-Kon. Note though that I will initially present J-Kon as a very deliberate, cognitively demanding updating procedure. This will help get the basic picture across without too much fuss. But the official version of J-Kon only involves updating *as if* you are deliberately following this procedure. It is much less cognitively demanding than it appears at first blush. We return to this issue in sections 3 and 6.

J-Kon proceeds in two stages. The first stage is the *expansion stage*. In response to any learning experience, $\mathcal{E}$, you ought to settle on a new conditional credence, $new(\mathcal{E}|\omega)$, for each world ω. These new conditional credences reflect how likely you think you are to have that very experience *conditional on being in this, that, or the other world*. Typically, you will not have any *prior* (pre-$\mathcal{E}$) credences about $\mathcal{E}$, conditional or not. $\mathcal{E}$ itself puts you in a position to have opinions about $\mathcal{E}$. So settling on these new conditional credences involves *expanding* the range of propositions that you have opinions about.

J-Kon updaters, however, do not expand willy nilly. Rather, they settle on new conditional credences by settling on *new conditional chance estimates*. They estimate the *chance* of having the experience $\mathcal{E}$ conditional on being in this, that, or the other world. Then they use these new conditional chance estimates as their new conditional credences.

The second stage is the *update stage*. Once you have expanded, you should input your *old unconditional credences* for atoms (worlds) and your *new conditional chance estimates* into Bayes' theorem. Then conditionalize on $\mathcal{E}$. This specifies new credences for each atom of your algebra. Together with the probability axioms, this fixes your entire new credal state.

In a little bit more detail, J-Kon says that you ought to accommodate uncertain learning experiences as follows:

J-Kon (Unofficial Version). Suppose you have prior credences *old* and have accommodated past learning experiences $\mathcal{P}$ via J-Kon using some set of conditional chance estimates EST_{old}. You now undergo learning experience $\mathcal{E}$. Then you ought to update *old* as follows.

1. **Expansion stage.** Expand EST_{old} to include new conditional chance estimates of the form:

$$est[ch(\mathcal{E}|\omega \cap \mathcal{P})|\omega \cap \mathcal{P}].$$

The only constraints on the newly expanded set of conditional estimates EST are: (i) EST should be **consistent**, in the sense that it never commits you to estimating that a variable will take a positive value if it cannot *possibly* do so (this is what

Peter Walley calls *avoiding uniform loss*; see appendix); (ii) *EST* should be consistent with the Principal Principle.[5]

2. **Update stage.** Use these new conditional chance estimates to update your credence for each atom ω of $\mathcal{F}$ as follows:

$$new(\omega) = \frac{est[ch(\mathcal{E}|\omega \cap \mathcal{P})|\omega \cap \mathcal{P}] \cdot old(\omega)}{\Sigma_{\omega' \in \Omega} est[ch(\mathcal{E}|\omega' \cap \mathcal{P})|\omega' \cap \mathcal{P}] \cdot old(\omega')}.$$

The best way to get a feel for J-Kon is to see it in action. But before we do, we should set aside a few potential concerns. First, a word about learning experiences and these heretofore nebulous propositions $\mathcal{E}$ that we have been using to describe them. Learning experiences are rich, complex events with a range of properties. An agent's learning experience might have a certain phenomenological character, for example. In addition, it might "directly affect" her doxastic, affective or conative state in various ways. For example, it might shift her credences over some partition, as Jeffrey imagined. Or it could push her conditional credences around, or her expectations, or other properties of her credal state. And of course learning experiences do not happen in a vacuum. Some learning experiences are shaped by years of training. Others are not. And on, and on, and on.

Given how rich and varied learning experiences are, it is a fool's errand to try to pin down any single property, or even a cluster of properties that we can always use to characterize them. Simply describing the phenomenological character of an agent's learning experience, or its direct effects on her credal state, etc., will almost certainly leave out epistemologically important information; information that ought to have some impact on how she accommodates that learning experience. To avoid this sort of concern, we will pick out learning experiences using demonstrative propositions. That is, we will describe learning experiences using propositions $\mathcal{E}$ of the form *agent A had* **that** *learning experience*. Of course, this is the sort of proposition that you are only in a position to have opinions about *once you have already had the learning experience*. This would be problematic if J-Kon required you to have *prior* credences about $\mathcal{E}$. But it does not.

Second, J-Kon may seem to just dress up an old Bayesian story in new garb. After all, the unofficial version says that if you undergo a non-dogmatic learning experience $\mathcal{E}$—one that does not make you *certain* of anything, but nevertheless shifts your credences around in some way or other—then even though you cannot

[5] *EST* is consistent with the Principal Principle iff expanding it to include conditional estimates of the form $est[X|(CH = ch) \cap Y] = ch(X|Y)$ preserves consistency, *i.e.*, does not make it subject to a uniform loss. See the appendix for more detail.

conditionalize straighaway (because there is no proposition learned with certainty to conditionalize on), you should nonetheless (i) put yourself in a position to conditionalize (on $\mathcal{E}$ in particular) and then (ii) conditionalize. But this concern misses the mark in two ways. First, the unofficial version of J-Kon recommends responding to non-dogmatic learning experiences by *expanding*. Moreover, it constrains *how* you should expand (at least if there are interesting constraints on the space of possible chance functions). None of this is standard Bayesian fare. Second, the official version of J-Kon (§3) ditches the recommendation to explicitly expand and conditionalize, and rather recommends updating *as if* you were expanding and conditionalizing. As will be abundantly clear by the end of §3, what we end up with is a genuinely new story about rational updating; more than just an old tune in a new key.

So much for the preliminary remarks. Onto the applications!

2.2 Applications

1. **Dogmatic learning.** Vanji is having a routine sexual health check-up. Though she does not suspect that she is at risk for HIV, she decides to have an HIV test anyway. She has prior credences over the power set $\mathcal{F}$ of Ω, which contains:

$$\omega_1 = HIV \,\&\, Test+ \qquad \omega_2 = HIV \,\&\, Test-$$
$$\omega_3 = NoHIV \,\&\, Test+ \qquad \omega_4 = NoHIV \,\&\, Test-$$

Her prior credences are as follows:

$$old(\omega_1) = 0.00095 \quad old(\omega_2) = 0.00005$$
$$old(\omega_3) = 0.04995 \quad old(\omega_4) = 0.94905$$

So Vanji's prior credence that she has HIV is 0.001. Her prior credence that the test will come back positive given that she has HIV is 0.95. Her prior credence that the test will come back negative given that she has does not have HIV is also 0.95. Finally, her prior credence that she has HIV given that the test comes back positive is about 0.019 (19 times higher than her unconditional prior for HIV, but still rather low).

The doctor hands her the results of the test. This causes her to have a learning experience $\mathcal{E}$ that pushes her credence that the test is positive up to 1 (*i.e.*, a dogmatic learning experience).

Question: What should Vanji's new credences be after $\mathcal{E}$?
Answer: According to J-Kon, she ought to update as follows. First, adopt conditional chance estimates of the form:

$$est[ch(\mathcal{E}|\omega)|\omega]$$

(To simplify the problem, we will imagine that this learning experience is first of Vanji's epistemic life. So the proposition $\mathcal{P}$ describing her past learning experiences is just the tautology. We will make the same assumption in subsequent examples. But the results in the appendix do not make this assumption.) For example, Vanji might adopt the following conditional chance estimates:

$$est[ch(\mathcal{E}|\omega_1)|\omega_1] = est[ch(\mathcal{E}|\omega_3)|\omega_3] = 1$$

and

$$est[ch(\mathcal{E}|\omega_2)|\omega_2] = est[ch(\mathcal{E}|\omega_4)|\omega_4] = 0.$$

These estimates reflect the opinion that Vanji is an *infallible learner*, at least on this occasion. There is *no* chance of failing to have this sort of learning experience—one which sends her credence in a positive test result up to 1—if the test does in fact come back positive. Likewise, there is *no* chance of mistakenly having this sort of learning experience if the test comes back negative.

Next, she should treat these new conditional chance estimates, $est[ch(\mathcal{E}|\omega_i)|\omega_i]$, as her old conditional credences, $old(\mathcal{E}|\omega_i)$, and conditionalize on $\mathcal{E}$. This yields a new credal state given by:

$$new(\omega_i) = \frac{est[ch(\mathcal{E}|\omega_i)|\omega_i] \cdot old(\omega_i)}{\Sigma_j est[ch(\mathcal{E}|\omega_j)|\omega_j] \cdot old(\omega_j)}.$$

So, for example, Vanji's new credence for ω_1 is:

$$\begin{aligned} new(\omega_1) &= \frac{est[ch(\mathcal{E}|\omega_1)\omega_1] \cdot old(\omega_1)}{\Sigma_j est[ch(\mathcal{E}|\omega_j)|\omega_j] \cdot old(\omega_j)} \\ &= \frac{1.0.00095}{1 \cdot 0.00095 + 0 \cdot 0.00005 + 1 \cdot 0.04995 + 0 \cdot 0.94905} \\ &= 0.018664. \end{aligned}$$

More generally, her new credal state is given by:

$$\begin{array}{ll} new(\omega_1) = 0.018664 & new(\omega_2) = 0 \\ new(\omega_3) = 0.981336 & new(\omega_4) = 0 \end{array}$$

This is precisely the same posterior credal state that Vanji would end up with if she updated by conditioning on the proposition that the test came back positive. This is no coincidence. **Orthodox conditionalization is equivalent to J-Kon for infallible dogmatic learners.** For agents whose learning experiences always push their credences up to 1 in some proposition E (and nothing more), and who are infallible in the sense that (i) there is *no* chance of this occurring when E is false, and (ii) *no* chance of it *not* occurring when E is true, Orthodox Bayesian conditionalization is the way to go.

But even dogmatic learners are not always infallible. For example, Vanji might be extermely nervous about a positive test result. She might think: there is a marginal chance that I will mistakenly have $\mathcal{E}$ even if the test comes back negative. Perhaps her anxiety will cause her to not properly register the words printed on the report. In that case, the following conditional chance estimates might seem appropriate:

$$est[ch(\mathcal{E}|\omega_1)|\omega_1] = est[ch(\mathcal{E}|\omega_3)|\omega_3] = 1$$

and

$$est[ch(\mathcal{E}|\omega_2)|\omega_2] = est[ch(\mathcal{E}|\omega_4)|\omega_4] = .01.$$

And if she uses *those* estimates to accommodate $\mathcal{E}$ via J-Kon, she will end up with a different posterior credal state:

$$\begin{array}{ll} new^*(\omega_1) = 0.0157308 & new^*(\omega_2) = 8.27938 \cdot 10^{-6} \\ new^*(\omega_3) = 0.82711 & new^*(\omega_4) = 0.157151 \end{array}$$

This is the same posterior credal state that Vanji would end up with if $\mathcal{E}$ "directly" affected her credences for $Test+$ and $Test-$, pushing them to 0.842841 and 0.157159, respectively, and she then updated by J-Con. The moral: her conditional estimates reflect the opinion that there is a marginal chance of mistakenly having $\mathcal{E}$. J-Kon tells Vanji that, in light of this, she should hedge her epistemic bets that $\mathcal{E}$ is on the money by not quite conditioning, but Jeffrey conditioning instead. As is clear from this example, such hedging can have a *big* impact on your posterior credences. *Marginal* chances of error are not necessarily *negligible.*

2. **Uncertain learning with Jeffrey shifts.**[6] Nahdika is a histopathologist. She recently received a section of tissue surgically removed from a pancreatic tumor. She hopes to settle on a diagnosis by examining the tissue under a microscope. (To simplify matters, suppose that exactly one of the three diagnoses is correct.) Nahdika has prior credences over the power set $\mathcal{F}$ of Ω, which contains:

$$\begin{array}{ll} \omega_1 = A\&\neg B\&\neg C\&L & \omega_2 = A\&\neg B\&\neg C\&\neg L \\ \omega_3 = \neg A\&B\&\neg C\&L & \omega_4 = \neg A\&B\&\neg C\&\neg L \\ \omega_5 = \neg A\&\neg B\&C\&L & \omega_6 = \neg A\&\neg B\&C\&\neg L \end{array}$$

[6] This case is adapted from (Jeffrey 1992: 7–9).

where

$$A = \text{Islet cell carcinoma} \qquad B = \text{Ductal cell carcinoma}$$
$$C = \text{Benign tumor} \qquad L = \text{Patient lives}$$

Her prior credences are as follows:

$$old(\omega_1) = 0.2 \qquad old(\omega_2) = 0.3$$
$$old(\omega_3) = 0.15 \qquad old(\omega_4) = 0.1$$
$$old(\omega_5) = 0.225 \qquad old(\omega_6) = 0.025$$

So Nadhika's priors for A, B and C are as follows:

$$old(A) = 0.5 \text{ and } old(B) = old(C) = 0.25.$$

Likewise, her priors for L conditional on A, B and C, respectively, are as follows:

$$old(L|A) = 0.4,\ old(L|B) = 0.6 \text{ and } old(L|C) = 0.9.$$

Nadhika looks in the microscope. This causes her to have a learning experience $\mathcal{E}$ that pushes her credence for A, B and C to 1/3, 1/6 and 1/2, respectively.

Question: What should Nadhika's new credences be after $\mathcal{E}$?
Answer: According to J-Kon, she ought to update as follows. First, adopt conditional chance estimates of the form $est[ch(\mathcal{E}|\omega)|\omega]$. For example, Nahdika might adopt the following conditional chance estimates:

$$est[ch(\mathcal{E}|\omega_1)|\omega_1] = est[ch(\mathcal{E}|\omega_2)|\omega_2] = est[ch(\mathcal{E}|\omega_3)|\omega_3] = est[ch(\mathcal{E}|\omega_4)|\omega_4] = 0.3$$

as well as:

$$est[ch(\mathcal{E}|\omega_5)|\omega_5] = est[ch(\mathcal{E}|\omega_6)|\omega_6] = 0.9.$$

(We will explore why these might be sensible conditional chance estimates shortly.) Next, she should use these new conditional chance estimates to update her old credences as follows:

$$new(\omega_i) = \frac{est[ch(\mathcal{E}|\omega_i)|\omega_i] \cdot old(\omega_i)}{\Sigma_j est[ch(\mathcal{E}|\omega_j)|\omega_j] \cdot old(\omega_j)}.$$

This yields:

$$new(\omega_1) = 0.133333 \qquad new(\omega_2) = 0.2$$
$$new(\omega_3) = 0.1 \qquad new(\omega_4) = 0.0666667$$
$$new(\omega_5) = 0.45 \qquad new(\omega_6) = 0.05$$

So Nahdika's posteriors for A, B and C are:

$$new(A) = 1/3,\ new(B) = 1/6 \text{ and } new(C) = 1/2.$$

Her posteriors for L conditional on A, B and C remain unchanged:

$$new(L|A) = 0.4,\ new(L|B) = 0.6 \text{ and } new(L|C) = 0.9.$$

This is precisely the same posterior credal state that Nahdika would end up with if she accommodated the Jeffrey shift induced by $\mathcal{E}$ via J-Con. But what is it about Nahdika's conditional chance estimates that forces J-Kon to agree with J-Con? And when might it make sense to adopt conditional chance estimates like Nahdika's?

The answer to the first question is given by ($\star$). Choose any learning experience $\mathcal{E}$ that induces a Jeffrey shift over a partition $\{E_1,\dots, E_n\}$. To keep the new credences recommended by J-Kon separate from the "direct" effects of $\mathcal{E}$, let *dir* capture the latter. So in Nahdika's case we have:

$$dir(A) = 1/3,\ dir(B) = 1/6 \text{ and } dir(C) = 1/2.$$

Then J-Kon agrees with J-Con if and only if:

($\star$) For all $X \in \{E_1,\dots, E_n\}$ and $\omega_i \in X$, if $old(\omega_i) = 0$ then $new(\omega_i) = 0$, and if $old(\omega_i) > 0$ then

$$\frac{dir(X)}{old(X)} = \frac{est[ch(\mathcal{E}|\omega_i)|\omega_i]}{\Sigma_j est[ch(\mathcal{E}|\omega_j)|\omega_j] \cdot old(\omega_j)}.$$

The second question, then, amounts to the following: When might it make sense to adopt conditional chance estimates that satisfy ($\star$), as Nahdika's do? The answer is not obvious. ($\star$) is a strong condition. Spelling out its consequences requires work. Here is one such consequence. ($\star$) implies (♥):

(♥) For all $X \in \{E_1,\dots, E_n\}$ and $\omega_i,\ \omega_j \in X$ with $old(\omega_i) > 0$ and $old(\omega_j) > 0$

$$est[ch(\mathcal{E}|\omega_i)|\omega_i] = est[ch(\mathcal{E}|\omega_j)|\omega_j].$$

Having conditional chance estimates that satisfy (♥) is only appropriate if you take a particular view of the credence formation process $\wp$ that induces the Jeffrey shift; the one that translates perceptive and proprioceptive inputs into new credences for elements of $\{E_1,\ldots, E_n\}$. In particular, you must think that $\wp$ is transparent about what it is causally sensitive to. You must think that if $\wp$ is causally sensitive to the differences between ω_i and ω_j, in the sense that the chance that $\wp$ produces $\mathcal{E}$ if you are in ω_i is *different*, in your view, than the chance if you are in ω_j—*i.e.*, $est[ch(\mathcal{E}|\omega_i)|\omega_i] \neq est[ch(\mathcal{E}|\omega_j)|\omega_j]$—then $\wp$ will be transparent about this fact. It will announce it to the world by inducing a shift over a sufficiently fine partition; one that slots ω_i and ω_j into different cells.

But when is it appropriate to adopt conditional chance estimates that reflect this sort of opinion about $\wp$? Partial answer: not if $\mathcal{E}$ introduces a new undercutting defeater D for one of the E_i. Consider, for example, the learning experience $\mathcal{E}^*$ in our heart attack example (section 1). Recall, $\mathcal{E}^*$ involved a tingling arm which caused your credence that you are about to have a heart attack to shoot up toward 1. $\mathcal{E}^*$ ought to cause the proposition L (that you lean on your elbow for an hour) to become an undercutting defeater for the proposition H (that you will have a heart attack) only if leaning on your elbow makes a difference to the chance of having a tingling arm and subsequent credence-in- H boost. If leaning on your elbow makes no difference to the chance of all that (*i.e.*, to $\mathcal{E}^*$), then learning L ought to leave your post-$\mathcal{E}^*$ credence in H intact.

The upshot: whenever $\mathcal{E}$ introduces a new undercutting defeater D for one of the E_i, (♥) will fail. And whenever (♥) fails, J-Kon and J-Con come apart. This helps to explain how J-Kon might naturally introduce new undercutting defeaters where J-Con stumbles.

($\star$) has other consequences too. For example, it implies (♦):

(♦) For all $X, Y \in \{E_1,\ldots, E_n\}$, $\omega_i \in X$ and $\omega_j \in Y$ with $old(w_i) > 0$ and $old(w_j) > 0$:

$$\frac{est[ch(\mathcal{E}|\omega_i)|\omega_i]}{est[ch(\mathcal{E}|\omega_j)|\omega_j]} = \frac{dir(X)/dir(Y)}{old(X)/old(Y)}.$$

Having conditional chance estimates that satisfy (♦) is only appropriate if you think that $\wp$ "tracks the chances" in a certain sense. For example, if you used to think that X and Y were equally likely (*i.e.*, $old(X)/old(Y) = 1$), then you must think that $\wp$ will produce an experience $\mathcal{E}$ that makes you think that X is twice as likely as Y just in case the *chance* of having $\mathcal{E}$ in any X-world is, in your view, twice as great as the chance of having $\mathcal{E}$ in any Y-world. In this sense, $\wp$ must "track the chances." More generally, you must think that $\wp$ will produce an $\mathcal{E}$ that sets your new odds for X and Y (*i.e.*, $dir(X)/dir(Y)$) to be k times your old odds (*i.e.*, $old(X)/old(Y)$) just in case the chance of having $\mathcal{E}$ in any X-world is, in your view, k-times as great as the chance of having $\mathcal{E}$ in any Y-world (*i.e.*, $est[ch(\mathcal{E}|\omega_i)|\omega_i]/est[ch(\mathcal{E}|\omega_j)|\omega_j] = k$).

Back to our second question then. When might it make sense to adopt conditional chance estimates that satisfy $(\star)$? We now have an informative partial answer: only if you think that the credence formation process $\wp$ in play is "transparent about what it is causally sensitive to" in the sense of (♥), and "tracks the chances" in the sense of (♦).

Now consider Nahdika again. In particular, consider her view about the chance of having a learning experience $\mathcal{E}$ that impacts her like so:

$$dir(A) = 1/3,\ dir(B) = 1/6 \text{ and } dir(C) = 1/2.$$

She might well think that the chance of $\mathcal{E}$ is greater in A-worlds (the patient has Islet cell carcinoma) than in B-worlds (the patient has Ductal cell carcinoma). In that case, Nahdika's original chance estimates are inapproprate. They do not reflect this opinion. After all, ω_1 is an A-world, ω_3 a B-world, but nevertheless:

$$\frac{est[ch(\mathcal{E}|\omega_1)|\omega_1]}{est[ch(\mathcal{E}|\omega_3)|\omega_3]} = \frac{0.3}{0.3} = 1.$$

Instead, Nahdika might opt for the following:

$$\begin{aligned}
est^*[ch(\mathcal{E}|\omega_1)|\omega_1] &= est^*[ch(\mathcal{E}|\omega_2)|\omega_2] = 0.6\\
est^*[ch(\mathcal{E}|\omega_3)|\omega_3] &= est^*[ch(\mathcal{E}|\omega_4)|\omega_4] = 0.3\\
est^*[ch(\mathcal{E}|\omega_5)|\omega_5] &= est^*[ch(\mathcal{E}|\omega_6)|\omega_6] = 0.9
\end{aligned}$$

And if she uses *those* estimates to accommodate $\mathcal{E}$ via J-Kon, she will end up with a different posterior credal state:

$$\begin{aligned}
&new^*(\omega_1) = 0.2 && new^*(\omega_2) = 0.3\\
&new^*(\omega_3) = 0.075 && new^*(\omega_4) = 0.05\\
&new^*(\omega_5) = 0.3375 && new^*(\omega_6) = 0.0375
\end{aligned}$$

So Nahdika's posteriors for A, B and C are:

$$new^*(A) = 1/2,\ new^*(B) = 1/8 \text{ and } new^*(C) = 3/8.$$

Indeed, new^* is the same posterior credal state that Nahdika would end up with if she used this distribution over $\{A, B, C\}$, rather than the "direct effect" of $\mathcal{E}$, as an input to J-Con. The moral seems to be this: by taking the "direct effect" of $\mathcal{E}$ at face value—using it as an input to updating—J-Con tacitly presupposes that the credence formation process $\wp$ that produced $\mathcal{E}$ satisfies $(\star)$. This means presupposing that $\wp$ is "transparent about what it is causally sensitive to" in the sense of (♥), and "tracks the chances" in the sense of (◆). If ($\star$) holds, and consequently (♥) and (◆) hold, then J-Kon and J-Con agree. If not, not.

When (◆) fails, but (♥) holds, J-Kon says: use your views about the *way* in which $\wp$ fails to track the chances to adjust the *input* to J-Con. (More specifically, keep the input *partition* fixed, but adjust the *distribution* over that partition.) When (♥) fails, J-Kon recommends more radical departures from J-Con; departures which are inconsistent with any naïve application of J-Con.

3. **Uncertain learning without Jeffrey shifts**. Aamilah is walking past the abandoned coin factory at night. She picks up an old coin. She plans to flip it three times. She has prior credences over the power set $\mathcal{F}$ of Ω, which contains:

$$\begin{array}{ll} \omega_1 = H_1\&H_2\&H_3 & \omega_2 = H_1\&H_2\&T_3 \\ \omega_3 = H_1\&T_2\&H_3 & \omega_4 = H_1\&T_2\&T_3 \\ \omega_5 = T_1\&H_2\&H_3 & \omega_6 = T_1\&H_2\&T_3 \\ \omega_7 = T_1\&T_2\&H_3 & \omega_8 = T_1\&T_2\&T_3 \end{array}$$

Her prior credences are as follows:

$$\begin{array}{ll} old(\omega_1) = .25 & old(\omega_2) = .08\bar{3} \\ old(\omega_3) = .08\bar{3} & old(\omega_4) = .08\bar{3} \\ old(\omega_5) = .08\bar{3} & old(\omega_6) = .08\bar{3} \\ old(\omega_7) = .08\bar{3} & old(\omega_8) = .25 \end{array}$$

(There are just the credences she would have if she had a uniform distribution over hypotheses about the bias of the coin.) Aamilah flips the coin three times. In the black of night, she glimpses the outcome of each flip. The first flip causes her to have a fairly ambiguous heads-ish visual experience $\mathcal{E}_1$. The second and third flips cause her to have fairly ambiguous tails-ish visual experiences, $\mathcal{E}_2$ and $\mathcal{E}_3$.

ε_1 ε_2 ε_3

Question: What should Aamilah's new credences be after $\mathcal{E}_1$? $\mathcal{E}_2$? $\mathcal{E}_3$?
Answer: According to J-Kon, she ought to update as follows. First, adopt conditional chance estimates of the form:

$$est[ch(\mathcal{E}_1|\omega)|\omega].$$

For example, Aamilah might adopt the following conditional chance estimates:

$$est[ch(\mathcal{E}_1|\omega_1)|\omega_1] = est[ch(\mathcal{E}_1|\omega_2)|\omega_2] = est[ch(\mathcal{E}_1|\omega_3)|\omega_3] = est[ch(\mathcal{E}_1|\omega_4)|\omega_4] = 0.8$$

as well as:

$$est[ch(\mathcal{E}_1|\omega_5)|\omega_5] = est[ch(\mathcal{E}_1|\omega_6)|\omega_6] = est[ch(\mathcal{E}_1|\omega_7)|\omega_7] = est[ch(\mathcal{E}_1|\omega_8)|\omega_8] = 0.2.$$

Such estimates seem appropriate if you think (i) that there is a high (low) chance of having an ambiguously heads-ish visual experience in a dark environment given that the first flip comes up heads (tails), and (ii) the chance of having that experience is independent of the outcome of the second and third toss conditional on the outcome of the first.

Next, she should use these conditional chance estimates to update her old credences as follows:

$$new_1(\omega_i) = \frac{est[ch(\mathcal{E}|\omega_i)|\omega_i] \cdot old(\omega_i)}{\Sigma_j est[ch(\mathcal{E}|\omega_j)|\omega_j] \cdot old(\omega_j)}.$$

This yields:

$$\begin{aligned} new_1(\omega_1) &= .4 \; new_1(\omega_2) &= .1\bar{3} \\ new_1(\omega_3) &= .1\bar{3} \; new_1(\omega_4) &= .1\bar{3} \\ new_1(\omega_5) &= .0\bar{3} \; new_1(\omega_6) &= .0\bar{3} \\ new_1(\omega_7) &= .0\bar{3} \; new_1(\omega_8) &= .1 \end{aligned}$$

So Aamilah's ambiguously heads-ish learning experience makes her fairly confident (credence 0.8) that the coin came up heads on the first flip. This, in turn, is evidence that the coin is biased towards heads, and hence increases her confidence that it will come up heads on flips two and three.

$$new_1(H_1) = .8 \text{ and } new_1(H_2) = new_1(H_3) = .6.$$

This is precisely the same posterior credal state that Aamilah would end up with if $\mathcal{E}_1$ "directly" affected her credences for H_1 and T_1, pushing them to 0.8 and 0.2, respectively, and she then updated by J-Con.

What credences should Aamilah have after $\mathcal{E}_2$? According to J-Kon, she ought to adopt new conditional chance estimates of the form:

$$est[ch(\mathcal{E}_2|\omega \cap \mathcal{E}_1)|\omega \cap \mathcal{E}_1].$$

And she ought to do so in a way that preserves coherence, so that her new expanded set of conditional chance estimates satisfies the laws of conditional estimation. For example, Aamilah might adopt the following:

$$
\begin{aligned}
& est[ch(\mathcal{E}_2|\omega_1 \cap \mathcal{E}_1)|\omega_1 \cap \mathcal{E}_1] && (1)\\
&= est[ch(\mathcal{E}_2|\omega_2 \cap \mathcal{E}_1)|\omega_2 \cap \mathcal{E}_1] && (2)\\
&= est[ch(\mathcal{E}_2|\omega_7 \cap \mathcal{E}_1)|\omega_7 \cap \mathcal{E}_1] && (3)\\
&= est[ch(\mathcal{E}_2|\omega_8 \cap \mathcal{E}_1)|\omega_8 \cap \mathcal{E}_1] && (4)\\
&= .001 && (5)
\end{aligned}
$$

as well as:

$$
\begin{aligned}
& est[ch(\mathcal{E}_2|\omega_3 \cap \mathcal{E}_1)|\omega_3 \cap \mathcal{E}_1] && (6)\\
&= est[ch(\mathcal{E}_2|\omega_4 \cap \mathcal{E}_1)|\omega_4 \cap \mathcal{E}_1] && (7)\\
&= .8 && (8)
\end{aligned}
$$

and:

$$
\begin{aligned}
& est[ch(\mathcal{E}_2|\omega_5 \cap \mathcal{E}_1)|\omega_5 \cap \mathcal{E}_1] && (9)\\
&= est[ch(\mathcal{E}_2|\omega_6 \cap \mathcal{E}_1)|\omega_6 \cap \mathcal{E}_1] && (10)\\
&= .2 && (11)
\end{aligned}
$$

(1)–(5) seem appropriate if you think your visual system is stable. In what sense? The following: if you had an ambiguously heads-ish visual experience in response to a heads on the first flip, then there is almost no chance that you will have a different (tails-ish) experience in response to the same outcome (heads) on the second. Ditto for tails. If you had a heads-ish experience in response to a *tails* on the first flip, there is almost no chance that you will have a different (tails-ish) experience in response to the same outcome (tails) on the second.

(6)–(8) seem appropriate if you think that having a heads-ish visual experience in response to heads on the first flip is good evidence that the lighting conditions are just good enough for your visual system to be sensitive to the outcome. In that case, you think: there is a reasonably high chance of having a tails-ish experience if you get tails on the second.

(9)–(11) seem appropriate if you think that having a heads-ish visual experience in response to *tails* on the first flip is good evidence that the lighting conditions are just *bad* enough for your visual system to *not* be sensitive to the outcome. In that case, you think: there is a high chance of having the same heads-ish experience even if you get tails on the second. So there is a *low* chance of having the tails-ish experience described by $\mathcal{E}_2$.

With these estimates in hand, Aamilah ought to update as follows:

$$new_2(\omega_i) = \frac{est[ch(\mathcal{E}_2|\omega_i \cap \mathcal{E}_1)|\omega_i \cap \mathcal{E}_1] \cdot new_1(\omega_i)}{\Sigma_j est[ch(\mathcal{E}_2|\omega_j \cap \mathcal{E}_1)|\omega_j \cap \mathcal{E}_1] \cdot new_1(\omega_j)}.$$

This yields:

$$\begin{array}{ll} new_2(\omega_1) = 0.00175953 & new_2(\omega_2) = 0.00058651 \\ new_2(\omega_3) = 0.469208 & new_2(\omega_4) = 0.469208 \\ new_2(\omega_5) = 0.0293255 & new_2(\omega_6) = 0.0293255 \\ new_2(\omega_7) = 0.000146628 & new_2(\omega_8) = 0.000439883 \end{array}$$

So Aamilah's credence that the first and second flips resulted in heads and tails, respectively, are now roughly 0.94. Her credence that the third flip will come up heads still hovers around 0.5.

$$new_2(H_1) = 0.940762,\ new_2(T_2) = 0.939003,\ new_2(H_3) = 0.50044.$$

But why would Aamilah's credence that the *first* flip came up heads shoot up (from 0.8 to 0.94) in response to an ambiguously tails-ish visual experience following the *second* flip? The reason: her conditional chance estimates reflect the opinion that having *different* visual experiences in response to the first two flips is good news about the reliability of her visual system. It is evidence that the lighting conditions are just good enough for her visual system to track the outcome. Wiping away this uncertainty about the reliability of her visual system pushes her credence in H_1 up from 0.8 to 0.94.

Finally, what credences should Aamilah have after $\mathcal{E}_3$? According to J-Kon, she ought to adopt new conditional chance estimates of the form:

$$est[ch(\mathcal{E}_3|\omega \cap \mathcal{E}_1 \cap \mathcal{E}_2)|\omega \cap \mathcal{E}_1 \cap \mathcal{E}_2]$$

while again ensuring to preserve coherence. She might, for example, adopt the following:

$$est[ch(\mathcal{E}_3|\omega_1 \cap \mathcal{E}_1 \cap \mathcal{E}_2)|\omega_1 \cap \mathcal{E}_1 \cap \mathcal{E}_2] = .4 \quad (12)$$
$$est[ch(\mathcal{E}_3|\omega_2 \cap \mathcal{E}_1 \cap \mathcal{E}_2)|\omega_2 \cap \mathcal{E}_1 \cap \mathcal{E}_2] = .6 \quad (13)$$
$$est[ch(\mathcal{E}_3|\omega_3 \cap \mathcal{E}_1 \cap \mathcal{E}_2)|\omega_3 \cap \mathcal{E}_1 \cap \mathcal{E}_2] = .0001 \quad (14)$$
$$est[ch(\mathcal{E}_3|\omega_4 \cap \mathcal{E}_1 \cap \mathcal{E}_2)|\omega_4 \cap \mathcal{E}_1 \cap \mathcal{E}_2] = .9999 \quad (15)$$
$$est[ch(\mathcal{E}_3|\omega_5 \cap \mathcal{E}_1 \cap \mathcal{E}_2)|\omega_5 \cap \mathcal{E}_1 \cap \mathcal{E}_2] = .8 \quad (16)$$
$$est[ch(\mathcal{E}_3|\omega_6 \cap \mathcal{E}_1 \cap \mathcal{E}_2)|\omega_6 \cap \mathcal{E}_1 \cap \mathcal{E}_2] = .2 \quad (17)$$
$$est[ch(\mathcal{E}_3|\omega_7 \cap \mathcal{E}_1 \cap \mathcal{E}_2)|\omega_7 \cap \mathcal{E}_1 \cap \mathcal{E}_2] = .4 \quad (18)$$
$$est[ch(\mathcal{E}_3|\omega_8 \cap \mathcal{E}_1 \cap \mathcal{E}_2)|\omega_8 \cap \mathcal{E}_1 \cap \mathcal{E}_2] = .6 \quad (19)$$

(12)–(13) and (18)–(19) seem appropriate if having *different* visual experiences (a heads-ish and tails-ish experience, respectively) in response to the *same* outcome on flips 1 and 2—which is precisely what happens in ω_1/ω_2 and ω_7/ω_8—makes you think that, in the current lighting conditions, a small tilt of the head this way, or a half step that way might well make you have an entirely different experience regardless of how the coin lands. The output of your visual system in current conditions is rather fragile. In that case, one "success" (*e.g.*, head-ish experience in response to heads on trial (1) and one "failure" (*e.g.*, tails-ish experience in response to heads on trial (2) might cause you to think that your chance of success is not much better than 0.5, *e.g.*, 0.6 (down from $est[ch(\mathcal{E}_1|\omega_1)|\omega_1] - 0.8$.)

(14)–(15) seem appropriate if you think that having a heads-ish visual experience in response to heads on the first flip, and a tails-ish experience in response to tails on the second flip provide overwhelming evidence that the lighting conditions are good enough for your visual system to reliably track the outcome.

(16)–(17) seem appropriate if you think that having a heads-ish visual experience in response to *tails* on the first flip, and a tails-ish experience in response to *heads* on the second flip provide good evidence that (i) there is enough light for your visual system to be sensitive to *something*, but (ii) it is sensitive to an oddly misleading set of features; a set of features that renders your visual system *anti-reliable*.

Then yet again Aamilah ought to update as follows:

$$new_3(\omega_i) = \frac{est[ch(\mathcal{E}_3|\omega_i \cap \mathcal{E}_1 \cap \mathcal{E}_2)|\omega_i \cap \mathcal{E}_1 \cap \mathcal{E}_2] \cdot new_2(\omega_i)}{\sum_j est[ch(\mathcal{E}_3|\omega_j \cap \mathcal{E}_1 \cap \mathcal{E}_2)|\omega_j \cap \mathcal{E}_1 \cap \mathcal{E}_2] \cdot new_2(\omega_j)}.$$

This yields:

$$\begin{array}{ll} new_3(\omega_1) = 0.00140787 & new_3(\omega_2) = 0.000703936 \\ new_3(\omega_3) = 0.0000938582 & new_3(\omega_4) = 0.938488 \\ new_3(\omega_5) = 0.0469291 & new_3(\omega_6) = 0.0117323 \\ new_3(\omega_7) = 0.000117323 & new_3(\omega_8) = 0.000527953 \end{array}$$

So Aamilah's post-$\mathcal{E}_3$ credences for heads on the first flip, tails on the second flip, and tails on the third flip are as follows:

$$new_3(H_1) = 0.940693,\ new_3(T_2) = 0.939227,\ new_3(T_3) = 0.951452.$$

Of course, the conditional chance estimates that we imagined Aamilah adopting at each stage of our little inference problem are merely illustrative. Nothing in J-Kon *forces* you to adopt such estimates. J-Kon permits using *any* conditional chance estimates as inputs to updating so long as (i) each time you expand that set of chance estimates you preserve consistency (avoid uniform loss), and (ii) your estimates are consistent with the Principal Principle, in the sense that expanding to include estimates of the form

$$est[X|(CH = ch) \cap Y] = ch(X|Y)$$

(where $CH = ch$ is the proposition that ch is the true chance function) also preserves consistency. So the examples in section 2 describe only *one* way you might apply J-Kon, not *the* way.

3. Equivalence to Gilded Superconditioning

We now have a new policy for rational learning on the table. To recap, J-Kon in its unofficial form says: when you have a learning experience, $\mathcal{E}$, you ought to estimate the chance of having that very experience conditional on being in this, that, or the other world (*expansion stage*). Then you ought to treat these new conditional chance estimates, $est[ch(\mathcal{E}|\omega)|\omega]$, as your old conditional credences, $old(\mathcal{E}|\omega)$ (conditional credences which you in fact lack, since you have no pre-$\mathcal{E}$ opinions about $\mathcal{E}$). Input your old unconditional credences, $old(\omega)$, and your new conditional chance estimates, $est[ch(\mathcal{E}|\omega)|\omega]$, into Bayes' theorem. Then conditionalize on $\mathcal{E}$. In its official form (detailed shortly), J-Kon says that you ought to update *as if* you were expanding and conditioning in this way.

This updating policy might seem as if it was plucked out of thin air. But in fact it characterizes a brand of what Jeffrey called "superconditioning." Your new credences $new : \mathcal{F} \to \mathcal{R}$ come from your old credences $old : \mathcal{F} \to \mathcal{R}$ by superconditioning when you can:

(i) Expand $\mathcal{F}$ to a larger σ-algebra $\mathcal{F}^+$
(ii) Extend $old : \mathcal{F} \to \mathcal{R}$ to $old^+ : \mathcal{F}^+ \to \mathcal{R}$
(iii) Obtain new^+ from old^+ by conditioning on some proposition E in the larger algebra $\mathcal{F}^+$, so that $new^+(\cdot) = old^+(\cdot|E)$
(iv) Recover new by restricting new^+ to $\mathcal{F}$.

Figure 1 shows what superconditioning looks like in pictures.

Diaconis and Zabell (1982: 824) provide necessary and sufficient conditions for your new credences to come from your old ones by superconditioning. They prove that $new : \mathcal{F} \to \mathcal{R}$ comes from $old : \mathcal{F} \to \mathcal{R}$ by superconditioning just in case there is some upper bound $b \geq 1$ on your probability ratios, so that for every $X \in \mathcal{F}$ we have

$$b \geq \frac{new(X)}{old(X)}.$$

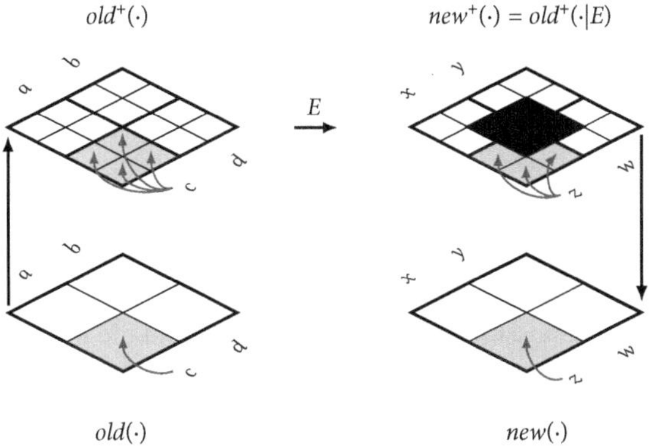

Figure 4.1 *old*(·) can be extended to *old*⁺(·) defined on $\mathcal{F}^+$ and *new*(·) can be recovered by cutting *old*⁺(·|*E*) back down to $\mathcal{F}$.

Diaconis and Zabell are concerned with what you might call *austere superconditioning.* Austere superconditioning places no constraints at all on what the larger algebra $\mathcal{F}^+$ looks like. Neither does it place any constraints on the extended prior old^+, save for probabilistic coherence.

But we might hope that old^+ satisfies norms of epistemic rationality beyond probabilism. For example, we might require old^+ to satisfy Lewis' Principal Principle (PP), so that once chance is brought up to speed on your past learning experiences $\mathcal{P}$, old^+ treats it as an expert worthy of full deference:[7]

$$old^+(X|Y \cap (CH = ch)) = ch(X|Y \cap \mathcal{P}).$$

We might also hope that we can recover *new* not simply by conditioning old^+ on *some* proposition or other in $\mathcal{F}^+$ and then cutting back down to $\mathcal{F}$, but rather by conditioning old^+ on the proposition $\mathcal{E}$ describing *your learning experience.*

Finally, we might hope that not only can we obtain *new* (your post-$\mathcal{E}$ credences) from *old* (your pre-$\mathcal{E}$ credences) in this way, but moreover that your *entire epistemic life* hangs together in the right way. Let $c_0 : \mathcal{F} \to \mathcal{R}$ be your initial credence function, $c_1 : \mathcal{F} \to \mathcal{R}$ be your credence function after learning experience $\mathcal{E}_1$, $c_2 : \mathcal{F} \to \mathcal{R}$ be your credence function after learning experience $\mathcal{E}_2$, and so on. Let $\mathfrak{c} = \langle c_0, \ldots, c_n \rangle$ be the sequence of credal states that you adopt over the course of your life. Call $\mathfrak{c}$ your *epistemic life.* Then we might hope that the various stages of your epistemic life hang together in the following sense: we can extend c_0 to some Principal Principle satisfying c_0^+ defined on $\mathcal{F}^+$ and recover each c_i by

[7] This is a variant of what (Pettigrew 2016: 135) calls the "Extended Principal Principle." See chapters 9 and 10 of Pettigrew (2016) for a careful discussion of the strengths and weaknesses of various formulations of the Principal Principle.

conditioning c_0^+ on the proposition $\mathcal{E}_1 \cap \ldots \cap \mathcal{E}_i$ describing your learning experiences to that point in your life and cutting back down to $\mathcal{F}$.

When $\mathfrak{c}$ hangs together in this way, call it a *gilded superconditioning life*. More carefully, say that $\mathfrak{c}$ is a gilded superconditioning life when you can:

(v) Refine the possibilities $\omega \in \Omega$ into new, more finely-grained possibilities $\alpha \in \Omega^+$ which specify whether $\mathcal{E}_1, \ldots, \mathcal{E}_n$ are true and which chance function $ch \in C$ is true;
(vi) Collect these possibilities into a new set Ω^+ and the propositions expressible as subsets of Ω^+ into a new σ-algebra, $\mathcal{F}^+$;
(vii) Extend $c_0 : \mathcal{F} \to \mathcal{R}$ to $c_0^+ : \mathcal{F}^+ \to \mathcal{R}$, where c_0^+ is not only probabilistically coherent, but also satisfies the Principal Principle;
(viii) Obtain c_i^+ from c_0^+ by conditioning on $\mathcal{E}_1 \cap \ldots \cap \mathcal{E}_i$, for all $i \leq n$, so that $c_i^+(\cdot) = c_0^+(\cdot|\mathcal{E}_1 \cap \ldots \cap \mathcal{E}_i)$;
(iv) Recover c_i by restricting c_i^+ to $\mathcal{F}$.

A natural question, then: when exactly is your epistemic life a gilded superconditioning life? The answer: exactly when you update by the official version of J-Kon.

J-Kon (Official Version). Suppose $\mathfrak{c} = \langle c_0, \ldots, c_n \rangle$ is your epistemic life. So $c_0: \mathcal{F} \to \mathcal{R}$ is your initial credence function, $c_1: \mathcal{F} \to \mathcal{R}$ is the credence function you adopt in response to learning experience $\mathcal{E}_1$, and so on. Let Ω be the set of atoms of $\mathcal{F}$, Ω^+ be the set of atoms of $\mathcal{F}^+$, and $\mathcal{L}_i$ be shorthand for $\mathcal{E}_1 \cap \ldots \cap \mathcal{E}_i$. Then there ought to be some set of conditional chance estimates, *EST*, of the form

$$est[ch(\omega|\Omega^+)|\Omega^+]$$

and

$$est[ch(\mathcal{E}_i|\omega \cap \mathcal{L}_{i-1})|\omega \cap \mathcal{L}_{i-1}]$$

which are both consistent (avoid uniform loss) and PP-consistent such that

$$c_0(\omega) = est[ch(\omega|\Omega^+)|\Omega^+]$$

and

$$c_i(\omega) = \frac{est[ch(\mathcal{E}_i|\omega \cap \mathcal{L}_{i-1})|\omega \cap \mathcal{L}_{i-1}] \cdot c_{i-1}(\omega)}{\Sigma_{\omega' \in \Omega} A est[ch(\mathcal{E}_i|\omega' \cap \mathcal{L}_{i-1})|\omega' \cap \mathcal{L}_{i-1}] \cdot c_{i-1}(\omega')}$$

for all $\omega \in \Omega$ and $0 < i \leq n$.

Your epistemic life satisfies J-Kon just in case it is a gilded superconditioning life (proposition 4, appendix).

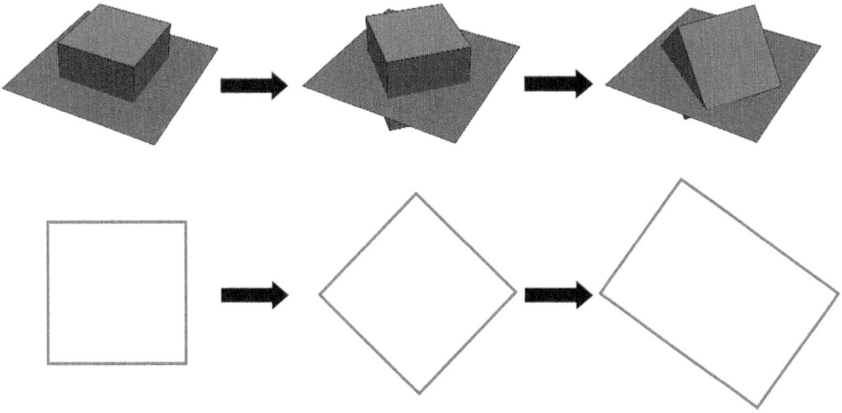

Figure 4.2 3D dynamics (top) vs. 2D cross-section dynamics (bottom).

What this means is that even when you are not in a position to condition on the proposition $\mathcal{E}$ describing your learning experience—perhaps because you have no prior opinions about $\mathcal{E}$ (it is not in your algebra)—you should nonetheless, according to J-Kon, update your "small space credences," *i.e.*, your credences over "first order" propositions in $\mathcal{F}$, just as a more opinionated Bayesian agent would. Such an agent would update her Principal Principle satisfying "big space credences" for propositions in $\mathcal{F}^+$—which include all of the propositions that you have opinions about and more—by conditioning on $\mathcal{E}$. You should mimic her in your small space. Your update should be something like a 2D cross-section of her 3D update (see Figure 2).

Of course, there are *many* ways of extending your old small space credences to PP-satisfying big space credences. Accordingly, there will be *many* ways of mimicking a big space Bayesian agent. This is why there is slack in J-Kon that there is not in J-Con. Every PP-consistent set of conditional chance estimates corresponds to a different PP-satisfying extension (or rather, an equivalence class of extensions). J-Kon simply recommends mimicking a big space Bayesian agent *somehow*, using *some* PP-consistent set of conditional chance estimates. It does not specify *which* set to use.

Given how complicated this all seems, you might reasonably wonder whether J-Kon is within our epistemic ken. J-Kon says that you should update *as if* you were explicitly settling on new, PP-consistent conditional chance estimates (expanding), treating them as your old conditional credences, and conditionalizing on $\mathcal{E}$. If it turned out that testing the consistency of a set of conditional estimates was *really* computationally difficult, then you might worry that updating *as if* you were choosing such estimates would be practically impossible for agents like us. Two points are worth bearing in mind here. First, we often behave *as if* we were solving computationally intensive problems by employing low-cost strategies. For example, when we catch a ball, we behave *as if* we were projecting its trajectory and estimating both when and where it will land. But we do so by employing a low-cost strategy: run in a way that keeps the ball moving at a constant speed through your visual field (Clark 2016: 247). Of course, that is no guarantee that there is a low-cost strategy available for updating via J-Kon. But it would be a mistake to simply assume that there is not, given how often nature finds elegant solutions to seemingly computationally difficult problems. Second, and more to the point, it is *not* computationally difficult to check the consistency of a set of conditional estimates. Walley et al. (2004) provide algorithms for checking consistency (avoiding uniform loss) that only require solving one or two linear programming problems, which can be done efficiently. Human brains (and indeed artificial neural networks) are perfectly capable of solving such problems.

Now we have a better understanding of *what* J-Kon demands of us, and *whether* agents like us can meet those demands. But you might still wonder *why* any of this is a good idea. There are good epistemic reasons to condition when you have infallible dogmatic learning experiences. For example, Greaves and Wallace (2006) provide an expected accuracy argument for conditioning, and Briggs and Pettigrew (2020) provide an accuracy-dominance argument.[8] Likewise, there are good epistemic reasons to satisfy the Principal Principle. Pettigrew (2016), for example, provides an objective expected accuracy (*i.e.*, chance-dominance) argument for PP. But these are all reasons for *actually being* a PP-satisfying conditioner. Is there any reason to *mimic* such an agent? Does small-space updating that mimics PP-satisfying big-space conditioning enjoy any of the epistemic benefits that the latter is privy to?

The answer is *yes*. In the next section I will provide a *chance-dominance* argument for J-Kon, or equivalently, gilded superconditioning. Put roughly: failing to update by J-Kon/gilded superconditioning reduces your chances of living the epistemic good life, or accruing accuracy over the course of your life.

4. Chance-Dominance Argument for J-Kon

Here is how we will proceed. First, we will attempt to pin down what it is that makes one's credences epistemically valuable at a world, and specify "epistemic utility functions" that measure this sort of value. Second, we will use the machinery of decision theory to show that J-Kon can be given an epistemic-value-based rationale. The story in a nutshell is this: if you fail to update by J-Kon, your epistemic life is *chance-dominated* by some other J-Kon satisfying life, *i.e.*, *every possible chance function* expects your life to accrue strictly less total epistemic

[8] Both Greaves and Wallace (2006) and Briggs and Pettigrew (2020) tacitly assume that rational agents are infallible dogmatic learners. They measure the epistemic value of an updating plan at a world by the accuracy of the credal state that the plan recommends at the world. But this only makes sense if there is no chance that the agent will mis-execute the plan. In this way, they bake infallibility into their measure of epistemic value.

value than the J-Kon satisfying life. In this sense, you are *guaranteed* to have a worse chance of living the epistemic good life than you could have had by satisfying J-Kon. If you update by J-Kon, in contrast, you are never chance-dominated in this way. This reveals an *evaluative* defect—chance-dominance—that mars the epistemic lives of J-Kon violators. And facts about such defects ought to inform your preferences over epistemic lives. They give you reason to prefer updating via J-Kon to not.

Here is our main argument:

1. **Veritism**: The ultimate source of epistemic value is accuracy. So the epistemic value of an unconditional credence function $c: \mathcal{F} \to \mathcal{R}$ at a world $\alpha \in \Omega^+$ is given by $-\mathcal{I}(c, \alpha)$, where $\mathcal{I}$ is some reasonable measure of inaccuracy. We assume that $\mathcal{I}$ is an additive inaccuracy score generated by a continuous, bounded, strictly proper component function. Moreover, the epistemic value of an epistemic life, or sequence of credal states $\mathfrak{c} = \langle \mathfrak{c}_0, \ldots, \mathfrak{c}_n \rangle$ at α is given by

$$\mathcal{I}(\mathfrak{c}, \alpha) = \sum_{i:\alpha \in \mathcal{L}_i} \mathcal{I}(c_i, \alpha)$$

where $\mathcal{L}_i = \mathcal{E}_1 \cap \ldots \cap \mathcal{E}_i$. $\mathcal{I}$ reflects the view that life stages c_i ought to be evaluated as conditional credence functions. More carefully, $c_i(X)$ should be evaluated as your credence for X *conditional on the learning experiences that produced* c_i. As such, c_i is evaluable for accuracy only at worlds α in which the learning experiences that produced that stage take place, *viz.*, $\alpha \in \mathcal{L}_i$. The total inaccuracy of your epistemic life $\mathfrak{c}$ at α is the sum of the degrees of inaccuracy of the life stages c_i that are evaluable for accuracy at α.

2. **Chance-dominance**: If one option O **strictly chance-dominates** another option O', in the sense that every possible chance function ch expects O to be strictly more valuable than O', *i.e.*

$$\sum_{\alpha \in \Omega^+} ch(\alpha|\Omega^+)\mathcal{U}(O, \alpha) > \sum_{\alpha \in \Omega^+} ch(\alpha|\Omega^+)\mathcal{U}(O', \alpha)$$

then any rational agent ought to strictly prefer O to O'.

3. **Theorem**[9] If $\mathfrak{b}$ is not a J-Kon sequence (or gilded superconditioning sequence), then $\mathfrak{b}$ is **strictly chance-dominated** by a J-Kon sequence $\mathfrak{c}$, *i.e.*,

[9] We should note that the proof of this theorem makes a number of simplifying assumptions. For example, we assume that both "small space" and "big space" credence functions are defined on finite algebras. We also assume that all small space credence function are regular, in the sense that they assign positive probability to each world.

$$\sum_{\alpha \in \Omega^+} ch(\alpha|\Omega^+)\mathcal{I}(\mathfrak{b},\alpha) > \sum_{\alpha \in \Omega^+} ch(\alpha|\Omega^+)\mathcal{I}(\mathfrak{c},\alpha)$$

for every possible chance function *ch*. If $\mathfrak{b}$ is a J-Kon sequence, on the other hand, then it is not even **weakly chance-dominated**, *i.e.*, there is no $\mathfrak{c} \neq \mathfrak{b}$ such that

$$\sum_{\alpha \in \Omega^+} ch(\alpha|\Omega^+)\mathcal{I}(\mathfrak{b},\alpha) \geq \sum_{\alpha \in \Omega^+} ch(\alpha|\Omega^+)\mathcal{I}(\mathfrak{c},\alpha)$$

for all possible chance functions *ch*.

C. **J-Kon**: If a rational agent fails to update via J-Kon, then she ought to strictly prefer some other J-Kon satisfying epistemic life to her own.

Premise 1 identifies a theory of epistemic value: *veritism*. Veritists claim that accuracy is the principal epistemic good-making feature of credal states. Your credences may well be epistemically laudable for a range of reasons. They may be specific, informative, verisimilar, encode simple, unified explanations, be justified, etc. But these are all *instrumental* epistemic good-making features, on the veritist view. They are good, roughly speaking, as a means to the end of accuracy. Accuracy—how close your credences are to the truth—is the fundamental epistemic good. It is the primary source of epistemic value. The higher your credence in truths and the lower your credence in falsehoods, the more valuable your credal state is from the epistemic perspective.

And this applies not just to your credal state at a single time—to an epistemic time slice—but to your *whole epistemic life*. The principal epistemic good-making feature of your epistemic life—the *sequence* of credal states that you adopt over time—is the total accuracy that your life accrues. This really captures two distinct veritist thoughts. First, the epistemic value of your life supervenes on accuracy of the credal states you adopt over the course of your life. Second, the *shape* of your epistemic life does not contribute to its distinctively epistemic value. A life of gradual gains in accuracy is no better or worse, from the epistemic perspective, than a life of alethic ups and downs. Any two lives that accrue the same total accuracy are equally epistemically valuable. The shape of one's epistemic life is not the "right kind of alethic fact" to determine its epistemic value.

Premise 1 also delineates a class of reasonable measures of accuracy, or what's better for technical purposes, *in*accuracy. We will assume that inaccuracy is measured by an additive, continuous, bounded, strictly proper inaccuracy score $\mathcal{I}$. **Additivity** says that $\mathcal{I}$ takes the following form:

$$\mathcal{I}(c, \alpha) = \sum_{X \in \mathcal{F}} s(c(X), \alpha(X))$$

where $s\colon \mathcal{R} \times \{0,1\} \to \mathcal{R}$ is what Joyce (2009) calls a *component function*; a function which measures the inaccuracy of an individual credence $c(X)$ when

X's truth value is $\alpha(X)$ (0 or 1). **Strict Propriety** says that every probabilistically coherent credence function expects itself to be strictly more accurate than any other credence function. See appendix for technical details. For a philosophical rich discussion of these properties, see Joyce (2009) and Pettigrew (2016).

Now extend $\mathcal{I}$ to measure not only the accuracy of individual credence functions c, but also epistemic lives $\mathfrak{c} = \langle c_0, \ldots, c_n \rangle$ as follows:

$$\mathcal{I}(\mathfrak{c}, \alpha) = \sum_{i:\alpha \in \mathcal{L}_i} \mathcal{I}(c_i, \alpha)$$

$\mathcal{I}$ reflects the view that epistemic time slices c_i ought to be evaluated as *conditional credence functions*. More carefully, $c_i(X)$ should be evaluated as an epistemic bet on the truth-value X, but only a conditional one; one which "takes for granted" the learning experiences $\mathcal{L}_i$ that produced it, and so is "called-off"—not evaluable for accuracy—at worlds α in which those learning experiences do not take place. According to $\mathcal{I}$, the total inaccuracy of your epistemic life $\mathfrak{c}$ at α is the sum of the degrees of inaccuracy of the epistemic time slices or life stages c_i that are evaluable for accuracy at α. When $\mathcal{I}$ takes this form, call it *temporally additive.*

Premise 2 identifies a constraint on rational preference. It specifies how rational agents structure their preferences over options in light of facts about their value, together with facts about the chances. In particular, it says that if every possible chance function expects one option to be better than another, then you ought to prefer the one to the other.

Imagine, for example, that a friend tells you that she is going to pick a ball from one of two urns, *A* or *B*. Whichever urn she draws from, she will pick the ball at random. Both urns contain red and blue balls in the exact same proportion. But you have no idea what that proportion is. Finally, your friend drops one additional red ball into urn B. Now she gives you a choice. You can select the urn, *A* or *B*, and she will give you 100 if she draws a red. (What a friend!) Which should you prefer? Urn *B*, of course. Whatever proportion you started with, urn *B* now has a higher objective expected payout than urn *A*. You have a better chance of making off with the goods if you go with *B*. Chance dominance says: in light of these facts, you ought to prefer *B* to *A*.

Premise 3 is the spine of the argument. It shows that if you violate J-Kon, then your epistemic life is chance-dominated. There is some other J-Kon satisfying life that has higher objective expected value relative to every possible chance function. (See proposition 8 in the appendix.) In conjunction with premises 1 and 2, this establishes that J-Kon violators should prefer some other J-Kon satisfying life to their own.

This argument provides a purely alethic (rather than evidential or pragmatic) rationale for abiding by J-Kon. The epistemic lives of J-Kon violators are marred by a particular sort of evaluative defect. They are chance-dominated. This is a "wide scope" defect; a defect of epistemic lives which may not be reflected in "lower level defects." Each stage of an agent's epistemic life—the credal state that she adopts at any particular time—may be epistemically unimpugnable considered individually. But nevertheless, those stages may together constitute an epistemically defective life.

Upon reflection, this is perhaps not very surprising. Wide scope evaluative defects are precisely the sorts of defects you would *expect* to underpin a genuinely diachronic updating policy like J-Kon.

5. Confirmational Holism

To recap, we began our journey in section 1 by outlining Weisberg's concern. J-Con bungles the introduction of new undercutting defeaters. Since nearly all learning experiences introduce new undercutting defeaters, J-Con almost never applies. We then introduced a new updating policy, J-Kon, designed to apply where J-Con does not. After seeing how J-Kon works in practice, we explored its equivalence to gilded superconditioning. We also provided a purely alethic (accuracy-centred) rationale for abiding by J-Kon. Now we will return to the issues surrounding confirmational holism that set us on this path.

Consider our heart attack case again. For the last hour you have been sitting on the train, reading the news, and, unbeknownst to you, leaning lazily on your left elbow. You have prior credences over the power set $\mathcal{F}$ of Ω, which contains:

$$\omega_1 = L\&H \qquad \omega_2 = L\&\neg H$$
$$\omega_3 = \neg L\&H \qquad \omega_4 = \neg L\&\neg H$$

where

L = You have been leaning on your elbow for an hour
H = You will have a heart attack.

Your prior credence that you will have a heart attack is low—maybe 0.001. You have no idea whether you have been leaning on your elbow for an hour. So we will say that you are 50–50. Your prior credence for L is 0.5. Finally, you think that leaning lazily on your left elbow is *irrelevant* to your prospects of having a heart attack. Taking on the supposition that you have been leaning on your elbow does nothing to raise or lower your credence that you will have a heart attack:

$$old(H|L) = old(H) = 0.001.$$

This fixes your prior credal state:

$$old(w_1) = 0.0005 \qquad old(w_2) = 0.4995$$
$$old(w_3) = 0.0005 \qquad old(w_4) = 0.4995$$

Then you feel your left arm tingling. This learning experience $\mathcal{E}$ "directly affects" your credence for *H*, pushing it up to 0.99. But what *should* your new credences be after $\mathcal{E}$? Should you take this "direct product" of $\mathcal{E}$ at face value? Should you stick with 0.99 as your new credence for *H*, rather than sloughing it off as you would if it were the aberrant result of momentary mania? Or should you correct for biases in your credence-producing processes in some other way? And what about the rest of your new credences? What should they be?

According to Christensen, the doxastic effects of experience should almost always be mediated by your background beliefs. This is one of confirmational holism's great insights. Whether the tingling in your arm pushes your credence that you are going to have a heart attack up, or down, or leaves it unchanged, ought to depend for example on your background beliefs about your cardiovascular health, what exactly the symptoms of a heart attack are, whether you have been leaning on your left elbow, etc. But J-Con treats the doxastic effects of experience as an exogenous factor; an output of some "black box" process that serves as an input to J-Con. So it fails to vindicate this insight.

The inputs to J-Kon, on the other hand, are not the *direct effects* of experience. Rather, they are quantities that might plausibly be mediated by your background beliefs. Recall, two types of quantities serve as inputs to J-Kon. The first quantity is your old credence function. The second quantity is a set of conditional chance estimates of the form:

$$est[ch(\mathcal{E}|\omega \cap \mathcal{P})|\omega \cap \mathcal{P}].$$

The conditional chance estimates that you are disposed to adopt (or behave *as if* you were adopting) reflect your background beliefs. In particular, they reflect your beliefs about how various factors causally influence your learning experiences. For example, you might estimate the chance of having an arm-tingling experience conditional on being in a heart-attack world to be roughly 0.999. This reflects your background belief that heart attacks cause arm tingling. Of course, conditional chance estimates will often reflect background beliefs in varied and complex ways. But the basic point stands: background beliefs influence which conditional chance estimates you are disposed to adopt (or behave as if you were adopting). (Maybe such dispositions even *constitute* background beliefs.) Conditional chance estimates, in turn, serve as an input to J-Kon. As such, they provide a vehicle for background beliefs to systematically influence the doxastic effects of experience.

Of course, J-Kon does not specify precisely *how* an agent's background beliefs ought to determine how she expands; which conditional chance estimates she ought to adopt. But we side with Jeffrey here. Learning how to change one's mind involves training the messy network of neurons in your skull to translate perceptive and proprioceptive inputs into sensible inputs to updating—in our case, sensible conditional chance estimates. This will undoubtedly involve domain-specific skill; skill that goes far beyond the skills one might be said to have simply in virtue of being epistemically rational. As such, it will not be something that constraints on *rational updating* will speak to.

Importantly, though, J-Kon makes sensible updating rather less mysterious than J-Con does. It leaves less to domain-specific skill than J-Con. According to Jeffrey, settling on a sensible input to J-Con (a sensible input partition and distribution) is a matter of skill; outside the purview of epistemic rationality. But according to J-Kon, this is only half right. Settling on sensible conditional chance estimates may be a matter of domain-specific skill. From there, however, J-Kon determines whether you should update by J-Con, and if so, what the input partition and distribution ought to be. So we have a story about where the inputs to J-Con come from (at least in those situations where J-Kon agrees that J-Con applies). We have lightened how much of the explanatory burden we offload onto domain-specific skill, just as Christensen requested.

Back to our heart attack case. What *should* your new credences be after $\mathcal{E}$? According to J-Kon, you ought to update as follows. First, adopt conditional chance estimates of the form $est[ch(\mathcal{E}|\omega_i)|\omega_i]$. For example, you might adopt the following conditional chance estimates:

$$est[ch(\mathcal{E}|\omega_1)|\omega_1] = est[ch(\mathcal{E}|\omega_3)|\omega_3] = 0.99$$

as well as

$$est[ch(\mathcal{E}|\omega_2)|\omega_2] = 0.1$$

and

$$est[ch(\mathcal{E}|\omega_4)|\omega_4] = 0.01.$$

The first two estimates seem appropriate if you think that there is a high ($\approx 99\%$) chance of having an arm-tingling, credence-pushing learning experience if you are indeed having a heart attack. The third estimate seems appropriate if you think that there is a significant, but nevertheless fairly low ($\approx 10\%$) chance of having an arm-tingling, credence-pushing experience if you have been leaning on your elbow, potentially pinching your ulnar nerve, even if you are *not* having a heart attack. The final estimate seems appropriate if you think there is a rather low chance ($\approx 1\%$) of having such an experience otherwise.

Next, you should use these conditional chance estimates to update as follows:

$$new(\omega_i) = \frac{est[ch(\mathcal{E}|\omega_i)|\omega_i] \cdot old(\omega_i)}{\Sigma_j est[ch(\mathcal{E}|\omega_j)|\omega_j] \cdot old(\omega_j)}.$$

This yields:

$$\begin{array}{ll} new(\omega_1) = 0.00884956 & new(\omega_2) = 0.893001 \\ new(\omega_3) = 0.00884956 & new(\omega_4) = 0.0893001 \end{array}$$

So your posteriors for H and L are:

$$new(H) = 0.0176991 \text{ and } new(L) = 0.90185.$$

So despite the fact your learning experience $\mathcal{E}$ "directly affects" your credence for H, pushing it up to 0.99, J-Kon recommends adopting a significantly lower (≈ 0.02) credence for H. Why? Because your conditional chance estimates reflect the opinion that there is a significant ($\approx 10\%$) chance of having $\mathcal{E}$ even if H is false—in particular, if L is true. In light of this and your prior near-certainty in $\neg H$ (before $\mathcal{E}$, you were 99.9% confident that you are *not* going to have a heart attack), J-Kon recommends hedging your epistemic bets that $\mathcal{E}$ is on the money by only bumping up your credence in H to roughly 0.02.

More importantly, your posterior for H conditional on L is:

$$new(H|L) = 0.00981267.$$

So J-Kon naturally predicts that $\mathcal{E}$ turns L into an undercutting defeater for H. Prior to $\mathcal{E}$, L is irrelevant to H. And irrelevant propositions do not undercut anything. But *after* $\mathcal{E}$, you *do* see L as an undercutting defeater for H. After $\mathcal{E}$ you think: learning L would be good reason to cut your posterior confidence in H in half, dropping it from roughly 0.02 to 0.01.

J-Kon does not do this by hand, in some ad hoc fashion. Take yourself back to the moment when you feel your arm tingling and your credence in H shoots up to 0.99. Ask yourself about the chance of having that experience if you are in ω_2 (no heart attack, but leaning on elbow). What's your best estimate of that chance? Now ask yourself about the chance of having that experience if you are in ω_4 (no heart attack, no leaning). What's your best estimate? Is it different from your earlier estimate? If so—and I am betting it is—then J-Kon *demands* that you accommodate your experience by applying J-Con to a sufficiently fine partition;

one that slots ω_2 and ω_4 into different cells.[10] (See our discussion of (♥) in §2.2.) But then *new* cannot come from *old* by applying J-Con naïvely to any Jeffrey shift over $\{H,\neg H\}$. And it is precisely this fact—that we were applying J-Con to some Jeffrey shift over $\{H,\neg H\}$ —that prevented $\mathcal{E}$ from turning L into an undercutting defeater for H.

The moral: J-Kon handles the introduction of new undercutting defeaters in a natural and principled fashion, just as Weisberg requested. J-Kon also specifies the sense in which the doxastic effects of experience are mediated by one's background beliefs, just as Christensen required. So J-Kon is pretty holism-friendly![11] Even more importantly, there is a purely alethic (accuracy-centred) justication for updating via J-Kon.

6. Objections

Before wrapping up, let's address a few pressing concerns.

Objection. If you start your epistemic life with an initial credence function and an extremely rich set of conditional chance estimates, as J-Kon requires, then you never really *learn to learn*. How you update over the course of your epistemic life is fixed by (i) those estimates, which do not change with domain-specific training, and (ii) one's experiences, which do not obviously change with training either. So it seems as though we have lost Jeffrey's insight that learning to translate perceptive and proprioceptive inputs into the sort of information that feeds into your updating policy is a matter of acquiring a domain-specific skill.

Reply. J-Kon does *not* require you to start your epistemic life with an extremely rich set of conditional chance estimates. It just requires you to consistently expand that set after each learning experience (or rather to update as if you were doing so). Becoming skilled at settling on sensible inputs is a matter of becoming skilled at estimating the conditional chance of having various types of experience. And that *is* something you can plausibly improve on with domain-specific training.

Objection. If J-Kon is equivalent to gilded superconditioning, then it in effect requires having prior credences over an extremely rich algebra $\mathcal{F}^+$. $\mathcal{F}^+$ must include demonstrative propositions describing all possible learning experiences. But that is massively implausible! You are only in a position to have opinions about those demonstrative propositions (I had *that* learning experience) *after* you have the experience. Second, *even if* you somehow have such prior credences, then

[10] *Any* shift from *old* to *new* can be accommodated by applying J-Con to a sufficiently fine partition. The question is simply: How fine? And is there a principled story about why to choose *that* input distribution over *that* input partition?

[11] Gallow's (2013) HCondi is also holist-friendly. An extended comparison of J-Kon and HCondi is beyond the scope of this paper.

J-Kon just recommends conditioning on the proposition describing your learning experience. But this is just Bayesian orthodoxy!

Reply. J-Kon/gilded superconditioning is not conditioning. It does *not* require you to have prior credences over propositions describing all possible learning experiences. It merely requires that in response to any learning experience, you "settle on" conditional chance estimates that are consistent with the conditional chance estimates that you used earlier. And it only requires you to "settle on" and "use" conditional chance estimates in an extremely thin sense. J-Kon updaters only need to be causally sensitive to learning experiences in such a way that they transition from old to new credences *as if* they are explicitly estimating conditional chances. But those conditional chance estimates, which are in this thin sense available for the purposes of updating, *need not be available for other purposes*. You need not be able to announce those estimates, for example. You need not be able to use them to guide action (*e.g.*, to decide whether to accept or reject a bet). So while these estimates reflect your opinions *in some weak sense*, they need not play the theoretical roles characteristic of *credences* or *expectations* in the Bayesian tradition. This more subtle story is quite clearly not standard Bayesian orthodoxy.

Objection. J-Kon recommends updating as if you were (i) generating new conditional chance estimates $est[ch(\mathcal{E}|\omega)|\omega]$ and then (ii) conditionalizing on $\mathcal{E}$. In this second step, $est[ch(\mathcal{E}|\omega)|\omega]$ functions as your old credence for $\mathcal{E}$ conditional on ω (a conditional credence which you lack). Why take this detour through conditional chance estimates? Why not simply update by expanding your old credal state to include new credences for $\mathcal{E}$ conditional on ω, and then updating as if you were conditionalizing on $\mathcal{E}$?

Reply. J-Kon is equivalent to gilded superconditioning. Gilded superconditioning requires that your new credences for $\mathcal{E}$ conditional on ω take a particular form, *viz.*, the form of conditional chance estimates. This makes J-Kon more restrictive than austere superconditioning (at least if there are interesting constraints on the space of possible chance functions). And gilded superconditioning, not austere conditioning, is what our chance dominance argument yields. So this restriction is forced on us by accuracy considerations.

Objection. Garber (1980) objected to Field's (1978) reformulation of J-Con—Field conditioning—on (roughly) the following grounds. Suppose that you have phenomenologically identical uncertain learning experiences (glimpsing a coin in poor lighting conditions, hearing a voice that sounds familiar but you cannot quite place, etc.) back to back to back—9 times instead of once, let's say. Then you get no more information from the last 8 than you do from the first. Nevertheless, Field conditioning predicts that your credence in some cell of the input partition will keep going up and up and up, in the end rendering you "virtually certain" that the given cell is the true one (that the coin came up heads, that the distant voice belongs to a particular friend, etc.). But J-Kon is just a species of Field conditioning! It is what you get when you set the e^{α_i} 's in (5′) of (Field 1978: 367) as follows:

$$e^{\alpha_i} = est[ch(\mathcal{E}|\omega_i \cap \mathcal{P})|\omega_i \cap \mathcal{P}]$$

But then surely J-Kon falls to the same objection.

Reply. It does not. Garber and Field both assume that the α_i s are "given by experience." Since you have phenomenologically identical uncertain learning experiences in Garber's example, he uses the same α_i s as inputs to Field conditioning after each experience. J-Kon does not use the same inputs after each experience. And rightly so. Garber's intuition that you get no more information from the last 8 experiences than you do from the first is undergirded by the thought that *if you had a certain type of experience the first time around, and nothing relevant has changed, then you are virtually certain—chance of 1—to have the same type of experience the next 8 times*. This information is reflected in the conditional chance estimates that serve as inputs to J-Kon, and prevent the sort of compounding that plagues naïve applications of Field conditioning. (In fact, we already saw J-Kon handle this sort of case in section 2.2, example 3.)

7. Summary and Epilogue

Confirmational holism causes fits for J-Con. According to holism, the effects of experience ought to be mediated by one's background beliefs. J-Con fails to adequately explain how the latter influences the former. Holism also maintains that learning experiences ought nearly always to introduce new undercutting defeaters. But J-Con bungles the introduction of new undercutting defeaters.

Our question was this: Can we provide a more holism-friendly alternative to J-Con? And if so, can we provide a purely epistemic rationale for employing this alternative updating rule?

To that end, we detailed and defended J-Kon. J-Kon says, roughly, that when you have a learning experience, $\mathcal{E}$, you should *expand* by settling on new conditional chance estimates, $est[ch(\mathcal{E}|\omega)|\omega]$; estimates of the chance of having that very experience conditional on being in this, or that, or the other world. Then you should to treat these new conditional chance estimates, $est[ch(\mathcal{E}|\omega)|\omega]$, as your old conditional credences, $old(\mathcal{E}|\omega)$ (conditional credences which you in fact lack, since you have no pre-$\mathcal{E}$ opinions about $\mathcal{E}$). Input your old unconditional credences, $old(\omega)$, and your new conditional chance estimates, $est[ch(\mathcal{E}|\omega)|\omega]$, into Bayes' theorem. Then conditionalize on $\mathcal{E}$. This specifies new credences for each atom of your algebra. Together with the probability axioms, this fixes your entire new credal state.

After putting J-Kon to work in a range of applications, we showed that J-Kon was in fact equivalent to what we called *gilded superconditioning*. Then we used this equivalence to provide a purely alethic (accuracy-centred) rationale for updating via J-Kon (rather than an evidential or pragmatic rationale). Finally, we showed that J-Kon is indeed more holism-friendly than J-Con. It pins down a precise sense in which the effects of experience are mediated by one's background beliefs. It also elegantly handles the introduction of new undercutting defeaters.

At the end of his life, Jeffrey rejected the claim that epistemic rationality requires you to update in accordance with any particular updating policy. As he himself put it, "it no longer goes without saying that you will change your mind by conditioning or generalized conditioning (probability kinematics)," *i.e.*, J-Con, "any more than it goes without saying that your changes of mind will be quite spontaneous or unconsidered... these are questions about which you may make up your mind about changing your mind in specific cases." (Jeffrey 1992: 6). This was part of Jeffrey's "radical probabilism."

Our project here shows us that accuracy considerations seem to push us toward something of a middle ground. Gone are the old days of Bayesian orthodoxy. In the old days, there was conditioning and Jeffrey conditioning (and perhaps minimization of Kullback-Leibler divergence). And according to each of these updating policies, one's old credences and learning experience *uniquely determines* one's new credences. Rational agents have no wiggle room in updating.

In Jeffrey's radical paradise, quite the opposite is true. In this paradise, rational agents have nothing *but* wiggle room. They may choose which properties of their old credal state to preserve, choose which new properties seem appropriate in light of their learning experience, and adopt any new coherent credal state that has the whole lot of them. Sometimes these properties, together with the probability axioms, will be sufficient to single out a unique new credal state. Sometimes not. Of course, that does not mean that just anything goes. They may make these choices well or poorly. And their skill at making these choices will often be the product of hard-earned domain-specific skill. But as we emphasized earlier, such skill will far outstrip the skill one might be said to have in virtue of being epistemically rational. As such, it will simply not be reflected in constraints of rationality.

The accuracy considerations that motivate J-Kon seem to land us somewhere in the middle. Unlike the old days of Bayesian orthodoxy, J-Kon permits significant wiggle room in updating. Rational agents can accommodate new learning experiences using *any* set of conditional chance estimates that are consistent with the Principal Principle and their past updates. And there are *many* such sets. But unlike Jeffrey's radical paradise, the wiggle room does not stretch all the way to the horizon. If there are interesting constraints on the space of possible chance functions, these will also constrain how you can update. So while you have quite a bit of wiggle room in updating, according to J-Kon, you do not have all the room in the world.

J-Kon also clears up a mystifying bit of Jeffrey's radical probabilism. Learning to change one's mind, on Jeffrey's picture, involves acquiring skill at deciding which properties of one's old credal state to preserve, and which new properties seem appropriate in light of their learning experience. But without some insight into what makes properties of credal states good or bad quite generally—without a theory of value for properties of credal states (not for credal states *themselves*, but for *properties* of credal states)—it is slightly perplexing what it might mean to make such choices well or poorly.

J-Kon swaps out this perplexing skill for a more understandable one. Learning to change one's mind does not involve acquiring skill at choosing properties of credal states. Instead, it involves acquiring skill at estimating conditional chances. But we already have a theory of value for estimates! According to veritism, estimates are good exactly to the extent that they are accurate; exactly to the extent that they are close to the true value of the estimated quantity. The upshot: it is much easier to wrap one's head around what learning to change one's mind might actually amount to.

To conclude, it is worth pointing to a number of exciting new questions that J-Kon raises. First, J-Kon makes room for a healthy subjectivism/objectivism debate about rational learning. Subjectivists might be swayed only by accuracy-dominance considerations, rather than chance-dominance considerations. Such considerations seem to support superconditioning, rather then gilded superconditioning, or J-Kon. And plain old superconditioning *really does* permit epistemic lives comprising nearly any sequence of coherent credal states. On the other hand, objectivists might be swayed by considerations of worst-case epistemic loss avoidance (*cf.* Pettigrew (2016)). Such considerations seem to support an even more restrictive form of superconditioning than gilded superconditioning; one that requires old^{+} to maximize entropy, perhaps. As a result, objectivists will tighten up what slack J-Kon permits.

Second, J-Kon opens up new questions about *diachronic deference principles*. Synchronic deference principles answer the following question: When I learn that another agent's credence for X is x (maybe she is an expert, maybe an epistemic peer), how should I adjust my credence in X? Diachronic deference principles, in contrast, answer this question: When I learn that another agent accommodated learning experiences $\mathcal{E}_1,\ldots,\mathcal{E}_n$ by adopting a particular sequence of credal states, how should that influence how I update in the future? Perhaps the tools used to provide an alethic justification for J-Kon can help answer this question.

Finally, J-Kon raises questions about *diachronic aggregation principles*. Synchronic aggregation principles answer the following question: Given the credal states of some group members, how can we arrive at a single credal state that captures not the members' individual opinions, but the group's opinions as a whole? Diachronic aggregation principles answer a slightly different question: Given how different group members accommodated past learning experiences, how we can we arrive at a single updating rule that captures not the members' individual inductive dispositions, but the group's inductive dispositions as a whole? For a group of J-Kon updaters, you might aggregate the conditional chance estimates that the members used to update in the past, and then accommodate group learning experiences by expanding that aggregated set going forward. Or perhaps the tools used to provide an alethic justification for J-Kon will offer up a different solution.

Appendix

Appendix A.1 The Framework

Let Ω be a finite sample space. Let

$$\Omega^+ = \Omega \times \{a_1, b_1\} \times \ldots \times \{a_n, b_n\} \times \{c_1, \ldots, c_m\}$$

Let $\mathcal{F}$ be the power set of Ω and $\mathcal{F}^+$ be the power set of Ω^+. Intuitively, Ω contains all of the "possible worlds" ω that you can distinguish and $\mathcal{F}$ contains all of the propositions that you have opinions about. Ω^+ contains more refined possibilities and consequently $\mathcal{F}^+$ contains additional propositions that you do not have opinions about. The way to think about Ω^+ is as follows. In the actual world, you have learning experiences $E_1, \ldots, E_n$ at times $t_1, \ldots, t_n$. We introduce variables $\mathcal{E}_1, \ldots, \mathcal{E}_n$ that indicate whether you have these experiences at any "world" α in Ω^+. $\mathcal{E}_i = a_i$ means that you have experience E_i at t_i. $\mathcal{E}_i = b_i$ means that you do not have experience E_i at t_i. Finally, we introduce a variable CH that indicates which of a finite number of possible conditional chance functions obtains. $CH = ch_j$ means that ch_j: $\mathcal{F}^+ \times \mathcal{F}^+ \rightarrow \mathcal{R}$ is the true chance function. So, for example, the "fine-grained world"

$$\alpha = \langle \omega, a_1, a_2, \ldots, b_n, ch_j \rangle$$

in Ω^+ says not only that the "coarse-grained world" ω in Ω is true, but also that you have learning experience E_1 at t_1 ($\mathcal{E}_1 = a_1$), E_2 at t_2 ($\mathcal{E}_2 = a_2$), and so on, but do not have learning experience E_n at t_n ($\mathcal{E}_n = b_n$). In addition, $ch_j : \mathcal{F}^+ \times \mathcal{F}^+ \rightarrow \mathcal{R}$ is the true chance function ($CH = ch_j$).

In what follows, we will abuse notation by using '$\mathcal{E}_i$' to refer to the set of all $\alpha \in \Omega^+$ with $\mathcal{E}_i = a_i$. Also for convenience let $\mathcal{L}_i = \mathcal{E}_1 \cap \ldots \cap \mathcal{E}_i$ for $1 \leq i \leq n$.

Let $C = \{ch_1, \ldots, ch_m\}$ be the set of possible conditional chance functions. We assume that every $ch_j \in C$ is coherent (*i.e.*, satisfies the Rényi-Popper axioms) and *non-self-undermining*, in the sense that $ch_j(CH = ch_j | \Omega^+) = 1$. We also assume that $ch_j(\mathcal{L}_n | \Omega^+) > 0$.

Let $\mathcal{S}$ be the set of all sequences $\mathfrak{b} = \langle b_0, \ldots, b_n \rangle$ of "small space" credence functions $b_i : \mathcal{F} \rightarrow [0,1]$. We will assume that every $\mathfrak{b} \in \mathcal{S}$ is **regular** in the sense that $b_i(\{\omega\}) > 0$ for all $i \leq n$ and $\omega \in \Omega$. (Henceforth we write $b_i(\omega) > 0$.)

Let $\mathcal{B}$ be the set of all sequences $\mathfrak{p} = \langle p_0, \ldots, p_n \rangle$ of "big space" credence functions $p_i : \mathcal{F}^+ \rightarrow [0,1]$.

Definition 1. $\mathfrak{p}$ is **coherent** iff p_i is a finitely additive probability function for all $i \leq n$.
Definition 2. $\mathfrak{p}$ is **quasi-regular** iff $p_0(\mathcal{L}_n) > 0$.
Definition 3. $\mathfrak{p}$ is a **condi sequence** iff

$$p_i(X)p_0(\mathcal{L}_i) = p_0(X \cap \mathcal{L}_i)$$

for all $X \in \mathcal{F}^+$ and $i \leq n$.

For any $ch \in \mathcal{C}$, let

$$\mathfrak{ch} = \langle ch(\cdot|\Omega^+), ch(\cdot|\mathcal{L}_1), \ldots, ch(\cdot|\mathcal{L}_n) \rangle$$

Let $\mathfrak{C}$ be the set of all $\mathfrak{ch}$ with $ch \in \mathcal{C}$. Then every $\mathfrak{ch} \in \mathfrak{C}$ is a coherent, quasi-regular, condi sequence.

Definition 4. $\mathfrak{p}$ is a **PP sequence** iff

$$p_i(Y \cap (CH = ch_j))ch_j(X|Y \cap L_i) = p_i(X \cap Y \cap (CH = ch_j))$$

for all $i \leq n$, $ch_j \in \mathbb{C}$ and $X, Y \in \mathcal{F}^+$.

Let $\mathcal{Q} \subseteq \mathcal{B}$ be the set of coherent, quasi-regular, condi sequences.

Let $\wp \subseteq \mathcal{Q} \subseteq \mathcal{B}$ be the set of coherent, quasi-regular, condi, PP sequences.

Now choose any "small space" sequence $\mathfrak{b} = \langle b_0, \ldots, b_n \rangle \in \mathcal{S}$.

Definition 5. $\mathfrak{b}$ is **coherent** iff b_i is a finitely additive probability function for all $i \leq n$.

Definition 6. $\mathfrak{b} = \langle b_0, \ldots, b_n \rangle$ is a **superconditioning sequence** iff there is some coherent condi sequence $\mathfrak{p} = \langle p_0, \ldots, p_n \rangle$ that extends $\mathfrak{b}$ to $\mathcal{F}^+$, i.e., p_i extends b_i for all $i \leq n$.

Definition 7. $\mathfrak{b}$ is a **quasi-regular superconditioning sequence** iff there is some coherent, quasi-regular, condi sequence $\mathfrak{p}$ that extends $\mathfrak{b}$ to $\mathcal{F}^+$.

Definition 8. $\mathfrak{b}$ is a **gilded superconditioning sequence** iff there is some coherent, quasi-regular, condi, PP sequence $\mathfrak{p}$ that extends $\mathfrak{b}$ to $\mathcal{F}^+$.

For any $1 \leq i \leq n$ and $\omega \in \Omega$, let $CH_{\omega,i} : \Omega^+ \to \mathcal{R}$ be defined by

$$CH_{\omega,i}(\omega^*, a_1/b_1, \ldots, a_n/b_n, ch_j) = ch_j(\mathcal{E}_i|\omega \cap \mathcal{L}_{i-1})$$

$CH_{\omega,i}(\alpha)$ specifies the chance of $\mathcal{E}_i$ conditional on $\omega \cap \mathcal{L}_{i-1}$ at $\alpha = \langle \omega^*, a_1/b_1, \ldots, a_n/b_n, ch_j \rangle$. Similarly, let $CH_{\bar{\omega}} : \Omega^+ \to \mathcal{R}$ be defined by

$$CH_\omega(\omega^*, a_1/b_1, \ldots, a_n/b_n, ch_j) = ch_j(\omega|\Omega^+)$$

CH_ω specifies the "ur-chance" of ω at $\alpha = \langle \omega^*, a_1/b_1, \ldots, a_n/b_n, ch_j \rangle$.

Let *EST* be a (finite) set of conditional chance estimates of the form

$$est[CH_{\omega,i}|\omega \cap \mathcal{L}_{i-1}] = x$$

and

$$est[CH_\omega|\Omega^+] = y$$

for all $1 \leq i \leq n$ and $\omega \in \Omega$. Formally, each such estimate is a tuple

$$\langle \langle \mathcal{V}, E \rangle, x \rangle$$

consisting of a variable $\mathcal{V}:\Omega^{+}\rightarrow\mathcal{R}$ (in our case, $\mathcal{V}=CH_{\omega,i}$ or $\mathcal{V}=CH_{\omega}$), a condition $E\subseteq\Omega^{+}$ (in our case, $E=\omega\cap\mathcal{L}_{i-1}$ or $E=\Omega^{+}$), and an estimate $x\in\mathcal{R}$. In what follows, we will sometimes write

$$est[ch(\mathcal{E}_i|\omega\cap\mathcal{L}_{i-1})|\omega\cap\mathcal{L}_{i-1}]=x,\ est[ch(\omega|\Omega^{+})|\Omega^{+}]=y$$

rather than $est[CH_{\omega,i}|\omega\cap\mathcal{L}_{i-1}]=x$ or $est[CH_{\omega}|\Omega^{+}]=y$, just to make it easier to remember what $CH_{\omega,i}$ and CH_{ω} mean.

For any $i\leq n$ and $\omega\in\Omega$, let

$$M_{\omega,i}=\omega\cap\mathcal{L}_{i-1}(CH_{\omega,i}-est[CH_{\omega,i}|\omega\cap\mathcal{L}_{i-1}])$$

Here again we abuse notation and use '$\omega\cap\mathcal{L}_{i-1}$ 'to refer to the indicator function which returns 1 if $\alpha\in\omega\cap\mathcal{L}_{i-1}$ and 0 otherwise. So

$$M_{\omega,i}(\alpha)=\begin{cases}CH_{\omega,i}(\alpha)-est[CH_{\omega,i}|\omega\cap\mathcal{L}_{i-1}] & \text{if } \alpha\in\omega\cap\mathcal{L}_{i-1}\\ 0 & \text{otherwise}\end{cases}$$

Hence $M_{\omega,i}$ is "called off" if $\alpha\notin\omega\cap\mathcal{L}_{i-1}$ and "pays out" $CH_{\omega,i}-est[CH_{\omega,i}|\omega\cap\mathcal{L}_{i-1}]$ otherwise.

We will assume that adopting a precise conditional estimate $est[\mathcal{V}|E]$ requires judging the gamble $M=E(\mathcal{V}-est[\mathcal{V}|E])$, as well as the gamble $-M$, to both be "marginal gambles." M and $-M$ are marginal gambles, in your view, just in case you estimate them to pay out 0—no more or less than the status quo. Call M and $-M$ the **marginal gambles associated with** $est[\mathcal{V}|E]$.

Let $\mathcal{V}$ be the set of all (bounded) gambles/variables $\mathcal{V}:\Omega^{+}\rightarrow\mathcal{R}$. Let $\mathcal{V}_{<0}\subseteq\mathcal{V}$ be the set of gambles/variables $\mathcal{V}:\Omega^{+}\rightarrow\mathcal{R}$ with $\mathcal{V}(\alpha)<0$ for all $\alpha\in\Omega^{+}$.

Definition 9. For any $\mathcal{V}_1,\ldots,\mathcal{V}_k\in\mathcal{V}$, the **positive hull** of $\{\mathcal{V}_1,\ldots,\mathcal{V}_k\}$ is given by

$$\text{posi}\{\mathcal{V}_1,\ldots,\mathcal{V}_k\}=\{\sum_{i\leq k}\lambda_i\mathcal{V}_i|\lambda_i\geq 0\ for\ all\ i\leq k\ and\ \lambda_j\rangle 0\ for\ some\ j\leq k\}$$

i.e., $\text{posi}\{\mathcal{V}_1,\ldots,\mathcal{V}_k\}$ is the set of all positive linear combinations of $\mathcal{V}_1,\ldots,\mathcal{V}_k$.

Definition 10. A set $\mathcal{D}\subseteq\mathcal{V}$ is a **coherent set of desirable gambles** iff:

D1. $0\notin\mathcal{D}$

D2. If $\mathcal{V}(\alpha)\geq 0$ for all $\alpha\in\Omega^{+}$ and $\mathcal{V}(\alpha')>0$ for some $\alpha'\in\Omega^{+}$, then $\mathcal{V}\in\mathcal{D}$

D3. If $\mathcal{V}\in\mathcal{D}$ and $\lambda>0$, then $\lambda\mathcal{V}\in\mathcal{D}$

D4. If $\mathcal{V},\mathcal{Q}\in\mathcal{D}$, then $\mathcal{V}+\mathcal{Q}\in\mathcal{D}$

Let $\mathbb{D}$ be the set of all coherent sets of desirable gambles.

Definition 11. For any set $\mathcal{A}\subseteq\mathcal{V}$, the **natural extension** of $\mathcal{A}$ is

$$ext(\mathcal{A})=\bigcap_{\mathcal{D}\in\mathbb{D}:\mathcal{A}\subseteq\mathcal{D}}\mathcal{D}$$

Definition 12. A finite set of conditional estimates

$$X=\{est[\mathcal{V}_1|E_1]=x_1,\ldots,est[\mathcal{V}_k|E_k]=x_k\}$$

avoids uniform loss (AUL) iff the marginal gambles associated with X,

$$\mathcal{M}_X = \{M_i | i \leq k\} \cup \{-M_i | i \leq k\}$$

avoid uniform loss ($M_i = E_i[\mathcal{V}_i - x_i]$).

Definition 13. $\mathcal{M}_X$ **avoids uniform loss (AUL)** iff there is no set of non-negative reals

$$\{\lambda_i | i \leq k\} \cup \{\rho_i | i \leq k\} \subseteq \mathcal{R}_{\geq 0}$$

with some λ_i or ρ_i positive and some $\varepsilon > 0$ such that

$$\sum_{i \leq k} \lambda_i (M_i + \varepsilon E_i) + \sum_{i \leq k} \rho_i (-M_i + \varepsilon E_i) \leq 0$$

In English, $\mathcal{M}_X$ is subject to uniform loss if there is a positive linear combination of the acceptable variables/gambles $M_i + \varepsilon E_i$ and $-M_i + \varepsilon E_i$ (which are slight sweetenings of the marginal gambles M_i and $-M_i$) whose net reward cannot possibly be positive.

Definition 14. A finite set of conditional estimates X **avoids conditional negativity** iff for every subset $A \subseteq X$, the set of marginal gambles $\mathcal{A}$ associated with A avoids conditional negativity.

Definition 15. A finite set of marginal gambles $\mathcal{A} \subseteq \mathcal{M}_X$ **avoids conditional negativity** iff

$$\text{posi}\mathcal{A}|_{S(\mathcal{A})} \cap \mathcal{V}_{<0}|_{S(\mathcal{A})} = \varnothing$$

where

- $S(\mathcal{A}) = \cup_{\pm M_i \in \mathcal{A}} E_i$
- $M_i|_E$ is the restriction of M_i to $E \subseteq \Omega^+$
- $\mathcal{A}|_E = \{\pm M_i|_E | \pm M_i \in \mathcal{A}\}$

It is straightforward to show that X avoids conditional negativity iff it avoids uniform loss.

Lemma 1. *A finite set of conditional estimates*

$$X = \{est[\mathcal{V}_1 | E_1] = x_1, \ldots, est[\mathcal{V}_k | E_k] = x_k\}$$

avoids conditional negativity iff it avoids uniform loss.

Proof. Suppose that X avoids conditional negativity but does not avoid uniform loss. So there is some set of non-negative reals

$$\{\lambda_i | i \leq k\} \cup \{\rho_i | i \leq k\} \subseteq \mathcal{R}_{\geq 0}$$

with some λ_i or ρ_i positive and some $\varepsilon > 0$ such that

$$G = \sum_{i \leq k} \lambda_i (M_i + \varepsilon E_i) + \sum_{i \leq k} \rho_i (-M_i + \varepsilon E_i) \leq 0$$

Let

$$\mathcal{A} = \bigcup_{i \leq k : \lambda_i > 0 \text{ or } \rho_i > 0} \{M_i, -M_i\}$$

$\mathcal{A}$ is the set of marginal gambles associated with

$$A = \{est[\mathcal{V}_i|E_i] = x_i|\lambda_i\rangle 0 \text{ or } \rho_i > 0\} \subseteq X$$

Note that

$$G = \sum_{M_i \in \mathcal{A}} \lambda_i(M_i + \varepsilon E_i) + \sum_{-M_i \in \mathbb{A}} \rho_i(-M_i + \varepsilon E_i) \leq 0$$

Let

$$G' = \sum_{M_i \in \mathcal{A}} \lambda_i M_i + \sum_{-M_i \in \mathcal{A}} \rho_i(-M_i)$$

Then $G'(\alpha) < G(\alpha) \leq 0$ for any $\alpha \in S(\mathcal{A})$. Hence $G'|_{S(\mathcal{A})} \in \mathcal{V}_{<0}|_{S(\mathcal{A})}$. But also $G'|_{S(\mathcal{A})} \in \text{posi}\mathcal{A}|_{S(\mathcal{A})}$. So the set of marginal gambles $\mathcal{A}$ associated with $A \subseteq X$ does not avoid conditional negativity. $\Rightarrow\Leftarrow$.

For the other direction, suppose that X avoids uniform loss but does not avoid conditional negativity. So there is some subset $A \subseteq X$ whose associated marginal gambles

$$\mathcal{A} = \bigcup_{(est[\mathcal{V}_i|E_i]=x_i) \in A} \{M_i, -M_i\}$$

do not avoid conditional negativity, *i.e.*

$$\text{posi}\mathcal{A}|_{S(\mathcal{A})} \cap \mathcal{V}_{<0}|_{S(\mathcal{A})} \neq \emptyset$$

For notational convenience, let $\mathcal{A} = \{N_1,\ldots, N_t\}$. Then there is some $F = \sum_{i \leq t} \lambda_i N_i|_{S(\mathbb{A})}$ with $\lambda_i \geq 0$ for all $i \leq t$ and $\lambda_j > 0$ for some $j \leq t$ such that $F \in \mathcal{V}_{<0}|_{S(\mathbb{A})}$. Let

$$\mathcal{A}' = \{N_i \in \mathcal{A}|\lambda_i\rangle 0\}$$

Then $F = \Sigma_{N_i \in \mathcal{A}'} \lambda_i N_i|_{S(\mathcal{A})}$. Let $\varepsilon = \frac{1}{2} \cdot \min_{\beta \in S(\mathcal{A}')} - \dfrac{\Sigma_{N_i \in \mathcal{A}'} \lambda_i N_i|_{S(\mathcal{A}')}(\beta)}{\Sigma_{N_i \in \mathcal{A}'} \lambda_i E_i|_{S(\mathcal{A}')}(\beta)} > 0$. Let

$$\delta_i = \begin{cases} \lambda_i & \text{if } N_i \in \mathcal{A}' \\ 0 & \text{otherwise} \end{cases}$$

And let

$$F' = \sum_{i \leq t} \delta_i(N_i + \varepsilon E_i)$$

First choose $\alpha \notin S(\mathcal{A}')$. Then $(N_i + \varepsilon E_i)(\alpha) = 0$ for all $N_i \in \mathcal{A}'$ and $\delta_i = 0$ for all $N_i \notin \mathcal{A}'$. Hence $F'(\alpha) = 0$. Next choose $\alpha \in S(\mathcal{A}')$. Then

$$F'(\alpha) = \sum_{i \leq t} \delta_i(N_i + \varepsilon E_i)(\alpha) = \sum_{N_i \in \mathcal{A}'} \lambda_i(N_i|_{S(\mathcal{A}')} + \varepsilon E_i|_{S(\mathcal{A}')})(\alpha) < 0$$

iff

$$\sum_{N_i \in \mathcal{A}'} \lambda_i N_i|_{S(\mathcal{A}')}(\alpha) < -\varepsilon \sum_{N_i \in \mathcal{A}'} \lambda_i E_i|_{S(\mathcal{A}')}(\alpha)$$

iff

$$\varepsilon < -\frac{\Sigma_{N_i \in \mathcal{A}'} \lambda_i N_i|_{S(\mathcal{A}')}(\alpha)}{\Sigma_{N_i \in \mathcal{A}'} \lambda_i E_i|_{S(\mathcal{A}')}(\alpha)}$$

But by definition

$$\varepsilon < 2\varepsilon = \min_{\beta \in S(\mathcal{A}')} -\frac{\Sigma_{N_i \in \mathcal{A}'} \lambda_i N_i|_{S(\mathcal{A}')}(\beta)}{\Sigma_{N_i \in \mathcal{A}'} \lambda_i E_i|_{S(\mathcal{A}')}(\beta)} \leqslant -\frac{\Sigma_{N_i \in \mathcal{A}'} \lambda_i N_i|_{S(\mathcal{A}')}(\alpha)}{\Sigma_{N_i \in \mathcal{A}'} \lambda_i E_i|_{S(\mathcal{A}')}(\alpha)}$$

So $F'(\alpha) < 0$. Hence $F' \leq 0$. But then X does not avoid uniform loss. $\Rightarrow\Leftarrow$.

□

Lemma 2. *For any*

$$A \subseteq X = \{est[\mathcal{V}_1|E_1] = x_1, \ldots, est[\mathcal{V}_k|E_k] = x_k\}$$

the set of positive linear combinations of elements of $\mathcal{A}$ *(the marginal gambles associated with* A*) is the full set of linear combinations of elements of* $\mathcal{A}$*:* $\text{posi}(\mathcal{A}) = \text{span}(\mathcal{A})$.

Proof.

$$\mathcal{A} = \bigcup_{i \in I} \{M_i, -M_i\}$$

for some $I \subseteq \{1, \ldots, k\}$. Trivially $\text{posi}(\mathcal{A}) \subseteq \text{span}(\mathcal{A})$. Choose $F \in \text{span}(\mathcal{A})$. So there are reals λ_i and ρ_i for all $i \in I$ such that

$$F = \sum_{M_i \in \mathcal{A}} \lambda_i M_i + \sum_{-M_i \in \mathcal{A}} \rho_i(-M_i)$$

Assume WLOG that $\lambda_i \neq 0$ or $\rho_i \neq 0$ for some $i \in I$, since we already know that

$$0 = \sum_{M_i \in \mathcal{A}} M_i + \sum_{-M_i \in \mathcal{A}} (-M_i) \in \text{posi}(\mathcal{A})$$

Let

$$\langle \lambda_i^*, \rho_i^* \rangle = \begin{cases} \langle \lambda_i, \rho_i \rangle & \text{if } \lambda_i \geq 0,\ \rho_i \geq 0 \\ \langle \lambda_i - \rho_i, 0 \rangle & \text{if } \lambda_i \geq 0,\ \rho_i < 0 \\ \langle 0, \rho_i - \lambda_i \rangle & \text{if } \lambda_i < 0,\ \rho_i \geq 0 \\ \langle -\rho_i, -\lambda_i \rangle & \text{if } \lambda_i < 0,\ \rho_i < 0 \end{cases}$$

Let

$$F^* = \sum_{M_i \in \mathcal{A}} \lambda_i^* M_i + \sum_{-M_i \in \mathcal{A}} \rho_i^*(-M_i)$$

Clearly $F = F^*$ and $F^* \in \text{posi}(\mathcal{A})$. Hence $\text{span}(\mathcal{A}) \subseteq \text{posi}(\mathcal{A})$.

□

Corollary 3. *For any finite set of conditional estimates*

$$X = \{est[\mathcal{V}_1|E_1] = x_1, \ldots, est[\mathcal{V}_k|E_k] = x_k\}$$

the following conditions are equivalent:

- *X avoids conditional negativity*
- *X avoids uniform loss*
- *For every subset $A \subseteq X$, the marginal gambles $\mathcal{A}$ associated with A satisfy*

$$\text{span}(\mathcal{A}|_{S(\mathcal{A})} \cap \mathcal{V}_{<0}|_{S(\mathcal{A})} = \varnothing$$

Definition 16. A set of conditional chance estimates *EST* which avoids conditional negativity is **PP-consistent** iff

$$EST \cup \{est[X|Y \cap (CH = ch_j)] = ch_j(X|Y)|ch_j \in \mathcal{C} \text{ and } X,Y \in \mathcal{F}^+\}$$

also avoids conditional negativity.

Definition 17. A function $\underline{P} : \mathcal{V} \times \mathcal{F}^+ \to \mathcal{R}$ is a **coherent lower prevision** iff there is some coherent set of desirable gambles $\mathcal{D}$ such that

$$\underline{P}(\mathcal{V}|E) = sup\{x|E[\mathcal{V} - x] \in \mathcal{D}\}$$

for all $\mathcal{V} \in \mathcal{V}$ and $E \in \mathcal{F}^+$.

This is what De Bock (2019) calls "Williams coherence." It is inspired by the work of Williams (1975, 2007).

Definition 18. A function $P : \mathcal{V} \times \mathcal{F}^+ \to \mathcal{R}$ is a **conditional linear prevision** iff

P1. $P(\mathcal{V}|A) \geqslant \inf_{\alpha \in A} \mathcal{V}(\alpha)$
P2. $P(\lambda\mathcal{V}|A) = \lambda P(\mathcal{V}|A)$ for any $\lambda \in \mathcal{R}$
P3. $P(\mathcal{V} + \mathcal{Q}|A) = P(\mathcal{V}|A) + P(\mathcal{Q}|A)$
P4. $P(B\mathcal{V}|A) = P(\mathcal{V}|A \cap B)P(B|A)$ if $A \cap B \neq \varnothing$

Definition 19. $\mathfrak{b} = \langle b_0,..., b_n \rangle$ is a **J-Kon sequence** iff there is a finite set of conditional chance estimates, *EST*, which (i) avoids conditional negativity, (ii) is PP-consistent and satisfies (iii) for all $\omega \in \Omega$

$$b_0(\omega) = est[ch(\omega|\Omega^+)|\Omega^+]$$

and for all $0 < i \leq n$

$$b_i(\omega) = \frac{est[ch(\mathcal{E}_i|\omega \cap \mathcal{L}_{i-1})|\omega \cap \mathcal{L}_{i-1}] \cdot b_{i-1}(\omega)}{\sum_{\omega' \in \Omega} est[ch(\mathcal{E}_i|\omega' \cap \mathcal{L}_{i-1})|\omega' \cap \mathcal{L}_{i-1}] \cdot b_{i-1}(\omega')}$$

A.2 Characterizing J-Kon Sequences

Proposition 4. *For any sequence $\mathfrak{b} \in \mathcal{S}$, $\mathfrak{b}$ is a J-Kon sequence iff $\mathfrak{b}$ is a gilded super-conditioning sequence.*

Proof. Suppose that $\mathfrak{b} = \langle b_0,..., b_n \rangle$ is a J-Kon sequence. So there is a finite set of conditional chance estimates, *EST*, which (i) avoids conditional negativity, (ii) is PP-consistent and satisfies (iii) for all $\omega \in \Omega$

$$b_0(\omega) = est[ch(\omega|\Omega^+)|\Omega^+]$$

and for all $0 < i \leq n$

$$b_i(\omega) = \frac{est[ch(\mathcal{E}_i|\omega \cap \mathcal{L}_{i-1})|\omega \cap \mathcal{L}_{i-1}] \cdot b_{i-1}(\omega)}{\Sigma_{\omega' \in \Omega}\ est[ch(\mathcal{E}_i|\omega' \cap \mathcal{L}_{i-1})|\omega' \cap \mathcal{L}_{i-1}] \cdot b_{i-1}(\omega')}$$

Since *EST* is PP-consistent, we can assume WLOG that

$$\{est[X|Y \cap (CH = ch_j)] = ch_j(X|Y)|ch_j \in \mathcal{C} \text{ and } X,Y \in \mathcal{F}^+\} \subseteq EST$$

By corollary 3, *EST* avoids uniform loss. By (de Cooman and Quaeghebeur, 2012, Theorem 1), *EST* avoids uniform loss iff the natural extension of the set

$$\mathbb{A} = \bigcup_{(est[\mathcal{V}_i|E_i]=x_i) \in EST} \{M_i + \varepsilon E_i|\varepsilon > 0\} \cup \{-M_i + \varepsilon E_i|\varepsilon > 0\}$$

is a coherent set of desirable gambles (where $M_i = E_i[\mathcal{V}_i - x_i]$), in which case

$$\text{ext}(\mathcal{A}) = \text{posi}(\mathcal{A} \cup \{\mathcal{V} \geq 0|\mathcal{V}(\alpha)\rangle 0 \text{ for some } \alpha \in \Omega^+\}).$$

And as (Walley et al., 2004, section 3.2) notes, the function $P : \mathcal{V} \times \mathcal{F}^+ \rightarrow \mathcal{R}$ defined by

$$P(\mathcal{V}|E) := sup\{x|E[\mathcal{V} - x] \in \text{ext}(\mathcal{A})\}$$

is a coherent conditional lower prevision and

$$P(\mathcal{V}|E) = est(\mathcal{V}|E) = x$$

for all $(est[\mathcal{V}|E] = x) \in EST$. Indeed, since both $E[\mathcal{V} - x + \varepsilon]$ and $E[x - \mathcal{V} + \varepsilon]$ are in $\mathcal{A}$ for all $(est[\mathcal{V}|E] = x) \in EST$ and $\varepsilon > 0$, we must have

$$P(\mathcal{V}|E) = sup\{x|E[\mathcal{V} - x] \in \text{ext}(\mathcal{A})\} = inf\ \{x|E[x - \mathcal{V}] \in \text{ext}(\mathcal{A})\}$$

in which case P is a conditional *linear* prevision.

For any $i \leq n$ and $X \in \mathcal{F}^+$, let

$$p_i(X) := P(X|\mathcal{L}_i)$$

Since P is a conditional linear prevision, it follows trivially that p_i is a finitely additive probability function. So $\mathfrak{p}$ is coherent. And

$$\begin{aligned} p_0(\mathcal{L}_n) &= P(\mathcal{L}_n|\Omega^+) \\ &= \sum_{ch_i \in \mathcal{C}} P(\mathcal{L}_n|(CH = c_i) \cap \Omega^+)P(CH = c_i|\Omega^+) \\ &= \sum_{ch_i \in \mathcal{C}} est[\mathcal{L}_n|(CH = c_i) \cap \Omega^+]P(CH = c_i|\Omega^+) \\ &= \sum_{ch_i \in \mathcal{C}} ch_i(\mathcal{L}_n|\Omega^+)P(CH = c_i|\Omega^+) > 0 \end{aligned}$$

So $\mathfrak{p}$ is quasi-regular. To see that $\mathfrak{p}$ is a condi sequence, note that for any $X \in \mathcal{F}^+$ and $i \leq n$

$$p_i(X)p_0(\mathcal{L}_i) = p_0(X \cap \mathcal{L}_i)$$

iff

$$P(X|\mathcal{L}_i \cap \Omega^+)P(\mathcal{L}_i|\Omega^+) = P(X \cap \mathcal{L}_i|\Omega^+)$$

which follows immediately from axiom 4 for conditional linear previsions. To see that $\mathfrak{p}$ is a PP sequence, note that for any $i \leq n$, $ch_j \in \mathbb{C}$ and $X, Y \in \mathcal{F}^+$

$$p_i(Y \cap (CH = ch_j))ch_j(X|Y \cap L_i) = p_i(X \cap Y \cap (CH = ch_j))$$

iff

$$P(Y \cap (CH = ch_j)|L_i)ch_j(X|Y \cap L_i) = P(X \cap Y \cap (CH = ch_j)|L_i)$$

Given $ch_j(X|Y \cap \mathcal{L}_i) = est[X|(CH = ch_j) \cap Y \cap \mathcal{L}_i] = P(X|(CH = ch_j) \cap Y \cap \mathcal{L}_i)$ this holds iff

$$P(Y \cap (CH = ch_j)|L_i)P(X|(CH = ch_j) \cap Y \cap \mathcal{L}_i) = P(X \cap Y \cap (CH = ch_j)|L_i)$$

which follows immediately from axiom 4 for conditional linear previsions.

To show that $\mathfrak{b}$ is a gilded superconditioning sequence, it only remains to show that $\mathfrak{p}$ extends $\mathfrak{b}$ to $\mathcal{F}^+$. Choose $\omega \in \Omega$. First note that

$$\begin{aligned} p_0(\omega) &= P(\omega|\Omega^+) \\ &= \sum_{ch_j \in C} P(\omega|(CH = ch_j) \cap \Omega^+)P(CH = ch_j|\Omega^+) \\ &= \sum_{ch_j \in C} est[\omega|(CH = ch_j) \cap \Omega^+]P(CH = ch_j|\Omega^+) \\ &= \sum_{ch_j \in C} ch_j(\omega|\Omega^+)P(CH = ch_j|\Omega^+) \\ &= P(ch(\omega|\Omega^+)|\Omega^+) \\ &= est[ch(\omega|\Omega^+)|\Omega^+] \\ &= b_0(\omega) \end{aligned}$$

Now suppose that p_{i-1} extends b_{i-1} to $\mathcal{F}^+$. We will show that p_i must extend b_i to $\mathcal{F}^+$ as well.

$$\begin{aligned} b_i(\omega) &= \frac{est[ch(\mathcal{E}_i|\omega \cap \mathcal{L}_{i-1})|\omega \cap \mathcal{L}_{i-1}] \cdot b_{i-1}(\omega)}{\sum_{\omega' \in \Omega} est[ch(\mathcal{E}_i|\omega' \cap \mathcal{L}_{i-1})|\omega' \cap \mathcal{L}_{i-1}] \cdot b_{i-1}(\omega')} \\ &= \frac{P(ch(\mathcal{E}_i|\omega \cap \mathcal{L}_{i-1})|\omega \cap \mathcal{L}_{i-1}) \cdot p_{i-1}(\omega)}{\sum_{\omega' \in \Omega} P(ch(\mathcal{E}_i|\omega' \cap \mathcal{L}_{i-1})|\omega' \cap \mathcal{L}_{i-1}) \cdot p_{i-1}(\omega')} \\ &= \frac{(\sum_{ch_j \in C} ch_j(\mathcal{E}_i|\omega \cap \mathcal{L}_{i-1})P(CH = ch_j|\omega \cap \mathcal{L}_{i-1})) \cdot P(\omega|\mathcal{L}_{i-1})}{\sum_{\omega' \in \Omega} (\sum_{ch_j \in C} ch_j(\mathcal{E}_i|\omega' \cap \mathcal{L}_{i-1})P(CH = ch_j|\omega' \cap \mathcal{L}_{i-1})) \cdot P(\omega'|\mathcal{L}_{i-1})} \\ &= \frac{(\sum_{ch_j \in C} P(\mathcal{E}_i|(CH = ch_j) \cap \omega \cap \mathcal{L}_{i-1})P(CH = ch_j|\omega \cap \mathcal{L}_{i-1})) \cdot P(\omega|\mathcal{L}_{i-1})}{\sum_{\omega' \in \Omega} (\sum_{ch_j \in C} P(\mathcal{E}_i|(CH = ch_j) \cap \omega' \cap \mathcal{L}_{i-1})P(CH = ch_j|\omega' \cap \mathcal{L}_{i-1})) \cdot P(\omega'|\mathcal{L}_{i-1})} \\ &= \frac{P(\mathcal{E}_i|\omega \cap \mathcal{L}_{i-1}) \cdot P(\omega|\mathcal{L}_{i-1})}{\sum_{\omega' \in \Omega} P(\mathcal{E}_i|\omega' \cap \mathcal{L}_{i-1}) \cdot P(\omega'|\mathcal{L}_{i-1})} \\ &= P(\omega|\mathcal{E}_i \cap \mathcal{L}_{i-1}) = P(\omega|\mathcal{L}_i) = p_i(\omega) \end{aligned}$$

Therefore $\mathfrak{b}$ is a gilded superconditioning sequence.

For the other direction, suppose that $\mathfrak{b}$ is a gilded superconditioning sequence. So there is some coherent, quasi-regular, condi, PP sequence $\mathfrak{p}$ that extends $\mathfrak{b}$ to $\mathcal{F}^+$. Let $P : \mathcal{V} \times \mathcal{F}^+ \rightarrow \mathcal{R}$ be the partial assignment of conditional estimates defined by

$$P(\mathcal{V}|A) := \begin{cases} E_{p0}(\mathcal{V}|A) & \text{if } A \in \mathcal{F}^+ \text{ and } p_0(A) > 0 \\ E_{ch_j}(\mathcal{V}|A) & \text{if} A = Y \cap (CH = ch_j) \text{ for some } Y \in \mathcal{F}^+, ch_j \in C \text{ and } p_0(Y \cap (CH = ch_j)) = 0 \end{cases}$$

where

$$E_{p_0}(\mathcal{V}|A) := \Sigma_{\omega \in \Omega} \mathcal{V}(\omega) \frac{p_0(\omega \cap A)}{p_0(A)}$$

and

$$E_{ch_j}(\mathcal{V}|A) := \Sigma_{\omega \in \Omega} \mathcal{V}(\omega) ch_j(\omega|A)$$

Since both $E_{p_0}(\cdot|A)$ and $E_{ch_j}(\cdot|A)$ satisfy (P1)-(P3) whenever they are defined, so too does P whenever $P(\cdot|A)$ is defined. It is also easy to verify that P satisfies (P4) whenever the relevant terms are defined. In that case, (Williams, 2007, Thm 3) guarantees that P is extendable to a full conditional linear prevision, so that $P(\mathcal{V}|A)$ is defined for all $\mathcal{V} \in \mathcal{V}$ and $A \in \mathcal{F}^+$. We assume WLOG that P is so defined.

Let EST be the following (finite) set of conditional chance estimates

$$EST = \{P(CH_{\omega,i}|\omega \cap \mathcal{L}_{i-1})|\omega \in \Omega, 1 \leq i \leq n\} \cup \{P(CH_\omega|\Omega^+)|\omega \in \Omega\}$$

Since P is a conditional linear prevision, it is coherent (De Bock, 2019, Prop 35), and hence avoids uniform loss (de Cooman and Quaeghebeur, 2012, Thm 1) and conditional negativity (corollary 3).

To see that EST is PP-consistent, note that if $p_0(Y \cap (CH = ch_j)) > 0$, then

$$\begin{aligned} P(X|Y \cap (CH = ch_j)) &= E_{p_0}(X|Y \cap (CH = ch_j)) \\ &= \sum_{\omega \in \Omega} 1_X(\omega) \frac{p_0(\omega \cap Y \cap (CH = ch_j))}{p_0(Y \cap (CH = ch_j))} \\ &= \sum_{\omega \in \Omega} 1_X(\omega) ch_j(\omega|Y) = ch_j(X|Y) \end{aligned}$$

where $1_X : \Omega^+ \rightarrow \{0,1\}$ is the indicator function for X. And if $p_0(Y \cap (CH = ch_j)) = 0$, then

$$P(X|A) = E_{ch_j}(X|Y \cap (CH = ch_j)) = ch_j(X|Y)$$

To show that $\mathfrak{b}$ is a J-Kon sequence, it only remains to show that for all $\omega \in \Omega$

$$b_0(\omega) = est[ch(\omega|\Omega^+)|\Omega^+]$$

and for all $0 < i \leq n$

$$b_i(\omega) = \frac{est[ch(\mathcal{E}_i|\omega \cap \mathcal{L}_{i-1})|\omega \cap \mathcal{L}_{i-1}] \cdot b_{i-1}(\omega)}{\Sigma_{\omega' \in \Omega}\, est[ch(\mathcal{E}_i|\omega' \cap \mathcal{L}_{i-1})|\omega' \cap \mathcal{L}_{i-1}] \cdot b_{i-1}(\omega')}$$

Choose $\omega \in \Omega$. Then

$$\begin{aligned}
b_0(w) &= p_0(w) \\
&= \sum_{ch_j \in C: p_0(CH=ch_j)>0} \frac{p_0(\omega \cap (CH = ch_j))}{p_0(CH = ch_j)} p_0(CH = ch_j) \\
&= \sum_{ch_j \in C: p_0(CH=ch_j)>0} ch_j(\omega|\Omega^+) p_0(CH = ch_j|\Omega^+) \\
&= E_{p_0}(ch(\omega|\Omega^+)|\Omega^+) \\
&= P(ch(\omega|\Omega^+)|\Omega^+) \\
&= est[ch(\omega|\Omega^+)|\Omega^+]
\end{aligned}$$

Now choose $0 < i \leq n$. Suppose WLOG that $b_{i-1}(\omega) = p_{i-1}(\omega) > 0$.

$$b_i(\omega) = p_i(\omega) = \frac{p_{i-1}(\mathcal{E}_i \cap \omega)}{p_{i-1}(\mathcal{E}_i)} = \frac{\frac{p_{i-1}(\mathcal{E}_i \cap \omega)}{p_{i-1}(\omega)} \cdot b_{i-1}(\omega)}{\sum_{\omega' \in \Omega: p_{i-1}(\omega')>0} \frac{p_{i-1}(\mathcal{E}_i \cap \omega')}{p_{i-1}(\omega')} \cdot b_{i-1}(\omega')}$$

$$= \frac{\left(\sum_{ch_j \in C: p_{i-1}(\omega \cap (CH=ch_j))>0} \frac{p_{i-1}(\mathcal{E}_i \cap \omega \cap (CH = ch_j))}{p_{i-1}(\omega \cap (CH = ch_j))} \frac{p_{i-1}(\omega \cap (CH = ch_j))}{p_{i-1}(\omega)} \right) \cdot b_{i-1}(\omega)}{\sum_{\omega' \in \Omega} \left(\sum_{ch_j \in C: p_{i-1}(\omega' \cap (CH=ch_j))>0} \frac{p_{i-1}(\mathcal{E}_i \cap \omega' \cap (CH = ch_j))}{p_{i-1}(\omega' \cap (CH = ch_j))} \frac{p_{i-1}(\omega' \cap (CH = ch_j))}{p_{i-1}(\omega')} \right) \cdot b_{i-1}(\omega')}$$

$$= \frac{\left(\sum_{ch_j \in C} ch_j(\mathcal{E}_i|\omega \cap \mathcal{L}_{i-1}) P(CH = ch_j|\omega \cap \mathcal{L}_{i-1}) \right) \cdot b_{i-1}(\omega)}{\sum_{\omega' \in \Omega} \left(\sum_{ch_j \in C} ch_j(\mathcal{E}_i|\omega' \cap \mathcal{L}_{i-1}) P(CH = ch_j|\omega' \cap \mathcal{L}_{i-1}) \right) \cdot b_{i-1}(\omega')}$$

$$= \frac{P(ch(\mathcal{E}_i|\omega \cap \mathcal{L}_{i-1})|\omega \cap \mathcal{L}_{i-1}) \cdot b_{i-1}(\omega)}{\sum_{\omega' \in \Omega} P(ch(\mathcal{E}_i|\omega' \cap \mathcal{L}_{i-1})|\omega' \cap \mathcal{L}_{i-1}) \cdot b_{i-1}(\omega')}$$

$$= \frac{est[ch(\mathcal{E}_i|\omega \cap \mathcal{L}_{i-1})|\omega \cap \mathcal{L}_{i-1}] \cdot b_{i-1}(\omega)}{\sum_{\omega' \in \Omega} est[ch(\mathcal{E}_i|\omega' \cap \mathcal{L}_{i-1})|\omega' \cap \mathcal{L}_{i-1}] \cdot b_{i-1}(\omega')}$$

This establishes that $\mathfrak{b}$ is J-Kon sequence.

□

A.3 Quasi Bregman Divergences

Let $\mathcal{I} : \mathcal{S} \times \Omega^+ \rightarrow \mathcal{R}_{\geq 0}$ be an **inaccuracy measure**

$$\mathcal{I}(b, \alpha) = \Sigma_{X \in \mathcal{F}}\, s(b(X), \alpha(X))$$

defined by a continuous, bounded, strictly proper **component function**

$$s: [0,1] \times \{0,1\} \rightarrow \mathcal{R}_{\geq 0}$$

s is **strictly proper iff**

$$x \cdot s(x, 1) + (1 - x) \cdot s(x, 0) < x \cdot s(y, 1) + (1 - x) \cdot s(y, 0)$$

for any $x,y \in [0,1]$ with $x \neq y$. A component function s measures the inaccuracy of the credence $b(X)$ when X 's truth-value is $\alpha(X)$. When $\mathcal{I}$ is defined by a component function in this way, we call it *additive*.

Now extend $\mathcal{I}$ to measure not only the accuracy of individual credence functions b, but also epistemic lives $\mathfrak{b} = \langle \mathrm{b}_0,\ldots, \mathrm{b}_\mathrm{n} \rangle \in \mathcal{S}$ as follows:

$$\mathcal{I}(\mathfrak{b}, \omega) = \Sigma_{i:\alpha \in \mathcal{L}} \mathcal{I}(b_i,\alpha)$$

$\mathcal{I}$ reflects the view that life stages b_i ought to be evaluated as conditional credence functions. More carefully, $b_i(X)$ should be evaluated as your credence for X *conditional on the learning experiences that produced* b_i. As such, b_i is evaluable for accuracy only at worlds α in which the learning experiences that produced that stage take place, viz., $\alpha \in \mathcal{L}_i$.

According to $\mathcal{I}$, the total inaccuracy of your epistemic life $\mathfrak{b}$ at α is the sum of the degrees of inaccuracy of the life stages b_i that are evaluable for accuracy at α. When $\mathcal{I}$ takes this form, call it *temporally additive*.

For any temporally additive $\mathcal{I}$ defined by a continuous, bounded, strictly proper component function, we can generate a divergence between big space lives, $\mathfrak{p} = \langle \mathrm{p}_0,\ldots, \mathrm{p}_\mathrm{n} \rangle$ and $\mathfrak{q} = \langle \mathrm{q}_0,\ldots, \mathrm{q}_\mathrm{n} \rangle$, as follows.

Let $\mathfrak{b} = \langle \mathrm{b}_0,\ldots, \mathrm{b}_\mathrm{n} \rangle$ be the restriction of $\mathfrak{p}$ to $\mathcal{F}$, *i.e.*, b_i is the restriction of p_i to $\mathcal{F}$ for all $i \leq n$. Similarly, let $\mathfrak{c}$ be the restriction of $\mathfrak{q}$ to $\mathcal{F}$. Now let

$$H(\mathfrak{p}, \mathfrak{q}) = \Sigma_{\alpha \in \Omega^+} p_0(\alpha) \mathcal{I}(\mathfrak{c},\alpha)$$

Then let

$$\mathcal{D}(\mathfrak{p}, \mathfrak{q}) = H(\mathfrak{p}, \mathfrak{q}) - H(\mathfrak{p}, \mathfrak{p})$$

So the divergence from $\mathfrak{p}$ to $\mathfrak{q}$ is given by the difference between the expected inaccuracy of their respective restrictions, from p_0 's perspective.

Say that $\mathfrak{p}$ and $\mathfrak{q}$ are **small space equivalent** iff $p_i(X) = q_i(X)$ for all $i \geq 0$ and all $X \in \mathcal{F}$. When $\mathfrak{p}$ and $\mathfrak{q}$ are small space equivalent, we write $\mathfrak{p} \approx \mathfrak{q}$.

Say that $\mathcal{D}$ is a **Quasi Bregman divergence** iff

(I) For any $\mathfrak{p}$ and $\mathfrak{q}$ in the set $\mathbb{Q} \subseteq \mathbb{B}$ of coherent, quasi-regular, conditioning sequences

- $\mathcal{D}(\mathfrak{p}, \mathfrak{q}) = 0$ if $\mathfrak{p} \approx \mathfrak{q}$
- $\mathcal{D}(\mathfrak{p},\mathfrak{q}) > 0$ if $\mathfrak{p} \not\approx \mathfrak{q}$

(II) $\mathcal{D}(\cdot,\mathfrak{r})$ is **quasi convex** on the set $\mathcal{Q}$ of coherent, quasi-regular, conditioning sequences in the following sense. Choose $\mathfrak{r} \in \mathcal{B}$ and $\mathfrak{p},\mathfrak{q}^1,\ldots,\mathfrak{q}^k \in \mathcal{Q}$. If (i) $p_0 = \Sigma_{i \leq k} \mu^i q_0^i$ for some $\mu^i \in [0,1]$ with $\Sigma_{i \leq k} \mu^i = 1$ and (ii) $\mathfrak{q}^a \not\approx \mathfrak{q}^b$ for some $a,b \leq k$ with μ^a, $\mu^b > 0$, then

$$\mathcal{D}(\mathfrak{p}, \mathfrak{r}) < \Sigma_{i \leq k}\, \mu^i \mathcal{D}(\mathfrak{q}^i, \mathfrak{r})$$

(III) There is some $\Phi : \mathcal{B} \to [0, \infty]$ that is bounded and continuously differentiable on $\mathcal{Q}$, and moreover

$$\mathcal{D}(\mathfrak{p},\mathfrak{q}) = \Phi(\mathfrak{p}) - \Phi(\mathfrak{q}) - \nabla\Phi(\mathfrak{q}) \cdot (\mathfrak{p} - \mathfrak{q})$$

for any $\mathfrak{p}, \mathfrak{q} \in \mathcal{Q}$.

Proposition 5. *For any temporally additive inaccuracy measure $\mathcal{I}$ defined by a continuous, bounded, strictly proper component function*

$$\mathcal{D}(\mathfrak{p}, \mathfrak{q}) = H(\mathfrak{p}, \mathfrak{q}) - H(\mathfrak{p}, \mathfrak{p})$$

is a Quasi Bregman divergence.

Proof. Let $\mathcal{I}$ be a temporally additive inaccuracy measure defined by a continuous, bounded, strictly proper component function. Let

$$\mathcal{D}(\mathfrak{p}, \mathfrak{q}) = H(\mathfrak{p}, \mathfrak{q}) - H(\mathfrak{p}, \mathfrak{p})$$

Proof of (I). Choose $\mathfrak{p}, \mathfrak{q} \in \mathcal{Q}$. Let $\mathfrak{b}$ and $\mathfrak{c}$ be the restrictions of $\mathfrak{p}$ and $\mathfrak{q}$ to $\mathcal{F}$, respectively.

Case 1. $\mathfrak{p} \approx \mathfrak{q}$. Then $\mathfrak{b} = \mathfrak{c}$. Hence

$$H(\mathfrak{p}, \mathfrak{q}) = \Sigma_{\alpha \in \Omega^+} p_0(\alpha)\mathcal{I}(\mathfrak{c}, \alpha) = \Sigma_{\alpha \in \Omega^+} p_0(\alpha)\mathcal{I}(\mathfrak{b}, \alpha) = H(\mathfrak{p}, \mathfrak{p})$$

So

$$\mathcal{D}(\mathfrak{p}, \mathfrak{q}) = H(\mathfrak{p}, \mathfrak{q}) - H(\mathfrak{p}, \mathfrak{p}) = 0$$

Case 2. $\mathfrak{p} \not\approx \mathfrak{q}$. Then $\mathfrak{b} \neq \mathfrak{c}$.

Since s is strictly proper, for any $i \leq n$ and any $X \in \mathcal{F}$ we have

$$p_i(X)s(q_i(X),1) \quad + (1 - p_i(X))s(q_i(X),0)$$

$$\geq p_i(X)s(p_i(X),1) + (1 - p_i(X))s(p_i(X),0)$$

with equality iff $p_i(X) = q_i(X)$. Moreover, since $\mathfrak{p}$ is a coherent, quasi-regular, condi sequence we have

$$p_i(X) = \frac{p_0(X \cap \mathcal{L}_i)}{p_0(\mathcal{L}_i)}$$

So the above inequality holds iff

$$p_0(X \cap \mathcal{L}_i)s(q_i(X),1) + p_0(\neg X \cap \mathcal{L}_i) \cdot s(q_i(X),0)$$
$$\geq p_0(X \cap \mathcal{L}_i)s(p_i(X),1) + p_0(\neg X \cap \mathcal{L}_i)s(p_i(X),0)$$

In addition, since $\mathfrak{p} \not\approx \mathfrak{q}$, $q_j(Y) \neq p_j(Y)$ for some $j \leq n$ and $Y \in \mathcal{F}$. Hence

$$p_0(Y \cap \mathcal{L}_j)s(q_j(Y),1) + p_0(\neg Y \cap \mathcal{L}_j) \cdot s(q_j(Y),0)$$
$$> p_0(Y \cap \mathcal{L}_j)s(p_j(Y),1) + p_0(\neg Y \cap \mathcal{L}_j)s(p_j(Y),0)$$

Finally we have

$$\begin{aligned} H(\mathfrak{p}, \mathfrak{q}) &= \sum_{\alpha \in \Omega^+} p_0(\alpha)\mathcal{I}(\mathfrak{c},\alpha) \\ &= \sum_{\alpha \in \Omega^+} p_0(\alpha) \sum_{i:\alpha \in \mathcal{L}_i} \mathcal{I}(c_i,\alpha) \\ &= \sum_{i \leqslant n} \sum_{\alpha \in \mathcal{L}_i} p_0(\alpha)\mathcal{I}(c_i,\alpha) \\ &= \sum_{i \leqslant n} \sum_{\alpha \in \mathcal{L}_i} p_0(\alpha) \sum_{X \in \mathcal{F}} s(c_i(X),\alpha(X)) \\ &= \sum_{i \leqslant n} \sum_{\alpha \in \mathcal{L}_i} p_0(\alpha) \sum_{X \in \mathcal{F}} s(q_i(X),\alpha(X)) \\ &= \sum_{i \leqslant n} \sum_{X \in \mathcal{F}} p_0(X \cap \mathcal{L}_i)s(q_i(X),1) + p_0(\neg X \cap \mathcal{L}_i)s(q_i(X),0) \\ &> \sum_{i \leqslant n} \sum_{X \in \mathcal{F}} p_0(X \cap \mathcal{L}_i)s(p_i(X),1) + p_0(\neg X \cap \mathcal{L}_i)s(p_i(X),0) \\ &= H(\mathfrak{p}, \mathfrak{p}) \end{aligned}$$

Therefore $\mathcal{D}(\mathfrak{p}, \mathfrak{q}) = H(\mathfrak{p}, \mathfrak{q}) - H(\mathfrak{p}, \mathfrak{p}) > 0$.

Proof of (II). Choose $\mathfrak{r} \in \mathcal{B}$ and $\mathfrak{p}, \mathfrak{q}^1,\ldots,\mathfrak{q}^k \in \mathcal{Q}$. Suppose that (i) $p_0 = \Sigma_{i \leq k}\mu^i q_0^i$ for some $\mu^i \in [0,1]$ with $\Sigma_{i \leq k}\mu^i = 1$ and (ii) $\mathfrak{q}^a \not\approx \mathfrak{q}^b$ for some $a,b \leq k$ with $\mu^a, \mu^b > 0$. We must show that

$$\mathcal{D}(\mathfrak{p}, \mathfrak{r}) < \sum_{i \leq k} \mu^i \mathcal{D}(\mathfrak{q}^i, \mathfrak{r})$$

Note that

$$\begin{aligned} \mathcal{D}(\mathfrak{p}, \mathfrak{r}) &= H(\mathfrak{p}, \mathfrak{r}) - H(\mathfrak{p}, \mathfrak{p}) \\ &= \sum_{i \leqslant n} \sum_{X \in \mathcal{F}} p_0(X \cap \mathcal{L}_i)s(r_i(X),1) + p_0(\neg X \cap \mathcal{L}_i)s(r_i(X),0) \\ &\quad - \sum_{i \leqslant n} \sum_{X \in \mathcal{F}} p_0(X \cap \mathcal{L}_i)s(p_i(X),1) + p_0(\neg X \cap \mathcal{L}_i)s(p_i(X),0) \\ &= \sum_{i \leqslant n} \sum_{X \in \mathcal{F}} \left[\sum_{j \leqslant k} \mu^j q_0^j(X \cap \mathcal{L}_i)\right] s(r_i(X),1) + \left[\sum_{j \leqslant k} \mu^j q_0^j(\neg X \cap \mathcal{L}_i)\right] s(r_i(X),0) \\ &\quad - \sum_{i \leqslant n} \sum_{X \in \mathcal{F}} \left[\sum_{j \leqslant k} \mu^j q_0^j(X \cap \mathcal{L}_i)\right] s(p_i(X),1) + \left[\sum_{j \leqslant k} \mu^j q_0^j(\neg X \cap \mathcal{L}_i)\right] s(p_i(X),0) \\ &= \sum_{j \leqslant k} \mu^j \sum_{i \leqslant n} \sum_{X \in \mathcal{F}} q_0^j(X \cap \mathcal{L}_i)s(r_i(X),1) + q_0^j(\neg X \cap \mathcal{L}_i)s(r_i(X),0) \\ &\quad - \sum_{j \leqslant k} \mu^j \sum_{i \leqslant n} \sum_{X \in \mathcal{F}} q_0^j(X \cap \mathcal{L}_i)s(p_i(X),1) + q_0^j(\neg X \cap \mathcal{L}_i)s(p_i(X),0) \end{aligned}$$

Similarly

$$\begin{aligned} \mathcal{D}(\mathfrak{q}^j, \mathfrak{r}) &= H(\mathfrak{q}^j, \mathfrak{r}) - H(\mathfrak{q}^j, \mathfrak{q}^j) \\ &= \sum_{i \leqslant n} \sum_{X \in \mathcal{F}} q_0^j(X \cap \mathcal{L}_i)s(r_i(X),1) + q_0^j(\neg X \cap \mathcal{L}_i)s(r_i(X),0) \\ &\quad - \sum_{i \leqslant n} \sum_{X \in \mathcal{F}} q_0^j(X \cap \mathcal{L}_i)s(q_i^j(X),1) + q_0^j(\neg X \cap \mathcal{L}_i)s(q_i^j(X),0) \end{aligned}$$

So

$$\mathcal{D}(\mathfrak{p}, \mathfrak{r}) < \sum_{j \leq k} \mu^j \mathcal{D}(\mathfrak{q}^j, \mathfrak{r})$$

iff

$$\Sigma_{j \leq k} \mu^j \, \Sigma_{i \leq n} \Sigma_{X \in \mathcal{F}} q_0^j(X \cap \mathcal{L}_i) s(p_i(X),1) + q_0^j(\neg X \cap \mathcal{L}_i) s(p_i(X),0)$$
$$> \Sigma_{j \leq k} \mu^j \, \Sigma_{i \leq n} \Sigma_{X \in \mathcal{F}} q_0^j(X \cap \mathcal{L}_i) s(q_i^j(X),1) + q_0^j(\neg X \cap \mathcal{L}_i) s(q_i^j(X),0)$$

Since s is strictly proper, and $\mathfrak{q}^j$ is a coherent, quasi-regular, condi sequence

$$q_0^j(X \cap \mathcal{L}_i) s(p_i(X),1) + q_0^j(\neg X \cap \mathcal{L}_i) s(p_i(X),0)$$
$$\geq q_0^j(X \cap \mathcal{L}_i) s(q_i^j(X),1) + q_0^j(\neg X \cap \mathcal{L}_i) s(q_i^j(X),0)$$

with equality iff $p_i(X) = q_i^j(X)$. Now recall that $\mathfrak{q}^a \not\approx \mathfrak{q}^b$ for some $a,b \leq k$ with $\mu^a,\mu^b > 0$. So $q_i^a(X) \neq q_i^b(X)$ for some $i \leq n$ and $X \in \mathcal{F}$. Hence either $p_i(X) \neq q_i^a(X)$ or $p_i(X) \neq q_i^b(X)$. This ensures that

$$\Sigma_{j \leq k} \mu^j \, \Sigma_{i \leq n} \Sigma_{X \in \mathcal{F}} q_0^j(X \cap \mathcal{L}_i) s(p_i(X),1) + q_0^j(\neg X \cap \mathcal{L}_i) s(p_i(X),0)$$
$$> \sum_{j \leq k} \mu^j \sum_{i \leq n} \sum_{X \in \mathcal{F}} q_0^j(X \cap \mathcal{L}_i) s(q_i^j(X),1) + q_0^j(\neg X \cap \mathcal{L}_i) s(q_i^j(X),0)$$

Therefore

$$\mathcal{D}(\mathfrak{p}, \mathfrak{r}) < \sum_{j \leq k} \mu^j \mathcal{D}(\mathfrak{q}^j, \mathfrak{r})$$

Proof of (III). Represent any $\mathfrak{p} \in \mathcal{B}$ as a vector in $[0,1]^{t(n+1)}$

$$\langle p_0(X_1),\ldots,p_0(X_t),\ldots,p_n(X_1),\ldots,p_n(X_t) > \in [0,1]^{t(n+1)}$$

where $\mathcal{F}^+ = \{X_1,\ldots,X_t\}$. Assume WLOG that $\Omega^+ = \{\alpha_1,\ldots,\alpha_s\}$ and that $X_1 = \alpha_1,\ldots,X_s = \alpha_s$.

Now let

$$\Phi(\mathfrak{p}) = -H(\mathfrak{p},\mathfrak{p})$$

Let $\mathfrak{b}$ be the restriction of $\mathfrak{p}$ to $\mathcal{F}$. And let

$$\Psi(\mathfrak{p}) = -\sum_{i:\alpha_1 \in \mathcal{L}_i} \mathcal{I}(b_i, \alpha_1),\ldots, -\sum_{i:\alpha_s \in \mathcal{L}_i} \mathcal{I}(b_i, \alpha_s),0,\ldots,0$$

We will now show that (i) Φ is bounded and continuously differentiable on $\mathcal{Q}$, (ii) $\nabla \Phi = \Psi$, and (iii) for any $\mathfrak{p},\mathfrak{q} \in \mathcal{Q}$

$$\mathcal{D}(\mathfrak{p}, \mathfrak{q}) = \Phi(\mathfrak{p}) - \Phi(\mathfrak{q}) - \Psi(\mathfrak{q}) \cdot (\mathfrak{p} - \mathfrak{q})$$

The continuity and boundedness of Φ follows trivially from the fact that $\mathcal{I}$ is defined by a continuous, bounded component score.

Choose $\mathfrak{p} \in \mathcal{Q}$. We will show that Φ is partially differentiable with respect to x_j at $\mathfrak{p}$, for each $j \leq t(n+1)$, and moreover that these partial derivatives ensure that $\nabla \Phi(\mathfrak{p}) = \Psi(\mathfrak{p})$.

Case 1: $1 \leq j \leq s$. Choose $\varepsilon > 0$. Let $\mathfrak{q}$ be

$$\langle p_0(\alpha_1), \ldots, p_0(\alpha_j) + \varepsilon, \ldots, p_0(\alpha_s), \ldots, p_0(X_t), \ldots, p_n(X_1), \ldots, p_n(X_t)\rangle$$

Let $\mathfrak{b}$ and $\mathfrak{c}$ be the restrictions of $\mathfrak{p}$ and $\mathfrak{q}$ to $\mathcal{F}$. Then

$$\begin{aligned}
&\frac{1}{\varepsilon}[\Phi(\mathfrak{q}) - \Phi(\mathfrak{p})] \\
&= \frac{1}{\varepsilon}[H(\mathfrak{p},\mathfrak{p}) - H(\mathfrak{q},\mathfrak{q})] \\
&= \frac{1}{\varepsilon}\left[\sum_{\alpha \in \Omega^+} p_0(\alpha) \sum_{i:\alpha \in \mathcal{L}_i} \mathcal{I}(b_i,\alpha) - \sum_{\alpha \in \Omega^+} q_0(\alpha) \sum_{i:\alpha \in \mathcal{L}_i} \mathcal{I}(c_i,\alpha)\right] \\
&= \frac{1}{\varepsilon}\left[\sum_{\alpha \in \Omega^+} p_0(\alpha) \sum_{i:\alpha \in \mathcal{L}_i} \mathcal{I}(b_i,\alpha) - \sum_{\alpha \in \Omega^+} p_0(\alpha) \sum_{i:\alpha \in \mathcal{L}_i} \mathcal{I}(c_i,\alpha) - \varepsilon \sum_{i:\alpha_j \in \mathcal{L}_i} \mathcal{I}(c_i,\alpha_j)\right] \\
&= -\sum_{i:\alpha_j \in \mathcal{L}_i} \mathcal{I}(c_i,\alpha_j) + \frac{1}{\varepsilon}\left[\sum_{\alpha \in \Omega^+} p_0(\alpha) \sum_{i:\alpha \in \mathcal{L}_i} \mathcal{I}(b_i,\alpha) - \sum_{\alpha \in \Omega^+} p_0(\alpha) \sum_{i:\alpha \in \mathcal{L}_i} \mathcal{I}(c_i,\alpha)\right]
\end{aligned}$$

Since $\mathcal{I}$ is defined by a strictly proper component score, and $\mathfrak{p}$ is a coherent, quasi-regular, condi sequence, this second term is less than or equal to zero. Hence

$$\begin{aligned}
\lim_{\varepsilon \to 0} \frac{1}{\varepsilon}[\Phi(\mathfrak{q}) - \Phi(\mathfrak{p})] &\leqslant \lim_{\varepsilon \to 0} - \sum_{i:\alpha_j \in \mathcal{L}_i} \mathcal{I}(c_i,\alpha_j) \\
&= - \sum_{i:\alpha_j \in \mathcal{L}_i} \mathcal{I}(b_i,\alpha_j)
\end{aligned}$$

Now let $\mathfrak{r}$ be

$$\langle p_0(\alpha_1), \ldots, p_0(\alpha_j) - \varepsilon, \ldots, p_0(\alpha_s), \ldots, p_0(X_t), \ldots, p_n(X_1), \ldots, p_n(X_t)\rangle$$

A similar argument shows that

$$\begin{aligned}
\lim_{\varepsilon \to 0} \frac{1}{\varepsilon}[\Phi(\mathfrak{p}) - \Phi(\mathfrak{r})] &\geqslant \lim_{\varepsilon \to 0} - \sum_{i:\alpha_j \in \mathcal{L}_i} \mathcal{I}(c_i,\alpha_j) \\
&= - \sum_{i:\alpha_j \in \mathcal{L}_i} \mathcal{I}(b_i,\alpha_j)
\end{aligned}$$

Since Φ is continuous, this shows that Φ is partially differentiable with respect to x_j at $\mathfrak{p}$, and that

$$\frac{\partial \Phi}{\partial x_j}(\mathfrak{p}) = - \Sigma_{i:\alpha_j \in \mathcal{L}_i} \mathcal{I}(b_i,\alpha_j)$$

Case 2: $s < j$. Choose $\varepsilon > 0$. Let $\mathfrak{q}$ be

$$\langle p_0(X_1), \ldots, p_0(X_t), \ldots, p_a(X_b) + \varepsilon, \ldots, p_n(X_1), \ldots, p_n(X_t)\rangle$$

where $p_a(X_b)$ is the jth entry of $\mathfrak{p}$. Let $\mathfrak{b}$ and $\mathfrak{c}$ be the restrictions of $\mathfrak{p}$ and $\mathfrak{q}$ to $\mathcal{F}$. Then

$$\begin{aligned}\frac{1}{\varepsilon}[\Phi(\mathfrak{q}) - \Phi(\mathfrak{p})] &= \frac{1}{\varepsilon}[H(\mathfrak{p}, \mathfrak{p}) - H(\mathfrak{q}, \mathfrak{q})] \\ &= \frac{1}{\varepsilon}\left[\sum_{\alpha\in\Omega^+} p_0(\alpha) \sum_{i:\alpha\in\mathcal{L}_i} \mathcal{I}(b_i,\alpha) - \sum_{\alpha\in\Omega^+} q_0(\alpha) \sum_{i:\alpha\in\mathcal{L}_i} \mathcal{I}(c_i,\alpha)\right] \\ &= \frac{1}{\varepsilon}\left[\sum_{\alpha\in\Omega^+} p_0(\alpha) \sum_{i:\alpha\in\mathcal{L}_i} \mathcal{I}(b_i,\alpha) - \sum_{\alpha\in\Omega^+} p_0(\alpha) \sum_{i:\alpha\in\mathcal{L}_i} \mathcal{I}(c_i,\alpha)\right]\end{aligned}$$

Since $\mathcal{I}$ is defined by a strictly proper component score, and $\mathfrak{p}$ is a coherent, quasi-regular, condi sequence, the term in brackets is less than or equal to zero. Hence

$$\lim_{\varepsilon\to 0} \frac{1}{\varepsilon}[\Phi(\mathfrak{q}) - \Phi(\mathfrak{p})] \leqslant 0$$

Let $\mathfrak{r}$ be

$$\langle p_0(X_1),\ldots,p_0(X_t),\ldots,p_a(X_b) - \varepsilon,\ldots,p_n(X_1),\ldots,p_n(X_t)\rangle$$

where again $p_a(X_b)$ is the jth entry of $\mathfrak{p}$. A similar argument shows that

$$\lim_{\varepsilon\to 0} \frac{1}{\varepsilon}[\Phi(\mathfrak{p}) - \Phi(\mathfrak{r})] \geqslant 0$$

Since Φ is continuous, this shows that Φ is partially differentiable with respect to x_j at $\mathfrak{p}$, and that

$$\frac{\partial\Phi}{\partial x_j}(\mathfrak{p}) = 0$$

Together cases 1 and 2 establish that

$$\nabla\,\Phi(\mathfrak{p}) = \Psi(\mathfrak{p}) = -\textstyle\sum_{i:\alpha_1\in\mathcal{L}_i}\mathcal{I}(b_i,\,\alpha_1),\ldots,-\sum_{i:\alpha_s\in\mathcal{L}_i}\mathcal{I}(b_i,\,\alpha_s),0,\ldots,0$$

Finally we must show that for any $\mathfrak{p}$, $\mathfrak{q} \in \mathcal{Q}$

$$\mathcal{D}(\mathfrak{p},\mathfrak{q}) = \Phi(\mathfrak{p}) - \Phi(\mathfrak{q}) - \Psi(\mathfrak{q})\cdot(\mathfrak{p} - \mathfrak{q})$$

Choose $\mathfrak{p}$, $\mathfrak{q} \in \mathcal{Q}$.

$$\begin{aligned}\mathcal{D}(\mathfrak{p},\mathfrak{q}) &= H(\mathfrak{p},\mathfrak{q}) - H(\mathfrak{p},\mathfrak{p}) \\ &= \sum_{\alpha\in\Omega^+} p_0(\alpha) \sum_{i:\alpha\in\mathcal{L}_i} \mathcal{I}(c_i,\,\alpha) - \sum_{\alpha\in\Omega^+} p_0(\alpha) \sum_{i:\alpha\in\mathcal{L}_i} \mathcal{I}(b_i,\,\alpha) \\ &= \sum_{\alpha\in\Omega^+} [p_0(\alpha) - q_0(\alpha)] \sum_{i:\alpha\in\mathcal{L}_i} \mathcal{I}(c_i,\alpha) + \sum_{\alpha\in\Omega^+} q_0(\alpha) \sum_{i:\alpha\in\mathcal{L}_i} \mathcal{I}(c_i,\alpha) \\ &\quad - \sum_{\alpha\in\Omega^+} p_0(\alpha) \sum_{i:\alpha\in\mathcal{L}_i} \mathcal{I}(b_i,\alpha) \\ &= -\Psi(\mathfrak{q})\cdot(\mathfrak{p} - \mathfrak{q}) - \Phi(\mathfrak{q}) + \Phi(\mathfrak{p})\end{aligned}$$

Hence $\mathcal{D}$ is a Quasi Bregman divergence.

□

A.4 Chance-Dominance Argument for J-Kon

Proposition 6. *Let $\mathcal{D}$ be a Quasi Bregman divergence. Then for any $\mathfrak{q} \in \mathcal{Q} - \wp$ there is a point $\pi^{\mathfrak{q}} \in \wp$, called the projection of $\mathfrak{q}$ onto $\wp$, such that*

$$\mathcal{D}(\pi^{\mathfrak{q}}, \mathfrak{q}) \leq \mathcal{D}(\mathfrak{p}, \mathfrak{q})$$

for any $\mathfrak{p} \in \wp$. Moreover, $\pi^{\mathfrak{q}}$ is unique up to small space equivalence.

Proof. Recall $\mathcal{Q}$ is the set of coherent, quasi-regular, condi sequences. And $\wp \subseteq \mathcal{Q}$ is the set of coherent, quasi-regular, condi, PP sequences. (Pettigrew, 2012, Thm 5.3) shows that

$$\{p_0 | \mathfrak{p} = \langle p_0, \ldots, p_n \rangle \in \mathbb{P}\}$$

is the closed (and bounded) convex hull of $\mathbb{C}$. Let Γ map any point p_0 in this set to $\mathfrak{p} = \langle \mathfrak{p}_0, \ldots, \mathfrak{p}_n \rangle$. Γ is continuous. And the image of Γ is $\wp$. (Arkhangel'skii and Fedorchuk 1990, Thm 5.2.2) then implies that $\wp$ is closed and bounded.

Choose $\mathfrak{q} \in \mathcal{Q} - \wp$. Note that $\mathcal{D}(\cdot, \mathfrak{q})$ is continuous for fixed $\mathfrak{q}$. Hence $\mathcal{D}(\cdot, \mathfrak{q})$ takes a minimum $\pi^{\mathfrak{q}}$ on the closed bounded set $\wp$.

To see that this minimum is unique up to small space equivalence, suppose that $\mathcal{D}(\cdot, \mathfrak{q})$ takes a minimum at both $\pi^{\mathfrak{q}}$ and $\mathfrak{r}$, where the restrictions of $\pi^{\mathfrak{q}}$ and $\mathfrak{r}$ to $\mathcal{F}$ are distinct. Since $\pi^{\mathfrak{q}} \in \wp$, there are $\mu_j \in [0,1]$ with $\Sigma_{ch_j \in \mathbb{C}} \mu_j = 1$ such that $\pi_0^{\mathfrak{q}} = \Sigma_{ch_j \in \mathcal{C}} \mu_j ch_j(\cdot | \Omega^+)$. Likewise, there are $\theta_j \in [0,1]$ with $\Sigma_{ch_j \in \mathcal{C}} \theta_j = 1$ such that $r_0^{\mathfrak{q}} = \Sigma_{ch_j \in \mathcal{C}} \theta_j ch_j(\cdot | \Omega^+)$. Let $\mathfrak{p}$ be the coherent, quasi-regular, condi sequence with $p_0 = \frac{1}{2}\pi_0^{\mathfrak{q}} + \frac{1}{2} r_0$. Then $p_0 = \Sigma_{ch_j \in \mathcal{C}} (\frac{1}{2}\mu_j + \frac{1}{2}\theta_j) ch_j(\cdot | \Omega^+)$. So $\mathfrak{p} \in \wp$. But since $\mathcal{D}$ is quasi convex, we have

$$\mathcal{D}(\mathfrak{p}, \mathfrak{q}) < \frac{1}{2}\mathcal{D}(\pi^{\mathfrak{q}}, \mathfrak{q}) + \frac{1}{2}\mathcal{D}(\mathfrak{r}, \mathfrak{q}) = \mathcal{D}(\pi^{\mathfrak{q}}, \mathfrak{q})$$

which contradicts the assumption that $\mathcal{D}(\cdot, \mathfrak{q})$ takes a minimum on $\wp$ at $\pi^{\mathfrak{q}}$.

□

Proposition 7. *Let $\mathcal{D}$ be a Quasi Bregman* divergence. Then for any $\mathfrak{q} \in \mathcal{Q} - \wp$, *the projection of $\mathfrak{q}$ onto $\wp$, $\pi^{\mathfrak{q}}$, is such that*

$$\mathcal{D}(\mathfrak{p}, \pi^{\mathfrak{q}}) \leq \mathcal{D}(\mathfrak{p}, \mathfrak{q}) - \mathcal{D}(\pi^{\mathfrak{q}}, \mathfrak{q})$$

for all $\mathfrak{p} \in \wp$.

Proof. Choose $\mathfrak{q} \in \mathcal{Q} - \wp$ and $\mathfrak{p} \in \wp$. Let $\pi^{\mathfrak{q}}$ be the projection of $\mathfrak{q}$ onto $\wp$. We will show that

$$\mathcal{D}(\mathfrak{p}, \pi^{\mathfrak{q}}) \leq \mathcal{D}(\mathfrak{p}, \mathfrak{q}) - \mathcal{D}(\pi^{\mathfrak{q}}, \mathfrak{q})$$

Let $\mathfrak{m} \in \wp$ be the coherent, quasi-regular, condi, PP sequence with

$$m_0 = (1 - \varepsilon)\pi_0^{\mathfrak{q}} + \varepsilon p_0$$

for some $0 < \varepsilon \leq 1$. Then since $\mathcal{D}(\cdot, \mathfrak{q})$ takes a minimum on $\wp$ at $\pi^{\mathfrak{q}}$ (unique up to small space equivalence) we have

$$0 \leq \mathcal{D}(\mathfrak{m}, \mathfrak{q}) - \mathcal{D}(\pi^{\mathfrak{q}}, \mathfrak{q})$$

This gives us

$$
\begin{aligned}
0 &\leqslant \mathcal{D}(\mathfrak{m},\mathfrak{q}) - \mathcal{D}(\pi^{\mathfrak{q}},\mathfrak{q}) \\
&= [\Phi(\mathfrak{m}) - \Phi(\mathfrak{q}) - \nabla\Phi(\mathfrak{q})\cdot(\mathfrak{m}-\mathfrak{q})] - [\Phi(\pi^{\mathfrak{q}}) - \Phi(\mathfrak{q}) - \nabla\Phi(\mathfrak{q})\cdot(\pi^{\mathfrak{q}}-\mathfrak{q})] \\
&= -\nabla\Phi(\mathfrak{q})\cdot(\mathfrak{m}-\pi^{\mathfrak{q}}) + [\Phi(\mathfrak{m}) - \Phi(\pi^{\mathfrak{q}})] \\
&= -\varepsilon\nabla\Phi(\mathfrak{q})\cdot(\mathfrak{p}-\pi^{\mathfrak{q}}) + [\Phi(\mathfrak{m}) - \Phi(\pi^{\mathfrak{q}})]
\end{aligned}
$$

We also have

$$
\begin{aligned}
\lim_{\varepsilon\to 0}\frac{\Phi(\mathfrak{m}) - \Phi(\pi^{\mathfrak{q}})}{\varepsilon} &= \lim_{\varepsilon\to 0}\frac{\nabla\Phi(\pi^{\mathfrak{q}})\cdot(\mathfrak{m}-\pi^{\mathfrak{q}})}{\varepsilon} \\
&= \lim_{\varepsilon\to 0}\frac{\nabla\Phi(\pi^{\mathfrak{q}})\cdot(\varepsilon\mathfrak{p}-\varepsilon\pi^{\mathfrak{q}})}{\varepsilon} \\
&= \nabla\Phi(\pi^{\mathfrak{q}})\cdot(\mathfrak{p}-\pi^{\mathfrak{q}})
\end{aligned}
$$

Hence

$$
\begin{aligned}
0 &\leqslant \lim_{\varepsilon\to 0}\frac{1}{\varepsilon}[-\varepsilon\nabla\Phi(\mathfrak{q})\cdot(\mathfrak{p}-\pi^{\mathfrak{q}}) + [\Phi(\mathfrak{m}) - \Phi(\pi^{\mathfrak{q}})]] \\
&= -\nabla\Phi(\mathfrak{q})\cdot(\mathfrak{p}-\pi^{\mathfrak{q}}) + \lim_{\varepsilon\to 0}\frac{\Phi(\mathfrak{m}) - \Phi(\pi^{\mathfrak{q}})}{\varepsilon} \\
&= -\nabla\Phi(\mathfrak{q})\cdot(\mathfrak{p}-\pi^{\mathfrak{q}}) + \nabla\Phi(\pi^{\mathfrak{q}})\cdot(\mathfrak{p}-\pi^{\mathfrak{q}}) \\
&= [\nabla\Phi(\pi^{\mathfrak{q}}) - \nabla\Phi(\mathfrak{q})]\cdot(\mathfrak{p}-\pi^{\mathfrak{q}})
\end{aligned}
$$

Finally note that

$$
\mathcal{D}(\mathfrak{p},\mathfrak{q}) - \mathcal{D}(\pi^{\mathfrak{q}},\mathfrak{q}) - \mathcal{D}(\mathfrak{p},\pi^{\mathfrak{q}}) = [\nabla\Phi(\pi^{\mathfrak{q}}) - \nabla\Phi(\mathfrak{q})]\cdot(\mathfrak{p}-\pi^{\mathfrak{q}})
$$

So

$$
0 \leq \mathcal{D}(\mathfrak{p},\mathfrak{q}) - \mathcal{D}(\pi^{\mathfrak{q}},\mathfrak{q}) - \mathcal{D}(\mathfrak{p},\pi^{\mathfrak{q}})
$$

and therefore

$$
\mathcal{D}(\mathfrak{p},\pi^{\mathfrak{q}}) \leq \mathcal{D}(\mathfrak{p},\mathfrak{q}) - \mathcal{D}(\pi^{\mathfrak{q}},\mathfrak{q})
$$

□

Proposition 8. *Let $\mathcal{I}$ be a temporally additive inaccuracy measure defined by a continuous, bounded, strictly proper component function. Then for any $\mathfrak{b} \in \mathcal{S}$ we have the following:*

(I) *If $\mathfrak{b}$ is not a J-Kon sequence, then $\mathfrak{b}$ is* ***strictly chance-dominated*** *by a J-Kon sequence $\mathfrak{c}$, i.e.,*

$$
\Sigma_{\alpha\in\Omega^{+}}\, ch_j(\alpha|\Omega^{+})\mathcal{I}(\mathfrak{b},\alpha) > \Sigma_{\alpha\in\Omega^{+}}\, ch_j(\alpha|\Omega^{+})\mathcal{I}(\mathfrak{c},w)
$$

for all $ch_j \in \mathcal{C}$.

(II) *If* $\mathfrak{b}$ is a J-Kon sequence, then it is not even **weakly chance-dominated**, i.e., there is no $\mathfrak{c} \neq \mathfrak{b}$ *such that*

$$\sum_{\alpha \in \Omega^+} ch_j(\alpha|\Omega^+)\mathcal{I}(\mathfrak{b},\alpha) \geq \sum_{\alpha \in \Omega^+} ch_j(\alpha|\Omega^+)\mathcal{I}(\mathfrak{c},w)$$

for all $ch_j \in \mathcal{C}$.

Proof. Choose $\mathfrak{b} \in \mathcal{S}$. Suppose that $\mathfrak{b}$ is not a J-Kon sequence. Then by proposition 4, $\mathfrak{b}$ is not a gilded superconditioning. So no extension of $\mathfrak{b}$ to $\mathcal{F}^+$ is a coherent, quasi-regular, condi, PP sequence.

Case 1. No extension of $\mathfrak{b}$ *to* $\mathcal{F}^+$ *is coherent.* de Finetti (1949) shows that any coherent b_i is coherently extendable to $\mathcal{F}^+$. So $\mathfrak{b} = \langle b_0,\ldots,b_n \rangle$ must be incoherent. Suppose WLOG that b_i is incoherent, but b_j is coherent for all $j \neq i$. Then theorem 1 of Predd et al. (2009) implies that there is some coherent c such that

$$\mathcal{I}(b_i, \alpha) > \mathcal{I}(c, \alpha)$$

for all $\alpha \in \Omega^+$. Let $\mathfrak{c}$ be

$$\mathfrak{c} = \langle b_0,\ldots, b_{i-1}, c, b_{i+1},\ldots, b_n \rangle$$

Choose $\alpha \in \mathcal{L}_i$. Suppose WLOG that $\alpha \in \mathcal{L}_j$ for some $j \geq i$, but $\alpha \notin \mathcal{L}_k$ for any $k > j$. Then

$$\begin{aligned}
\mathcal{I}(\mathfrak{c},\alpha) &= \sum_{k \leqslant j} \mathcal{I}(c_k,\alpha) \\
&= \mathcal{I}(c,\alpha) + \sum_{k \leqslant j : k \neq i} \mathcal{I}(b_k,\alpha) \\
&< \mathcal{I}(b_i,\alpha) + \sum_{k \leqslant j : k \neq i} \mathcal{I}(b_k,\alpha) \\
&= \mathcal{I}(\mathfrak{b},\alpha)
\end{aligned}$$

Now choose $\alpha \notin \mathcal{L}_i$. Suppose WLOG that $\alpha \in \mathcal{L}_j$ for some $j < i$, but $\alpha \notin \mathcal{L}_k$ for any $k > j$. Then

$$\mathcal{I}(\mathfrak{c},\alpha) = \sum_{k \leq j} \mathcal{I}(c_k,\alpha) = \sum_{k \leq j} \mathcal{I}(b_k,\alpha) = \mathcal{I}(\mathfrak{b},\alpha)$$

Since $ch_j(\mathcal{L}_i|\Omega^+) > 0$ for all $ch_j \in \mathcal{C}$, this implies

$$\begin{aligned}
\sum_{\alpha \in \Omega^+} ch_j(\alpha|\Omega^+)\mathcal{I}(\mathfrak{b},\alpha) &= \sum_{\alpha \in \mathcal{L}_i} ch_j(\alpha|\Omega^+)\mathcal{I}(\mathfrak{b},\alpha) + \sum_{\alpha \notin \mathcal{L}_i} ch_j(\alpha|\Omega^+)\mathcal{I}(\mathfrak{b},\alpha) \\
&> \sum_{\alpha \in \mathcal{L}_i} ch_j(\alpha|\Omega^+)\mathcal{I}(\mathfrak{c},\alpha) + \sum_{\alpha \notin \mathcal{L}_i} ch_j(\alpha|\Omega^+)\mathcal{I}(\mathfrak{c},\alpha) \\
&= \sum_{\alpha \in \Omega^+} ch_j(\alpha|\Omega^+)\mathcal{I}(\mathfrak{c},\alpha)
\end{aligned}$$

Case 2. Some extension $\mathfrak{q}$ *of* $\mathfrak{b}$ *to* $\mathcal{F}^+$ *is coherent, but no coherent extension is a quasi-regular, condi, PP sequence.*

Since $\mathfrak{q}$ is coherent, $\mathfrak{b}$ must be coherent. Since $\mathfrak{b}$ is regular, the support of b_i

$$\text{supp}(b_i) = \{X \in \mathcal{F} | p_i(X) \neq 0\}$$

is trivially a superset of the support of b_j for all $i \leq n$ and $j > i$, *i.e.*, $\text{supp}(b_j) \subseteq \text{supp}(b_i)$ (since both $= \mathcal{F}$). In that case, (Diaconis and Zabell, 1982, Thm 2.1) guarantees that $\mathfrak{b}$ is extendable to a coherent, quasi-regular, condi sequence. So we can assume WLOG that $\mathfrak{q}$ is a coherent, quasi-regular, condi sequence, but not a PP sequence. That is, $\mathfrak{q} \in \mathcal{Q} - \wp$.

By proposition 7, the projection of $\mathfrak{q}$ onto $\wp$, $\pi^{\mathfrak{q}}$, is such that

$$\mathcal{D}(\mathfrak{p},\pi^{\mathfrak{q}}) \leq \mathcal{D}(\mathfrak{p},\mathfrak{q}) - \mathcal{D}(\pi^{\mathfrak{q}},\mathfrak{q})$$

for all $\mathfrak{p} \in \wp$. So in particular

$$\mathcal{D}(\mathfrak{ch},\pi^{\mathfrak{q}}) \leq \mathcal{D}(\mathfrak{ch},\mathfrak{q}) - \mathcal{D}(\pi^{\mathfrak{q}},\mathfrak{q})$$

for all $\mathfrak{ch} \in \mathfrak{C} \subseteq \wp$.

Let $\mathfrak{c}$ be the restriction of $\pi^{\mathfrak{q}}$ to $\mathcal{F}$.

Since $\mathfrak{b}$ is not extendable to any $\mathfrak{p} \in \wp$, $\pi^{\mathfrak{q}} \not\approx \mathfrak{q}$. So $\mathcal{D}(\pi^{\mathfrak{q}},\mathfrak{q}) > 0$ and hence

$$\mathcal{D}(\mathfrak{ch}, \pi^{\mathfrak{q}}) < \mathcal{D}(\mathfrak{ch}, \mathfrak{q})$$

for all $\mathfrak{ch} \in \mathfrak{C}$. But this inequality holds iff

$$H(\mathfrak{ch}, \pi^{\mathfrak{q}}) < H(\mathfrak{ch}, \mathfrak{q})$$

And this is the case iff

$$\sum_{\alpha \in \Omega^+} ch_j(\alpha|\Omega^+)\mathcal{I}(\mathfrak{c},\alpha) < \sum_{\alpha \in \Omega^+} ch_j(\alpha|\Omega^+)\mathcal{I}(\mathfrak{b},\alpha)$$

for all $ch_j \in \mathcal{C}$. This suffices to establish (I).

We will now prove (II). Choose $\mathfrak{b} \in \mathcal{S}$. Suppose that $\mathfrak{b}$ is a J-Kon sequence. Suppose for reductio that there is some $\mathfrak{c} \neq \mathfrak{b}$ such that

$$(\bigstar) \sum_{\alpha \in \Omega^+} ch_j(\alpha|\Omega^+)\mathcal{I}(\mathfrak{b},\alpha) \geq \sum_{\alpha \in \Omega^+} ch_j(\alpha|\Omega^+)\mathcal{I}(\mathfrak{c},\alpha)$$

for all $ch_j \in \mathcal{C}$.

Since $\mathfrak{b}$ is a J-Kon sequence, $\mathfrak{b}$ is extendable to some $\mathfrak{p} \in \wp$, by proposition 4. Let $\mathfrak{q}$ be any extension of $\mathfrak{c}$ to $\mathcal{F}^+$. ($\bigstar$) implies

$$\sum_{ch_j \in \mathcal{C}} p_0(CH = ch_j) \sum_{\alpha \in \Omega^+} ch_j(\alpha|\Omega^+)\mathcal{I}(\mathfrak{b},\alpha) \geq \sum_{ch_j \in \mathrm{C}} p_0(CH = ch_j) \sum_{\alpha \in \Omega^+} ch_j(\alpha|\Omega^+)\mathcal{I}(\mathfrak{c},\alpha)$$

Since $\mathfrak{p}$ is a PP sequence, this holds iff

$$\sum_{\alpha \in \Omega^+} \sum_{ch_j \in \mathcal{C}} p_0(\alpha \cap (CH = ch_j))\mathcal{I}(\mathfrak{b},\alpha) \geq \sum_{\alpha \in \Omega^+} \sum_{ch_j \in \mathcal{C}} p_0(\alpha \cap (CH = ch_j))\mathcal{I}(\mathfrak{c},\alpha)$$

iff

$$\sum_{\alpha \in \Omega^+} p_0(\alpha)\mathcal{I}(\mathfrak{b},\alpha) \geq \sum_{\alpha \in \Omega^+} p_0(\alpha)\mathcal{I}(\mathfrak{c},\alpha)$$

And this implies

$$0 = \mathcal{D}(\mathfrak{p},\mathfrak{p}) \geq \mathcal{D}(\mathfrak{p},\mathfrak{q}) > 0$$

Hence there is no $\mathfrak{c} \neq \mathfrak{b}$ such that

$$\sum_{\alpha \in \Omega^+} ch_j(\alpha|\Omega^+)\mathcal{I}(\mathfrak{b}, \alpha) \geq \sum_{\alpha \in \Omega^+} ch_j(\alpha|\Omega^+)\mathcal{I}(\mathfrak{c}, \alpha)$$

for all $ch_j \in \mathcal{C}$.[12]

References

Arkhangel'skii, A.V., and V.V. Fedorchuk. *General topology I.* Springer, 1990.

Briggs, R.A., and Richard Pettigrew. An Accuracy-Dominance Argument for Conditionalization. *Nous*, 54(1): 162–81, 2020.

Christensen, David. Confirmational Holism and Bayesian Epistemology. *Philosophy of Science*, 59(4): 540–57, 1992.

Clark, Andy. *Surfing Uncertainty.* Oxford University Press, 2016.

De Bock, Jasper. Independent Natural Extension for Infinite Spaces. *International Journal of Approximate Reasoning*, 104: 84–107, 2019.

de Cooman, Gert, and Erik Quaeghebeur. Exchangeability and Sets of Desirable Gambles. *International Journal of Approximate Reasoning*, 53(3): 363–95, 2012. Special issue in honour of Henry E. Kyburg, Jr.

de Finetti, Bruno. Sull'impostazione assiomatica del calcolo delle probabilit. *Annali Triestini dell'Universita di Trieste XIX*, 2: 29–81, 1949.

de Finetti, Bruno. *Theory of Probability. A Critical Introductory Treatment.* John Wiley & Sons, 1974.

Diaconis, Persi, and Sandy Zabell. Updating Subjective Probability. *Journal of the American Statistical Association*, 77: 822–30, 1982.

Field, Hartry. A Note on Jeffrey Conditionalization. *Philosophy of Science*, 45(3): 361–7, 1978.

Gallow, Dmitri. How to Learn from Theory-Dependent Evidence; or Commutativity and Holism: A Solution for Conditionalizers. *British Journal for the Philosophy of Science*, 65(3): 493–519, 2013.

Garber, Daniel. Field and Jeffrey Conditionalization. *Philosophy of Science*, 47(1): 142–5, 1980.

Greaves, Hilary, and David Wallace. Justifying Conditionalization: Conditionalization Maximizes Expected Epistemic Utility. *Mind*, 115(459): 607–32, 2006.

[12] Many thanks to Ray Briggs, Catrin Campbell-Moore, David Corfield, Billy Dunaway, Kenny Easwaran, Branden Fitelson, Graeme Forbes, Pavel Janda, Jim Joyce, Ben Levinstein, Hanti Lin, Samir Okasha, Richard Pettigrew, Miriam Schoenfield, Jon Williamson, and participants of the Epistemic Utility Theory Conference at the University of Bristol (2016) for very helpful comments and questions on earlier versions of this work. This research was partially supported by the Epistemic Utility for Imprecise Probability project which is funded by the European Research Council (ERC) under the European Union's Horizon 2020 research and innovation programme (grant agreement no. 852677).

Jeffrey, Richard. Probabilism and Induction. *Topoi*, 5(1): 51–8, 1986.

Jeffrey, Richard. *The Art of Judgment*. Cambridge University Press, 1992.

Joyce, James M. Accuracy and coherence: Prospects for an alethic epistemology of partial belief. In Franz Huber and Christoph Schmidt-Petri (Eds.), *Degrees of Belief*, volume 342. Springer, Dordrecht, 2009.

Konek, Jason. Comparative probabilities. In Jonathan Weisberg and Richard Pettigrew (Eds.), *The Open Handbook of Formal Epistemology*. PhilPapers, 2019.

Pettigrew, Richard. Accuracy, Chance, and the Principal Principle. *Philosophical Review*, 121(2): 241–75, 2012.

Pettigrew, Richard. Accuracy, Risk, and the Principle of Indifference. *Philosophy and Phenomenological Research*, 92(1): 35–59, 2016.

Pettigrew, Richard. *Accuracy and the Laws of Credence*. Oxford University Press, Oxford, 2016.

Predd, Joel, Robert Seiringer, Elliott Lieb, Daniel Osherson, H. Vincent Poor, and Sanjeev R. Kulkarni. Probabilistic Coherence and Proper Scoring Rules. *IEEE Transaction on Information Theory*, 55(10): 4786–92, 2009.

Walley, Peter, Renato Pelessoni, and Paolo Vicig. Direct Algorithms for Checking Coherence and Making Inferences from Conditional Probability Assessments. *Journal of Statistical Planning and Inference*, 126(1): 119–51, 2004.

Weisberg, Jonathan. Updating, Undermining, and Independence. *British Journal for the Philosophy of Science*, 66(1): 121–59, 2015.

Weiskrantz, L. *Blindsight, a Case Study and Implication*. Clarendon Press, Oxford, 1986.

Williams, Peter M. Coherence, strict coherence and zero probabilities. In *Proceedings of the Fifth International Congress on Logic, Methodology and Philosophy of Science*, volume VI, pages 29–33. Dordrecht, 1975. Proceedings of a 1974 conference held in Warsaw.

Williams, Peter M. Notes on Conditional Previsions. *International Journal of Approximate Reasoning*, 44(3): 366–83, 2007.

5

Conceptions of Genuine Knowledge in Wang Yangming

Harvey Lederman

1. Introduction

Wang Shouren (王守仁, Yangming 陽明 1472–1529) is widely recognized as the most influential philosopher of the Ming dynasty (1368–1644) and one of the most important philosophers in the whole tradition now called "Confucian." Some of Wang's most celebrated doctrines concern the relationship between knowledge and virtuous action. He claimed that his Song dynasty predecessors had held that a person can act virtuously only if they first determine that their action will be virtuous, by applying their knowledge of general moral laws to their predicament. Since on this picture, knowledge of moral laws must precede virtuous action, the view was associated with the slogan that knowledge comes first, and action later.

Wang rejected this picture. According to him, virtuous action does require an important cognitive achievement, but this cognitive achievement—which he sometimes called "genuine knowledge" (*zhen zhi* 真知)—does not precede action. Where his predecessors were associated with the slogan that knowledge comes first and action later, Wang described his own view as centered on "the unity of knowledge and action" (知行合一).

A key component of Wang's radical reconceptualization of the relationship between knowledge and virtuous action was a distinctive understanding of the cognitive achievement associated with virtuous action, that is, of "genuine knowledge." The last five centuries of extensive scholarly discussion of Wang's doctrine have produced many different proposals about how to understand this important notion. But we lack a systematic assessment of possible interpretations of the notion. In this chapter, I take some steps toward providing such an assessment. I identify and develop four different interpretations of genuine knowledge: the perceptual model, the practical model, the normative model, and the introspective model. The main aim of the chapter is to present these four views in more detail than has been done before, and to clarify some advantages and disadvantages of each of them. But at the end of the chapter, I suggest that the balance of considerations favors my own, introspective model.

Harvey Lederman, *Conceptions of Genuine Knowledge in Wang Yangming* In: *Oxford Studies in Epistemology, Volume 7*. Edited by: Tamar Szabó Gendler, John Hawthorne, and Julianne Chung, Oxford University Press. © Harvey Lederman 2023. DOI: 10.1093/oso/9780192868978.003.0005

In outline, the chapter proceeds as follows. Section 2 presents some key background. Section 3 considers what is arguably the most prominent position in the Anglophone scholarship on Wang—the *perceptual model*—according to which genuine knowledge sometimes has perception of the environment as a part of it. On this view, the unity of knowledge and action is taken to concern in part how a virtuous person will perceive ethically significant facts in their environment, and seamlessly respond on the basis of this perception with appropriate demeanor and affect (Nivison 1973; Cua 1982; Angle 2005, 2009; Ivanhoe 2002, 2009, 2011). I present some passages in support of this view and consider a simple, natural way of developing it. But I argue that this simple development is incorrect. My argument against this particular development of the perceptual model is not a direct argument against that model itself—and I later consider a more sophisticated version of that model which escapes the argument—but it does tell against the overarching interpretation of the unity of knowledge and action which the perceptual model has been supposed to support.

Section 4 turns to two further interpretations of genuine knowledge, the practical model and the normative model. According to the *practical model*, genuine knowledge is a form of "knowledge how," for instance, knowing how to be filially pious. On this view, the unity of knowledge and action concerns the claim that knowledge of how to be virtuous is acquired through, manifested in, and even constituted by virtuous action (Chen 1991, section 5.3; Yu 2014; Yu 2016; Shi 2017). According to the *normative model*, by contrast, genuine knowledge is understood as "knowledge-to" (as in, "a good child knows to care for their parents"). On this view, the unity of knowledge and action concerns the claim that if a person knows to do something, then they will do it in the appropriate circumstances (Huang 2016b, 2017; cf. Huang 2013, 2016a). I argue that the simplest view of the metaphysics of genuine knowledge which makes good on these two ideas does not sit well with the texts. Wang often emphasizes that introspective knowledge is a key component of the knowledge a fully virtuous person has, and the simplest versions of the practical and normative models cannot explain why he would do this.[1] In response to this argument, I present a more sophisticated view of the metaphysics of genuine knowledge, which does accommodate Wang's remarks about introspection in a manner consistent with the practical and normative models. But, I argue, even such a sophisticated view cannot escape a deeper problem for these models. Since a person often knows how to do something or knows to do it before they do it, both models struggle to make

[1] Sometimes in ordinary English "introspection" describes an effortful process of directing one's attention toward one's own mind, and considering its contents. I am not using the word in this way. Rather, I am following a standard philosophical usage according to which any knowledge of one's own mind counts as introspective knowledge.

sense of Wang's repeated, strenuous insistence that the form of knowledge which interests him does not precede action.

In arguing against the practical and normative models I suggest that an adequate understanding of genuine knowledge should take account of Wang's remarks about introspection. This suggestion raises the question: what if genuine knowledge just is a form of introspective knowledge? Section 5 develops this idea, and shows how it can accommodate some initially puzzling passages, including those which have been taken to motivate the perceptual, practical and normative models. At the end of the section, I argue that, on balance, the introspective model is to be preferred over the alternatives. A brief conclusion, section 6, takes stock, and discusses an important methodological question: the extent to which we should think that Wang himself held systematic views about genuine knowledge.

A companion paper, "The Introspective Model of Genuine Knowledge in Wang Yangming" (Lederman 2022), takes a different approach to the introspective model. There, I motivate the introspective model directly from the primary texts, focusing on the sense in which genuine knowledge can be thought of as an elevated form of knowledge. I say little there about how the introspective model compares to others' interpretations of genuine knowledge. In the present chapter, by contrast, I focus to a great extent on the viability of alternative interpretations of genuine knowledge, and argue for the introspective model primarily by comparing it to those alternatives. The two papers are intended to be free-standing, but the considerations they adduce in favor of the introspective model are complementary.

2. Background

In this section I introduce some key background for the remainder of the chapter, starting from what are arguably Wang's most famous remarks about the unity of knowledge and action. In this passage, one of Wang's students, Xu Ai (徐愛, Riren 曰仁 1487–1517), initiates a discussion of the doctrine by presenting a putative counterexample to it. Xu says: "Today everyone knows that they should be filial to their parents, and that they should be respectful to their older brothers, but they are unable to be filial, and unable to be respectful. So in this case knowledge and action are separated and are clearly two things."[2] Wang's response to this comment is worth quoting at some length:

[2] *IPL* 5, *QJ* 4, 如今人儘有知得父當孝、兄當弟者,却不能孝、不能弟,便是知與行分明是兩 件。 Throughout the chapter, I cite passages from the *Instructions for Practical Living* (hereafter, *IPL*, 傳習錄) by the section number of Chan's editions (Chan 1963, 1983), followed by a page number in Wu et al. 2011 (indicated by "*QJ*"). Passages in Wang's works outside the *IPL* are cited by the *juan* number and page number (e.g. "*QJ* 6.242"); I cite passages from Shu and Zha 2016 using "*QJBB*" and then a page

[T1] 此已被私慾隔斷, 不是知行的本體了。未有知而不行者。知而不行, 只是未 知。聖賢教人知行, 正是安復那本體, 不是着你只恁的便罷。故《大學》指個真知行與人看, 說『如好好色, 如惡惡臭』。見好色屬知, 好好色屬行。只見那好色時已自好了, 不是見了後又立個心去好。聞惡臭屬知, 惡惡臭屬行。只聞那惡臭時已自惡了, 不是聞了後別立個心去惡。如鼻塞 人雖見惡臭在前, 鼻中不曾聞得, 便亦不甚惡, 亦只是 不曾知臭。就如稱某 人知孝、某 人知弟, 必是其 人已曾行孝行弟, 方可稱 他知孝知弟, 不成只是曉得說 些孝弟的話, 便可稱為知孝弟。又如知痛, 必已自痛 了方知 痛, 知寒, 必已自寒 了; 知饑, 必已自饑了; 知行如何分得開 ?此便是知行的本體, 不曾有私意隔斷的。聖 人教人, 必要是如此, 方可謂 之知。不然, 只是 不曾知。

In this case, knowledge and action have already been divided by selfish desires; they are no longer in the original natural condition (*ben ti*) of knowledge and action.[3] No one has ever known but failed to act. If one knows but does not act, one simply does not yet know. In regard to knowledge and action, the sages and worthies taught people to stabilize and restore this original natural condition; they did not order one to do any old thing and then just stop.

For this reason, the *Great Learning* points to genuine knowledge and action for people to see. It says they are "like loving lovely sights and hating hateful odors."

Seeing a lovely sight belongs to knowledge, while loving a lovely sight belongs to action. But when someone sees a lovely sight, he already at that time automatically loves it. It is not that after seeing it he additionally makes up his mind to love it. Smelling a hateful odor belongs to knowledge, while hating a hateful odor belongs to action. When someone smells a hateful odor, he already at that time automatically hates it. It is not that after smelling it he separately makes up his mind to hate it. It's like a person with his nose blocked: even if he sees something with a hateful smell in front of him, in his nose, he has not smelt it. So while he doesn't really hate it, this is only because he does not yet know the odor.

The same goes for saying that someone knows filial piety or that someone knows fraternal respect. They must have at some point acted filially or acted respectfully, before they can be said to know filial piety or fraternal respect. If a person merely knows how to say some filial or respectful words, that's not enough for it to be acceptable to say that they know filial piety or fraternal respect. Knowledge of pain is also like this. One must have been in pain oneself to know pain. One must

number. Where available, I also cite pages in the translations of Ching 1972. Some of these texts are also translated in Ivanhoe 2009, and in Tiwald and Van Norden 2014. I recommend that interested readers consult these more recent translations as well.

[3] I will use the translation "original natural condition" for *ben ti* 本體 throughout the chapter. Fortunately very little will hinge here on the exegesis of this difficult term, and the reader can largely treat this expression as a black box in what follows.

> have been cold oneself to know cold. One must have been hungry oneself to know hunger. How then can knowledge and action be separated? This is the original natural condition of knowledge and action, which have not been divided by selfish inclinations. The sage taught people that only a person in this state can be said to know. If they are not in this state, then they do not yet know.
>
> (*IPL* 5, *QJ* 4)

This passage gives us a general sense for the shape of the doctrine of the unity of knowledge and action. In a moment, I will turn to specific interpretations of the key notion of genuine knowledge which appears in it. But first I will use this passage to introduce four points of background that will help to mark out the target of such interpretations: first, about which expressions I understand to be relevant to Wang's notion of "genuine knowledge"; second, about how I understand the metaphysics of genuine knowledge; third, about which cases of genuine knowledge I will focus on; and fourth, about how I will understand the relationship between genuine knowledge and Wang's famous notion of *liangzhi*.

First, then, on "genuine knowledge": Wang's opening move in his response to Xu Ai is to clarify the scope of the unity of knowledge and action. He accepts Xu's description of Xu's example, but denies that the example is a counterexample to his doctrine. Wang says that the people in Xu's case do not exhibit "the original natural condition" of knowledge and action; they do not display what he later calls "genuine knowledge and action." Wang uses the expression "genuine knowledge" on its own, separated from "genuine action," in several passages to describe a form of knowledge connected to the unity of knowledge and action.[4] Especially in later writing, Wang begins to use the expression "extended knowledge" (*zhi zhi* 致知) on occasion in a closely related way, to describe a distinctive form of knowledge connected to the unity of knowledge and action.[5] As I will discuss in more detail later, Wang can use the expression "extended knowledge" quite broadly to describe a condition of the mind which is not directly connected to the unity of knowledge and action. But when Wang does connect this "extended knowledge" to the unity of knowledge and action, it is natural to suppose that he is describing the same elevated form of knowledge that he describes with "genuine knowledge." Accordingly, I will use "genuine knowledge" throughout as my technical term for this distinctive form of knowledge, though I take uses of "the original natural condition" of knowledge and "extended knowledge," *when these are explicitly connected to the unity of knowledge and action* to describe the same mental state or mental event.

[4] *IPL* 125 *QJ* 42 (where it is in fact used by Xu Ai, not by Wang himself); *IPL* 133 *QJ* 47–8. For further citations and discussion see Lederman 2022, n. 11.

[5] *IPL* 139 *QJ* 56; *IPL* 140, *QJ* 58; *IPL* 321, *QJ* 137; *QJ* 5.211, Ching 1972: 68–9; *QJ* 8.308; and *QJ* 27.1100; cf. *QJ* 6.234, Ching 1972: 106–8.

Second, on the metaphysics of genuine knowledge: the most usual way of understanding *knowledge* is as a long-lasting state. Adults know many facts that they learned as children, even if they have not thought about them for many years. Indeed, they may know such facts even when they are asleep or unconscious. But there is some evidence that, in his more theoretical remarks on knowledge (*zhi*), Wang thought of it as more similar to a short-lived episode of apprehending or grasping, than to a long-lasting state.[6] Officially in this chapter, I will remain neutral on whether Wang thought "genuine knowledge" and related terms discussed in the previous paragraph denote a long-lasting state, whether he thought they denote a short-lived episode, or whether he could use the term to refer to states in some contexts, and episodes in other contexts. But I will be making two background assumptions about the metaphysics of mind associated with genuine knowledge. First, I will be assuming that there are two kinds of mental events in the vicinity of genuine knowledge: one, a longer-lasting state; and the other a short-lived episode. Second, I will be assuming that the longer-lasting state can be thought of as in part a disposition, and that the short-lived episodes are parts of the exercise of that disposition. So, for example, I assume that a person who has the longer-lasting state which is related to genuine knowledge of filial piety will be disposed to experience episodes related to genuine knowledge of filial piety in a particular array of circumstances. I will call these short-lived episodes "episodes of genuine knowledge," an expression which is intended to be neutral on the question of whether the episodes are themselves genuine knowledge or simply episodes of the exercise of genuine knowledge, understood as a disposition.

Third, on the scope of genuine knowledge: there is some debate about whether the unity of knowledge and action is supposed to apply to all knowledge, or only to knowledge that is relevant to virtuous action.[7] I will not attempt to make progress on this debate here, but will focus on uncontroversial examples of genuine knowledge. In [T1] Wang describes knowledge of filial piety (*xiao* 孝 hereafter "filiality") and fraternal respect (*ti* 悌 hereafter, "respect").[8] In the context of his reply to Xu Ai, it is clear that Wang means to describe what he earlier called "knowledge in its original natural condition," or "genuine

[6] In a series of passages where Wang describes the relationship between *zhi* and inclinations (*yi* 意), Wang quite clearly describes these inclinations as short-lived episodes (*IPL* 6 *QJ* 6; *IPL* 78 *QJ* 27; *IPL* 137 *QJ* 53; *IPL* 174 *QJ* 86–7; *IPL* 201 *QJ* 103). In two of these passages, Wang describes *zhi* as a property or aspect of such inclinations (*IPL* 174 *QJ* 86–7; *IPL* 201 *QJ* 103). Instances of properties of such short-lived episodes are presumably themselves short-lived.

[7] Cua 1982 and Yang 2009, for instance, see it as restricted to ethically relevant knowledge; Frisina (2002, Ch. 4) and Zheng 2018 argue that it applies to all knowledge.

[8] The phrase I've translated as "know filiality," could instead be rendered as "know how to be filial" or "know to be filial" (and similarly for respect). I discuss this point in detail in section 4.

knowledge." In different passages ([T3] and [T4] below), Wang makes similar remarks about compassion (*ce yin* 惻隱), humaneness (*ren* 仁) and conscientiousness (*zhong* 忠), so it is natural to think that he held that there can be genuine knowledge related to these notions as well.[9] In an attempt to sidestep the debates just mentioned, I will focus exclusively on interpretations of genuine knowledge in connection to these five examples: filiality, respect, conscientiousness, compassion, and humaneness.

Fourth, and finally, on the relationship between genuine knowledge and *liangzhi* (良知): the *Mencius* (7A.15) uses the expression "*liangzhi*" to describe innate, ethically relevant knowledge (see below [T3]).[10] Wang took inspiration from this passage of the *Mencius*, and elevated the notion of *liangzhi* to a central component of his moral psychology. He ascribes broad powers to *liangzhi*: it acquires introspective knowledge of the ethical qualities of mental events,[11] and also produces appropriate thoughts (*si* 思) and affective responses (*qing* 情) (*IPL* 169 *QJ* 81-2; *IPL* 290 *QJ* 126). In some places, Wang suggests that *liangzhi* can even be responsible for perception of the environment (*IPL* 168 *QJ* 80 cf. *QJ* 6.235; Ching 1972: 110) or for divining others' future actions on the basis of their present behavior and mental states (*IPL* 171; *QJ* 83). There is a great deal of controversy about how *liangzhi* should be understood: some think of it as a body of knowledge; others think of it as a class of mental events (e.g. Angle and Tiwald 2017: 103–6); and still others think of it in the first instance as a faculty with important similarities to the conscience. Though I will sometimes speak about *liangzhi* in line with this last position (which is closest to my own view), nothing essential will turn on this: officially I will not be taking a stand on how this important issue should be resolved. I will however be taking a stand on

[9] The expression I will follow tradition in translating "compassion" here does not mean "compassion." Unlike compassion (or empathy, or sympathy), the emotion described here is one that is directed at situations, not people, and it can even be directed at oneself, not others (see Shun 2018: 90 for these points). The expression might be better translated "being pained by" or "being unable to bear." These alternative translations (and their associated interpretation) would not affect my arguments below, which will not turn on substantive claims about the content of this "compassion."

[10] Wang did not begin to espouse his distinctive views about *liangzhi* until 1520–21, approximately twelve years after he first proposed the unity of knowledge and action. But he continued to discuss the unity of knowledge and action after 1521, and there is good evidence that he understood his views before 1521 to be consistent with his views after that year. (For details, see Lederman 2022, n. 5.) In this chapter, I will use passages after 1521 freely; the project can be thought of as aiming at an exegesis of Wang's post-1521 views of the unity of knowledge and action. I take the general idea that Wang's later views about the unity of knowledge and action were consistent with his earlier ones to be compatible with the idea that his thinking about *liangzhi* underwent important development over the course of his career, which it clearly did. For a detailed story about this development, see Kern (2010: 87–355), though Kern himself acknowledges that the aspects of Wang's thinking about *liangzhi* which he identifies were all still discussed in a later period (for discussion of the relationship between them, see Kern 2010: 344–55).

[11] Wang emphasizes this kind of introspection in a host of other passages as well, e.g. in: *IPL* 162 *QJ* 76, *IPL* 169 *QJ* 81–2; *IPL* 206 *QJ* 105; *IPL* 290 *QJ* 126; the second and third sentences of the "Four Sentence Teaching" (四句教) (*IPL* 315 *QJ* 133–4); *IPL* 318 *QJ* 135–6; *QJ* 6.242 Ching 1972: 114; and *QJ* 8.307. Wang makes similar points in his pre- *liangzhi* period, in the 1515 "Preface to the Old Version of the Great Learning" *QJ* 7.271. Chen Jiuchuan (陳 九川) also makes related points in *IPL* 201 *QJ* 102.

the relationship between *liangzhi* and genuine knowledge. In particular, I believe that not all knowledge acquired by or possessed by *liangzhi* is genuine knowledge. This claim is controversial; some authors, for instance, say that genuine knowledge just is *liangzhi*. But there is in my view a very strong argument for the claim: Wang says in many places that even people who are acting viciously acquire ethically relevant knowledge by the exercise of their *liangzhi* (e.g. *IPL* 152 *QJ* 69, *IPL* 207 *QJ* 105, *QJ* 27.1112-1113 Ching 1972: 121; see Lederman 2022, n. 21 for more citations). But as we have seen, Wang is clear that only people who act in accord with what they know have genuine knowledge. So he clearly does not hold that people who are acting viciously have genuine knowledge. Genuine knowledge and the knowledge *liangzhi* always acquires must therefore be distinct.[12]

These points set the stage for the development of our different interpretations of genuine knowledge, to which I now turn in earnest.

3. The Perceptual Model

According to arguably the most prominent interpretation of the unity of knowledge and action in the scholarship on Wang written in English, the doctrine concerns in part a rich form of perception (Nivison 1973; Cua 1982; Ivanhoe 2002, 2009, 2011; Angle 2005, 2009). On this interpretation, Wang holds that appropriately acknowledging features of the world around one consists in part in having an appropriate affective response to them, and this appropriate affective response in turn results in an appropriate action. Proponents of this broad interpretation of the unity of knowledge and action have typically not offered a detailed analysis of genuine knowledge. But they all seem committed to what I will call the *perceptual model*, characterized by adherence to the following claim:

[12] In **[T1]** Wang uses the expression "original natural condition of knowledge and action" (知行本體) quite clearly to describe what he then calls "genuine knowledge and action." In *IPL* 165 *QJ* 78 Wang directly identifies *liangzhi* and *liangneng* (良能, see **[T3]** below) with this same "original natural condition of knowledge and action." This pattern of usage might seem to flatly contradict my claim that genuine knowledge must be distinguished from *liangzhi*. But there is no contradiction, because the expression I translate "original natural condition" (本體) is clearly used in two different ways in these two passages. In *IPL* 5 (**[T1]**) Wang uses "'the original natural condition of knowledge and action" explicitly to describe something which can be lost (失) and must be restored (復), whereas in *IPL* 165, when he says that *liangzhi* is the original natural condition of knowledge, he clearly means something which can never be lost, and which all people possess. Wang often uses the expression "original natural condition" to describe the "original natural condition of the mind" (心之本體), and his usage of this expression exhibits exactly the same ambiguity we see in *IPL* 5 and *IPL* 165. Wang can describe the original natural condition of the mind both as something which can be "lost" (失, *IPL* 34 *QJ* 17, *IPL* 222 *QJ* 108–9, cf. *IPL* 204 *QJ* 104) and hence must be "restored" (復) (e.g. *IPL* 121 *QJ* 40, *IPL* 127 *QJ* 43 (性之本體); *IPL* 145, *QJ* 66 (repeated in *IPL* 169, *QJ* 81); *IPL* 237 *QJ* 112–13; *QJ* 5.216 Ching 1972: 87, cf. *IPL* 101 *QJ* 34). But he can also speak of it as something which everyone has, and can only be obstructed, not lost (*IPL* 48 *QJ* 20, *IPL* 152 *QJ* 69, *IPL* 155 *QJ* 70–71, *IPL* 221 *QJ* 108, cf. *QJ* 7.271 (本體之知)). In *IPL* 76 (*QJ* 26–27) the two uses are especially close to the surface.

Perceptual Part Some episodes of genuine knowledge of filiality have episodes of perceiving the environment as a part of them.

In displayed principles like this one, I will always present only the one example of "filiality," although I mean such principles to apply also to the other examples mentioned in the previous section: to respect, compassion, conscientiousness and humaneness. In this principle, I have used "episode of perceiving" in part to highlight the fact that I mean the word "part" quite literally. Events like parties have multiple parts: they have parts which are separated in time—the first part of the party, when only a few guests have arrived, and later parts when things are buzzing—as well as simultaneous parts—the part of the party outside where people are playing lawn games, and the part inside, where people are talking. In Perceptual Part, the "episodes of perceiving" are taken to be literally parts of the episodes of genuine knowledge, just as the playing of lawn games outside may be part of a party. Moreover, I allow the special case where the party is a part of itself, namely, the part that makes up all of it. A person who holds that some episodes of genuine knowledge just are episodes of perceiving would count as endorsing Perceptual Part. Finally, it is worth reiterating that genuine knowledge (*zhen zhi* 真知) is not *liangzhi*. Everyone should agree that *liangzhi* is sometimes responsible for perception of the environment. Wang says as much in at least one place (*IPL* 168, *QJ* 80). The distinctive thesis of the perceptual model is a claim about the connection between perception and *genuine knowledge*, not this completely uncontroversial claim about the connection between perception and *liangzhi*.[13]

Let us start by considering the main passages which motivate the idea that genuine knowledge is closely connected to perception. **[T1]** is perhaps the most important. Just like the word "like" in English, the word I have translated "like" (*ru* 如) in "The *Great Learning* points to genuine knowledge and action for people

[13] Philosophers often use the words "see" and "perceive" in such a way that (in their usage) a person who hallucinates a dagger does not see or perceive a dagger, but merely seems to see or perceive one, or merely experiences a perceptual seeming as of there being one. The proponents of the perceptual model cited above do not consider the distinction between perception and perceptual seemings, and do not take a stand on whether their view is best articulated in terms of perception (in this sense) or in terms of perceptual seemings. But I believe that many proponents of the position would not see an important difference between Perceptual Part and the claim that some episodes of genuine knowledge have perceptual seemings as a part of them, so I won't consider objections which turn on this distinction in what follows. With that said, when I speak of perception here and throughout the chapter, I mean perception by the five senses, not further aspects of cognition which might metaphorically be described as "perception." An interpretation (like those of Liu (2018: 253–4) or Zheng (2019: 1358, 1360)) which uses the word "perceive" to describe what *liangzhi* knows on the basis of introspection, taking introspection to be something like an "inner sense," would therefore not count as an instance of the perceptual model in my terminology. As I will discuss later (see n. 45), Wang certainly thought that there were important analogies between (ordinary) sense-perception and the introspection of *liangzhi*. But I know of only a single passage where he directly uses the word "see" (見) to describe what the mind "sees" in introspection (*IPL* 96 *QJ* 30–31). Given that Wang himself does not seem particularly attracted to this metaphorical way of speaking, it is not clear to me how helpful or faithful it is to describe *liangzhi* as "perceiving" what it knows on the basis of introspection.

to see. It says they are 'like loving lovely sights and hating hateful odors'" can be used to introduce either an example or a simile. A proponent of the perceptual model will naturally adopt the first of these interpretations, taking these examples to be examples of genuine knowledge and action, not merely analogues for them. On this view, Wang's subsequent discussion of seeing and smelling describes episodes of genuine knowledge or parts of such episodes, so genuine knowledge at least sometimes is either identical to perception or has perception as a part of it.

This conclusion does not on its own establish Perceptual Part, since that thesis concerns genuine knowledge of filiality, respect, compassion, humaneness and conscientiousness, and not other putative examples of genuine knowledge, such as of a sight or a smell. But proponents of the perceptual model who take seeing and smelling to be examples of genuine knowledge will naturally understand these examples as intended to illustrate a more general point, that the core examples of genuine knowledge can also have perception of the environment as a part of them.[14] And indeed this reading of [T1] might seem to be confirmed by the following passage, which can be read as describing a more direct relationship between perception and (genuine) knowledge of ethical qualities such as filiality:

> **[T2]** 知是心之本體, 心自然會知: 見父自然知孝, 見兄自然知弟, 見孺子入井自 然知惻隱, 此便是良知 不假外求。若良知之發, 更無私意障礙, 即所謂『充 其惻隱 之心, 而 仁 不可勝用矣』。然在常 人 不能無私意障礙, 所 以須用致 知。 。 。之功。 。 。即心 之良知更無障礙, 得 以充塞流行, 便是致其知。知致則 意誠。
>
> Knowing is the original natural condition of the mind. The mind is automatically able to know. When it sees one's parents, it automatically knows filiality. When it sees one's elder brother, it automatically knows respect. When it sees a child fall into a well, it automatically knows compassion.[15] This is *liangzhi*, and should not be sought outside. If *liangzhi* is aroused, and there is furthermore no obstruction of selfish inclinations, it will be like the saying "If one fulfills one's mind which is compassionate, then one's humaneness will function inexorably." But ordinary people are unable not to have the obstructions of selfish inclinations. That is why they must use the practice of the extension of knowledge (*zhi zhi* 致知)... Then the mind's *liangzhi* will furthermore have no obstructions and will be able to

[14] Not all proponents of the perceptual model agree that the examples in [T1] are examples of genuine knowledge. Cua 1982 for instance takes them merely to be analogous to genuine knowledge, and motivates the perceptual model primarily on the basis of our next passage, [T2].

[15] This passage alludes to a famous example from *Mencius* 2A.6. In Mencius's example, the child was on the verge of falling into the well (將入於 井), and it is plausible that, although Wang says "fall into a well," he means "on the verge of" falling into a well, relying on the reader's knowledge of the original text. See n. 9 on the word I translate as "compassion."

> operate smoothly everywhere. This then is the extension of knowledge. And if one's knowledge is extended, one's inclinations will be wholehearted.
>
> (*IPL* 8, *QJ* 7)

My criterion for determining which passages describe genuine knowledge does not logically imply that this one does. Wang does not use the expression "genuine knowledge" here, and although he does use "extended knowledge," he does not tie it explicitly to the unity of knowledge and action. But everyone should agree that Wang has genuine knowledge in mind in the passage. He describes an elevated form of knowledge, since he says that ordinary people do not achieve this state, in spite of the automatic knowledge of which their mind is capable. And he implicitly ties this elevated form of knowledge to action, since he explicitly connects it to the possibility of being fully virtuous, which at least in normal circumstances requires some virtuous action. So the passage can be understood to support the idea that genuine knowledge is closely connected to perception. In particular, when Wang says that, on seeing one's parents, seeing one's brother, or seeing a child fall into a well, the mind "automatically knows" (自然知) filiality, respect or compassion, one might take him to mean that this automatic knowledge is identical with the perception of filiality, respect or compassion, or at least that it has some perception as a part of it.

These two passages are the primary evidence that Wang connects genuine knowledge to perception.[16] But how exactly should we understand that connection? Perceptual Part is a fairly weak thesis, and it is natural to wonder how it might be strengthened to yield a richer analysis of the connection. Perhaps the most obvious such strengthening is the idea that (at least sometimes) genuine knowledge just is perception:

> **Genuine Perception** Some episodes of genuinely knowing filiality are episodes of perceiving filiality.

Genuine Perception entails Perceptual Part, but it is stronger than Perceptual Part. I will first examine this stronger thesis before considering the prospects of a weaker view which centers on Perceptual Part itself.

[16] A third passage not by Wang Yangming has played an important role in scholars' understanding of what Wang himself might mean by "genuine knowledge." In a famous passage, Cheng Yi (程頤, Yichuan 伊川, 1033–107), is reported as saying fairly clearly that a fieldhand, who was previously harmed by a tiger, has genuine knowledge of a tiger's ability to harm people (Wang 2004: 2A.16, cf. also 18.188). This passage doesn't directly support the idea that episodes of genuine knowledge have episodes of perceiving as parts. But it does strongly suggest that Cheng held that we can have genuine knowledge of objects or facts outside our minds. If Wang agreed with Cheng on this point, then it would be natural for him to endorse the idea that perception can be a part of that knowledge. For some further English language discussion of this passage see Huang (2015, Ch. 3). For other precedents of Wang's ideas, see Shun (2010: 188), Angle (2018: 166).

Genuine Perception is consistent with quite different understandings of genuine knowledge, depending on how one understands what it is to perceive qualities such as filiality. The most obvious, flatfooted way of thinking about this perception yields what I will call the *flashlight model.* On this view, properties such as filiality are instantiated in the environment in the same straightforward way that properties like sizes or shapes are, and people perceive filiality in the environment in the same straightforward way that they perceive sizes or shapes. This flashlight model offers a simple, natural way of developing the idea that genuine knowledge is a form of perception.[17] But there is an important problem with it. Wang repeatedly and strenuously argues that qualities such as filiality and respect are not external to the mind; he clearly does not hold that filiality or respect are instantiated in the environment in the straightforward way that sizes or shapes are.[18] So he cannot hold that genuine knowledge of filiality or respect is identical with perception of qualities instantiated in the environment in the straightforward way that sizes or shapes are.

This argument motivates interpreting Genuine Perception using a subtler conception of what it is to perceive ethical qualities like filiality, which does not require that these qualities be instantiated in the environment in a straightforward way. On a very particular (and perhaps idiosyncratic) version of what is sometimes called "projectivism," the mental states or events involved in perceiving qualities such as beauty or repulsiveness are not at all like the mental states or events involved in perceiving qualities such as size and shape. Instead, to perceive a quality like beauty or repulsiveness in an object just is to have an appropriate affective response to the object. Moreover, for an object to instantiate these qualities is for it to be disposed to cause these affective responses in those who encounter it. Our second development of Genuine Perception, the *affective*

[17] A natural reading of Nivison 1973 suggests that Nivison endorses the flashlight model. He writes: "My perception of a thing as having visible and value qualities is total and unitary. Just as when I look at a tree I see not only a shape but a solid extended object with a front and a back side, so here I 'see' an object with a visible and a 'value side'" (Nivison 1973: 132, reprinted in Nivison 1996: 243). Nivison says that the things which are "seen" (in scare-quotes) have both "visible and value qualities" and (again) that the "object" which has a "value side," *also* has a "visible" side. It is clear then that Nivison thinks that the objects which possess the "value qualities" that we "see" are objects *visible* to the person in question; they are not (for instance) the internal objects of an inner sense. So it is natural to read Nivison as committing himself to something quite close to Genuine Perception here. Moreover, earlier in the paper Nivison writes: "For Wang Yang-ming there is no effective difference between perceiving a sensible quality with a sense (for example, sight) and 'perceiving' a value-quality with the mind in the noninclusive sense of the mind that thinks and conceives" (Nivison 1973: 132, reprinted in Nivison 1996: 242–3). This passage, together with Nivison's use of the examples of shape in the previous quotation, strongly suggests that he has something like the flashlight model in mind. If he thought that objects' "value qualities" are mind-dependent in a way in which qualities like shape are not, that would be an extremely important "effective difference" between Nivison's two forms of "sight." So these passages seem to me to commit Nivison to the flashlight model. Others may disagree with that interpretation. Whether or not Nivison endorsed this model, the flashlight model is worth discussing, since it illustrates important constraints on the interpretation of Wang.

[18] *IPL* 3 *QJ* 2–3, *IPL* 101 *QJ* 33–4, *IPL* 133 *QJ* 48, *IPL* 135 *QJ* 50–1; cf. *QJ* 4.175 Ching 1972: 29–30.

perceptual model, takes inspiration from this idea. According to this model, what it is to perceive filiality in the environment just is to exhibit a certain affective response to it.

This new position escapes my argument against the flashlight model. If the affective perceptual model is correct, it would be natural for Wang to deny that filiality or respect are "out there in the world," since they partly depend on a person's responses to the world. Moreover, proponents of the affective perceptual model can understand Wang's comments that ethical qualities are "in the mind" as intended to highlight that the presence of these qualities in our environment at leas partly depends on the ways in which we respond psychologically to the environment.

The affective perceptual model gives us one example of how a subtler conception of perception can be used to avoid the problem with the flashlight model that I described above. Other sophisticated conceptions of perception might do the trick as well. But I will now argue that the question of how they might do so is moot. For there is a deeper problem with Genuine Perception, which neither the affective perceptual model, nor any other sophisticated view of the perception of ethical qualities can avoid. The problem is that it does not make sense to say that a person sees filiality or respect in the circumstances Wang describes in [T2]. In general, it is reasonable to say that people can see the beauty of beautiful sights,[19] and I can imagine a position according to which, when a son or younger brother responds correctly to his parents or older brother, his filiality or respectfulness is similarly visible on the surface; by looking at him we can just see these qualities. But these are not the circumstances Wang has in mind. He speaks of a son seeing his parents and, when he responds filially, knowing filiality. He speaks of a younger brother seeing his older brother and, when he responds respectfully, knowing respect. In these cases the son is not perceiving filiality or the younger brother perceiving respect in the environment in any natural sense. The parents may be *worthy* of filiality, but Wang does not tell us that the parents are themselves filial, and they might well not be. Similarly, the older brother may be worthy of respect, but Wang does not tell us that the brother himself is respectful, and he might well not be. Wang clearly says that when we see our parents or brothers we have (genuine) knowledge of filiality and respect, not that we have (genuine) knowledge of worthiness-of-filiality, or of worthiness-of-respect. So, at least in these examples Wang does not identify genuine knowledge of these qualities with a person's perception of them.[20]

[19] In [T1] Wang in fact says only that the person sees the beautiful sight, not its beauty, but we may suppose for the sake of argument here that he could have said that people can see the beauty itself.

[20] Antonio Cua takes genuine knowledge to involve a rich form of perception, which he connects to a Wittgensteinian notion of "seeing as." He takes this seeing as to include an acknowledgement that the

Genuine Perception does not sit well with the key examples in [T2]. And in light of the straightforward way in which Genuine Perception fails to apply to these examples, it is hard to see what motivation one might have for claiming that there are some further examples (not discussed by Wang) where in fact genuine knowledge of filiality, respect, or compassion is a form of perception.

This argument against Genuine Perception, importantly, does not tell directly against the weaker Perceptual Part. Perceptual Part says only that perception is a part of episodes of genuine knowledge. The principle does not require that the relevant perception be perception of qualities such as filiality; it could instead be an episode of perceiving something else entirely. Perceptual Part does not entail that filiality, respect or compassion are instantiated in the environment. It also does not entail that a virtuous person sees filiality when they see their parents.

But the argument against Genuine Perception does point toward a problem with one of the guiding ideas of the perceptual model, and thereby undermines some of its appeal. A core idea behind the perceptual model is that the unity of knowledge and action is intended to describe the way in which a virtuous person is distinctively sensitive to features of their environment. Angle (2005: 41) spells out this idea, for example, by connecting Wang's views to contemporary neo-Aristotelian discussions of moral perception.[21] He cites the following passage from Martha Nussbaum to illustrate what he takes Wang to be getting at:

> Perception is not merely aided by emotion but is also in part constituted by appropriate response. Good perception is a full recognition or acknowledgment of the practical situation; the whole personality sees it for what it is. The agent who discerns intellectually that a friend is in need or that a loved one has died, but who fails to respond to these facts with appropriate sympathy or grief, clearly lacks a part of Aristotelian virtue. It seems right to say, in addition, that a part of discernment or perception is lacking. This person doesn't really, or doesn't fully, see what has happened. (Nussbaum 1990: 79)

Nussbaum's examples of what a person perceives in this passage—that a friend is in need, or that a loved one has died—are clearly facts that the person discerns in the environment, in the world around them. Nussbaum closes by saying that a person who does not respond to these facts "doesn't really, or doesn't fully, see

object falls under a particular category—an acknowledgement which involves an affective response of what one sees (Cua 1982: 7; cf. Cua 1998: 181–3). This position falls to a closely related objection: Wang is clearly not describing acknowledging one's parents as falling under the category of filiality.

[21] Angle (2005: 40–4) draws heavily on an Aristotelian tradition in contemporary discussion, citing Murdoch 1970, Wiggins 1975, McDowell 1979, Nussbaum 1990, and Blum 1991. Ivanhoe 2011 investigates the relationship between McDowell and Wang Yangming in detail.

what has happened." In her view, virtuous people exhibit a distinctive form of sensitivity to the environment. Angle sees a related idea in Wang Yangming.

Crucially this basic thought seems to motivate not just proponents of Genuine Perception, but also those who endorse only the weaker Perceptual Part. P. J. Ivanhoe explicitly denies Genuine Perception and on one reading may endorse Perceptual Part instead, taking perception to be just a part of episodes of genuine knowledge. But he still understands Wang to hold that a person who acts virtuously exhibits an elevated form of sensitivity to their environment, and describes genuine knowledge as "true seeing" or "true perception." He writes that, according to Wang: "the necessary and sufficient condition for moral action is *true perception* of a situation. When we truly see, we don't just believe—we act. For Wang, true perception involves an understanding not only of what is being perceived but how it relates to the greater context of the Way. This larger understanding in turn entails the appropriate affective reaction to such a state of affairs, and this sets into motion a proper response or action" (Ivanhoe 2002: 99, emphasis his).[22]

Wang's examples in [T2] do not show that Perceptual Part is incorrect. But they strongly suggest that Wang's thought is different from Nussbaum's, and therefore undermine at least some of the motivation for Perceptual Part. Wang does not say that people who are not virtuous do not "really" or "fully" see their parents, their elder brothers, or the child who is about to fall into a well; he does not call into question their ability to see the environment around them at all. He only says that they do not really know filiality, respect, or compassion. While Wang certainly distinguishes between different grades of knowledge of filiality, the cases he considers (as we have seen) are not ones where a person perceives filiality in the environment, so these gradations in a person's knowledge of filiality should not be understood as gradations in their perception of a situation. More generally, and looking beyond these examples, I am unaware of cases where Wang clearly distinguishes between grades of perception in the way that Nussbaum and Ivanhoe do.[23]

[22] Elsewhere Ivanhoe writes that "genuine knowledge...is substantially constituted by a disposition to attend and respond affectively to ethical situations and act properly and without hesitation" (Ivanhoe 2009: 113). The "ethical situations" to which Ivanhoe says we "attend" are clearly mind-external, and he says explicitly that genuine knowledge is "substantially constituted by" a disposition to experience such episodes of attention. To me, this suggests that he is committed to Perceptual Part (cf. also Ivanhoe 2011: 282–3). Other remarks of Ivanhoe's might seem to suggest the flashlight model (and hence Genuine Perception), as opposed to Perceptual Part. For instance, in introducing a "spectrum" of meta-ethical views, Ivanhoe writes that "Wang Yangming's view, which claims that moral qualities are out there in the world and available to us through a special faculty of moral sapience...defines the 'moral faculty' pole," which is opposed to the "projectivist" pole of his spectrum (Ivanhoe 2011: 274). One might read "out there in the world" to mean that the qualities are instantiated by objects outside the mind, in line with the flashlight model. But in the context of Ivanhoe's other writings, quoted above, the expression is better understood to mean only that Wang understands moral properties in a mind-independent way.

[23] In the closing sentences of the first paragraph of [T1] Wang does say that a person who does not smell an odor does not hate it only because they do not know it. One might claim that, by focusing on

Where does this leave the perceptual model? Many aspects of the mind, with quite different characteristics, may have episodes of perception as a part of them. On its own, Perceptual Part is too weak to be the basis of a distinctive understanding of genuine knowledge. As we have seen, the most explicit proponents of something like the perceptual model—whether they endorse Genuine Perception or only Perceptual Part—have supplemented this thesis with the proposal that Wang holds that virtuous people enjoy a distinctive sensitivity to their environment. Indeed, while I officially defined the perceptual model in terms of an endorsement of Perceptual Part, commitment to this broader claim about the sensitivity of virtuous people is so prominent that I might as well have included it too. But this broader claim, I have argued, should be rejected. If Perceptual Part is true, it is not because Wang holds that virtuous people exhibit a distinctive form of sensitivity to their environment. And, given this conclusion, it is unclear what hangs on the question of whether Wang does, or does not, endorse Perceptual Part, since perception will not have a distinctive place in the unity of knowledge and action.

In short: although my arguments leave the letter of Perceptual Part untouched—for all I have said, it may still be that perception is a part of genuine knowledge—they do suggest that the perceptual model does not have the broad significance for our understanding of the unity of knowledge and action it has been supposed to have.

[T2], I am ignoring this key passage where Wang does sound more like Nussbaum or Ivanhoe. But while I agree that in this passage Wang describes different forms of knowledge, he does not describe different forms of *perception*, in line with Nussbaum's "really" or "fully" seeing or Ivanhoe's "true perception." Wang says that the person's nose is blocked, so that they do not smell the odor *at all*; he does not draw a contrast between a person who "really" smells and someone who in some sense can smell but cannot really smell in this more discerning way. Moreover, immediately after the example, Wang begins to discuss explicitly the idea that one cannot know something unless one has experienced it. In context, the most natural reading of the example of the blocked nose is as intended to illustrate this next point. It seems then that Wang's goal in this passage is to emphasize that different sense modalities can result in knowledge of different kinds. If a person hasn't smelled an odor then even if they know it is there (say, on the basis of testimony) they still do not know it in the way that interests Wang, because they have not experienced it directly. This contrast is quite different from the contrast between the way a discerning person smells, and the way an undiscerning person does.

In *IPL* 171 *QJ* 83, Wang says that extending one's *liangzhi* allows one to know on the basis of others' current behavior and mental states what they will do in the future. As I said in the previous section, it is not obvious that every instance of "extended knowledge" is relevant to our understanding of genuine knowledge. But a proponent of Perceptual Part might take this instance to describe genuine knowledge, and hence take it to support the idea that genuine knowledge does involve a distinctive sensitivity to the environment. Perhaps. In my view, a better interpretation of this passage takes it to be an example of "extended knowledge" used in a broad sense to describe the "full functioning of *liangzhi*," not in a narrow sense to describe genuine knowledge. First, it is noteworthy that Wang does not apply the ideas he develops in this passage to knowledge of ethical qualities such as filiality, respect and compassion. Second, this passage is the only one I know of where Wang describes extended knowledge explicitly as involving increased ability to know this kind of claim. If it were central to the unity of knowledge and action, one might have expected him to discuss it considerably more often.

4. The Practical and Normative Models

I turn now to two quite different views of the character of genuine knowledge, based, first, on the idea that genuine knowledge is a form of knowledge-how (the *practical model*) and, second, on the idea that it is a form of knowledge-to (the *normative model*).

As in my discussion of the perceptual model, I will begin by considering the key passages which motivate these models. But before we do, we must start with two linguistic points about classical Chinese. First, like the English word "know," the character *zhi* 知 can take syntactically different expressions as its complement, and when it does so it describes what we may think of as at least *prima facie* different kinds of knowledge: if it takes a sentential complement, it describes propositional knowledge ("know that");[24] if it takes a simple noun-phrase as its complement ("arithmetic"), it describes objectual knowledge ("know arithmetic"); and if it takes a verb-phrase as its complement ("run," "say thank you"), it describes knowing-how ("know how to run"), or knowing-to ("know to say thank you"). So far, so familiar. But, second, and much less familiarly to those accustomed to English or Romance languages, many characters in classical Chinese can have a diverse array of syntactic roles, making it difficult to determine what kind of complement *zhi* ("know") in fact takes in a given instance. For example, the character *xiao* 孝 can be used as a noun ("filiality"), as an adjective ("filial"), or as a verb-phrase ("be filial") without any change in the way it is written. As a result, the expression I have translated in [T1] and [T2] as "know filiality" might instead be translated as "know how to be filial" or "know to be filial." And this same pattern is exhibited by the characters I have translated as "respect" and "compassion," so the expressions I have translated "know respect" and "know compassion" might be rendered instead as "know how to be respectful" or "know to be respectful" and "know how to be compassionate" or "know to be compassionate."[25]

Proponents of the practical and normative models will claim that my earlier translations of [T1] and [T2] are incorrect: Wang does not there describe knowledge *of* filiality, respect or compassion, but instead describes knowing (how) to be filial, respectful or compassionate. In their view, in the key sentence of [T2], for example, Wang says that when a person sees their parents, they

[24] A common way of expressing propositional knowledge in classical Chinese involves a special construction where a nominalized sentence is the complement of the verb "know." At least in Wang's corpus, there does not seem to me a significant semantic difference between this construction and those in which the complement is an un-nominalized sentence. See Harbsmeier 1993 for discussion of a related issue in pre-Han texts.

[25] In principle they might also be understood as "know that one is filial," "know that one is respectful" and "know that one is compassionate," but I know of no one who has advocated this construal, so I won't consider it here.

automatically know (how) to be filial, that when a person sees their brother, they automatically know (how) to be respectful, and when a person sees a child about to fall into a well, they automatically know (how) to be compassionate (see e.g. Shi 2017: 55–6, and Huang 2017: 87). The passage does not on its own support the knowing-how or knowing-to construal by comparison to the objectual construal, but proponents of the practical and normative models will naturally seek to support their translation on the basis of parallels with other passages. One way of doing so would start from the passage in the *Mencius* which first uses the notion of *liangzhi*:

> **[T3]** 孟子曰:「人之所 不學而能者, 其良能也; 所 不慮而知者, 其良知 也。孩提之童, 無 不知愛其親者; 及其長 也, 無 不知敬其兄 也。。。
>
> Mencius said: "what people are able to do without learning is their *liangneng* [lit: "good ability"]; what they know without reflection is their *liangzhi* [lit: "good knowledge"]. Infants all know (how) to love their parents; when they are grown, they all know (how) to respect their older brothers..." (7A.15)

As *the* locus classicus for the use of *liangzhi*—a notion which, as we saw above, Wang elevated to a central position in his moral psychology—this passage had outsized importance for Wang. And, interestingly, the complements of the word "know" in this passage are not as syntactically flexible as the expressions we considered above: the expressions I have translated as "love their parents" (愛其親) and "respect their older brother" (敬其兄) are hard to understand in any way other than as verb-phrases. So the *Mencius* clearly describes knowing (how) to love one's parents and knowing (how) to respect one's older brother.[26]

These observations are especially relevant to [T2] because in one passage (*IPL* 118 *QJ* 39), Wang uses the exact examples from the *Mencius* as part of an explanation of how "knowledge is the original natural condition of the mind" (知是心 之本體), the very same idea with which he begins [T2]. On the basis of this parallel—and given the fact that the Mencian examples strongly favor the knowing-how or knowing-to construals—proponents of the practical and normative models might argue that "know" in [T2] should also be understood as "know how" or "know to." According to them, [T2] goes beyond the *Mencius*'s claims about knowing (how) to love one's parents and knowing (how) to respect one's

[26] I confess that I find the "knowing-to" construal considerably more natural here; it is odd without further context to say that a child "knows how to love their parents." I will return to this point later on. But those who hope to understand genuine knowledge as knowing-how might emphasize that Wang preserves a tight relationship between *liangzhi* and *liangneng* in his writings: for instance, in the passage just quoted, he quickly moves from discussing knowledge to citing the "ability" of the children he describes. Since ability is closely connected to knowing how, this fact could be thought of as supporting the construal as knowing-how here. For this idea, see Yu (2014: 33–4).

brother, to the further claims that people also know in general (how) to be filial, know (how) to be respectful and know (how) to be compassionate.[27]

This striking reading of [T2]—and the possibility of understanding that passage as parallel to the key examples from the *Mencius*—is a first important line of support for the practical and the normative models. A second can be found in two passages from Wang's letter to Gu Lin (顧璘, Dongqiao 東橋, 1476–1545). In the first of these passages (*IPL* 138 *QJ* 55–6), Wang says that "to know the detailed rites for how to warm and cool one's parents and to know what is appropriate for how to serve and nourish them is what is called knowledge but it is not yet admissible to say that it is the extension of knowledge" (知如何而爲温凊 之節, 知如何而爲奉養之宜者, 所謂 知也, 而未可謂 之致知). He goes on to say that one's knowledge is extended only if one acts in warming or cooling one's parents and in serving or nourishing them, and then closes by twice discussing "extending *liangzhi* which knows (how) to warm and cool" (致其知温凊之良知) and "extending *liangzhi* which knows (how) to serve and nurture"(致其知奉養之良知 cf. *QJ* 8.308 for similar points). As I have said before, it is not obvious that every time Wang discusses the "extension of knowledge," and in particular the extension of *liangzhi*, he is also discussing a state which is relevant to the unity of knowledge and action. But it seems plausible that, in this case, where he discusses how knowledge requires action if it is to count as an elevated form of knowledge, he is. So, his explicit discussion of knowledge-how in this passage supports the claim that genuine knowledge is a form of knowledge-how.

In the next section of his reply to Gu's letter, Wang explicitly connects the extension of knowledge to the unity of knowledge and action, so that it is not only plausible, but in fact entailed by my criterion for when he counts as discussing genuine knowledge that he does so here:

[27] My presentation of the practical and normative models differs substantially from two of these models' most important proponents, Shi 2017 and Huang 2017. These authors (and especially Huang) present their own views as views about the knowledge *liangzhi* has, and not specifically about genuine knowledge (although they do claim that their hypotheses are relevant to the unity of knowledge and action). But it seems to me that the hypotheses are in fact more plausible if they are restricted to genuine knowledge, than if they are supposed to cover all of the knowledge of *liangzhi*. As we saw above, in *IPL* 168 (*QJ* 80), Wang says that *liangzhi* is responsible for sense perception. It is hard to understand this as a form of knowing-to, and while it *could* be that Wang intends us to think of "knowing how to perceive" this seems a stretch. Similarly, in *IPL* 171 (*QJ* 83), Wang says that *liangzhi* can be the basis of predicting what others will do. Again, this is hard to understand as a form of "knowledge-to," and while it could be that Wang intends us to think of "knowing how to predict," this doesn't seem to be his idea. In a further array of passages, most notably in the "Four Sentence Teaching" (*IPL* 315 *QJ* 133–4), Wang says that *liangzhi* knows good and bad. There is some basis (most notably *IPL* 288 *QJ* 126) for thinking that he understood knowing good and bad to be exhibited by knowing to approve the good and knowing to disapprove the bad, but it is hard to understand this latter form of knowledge as knowledge-how. Together, then, these passages challenge both of these ways of thinking about *liangzhi*: the first two of the passages make it hard to understand the knowledge of *liangzhi* uniformly as knowledge-to, and the last of them makes it hard to understand it as knowledge-how. So, as I have said, the restriction to genuine knowledge seems to make the theses more plausible, not less so.

[T4] 吾子謂:「語孝於温凊定省, 孰 不知 之?」然而能致其知者鮮矣。若謂粗知 温凊定省之儀節, 而遂謂 之能致其知, 則凡知君 之當 仁者皆可謂 之能致其 仁之知, 知臣 之當忠者皆可謂 之能致其忠 之知, 則天下孰非致知者邪 ?以是 而言, 可以知致知 之必在於行, 而 不行 之 不可 以爲致知 也明矣。知行合 一 之 體, 不益較然矣 乎?

You say: "who does not know to say that filiality consists in warming and cooling [one's parents bed] and settling them and inquiring after [their health]?"[28] But those who are able to extend their knowledge are few. If we describe someone who roughly knows the detailed rites for how to warm and cool, to settle and inquire after, and for this reason say that they can extend their knowledge, then it would be admissible to say that anyone who knows that the ruler should be humane can extend his knowledge of humaneness [or: knowing (how) to be humane], and admissible to say that anyone who knows that the subject should be conscientious is able to extend his knowledge of conscientiousness [or: knowing (how) to be conscientious]. Who in the world would not extend his knowledge? If we consider the matter from this perspective, we know that extending knowledge must consist in acting, and it is clear also that if a person is not acting then they cannot be regarded as extending their knowledge. Is the natural condition of the unity of knowledge and knowledge and action not still more evident now? (*IPL* 139 *QJ* 56; cf. *QJ* 8.308)

In this passage, the two key expressions which I have rendered in the first instance as "knowledge of humaneness" and "knowledge of conscientiousness" are ambiguous in the same way that the expression I translated as "knowledge of filiality" was in [T1] and [T2]. As before, proponents of the practical and normative models will prefer to translate these phrases as: "knowing (how) to be humane" and "knowing (how) to be conscientious." Those who favor the practical model will naturally say that Wang means here to make a similar point to the one he made in the previous section of his reply (*IPL* 138), where (as we saw) he says that a person's knowledge of the details of how to enact filiality (a form of knowledge-how) counts as extended knowledge only if they have acted filially. Proponents of the normative model will offer a slightly different spin on the passage. They will naturally see it as quite significant that, when it comes time to discuss the unity of knowledge and action explicitly, Wang shifts his example

[28] The passage says only "warming and cooling, settling and inquiring," but it clearly alludes to a famous passage in the *Book of Rites*, "Summary of the Rules of Propriety" (曲禮 上), which Legge (1885) translates as: " For all sons it is the rule :–In winter, to warm (the bed for their parents), and to cool it in summer; in the evening, to adjust everything (for their repose), and to inquire (about their health) in the morning; and, when with their companions, not to quarrel" (凡為 人子 之禮:冬溫而夏凊, 昏定而晨省, 在醜夷不爭). The original text of the *Rites* itself also does not explicitly mention the bed of parents or their health, but the standard traditional commentaries (which Wang would have known, and which Legge follows) understood the text in this way.

away from "knowing how" and begins to discuss knowledge that the ruler should be humane, and knowledge that the subject should be conscientious, just the kind of normative claims about what one should do that were also at issue in Xu Ai's discussion of people who know that they should be filial to their parents (quoted in the text before [**T1**]). While proponents of the normative model must of course acknowledge that in the previous section Wang did discuss "knowing how," they will say that he here turns to the form of knowledge which is actually key to his doctrine, and draws a sharp contrast between those who merely know *that* people should be humane or conscientious on the one hand, and those who know *to* be humane or conscientious on the other. The latter, but not the former (they will say) is what Wang takes to be closely tied to action.

In either case, proponents of the practical and normative models will both see something to support their overall position in this passage, whether stemming from Wang's explicit discussion of knowing-how, or from his explicit discussion of knowledge of normative claims.

A third, and final line of support for these models is less direct, but on the face of it no less significant. In two important passages, Wang explicates the unity of knowledge and action by emphasizing that concerns (*nian* 念) and inclinations (*yi* 意) are either actions themselves or parts of actions ("the beginning of action") (*IPL* 226 *QJ* 109-110, *IPL* 132 *QJ* 46–7). In a further set of passages, Wang ties inclinations closely to knowledge.[29] (For simplicity in what follows I will treat inclinations (*yi* 意), concerns (*nian* 念) and "motivating concerns" (*yinian* 意念)—a compound expression formed from the word I have translated "inclination" and the word I have translated "concern"—as interchangeable.) These passages suggest that the two-sided relationship of inclinations/concerns to knowledge on the one hand and action on the other is at the heart of Wang's understanding of the unity of knowledge and action. A remarkable further passage seems to offer striking confirmation of this bold idea. In response to a question about the unity of knowledge and action, Wang says:

> [**T5**] 你說固是。但要曉得 一念動處便是知, 亦便是行。
>
> What you say is indeed correct. But you must understand that insofar as a single concern is moved it is already knowledge, and it is also already action. (*QJBB* 323; cf. *QJ* 1292)[30]

[29] *IPL* 6 *QJ* 6, *IPL* 78 *QJ* 27, *IPL* 137 *QJ* 53, *IPL* 174 *QJ* 86–7, *IPL* 201 *QJ* 103.

[30] For discussion, see also Wu (2018: 50). Wu goes on to suggest that "a single concern" (*yi nian* 一念) here is a technical term, and takes inspiration from Wang's student Wang Ji (王幾, Longxi 龍溪 1498–1583) in giving an exegesis of the notion. But while I agree that Wang could use this expression as a technical term, I am unsure whether it is one in this instance. Wang (in my view, undeniably) uses this expression as a technical term in the set phrase "one-concern *liangzhi* (一念良知)" (e.g. in *IPL* 139 *QJ* 56; *IPL* 162 *QJ* 76). In these cases, he seems to be imagining people *singlemindedly* set on a positive goal, and I think "singleminded" might be a good translation. But in the reconstruction of this conversation which Wu relies on, immediately following [**T5**], Wang describes how a thief's thought

The practical and normative models promise an elegant interpretation of this passage. Proponents of the practical model can say that what it is to know how to be filial is to produce filial inclinations when it is appropriate to do so: episodes of knowing how to be filial are thus understood as identical to inclinations to perform filial actions (Shi 2017: 54–5). Proponents of the normative model can say something similar: they can say that episodes of knowing to be filial are again identical to inclinations to perform filial actions. Proponents of both models may thus endorse the following bold thesis about the metaphysics of genuine knowledge:

> **Simple Knowledge** All episodes of genuinely knowing (how) to be filial are inclinations to perform filial actions.[31]

Simple Knowledge says that episodes of genuine knowledge are episodes of a certain motivational kind: they are inclinations to perform particular actions. On the assumption—which Wang seems to endorse—that inclinations are parts of actions (or even actions themselves), this principle would allow us to vindicate a remarkable thesis in the vicinity of the unity of knowledge and action: inclinations which are episodes of knowing (how) to be filial would be understood at once as episodes of knowledge and parts of action. If the practical and normative models vindicate this thesis, they would offer us a deep understanding of the doctrine and why it was seen as so revolutionary—an important point in favor of both models.

This completes my presentation of the motivations for the practical and normative models. In the remainder of this section I will turn to criticize these models. I first present an argument against Simple Knowledge, which suggests that proponents of the practical and normative models should endorse an alternative thesis about the metaphysics of genuine knowledge, and give up their hope of vindicating the striking understanding of the unity of knowledge and action just described. I then turn to a more direct assault on the practical and normative models, which applies regardless of how proponents of these models understand the metaphysics of genuine knowledge.

My argument against Simple Knowledge is based on the following important passage, where Wang emphasizes *liangzhi*'s introspective knowledge of the ethical qualities of mental events (see n. 2) in connection with "extended knowledge":

of stealing also coincides with knowledge. This example makes it in my mind unlikely that he wants to describe the positive state of mind denoted by his semi-technical use of "singlemindedness." Instead, it seems to me that he is emphasizing that even if *a single* concern arises, knowledge also does.

[31] This principle is presented as part of an analysis of knowing (how) to be filial, but an analogous principle analyzing objectual knowledge of filiality would also fall to my arguments below. That analogous principle for objectual knowledge is partly of interest because it could be understood as part of a development of the affective perceptual model discussed in the previous section, provided one endorses something like the further claim that episodes of perceiving filiality in an object just are inclinations to perform filial actions in response to the object.

[T6] 凡意念之發, 吾心之良知無有不自知者。其善歟, 惟吾心之良知自知之; 其不善歟, 亦惟吾心之良知自知之。。。

今欲別善惡以誠其意, 惟在致其良知之所知焉爾。何則?意念之發, 吾心之良知既知其為善矣, 使其不能誠有以好之, 而復背而去之, 則是以善為惡, 而自昧其知善之良知矣。意念之所發, 吾之良知既知其為不善矣, 使其不能誠有以惡之, 而覆蹈而為之, 則是以惡為善, 而自昧其知惡之良知矣。若是, 則雖曰知之, 猶不知也, 意其可得而誠乎! 今於良知之善惡者, 無不誠好而誠惡之, 則不自欺其良知而意可誠也已。

Whenever a motivating concern arises, your mind's *liangzhi* automatically knows it. [If it is good] your mind's *liangzhi* automatically knows that it is good; [if it is bad], your mind's *liangzhi* also automatically knows that it is bad....

Now, if you want to discriminate good and evil in order to make your inclinations wholehearted, this just depends on extending what your *liangzhi* knows about them and nothing more. Why is this? When a [good] motivating concern arises, the *liangzhi* of your mind already knows that it is good. Suppose you do not wholeheartedly love it but instead turn away from it and diminish it. You would then be taking what is good to be bad and obscuring your *liangzhi* which knows that it is good. When a [bad] motivating concern arises, the *liangzhi* of your mind already knows that it is bad. Suppose you do not wholeheartedly hate it but instead backslide and promote it. You would then be taking what is bad to be good and obscuring your *liangzhi* which knows that it is bad. In such cases one says that you know it, but in fact you do not know – how could your inclinations have become wholehearted! [But] now if what *liangzhi* [recognizes as] good or bad is wholeheartedly loved or hated, one's *liangzhi* is not deceived and one's inclinations can be wholehearted. (*QJ* 26.1070–1, cf. Chan 1963: 279)

My main observation is that, if Wang is discussing something related to genuine knowledge here, and if he endorses Simple Knowledge, this passage is bizarre. One would have expected Wang to emphasize not *liangzhi*'s knowledge that the relevant inclinations are good or bad, but instead the fact that *liangzhi produces* the relevant inclinations, and that this manifests its knowing (how) to act virtuously. But Wang says nothing of the kind: instead he talks about extending *liangzhi*'s knowledge *about* the relevant inclinations and motivating concerns.

This argument is rough. But one can think of the rough argument as resting on a more exact claim. Wang's remarks strongly suggest that the extended knowledge he considers does not merely correlate with *liangzhi*'s introspective knowledge that relevant inclinations are good, but that it has *liangzhi*'s (unobscured) knowledge that the inclinations are good as *a part* of it (where "part" is meant literally, as in the example of a party used at the opening of section 3). If Wang did not believe that *liangzhi*'s knowledge was a part of this extended knowledge, it is unclear why he would connect the fact that a person's *liangzhi* is "obscured" so closely to the fact that "one says that [they] know it, but in fact [they] do not know it." If Wang is discussing genuine knowledge here, the passage supports the idea that *liangzhi*'s introspective knowledge of the ethical qualities of mental events can be a part of episodes of genuine knowledge. The problem for Simple Knowledge is that Wang clearly holds that the event of *liangzhi* knowing the ethical qualities of inclinations is distinct from the (first-order) motivating concern or inclination itself.[32] So Simple Knowledge is incompatible with the claim—supported by this passage—that genuine knowledge has *liangzhi*'s knowledge that inclinations are good as a part.

Both versions of the argument rest on the assumption that **[T6]** describes genuine knowledge, or at least something closely related to it. The case for this assumption rests on some further background. In this passage, Wang discusses a connection between "extending knowledge" (*zhi zhi* 致知) and "making inclinations wholehearted" (*cheng yi* 誠意, often translated as "making the will sincere" or "making intentions sincere"). These terms come from a central section of the *Great Learning*, one of the most important canonical texts for scholars working in Wang's tradition. In the *Great Learning*, the extension of knowledge and making inclinations wholehearted first appear as two items on what was understood by later scholars to be a list of four stages of or tasks in a person's progress toward becoming fully virtuous. Essentially everyone in Wang's tradition accepts the claim that a person can be fully virtuous if and only if they have performed all four of these tasks. But Wang holds a further distinctive view about their relationship: that in fact one cannot complete any one of the four without completing them all. So in particular, Wang holds that a person can have extended their knowledge if and only if they have made their inclinations wholehearted.[33]

I emphasized in section 2 that Wang can sometimes use "extending knowledge" to describe cultivating abilities which are distinct from and broader than genuine knowledge (e.g. in *IPL* 171 *QJ* 83). But, in general, when Wang talks about a connection between an elevated form of knowledge and wholeheartedness of the inclinations, there should be a presumption that he has genuine knowledge in

[32] Two other passages provide further support for this claim. First, in *IPL* 169 (*QJ* 81–2), after discussing thoughts that are the "aroused functioning" of *liangzhi* (良知之發用), Wang says that "*liangzhi* also is automatically able to know" (良知 亦自能知得). This "also" strongly suggests that Wang takes the relevant knowledge to be distinct from the thoughts *liangzhi* produces. Second, in *IPL* 206 (*QJ* 105) Wang says: "Insofar as your motivating concerns (*yinian*) are attached, it [viz. *liangzhi*] knows that they are right if they are right, and that they are wrong if they are wrong" (爾意念著處, 他是便知是, 非便知非); here, he clearly takes the knowledge of the rightness and wrongness of the motivating concerns to be distinct from those motivating concerns themselves. It is worth emphasizing that my argument here does not require the claim that knowing that an inclination is good is a non-affective state itself; for all I have said the event of knowing could be an affective internal response to the relevant inclination. The argument only requires the mental event of knowing that the mental event is good is distinct from the underlying mental event itself.

[33] *IPL* 137 *QJ* 54, *QJ* 26.1069–70 Chan 1963: 277. See Shun (2011: Section IV) and Ching (1976: 82–4) for discussion.

mind. In such passages, Wang is thinking of the state of a fully virtuous person, not about the capacities *liangzhi* might have for acquiring different forms of knowledge. So, given Wang's detailed analysis of the relationship between extended knowledge and wholehearted inclinations in the present passage, it is natural to think that Wang has something related to genuine knowledge in view here as well, that is, it is natural to make the assumption we set out to defend.[34]

So, it seems to me, Simple Knowledge does not correctly describe Wang's views about the metaphysics of genuine knowledge. And, as a result, the practical and normative models cannot be motivated on the grounds that, by appealing to Simple Knowledge, they can give a neat account of [T5] and related passages. This conclusion, of course, does not entail that the practical or the normative models are incorrect. There are many different positions one could develop that understand genuine knowledge as a form of knowledge how or knowledge-to, but which respect the constraint introduced by [T6], namely, that *liangzhi*'s introspective knowledge that an inclination is good be a *part* of episodes genuine knowledge. In what follows, for ease of exposition, I will focus on one such thesis, which takes the event of genuine knowledge to be a *total mental event*, that is, an event composed of all mental events ongoing for a person at a given time:

Total Knowledge Episodes of a person's genuinely knowing (how) to be filial are total mental events of that person which have as a part an inclination to perform a filial action, as well as an episode of their *liangzhi*'s knowing that the relevant inclination is good.[35]

Unlike Simple Knowledge, Total Knowledge is consistent with the claim that *liangzhi*'s introspective knowledge can be a part of genuine knowledge. It thus

[34] One might try to argue that Wang does not speak of genuine knowledge in this passage by alleging that he had changed his mind about the unity of knowledge and action by this point in his career, in part on the basis of the fact that [T6] comes from a much later work (1527) than [T1] does (a conversation which must have taken place before 1517 and is usually reported as a record of conversations in 1512/13). But this response to the argument should not be attractive to proponents of the practical and normative models. First, [T6] is not much later than [T4] and proponents of the practical and normative models will want to emphasize the importance of the latter passage, so they cannot discount Wang's later writings altogether. Second, Wang continued to speak of the unity of knowledge and action until quite late in his life; he still mentioned it in the year before [T6] was written (see Lederman (2022, n. 5) for more discussion). Third, Qian Dehong (錢德洪, Xushan 緒山 1496–1574) tells us that [T6] comes from a set of ideas that Wang used to introduce students to his system well before it was written down (*QJ* 26.1066).

[35] An alternative is

Complex Knowledge Episodes of a person's genuinely knowing (how) to be filial are complex events consisting of exactly an inclination to perform a filial action, and *liangzhi*'s introspective knowledge that that inclination is good.

Total Knowledge could be thought of as the "maximal' extension of the idea that the first-order inclination is itself an episode of genuine knowledge, by contrast to this "minimal" extension of that idea.

allows us to uphold the practical and normative models in a way which escapes the problem that [T6] poses for Simple Knowledge.[36]

Before turning to my main objection to the practical and normative models, I want to pause for a moment to consider the relationship between the different models we have considered to this point. As the reader may already have noticed, there is an important sense in which the practical and normative models answer a different kind of question than the perceptual model does. One question is: is genuine knowledge best understood as knowledge-that, objectual knowledge, knowledge-how, or knowledge-to? Answers to this question might be called *construals* of genuine knowledge. A different question is: granting a construal of genuine knowledge, what kind of events are episodes of genuine knowledge? Answers to this question might be called *metaphysical analyses* of genuine knowledge. The distinction between construals and metaphysical analyses is not always clear. For instance, Genuine Perception is best understood as combining an

[36] In his magisterial paper Shun (2011), Kwong-loi Shun does not discuss genuine knowledge in the terms I use in this chapter, but he does seem to endorse something quite close to Total Knowledge as part of a general picture which is quite close to the normative model. He writes:

> It follows from Wang's teaching that knowledge and action are not separate when the heart/mind responds in its original state. While one might have the thought that one should so respond and in that sense have knowledge, that knowledge is part of and does not guide the response. Action is constituted by that response, which also includes the thought of so responding. Thus, the terms *zhi* (knowledge) and *xing* (action) are just two different ways of describing the same response, one emphasizing the thought that is part of the response and the other emphasizing the actualization of the response. Thus, for Wang, the terms *zhi* and *xing* refer to the same thing, the former emphasizing the conscious discernment (*ming jue jing cha chu* 明覺精察處) and the latter the intimate actualization (*zhen qie du shi chu* 真切篤實處). (Shun 2011: 99–100)

Shun typically translates *yi* (意, my "inclination"), by "thought," and I'll assume that when he uses "thought" here he also means what I would translate as "inclination."

I want to highlight two points about this passage. First, I earlier described the normative model as endorsing the claim that genuine knowledge is a form of "knowing to," but one could consider it as a more general position, according to which genuine knowledge can also be a special form of knowledge of a normative proposition, for instance that one should do something. Huang Yong, the most vocal proponent of this normative model, emphasizes the importance of distinguishing "knowing to" from knowledge of normative propositions (see, e.g. Huang (2017: 85–8) for discussion), but this aspect of Huang's view could be seen as incidental to the core idea behind the position. And, if we adopt this broader understanding of the normative model, then when Shun describes knowledge as "the thought that one should so respond," this could be understood as an endorsement of the normative model. Second, it seems plausible that Shun has something like Total Knowledge in mind in this passage. When Shun concludes ("thus") that "the terms *zhi* and *xing* refer to the same thing" he cannot any longer have in view the relationship between what he earlier described as the response (the total mental event) and the knowledge which he said was just a (proper) "part of the response" (since by definition nothing is identical to one of its proper parts). Instead, he is best understood to have shifted his attention to genuine knowledge, and to be taking genuine knowledge to be distinct from the knowledge which is merely a part of the response, and identical with the person's total mental event. (The shift is suggested by his citation of passages like *IPL* 133 (*QJ* 47–8) in the final sentences, since there Wang explicitly discusses genuine knowledge.) The basic idea seems to be that the whole response is understood to be knowledge because a part of it is, and that the part which is understood as knowledge is "the thought that one should respond." While it is not easy to categorize Shun's detailed and rich exegesis in any simple way, these two points suggest that his position could be seen as combining the normative model with Total Knowledge.

objectual construal of genuine knowledge (plausibly there is no "seeing how" or "seeing to," if "see" is understood as a form of sensory perception) with a metaphysical analysis of genuine knowledge. But in some cases the difference is quite clear: I presented Perceptual Part above as assuming that genuine knowledge is construed as objectual knowledge (i.e. knowledge of filiality), but the main idea behind Perceptual Part is a constraint on a metaphysical analysis of genuine knowledge—that perception is a part of genuine knowledge—and this idea is also compatible with a construal of genuine knowledge as knowledge-how or knowledge-to. Understood in this broader way, which allows a construal of genuine knowledge as knowing-how or knowing-to, Perceptual Part is compatible with Total Knowledge. In fact, on the natural assumption that events of perceiving can be parts of the total mental events of people who genuinely know filiality or (how) to be filial, Total Knowledge *entails* Perceptual Part. Total Knowledge thus illustrates that the practical and normative models need not be seen as competitors to the perceptual model; if developed in the right way, they are in fact compatible with Perceptual Part. And this result supports the point that I made at the end of the last section: that on its own Perceptual Part is too weak to be the basis of a distinctive understanding of genuine knowledge. It must be supplemented in some way, if it is to yield an interesting thesis about the character of genuine knowledge.

These points about the relationship between the three models will be important again in the next section. But for now let us turn back to the main thread, and in particular to what I see as a crucial objection to both the practical and normative models. The objection turns on [**T1**], the passage which I used to introduce the unity of knowledge and action in section 2 (for the following points, see also Lederman 2022: 176–7). Wang's first two examples in this passage—knowledge of a sight and knowledge of a smell—do not exhibit the ambiguity between objectual knowledge, knowing-how and knowing-to that I emphasized at the start of this section in the cases of knowledge of filiality, respect, compassion, humaneness and conscientiousness; the expressions Wang uses in this case can only describe objectual knowledge. The examples come from the *Great Learning*, but Wang was free to choose which aspects of the example he described as knowledge. And he did not choose to describe this knowledge as knowing (how) to love a sight, or knowing (how) to hate an odor; instead the passage speaks of knowing the sight, and knowing the odor. Later in the passage, Wang presents three further examples: of pain, cold, and hunger. These examples are less grammatically straightforward than the examples of the sight and the odor, but in the context, it is clear that they too must be read as describing objectual knowledge. Like the characters for "filiality" and "respect," the characters for "pain," "cold" and "hunger" can in general be understood either as nouns, *or* as verb-phrases ("be in pain," "be cold," "be hungry"). So in principle, one might take these examples to be intended as examples of knowing-to or knowing-how. But the way in which

Wang uses these examples clearly favors understanding them as describing objectual knowledge. Wang says that one must experience pain, cold, or hunger in order to know them in the way that interests him. This claim would be strange if he had knowledge-how or knowledge-to in mind: it is plausible that without previous experience, infants *do* know how to be in pain, how to be cold, and certainly how to be hungry. Moreover, without any prior experience they also know *to* be in pain, to be cold, and to be hungry. By contrast to the odd, implausible claims Wang would be making if he had knowledge-how or knowledge-to in mind, the claim that people can acquire objectual knowledge of pain, cold, or hunger only through experience is intuitively plausible. Since Wang does not give any argument to defend his claims about these three examples, it is far preferable to interpret him as speaking of objectual knowledge, and making these intuitively plausible claims.

Given that these examples all describe objectual knowledge, there is a strong case that Wang intends to describe objectual knowledge also when he speaks of filiality and respect. Wang uses the examples discussed in the previous paragraph to illustrate cases where knowledge arises simultaneously with or later than action. If he understands knowledge of filiality and respect as objectual knowledge, then the examples directly support his claim that knowledge of filiality and respect must come after filial or respectful action. If, however, he means to speak of knowing (how) to be filial or respectful, the examples which seem designed to support his claim are a non-sequitur.[37] The observation that acquiring objectual knowledge may require prior experience provides little or no support for the claim that knowing-how, or knowing-to requires prior experience. And the latter claim would be badly in need of some defense. It is not only intuitively plausible that both knowing-how and knowing-to often precede action, but this point is central to the canonical discussion in the *Mencius* ([T3]), of the fact that children know (how) to love their parents without prior experience. It is hard to imagine that Wang failed to appreciate this aspect of knowing-how and/or knowing-to given its importance in one of his favorite passages of the *Mencius*. So there is a strong case that Wang also means to describe objectual knowledge when he speaks about filiality and respect.[38]

[37] Yu (2014: 30–1) suggests that the examples of filiality and respect are examples of knowledge-how, while acknowledging that the surrounding examples are examples of objectual knowledge.

[38] In *IPL* 136 (*QJ* 51), Wang says that in order to learn archery or writing one must first perform various actions—indeed he says that all learning requires some form of action. A proponent of the practical model in particular might seek to use these examples to argue that Wang does think that knowing how comes after action. But this claim overlooks an important fact. As I discuss in detail in Lederman (forthcoming), Wang sees his doctrine as having two distinct aspects: one of which concerns training (*gong fu* 功/工夫), and the other of which concerns the original natural condition of knowledge and action (*ben ti* 本體). In the present chapter, I have focused only on the latter of these, but in the passage from *IPL* 136, Wang is explicit that he is focused on the former aspect of the doctrine, about "training" (知行 並進 之功, *QJ* 52).

The practical and normative models do not offer a satisfying interpretation of this passage, and this is an important mark against them, since the passage is central to our understanding of the unity of knowledge and action. Still, this observation does not show conclusively that the models are incorrect. It may be that, by comparison to the problems alternative models face, this one is not particularly deep, and that on balance, the practical and normative models offer the best overall account of what Wang says. I will return to this issue, and offer some comparison of the costs and benefits of different interpretations later on, after I have presented a fourth and final model of genuine knowledge.

5. The Introspective Model

This fourth, introspective model, can be motivated by considering the two arguments I have just given against the practical and normative models. First, consider the series of passages where Wang emphasizes the fact that *liangzhi* acquires introspective knowledge of the ethical quality of mental events (n. 11), and in particular [**T6**], which led to the idea that episodes of genuine knowledge have *liangzhi*'s introspective knowledge of the ethical qualities of mental events as a part of them. In the context of the practical and normative models, this last idea was something of a problem: it forced proponents of those models to abandon Simple Knowledge and complicate their understanding of the metaphysics of genuine knowledge. But a proponent of the introspective model will see these texts as a starting point for their own understanding of genuine knowledge. They will see the passages as supporting not only the weak claim that genuine knowledge has the introspective knowledge of *liangzhi* as a part, but in fact the stronger claim that episodes of genuine knowledge *just are* episodes of introspective knowledge, that is:

> **Introspective Knowledge** Episodes of a person's genuinely knowing filiality are episodes of their *liangzhi*'s knowing that an inclination to perform a filial action is good.

I will take the introspective model to be characterized by adherence to this claim.[39]

Second, the practical and normative models stumbled on the fact that, in [**T1**], Wang emphasizes that the kind of knowledge which interests him is acquired

[39] In Lederman (2022, section 5), I characterize the "introspective model" slightly differently, as including some further commitments as well. There, I focus on the sense in which genuine knowledge can be understood as an elevated form of knowledge, and also use the name "Introspective Knowledge" for a stronger principle, which connects genuine knowledge to freedom from doxastic conflict (and hence to having wholehearted inclinations). Independently, I also discuss in detail there what is at stake in stating Introspective Knowledge in terms of *liangzhi*'s knowledge that an inclination is good, rather than its knowledge that an inclination is filial.

through first-hand experience: one knows pain, cold, and hunger, only after one has been in pain, been cold or been hungry. This basic point is not restricted to a single passage. Elsewhere Wang tells a student that the "mean before the feelings are aroused" can be known only by experiencing it: "it is like a mute person who eats a bitter melon; I can't describe it to you. If you want to know this bitterness, you will have to eat it for yourself" (*IPL* 125, *QJ* 42, 啞子吃苦瓜, 與你說不得。你要知此苦, 還須你自吃). (Xu Ai, the student we encountered in [T1], follows Wang's remark by saying that this example illustrates the character of genuine knowledge (*zhen zhi* 真知), and the recorder of this conversation approvingly tells us that on this day all present gained a little enlightenment.) These examples pose a problem for the practical and normative models, but the introspective model has a natural way of accounting for them. First, there is an obvious sense in which a person can have knowledge of features of their own mind only if their mind exhibits those features. So the general point that Wang is making—that certain forms of knowledge require experience—fits well with the idea that genuine knowledge is a form of knowledge of qualities of one's own mental states. And, second, it is possible that Wang means to draw an even more exact parallel. Especially the later examples in [T1]—which he did not simply inherit from the *Great Learning*, but developed himself—seem carefully chosen to use terms ("pain," "cold," "hunger") which may be (or in some cases must be) used to describe properties of sensations as opposed to properties of the objects which cause those sensations. Wang may be saying that these properties of sensations are exactly analogous to the goodness (or even filiality) instantiated by a person's inclinations. Just as one can acquire direct knowledge of the relevant properties of sensations only by having sensations which instantiate them, so too, one can directly know filiality and respect in the relevant way only by having inclinations which are filial or respectful.

In the terms introduced in the previous section, the introspective model combines a construal of genuine knowledge as objective knowledge with a metaphysical analysis of genuine knowledge as the introspective knowledge that *liangzhi* has of the ethical qualities of mental events. According to the introspective model, genuine knowledge is a form of objectual knowledge. This objectual knowledge of filiality—which is understood to be identical with *liangzhi*'s introspective knowledge—cannot be understood as knowing-how, or knowing-to, so the introspective model is incompatible with the practical and normative models.[40]

[40] On the basis of *IPL* 288 (*QJ* 126), one might argue that *liangzhi*'s introspective knowledge that an inclination is good or bad is its loving or hating the inclination. Accordingly one might think that *liangzhi*'s introspective knowledge is constituted by its knowing (how) to love the good and (how) to hate the bad. But even granting this sense in which *liangzhi*'s knowledge might be understood as practical or normative knowledge, genuine knowledge of filiality would still not be a form of knowing (how) *to be filial*.

Introspective Knowledge is also incompatible with the alternative metaphysical analyses and constraints on such analyses considered above. An example will help to illustrate this point. Suppose a person who sees their parents has an inclination to perform a filial action (say, to cool their parents' bed in the summer), and that their *liangzhi* knows on the basis of introspection that this filial inclination is good. Supposing furthermore that they experience an episode of genuine knowledge, our different theories will give different verdicts about which mental event counts as that episode. Simple Knowledge says that the episode of genuine knowledge is the first-order inclination to perform a filial action, their inclination to cool their parents' bed. Introspective Knowledge says that it is their *liangzhi*'s introspective knowledge of the goodness of this first-order inclination. And Total Knowledge says that it is their total mental event, including not only the first-order inclination and the episode of *liangzhi*'s introspective knowledge, but also (compatibly with Perceptual Part) the episode of their perceiving their parents. Since the episode of introspective knowledge is distinct from the first-order inclination to cool the person's parents, and also distinct from the total mental event which has the introspective knowledge as a proper part, Introspective Knowledge is incompatible with both Simple Knowledge and Total Knowledge.[41] And Introspective Knowledge is also incompatible with Perceptual Part, since the episodes of *liangzhi*'s introspective knowledge that certain mental events are good or bad in fact will never have perception as a part of them.[42]

So the introspective model offers an understanding of genuine knowledge that is distinct from the models we have considered so far. But how well-supported is this model? The remainder of this section will examine this question, by working through the passages we have encountered in the chapter to this point.

[41] In n. 35 I discussed Complex Knowledge, according to which episodes of genuine knowledge are complex mental events, consisting in part of first-order inclinations and in part of episodes of introspective knowledge. Introspective Knowledge is on its face distinct from this thesis as well, since it identifies the episode of genuine knowledge solely with the episode of introspective knowledge. But one might wonder how different they really are. Since having introspective knowledge that a filial inclination is good requires having a filial inclination, it might seem that proponents of Introspective Knowledge are committed to thinking that the filial inclination is in fact a component of the episode of genuine knowledge. But the thesis should not be understood in this way. To illustrate the point, consider a different example. I know that Beijing is the capital of the PRC. The existence of the city of Beijing (and its being the capital of the PRC) is required for my mental state to count as knowledge, but there is a salient sense in which the city itself is not a part of my mental state of knowing. Similarly, it is a precondition for the relevant introspective knowledge to be knowledge of filiality that the relevant inclination be filial, but the inclination itself need not be a part of the mental event of *liangzhi*'s knowing that it is good.

[42] This conclusion is consistent with a number of other claims that might tie perception to genuine knowledge. Perhaps most obviously, one might hold that perception of the environment is a precondition of genuine knowledge. To illustrate the idea, suppose that, necessarily, any party must be preceded by some form of invitation. Plausibly the invitations—unlike the lawn games or the conversations—would not be parts of the party, even though they would be required for the party to take place. The view in the main text is consistent with the claim that a person can have genuine knowledge only if they perceive the environment around them. For even given this strong claim, the perception, like the invitations, need not be a *part* of the episode of genuine knowledge.

Let us start at the beginning, then, with [T1]. We saw above how the introspective model handles the second half of that passage, and in particular the five examples Wang discusses there (filiality, respect, pain, cold, and hunger). But one might wonder whether it can help to explain the first half of the passage, and in particular the two perceptual examples of loving a lovely sight and hating a hateful odor. I noted early on that the introduction of these examples can be read in two different ways, depending on how one understands the word I have translated "like" (如)—whether as "for example" or "similar to." On the reading preferred by proponents of the perceptual model, loving a lovely sight and hating a hateful odor are understood as *examples* of genuine knowledge, so some perceptual knowledge counts as genuine knowledge. But there is another reading available—which is equally natural linguistically—according to which Wang merely intends the examples as illustrative analogues for genuine knowledge, and not examples of it. On this reading, Wang says that having genuine knowledge is *similar to* loving a lovely sight or hating a hateful odor, insofar as action and knowledge are closely connected in both cases. Importantly, on this interpretation, his remarks do not imply that seeing a lovely sight or smelling a hateful odor are instances of genuine knowledge. So, there is a perfectly natural way of reading these examples on which they too are compatible with the introspective model.[43]

According to the introspective model, the examples of loving a lovely sight and hating a hateful odor do not illustrate the role of perception in genuine knowledge, but they do illustrate an important aspect of Wang's view of the mechanics of genuine knowledge. In the lead-up to the key passage [**T6**], Wang uses these examples from the *Great Learning* again, this time to illustrate the way in which *liangzhi* loves good motivating concerns and hates bad ones. Just as, when a person sees a lovely color or smells a hateful odor, they spontaneously and automatically love or hate, so too, Wang says, when a person's *liangzhi* recognizes that an inclination is good or bad, it spontaneously and automatically loves or hates it. Wang clearly holds that *liangzhi*'s recognizing that an inclination is good or bad is tightly tied to *liangzhi*'s loving and hating, just as, in [T1] he says that seeing the sight is closely connected to loving it, and smelling the odor is closely connected to hating it.[44] Thus, proponents of the introspective model

[43] Elsewhere I argue that evidence from one of Wang's letters strongly suggests that he himself favored the second reading, in line with the introspective model, but I will not press this point here. See Lederman (2022, section 5), discussing *QJ* 5.218, Ching (1972: 91).

[44] More strongly than this, Wang may even hold that for *liangzhi* to know that a motivating concern is good (or bad) just is for *liangzhi* to love (hate) the motivating concern (*IPL* 288 *QJ* 126). (This passage is framed in terms of knowing that the relevant mental event is right/correct (是) or wrong/incorrect (非), not in terms of its knowing that it is good or bad, but we may suppose this difference is unimportant, at least for present purposes.) This claim could be thought of as a version of Simple Knowledge, transposed to the key of introspection. Instead of saying that a person's affective responses count as knowledge, Wang would be saying instead that *liangzhi*'s affective responses to their mental events count as knowledge of qualities they instantiate. Lee (1994: 433) emphasizes this point in a slightly different context.

can make sense of Wang's emphasis on these examples from the *Great Learning* by holding that Wang sees the examples as important models for the way in which, when *liangzhi* acquires introspective knowledge that an inclination is good or bad (i.e. the kind of knowledge which constitutes genuine knowledge), it spontaneously and automatically loves or hates the relevant inclination.[45]

Our second text, [T2], also does not pose a serious challenge to the introspective model. As we saw above, Wang's key remarks about perception and knowledge in this passage ("when it sees the parents, it automatically knows filiality [or: (how) to be filial]," and so on) can be understood in at least two different ways: first, as claiming that knowledge of filiality, respect or compassion can have perception as a part; or, second, as claiming that perception is a precursor to the separate, automatic achievement of genuine knowledge. Proponents of the perceptual model have found the first of these claims in the passage; proponents of the practical and normative models have found the second there. For the second group of interpreters, perceiving one's parents is simply the occasion for *liangzhi* to exhibit its knowing (how) to be filial in the circumstances, presumably by producing a filial inclination or concern. Proponents of the introspective model should offer a similar reading of this passage: they should say that Wang means that (for example) when a person sees their parents, their mind produces an inclination to perform a filial action, and, as a result *liangzhi* comes to know that this inclination is good. Wang of course does not elucidate this picture in detail in the passage, but what he says is consistent with it.[46]

[45] As noted above in n. 13, some authors who speak of genuine knowledge as a form of perception understand "perception" to include the operation of an inner sense. It may be that, if pressed, many who have defended the perceptual model in print would say that they did not intend to endorse the claim that perception was a part of genuine knowledge, but only the claim that the automatic, spontaneous way in which a person exhibits or acquires genuine knowledge is analogous to the automatic and spontaneous way in which people acquire knowledge on the basis of perception. I want to emphasize that my arguments against the perceptual model are *not* arguments against this claim: as the discussion in the main text illustrates, I in fact endorse it. But even if some proponents of the perceptual model would retreat to this claim when pressed, abandoning the claim that perception is really a part of genuine knowledge seems to me an important change of view. I hope my discussion here at least helps to clarify the difference between the relevant positions.

[46] One might try to decide between these interpretations on the basis of Wang's comment in the passage that "this is *liangzhi* and should not be sought outside," since it might seem that this comment explicitly states that the object of the knowledge is not external to the mind, and thus that perceiving one's parents or brothers is an *occasion* for having genuine knowledge, but not itself part of genuine knowledge (since the perception, but not the knowledge, has an external object). At times I have been attracted to this idea. But I note that it is not the only reading of the remark: proponents of the perceptual model can instead read the remark as emphasizing *liangzhi*'s self-sufficient role in the apprehension of ethical qualities, as opposed to the physical location of the qualities which are apprehended. On this reading, the point would be that a person need not have acquired other knowledge in order for *liangzhi* to operate in the right way.

So the introspective model can make sense of the main passages that were supposed to support the perceptual model.[47] How does it fare on the passages which seemed to favor the practical and normative models?

First, there is the canonical passage from the *Mencius* ([T3]), together with Wang's explicit discussions of it, especially in *IPL* 118 (*QJ* 39). I suggested earlier that proponents of both the practical and normative models might want to emphasize the parallel between these examples and Wang's discussion in [T2]. Proponents of the introspective model, by contrast, should reject the proposed parallel. They will agree with proponents of the practical and normative models (as everyone should) that among many other things, *liangzhi* is the basis of a person's knowing to love their parents, and also of their knowing how to take care of their parents (as emphasized in *IPL* 138 (*QJ* 55-6), for instance). They will also agree that Wang ascribes these powers to *liangzhi* in part on the basis of *Mencius* 7A.15 ([T3]). But they will naturally hold that, in [T2], Wang is not focused on *these* capacities of *liangzhi*, but is rather interested in *liangzhi* as the basis of the elevated form of knowledge which is closely related to action, that is, of genuine knowledge. They will then argue that this genuine knowledge is best understood not as knowing-how or knowing-to, but instead as introspective knowledge of the ethical qualities of mental events. So, while proponents of the introspective model will accept that [T3] provides important constraints on how we should understand *liangzhi*, they will deny that the fact that we should understand "know" as "know how" or "know to" in [T3], and *IPL* 118 (*QJ* 39), creates significant pressure to understand "know" in either of these ways in [T2], or to understand genuine knowledge more broadly as a form of knowing how or knowing to.

Next, skipping over for a moment the passages from the letter to Gu Donqiao ([T4] and the preceding discussion from *IPL* 138), let us turn to [T5] and related passages which seemed to support Simple Knowledge. The introspective model offers a simple, natural account of the passages other than [T5] which I cited in the lead-up to that text. The first two passages I cited there (*IPL* 132 *QJ* 46–7, *IPL* 226 *QJ* 109–110) focus on the fact that inclinations or concerns are already action; they do not themselves explain how knowledge might accompany these mental events. According to the introspective model, Wang's point is clear: he emphasizes that a person's mental events are actions or parts of actions because, once one recognizes that actions start with mental events, it becomes obvious that the relevant form of knowledge—introspective knowledge of the quality of these

[47] How should we understand the relationship between Wang's notion of genuine knowledge and the example of genuine knowledge which Cheng Yi uses described in n. 16? The introspective model—unlike the perceptual model—seems committed to denying that Wang held that this example was an example of genuine knowledge. But there is no obvious problem for the introspective model here. Cheng lived four centuries before Wang, and while there was undoubtedly a preference for conforming with the remarks of eminent predecessors in Wang's tradition, Wang did not hesitate to diverge from them in many cases. The fact that the introspective model sees a divergence in the analysis of this example does not seem to me a serious cost to the view.

mental events—will arise at the same time as the action begins. And, similarly, the second set of passages which connect knowledge and inclinations (see n. 29), can be read as emphasizing that, although inclinations are not themselves (or at least not always) identical to knowledge, they are the objects of an important form of knowledge. So, in both cases, the introspective model can offer a natural account of what Wang wants to achieve.

[T5] itself, however, does seem to present a challenge for the introspective model. Understood literally, the passage says that a concern—in context, a first-order concern to perform some action—*itself* is the form of knowledge that is relevant to the unity of knowledge and action. The introspective model cannot make sense of this claim, since a first-order concern cannot be understood as the kind of introspective knowledge which the introspective model takes genuine knowledge to be. But the introspective model is not alone in this regard. The only natural theory I am aware of which can make sense of the literal content of what Wang says in the passage is Simple Knowledge. And, as we have seen, Simple Knowledge itself should be rejected. So every natural, live interpretation of Wang must offer a non-literal interpretation of this passage. The most obvious idea is that Wang says that the concern *just is* knowledge not because he means that it is, but because he wants to emphasize the close connection between a concern and knowledge. Proponents of Total Knowledge, for instance, might say that Wang's goal is to emphasize that a single concern can be the basis for (genuine) knowledge if one's total mental event is relevantly coherent.[48] And proponents of Introspective Knowledge can say much the same thing: they can say that Wang holds that the single concern is the occasion for introspective knowledge, which coincides with the arising of the concern in the mind. This interpretation does not capture the full force of Wang's claim that the concern itself *is* knowledge. But this is not a problem for Introspective Knowledge in particular, since—as I have said—I do not know of an interpretation which can capture the full force of this remark. And in general it is reasonable to think that Wang might make the strong claim about the identity of the concern and knowledge in order to draw our attention to something like the claim "when the concern arises, knowledge does too."

This brings us at last to what are in my view the hardest passages for the introspective model, the two passages I discussed from the letter to Gu Dongqiao: *IPL* 138 (*QJ* 55–6), and [T4] (*IPL* 139 *QJ* 56). As we saw, in *IPL* 138 Wang explicitly describes extending one's knowledge of how to take care of one's parents, and in [T4] he discusses knowledge-how and knowledge of what one should do, in the lead-up to an explicit discussion of the unity of knowledge and

[48] Proponents of Total Knowledge might hope to make this point more explicit by claiming that Wang uses the expression "single concern" (*yi nian* 一念) in a semi-technical way in this passage to mean something like "singleminded state of mind." But as I argued above in n. 30, I am not convinced that we can find this point in the passage.

action. I will first lay out what I see as the best interpretive strategy for proponents of the introspective model here, before turning to the costs and benefits of this approach.

Proponents of the introspective model should argue that in the passage from *IPL* 138, Wang discusses extending a capacity of *liangzhi* whose extension does not result in genuine knowledge properly understood. Everyone agrees that Wang holds not only that *liangzhi* produces introspective knowledge, but also that it produces appropriate thoughts and emotions in the right circumstances (*IPL* 169 *QJ* 81–2; *IPL* 290 *QJ* 126). So it is not surprising that Wang might speak of acting on the inclinations that *liangzhi* produces as "extending *liangzhi*." But, crucially, this claim does not entail that this form of "extending one's *liangzhi* which knows how to warm and cool" or "extending one's *liangzhi* which knows how to serve and nourish" itself counts as genuine knowledge (*zhen zhi* 真知). Instead, this "extended knowledge" can be thought of as a separate mental state which goes along with or precedes the acquisition of genuine knowledge.

The situation is slightly different with [T4] (*IPL* 139). Here, proponents of the introspective model should hold that Wang does describe genuine knowledge, but they should argue that, when he does, he means to describe objectual knowledge. In the passage, Wang starts out by discussing knowing-how, but, as we saw above, in the course of his discussion he changes his example, and explicitly speaks of (normative) knowledge that the ruler should be humane, and that the subject should be conscientious. When he turns to the knowledge that would count as extended knowledge in that passage, he uses an expression which is crucially ambiguous, and can be understood as describing objectual knowledge. Proponents of the introspective model should argue that he is describing objectual knowledge here, and making a point similar to the one we saw in the examples of pain, cold, and hunger in [T1], namely, that one can acquire knowledge of the relevant virtues only by experiencing them oneself.

This interpretive strategy allows us to read these two passages in a way that is consistent with the introspective model. But the interpretations I have just described are certainly not how one would understand these passages on a first reading. I want to acknowledge, then, that these passages do provide evidence against the introspective model.[49] But I want now to argue that this

[49] I should note that there is also some evidence that in fact this interpretation of [T4] is on the right track. Earlier in *IPL* 139 (*QJ* 57), Wang says "If one does not examine the subtleties of the one concern of the mind's *liangzhi*, then what use would learning be?" (不於吾心良知一念之微而察之，亦將何所用其學乎?) (In this passage, by contrast to the one discussed in 30, I think it plausible that "one concern" 一念 is meant as a technical term; a better translation might be "the subtleties of the singlemindedness of the mind's *liangzhi*.") The fact that Wang speaks here of *examining* one's own *liangzhi*, seems to me to support the interpretation of [T4] I sketched in the previous two paragraphs. While Wang focuses throughout the discussion here on the fact that *liangzhi* produces the appropriate inclinations and concerns in response to one's changing circumstances, there are still suggestions (as in this quote) that he takes the relevant form of knowledge to be acquired by investigating the concerns produced by *liangzhi*, that is, that the relevant form of knowledge is introspective knowledge.

evidence against the introspective model is much weaker than the evidence against the practical and normative models, and that, on balance, the introspective model remains the most attractive of the interpretations we have considered.

I will make two points in defense of this claim. First, by presenting the practical and normative models together, there is an important way in which I have made these models seem more attractive than they are. There are a number of passages supporting the disjunction of the practical model and the normative model. But the support for each of these models on their own is not particularly strong. For instance, the passage from the *Mencius* ([T3]), is naturally read as describing knowing-to, but not naturally read as describing knowing-how (see n. 26). So, while the normative model is in a strong position to invoke the parallel between that passage and [T3] to motivate their view, the practical model is not. But other passages exhibit the reverse pattern, supporting the practical model but not the normative one. *IPL* 138, which we have just been discussing, provides strong support for the practical model, since Wang discusses knowing-how there explicitly. But the normative model cannot explain his emphasis on knowing-how in this passage, and in fact it faces exactly the same problem the introspective model faces in trying to make sense of this passage. More generally, the practical model does not offer a good account of the normative model's favorite passages, while the normative model does not offer a good account of the practical model's favorite passages, and as a result, neither has as broad support in the texts as they might have seemed to have in the discussion above.

Second, the introspective model's challenges with the passages from *IPL* 138 and *IPL* 139 are far less troubling than the practical and normative model's challenges with [T1]. The introspective model has a way of explaining what Wang is doing in *IPL* 138, by emphasizing the distinction between the capacities of *liangzhi* and the achievement of genuine knowledge. By contrast, I do not see how the practical or normative models can offer a natural account of what Wang says in [T1]. And there is an important difference between the aspects of the passages which give these models trouble. The introspective model struggles to make sense of examples in *IPL* 138 which are not typically thought to be central to Wang's thought about the unity of knowledge and action. By contrast, the practical and normative models struggle to make sense of what is arguably *the* central claim of the unity of knowledge and action: the claim that the relevant form of knowledge does not precede action. Conceding that we cannot make sense of this claim comes close to giving up on the exegesis of the unity of knowledge and action altogether.[50]

[50] A third, more involved argument against the practical and normative models aims at Total Knowledge. Total Knowledge is not an obvious metaphysical thesis that any person casually considering the question of what it is to know filiality would come up with on their own. If Wang endorsed

This completes my arguments in favor of the introspective model by comparison to the normative and practical models. Together with my arguments in section 3, that the perceptual model does not on its own constitute a distinctive understanding of genuine knowledge, these arguments lead me to conclude that the introspective model should be preferred over the other models of genuine knowledge I have considered in this chapter.[51]

6. Conclusion

The main aim of this chapter has been to develop detailed versions of the perceptual, practical, normative, and introspective models of genuine knowledge. In the course of developing these models, I have also presented a series of arguments which impose constraints on them. For example, I argued that Wang does not hold that genuine knowledge is an elevated form of perception, and that the unity of knowledge and action should not be understood to concern the putatively distinctive perceptual capacities of fully virtuous people. Similarly, I argued that some examples where Wang discusses genuine knowledge should not be understood to describe knowing-how or knowing-to. In the previous section, I went beyond these piecemeal constraints, and argued that my own introspective model of genuine knowledge is on balance preferable to the alternatives considered here.

The four interpretations I have considered in this chapter are certainly not the only interpretations which have been offered in the voluminous literature on Wang Yangming. I have discussed these four because they seemed most salient to me, whether because of recent scholarly attention they have received, or because they strike me as naturally suggested by one passage or another. But it may well be

this view, one would expect him to have said much more about how we can understand a total mental event as knowledge, and what a total mental event is. But we find no such explanations in the text. Moreover, some comments he makes seem to flatly contradict Total Knowledge. In **[T6]**, Wang discusses an elevated form of knowledge, and specifically describes a barrier to that elevated form of knowledge as "obscuring one's *liangzhi* which knows goodness." Earlier I extracted from this passage only the weak claim that introspective knowledge is a part of genuine knowledge. But this reading is a bit of a stretch to make space for the practical and normative models. By far the more natural reading of this passage takes it to say, more strongly, that *liangzhi*'s knowledge of goodness would *be* the elevated form of knowledge (i.e. genuine knowledge) were these obstacles absent. On this reading Wang essentially asserts Introspective Knowledge. By contrast, it is unclear how proponents of Total Knowledge should make sense of Wang's remarks here. Perhaps there are other metaphysical analyses of genuine knowledge that could vindicate the practical and normative models. But to me these problems for Total Knowledge are at least an important challenge for the practical and normative models.

[51] I have not discussed interpretations which attribute to Wang different construals or different metaphysical analyses of genuine knowledge across different passages. While it may be worth exploring interpretations of this kind further, those who (like me) believe that Wang's views on the unity of knowledge and action were largely consistent over the course of his career will see them as something of a last resort. Those who think that Wang's views about the unity of knowledge and action underwent significant changes, for instance, after 1521 will of course see the costs of such an interpretation very differently.

that some other historical interpretation—or a new one that I have not been able to imagine—can make better sense of the texts. I would consider this chapter a success if it inspires others to revive or develop an alternative interpretation which does better than the ones I have chosen to focus on here.

In closing, I want to address a methodological assumption I have made throughout. My investigation has been premised on the assumption that Wang held systematic views about genuine knowledge. But there is a case to be made, to the contrary, that Wang was not interested in advancing detailed or systematic theories of any kind, whether about genuine knowledge or anything else. What should we make of these conflicting perspectives? My own view is that an important strategy for making progress on this question is to study his writings on the assumption that he was, indeed, a systematic thinker. In some cases, it makes sense to investigate a hypothesis because it is most likely to be true out of the reasonable alternatives. But in other cases, it can make to investigate a hypothesis because it is in an intuitive sense stronger than the reasonable alternatives. Since intuitively stronger hypotheses make more predictions than weaker ones, in general they are easier to falsify than weaker hypotheses are. If we succeed in falsifying a strong hypothesis, we learn the important fact that it is false. But even if we do not falsify the hypothesis, we learn more than we would have by investigating a weaker one. Since we are more likely to falsify a stronger hypothesis, the fact that we have failed to do so is more evidence in favor of that hypothesis than we could have obtained in favor of a weaker one by the same methods.

We thus have good reason to begin our inquiry with the hypothesis that Wang had coherent and consistent views about genuine knowledge, since this hypothesis is intuitively stronger than the alternative hypothesis that Wang did not have coherent or consistent views. Whether or not it turns out to be true, this hypothesis is worth exploring first, if we wish to learn more about the philosophy of Wang Yangming.[52]

References

Angle, Stephen C. 2005. Sagely Ease and Moral Perception. *Dao*, 5(1): 31–55.

Angle, Stephen C. 2009. *Sagehood: The Contemporary Significance of Neo-Confucian Philosophy*. New York: Oxford University Press.

Angle, Stephen. 2018. Buddhism and Zhu Xi's Epistemology of Discernment. In John Makeham (ed.), *The Buddhist Roots of Zhu Xi's Philosophical Thought* (pp. 156–92). Oxford: Oxford University Press.

[52] Many thanks to Jennifer Eichman, P. J. Ivanhoe, Justin Tiwald, and two anonymous referees for detailed and incisive comments on earlier versions of this chapter.

Angle, Stephen C, and Tiwald, Justin. 2017. *Neo-Confucianism: A Philosophical Introduction*. Cambridge: Polity Press.

Blum, Lawrence. 1991. Moral Perception and Particularity. *Ethics*, 101(4): 701–25.

Chan, Wing-tsit. 1963. *Instructions for Practical Living and other Neo-Confucian Writings by Wang Yang-ming*. New York: Columbia University Press.

Chan, Wing-tsit (陳榮捷). 1983. 王陽明傳習錄詳註集評 *Wang Yangming's* Instructions for Practical Living *with detailed notes and collected discussions*. 臺灣學生書局 Taiwan Xuesheng Shuju.

Chen, Lai (陈来). 1991. 有无之境:王阳明哲学的精神 *The Boundary between Being and Non-Being: The Spirit of Wang Yangming's Philosophy*. 北京 Beijing: 人民出版社 Renmin Chubanshe.

Ching, Julia. 1972. *The Philosophical Letters of Wang Yang-ming*. Canberra: Australian National University Press.

Ching, Julia. 1976. *To Acquire Wisdom: The Way of Wang Yang-ming*. New York: Columbia University Press.

Cua, A. S. 1998. *Moral Vision and Tradition Essays in Chinese Ethics*. Washington: Catholic University of America Press.

Cua, Antonio S. 1982. *The Unity of Knowledge and Action: A Study in Wang Yang-ming's Moral Psychology*. Honolulu: University Press of Hawaii.

Frisina, Warren G. 2002. *The Unity of Knowledge and Action: Toward a Nonrepresentational Theory of Knowledge*. State University of New York Press.

Harbsmeier, Christoph. 1993. Conceptions of knowledge in ancient China. *Pages 11–30 of*: Lenk, Hans, & Paul, Gregor (eds), *Epistemological issues in classical Chinese philosophy*. Albany, NY: State University of New York Press.

Huang, Yong. 2013. Why "Besire" Is Not Bizarre. *Brahman and Dao: Comparative Studies of Indian and Chinese Philosophy and Religion*, 119.

Huang, Yong. 2015. *Why Be Moral?* New York: State University of New York Press.

Huang, Yong (黄勇). 2016a. 再论动力之知: 回应郁振华教授 "Knowing To" Revisited: A Reply to Professor Yu Zhenhua. 学术月刊 *Xueshu Yuekan*, 48(12): 24–30.

Huang, Yong (黄勇). 2016b. 王阳明的良知概念: 命题性知识, 能力之知, 抑或动力之知? Knowing-that, Knowing-how, or Knowing-to: Wang Yangming's Conception of Moral Knowledge. 学术月刊 *Xueshu Yuekan*, 48(1): 49–66.

Huang, Yong (黄勇). 2017. Knowing-That, Knowing-How, or Knowing-To? *Journal of Philosophical Research*, 42: 65–94.

Ivanhoe, Philip J. 2002. *Ethics in the Confucian Tradition: The Thought of Mengzi and Wang Yangming*. Indianapolis: Hackett Publishing.

Ivanhoe, Philip J. 2009. *Readings from the Lu-Wang school of Neo-Confucianism*. Indianapolis: Hackett Publishing.

Ivanhoe, Philip J. 2011. McDowell, Wang Yangming, and Mengzi's contributions to understanding moral perception. *Dao*, 10(3): 273.

Kern, Iso (耿宁). 2010. *Das Wichtigste im Leben: Wang Yangming (1427–1529) und seine Nachfolger über die "Verwirklichung des ursprünglichen Wissens" (The most important thing in life: Wang Yangming [1472–1529] and his successors on the "Realization of Original Knowledge")*. Schwabe Verlag. Translated as 人生第 一等事——王阳明及其后学论 "致良知" by 倪梁康, published by 务印书馆, 北京 2016; citations are to the translation.

Lederman, Harvey. (forthcoming). What is the "unity" in the "unity of knowledge and action"? *Dao*.

Lederman, Harvey. 2022. The Introspective Model of Genuine Knowledge in Wang Yangming. *The Philosophical Review*, 131(2): 169–213.

Lee, Ming-huei 李明輝. 1994. "WANG Yangming's Doctrine of the 'Unity of Knowing and Acting' in the Light of Kant's Practical Philosophy 從康德的實踐哲學論王陽明的 '知行合一' 說." *Bulletin of the Institute of Chinese Literature and Philosophy* 中國文哲研究集刊 4: 415–440.

Legge, James. 1885. *The Lî Kî ["Li Ji" or "The Book of Rites"]*. Sacred Books of the East, vol. 27–28. Oxford: Clarendon Press.

Liu, JeeLoo. 2018. *Neo-Confucianism: Metaphysics, Mind, and Morality*. New York: John Wiley & Sons.

McDowell, John. 1979. Virtue and Reason. *The Monist*, 62(3): 331–50.

Murdoch, Iris. 1970. The Idea of Perfection. In Murdoch Iris (ed.), *The Sovereignty of Good*. New York: Schocken Books.

Nivison, David S. 1973. Moral Decision in Wang Yang-ming: The Problem of Chinese "Existentialism." *Philosophy East and West*, 23(1/2): 121–37.

Nivison, David S. 1996. *The Ways of Confucianism: Investigations in Chinese philosophy*. Open Court Publishing.

Nussbaum, Martha Craven. 1990. The Discernment of Perception: An Aristotelian Conception of Private and Public Rationality. In Nussbaum, Martha Craven (ed.), *Love's Knowledge: Essays on Philosophy and Literature*. Oxford: Oxford University Press.

Shi, Weimin. 2017. The Quest for Ethical Truth: Wang Yangming on the Unity of Knowing and Acting. *Comparative Philosophy*, 8(2): 7.

Shu, Jingnan (束景南), & Zha, Minghao (查明昊) (eds). 2016. 王陽明全集補 編 *Wang Yangming quanji bubian*. 上海 Shanghai: 上海古籍出版社 Shanghai Guji Chubanshe.

Shun, Kwong-loi. 2010. Zhu Xi's Moral Psychology. *Pages 177–95 of: Dao Companion to Neo-Confucian Philosophy*. Dordrecht: Springer.

Shun, Kwong-loi. 2011. Wang Yang-ming on Self-Cultivation in the *Daxue*. *Journal of Chinese Philosophy*, 38(s1): 96–113.

Shun, Kwong-loi. 2018. On the Idea of 'No Self'. *Proceedings and Addresses of the American Philosophical Associations*, 92, 78–107.

Tiwald, J., and B.W. Van Norden. 2014. *Readings in Later Chinese Philosophy.* Indianapolis: Hackett.

Wang, Xiaoyu (王孝魚) (ed.). 2004. 二程集 *Collected Works of the Cheng Brothers.* 北 京 Beijing: 中華書局 Zhonghua Shuju.

Wiggins, David. 1975. II—Deliberation and Practical Reason. *Proceedings of the Aristotelian Society*, 76(1): 29–52.

Wu, Guang (吳光), Qian, Ming (錢明), Dong, Ping (董平), and Yao, Yanfu (姚延福) (eds). 2011. 王陽明全集 *Collected Works of Wang Yangming.* 上海 Shanghai: 上海古籍出版社 Shanghai Guji Chubanshe.

Wu, Zhen (吴震). 2018. 作為良知倫理學的 '知行合一' 論——以 '一念動處便是知亦便是行'爲中心." The Theory of 'The Unity of Knowledge and Action' As *Liangzhi* Ethics. 學術月刊 *Xueshu Yuekan* 5: 14–24.

Yang, Xiaomei. 2009. How to Make Sense of the Claim "True Knowledge is What Constitutes Action": A New Interpretation of Wang Yangming's Doctrine of Unity of Knowledge and Action. *Dao: A Journal of Comparative Philosophy*, 8(2): 173–88.

Yu, Zhenhua (郁振华). 2014. 论道德-形 上学的能力 之知-基 于赖尔 与王阳明的探讨 On Knowing How in Morality and Metaphysics: An Exploration of Gilbert Ryle and Wang Yangming. 中国社会科学 Zhongguo Shehui Kexue, 12: 22–41.

Yu, Zhenhua (郁振华). 2016. 再论道德的能力之知——评黄勇教授的良知诠释 Moral Knowing How Revisited: A Critical Examination of Professor Huang Yong's Interpretation of Wang Yangming's Notion of "Liangzhi." 学术月刊 *Xueshu Yuekan*, 48(12): 14–24.

Zheng, Zemian. 2019. An Alternative Way of Confucian Sincerity: Wang Yangming's "Unity of Knowing and Doing" as a Response to Zhu Xi's Puzzle of Self-Deception. *Philosophy East and West*, 68(4): 1345–68.

Zheng, Zongyi (Cheng Chong-yi, 郑宗义). 2018. 再论王阳明的知行合 一 A New Interpretation of Wang Yangming's Doctrine of the Unity of Knowing and Acting. 学术月刊 *Xueshu Yuekan*, 50(8), 5–19.

6
Knowledge and Legal Proof

Sarah Moss

1. An Overview of the Knowledge Account

What does it take to prove guilt beyond a reasonable doubt? Consider the following example from Nesson 1979, well-known among scholars of evidence:

> *Prisoners*: 25 prisoners are exercising in a prison yard, when 24 of them suddenly join together in a planned attack on the prison guards. The remaining prisoner tries to stop the attack. There is no available evidence distinguishing the innocent prisoner from the rest. Local prosecutors randomly select one of the prisoners and bring him to trial for participating in the attack.

It is widely agreed that the merely statistical evidence in *Prisoners* cannot sustain a verdict of guilt. But why not? After all, the evidence justifies a high degree of confidence in guilt. On the basis of this evidence, it would be reasonable to have .96 credence that the defendant participated in the attack. Increase the numbers, and the same evidence may justify having an arbitrarily high credence that the defendant is guilty. Yet something will be missing—something, apart from mere confidence in guilt, that we must have in order to convict.

Now consider the following example derived from Harman 1986, well-known among epistemologists:

> *Lottery*: Jones has purchased a ticket in a small lottery. There are 25 tickets in all. The winning number has already been selected at random, but it hasn't been announced yet.

Before the winning number is announced, Jones is justified in being confident that she lost the lottery. Increase the size of the lottery, and she may be justified in having an arbitrarily high credence that she lost. But there will still be one respect in which her mental state will fall short, epistemically speaking. As epistemologists are fond of pointing out, as long as Jones can't rule out the possibility that she has the winning ticket, she can't *know* that she lost the lottery.

Sarah Moss, *Knowledge and Legal Proof* In: *Oxford Studies in Epistemology, Volume 7.* Edited by: Tamar Szabó Gendler, John Hawthorne, and Julianne Chung, Oxford University Press.
DOI: 10.1093/oso/9780192868978.003.0006

Prisoners demonstrates that justified high confidence in a proposition does not suffice for proving it beyond a reasonable doubt. *Lottery* demonstrates that justified high confidence in a proposition does not suffice for knowing it. The examples are strikingly similar. In this chapter, I defend the most straightforward explanation for their similarity. At a first pass, my central thesis is just this: *legal proof requires knowledge*. Conviction requires proving beyond a reasonable doubt that the defendant is guilty, and this conclusion is proved if and only if the judge or jury knows it. Since the jury in *Prisoners* can't rule out the possibility that the defendant is the innocent prisoner who tried to stop the attack, they don't know that he is guilty, and that is why it is improper for them to convict.[1]

Right off the bat, the idea that legal proof requires knowledge has a lot to recommend it. Besides the striking similarity between *Prisoners* and *Lottery*, there is something unsettling about a jury deciding, "For all we know, the defendant might be innocent. But let's vote to convict him anyway." It would sound odd for them to say, "The defendant might be innocent. We find him guilty." When a jury delivers a guilty verdict, they are engaging in a speech act similar to declaring or asserting that the defendant is guilty. As Thomson 1986 points out, "their agreeing to say those words is not made acceptable by the mere fact that the defendant actually is guilty of what he is charged with" (213). In other words, mere truth is not the correct norm of assertion at a criminal trial, just as it is not the correct norm of assertion, more generally speaking. A more promising proposal is that knowledge is the norm of assertion, including legal assertions of guilt.[2]

If the knowledge account of legal proof has a lot to recommend it, why isn't it more widely accepted?[3] There are several stumbling blocks for the knowledge account, objections that may already be on the minds of discerning readers. For starters, it might seem as if proof of guilt does not require jurors to have *knowledge-level* confidence in guilt, but merely to believe that the likelihood of guilt is beyond some high threshold. According to this objection, the knowledge

[1] A second pass: strictly speaking, a guilty verdict is proper only if the factfinder knows that the defendant is guilty *on the basis of the evidence presented at trial*. The criminal standard of proof is not met when a judge happens to arrive at the courthouse knowing that the defendant is guilty, if no evidence of guilt is ever given in court. For ease of exposition, I will take this qualification to be implicit throughout.

[2] For a canonical defense of the knowledge norm of assertion, see chapter 11 of Williamson 2000. Additional proponents of the norm include Moore 1962, Unger 1975, DeRose 2002, Hawthorne 2004, and Stanley 2005.

[3] There are a few notable exceptions. Pardo 2005 and Duff et al. 2007 accept that some instances of legal proof require knowledge; in section 3 of this chapter, I contrast their accounts with mine. Knowledge also plays an interesting role in accounts of legal proof defended by Blome-Tillmann 2017 and Littlejohn 2020, though these accounts are much further from mine.

account imposes an overly strict demand on the subjective state of the factfinder—that is, the judge or jury. A second objection is that the knowledge account seems to impose an overly strict *objective* demand on legal proof. Knowledge is factive, i.e., only true contents can be known. If someone is innocent, you can't know that they are guilty; therefore, on the knowledge account, you can't convict them. Yet at first glance, it might seem obvious that our criminal standard of proof permits false convictions, provided they are justified by the evidence. Furthermore, factive standards of proof might appear ill-suited to guide jurors in their decision making. If it is hard for a jury to tell whether a defendant is innocent, then it may also be hard for them to tell whether they *know* that a defendant is innocent. And so, on the knowledge account, it will be hard for them to tell whether the criminal standard of proof is met. But then what good is the criminal standard of proof, if the jury can't tell whether it is satisfied?

This chapter answers each of the foregoing objections, as well as several others. In addition, the main part of this chapter sets out a positive case for the knowledge account, arguing that it provides illuminating answers to widely debated questions in the theory of evidence. In section 2, I use the knowledge account to explain why the standard of proof beyond a reasonable doubt seems to elude precise definition. In section 3, I discuss why statistical evidence is generally insufficient for legal proof, and why courts are sometimes reluctant even to admit statistical evidence at trial. I present objections to several leading accounts of legal proof, arguing that they make unacceptable predictions about when statistical evidence suffices for proof. I answer some objections to my account along the way, and I address remaining objections in the fourth and final section.

This chapter has two limits that I should flag up front. First, my primary aim in this chapter is to build a positive case for the knowledge account. I discuss the most prominent alternatives to my account, and I explain why they have problems. But my discussion of existing accounts is not comprehensive. A more thorough defense of my account would include an encyclopedic survey of all existing accounts of legal proof, along with my arguments against each. Second, this chapter is more theoretical than prescriptive. I am arguing that a conclusion is legally proved if and only if is knowledge, but I am not defending substantive claims about what sort of evidence is necessary and sufficient for knowledge. For example, I do not defend any claims about exactly when eyewitness testimony is capable of generating knowledge. This chapter calls attention to structural features of knowledge that make it especially apt for defining what legal proof requires. A recurring theme of the chapter is that legal proof requires ruling out relevant epistemic possibilities, where the relevance of a possibility is not determined by its probability. Since this same feature distinguishes knowledge from mere justified confidence, our discussion of it will help to illuminate why legal proof requires the former attitude, rather than the latter.

2. The Elusiveness of Reasonable Doubt

2.1 Attempts to Define the Reasonable Doubt Standard

The reasonable doubt standard has long served as the standard of proof in common law criminal trials.[4] For just as long as it has been around, the standard has been notoriously difficult to define. As Wigmore observes in his *Treatise on Evidence*, "when anything more than a simple caution and a brief definition is given . . . the actual effect upon the jury, instead of being enlightenment, is rather confusion or at least continued incomprehension."[5] The United States Supreme Court has held that "[a]ttempts to explain the term 'reasonable doubt' do not result in making it any clearer to the minds of the jury."[6] The difficulty of explaining the term has not deterred judges from trying, though, and over the past several decades, there has been a gradual accumulation of "a considerable corpus of case law in which judges flounder unhappily over the definition of 'reasonable doubt,'"[7] often leading to verdicts that are overturned on appeal. A number of appellate courts are not merely pessimistic about defining reasonable doubt, but openly hostile to the project. In some jurisdictions, giving any definition constitutes grounds for appeal. To quote one representative opinion from the Oklahoma Court of Criminal Appeals, "We are at a loss to understand why trial courts in this jurisdiction continue to give such an instruction when we have condemned them from territorial days to the present. . . . [I]t is error for the trial judge to try to define reasonable doubt."[8]

Given the importance of the criminal standard of proof, it is disconcerting, to say the least, that it often goes without definition. As Judge Posner puts it, "The question whether the prosecution has proved the defendant guilty beyond a reasonable doubt is central to every criminal trial. Can it be that the term should *never* be defined? Is it a mystical term, a talisman, somehow tarnished by attempts at definition?"[9] This exasperated question is not merely rhetorical, but illuminating. It is not just that it happens to be hard to figure out what it takes to prove something beyond a reasonable doubt. There seems to be something elusive about the standard itself, so that by its very nature, it is nearly impossible to define. As another author puts it,

[4] Although the reasonable doubt standard dates from the late eighteenth century, it was most recently clarified by the United States Supreme Court in *In re Winship*, 397 U.S. 358, 364 (1970). According to *Winship*, due process requires that each individual element of a crime be proved beyond a reasonable doubt. For simplicity, I talk about what it takes to prove that a defendant is guilty of a crime, but my arguments extend to the act of proving the individual elements that constitute this claim.

[5] Wigmore 1923, section 2497.

[6] *Holland v. United States*, 348 U.S. 121, 140 (1954) (quoting *Miles v. United States*, 103 U.S. 304, 312 (1880)).

[7] Whitman 2008: 2.

[8] *Jones v. Oklahoma*, 554 P.2d 830, 835 (1976).

[9] *United States v. Hall*, 854 F.2d 1036, 1043 (1988).

> This debate over definitions has raged as long as the term has been prominent. Although some might argue that the difficulty of the endeavor does not mean that it should be abandoned, "difficulty" is perhaps not the issue. Rather, the issue is the reasonable doubt concept's intrinsic incompatibility with the project of definition. The failure of the legal community to reach a consensus over the last one hundred years suggests that the nature of the concept defies attempts at more precise definition.[10]

Even the drafters of the Model Penal Code—which is, generally speaking, a wellspring of definitions—decline to define 'reasonable doubt' on the grounds that "definition can add nothing helpful to the phrase."[11]

Hence in addition to the traditional question—*what does it take to prove something beyond a reasonable doubt?*—there is a second question that deserves attention in its own right: *why is this first question so hard to answer?* Why is the criminal standard so elusive? Why have judges and scholars repeatedly concluded that when it comes to defining this standard for jurors, it is almost always better to say less rather than more? There have been few attempts to answer these questions. As Ho 2008 notes, "It is a mystery why a doctrine held in such high esteem should yet be so elusive" (455).

2.2 Explaining the Elusiveness of the Standard

To solve this mystery, it is helpful at this point to look at an analogous problem faced by the student of the theory of knowledge.[12] As Lewis 1996 famously puts it, knowledge is elusive. To give a simple example, consider the following attempt to ascribe some ordinary knowledge:

> It does sometimes happen that cars get stolen from driveways. But let's ignore that possibility. Now, we can truly say that you know that your car is in your driveway. After all, you can rule out plenty of ordinary possibilities in which your car isn't in your driveway, like the possibility that you parked it on the street.[13]

Having reflected on the possibility that your car has been stolen, it is difficult to say that you know it is in your driveway. Fogelin 2000 calls this the problem of

[10] Note, *Reasonable Doubt: An Argument Against Definition*, 108 *Harvard Law Review* 1955, 1970 (1995).

[11] Brief for the United States at 9, *Victor v. Nebraska*, 114 S.Ct. 1239 (1994), quoting Model Penal Code cmt. 190 (1985).

[12] With apologies to Judith Jarvis Thomson. See Thomson 1986: 206.

[13] The car theft example is due to Vogel 1990; it also serves as a focal point of the influential discussion of lottery knowledge in Hawthorne 2004.

"epistemic self-destruction," saying that "some sense should be made of this tendency of epistemic commitments to contract, perhaps to a near-vanishing point, under sustained philosophical scrutiny" (45). According to Lewis, the correct diagnosis of the problem is that philosophical scrutiny raises the epistemic standards for interpreting 'knowledge' at our context, where epistemic standards can be understood in terms of *relevant alternatives*—roughly speaking, possibilities that must be ruled out in order for a subject to count as knowing a proposition. By discussing possibilities, we make them relevant. As more possibilities become relevant, our epistemic standards become stricter, and it becomes harder for us to assert true knowledge ascriptions.[14]

Out of the epistemology classroom, back to the jury room. The knowledge account of legal proof connects the elusiveness of knowledge with the elusiveness of proof beyond a reasonable doubt, using the former to explain the latter. Suppose that Smith is on trial for murder. The prosecution has just presented an extremely compelling case, providing piles of evidence against Smith. Back in the jury room, a wacky juror could nevertheless manage to raise unreasonable doubts. The juror might insist, "Maybe these massive piles of evidence are part of a big conspiracy! Maybe Smith is actually being set up by the government, as part of a master plan hatched by the D.C. elite!" Or the jury might include an undergraduate philosophy major who insists, "We don't *know* that Smith is guilty! Maybe Smith is innocent, and we are all just victims of an evil demon, who is controlling our minds and feeding us false memories of evidence in order to get us to convict!" The reasonable doubt standard is meant to protect jury deliberation from exactly this sort of epistemic inflation. The standard places an important constraint on the context in which the jury should be deliberating—namely, it must be a context in which they are considering all and only doubts that it is reasonable for them to consider. It is important that jurors be able to act in good conscience when they vote to convict a defendant. The jury should not vote to convict Smith if they actually believe that he might be innocent. At the same time, there will always be far-fetched possibilities that jurors ought to set aside, such as possibilities involving evil mind-controlling demons. As the United States Supreme Court put it in *Hopt v. Utah*, "Persons of speculative minds may in almost every such case suggest possibilities of truth being different from that established by the most convincing proof. The jurors are not to be led away by such speculative notions as to such possibilities."[15] It is crucial that jury deliberations be guided by a reasonable epistemic standard, if there are to be any proper convictions at all.

[14] I have described one contextualist approach in the text, but the argument of this section does not rely on relevant alternatives contextualism, or indeed on any particular theory of the elusiveness of knowledge. For the purposes of my argument, what matters is simply that knowledge is elusive; given this fact, my knowledge account of proof entails that proof beyond a reasonable doubt is elusive as well.

[15] *Hopt v. Utah*, 120 U.S. 430, 440 (1886).

Now we can see why it is hard to define this reasonable epistemic standard in greater detail. The problem is that the more we say in an effort to spell out the difference between reasonable and unreasonable doubts, the more we call attention to the possibilities that jurors *shouldn't* be considering. As Lewis might have put it, the more we risk "destroying" the knowledge that would have sustained a conviction. For example, consider the following jury instruction:

> It does sometimes happen that a defendant is framed as part of a government conspiracy. But you should ignore this possibility, along with any other possibility it would be unreasonable for you to consider. Now, if you can truly say that you know that the defendant is guilty, you should return a guilty verdict.

A simple characterization of the reasonable doubt standard would instruct jurors to deliberate without considering unreasonable possibilities. But by mentioning those possibilities, we risk taking jurors out of the very context that we are telling them to be in.[16] The less that one says about unreasonable doubts, the easier it is for those doubts to be ignored. Insofar as attempts to clarify the reasonable doubt standard may undermine that standard, there is some reason for judges to refrain from clarifying the standard in jury instructions, and there is reason to expect that academic attempts to clarify the standard may be ill-fated.

We have explained why we can expect it to be difficult to define proof beyond a reasonable doubt. Is there anything that one *can* say to explicate this standard? A small number of strategies have been identified by courts as relatively promising. The good news is that most jurors are neither conspiracy theorists nor philosophy majors. As jurors go about their ordinary lives, they routinely set aside far-fetched possibilities and come to know things. As Lewis 1996 reminds us, "Maybe we do know a lot in daily life; but maybe when we look hard at our knowledge, it goes away. But only when we look at it harder than the sane ever do in daily life" (550). Accordingly, one might hope to clarify the reasonable doubt standard by comparing it with a more familiar epistemic standard. And indeed, in this spirit, courts have explicated the reasonable doubt standard with the following instruction:

> Proof beyond a reasonable doubt must, therefore, be proof of such a convincing character that a reasonable person would not hesitate to rely and act upon it in the most important of his own affairs.[17]

[16] If we are not careful, we do the same thing to ourselves in the context of academic discussions of reasonable doubt.

[17] *United States v. Savulj*, 700 F.2d 51, 69 (2nd Cir. 1983).

A reasonable person often relies on knowledge in making high-stakes decisions outside the courtroom. According to the above jury instruction, a similar state of knowledge should govern high-stakes decisions inside the courtroom.[18] Alternatively, some courts have managed to clarify the reasonable doubt standard by contrasting it with a stricter one—in particular, with a standard that is so strict that it is practically useless:

> Anything can be possible.... [A] planet could be made out of blue cheese. But that's really not in the realm of what we're talking about.[19]
>
> It is not a flimsy, fanciful, fictitious doubt which you could raise about anything and everything.[20]

These definitions work well because speakers generally presuppose that their context-sensitive expressions will be interpreted relative to *useful* standards. Although epistemic standards are often subject to inflation, they are somewhat more resilient against the sort of radical inflation that would leave speakers without any useful knowledge ascriptions at all. To sum up, the knowledge account not only explains why most attempts to describe reasonable doubt fail, but also why certain attempts are more likely to succeed.

2.3 Attractive Features of My Account

There is something surprising about my account of reasonable doubt. From a contemporary perspective, it is natural to assume that the requirement of proof beyond a reasonable doubt is meant to protect the accused against hasty conviction. But on my account, the reasonable doubt standard is intended to guard against epistemic inflation, thereby making it *easier* for jurors to convict. Interestingly, my account of the legal function of reasonable doubt reflects the historical origins of this notion. The reasonable doubt standard emerged in the late eighteenth century in response to an unreasonable inflation of epistemic

[18] This discussion raises an important question that I do not have space to address here—namely, can the criminal standard of proof vary depending on what is at stake in a criminal trial? Lillquist 2002 argues that "the reasonable doubt standard of proof is inevitably flexible in nature: in some cases juries will require more proof than in other cases" (85); Sand and Rose 2003 argue that a higher standard should apply in death-eligible cases; Laudan and Saunders 2009 argue that "differences in the seriousness of crimes and in the severity of their associated sentences make it questionable whether we should continue to seek a single standard for all seasons instead of a set of standards of varying degrees of severity" (1). These theories are naturally motivated and explained by my account of legal proof.

[19] *Victor v. Nebraska*, 511 U.S. 1, 17 (1994), quoted approvingly by Justice O'Connor as an accurate elaboration of the notion of reasonable doubt.

[20] *People v. Davis*, 171 Mich. 241, 137 N.W. 61 (1912).

standards in jury trials around that time. Just as our conspiracy theorist is in the grips of ideological message boards, and our philosophy major is in the grips of Descartes' First Meditation, so the jurors of the eighteenth century were in the grips of a popular literature of conscience that made them reluctant to deliver any guilty verdicts. As Whitman 2008 argues, jurors of the time believed that it was a mortal sin for them to convict an innocent person.[21] Accordingly, the potential consequences of false conviction were severe, including "vengeance of God upon his family and trade, body and soul, in this world and that to come."[22] With their own salvation at stake, jurors were understandably motivated to consider any conceivable possibility that the defendant might be innocent of the crime charged. In 1785, the moral philosopher William Paley describes the harmful result of these heightened epistemic standards:

> I apprehend much harm to have been done to the community, by the over-strained scrupulousness, or weak timidity of juries, which demands often such proof of a prisoner's guilt, as the nature and secrecy of his crime scarce possibly admit of; and which holds it the part of a *safe* conscience not to condemn any man, whilst there exists the minutest possibility of his innocence.[23]

As Whitman argues, the reasonable doubt standard emerged in this same time period in order to counteract the epistemic inflation described by Paley. The language of reasonable doubt was used to encourage jurors to deliberate using a more reasonable and more useful standard. As one judge put it,

> [For almost any crime,] there is a strict possibility, that somebody else might have committed it: But that the nature of evidence requires, that Juries should not govern themselves, in questions of evidence, that come before them, by that strictness, is most evident, for if it were not so, it is not possible that offenders of any kind should be brought to Justice.[24]

Insofar as the historical origins of the notion of reasonable doubt might shed light on its contemporary legal function, my account of the latter has the advantage of reflecting the former.

A second advantage to my discussion of reasonable doubt is that it can help answer an objection to the knowledge account of legal proof—namely, that the

[21] For instance, in a case where a defendant is falsely convicted and condemned to death, it was believed that "the Jury *in foro conscientiae* are certainly guilty of his murther" (Hawles 1680: 22).

[22] H.E. 1664: 1.

[23] Paley 1785: 550. For discussion of this passage and its historical context, see Green 1985.

[24] Trial of Thomas Hornsby (Theft with Violence, Highway Robbery) (1782). The Proceedings of the Old Bailey Ref: t17830430-67.

account imposes an overly strict demand on the subjective state of the factfinder. At first glance, one might be tempted to make the following objection:

> You do not have to know that the defendant is guilty before you can convict him. It is only necessary that you should believe from the evidence beyond a reasonable doubt, that he is guilty, and if you do so believe from all of the evidence, beyond a reasonable doubt, that the defendant is guilty, then it is your sworn duty to so find.

This passage is taken from a jury instruction given by a trial court judge in Mississippi and subsequently condemned by the Mississippi Supreme Court.[25] According to this instruction, knowledge requires eliminating *all doubts*, whereas conviction merely requires eliminating *all reasonable doubts*—and hence, conviction cannot require knowledge. There is something compelling about this line of thought, as it is indeed the case that eliminating all doubts means eliminating unreasonable doubts as well as reasonable ones. However, as long as jurors are being reasonable, there will not be any difference from their perspective between eliminating all doubts and eliminating reasonable ones. The objection itself is problematic because by considering it, one calls attention to this difference, and implicitly grants the existence of the very possibilities that the reasonable doubt standard calls jurors to set aside. That is what is wrong with issuing the above jury instruction, and why it was right for the Mississippi Supreme Court to reject it. The instruction takes the jurors out of the very context that they are being instructed to deliberate in.

There is a difference between being reasonable and merely acting as if you are being reasonable. We hold jurors to the former standard. Consider a jury made up entirely of unreasonable conspiracy theorists. No amount of evidence would convince them that the defendant is guilty. Should we encourage these jurors to say, "The defendant might be innocent, but we should convict him anyway"? This might be a decent response to a bad situation, but it wouldn't be the best response. A better jury instruction would not demand that jurors convict against their better judgment, but rather demand that they judge reasonably and then render their verdict accordingly. In a similar spirit, consider a jury of ignorant racists who are disposed to tune out any evidence that suggests that a white person is guilty. Should we encourage these jurors to acquit white defendants? In this case, the best response is obvious: jurors are not merely required to return the verdict that is proper given what they believe, but also required to be reasonable as they form their beliefs. In order to be reasonable, jurors must form their beliefs in accordance with the evidence. The reasonable doubt standard imposes a constraint with

[25] *Nobles v. State of Mississippi*, 241 So.2d 826 (1970).

a similar form: in order to be reasonable, jurors must consider only doubts that it is reasonable for them to consider.[26]

A third advantage of my account of the reasonable doubt standard is that it sheds light on fundamental problems with a certain sort of attempt to define the standard. I have argued that the standard is elusive in the sense that attempting to define it often makes it harder to follow. The reasonable doubt standard is also elusive in another very specific sense—namely, the standard is *impossible to quantify*. It it tempting to try to define the standard by throwing out numbers.[27] In fact, plenty of lawyers have done just that, making statements such as the following:

> I like to make it kind of like a football field where you start at one end and you go to the other. If you go all the way and make a touchdown, that's like a hundred percent. That's beyond no doubt. I like to say reasonable doubt is kind of like 75 percent. Somewhere—75 and 90.[28]
>
> It's beyond a reasonable doubt, so it's beyond the 50 yard line. You have to take it to the opponent's 20, the red zone. You got to get it in the red zone for beyond a reasonable doubt.[29]

Appellate courts routinely condemn analogies like these, stating that the criminal standard of proof cannot be defined in terms of any threshold notion of confidence.[30] As we have seen, the example of *Prisoners* is intended to make just this point. *Prisoners* demonstrates that justified high credence in a proposition does not suffice for proving it beyond a reasonable doubt.

The knowledge account of the criminal standard helps us better understand this fact. It is impossible to quantify reasonable doubt because whether a doubt is *probable* and whether it is *capable of undermining knowledge* are distinct

[26] This discussion calls attention to one sort of misconduct that the defense might engage in—namely, the act of raising possibilities *in order to prevent jurors from being able to engage in reasonable deliberation*. The correct response to such misconduct is not to instruct jurors to convict someone that they sincerely believe might be innocent. Rather, the correct response to defense misconduct will always depend on a range of pragmatic factors, including the costs of declaring a mistrial and the feasibility of proceeding as if the misconduct had not occurred—as Lewis puts it, whether jurors can "bend the rules of cooperative conversation" so that "they may rightly be said to know that the accused is guilty" (560, 556).

[27] For instance, McCauliff 1982 reports that among 171 federal judges and United States Supreme Court justices, the average probability threshold associated with proof beyond a reasonable doubt was.90. According to Magnussen et al. 2014, trial judges report intentions to return guilty verdicts in mock trial settings when their credences in guilt exceed .83.

[28] *State v. Casey*, No. 19940, 2004 WL 405738, at para. 43 (Ohio App. Mar. 5, 2004).

[29] *People v. Lewis*, 2015 IL App (1st) 130, 171, 33 N.E.3d 212, 392 Ill. Dec. 663.

[30] *Commonwealth v. Rosa*, 661 N.E.2d 56, 63 (Mass. 1996) ("it is best for judges to avoid examples that have numeric or quantifiable implications"); *State v. Rizzo*, 833 A.2d 363, 399 (Conn. 2003) ("it is improper for a trial court to attempt to explain the concept of reasonable doubt by metaphors or analogies that are quantified in nature").

questions. As Posner observes, "It is one thing to tell jurors to set aside unreasonable doubts, another to tell them to determine whether the probability that the defendant is guilty is more than 75, or 95, or 99 percent."[31] Following Lewis 1996, one might say that knowledge of guilt requires ruling out relevant possibilities in which the defendant is innocent, where the relevance of a possibility may depend on its non-probabilistic structural features. To return to our earlier example, suppose 25 separate trials are conducted in *Prisoners*, one for each prisoner in the yard. If each jury could reasonably set aside the possibility that the defendant is innocent, then our standard of proof would demand 25 convictions and ensure the conviction of an innocent person. Even if false convictions are prevalent in practice, it is counterintuitive to think that they could ever be required in certain circumstances. As Lewis would put it, the Rule of Actuality and Rule of Resemblance together constrain the possibilities that jurors may properly ignore. Since one of the prisoners is innocent, and his innocence is just like that of any other prisoner, we must acquit all 25. As Zuckerman 1986 observes, convicting all 25 prisoners would have us "openly acknowledge that the individual defendant may well belong to the innocent minority, and therefore undermine the citizen's confidence that the legal system will protect him from mistaken conviction of crime or mistaken imposition of liability" (499). Hence non-probabilistic features of possibilities can make a difference to their relevance—and from this fact, it follows that the reasonable doubt standard cannot be quantified.

3. Statistical Evidence

3.1 The General Problem of Statistical Evidence

So far, we have been focusing on the criminal standard of proof. At this point, we should broaden our discussion to include other standards, such as proof by clear and convincing evidence, proof by a preponderance of the evidence, and so on.[32] In other words, we should turn to discussing the notion of *legal proof* in general.

Although standards of proof differ in strength, they all require the factfinder to have at least some amount of confidence in the conclusion to be proved. As Justice Harlan states, "Although the phrases 'preponderance of the evidence' and 'proof beyond a reasonable doubt' are quantitatively imprecise, they do communicate to the finder of fact different notions concerning the degree of confidence he is expected to have in the correctness of his factual conclusions."[33] Bentham 1843

[31] *United States v. Hall*, 854 F.2d 1036, 1044 (7th Cir. 1988) (Posner, J., concurring).

[32] See McCauliff 1982 for an overview of standards of proof, including several that are less demanding than the preponderance standard. For instance, the standard of reasonable suspicion—applied in stop-and-frisk searches—is commonly associated with a probability threshold around .3.

[33] *In re Winship*, 397 U.S. 358, 370 (1970).

was among the first to clarify this notion of confidence, stating that legal proof "admits of, and exists in, different degrees of strength," where "the practice of wagering affords at the same time a proof of the existence, and a mode of expression or measurement for [these] quantities or degrees" (223). In the parlance of contemporary epistemologists, Bentham is talking about credences. The odds at which you are willing to bet on a proposition reflects how much credence you have in it. Proving a fact by a certain standard requires the factfinder to have at least a certain amount of credence in that fact. For instance, proof of liability by a preponderance of the evidence requires the factfinder to have greater than .5 credence that the defendant is liable. Proof by clear and convincing evidence imposes a more stringent standard, requiring the factfinder to believe that the claim to be proved is substantially more likely than not, where this is commonly associated with a probability threshold of .75.[34]

This sort of subjective requirement on credences is necessary but not sufficient for legal proof. As we have seen, merely statistical evidence can justify having a certain credence in a claim, without proving it beyond a reasonable doubt. This is another feature common to all standards of proof, as statistical evidence is also insufficient to establish proof by more lenient standards. Consider the following example from Cohen 1977:

> *Gatecrasher*: [I]t is common ground that 499 people paid for admission to a rodeo, and that 1,000 are counted on the seats, of whom *A* is one. Suppose no tickets were issued and there can be no testimony as to whether *A* paid for admission or climbed over the fence. So by any plausible criterion of mathematical probability there is a .501 probability, on the admitted facts, that he did not pay. (74)

Just as in *Prisoners*, the merely statistical evidence in *Gatecrasher* is insufficient to sustain a verdict. As Cohen 1981 puts it, "our intuitions of justice revolt against the idea that the plaintiff should be awarded judgment" (627). The insufficiency of statistical evidence must be explained not by some feature of the reasonable doubt standard in particular, but rather by some feature that all standards of proof have in common. That is, the problem of statistical evidence must be solved by a general account of what legal proof requires. I have argued that the evidence in *Prisoners* cannot prove guilt beyond a reasonable doubt because it cannot provide the factfinder with knowledge. In what follows, I extend the knowledge account to

[34] As reported in *United States v. Fatico*, 458 F. Supp. 388, 410 (1978), an informal study conducted by US District Judge Weinstein found that judges in the Eastern District of New York associated proof by clear and convincing evidence with probability thresholds ranging from .6 to .75. A subsequent study by McCauliff 1982 found that hundreds of federal judges and United States Supreme Court justices associated this standard with an average probability threshold of .75.

other standards of proof. Generally speaking, statistical evidence fails to provide legal proof because it fails to provide the factfinder with a certain sort of knowledge.

To clarify what I am aiming to explain: our hostility to statistical evidence is not without qualification. Courts have also been increasingly willing to issue convictions on the basis of random match DNA evidence.[35] Some courts have been willing to assign liability in civil cases that look remarkably like *Gatecrasher*.[36] In addition, courts have been willing to base verdicts on statistical evidence in market-share liability cases. Suppose that a plaintiff proves that multiple manufacturers were selling defective products and that one of these products harmed her, but she cannot prove that any particular manufacturer specifically caused her harm. In *Sindell v. Abbott Laboratories*, the California Supreme Court held that in such cases, the court may assign liability to manufacturers in proportion with their share of the market for the defective product.[37] For any company with a small market share, the statistical evidence suggests that it is very unlikely that they are liable for the harm in question. Hence the evidence is obviously insufficient to prove by a preponderance of the evidence that the small company is liable, as the evidence does not even justify having a high credence that they caused the harm.[38] The problem of statistical evidence is not the problem of explaining why statistical evidence is never sufficient for a verdict, but rather why it is insufficient in many normal cases.

As a final note of clarification, I should mention that a small number of legal scholars reject the problem of statistical evidence altogether.[39] According to a more revisionary approach to the problem, there is nothing objectionable *per se* about basing verdicts on merely statistical evidence. Courts should aim to maximize the accuracy of verdicts, and any intuitive hostility to highly probative statistical evidence is misguided. For present purposes, I will set aside this approach and focus on the project of making sense of a widely held hostility to statistical evidence, rather than defending that hostility from more basic principles.

[35] See Roth 2010 for discussion of the recent rise in "pure cold hit" prosecutions.

[36] The canonical example is *Kaminsky v. Hertz Corp.* 288 N.W.2d 426 (1979). See section 3.5 for further discussion.

[37] *Sindell v. Abbott Laboratories* 26 Cal. 3d 588 (1980).

[38] Defendants have also been assigned market-share liability after introducing decisive evidence that they did not cause a specific harm; see *Hymowitz v. Eli Lilly & Co.*, 73 N.Y.2d 487, 541 N.Y.S.2d 941, 539 N.E.2d 1069 (1989). This further supports the conclusion that the doctrine of market-share liability constitutes a *sui generis* exception to the typical burden of proving causation by a preponderance of the evidence. For additional arguments in support of this conclusion, see Steel 2015.

[39] For sympathetic discussion of this approach, see Saks and Kidd 1980, Shaviro 1989, and Schauer 2003.

3.2 Objections to Moral Accounts

Before introducing my preferred solution to the problem of statistical evidence, I want to raise some objections to several existing proposals for solving it. Broadly speaking, existing accounts of statistical evidence fall into two categories. According to epistemic accounts, statistical evidence is incapable of providing the sort of proof that non-statistical evidence can provide. According to moral accounts, statistical evidence might turn out to prove conclusions just as well as any other evidence, but it is morally objectionable to act on those conclusions, or to use statistical evidence to prove them.

According to the moral account defended by Zuckerman 1986, punishing a defendant on the basis of statistical evidence is tantamount to punishing him for being a member of a group, most of whose members are guilty of a crime. Our moral and legal values resist verdicts based on statistical evidence in just the same way that they resist acts of corporate punishment, acts that hold an entire social group responsible for the transgressions of its individual members (499). In a similar spirit, Cohen 1987 argues, "A person who deliberately runs his life in such a way as not to commit torts or break contracts is not to be put at risk by the probative procedures of the system just because he falls into a category of which the majority happen to be tort-feasors or contract-breakers" (94). Both Zuckerman and Cohen are worried about the moral permissibility of acting on conclusions supported by statistical inferences. Another moral account is defended by Wasserman 1991, who argues that even just the practice of using statistical evidence to form beliefs about an individual is itself morally problematic:

> [W]hat is objectionable is the reliance on others' conduct, or the defendant's past conduct, to infer his commission of a wrongful act. We object to this inference because it ignores the defendant's capacity to diverge from his associates or from his past, thereby demeaning his individuality. (942–3)

All of these accounts raise moral concerns related to inferences like the following:

(1) a. Most *F*s are tort-feasors.
  b. *X* is an *F*.
  c. Therefore, it is more likely than not that *X* is a tort-feasor.

As these authors see it, an inference of this form may be perfectly capable of proving its conclusion. But the inference itself is morally suspect, or it is morally incapable of grounding a verdict. According to Wasserman, someone who infers as in (1) is failing to treat *X* as an individual. According to Zuckerman and Cohen, basing a verdict on (1) is tantamount to assigning liability to *X* *merely because*

X *is an F*, as opposed to assigning liability for some morally legitimate reason, such as the fact that *X* probably caused some particular harm.

These moral accounts are tempting. As we will later see, there is something right about them. But unfortunately, they do not solve the problem of statistical evidence, because they are not broad enough to explain our general hostility to verdicts based on statistical inferences. The accounts explain our judgments about *Prisoners* and *Gatecrasher*, but only because these examples have certain idiosyncratic features—namely, both involve profiling an individual person on the basis of his membership in a group that consists mainly of bad actors. But many other sorts of statistical inferences are just as incapable of providing legal proof. The subject of a problematic statistical inference need not be the defendant. The predicate need not be any negative property. Consider the following example:

> *Dog Bite*: There are ten dogs that roam the neighborhood—six owned by Jones, and four owned by Smith. The local pet ordinances do not require owners to keep their dogs on a leash, but owners are liable for any harm caused by dogs that roam freely. Little Bobby sees ten dogs in a local park. He randomly picks one to play with, and the dog bites him. It can be established that the dogs in the park were all and only the neighborhood dogs. But Bobby is too young to tell the dogs apart, so there is no available evidence as to which dog bit him.

Given the available evidence, it is reasonable to have .6 credence that the dog that bit Bobby was owned by Jones. But it is impermissible to hold Jones responsible for the dog bite, merely on the grounds that she happens to own a majority of the dogs in the neighborhood. Just as in *Gatecrasher*, the merely statistical evidence in *Dog Bite* is insufficient to sustain a verdict. Yet the statistical inference in *Dog Bite* has the following form:

(2) a. Most of the neighborhood dogs are owned by Jones.
  b. The dog that bit Bobby is a neighborhood dog.
  c. Therefore, it is more likely than not that the dog that bit Bobby is owned by Jones.

Whose individuality is demeaned by this inference? The subject of the inference is a dog. Jones is not being treated like an arbitrary dog owner; indeed, since there are only two dog owners in the neighborhood, it would be impossible to unfairly assign her liability on the basis of the fact that most local dog owners have some property.

Suppose we ask Jones why we shouldn't hold her responsible for the dog bite. She would be right to respond, "Look, the mere fact that I own most of the dogs in the neighborhood doesn't *prove anything*." And in a sense, she's right. The problem in *Dog Bite* is not that we have made some inference we shouldn't have. The problem is that there is an epistemic shortcoming to the case against Jones. Let us turn to epistemic accounts of statistical evidence, then, to see if they can do any better.

3.3 Objections to Epistemic Accounts

According to most leading epistemic accounts, legal proof requires a special sort of evidence, evidence that provides the factfinder with something more than mere justified belief. There are a number of features that could be the missing ingredient. Thomson 1986 defends a causal account, arguing that legal proof requires evidence that is "in an appropriate way causally connected with the fact that the defendant caused the harm" (203), where two facts are causally connected just in case one causes the other or they both share a common cause. For example, the testimony of an eyewitness can prove that a defendant is liable for trespass, since the fact that the defendant trespassed is a cause of her testimony. By contrast, the fact that most rodeo-goers trespassed is causally unconnected with the fact that any particular defendant trespassed, and so the former fact is insufficient to prove the latter, even by a preponderance of the evidence.[40]

According to a second epistemic account defended in Enoch et al. 2012, a verdict must be *sensitive* in the following sense:

> For *A*'s belief that *p* to be sensitive is for it to be the case that had *p* been false, *A* would probably not have believed that *p*. (210)[41]

Enoch et al. say that they intend to explain "the reluctance to rely on statistical evidence... in terms of Sensitivity" (220). Unfortunately, they do not give any precise statement of this general thought. However, they do elucidate their account in the following helpful passage, in which they contrast statistical evidence with reliable testimony:

> Our eyewitness is not infallible, of course, but she is pretty reliable, and so had it not been a Blue Bus bus, she would have probably not testified that it was; and in that case we would not have found the Blue Bus Company liable. So in this

[40] Another causal account is defended by Sorensen 2006, who argues that a crime justifies a verdict only by being a cause of that verdict—namely, by causing some evidence that causes the verdict (170).

[41] This condition is inspired by the definition of sensitive belief in Nozick 1981. For simplicity, I classify sensitivity-based accounts of statistical evidence as epistemic, since they are modeled on sensitivity-based accounts of knowledge. In another sense, the account offered by Enoch et al. is not epistemic, since Enoch et al. argue that statistical evidence should be excluded because it provides perverse incentives, not because it supports intrinsically deficient beliefs.

> scenario, the finding is appropriately sensitive. Things are different, though, if we base our finding solely on statistical evidence. (206)

Given these remarks, it is natural to interpret Enoch et al. as endorsing the following thesis:

> (Sensitive Verdict) A finding of liability is proper only if the following condition holds: if the defendant hadn't been liable, the factfinder probably wouldn't have found him liable.

Enoch et al. implicate that they accept the analogous claim for criminal verdicts: proper conviction requires that if the defendant had been innocent, the factfinder probably wouldn't have found him guilty.[42]

Before I raise my main objections to these epistemic accounts, a quick detour is necessary. There is one technical problem with the above sensitivity account. A lot of verdicts based on statistical evidence actually happen to be sensitive, but for trivial reasons. For instance, consider *Dog Bite*. Let us imagine that as a matter of fact, Bobby was bitten by a dog owned by Jones. Suppose that Jones hadn't been liable for any harm to Bobby. What would probably have been the case? Well, in the vast majority of scenarios in which Jones isn't liable for any harm to Bobby, that's because Bobby *isn't harmed at all*. After all, it's not as if the neighborhood dogs were all lining up to bite Bobby, and if he hadn't been bit by a dog owned by Jones, he would have been bit by a dog owned by Smith. Suppose the jurors find Jones liable for causing harm to Bobby. Their verdict is going to be sensitive to the fact that she is liable, since if Jones hadn't been liable, the jurors probably wouldn't have found her liable—namely, because there probably wouldn't have been a trial at all.

We need to fix up the sensitivity account to avoid this bad result. On behalf of Enoch et al., I propose the following: say that an evidence proposition p is sensitive to the defendant's liability if and only if it satisfies the following condition: if the defendant hadn't been liable, then p would probably have been false. Rather than saying that legal verdicts must be sensitive, let us say that legal verdicts must be based on sensitive evidence:

[42] Enoch et al. alternate between saying that the jury must *deliver sensitive verdicts* and that they must *have sensitive beliefs*. The latter vocabulary suggests a slight variation on the account given above—namely, that a finding of liability requires that if the defendant hadn't been liable, the factfinder probably wouldn't have believed that he was liable. This variation does not make a difference to my arguments.

(Sensitive Evidence) A finding of liability is proper only if the following condition holds: the factfinder believes that the defendant is probably liable, and they base their belief on at least one evidence proposition that is sensitive to his liability.

This version of the sensitivity account delivers the right verdict about *Dog Bite*. The jurors' belief that Jones is probably liable is based entirely on the evidence proposition that she owns most of the dogs in the neighborhood, and this evidence proposition is not sensitive to the fact that she is liable. By contrast, consider a case where Jones is found liable on the basis of reliable eyewitness testimony. In this case, the jurors' belief that Jones is probably liable is based on the content of the testimony offered by the eyewitness—namely, the proposition *that she saw one of Jones's dogs bite Bobby*. This evidence proposition does counterfactually depend on the dog biting Bobby, so the relevant sensitivity condition is satisfied.

Unfortunately, serious problems remain. Several examples make trouble for both the causation account and the sensitivity account of statistical evidence. In a number of cases, statistical evidence is insufficient to sustain a verdict, even though it is causally connected with the fact to be proved and also sensitive to that fact. For instance, sometimes the statistical evidence causes the fact to be proved:

> *Reluctant Prisoner*: 50 prisoners are in a prison yard. Some of them start a riot, and others start to join in. An especially reluctant prisoner decides that he will only join the riot if at least 48 others participate. Eventually this happens, and he joins in, leaving just one innocent prisoner who refuses to join the riot. Local prosecutors randomly select one of the prisoners from the yard and bring him to trial. By sheer coincidence, the randomly selected prisoner is the reluctant prisoner, the last to join the riot.

In other cases, the fact to be proved causes the statistical evidence:

> *Bold Prisoner*: 25 prisoners are in a prison yard. An especially bold prisoner attacks the prison guards and thereby causes a riot. 23 prisoners join in the riot, while the remaining prisoner tries to stop it. Local prosecutors randomly select one of the prisoners from the yard and bring him to trial. By sheer coincidence, the randomly selected prisoner is the bold prisoner responsible for the riot.[43]

Finally, the statistical evidence and the fact to be proved can have a common cause:

[43] For a structurally similar example, see section 4 of Blome-Tillmann 2015.

Playing Cards: The local prison has four teams of prison guards and thirteen buildings, with exactly 25 prisoners living in each building. Every afternoon, a playing card is drawn at random. The suit of the card determines which guard team is on yard duty, and the number determines which building of prisoners goes out.

All the prisoners hate the Team Diamond guards. They decide that there should be a riot in the prison yard on the next day that Team Diamond has yard duty. That afternoon, the five of diamonds is drawn. Team Diamond and Building Five enter the yard. 24 of the prisoners riot, while the remaining prisoner tries to stop them. Local prosecutors randomly select one of the Building Five prisoners and bring him to trial. As it happens, the selected prisoner was indeed part of the riot.

In each of these examples, the jury has statistical evidence that the defendant is guilty—namely, they know that the defendant was in the yard and that at least 96 percent of the prisoners in the yard are guilty. Furthermore, this evidence is not misleading; the defendant is indeed guilty of attacking the guards. In each case, this merely statistical evidence is insufficient to sustain a verdict of guilt. Unfortunately, the causal account of statistical evidence fails to deliver this result. As noted above, all of these examples involve causal connections obtaining between the statistical evidence and the fact to be proved.

Turning to sensitivity accounts, we can ask: if the defendant hadn't attacked the guards, what would probably have been the case? In two of the three cases, we get the wrong answer. In *Bold Prisoner*, the defendant caused the riot. We can suppose that if he hadn't started the riot, the guards wouldn't have been harmed at all. Hence the jurors are basing their verdict on evidence that is sensitive to the fact that the defendant is guilty, in virtue of being causally connected to it. In the case of *Playing Cards*, any of the other twelve buildings could easily have been selected to enter the prison yard. In the vast majority of counterfactual scenarios where the defendant isn't guilty, that's because some other card was picked, and some other prisoners entered the yard and rioted against the Team Diamond guards. In any such scenario, the evidence proposition that the actual defendant entered the yard would have been false. Hence the jurors in *Playing Cards* also base their guilty verdict on an evidence proposition that is sensitive to the guilt of the defendant. To sum up, the fact that statistical evidence is incapable of sustaining a verdict cannot be grounded in its lack of causal connection or in its insensitivity to the facts.

As I have interpreted the causal and sensitivity accounts, they each aim to state a necessary condition on evidence such that: (a) our total evidence must satisfy the condition in order for it to be sufficient for a verdict, and (b) any total evidence consisting merely of statistical facts fails to satisfy the condition. The foregoing examples challenge the second half of each account, demonstrating that some statistical evidence actually satisfies the proposed necessary conditions of causal connection and sensitivity. Some additional examples challenge the former half of each account, demonstrating that evidence can be sufficient for a verdict, even without being sensitive to the verdict or bearing any substantial causal connection to it. Here is an example of sufficiency without sensitivity:

> *Grand Canyon*: Acme Corp. is charged with dumping waste onto federal land without a permit. At trial, the prosecution presents video evidence of Acme employees heaving a trash bag into a chute that dumps out into the Grand Canyon.[44]

The video evidence in *Pollution* is intuitively sufficient for a verdict. But it is easy enough to fill out the details of the case such that if Acme Corp. had not in fact been guilty of dumping waste onto federal land, it would have been because the trash bag in the video had gotten stuck in the chute and remained on their private property. But in that case, the jury would have been presented with the very same evidence as they actually have. The video evidence is sufficient for legal proof without being sensitive to the fact that it proves.

Evidence can also be sufficient for a guilty verdict without bearing any substantial causal connection to the guilt of the defendant. Consider the following example:

> *Spit in the Sink*: Alice is found murdered in her bedroom. A detailed forensic study proves the following facts: (a) the murder took place in her apartment within the last month, (b) no one except for Alice entered her apartment during that time, except for one person who left some spit in her bathroom sink, and (c) that spit came from the defendant.[45]

Together with the fact that no one else entered her apartment, the presence of the spit in the sink is evidence that the defendant killed Alice. Assuming the forensic science is trustworthy enough, this evidence could sustain a guilty verdict. But what causal connection holds between the fact that the defendant killed Alice, and the fact that he left spit in her sink? Perhaps the murder was caused by greed and jealousy, while the spit was caused by a sneeze, which was itself caused by a cold virus. The murder and the spit have a common cause in only a very attenuated sense—namely, the event of the defendant entering Alice's apartment is a causal enabling condition of each. But in this attenuated sense, many pairs of events

[44] This case is modeled on the trash chute case in Sosa 1999, offered by Sosa as a counterexample to a sensitivity requirement on knowledge.

[45] For simplicity, this example involves some science fiction. Actual forensic science is not good enough to prove these facts. To flesh out the example, suppose that each person necessarily has a radically different gut biome, and that this has enabled the construction of a National Spit Registry that can link any sample of spit with its unique source.

count as having a common cause. In *Prisoners*, the event of a certain group of 25 prisoners entering the yard is an enabling condition of: (a) the event of 24 of those prisoners attacking the guard, and also (b) the event of the defendant attacking the guard. Yet this shared enabling condition does not render (a) capable of proving (b). This sort of attenuated causal connection is not useful for saying what it takes for evidence to be sufficient for a verdict.

3.4 Explaining the Insufficiency of Statistical Evidence

I have described several problems for existing accounts of statistical evidence. Happily, where other accounts fail, the knowledge account succeeds. The knowledge account does not rely on any assumptions about the form of statistical inferences that fail to sustain verdicts. The statistical evidence in *Dog Bite* may be just as incapable of grounding knowledge as the statistical evidence in *Gatecrasher*. The examples *Bold Prisoner*, *Reluctant Prisoner*, and *Playing Cards* are all paradigmatic lottery cases, featuring evidence that fails to provide the jury with knowledge that the defendant is guilty. The knowledge account correctly predicts that the evidence in these cases is insufficient to sustain a guilty verdict. By contrast, the factfinder in *Grand Canyon* can know on the basis of video evidence that Acme dumped waste onto federal land, and the factfinder in *Spit in the Sink* can know on the basis of the forensic evidence that the defendant murdered Alice. Hence the knowledge account correctly predicts that the evidence in these cases is sufficient to sustain a guilty verdict.

In addition to solving problems faced by existing accounts, the knowledge account explains a recurring observation in the literature on statistical evidence—namely, that legal proof seems to require *something that looks an awful lot like knowledge*. There are several concepts that figure prominently in traditional theories of knowledge. Traditional epistemologists have argued that knowledge is caused by the facts and that it is sensitive. It has also been argued that knowledge is not just the result of luck, that knowledge is safe, and that knowledge is absent in Gettier cases.[46] These same concepts figure prominently in theories of what legal proof requires. We have already examined causal and sensitivity accounts. In addition, Thomson 1986 argues that legal proof requires something that is *not the result of luck*:

> [I]t is required of a jury that it not impose liability unless it has, not merely good reason, but reason of a kind which would make it not be just luck for the jury if its verdict is true. (214)

[46] All five of these features of knowledge routinely figure in introductory epistemology texts. For example, see Dancy 1985, Nagel 2014, Goldman and McGrath 2015, and Ichikawa and Steup 2018.

Pritchard 2015 argues that proof requires *safety*:

> [A]n adequacy condition on the total evidence presented at trial in support of the defendant's guilt ought to be such that it satisfies the epistemic anti-risk condition . . . i.e., it is not an easy possibility that one's belief could have been false. (457)

Pardo 2010a argues that proof requires something that is *absent in Gettier cases*:

> [A]n appropriate connection among (1) fact finders' conclusions (however conceived), (2) the epistemic support they require, and (3) their truth, matters for legal proof. This connection arises in non-Gettier cases and is missing in Gettier cases. . . . [T]he goal of legal proof is *non-Gettier-ized* true and justified conclusions. (55, 57)

The common thread running throughout this literature speaks for itself. An elegant explanation of these several observations is that legal proof requires *knowledge*.

There is just one hitch. A small handful of scholars have endorsed the idea that the criminal standard of proof requires knowledge. But it has proven difficult to extend this idea to other standards of proof, such as proof by a preponderance of the evidence. Redmayne 2008 describes this difficulty in detail. Redmayne agrees with Thomson that the strong parallels between examples like *Lottery* and *Prisoners* suggest that legal proof requires knowledge. But he goes on to object that this solution to the problem of statistical evidence cannot be extended to civil cases:[47]

> There is an obvious problem with this view, however. It is plausible that whatever prevents a liability verdict in Prisoners also prevents a liability verdict in Blue Bus. If Prisoners is explained by a knowledge requirement for proof, then Blue Bus is too. But that would involve arguing that civil as well as criminal verdicts require knowledge, and that is not easy to accept. Civil verdicts require no more than proof on the balance of probabilities. This standard seems too low to satisfy the degree of justification required for knowledge. (299)

[47] The Blue Bus case mentioned here by Redmayne is a hypothetical civil case modeled after *Smith v. Rapid Transit* 58 N.E.2d 754 (1945). A car is negligently run off the road by a blue bus. The driver of the car can't identify the exact bus that caused the accident, but she can prove that the Blue Bus Company operates 60 percent of the blue buses in town, while another company operates only the remaining 40 percent. The evidence is insufficient to sustain a verdict. For an early discussion of the implications of the Blue Bus case for theories of statistical evidence, see Tribe 1971.

As Redmayne sees it, the civil standard of proof cannot require knowledge, since the subjective component of this standard is merely that the factfinder has greater than .5 credence that the defendant is liable. By contrast, knowing that a defendant is liable requires the factfinder to fully believe that the defendant is liable, which is a much stricter constraint. A knowledge account of the criminal standard is plausible, since outright belief in guilt is a viable constraint on conviction. But a knowledge account of the civil standard is out.[48]

How to respond? Redmayne is correct that proof of liability by a preponderance of the evidence cannot require that the factfinder know *that the defendant is liable.* But there is another option available—namely, that proof by a preponderance of the evidence requires that the factfinder have knowledge of a significantly weaker content. Here is the thesis I want to defend: proof of liability by a preponderance of the evidence requires that the factfinder know that the defendant is *probably* liable.

What does it mean to know merely that the defendant is probably liable—or equivalently, that the defendant is *at least .5 likely* to be liable—as opposed to simply knowing that the defendant is liable? Fortunately, our answer to this question may be guided by recent literature on the formal semantics of knowledge ascriptions embedding probability operators. According to my preferred interpretation of these ascriptions, they are used to ascribe *probabilistic knowledge* in the sense of Moss 2018b. Rather than ascribing an outright belief to the factfinder, they say that the factfinder has certain credences and that those credences constitute knowledge.[49]

This interpretation of my thesis requires an epistemological assumption—namely, that credences, just like full beliefs, are among the kinds of attitudes that can constitute knowledge. Just as you can rule out relevant alternatives to your full beliefs, you can rule out relevant alternatives to your probabilistic beliefs. Rule out enough of them, and you can acquire knowledge. For example, suppose you have a sore throat, and you have greater than .5 credence that it is caused by a strep virus, and you have less than .5 credence that you are contagious. A doctor runs some tests and arrives at just the same conclusions. After talking with the doctor, you may come to *know* that you probably have strep throat and that you are probably not contagious. But before ruling out the possibility that her test

[48] For similar objections, see Stein 2015 and Blome-Tillmann 2017. Pardo 2005 discusses this objection and suggests that "one might therefore reject knowledge as the aim or goal of proof," retreating instead to the less precise claim that legal proof merely requires some "knowledge-like" attitude (55). This concession represents a significant difference between Pardo's account of legal proof and my own.

[49] To be more precise, these ascriptions say that the factfinder has a *probabilistic belief* that constitutes knowledge. A probabilistic belief can be a precise credence, such as .5 credence that a certain coin landed heads, or it can correspond to a range of credences, as with the belief that it is more than .5 likely that the coin landed heads. For further introductory discussion of probabilistic beliefs, see chapter 1 of Moss 2018b.

results would contradict your hunches, your probabilistic beliefs did not yet constitute knowledge.

Returning to a legal context, consider the civil standard of proof by a preponderance of the evidence. As discussed in section 3.1, the defendant is proven liable by this standard only if the judge or jury has greater than .5 credence that he is liable. The knowledge account adds an objective element to this condition: the defendant is proven liable by a preponderance of the evidence if and only if this probabilistic belief constitutes knowledge. Suppose you are the factfinder in *Gatecrasher*. The plaintiff has proved that most people at the rodeo climbed over the fence. But the defendant insists that he is not just any arbitrary person at the rodeo. In effect, the defendant is raising a certain possibility—namely, that he is an individual who is not represented by features of the group to which he belongs. Given the lottery-like similarity of all the possible defendants in the *Gatecrasher* scenario, this possibility is impossible to ignore. In the absence of other evidence, you may be *justified* in having .501 credence that the defendant is liable, and even justified in betting that he is liable. But your justified credence does not constitute knowledge. You do not know that this particular defendant is probably liable, because you can't rule out a relevant possibility that is inconsistent with this content—namely, that the defendant is an individual whose character makes him far less likely to trespass than just some arbitrary person at the rodeo. According to my account of the civil standard of proof, it follows that the plaintiff has failed to prove that the defendant is liable by a preponderance of the evidence.

The knowledge account similarly extends to other legal standards of proof. As discussed in section 3.1, each standard of proof corresponds to a distinct threshold of credence. A standard of proof is met just in case the factfinder has at least that much credence in a proposition, and this probabilistic belief constitutes knowledge. Apropos of this thesis, it is worth noting that in elucidating different standards of proof, Judge Weinstein does not merely say that they require different levels of confidence, but different levels of knowledge:

> The problem, then, is to determine what *level of knowledge* by the Marshal is necessary to permit this intrusion on the person [i.e. stop-and-frisk searches].[50]

Just as proof of liability by a preponderance of the evidence requires the factfinder to know that it is probable that the defendant is liable, proof by clear and convincing evidence requires the factfinder to know that it is *highly probable* that the defendant is liable. In other words, compared with the preponderance standard, proof of liability by clear and convincing evidence requires the factfinder

[50] *United States v. Lopez*, 328 F. Supp. 1077, 1094 (1971), my emphasis.

to have an even higher credence in liability, and also that this higher credence constitutes knowledge.

3.5 Accounting for Exceptional Cases

I have defended an account of legal proof that is based on knowledge and also solves the general problem of statistical evidence presented by all standards of proof. So far, I have focused on the traditional problem of statistical evidence—namely, explaining the fact that statistical evidence is generally insufficient for proof. Now we can turn our attention to two additional facts worth explaining.

The first fact is that our intuitions about the sufficiency of merely statistical evidence vary greatly from case to case. It seems unconscionable to convict the defendant in *Prisoners*. But in other cases, courts have been willing to treat statistical evidence as sufficient for legal proof, and it is not at all obvious that they shouldn't. For example, in *Kramer v. Weedhopper*, Kramer was injured in a plane crash which resulted from a defective bolt sold as part of a Weedhopper airplane kit. Weedhopper purchased 90% of its bolts from Lawrence and 10% from Hughes. Kramer filed a complaint alleging strict product liability against Lawrence. The circuit court granted summary judgment to Lawrence, arguing that the available statistical evidence was insufficient to prove that the bolt that injured Kramer probably came from Lawrence.[51] But an Illinois appellate court reversed the judgment, stating that "when two suppliers of an allegedly dangerous product exist, under circumstances which show that a defendant supplied 90% of the parts used, this evidence is sufficient to withstand a motion for summary judgment."[52]

Statistical evidence is also sometimes considered sufficient for a verdict in toxic tort cases where epidemiological evidence is used to prove specific causation claims. For example, in *Manko v. United States*, Manko developed Guillaim-Barré syndrome within weeks of receiving a swine flu vaccination. He alleged that the latter had caused the former. An expert testified that the relative risk of contracting the syndrome after vaccination was greater than 2, meaning that the syndrome was more than twice as prevalent in people who had received the vaccine as compared with those who hadn't. Based on this evidence, the court entered a judgment for the plaintiff, stating, "Because the relative risk of contracting GBS during the period 11–16 weeks after vaccination is greater than 2, it is more likely than not that plaintiff's swine flu vaccination caused his GBS."[53]

[51] A summary judgment is a judgment issued without a full trial, as when the court determines that the available evidence could not possibly sustain a verdict of liability.

[52] *Kramer v. Weedhopper of Utah, Inc.*, 141 Ill. App. 3d 217, 220 (1986). Another similar case often cited in the literature is *Kaminsky v. Hertz Corp.*, 288 N.W.2d 426 (Mich. App. 1979).

[53] *Manko v. United States*, 636 F. Supp. 1434 (W.D. Mo. 1986).

The use of relative risk to prove specific causation is controversial, to say the least.[54] But whether or not these judgments are correct, it is worth noting that they do not offend our intuitions as much as traditional cases of verdicts based on statistical evidence.

This variation in our intuitions about statistical evidence is unexpected on causal and sensitivity accounts of legal proof. The statistical facts used in *Weedhopper* and *Manko* are no more causally connected to individual claims in these cases than they are in *Gatecrasher*, nor are they more sensitive to the specific facts of causation that they are used to prove. By contrast, varying intuitions about statistical evidence are to be expected on the knowledge account. On my account, statistical evidence suffices to prove causation just in case the factfinder knows that causation is more than.5 likely. Put another way, the factfinder must rule out all relevant possibilities according to which causation is no more than.5 likely. Of course, this raises the central question of just what counts as a relevant possibility. As discussed in section 2.2, the answer to this question is highly context sensitive. We have seen that the relevance of a possibility may depend on its lottery-like structure. In addition, it is often held that whether a possibility is relevant depends partly on what is at stake—for instance, the cost of having a false belief if the possibility were to obtain.[55] Falsely profiling an individual person as having a negative character trait might be morally different from other instances of false profiling, such as falsely profiling inanimate objects or corporate defendants. False profiling that harms some specific person—as in *Dog Bite*, for instance—might also carry distinctive moral costs.[56] By contrast, false verdicts in some product liability and toxic tort cases may lack any similar costs. To sum up, differences in the stakes of a false verdict may naturally lead to some variation in how easy it is for jurors to have knowledge—which, on my account, explains the variation in our judgments about what is sufficient for legal proof.

This discussion of the moral stakes of profiling brings us to a second fact to be explained. Some statistical evidence is not only insufficient for proof, but inadmissible at trial. As Tribe 1971 reminds us, these are very different claims:

> [T]he fact that mathematical evidence taken alone can rarely, if ever, establish the crucial proposition with sufficient certitude to meet the applicable standard of proof does not imply that such evidence—when properly combined with other,

[54] See Haack 2014 for a detailed history of this practice, as well as several compelling arguments that relative risk factors are neither necessary nor sufficient for proof of specific causation claims.

[55] Compare the *Rule of High Stakes* from Lewis 1996: "when error would be especially disastrous, few possibilities are properly ignored" (556). See DeRose 1992 for a classic discussion of stakes and knowledge ascriptions, though see also Worsnip 2015 and Anderson and Hawthorne 2019 for important arguments that it is difficult to spell out the notion of stakes that is central to this literature.

[56] See Moss 2018a for a detailed discussion of how the moral stakes of a belief may have an epistemic impact on whether that belief constitutes knowledge.

more conventional, evidence in the same case—cannot supply a useful link in the process of proof. (1350)

Hence we need some additional explanation for why courts sometimes exclude statistical evidence as irrelevant, unable to serve even as a link in the process of proof. For example, statistical facts about crime rates among residents of a given neighborhood are irrelevant when it comes to proving the criminal behavior of a particular resident of that neighborhood. Similarly, the fact that most assaults in a given neighborhood involve illegal firearms is irrelevant when it comes to proving that some particular assault in that neighborhood involved an illegal firearm. On the basis of an examination of hundreds of state and federal cases, Koehler 2002 observes that "[c]ourts are likely to find base rates irrelevant when they smack of guilt by trait association" (383).

Again, it is hard for other epistemic accounts to explain these observations. Causal and sensitivity accounts merely impose a necessary condition on the sufficiency of evidence, and it is not obvious how to extend these accounts to provide an additional necessary condition for admissibility. By contrast, the knowledge account can explain why some statistical inferences are impermissible. Statistical evidence might justify the factfinder in having a higher credence in a claim. But whether this higher credence constitutes knowledge depends on whether the factfinder can rule out certain possibilities, and some possibilities may be epistemically resilient, such that no evidence could possibly rule them out. The possibility of being a brain in a vat is epistemically resilient in the context of an epistemology classroom, designed in order to be irrefutable by observation or reflection. In the context of a criminal trial, other possibilities are resilient, including the possibility that the defendant has individual traits that would undermine any alleged probative value of statistics having to do with racial categories. As with brain-in-a-vat hypotheses in a classroom context, there may be features of the courtroom context that prevent jurors from ruling out this possibility, thereby making it impossible for certain statistical facts to make even a minor contribution to an inference that could provide them with the knowledge they need to convict. Jurors are not morally compelled to assume that certain statistical inferences *are in fact* misleading, but only that they *might be* misleading—yet as long as this possibility is taken for granted, those same inferences cannot help ground knowledge.

A consistent theme has emerged from our discussion—namely, that moral considerations can play an important epistemic role in legal contexts. As a result of this fact, my knowledge account incorporates a lot of the desirable features of moral and epistemic accounts of legal proof. Although the knowledge account is itself epistemic, moral considerations play an important role in it, since there may be moral reasons why some possibilities of error involve high stakes, or can be safely ignored by jurors, or are especially resilient against further evidence.

This avenue of influence for moral facts underscores a broader theme of this chapter—namely, that legal proof is not merely a matter of justifying a subjective probability judgment. The epistemic relevance of a possibility does not depend only on its probability, but also on its moral features. Accordingly, on the knowledge account, moral features of statistical inferences can make a difference to their proper role in legal proof.

4. Responses to Objections

Having set out some positive arguments for my account, let me now address two important objections. The first objection, which is perhaps the prevailing objection in philosophical discussions of legal proof, is that the knowledge account delivers factive standards of legal proof. According my account, an innocent defendant cannot be proven guilty.[57] Some find this result unacceptable. As Gardiner 2019 puts it:

> [I]t is a desideratum of an account of legal evidence that—if evidence is compelling but misleading—the burden can be satisfied even if the judgment is false.... [A]n innocent defendant can appear guilty beyond reasonable doubt. (7)

Similarly, Blome-Tillmann 2015 argues:

> A final problem to be addressed here concerns wrongful convictions.... In some such cases of wrongful conviction, the defendant is found liable on the basis of very strong but ultimately misleading evidence. In such cases, the court is not at fault. The standards of proof have been met by strong, if misleading, evidence. Call such cases *no-fault wrongful convictions*.

Blome-Tillmann goes on to argue that no-fault wrongful convictions are impossible according to factive standards of proof, and he rejects factive standards for this reason. It is easy to appreciate this worry. Suppose that the prosecution has presented such a strong case that the only remaining possibilities of innocence involve far-fetched conspiracy theories. And now suppose that as it happens, the defendant *is* the innocent victim of a conspiracy. An opponent of the knowledge

[57] For simplicity, I focus on the criminal standard in this section. The civil standard of proof by a preponderance of the evidence is also factive, in the sense that a defendant cannot be proved probably liable unless the defendant is probably liable. For a detailed discussion of the notion of factivity as it applies to probabilistic knowledge, see chapter 5 of Moss 2018b.

account might say, "In situations like these, don't we *want* the jury to set aside the far-fetched conspiracy theory and find the defendant guilty?"[58]

The correct response is, "Well, we do and we don't." There are multiple dimensions along which we can evaluate jurors as they deliberate. There is one sense in which the jury should convict the defendant in the imagined case. But there is also a sense in which they shouldn't convict the innocent defendant—because there is a sense in which there is clearly something bad about false convictions, whether or not they result from misleading evidence. It is this second sort of intuitive judgment that is at work in the observation by Williams 1980 that "[t]here is a miscarriage of justice whenever an innocent man is convicted" (104), and also at work in the eighteenth-century judgment that convicting an innocent defendant was a mortal sin. In short, there is something good about convicting an innocent person on misleading evidence and also something bad about it. Any decent account of legal proof should offer explanations of both judgments.

The knowledge account of legal proof delivers both of these explanations. Suppose the jurors convict the innocent victim of the secret government conspiracy. Although they convict this defendant without proof that he is guilty, they are entirely blameless for doing so, since they are doing their subjective best to satisfy the objective legal rule they are following. They are subjectively in the right, despite being objectively in the wrong. This combination of normative judgments is familiar, as it can be found wherever we find externalist norms—which is to say, everywhere. Consider these ordinary norms:

(3) Turn off the stove as soon as the water starts boiling.
(4) Water the garden if and only if it doesn't rain.
(5) Set the Passover table for however many guests are coming, plus one.
(6) Call the tennis ball out if and only if it falls completely outside the line.
(7) Hang one light in the tower if they are coming by land, and two if by sea.
(8) Give your money to whichever charity has the lowest overhead.

You can have a justified belief that you are following these norms, even when you aren't actually following them. In that case, you are not doing the objectively right thing. But you may be blameless, and even praiseworthy, for doing what you believe is the objectively right thing to do. The same goes for the knowledge norm of conviction:

(9) Convict the defendant if and only if you know he is guilty.

[58] For additional discussion of this objection to the knowledge account, see section 2B of Beltrán 2006 and fn. 32 of Blome-Tillmann 2017. For a representative discussion of factivity in the context of civil litigation, see the distinction between material and procedural accuracy outlined in Pardo 2010b: 1470.

For every primary objective norm that tells you what you ought to do, there are secondary subjective norms, such as the instruction to do whatever you believe will result in the satisfaction of the primary norm. As far as the normative landscape goes, the subjective norms are grounded in the objective norms from which they are predictably derived.[59] Recall Gardiner's objection that "an innocent defendant can *appear* guilty beyond reasonable doubt" (7, my emphasis). Gardiner is right. But notice what Gardiner does not say—namely, that an innocent defendant can be *proved* guilty beyond a reasonable doubt. Gardiner does not say this because falsehoods cannot be proved. Proof in legal contexts is not entirely divorced from our more general notion of proof, which is factive.[60] In some cases of misleading evidence, an innocent defendant may appear guilty without being proved guilty. In such cases, the criminal standard of proof may appear to be satisfied. The apparent satisfaction of the standard of proof is sufficient to explain our intuition that there is a sense in which the jurors should convict, and that is enough to resolve the first objection to the knowledge account.

The second objection to my account is a broader worry about its externalist character. At first glance, it might seem unsettling that whether a jury ought to convict a defendant could depend on whether their evidence is misleading, when they have no way of determining whether that's true. Smith 2018 raises something like this internalist objection in the following passage:

> If two courts were presented with equivalent bodies of evidence against two individuals charged with equivalent crimes, could it really be acceptable for them to reach different verdicts—for one individual to be found guilty and the other innocent—even if there was some variation in external circumstances? (1205)

As stated, this objection is not hard to answer. In some cases, it might turn out that the evidence is *permissive*, in the sense that reasonable juries could disagree about what verdict it supports. In such cases, it should be acceptable for reasonable juries to reach different verdicts. But setting aside cases of permissive evidence, we can formulate an objection that is similar in spirit but harder to answer:

> If two courts are presented with equivalent bodies of evidence against two individuals charged with equivalent crimes, and the juries form exactly the same beliefs, and in fact the juries are *exact intrinsic duplicates*, could the juries

[59] The same response also applies to internalist objections to other knowledge norms, such as knowledge norms of belief and assertion. For further discussion, see Lasonen-Aarnio 2010, Hawthorne and Srinivasan 2013, and Williamson 2015.

[60] Beltrán 2006 suggests that "it is plausible that one could maintain an idea of proof according to which a false proposition could be proven" (302), but it is doubtful that this idea would capture our ordinary veridical notion of proof. For a more semantically informed discussion of our ordinary notion of proof, see White and Rawlins 2018.

> be *required* to reach different verdicts in virtue of some variation in external circumstances?

The knowledge account says that this is possible. But at first glance, it might seem inappropriate to hold juries to any standard of this sort, since the inscrutability of the standard necessarily entails that juries will not be able to control whether they are following it.

Here again, it is helpful to reflect on precedents provided by ordinary norms. In particular, it is helpful to think about legal statutes. Consider the following example involving statutes violated by drunk drivers:

> *Drunk Drivers*: Two drunk drivers pull out onto the highway. They are exact intrinsic duplicates, both with the same blurry field of vision and delayed reflexes. Both swerve unexpectedly into oncoming traffic. The unlucky drunk driver causes a fatal collision and is convicted of vehicular homicide. The lucky driver causes a minor collision and is convicted of negligent driving.

The drivers have no control over the circumstances that determine which offense they commit. The relevant offenses concern not just internal states, but also their external effects.[61] Legally speaking, it is not only important to avoid risky actions, but also important to avoid killing people as a result of undertaking risky actions. In short, many ordinary legal statutes are externalist norms, norms that give rise to legal luck.

We have arrived at an externalist thesis about legal statutes governing drivers on the highway. What about legal standards governing jurors in a courtroom? In fact, the dialectic is remarkably similar. Consider the following pair of cases:

> *Lucky Lucy*: Lucy is a juror in a criminal trial. She is not epistemically perfect. For instance, when she listens to people talk for a long time, she occasionally gets sleepy and, without realizing it, misses gathering some information. Despite her imperfections, Lucy comes to know that the defendant is guilty after listening to a lot of compelling evidence presented by the prosecution at trial.
>
> As it happens, Lucy could have easily failed to have this knowledge.[62] Lucy knows that the defendant is guilty only because she has done something epistemically blameworthy. At one point in the trial, she happened to miss hearing a false statement made by a friend of the defendant. If she had been paying closer

[61] Arguably, the same sort of luck adheres to moral judgments, though of course that's more controversial. For a radical discussion of legal and moral luck and the relationship between them, see Enoch 2018.

[62] To forestall confusion: my claim here—that Lucy could have easily failed to believe what she actually knows—is compatible with the claim that her knowledge is *safe*, i.e. that she couldn't have easily falsely believed that the defendant was guilty.

attention, Lucy would have been successfully tricked by the false testimony into believing that the defendant might be innocent.

Lucy is lucky. The evidence that she missed was misleading, and her epistemic imperfections have not prevented her from gaining knowledge. Since she knows that the defendant is guilty, she can correctly vote to convict. Unfortunately, her duplicate is not so lucky:

> *Unlucky Ursula*: Ursula is an intrinsic duplicate of Lucy, serving as a juror at a duplicate trial. Like Lucy, Ursula hears a lot of compelling evidence against the defendant, and on the basis of this evidence, she forms a justified belief that the defendant is guilty. She also misses hearing a brief statement made by a friend of the defendant, which would have caused her to believe that the defendant might be innocent.
>
> Unfortunately, in Ursula's case, the defendant is actually innocent. The prosecution's evidence is misleading, and the statement made by the friend of the defendant is genuinely exculpatory. Ursula is justified in believing that the defendant is guilty, but her belief is false, and it isn't knowledge. If she had just been paying closer attention, Ursula wouldn't have voted to convict an innocent person.

Lucky Lucy and *Unlucky Ursula* elicit just the same intuitive judgments as traditional illustrations of legal and moral luck. An imperfect juror who falsely convicts an innocent person is falling short of the ideal set by our legal standards. Unlucky Ursula deserves some blame for the false conviction that she helped cause, where Lucky Lucy is not blameworthy in this way. In order for there to be any such normative difference between intrinsically duplicate jurors, there must be at least some externalist legal standards governing their verdicts. The knowledge account succeeds in providing standards of proof of just this sort.

In defending the knowledge account, we have come across a novel variety of legal luck. In addition to first-order legal statutes that are sensitive to luck, our standards of proof are also sensitive to luck. And given that these standards are sensitive to luck, the second objection to the knowledge account fails. To be clear, it is not the case that the second objection fails *only if* our legal standards are luck-sensitive. It might turn out that there are externalist standards of proof but that there is no legal luck, i.e. that whether a juror is blameworthy for violating externalist legal standards depends only on internal characteristics that are under her control. In other words, I have defended a claim that is sufficient but not necessary to demonstrate that there are externalist standards of proof. Happily, my defensive argument also serves as a final positive argument for my account. Any account of proof should explain the fact that jurors with justified beliefs but epistemic shortcomings may be distinctively blameworthy in cases where their shortcomings lead to false convictions, and the knowledge account successfully explains this fact.

Having answered the foregoing objections, we can finally embrace the simple theory of legal proof that has seemed attractive from the start. We can explain the elusiveness of legal proof and the intimate connection of legal proof to knowledge, and we can accommodate a broad range of intuitive judgments about what legal proof requires. Legal proof requires knowledge.[63]

References

Anderson, Charity, and John Hawthorne. 2019. Knowledge, Practical Adequacy, and Stakes. In Tamar Szabó Gendler and John Hawthorne (Eds.), *Oxford Studies in Epistemology, Volume 6* (pp. 234–57). Oxford: Oxford University Press.

Beltrán, Jordi Ferrer. 2006. Legal Proof and Fact Finders' Beliefs. *Legal Theory*, 12(4): 293–314.

Bentham, Jeremy. 1843. *The Works of Jeremy Bentham, vol. 6 (The Rationale of Judicial Evidence).* William Tait, Edinburgh. Edited by John Bowring.

Blome-Tillmann, Michael. 2015. Sensitivity, Causality, and Statistical Evidence in Courts of Law. *Thought*, 4(2): 102–12.

Blome-Tillmann, Michael. 2017. 'More Likely Than Not'—Knowledge First and the Role of Bare Statistical Evidence in Courts of Law. In Adam Carter, Emma Gordon, and Benjamin Jarvis (Eds.), *Knowledge First: Approaches in Epistemology and Mind* (pp. 278–92). Oxford: Oxford University Press.

Cohen, L. Jonathan. 1977. *The Probable and the Provable*. Oxford: Clarendon.

Cohen, L. Jonathan. 1981. Subjective Probability and the Paradox of the Gatecrasher. *Arizona State Law Journal*, 2(2): 627–34.

Cohen, L. Jonathan. 1987. On Analyzing the Standards of Forensic Evidence: A Reply to Schoeman. *Philosophy of Science*, 54(1): 92–7.

Dancy, Jonathan. 1985. *Introduction to Contemporary Epistemology*. Oxford: Blackwell.

DeRose, Keith. 1992. Contextualism and Knowledge Attributions. *Philosophy and Phenomenological Research*, 52(4): 913–29.

[63] An early precursor of this chapter was discussed at the 2017 Analytic Legal Philosophy Conference, University of Texas–Austin, the Rutgers Value Theory Workshop, the Michigan Legal Theory Workshop, the UCLA Legal Theory Workshop, and the book symposia for *Probabilistic Knowledge* held at University of Hamburg and at King's College London. Thanks to these audiences for helpful comments. Thanks also to Nico Cornell, Marcello Di Bello, Mark Greenberg, Scott Hershovitz, Don Herzog, Gabe Mendlow, Michael Pardo, and Eric Swanson for thoughtful feedback on earlier drafts.

DeRose, Keith. 2002. Assertion, Knowledge, and Context. *Philosophical Review*, 111(2): 167–203.

Duff, Antony, Lindsay Farmer, Sandra Marshall, and Victor Tadros. 2007. *The Trial on Trial (vol. 3): Towards a Normative Theory of the Criminal Trial.* Oxford: Hart.

Enoch, David. 2018. Luck Between Morality, Law, and Justice. *Theoretical Inquiries in Law*, 9(1): 23–59.

Enoch, David, Levi Spectre, and Talia Fisher. 2012. Statistical Evidence, Sensitivity, and the Legal Value of Knowledge. *Philosophy and Public Affairs*, 40(3): 197–224.

Fogelin, Robert. 2000. Contextualism and Externalism: Trading in One Form of Skepticism for Another. *Philosophical Issues*, 10(1): 43–57.

Gardiner, Georgi. 2019. In David Coady and James Chase (Eds.), *Routledge Handbook of Applied Epistemology* (pp. 179—95). New York: Routledge.

Goldman, Alvin, and Matthew McGrath. 2015. *Epistemology: A Contemporary Introduction.* New York: Oxford University Press.

Green, Thomas. 1985. *Verdict According to Conscience: Perspectives on the English Criminal Trial Jury, 1200–1800.* Chicago, IL: University of Chicago Press.

Haack, Susan. 2014. Risky Business: Statistical Proof of Specific Causation. In *Evidence Matters: Science, Proof, and Truth in the Law* (pp. 264–93). Cambridge: Cambridge University Press.

Harman, Gilbert. 1986. *Change in View: Principles of Reasoning.* Cambridge, MA: MIT Press.

Hawles, John. 1680. *The Englishman's Right: A Dialogue between a Barrister at Law, and a Juryman.* Printed for Richard Janeway, in Queenshead Alley in Paternoster-Row, London. Reprinted New York: Garland, 1978.

Hawthorne, John. 2004. *Knowledge and Lotteries.* Oxford: Oxford University Press.

Hawthorne, John, and Amia Srinivasan. 2013. Disagreement Without Transparency: Some Bleak Thoughts. In David Christensen and Jennifer Lackey (Eds.), *The Epistemology of Disagreement: New Essays* (pp. 9–30). Oxford: Oxford University Press.

H.E. 1664. *The Juryman charged; or a Letter to a Citizen of London.* n.p., London.

Ho, Hock Lai. 2008. Book Review: The Origins of Reasonable Doubt—Theological Roots of the Criminal Trial by James Q. Whitman. *Singapore Journal of Legal Studies*, 2008(2): 455–62.

Ichikawa, Jonathan, and Matthias Steup. 2018. The Analysis of Knowledge. In Edward N. Zalta (Ed.), *The Stanford Encyclopedia of Philosophy (Summer 2018 Edition).* Available at https://plato.stanford.edu/archives/sum2018/entries/knowledge-analysis/.

Koehler, Jonathan J. 2002. When Do Courts Think Base Rate Statistics Are Relevant? *Jurimetrics*, 42(4): 373–402.

Lasonen-Aarnio, Maria. 2010. Unreasonable Knowledge. *Philosophical Perspectives*, 24(1): 1–21.

Laudan, Larry, and Harry Saunders. 2009. Re-Thinking the Criminal Standard of Proof: Seeking Consensus about the Utilities of Trial Outcomes. *International Commentary on Evidence*, 7(2): 1–34.

Lewis, David K. 1996. Elusive Knowledge. *Australasian Journal of Philosophy*, 74(4): 549–67.

Lillquist, Erik. 2002. Recasting Reasonable Doubt: Decision Theory and the Virtues of Variability. *U.C. Davis Law Review*, 36(1): 85–198.

Littlejohn, Clayton. 2020. Truth, Knowledge, and the Standard of Proof in Criminal Law. *Synthese* 197: 5253–86.

Magnussen, Svein, Dag Erik Eliertsen, Karl Halvor Teigen, and Ellen Wessel. 2014. The Probability of Guilt in Criminal Cases: Are People Aware of Being 'Beyond Reasonable Doubt'? *Applied Cognitive Psychology*, 28(2): 196–203.

McCauliff, C.M.A. 1982. Burdens of Proof: Degrees of Belief, Quanta of Evidence, or Constitutional Guarantees? *Vanderbilt Law Review*, 35(6): 1293–336.

Moore, G.E. 1962. *Commonplace Book: 1919–1953*. London: George Allen & Unwin Ltd.

Moss, Sarah. 2018a. Moral Encroachment. *Proceedings of the Aristotelian Society*, 118(2): 177–205.

Moss, Sarah. 2018b. *Probabilistic Knowledge*. Oxford: Oxford University Press.

Nagel, Jennifer. 2014. *Knowledge: A Very Short Introduction*. Oxford: Oxford University Press.

Nesson, Charles. 1979. Reasonable Doubt and Permissive Inferences: The Value of Complexity. *Harvard Law Review*, 92(6): 1187–225.

Nozick, Robert. 1981. *Philosophical Explanations*. Cambridge, MA: Harvard University Press.

Paley, William. 1785. *Principles of Moral and Political Philosophy*. Printed for R. Faulder, London.

Pardo, Michael. 2005. The Field of Evidence and the Field of Knowledge. *Law and Philosophy*, 24(4): 321–92.

Pardo, Michael. 2010a. The Gettier Problem and Legal Proof. *Legal Theory*, 16(1): 37–57.

Pardo, Michael. 2010b. Pleadings, Proof, and Judgment: A Unified Theory of Civil Litigation. *Boston College Law Review*, 51(5): 1451–510.

Pritchard, Duncan. 2015. Risk. *Metaphilosophy*, 46(3): 436–61.

Redmayne, Mike. 2008. Exploring the Proof Paradoxes. *Legal Theory*, 14(4): 281–309.

Roth, Andrea. 2010. Safety in Numbers? Deciding When DNA Alone Is Enough to Convict. *New York University Law Review*, 85(4): 1130–85.

Saks, Michael J., and Robert F. Kidd. 1980. Human Information Processing and Adjudication: Trial by Heuristics. *Law & Society Review*, 15(1): 123–60.

Sand, Leonard, and Danielle Rose. 2003. Proof Beyond All Possible Doubt: Is There a Need for a Higher Burden of Proof when the Sentence may be Death? *Chicago-Kent Law Review*, 78(3): 1359–75.

Schauer, Frederick. 2003. *Profiles, Probabilities, and Stereotypes*. Cambridge, MA: Harvard University Press.

Shaviro, Daniel. 1989. Statistical-Probability Evidence and the Appearance of Justice. *Harvard Law Review*, 103(2): 530–54.

Smith, Martin. 2018. When Does Evidence Suffice for Conviction? *Mind*, 127(508): 1193–218.

Sorensen, Roy. 2006. Future Law: Prepunishment and the Causal Theory of Verdicts. *Noûs*, 40(1): 166–83.

Sosa, Ernest. 1999. How to Defeat Opposition to Moore. *Philosophical Perspectives*, 13: 141–53.

Stanley, Jason. 2005. *Knowledge and Practical Interests*. Oxford: Oxford University Press.

Steel, Sandy. 2015. Justifying Exceptions to Proof of Causation in Tort Law. 78(5): 729–58.

Stein, Alex. 2005. *Foundations of Evidence Law*. Oxford: Oxford University Press.

Thomson, Judith Jarvis. 1986. Liability and Individualized Evidence. *Law and Contemporary Problems*, 49(3): 199–219.

Tribe, Laurence H. 1971. Trial by Mathematics: Precision and Ritual in the Legal Process. *Harvard Law Review*, 84(6): 1329–93.

Unger, Peter. 1975. *Ignorance: A Case for Scepticism*. Oxford: Clarendon Press.

Vogel, Jonathan. 1990. Are There Counterexamples to the Closure Principle? In Michael D. Roth and Glenn Ross (Eds.), *Doubting: Contemporary Perspectives on Skepticism* (pp. 13–25). Dordrecht: Kluwer.

Wasserman, David T. 1991. The Morality of Statistical Proof and the Risk of Mistaken Liability. *Cardozo Law Review*, 13(2–3): 935–76.

White, Aaron Steven, and Kyle Rawlins. 2018. The Role of Veridicality and Factivity in Clause Selection. In Sherry Hucklebridge and Max Nelson (Eds.), *Proceedings of the 48th Annual Meeting of the North East Linguistic Society* (pp. 221–34). Amherst, MA: GLSA Publications.

Whitman, James. 2008. *The Origins of Reasonable Doubt: Theological Roots of the Criminal Trial*. New Haven, CT: Yale University Press.

Wigmore, John Henry. 1923. *A Treatise on the Anglo-American System of Evidence in Trials at Common Law, 3rd edn*. Boston, MA: Little, Brown and Company.

Williams, Glanville. 1980. A Short Rejoinder. *Criminal Law Review*, 1980: 103–7.

Williamson, Timothy. 2000. *Knowledge and its Limits*. Oxford: Oxford University Press.

Williamson, Timothy. 2015. Justifications, Excuses, and Sceptical Scenarios. Ms., Department of Philosophy, Oxford University. Forthcoming in Julien Dutant and Daniel Dorsch (Eds.), *The New Evil Demon: New Essays on Knowledge, Rationality and Justification*. Oxford: Oxford University Press.

Worsnip, Alex. 2015. Two Kinds of Stakes. *Pacific Philosophical Quarterly*, 96(3): 307–24.

Zuckerman, Adrian A.S. 1986. Law, Fact or Justice? *Boston University Law Review*, 66(4): 487–508.

7
Trust as an Unquestioning Attitude

C. Thi Nguyen

1. Suspending Deliberation

In most accounts, trust is a conscious attitude, in which we attribute some particular attitude or mental state to another agent. In some such accounts, trust is supposed to be a belief that another person will properly support you. To trust somebody is to think that they have goodwill towards you, will be responsive to your needs, or something to that effect. In other accounts, trust turns out to be an attitude we adopt for various social reasons, which encourages us to rely on others and believe what they say. All these accounts share two features. First, trust is an attitude that is only directed towards other agents. Second, trust is supposed to be a clear and present rational force. It is an active participant in an ongoing deliberative process.

I would like to explore a very different alternative: that there is a form of trust which involves a suspension of the deliberative process. To trust something, in this sense, is to put its reliability outside the space of evaluation and deliberation. To trust something is to rely on it, without pausing to think about whether it will actually come through for you. To trust an informational source wholeheartedly is to accept its claims without pausing to worry or evaluate that source's trustworthiness. To trust, in short, is to adopt an unquestioning attitude. Which is not to say that one can't sometimes question one's trust, or reason about whether one ought to trust that source. Unquestioning trust can certainly arise out of deliberation and it can certainly be called into question. But when one has actually come to trust in this way, one has adopted, for the moment, an unquestioning attitude. And limited beings like us, I will suggest, must often take up such unquestioning attitudes as part of a reasonable strategy for coping with the cognitive onslaught of the world.

Crucially, we can take an unquestioning attitude towards non-agents: simple objects, body parts, and features of the natural world. I can trust my legs and I can trust the ground. To understand why this is a significant departure from other theories of trust, we need to look at the history of the philosophical work on trust. That literature springs from a couple of inquiries. First, philosophers have been interested in the morality of trust and how it plays out in various efforts of cooperation and social relationships (Baier 1986, 1992; Baker 1987; Holton

C. Thi Nguyen, *Trust as an Unquestioning Attitude* In: *Oxford Studies in Epistemology, Volume 7.* Edited by: Tamar Szabó Gendler, John Hawthorne, and Julianne Chung, Oxford University Press.
DOI: 10.1093/oso/9780192868978.003.0007

1994; Jones 1996, 2012; McLeod 2002; O'Neill 2002a, 2002b). This conversation tends to focus on how trust works in distinctively moral, social, and political settings. Second, philosophers have been concerned with the epistemology of trust and how we might acquire knowledge through testimony (Hardwig 1991; Hinchman 2005; Faulkner 2007a; 2011; Hieronymi 2008; Lackey 2008; Nickel 2012; Keren 2014). These discussions of trust all share a central presumption: that trust is agent-directed. That is, trust is taken to be an attitude of one agent *directed toward some other agent.*

We can find these presumptions articulated clearly in the opening moments of the modern conversation on trust. Annette Baier's pioneering work on trust sets the focus on agent-directed attitudes. There are, she says, two distinct attitudes which our colloquial use of "trust" blurs together. She proposes a terminological refinement: first, there is the attitude of *mere reliance*, in which we simply depend on something. Second, there is the more normatively loaded attitude of *trust.* Suppose I notice that you pass by my door every day at five minutes before noon, and I start to use your passing as my signal that it's time to go teach my class. In this case, I have merely come to rely on you. If you didn't pass by at noon one day, I might be disappointed, but I could make no reasonable criticism of you. But if you promised me you would knock on my door to remind me but failed to do so, I would feel, not only disappointed, but *betrayed.* I had trusted you and you let me down. Our relationship towards objects, says Baier, can be one of, at most, reliance. It is only other people that we might come to trust. And the possibility of betrayal is a telling sign of the presence of full-blooded trust (Baier 1986).

The ensuing conversation has largely followed Baier's basic framework. Philosophers have accepted her claim that trust is essentially agent-directed. And they have followed Baier in treating the possibility of betrayal as the sign that trust is present. Thus, they have studied betrayal in order to understand the content of trust. How might the reaction of betrayal be appropriate? In what might it be normatively grounded?

Baier suggests that trust involves ascribing goodwill to the trusted, and that our sense of betrayal comes from the discovery that there is no such goodwill after all. Baier's account has seen some notable counterexamples—such as Onora O'Neill's observation that you may trust a doctor simply for their professionalism, with no expectation of goodwill whatsoever (O'Neill 2002: 14). Most theorists have since abandoned Baier's particular emphasis on goodwill, but many new theories of trust still retain the basic shape of her proposal. Some theories replace Baier's focus on goodwill with a focus on *responsiveness.* According to responsiveness theories of trust, to trust somebody is to think that they will respond to your trust positively. As Karen Jones puts it, a trustworthy person "takes the fact that they are counted on to be a reason for acting as counted on" (Jones 2012: 66). For a trustworthy person, the very fact that you are putting your trust in them gives them a reason to fulfill that trust. Similarly, Paul Faulkner suggests that when one person trusts another, the truster knowingly depends on the trusted to do something, and expects the trusted's knowledge of this dependence to motivate them to do it (Faulkner 2007b: 313). Betrayal, then, is grounded in the betrayer's failure to be properly responsive. Katherine Hawley, on the other hand, rejects the details of the responsiveness account, but still analyzes trust in agent-directed terms. For Hawley, to trust somebody is to take them to have made a commitment to do something and to rely on them to fulfill that commitment (Hawley 2014). Hawley's account grounds the sense of betrayal in the trusted person's failure to live up to their commitments.

Note that Baier's account, Hawley's account, and the responsiveness account all share the presumption that trust is agent-oriented. To put it more precisely, the presumption is that the truster must *ascribe some complete agential state* to the trusted—be it a belief, motivation, disposition, or commitment. It follows, then, that trust is appropriately directed only towards things that can bear agential states: people and group agents, like nations and corporations (Hawley 2017). Perhaps we can also trust certain complex technological artifacts, like Google Search, precisely when we can attribute some form of agency to them. But we cannot trust or distrust dumb objects with no agencies of their own.

My proposed account rejects this presumption. I will describe a form of trust that need not ascribe any complete agential states to its target. We can, in fact, take the unquestioning attitude towards a wide variety of objects and artifacts. To trust, in this sense, is to have stepped back from the deliberative process; it is to have settled one's mind about something. It is to lower the barrier of monitoring, challenging, checking, and questioning—to let something inside, to let it play an immediate role in one's cognition and activity. When we trust, we give some external resource a direct line into our reasoning and agency. Trust is our mechanism for *integrating* other people and objects into our own functioning. This form of trust is still deeply bound up with agency, but it need not only be directed towards complete, external agents. We can be betrayed by objects, then, not because some distinct external agent in them has failed us, but because we have attempted to integrate them into our own agency, only to have them malfunction. Our response of betrayal towards those objects, then, is a close cousin of the betrayal we can feel towards our own recalcitrant, failing parts.

I do not suggest that this account of unquestioning trust be taken to replace, or subsume, the traditional agential accounts of trust. Rather, I will suggest that the unquestioning attitude is one form of trust; the agent-oriented accounts of trust chart another form. And these different forms of trust can interact. For example, I might take an unquestioning attitude towards somebody precisely because I take them to have goodwill towards me (or to be otherwise appropriately responsive). But they can also come apart. I trust the ground in the unquestioning attitude sense, and not any agent-directed sense. Finally, I will suggest that there is a reason that we group these various attitudes together under the umbrella of "trust": they are all ways we have of expanding our agency by integrating in bits of the external world. Responsive cooperation and the unquestioning attitude are two tools for agential expansion and integration. And I will suggest that the unquestioning attitude sense of trust is actually quite pervasive, and that, in many cases, when we say that we trust an agent, the indicated trust is partially or primarily of the unquestioning attitude variety.

2. Trusting the Ground

The trust literature shares a common founding presumption: that trust is a relationship we could only have towards other independent agents. Talk of trust towards simple, non-agential objects has been easily dismissed. After all, the colloquial language is fuzzy here. Everyday talk of trust in objects can simply be interpreted, in our newly technical language, as concerning mere reliance. After all, how could you ever be betrayed by an object? And isn't the response of betrayal only appropriate when it is directed towards other agents?

But if we look beyond the philosophical discussion of trust and morality—if we look to literature and to life—it's easy to find descriptions of trust in objects. I will, for the rest of this paper, use "trust" to refer to the full-blooded, normatively loaded sense and use "objects" to refer to non-agential objects. And I will take onboard Baier's diagnostic. A sign that we aren't merely relying on objects, but actually trusting them, is in the presence of that distinctive reaction to trust's breach: that sharply negative, normatively loaded response. We know we are in the presence of trust when we are willing to speak of betrayal.

A caveat: the goal here is not to show that we can somehow be betrayed by objects in precisely the same way that we can be betrayed by people. I am not trying to show that simple objects can somehow be the subject of moral criticism. Rather, I am groping towards a description of a genus of which there are at least two species. I am looking for the underlying similarities between trust in people and trust in objects that makes us so willing to reach for the same terms in both circumstances. Trust involves *something more* than mere reliance, and betrayal involves *something more* than mere disappointment—though those somethings might come in a variety of flavors.

Climbers speak of trusting the rope; they react with something far sharper than mere disappointment when a rope goes bad. And this form of trust is not just limited to human artifacts. We feel betrayed when the ladder gives way beneath us, but also by the collapse of that solid-seeming tree which we were climbing. We speak of trusting the ground and of being betrayed by it when good footing turns unexpectedly bad. And we speak of the shock of discovering the untrustworthiness of our own faculties and parts—of being betrayed by the shakiness of our hands or by our faltering memory. Superficially, these sorts of examples seem to weigh against the insistence that trust always be directed at agents. Our talk of betrayal seems to indicate that our relationship to our own parts is one of trust.

I will begin in the familiar mode of conceptual analysis, but that is only a starting point. My aim here is to key in on a real-world phenomenon, using our language and concepts as a pointer. And I have a larger purpose in this investigation. I think there is a distinctive relationship we can have with objects which goes beyond mere reliance—which is best described as a form of trust. Contemporary life is significantly marked by trust in technological artifacts and technologically-mediated social environments: Google's search algorithms, smart phones, the ranking algorithm behind Facebook and Twitter, and the emergent networks of interconnection on social media.[1] Our relationships with these objects, I suggest, is far more potent than mere reliance. One might respond that this is not really trust in objects, but trust in the designers behind those objects. Sanford Goldberg suggests that we can have normatively loaded relationships with designed artifacts, since we are willing to hold those designers to account when their artifacts fail us (Goldberg 2017). According to Goldberg, then, the sense of betrayal I feel when my iPhone fails me is really directed at the corporation and manufacturers.

But I think that there is a distinctive sense in which we can trust the object itself—in which we can trust even non-designed objects like the ground. And even with designed objects, I think our trust often cannot be wholly cashed out in terms of trust in the people and institutions which designed those objects. First, many of the artifacts we trust have run beyond their creators' abilities to understand or control. One of the pressing issues in the ethics of technology involves thinking about machine-learning algorithms, which have been built using evolutionary techniques, whose innards and proceedings aren't understood by those who have built them (Resch and Kaminski 2019; Carabantes 2019). Similarly, key features of the network architecture of online social structures, such as social media, have evolved beyond the intentional control of the institutions that have made them. Second, the question of our trust in a particular object is often distinct from that of our trust in its manufacturers. Climbers, for example, need to decide whether to trust an old rope. What matters is not the manufacturer's goodwill or intent in manufacturing its ropes. The question is whether this particular rope should still be trusted, after its particular life-history of use and abuse.

So let's start by thinking about our trust in obviously non-agential and undesigned parts of the world. When I walk, I usually trust the ground. This means more than simply relying on the ground. When I trust the ground, I walk

[1] For starters, see Pariser (2012); Miller and Record (2013); Frost-Arnold (2014); Frost-Arnold (2016); Rini (2017); Nguyen (2018b). Many of these accounts speak of how these technologies mediate trust in other agents, rather than speaking of trusting in the technologies themselves, but I think that is due, in part, to the lack of theoretical resources available to make sense of trust in objects.

without bothering to consider whether it will be steady beneath my feet. I don't evaluate the ground or ponder its supportiveness. I simply walk on it while thinking of other things. When I distrust the ground, on the other hand, I am constantly questioning its reliability. I worry about it; I test it. If I am walking across a muddy field, riddled with gopher holes, I'll examine the ground carefully before each step. And even when I do force myself to rely on that muddy ground—when I commit my weight to it—I don't, as yet, trust it. My reliance is tentative and demands constant reassurance. But when I trust the ground, I stop worrying about it. And the difference between mere reliance on the ground and the unquestioning attitude of trust tracks our different negative reactions. When I hesitantly rely on the ground, I am merely glumly disappointed when it gives way. But it is when I am walking without thinking about it—when the ground has become automatically and unthinkingly integrated into my background physical processes—that I react with shock and betrayal when the ground collapses beneath my feet.

I suggest that the form of trust here is best described as an unquestioning attitude. To trust something in this way is to rely on it while putting its reliability out of mind. When we don't trust, we question. Sometimes the answers to our questions might be positive; sometimes they might be negative. We may decide to rely after we've gone through the questioning process. But the lack of trust is shown in the very process of active investigation itself. It is only when we have settled our mind and stopped actively questioning something that we truly trust it, in this sense.

This does not mean that when you trust something, you never question it at all. To trust something is to have a general disposition not to question it. That disposition can be disrupted or overwhelmed for the moment, but we are still trusting it, so long as we are generally disposed to not question it. We only lose trust when we lose the disposition itself. And this explains how trust can exist on a spectrum: dispositions come in degrees.

I have found that philosophers who work on trust and testimony think that this use of "trust" is bizarre and unintuitive—especially locutions like "trusting the ground" and feeling "betrayed by the ground." But it seems to me, in fact, that these expressions are entirely natural and comprehensible, and it is only excess immersion in modern, narrowed philosophical theories of trust that renders these locutions odd to the ear.

We can find talk of trust in and betrayal by the ground throughout ordinary speech. Consider this advice from a manual on trail running.

> So pay attention ... Don't trust wooden structures. Stiles, bridges, fences, tiger traps, path edges: no matter how inviting they look, unless you have thoroughly tested them before, DON'T TRUST THEM.... Very few running mishaps result in such painful or long-lasting injuries as overconfident approaches to wooden

> structures. Just slow right down for a few strides and, if possible, find something to hold on to as you go... Oh yes, and don't trust the ground on either side of wooden structures either — in case you were thinking of leaping over one... The ground on either side will be much trodden and thus probably churned up, slippery, and generally untrustworthy. Just relax, take that extra second and speed up again when you're on the other side. (Askwith 2015: 150)

Notice that the runner here is not being told to avoid relying on the ground. Sometimes, you must rely, because there is no other place to step and nothing else to hold on to. The runner is being asked to suspend their unthinkingness, to pay attention, and to be careful. They are being asked to rely on the ground, but in a mode of interrogating, suspicious awareness. They are not being told to avoid any form of reliance; they are being told to suspend their trust even while they are forced to rely.

The presence of trust and betrayal are clear in certain experiences of profound violations of trust in one's environment. From a sociological investigation into the experience of war:

> The veteran also suffers from a problem of trust, a building block on which all of social life is erected. The everyday, taken-for-granted reality of civilian life ignores much; civility assumes the nonlethal intentions of others. In war, however, all such assumptions evaporate: one cannot trust the ground one walks on, the air one breathes, nor can one expect with full assuredness that tomorrow will come again. (Kearl 1989: 353)

The best explanation here is not that soldiers in war have suspended their reliance—after all, one cannot but rely on the ground and the air. What changes is their attitude towards that reliance. They become suspicious, unable to rest easy on the assurance that the ground and air will continue to support them. We reach for the language of trust here, I think, because we are trying to describe a relationship more loaded and more powerful than mere reliance.

Tellingly, the language of trust and betrayal often crops up in stories about the emotional aftermath of earthquakes. Douglas Kahn writes:

> I will never forget being in an earthquake near Seattle in which the ground itself became acoustic, with swelling waves traveling down through the road making houses I knew well bob up and down like ships on the sea. "A moment destroys the illusion of a whole life," writes Alexander von Humboldt in *Cosmos*. "Our deceptive faith run the repose of nature vanishes, and we feel transported as it were into a realm of unknown destructive forces. Every sound—the faintest motion in the air—arrests our attention, and we no longer trust the ground on which we stand." (Kahn 2013: 133)

And here is Betty Berzon's earthquake story:

> The house rocked and rolled, the glassware fell out of the cabinets, the pictures slid off the walls, the furniture skidded across the floor, and light fixtures came crashing down from the ceiling... I was frozen with fright and sure the house would topple over and end up in the street below. I was certainly going to die... The 6.6 earthquake and the aftershocks continue into the next day, but the house didn't fall down. There is something about being betrayed by the ground underneath you that feels like the ultimate treachery. It took weeks to regain my equilibrium. (Berzon 2002: 166)

These samplings make clear that we can trust objects in the more substantive sense. And the loss of trust can hit us in a similarly sharp register, whether it be in other people, the ground, or the air. These narratives make clear that this loss of trust must be something beyond the loss of mere reliance. After an earthquake, we must still rely on the ground. After war, we must still rely on the air. But suspicion intrudes upon us, and we find that we can no longer take their reliability for granted. Our mind is profoundly unsettled. (The fact that many philosophers find it odd to speak of being betrayed by their environment is perhaps partly explained by the fact that most philosophers have led, by and large, pretty cushy lives.)

Of course, one might continue to insist that these uses of "trust" and "betrayal" are merely metaphorical. They do not sound so to my ear. Saying that one felt betrayed by the ground after an earthquake, or by one's failing memory, strike me as paradigmatic invocations of the concept. But I do not think that we can settle the matter here just by comparing the intuitive rings of various locutions in our various ears. More importantly, even if this use is merely metaphorical, there is a reason why we reach for this particular metaphor—a reason why we reach for the terms "trust" and "betrayal" when we find ourselves profoundly perturbed by an earthquake. What's most important here is to understand the nature of the heightened form of relationship we sometimes hold towards objects, which goes beyond mere reliance, and which could ground the sharply negative response we have when it breaks.

3. Trust in the Background

Such an unquestioning attitude occurs in our relationships with other agents, too. I trust my doctor about medical advice when I take their medical suggestions as immediate reasons to act, without pausing to check their credentials or worrying about their ulterior motives for selling me this drug. I trust the newspaper when I simply accept its pronouncements without worrying about whether its staff might be financially biased or lazy. A soldier trusts their squad mates when they plunge ahead, accepting without question that their squad mates have their back.

I was once involved in a car accident; another driver lost control of their car and swerved across a narrow country highway, hitting me head-on. Afterwards, I lost my trust in other drivers. In fact, I hadn't realized how much I had been trusting other drivers until that trust had evaporated. What had changed? It wasn't my attributions of goodwill or responsiveness to other drivers. If you had asked me, I would have made the same evaluation of the relative goodwill and responsiveness of the average driver on the road, both before and after the accident. What changed, in the accident, was my ability to sink into that unquestioning state. The accident left me stuck in a constant state of suspicion. And note, once again: I relied on other drivers before the accident, and I still relied on other drivers just as much after the accident. Both before and after, I relied on them precisely because I took them to be responsive to my needs—and took myself to have reasons to think them properly responsive. What had changed—what had evaporated—was my easy, settled, unquestioning state of mind.

So I think that, when we say we trust agents, often much of that trust is actually to be cashed out in terms of the unquestioning attitude sense of trust, instead of strictly in terms of the various agent-directed accounts, which require that the trustor attribute to the trusted some agential state. But this is often misunderstood, because the conversation about trust has sometimes focused, I think, on the wrong sorts of cases. We often focus our analysis on those cases where trust comes to mind. But that focus may, in fact, be misleading. Trust is so common—it is such a background feature of our lives—that, much of the time, we don't even notice how much we trust. Often, it is only when our trust is threatened that we suddenly realize how much we have been trusting all along—as with my car accident. As Baier puts it, we inhabit trust like we inhabit the air, and we only notice it when it has departed (Baier 1986: 99; Jones 2004).

Thomas Simpson suggests that all our varied talk of trust descends from a simple root notion. We all partake of a kind of primitive ur-trust when we rely on others to act cooperatively. But this ur-trust is such a pervasive background feature of our lives that we barely notice it. Trust only comes to mind once it has been threatened. The fact that we are actively thinking and talking about our trust actually indicates that we are likely at the peripheries of the core phenomena (Simpson 2012: 560–1). This suggestion is quite striking. It means, for one thing, that if we only analyze those incidents where issues of trust have entered into our explicit conversation, then we might miss the real heart of the matter. And it explains why different conversations about trust can have very distinctive characters, even though they share a root phenomenon. Talk of trust arises in response to a particular threat; there are many different ways that trust can be threatened, which demand different flavors of response.

In this light, let's reconsider some of the standard examples that have fueled the literature on trust. Take Richard Holton's central case, from which he builds much of his account of trust: the trust fall, an exercise beloved of acting groups and management training consultants, where we make ourselves fall into the arms of others. When we take a trust fall, says Holton, we decide to trust. We will ourselves to trust. It is cases like this that suggest, to Holton, that trust can be voluntary, and that it can outrun the evidence. We do not know if people will catch us, but we decide to trust them in order to find out (Holton 1994). If we focused exclusively on cases like this, we might think that trust is not so unthinking, after all. The process of questioning and weighing considerations seem quite prominent with the trust fall. The novice climber, too, typically engages in such a tentative, conscious process as they learn to trust the rope. If we take these sorts of trust fall cases to be paradigmatic, then it would be a serious mark against my account. After all, here is a moment of trust in objects which is full of consciousness, indecisiveness, and questioning.

But notice that the management camp's staged trust fall is actually a case at the periphery of trust. Trust falls are done between people that do not trust, as an exercise in learning how to trust.[2] Similarly, the novice climber who nervously talks themselves into taking practice fall after practice fall onto the rope is not yet fully trusting; they are at an early stage on the long journey to trust. The paradigm of trust, in catching and falling, looks quite different. Consider the experienced rock climber's attitude toward their rope and their gear. A novice rock climber tests the rope gingerly, occasionally weighting it, telling themselves over and over again to trust it. While they are engaged in this process of self-negotiation and self-reassurance, we would say that they do not yet fully trust the rope. They are at the beginning of the process of learning to trust. It is the experienced rock climber who truly trusts their rope. Their trust is reflected in the fact that concerns about the rope's reliability occupies no mental space for them at all. And that trust lets them focus all their mental efforts on the climb itself (Ilgner 2006).

4. Trust and Resolve

In order to make out how trust in objects might work, we need to provide an account in which the trustor might reasonably trust objects, and reasonably expect something of those objects—in ways that might justify a sharply negative, normatively loaded response to failure. But, at the same time, that account should not demand that trust involve attributing any complete agential states to the trusted.

[2] Pamela Hieronymi offers a similar explanation of Holton's discussion: that what we are doing here is not full-blooded trust, but merely entrusting—acting *as if* we trusted, as part of the process of building trust (Hieronymi 2008).

I will now suggest such an account. But first, a caveat. I am quite confident of my claims up to this point: that there exists a distinctive form of trust, which involves taking on an unquestioning attitude. Now, I will make a first attempt at providing the detailed account of the unquestioning attitude. My confidence in the ensuing particulars is far more modest.

I take inspiration here from a very different sector of Holton's philosophical work: his analysis of weakness and strength of will. Let's examine his account in some depth. To exercise willpower, says Holton, is to close yourself to a certain kind of reconsideration. It is to decisively settle your mind in a certain direction, to armor yourself against re-opening further deliberation down the line. Holton is building here on Michael Bratman's account of intentions. Suppose I form an intention at one moment. Crucially, at a later moment, I can act directly from that previously formed intention. I don't treat my remembered intention as the mere issuances of some distinct past self. And I don't re-deliberate, treating my past self's decision as merely one input among many. In ordinary circumstances, I simply act on my past intentions. What it is to form an intention is to make up one's mind in a way that extends to one's future self. It is to have decided for one's future self. In order to perform that role, intentions must have a certain stability. They must exhibit *cognitive inertia*. This doesn't mean that they can't ever be re-considered, only that the standards for re-consideration are now much higher. All sorts of reasons that might play into deciding where I should go to dinner tonight—like the balance of my current desires or the exact state of our bank account. But once I form the intention to go to Roscoe's House of Chicken and Waffles, I don't re-consider it for minor fluctuations in these sorts of facts. I will only re-open deliberation on my intention if something major happens, like Roscoe's catching fire, or a violent case of the stomach flu.

Why do I close myself off in this way? First, says Bratman, we need to fix intentions in order to make plans, both with ourselves and with others.[3] But behind this lies a set of deeper considerations—ones which wrestle with our cognitive finitude. I only have so many cognitive resources to go around, and this is a way to conserve them. I decide certain things, and resist re-opening that decision for further deliberation, in order to free up cognitive resources. The cognitive inertia of intentions functions to conserve our cognitive resources. Limited beings need to settle their minds about some things in order to free up cognitive resources for other projects.

But sometimes, says Holton, we need something stronger than an intention: we need a *resolution*. We make resolutions when we need to steel ourselves against future temptations. A resolution, says Holton, is a pair of intentions: it is an intention to do something, and then a second-order intention not to let that first-

[3] Holton (2009: 2–4); Bratman (1987). My terminology and framing here draws on Holton's presentation of Bratman.

order intention be deflected (Holton 2009: 11). In other words, willpower includes the power to *actively refuse to reconsider* intentions. It is, we might say, willful inertia. And we breach a resolution when we open it up to the possibility of revision. The refusal to reconsider helps resolutions to play their particular role. As Holton puts it:

> ...Much of the point of a resolution, as with any other intention, is that it is a fixed point around which other actions — one's own and those of others — can be coordinated. To reconsider an intention is exactly to remove that status from it. (121–2)

I suggest that the unquestioning attitude of trust plays a similar role to that of resolutions in settling the mind. I do not mean that trust is a kind of resolution. I mean, instead, to indicate a functional similarity between trust and making resolutions. Trust is a strategy to cope with our cognitive finitude and manage our limited cognitive resources—to steel ourselves across time against new evidence by (defeasibly) closing our minds against re-consideration. Trust is a way of establishing fixed points in our deliberation. And trust is distinct from resolutions, because it is a way of establishing *external* fixed points—resources that we will always accept without question, resources that we will rely on without thought.

Here is the *unquestioning attitude* account of trust:

> To trust X to P is to have an attitude of not questioning that X will P.

We can also offer a specific instantiation of this unquestioning trust, for trusting informational sources:

> To trust X as an informational source in domain Z is to have an attitude of not questioning X's deliverances concerning Z.[4]

Let's take a look under the hood. I intend the notion of the "attitude of not questioning" to have a similar two-tiered structure as Holton's account of resolutions. To trust X to P is to have a first-order disposition to immediately accept that X will P, and a second-order disposition to deflect questioning about the first-order disposition.

[4] "Deliverances" here is meant to be a general term for transmitting propositional content. The deliverances of other people are usually what we call "testimony." But other cases of trusting informational sources' deliverances include: trusting my watch to tell the time; trusting my eyes to deliver accurate visual information; trusting my calendaring system to auto-sync between my phone, laptop, and tablet and report to me the events that I have entered into it; and trusting Google Search to deliver search results organized by relevance.

First, note that having an unquestioning attitude that X will P does not involve a disposition to come to a particular conclusion from deliberation about whether X will P, or to discount certain forms of evidence while deliberating about whether X will P. It is a disposition against deliberating, in the first place, about whether X will P.[5] Second, an unquestioning attitude is defeasible, but the reasons needed for defeating the unquestioning attitude that X will P need to be significantly stronger than merely being reasons that bear against belief that X will P. The unquestioning attitude towards X's doing P is thus *resistant*: it maintains itself against some classes of considerations that would normally weigh against my believing that X will P. Third, the account is intended to indicate a spectrum concept, with many shadings. Since one can hold the dispositions with varying degrees of force, one can trust with varying degrees of unreservedness. Finally, in almost all cases, the scope of trust in X will be restricted to particular functions of X. However, in colloquial usage, the specification of the domain of trust is often implicit and understood from context—usually because there is some understood role or standard function. When I say I trust my doctor, I can usually be understood to mean that I trust my doctor to perform their medical duties, and not that I trust them to successfully do modal logic or play jazz.

Next, notice that the account does not say that to trust X to P is to not question X in any way. It says, rather, that to trust X is *not to question that X will P*. That is, when I trust X to P, I don't question X's efficacy in particular instances of doing P. By the account I've given, it is possible to trust that X will P while asking questions about X in general—so long as we accept X's particular deliverances and affordances in regards to P. It's possible to trust something and, at the same time, to ask general questions about that thing's reliable functioning, *so long as we don't question particular instances of that functioning*. For example: suppose Esi is a memory researcher. Her research focuses on the fallibility of memory; she frequently asks questions about human memory in general and is willing to extend those theoretical worries to her own memory. But so far as she acts unquestioningly on the particular delivered content of her memory, then she still can be said to trust her memory. So long as she doesn't question her memories of what she had for breakfast, what time her doctor's appointment is, and what her grandparents were like, then she still trusts her memory to deliver information. Of course, questioning her memory in general may lead to questioning particular contents presented by her memory—but the two levels of questioning are distinct. Similarly, academic philosophers can ask as many questions as they like about the justifiability of accepting the deliverances of their senses and still be said to trust

[5] My account here shares certain thematic similarities to Lara Buchak's account of faith as steadfastness in the face of counter-evidence (Buchak 2017), but there is a key difference. Buchak's analysis concerns cases in which it is rational for me to commit myself in a way so as to ignore counter-evidence during deliberation; my analysis concerns when we suspend deliberation altogether.

their senses, so long as they accept the particular deliverances of their senses without questioning them. It is only when you begin to question whether this apparent car is really a car that you can be said to distrust your senses.

Importantly, trust is an unquestioning *attitude*—understood as a two-tiered set of dispositions—and not a total cessation of questioning. Those dispositions can be defeated in the moment and yet still remain dispositions. I may trust my friend about all movie trivia, and then come across good reason to think they have probably made a particular mistake about the casting history of Ozu's *Late Spring*—and so come to question my friend's claims about a particular narrow range of facts. That doesn't destroy my trust in my friend's encyclopedic movie knowledge, because it doesn't budge my overall disposition to accept their claims unquestioningly. I will still resist weighing most run-of-the-mill considerations. The inertia of trust can survive the occasional disturbance. I only lose trust when I lose that inertia—when I lose the dispositions against questioning, and let any sort of considerations trigger questioning and redeliberation about any of their claims.

Furthermore, the account specifies that trust is an unquestioning attitude, and not that it has gone unquestioned. The account is entirely compatible with my having questioned, sought justifications for, and deciding to trust, prior to my actually being in the trusting state. Don't confuse the issue of what it is to trust with the issue of the basis on which one has come to trust. I can decide to trust this rope to hold my weight because it has held it so many times in the past. But what it is to decide to trust the rope is to decide, henceforth, to stop questioning it.

The unquestioning attitude account is also compatible with forms of trust which have never been questioned, and for which I have no reasons. Naive trust in authority and in the physical environment often has such a character. As Baier says, any adequate account of trust has to take into account the trust of children for their caregivers (Baier 1986: 240–6). And I take it that, when my toddler eats the food I give him, he has no reasons for his unquestioning acceptance of what I hand him. He has always trusted me and he gobbles it all up without a moment's hesitation. A point in favor of the unquestioning attitude account is how well it models such naive, unconsidered trust. My toddler's trust in me is one of the paradigmatic instances of trust—but it is not best explained in terms of his attributing some commitment or benevolence to me. It is something more primitive than that. His trust, I suggest, is constituted by his unquestioning acceptance of my food offerings.

The unquestioning attitude account also explains why trust is often recalcitrant. I often find it hard to trust, even if all my reasons indicate that I should.[6] I may have every reason to think my belayer and my climbing rope trustworthy—but,

[6] The observation of recalcitrance comes from Baker (1987). Karen Jones has offered a different account of the recalcitrance of trust. She suggests that trust is an affective attitude of optimism about

still, I might find myself unable to trust. I have come to trust only when I actually have made the transition to the unquestioning attitude. Consider a well-documented exercise for learning to trust: Arno Ilgner's technique for training climbers to trust their gear and their belayer. A beginning climber has likely done their research and learned that modern ropes simply do not break in standard circumstances and that modern climbing gear is at least as trustworthy as, say, a car. They have, hopefully, also chosen a belayer who they have every reason to think trustworthy. But many beginning climbers find that they still cannot banish worries about the rope and the belayer from their mind, which limits their ability to climb fearlessly and efficiently.

Imagine a beginning climber, halfway up a wall, who is already depending on their rope and belayer to save their life, but who is suddenly beset by worries and questions. Here is a very natural way to describe their attitude: they, as a matter of fact, are currently relying on their rope and belayer to save their life, but they have not yet come to entirely trust their rope and belayer. Ilgner's solution to this mental difficulty is simply to practice falling, in enormous volume. The climber must climb a little bit above their last anchor point and jump off so many times that they simply become bored. Then they must climb a little higher, and jump off, over and over again. And, over time, the evidence they have that the rope will not break becomes something else: a confidence so complete that it recedes into the background. Falling—and being caught by the rope—becomes ordinary. Then the climber can focus entirely on the climb itself, without having to worry about their gear or having to rehearse to themselves all the reasons they have to think it reliable (Ilgner 2006). The transition from mere reliance to trust here is exactly the transition between having the reasons to trust and having the further attitude of unquestioning acceptance. And note, too, that this unquestioning trust applies to a complex system that includes both simple objects—the rope and belay device—along with an agent.

5. The Integrative Stance

Does the unquestioning acceptance account meet our desiderata for an account of trust? Let's start with Hawley's demand for a tripartite account of trust. Hawley notes that reliance has only two states: we either rely on something or we don't. But with trust, she says, there are three distinctive states. We can either actively trust, actively distrust, or be in a third, neutral state—what Hawley calls non-trust.

the trusted's goodwill and competence (Jones 1996). My reasons for thinking trust is an attitude, rather than a set of reasons, borrows from Jones' analysis. Obviously, we cannot generalize her account's particular references to goodwill and competence to understand trust in objects.

Actively distrusting somebody is a very different state from merely not trusting them. Any theory of trust needs to account for all three of these possible registers.

The unquestioning acceptance account meets Hawley's demand quite tidily. To trust is to have an unquestioning attitude. To distrust is to have an actively questioning attitude. And to non-trust is to have a neutral attitude, which is entirely open and unresistant to questioning and non-questioning, as the situation suggests. I trust the ground when I don't think about it, and when that unthinkingness has been adopted as an attitude with some weight and resistance behind it. One uneven bit of sidewalk doesn't, by itself, disrupt my trust in the ground. I come to distrust the ground only when I have begun to actively worry about and question each step. And I non-trust the ground when I maintain neither attitude with any cognitive inertia, but simply react to considerations as they arise. Most of the time, my trust settings are something like this: I trust the sidewalk and the highway; I distrust swampy and icy ground; and I non-trust natural grassy plains and the average backcountry hiking paths. To put it more technically: non-trust involves no disposition to avoid questioning. When I non-trust the hiking path, I may walk for a while without actively questioning every step, but I have no disposition to resist questioning if any relevant considerations arise, like a bumpy patch.

Now for the main event: we need to explain how this form of trust is something above and beyond mere reliance. And we need to do so in a way that could help explain why we might feel betrayal. On a first pass, our language is full of talk of betrayal by non-agents: of being betrayed by our body when it fails to do what we wish, of being betrayed by our memory when it starts to fail us; of rage and anger at our failing computers and recalcitrant devices. But is this merely a sloppy or metaphorical use of "betrayal"? To claim that it is a full-throated use of "betrayal," we would need to explain what might ground and make appropriate the reaction of betrayal. But how could it ever be reasonable to have normatively charged expectations of objects? How could objects ever be the appropriate subjects of criticism?

Thinking about how we can be betrayed by our sub-parts will shed some light on the matter. Betrayal by our body and mind seems to be a paradigmatic case of non-agential betrayal. We feel betrayed when one of our limbs were to suddenly resist our control—refusing to move in accordance with our intent, or lunging about of its own accord. We rage and blame when our memory starts to go. What could justify the sharpness of that reaction? It can't be that my faculty of memory has made some commitment or that it bears goodwill towards me. It can do no such thing. My memory isn't responding to my trust, either. My faculty of memory is too cognitively simple to recognize or be motivated by my trust. My memory has no significant agency of its own. Rather, I feel betrayed because my memory had been tightly integrated into my basic functioning—until it started to let me down.

The external objects that evoke the strongest sense of betrayal are those whose functions are most tightly integrated into our own thinking and functioning: our musical instruments, our wheelchairs, our smartphones, our social media networks, our walking sticks, or our cars. Even the more distant examples—like the ground—are part of our background system of affordances.[7] The ground's stability is a part of how I walk, and especially how I walk with ease. It is not exactly a part of myself, but it is tightly integrated into my background functionality. It is the loss of that effortless integration—the suggestion that the earth might have, so to speak, a mind of its own—that makes earthquakes so disturbing. Let me suggest, then, that the normativity here arises, not from there being any moral commitments in play, but from *teleological integration*. It is the normativity of integrated functionality, of parts knitted together into a functional whole. The negative reaction here towards the failure of one's trusted memory, I think, is one of alienation—a type (or at least close neighbor) of betrayal.[8] One feels alienated towards a part when one discovers that what one thought was a perfectly integrated piece of one's self is, in fact, failing to function as a smooth part of one's agency. That part is failing to be a good participant in one's functional whole. It seems perfectly appropriate for me to feel betrayed by my parts—my memory, my hands—for failing in their tasks. This reaction is, then, not entirely unrelated to agency. But it is not a reaction necessarily orientated towards independent, self-sufficient agents. It is a reaction directed at *parts of agents* by the whole agent—or by other parts of that agent—for failing the rest. And those parts need not be independent agencies in and of themselves, in order to merit our sense of alienation when they fail us. Reproaching one's own parts for their failures is appropriate, not on moral grounds, but on grounds of functional unity.

Some might think that it is odd to think of betrayal as a response to the failure of one's integrated parts. Betrayal, in most philosophical accounts, turns out to be a specifically moral notion, directed at other people. This is why various analyses of trust have tried to ground betrayal in such obviously morally-involved phenomena such as responsiveness and commitments. But betrayal, it seems to me, is even more intimately connected with notions of integration than it is with notions of commitment or responsiveness. After all, there are plenty of ways in which somebody can fail to be responsive to my needs or fail to live up to their commitments, but where I don't feel betrayed. I depend on the administrative

[7] Consider, for example, the well-known cases where an instrument seems to become an integrated part of one's perceptual system, like a walking stick. Classical discussions are in Merleau-Ponty (1962) and Gibson ([1979] 2014). The theme has been taken up by the extended mind literature, especially Clark (2008: 30–43). Notice that the argument I give here doesn't turn on any robust version of the extended mind thesis, that such external objects can become literally part of one's mind. My argument only depends on the weaker commonplace, that affordances can become phenomenally integrated into one's practical functioning and cognition.

[8] I don't mean alienation here in the very particular modern notion, such as the Marxist usage (Jaeggi 2014). I mean to be drawing on a more colloquial use of the term.

assistants in my university payroll department to be motivated by my needs; I depend on the manufacturing staff at Apple to live up to their commitments to make functional laptops. Their failures might leave me furious or angry, but not *betrayed*. Betrayal is a more intimate notion. We are betrayed by those that are close to us, with whom we work in intimate concert. We are betrayed when something we were trying to make into a part of ourselves shears away from us, or when we are let down by somebody with whom we were trying to form a collective unit. It is far more natural to speak of being betrayed by one's memory than of being betrayed by some distant bureaucrat on whose cooperation one's visa application depends. The primary axis around which betrayal revolves, I suggest, is that of agential integration. Moral criticism often comes into the picture in those cases where we use various moral apparatus—like commitments—to enable the integration.

Holton suggests that the responses of trust are part of what he calls the *participant stance*. This is the characteristic stance that one agent takes towards another agent, which involves entering into a network of agent-directed attitudes and actions: praise, blame, ascribing responsibility, or feeling betrayal. And interpersonal trust of this sort plausibly occurs against the background of the participant stance. But thinking about object-oriented trust reveals another kind of stance we might take up, which we might call the *integrative stance*. This is our attitude towards things that we take to be part of us, and towards things with which we are supposed to be integrating, to form some larger whole. I take the integrative stance to be my stance not only towards my own parts—like my hands and my memory—but also towards my fellow parts—like my fellow team-members, or fellow employees, or fellow citizens. And I think the integrative stance helps explain why we feel betrayed by the failure of some objects but not others. I may rely on my shelf to hold up my books, but I do not feel betrayed if it collapses—only annoyed. But I have a much sharper reaction if the steering on my car suddenly breaks down, or if my computer mouse begins to respond erratically to input, or if my smartphone begins to scroll at random, or when the files on my computer desktop suddenly rearrange themselves, unbidden. My car, my mouse, and my laptop—these objects have come to be functionally integrated with me to various extents, and the breakdown of that integration is a violation from the point of view of the integrative stance. When I integrate other objects into my agency, I, in a sense, extend my agency into them, and so invest them with such status so as to be the appropriate objects of a particular kind of reproach.

This suggests an account of the functional importance of the unquestioning attitude. For most of my sub-parts, a questioning attitude towards them would impede regular efficient functioning. For most daily functioning, I need to trust my parts. This means not just that I rely on them, but that I can take my reliance for granted. When I truly make something a well-integrated part of my functional system, I drop the barriers. When I trust my memory, I let my various cognitive processes use the deliverances of my memory without a moment's hesitation. The same is true, I suggest, when we begin to incorporate external resources into our functioning. The unquestioning attitude lets me give external resources a direct pipeline into my cognitive and practical functioning. When one member of an elite and tightly knit unit of soldiers shouts, "Duck!," the other members simply duck. I trust the calendaring function on my phone because I treat its alerts as immediate directives about where I am supposed to go, and its silence as an unquestioned indication that I have no immediate obligations for the moment. To trust something is to *let it in*, to let it muck about directly with one's practical and cognitive innards. To trust something is to attempt to bring it *inside* one's practical functioning. Again: such trust is not indestructible. The unquestioning attitude can be defeated if the right sorts of evidence and considerations arise. Rather, to trust is to be strongly disposed to take the unquestioning attitude—to make the unquestioning attitude a moderately sticky default stance.

So here is the answer to our question about how we might ground negative reactions towards objects—how we might explain their air of normative bite. Trust is an unquestioning attitude. The primary use of the unquestioning attitude is as cognitive grease for functional integration. This explains the sharply negative reaction that arises from failures of trust. Such reactive responses are ones of alienation, arising from the integrative stance, towards things we thought were well-integrated parts of our functioning, when they fail to be well-behaved parts of our integrated, functional whole.

Let me offer a sketch of an even larger thought. This sketch will take us quickly over some very heady philosophical terrain, but I think it might be useful to scout out where this line of thinking might take us. Many philosophers have suggested that there is a deep relationship between our intentions and the unity of our agency over time. As Edward Hinchman puts it, when I make up my mind to do something, I don't usually re-deliberate that decision later. This lack of re-deliberation arises from my self-trust. And it is this self-trust which binds me together as an agent over time, says Hinchman. Let's say that, this morning, I decide to make a chicken stir-fry for dinner. In the evening, I go to the store and simply buy chicken breast and bok choy. I don't re-deliberate in the present, treating my past self's decision as only one reason among many. What it is for my present self to trust my past self is for my present self to simply buy the bok choy, because my past self had settled on chicken stir-fry. My self-trust (defeasibly) preserves my decisiveness from past to present. As long as things are going as usual, and my intention hasn't been defeated, my past deliberation has closed the matter (Hinchman 2003).

But it is not just trust in my past self; it is trust in my present self's faculties to maintain the connection to the past self. I trust my memory. As Tyler Burge puts it, memory doesn't supply propositions about past events—"... it *preserves* [propositions], together with their judgmental force" (Burge 1993: 462). That is, if

I perceived something in the past such that my perception was conclusive to my past self, and my memory conveys that perception to my present self, I don't relate to that memory as one fact among many. The conclusiveness itself transmits. For this to work, my memory must transmit the force of my past self's conclusiveness, even if I don't remember the details of the process of reasoning that led to that remembered conclusion. So long as I trust my memory, it functions as a direct pipeline from my past self into my present self. And we, as cognitively finite beings, all need to trust in this way. We must often engage in chains of reasoning that are longer than our consciousness can grasp in any single moment. We must, then, have the capacity to use our memory to integrate past conclusions into present deliberations, even when those past conclusions are presented to us shorn of their accompanying evidence and reasoning. That is the only way we can manage to pass long chains of reasoning through the limited pinhole of our teeny little consciousness.

I simply don't have the cognitive resources to constantly question my parts. The unquestioning attitude is needed for the seamless, efficient functioning of my integrated parts. When we trust others, I suggest, we are bringing them into a relationship roughly analogous to that which we have towards our own faculties and body. Self-trust and other-trust, then, turn out to be very much of a kind. Trust extends to external informational sources the same cognitive permissions as one's memory and one's other internal cognitive resources. When my spouse, who I trust entirely, shouts to me that the child has gotten his hands on a knife, I just start sprinting towards the kid. Her testimony is simply entered instantly into my set of accepted beliefs, just as would be a belief presented to me through my own memory. When I trust Google, I let its ordering of the search results direct my attention almost as if they were part of my own cognitive processes.

One use of the unquestioning attitude, then, would be to let one agent integrate other bits of the world into its system of cognition and action—to plug them in directly. Another use would be for individual agents to integrate with each other, along with some non-agential resources, into a smoothly functioning collective agency. Trust can put these external individuals and individuals into something like the direct-pipeline relationships found between a single person's body parts and cognitive faculties.[9]

My relationship to evidence, when I acquire a belief through trust in another's testimony, would then turn out to be something like my relationship to the remembered conclusions of my past self. Often, I don't possess the evidence and epistemic reasons for those past conclusions at the present moment. Rather, the conclusive force of my past reasoning is transmitted to my present self—though

[9] For a compelling account of something like this, see Hutchins (1996) for a classic study of how submarine crews act as a single mind.

stripped of awareness of the actual evidence and reasons that my past self reasoned with. Thus, even when I am following the best norms of practical rationality (for a cognitively finite being), I can be in a position where my present belief outruns the evidence I presently grasp. Self-trust opens the door to having beliefs without having immediate access to the full body of supporting evidence and reasoning used to generate those beliefs. This may seem terrifying, but it is, in fact, the only way for cognitively limited beings to proceed. We must trust our past selves to have reasoned properly according to the relevant norms of deliberation. When our past selves have failed to do well by those norms, then our self-trust can lead us to unjustified beliefs—precisely because self-trust involves accepting the deliverances of our past self without re-checking our past self's reasoning.

My suggestion is that trust in others puts us in the same exquisitely vulnerable position, and for similar reasons. Trust transmits the conclusive force of their reasoning; it transmits the conclusion to me, shorn of its support.[10] By trusting somebody else as an informational source, I can enter them into my cognitive network and take up a relationship with them similar to the relationship I have to my own cognitive sub-faculties. So, when I accept testimony through trust without deliberation, it isn't that I have failed to go through a proper practical deliberation. I am *deferring to deliberation that was run elsewhere.*[11] Again, this makes us terrifyingly vulnerable and makes our deliberative procedures vastly open-ended. But, as has been often observed, trust in others is the only way to proceed in the modern era, where human knowledge has vastly outgrown the reach of a single mind—or even a single institution, or discipline. We are no longer capable of individual intellectual autonomy; at best, we can autonomously manage our participation in a vast and distributed community of inquiry (Hardwig 1985, 1991; Millgram 2015; Nguyen 2018a).

[10] Some have worried that this sort of extended-mind approach to knowledge leads to a kind of epistemic bloat, in which we "know" far too many things. Carter and Kallestrup (2019) provide a useful response to this worry, by distinguishing between what we have in principle access to via extended faculties, and what we have actually called forth into our awareness.

[11] Benjamin McMyler offers a somewhat similar view. According to McMyler, when we accept a belief through testimony, we defer the justification of that belief to the testifiers. However, McMyler situations the deference in a voluntary taking of responsibility by the testifier (McMyler 2017). McMyler here is offering what has been called an assurance view of trust—that what it is to trust somebody is to accept their assurances, in which they voluntarily take on responsibility for what follows from another's acceptance of their assurances. Such assurance theories make trust an essentially second-personal relationship—it is one where I trust you, because you gave me your assurances about that trust. My view doesn't depend on any such action on the part of the testifier, or on any second-personal relationship. I can decide to trust somebody who has no idea who I am, and no relationship towards me, by observing their actions and following them without question. Imagine, for instance, that I am following somebody else through treacherous terrain. I can trust them by following, unhesitatingly, and stepping where they step. They need not offer me second-personal assurance for me to trust; in fact, they may not know I am there at all. My trust in them is entirely a matter of my own attitude towards their actions.

My cognitive system typically runs with open pipelines, internally. What one part of me accepts, the other parts of me use without question.[12] The unquestioning attitude is the internal grease that lets me function quickly and efficiently. The unquestioning attitude, then, also lets me weld, into my cognitive and practical system, open pipelines from outside resources. And this also goes a long way to explaining my sharply negative reactive attitude when what's at the other ends of those pipelines lets us down. When we not only rely on a resource, but give it a direct pipeline into our thought and action, we are more profoundly alienated and disturbed when it goes awry.

Here's a real-life story—and an interpersonal echo of Hinchman's individualist story. My spouse and I keep a shared shopping list in a document file—a Google Doc—that we access from our phones. Each of us updates that list whenever they realize that we need some item. When one of us is in the store, they simply buy everything that's on that list. When I am at the grocery store, I don't question the list. I don't try to remember which items I entered and which she entered. I don't worry about whether or not she or I might have made some miscalculation or forgotten to update the list properly. I trust the list—which includes trusting my past self, my spouse, the software, and the processes that my spouse and I have put into place to maintain it. And since I trust the list, I simply let its contents direct my actions without question, under normal circumstances. I trust the list in the same way that I trust my own memory about my past decisions. And trusting that shared list gives my spouse the power to directly input certain things into my practical reasoning. And, since we are depending on Google to preserve the items on the list—just as I depend on my memory to preserve my past reasoning—this trust also opens the door for Google to enter or delete items from the list, and thus play with the direct inputs to my practical reasoning.

The unquestioning attitude account also helps to explain the divide between the sorts of objects with which we seem to engage in relationships of robust trust and the sorts of objects with which we don't. I have claimed that we can be betrayed by ropes, phones, computers, and the ground. On the other hand, I have seen far less talk of trust and betrayal towards the weather and the natural ecosystem. Farmers may rely on the weather, and when it fails them, they may be profoundly disappointed—but there seems to be no sense of profound betrayal. I may depend on the flowers in my garden to bloom, but if they do not, I am disappointed, but not betrayed. My account suggests a reason. The weather and my flowers are not immediately integrated into my system of practical affordances; I do not try to make them a part of my agential system. Likely, I don't try to integrate them because it is abundantly clear that they have some degree of agency of their own.

[12] The discussion of cognitive integration with external sources has been deeply inspired by Bryce Huebner's discussion of distributed cognition, and the kinds of integration required to count as distributed cognition (Huebner 2014).

The ground, on the other hand, is mute, simple, and seemingly easy to integrate. My smartphone is more complex, but it seems designed to be pliable and to conform itself to my will. These are the things that I try to integrate into my practical and cognitive self—which I invest with some of my own agency—making them into the kinds of things by which I can be betrayed.

The unquestioning attitude account also helps to explain the characteristic ways in which trust can go terribly wrong. Once we have welded together some cognitive pieces together with trust, errors can propagate easily. Cognitive elements that have been joined together with the unquestioning attitude are more efficient and more capable of seamless cooperation. But they are also more susceptible to infection as a whole.[13] According to the picture I've suggested, this is not a mere byproduct of trust. The efficiency and infectability both arise directly from the fact that trust welds open pipelines directly into our functioning. The unquestioning attitude permits both collective power and collective fragility.[14]

The unquestioning attitude account, then, could be taken as a first step towards a more radically non-individualist epistemology. The literature on trust has started from a presumption that the basic unit of analysis is the individual. This presumption is shared across a broad swathe of philosophy. Understanding our social and moral lives is about understanding relationships between autonomous individuals. Understanding our epistemic lives—even our social epistemic lives—is about understanding how information is processed by individuals and how it passes between individuals. But the unquestioning attitude account suggests a different take. The basic units could be larger collectives, and trust just might be the glue that holds them together and helps assemble them into a collective. And betrayal could be the response, not of one individual to another, but of a part of a collective towards a recalcitrant part.[15]

However, these more radically non-individual thoughts have only been intended as exploratory proposals, to feel out what a possible fuller account might be like. What matters most, for the present purpose, is to see that we have some need for cognitive and practical integration, and that the unquestioning attitude has a clear role to play in such integration. We usually not only take the unquestioning attitude towards our own parts, but also use it to integrate other

[13] For more, see my account of echo chambers as trust manipulators (Nguyen 2018b).

[14] I am inspired here by Charles Perrow's discussion of natural disasters. According to Perrow, some organizational systems have "loose linkages," where each functional unit questions and interprets what's passed to it. Systems where a person has active interpretational agency at each juncture are such systems. Other systems have "tight linkages," where each system simply takes what's been given without interpretation and operates on it directly. Computer subsystem that simply takes a variable from another computer system and plugs that number directly into its calculations and operations—that is a tight linkage. Tight linkages, says Perrow, are very efficient, but they don't fail well. He attributes many kinds of systems failures—like the Three Mile Island nuclear meltdown—to cascading unpredictable failures in large, complex, tightly linkaged systems (Perrow 1999).

[15] I have been influenced here by recent literature in group agency (List and Pettit 2011; Gilbert 2015), especially Carol Rovane's discussion of the metaphysics of groups (Rovane 2019).

resources into our functioning. And the stance of integration brings with it certain loaded expectations, the failure of which leads to a sharply negative reaction. That is enough to see how failures of such integration can ground sharply negative attitudes of betrayal, or something very close to it.

And this helps us to reunite our discussion of trust with concepts of intimacy. Baier, in her originating discussion, made note of the deep association between trust and intimacy (Baier 1986: 247, 252). But that connection has largely been lost—perhaps because philosophers seem to understand intimacy poorly and have usually avoided talking about it. But these thoughts about integration help us understand why trust and intimacy seem closely associated. Trust, here, is about agential integration—about letting something inside, about uniting with it. Closeness and unification are some of the key markers of intimacy (Inness 1996; Nguyen and Strohl 2019).

6. Gullibility and Agential Outsourcing

I have made a linguistic claim: that our natural use of "trust" includes the unquestioning attitude, and our natural use of "betrayal" includes disappointment from resources which we have taken the unquestioning attitude towards. But I don't want these linguistic claims to get in the way of the more substantive proposal. What is most important here is the description of the phenomenon itself. What I really care about is the unquestioning attitude and how it functions in our cognitive and practical lives.

And I think that it is vital that we get a handle on the unquestioning attitude, especially when it concerns our relationship to new and emerging technologies. Many of us, I think, have come to take the unquestioning attitude towards our smartphones, Google Search, and social media networks. And this means that we have integrated complex processes and structures into our agency—often without adequate reflection about how deep a change we are effecting. Each of these technologies structure our activities and cognitive processes in substantive ways. Google Search guides our attention. Social media networks filter what information gets to us, and what we pay attention to (Pariser 2012; Miller and Record 2013; Heersmink and Sutton 2020; Gillet and Heersmink 2019). Many of us seem to have integrated our portable music players into our systems of emotional self-regulation (Krueger 2013; Colombetti and Krueger 2015). Infrastructural features of technologies can suggest conceptual schemes—like the menu bar on a news site suggesting a basic division of the important categories of news (Alfano, Carter, and Cheong 2018). And technologies can even suggest goals and structure our motivations. Gamified technologies can change our goals with respect to an activity. A fitness tracker, such as Fitbit, highlights certain measures and, by giving the user daily scores and rankings based on those measures, invites the user to change their reasons and motivations for physical activity (Nguyen 2020).

This suggests an enlarged notion of gullibility. First, let's start with what gullibility looks like in agent-directed forms of trust. Trust, it is usually thought, should track trustworthiness. Gullibility, then, turns out to be trusting somebody more than their trustworthiness warrants.[16]

What, then, is the analogous mistake with the unquestioning attitude? What would gullibility look like for this form of trust? Gullibility here would involve being too ready to set up pipelines into our agency—of being too quick to weld external objects, sources, and agencies into our cognition and practicality. The results are familiar when we take the unquestioning attitude towards informational sources. As with traditional gullibility, the problem involves being too willing to accept the testimony of others. But thinking about the unquestioning attitude points us towards a distinctive form of gullibility. We can take the unquestioning attitude, not just towards informational sources, but towards processes that we incorporate into our agency. We can take an unquestioning attitude towards the agential infrastructure of the world. When we take an unquestioning attitude towards a news site, we integrate its conceptual schemas and ways of organizing the world into our thinking. When we take an unquestioning attitude towards, say, a streaming musical service and use its algorithmically generated playlists to help regulate our emotions, we are integrating its emotional content—and its algorithmic selection process—into our system of emotional self-regulation. When we take an unquestioning attitude towards our Fitbit, we are letting its embedded goals and metrics guide our valuing and decision-making.

I am not here urging categorical resistance to the unquestioning attitude. It is a powerful—and necessary—resource, which also carries enormous risks. And its powers are inseparable from the vulnerabilities it creates. Those vulnerabilities are part and parcel of the basic functioning of the unquestioning attitude: to create efficiency by removing checks. Taking the unquestioning attitude is something like one country deciding to have open borders with another country, with all the efficiency, freedom, and vulnerability that entails. We should certainly deploy it in the right circumstances—but we should also do so with great care.

Let's take a step back. Trust, in all its forms, runs far beyond our ability to manage or control. This is true even of mere reliance on testimony. Each person I rely on as an informational source has relied on others, who, in turn, rely on others. When I rely on my doctor's testimony, I am also thereby relying on

[16] One caveat: voluntarists like Holton think that our trust can exceed the trustworthiness of its target, when we have a reason to so exceed—like inspiring somebody to live up to our trust. Gullibility, in this case, would be trusting beyond what the trustworthiness of the target, combined with our good aspirational reasons, allow.

whoever my doctor relies on. And that reliance iterates, since I am also relying on whomever those latter people rely on. A doctor relies on some published research in a medical journal—in doing so, they are directly relying on the authors of that research, and on the journal's peer review process. But the doctor is thereby also relying on whoever those researchers relied on—including the statisticians whose methods were used in analyzing the research data, the engineers who made the research instrumentation, and on and on. Reliance on testimony is *fractally iterated*. And because of that, we usually have no idea about how far our reliance extends, and on whom we are relying.

The danger is compounded with the unquestioning attitude, especially since the unquestioning attitude can be taken towards processes and agencies. This is already true for simple environmental features: when I trust a particular path or a ladder, my movements and decisions are significantly conditioned by those features. But the consequences for my agency are particularly sharp when I take the unquestioning attitude towards complex technologies. When I take the unquestioning attitude towards Google Search or my social media network, I am permitting complex technological processes to play a crucial role in my cognition and practical activity. Google Search is actively ranking and filtering search results. My social media network is actively amplifying some forms of discourse and suppressing others, as ranking algorithms intrude into what each node-member sees and the network architecture encourages certain forms of expression to enter explosive viral feedback loops, while burying other expressions out of sight (Tufekci 2017, 2018). Importantly, the unquestioning attitude doesn't simply add discrete, self-contained functions to our own agency. It *outsources* our agency—and that outsourcing can be iterated. When I trust Google Search, I let it guide my attention, thus outsourcing a part of my agency. But I actually have very little idea who or what I'm outsourcing to—especially since Google Search itself outsources much of its own operations to external resources. Google Search is built from modules collected from thousands of different researchers and technological institutions. And these modules employ even more modules. And, what's more, those modules aren't adopted in some stable and finalized form. Contemporary computing technologies usually outsource dynamically, so that each integrated resource is up for constant revision and change.

This system is, of course, vastly powerful and efficient. (Try asking anybody who's lived with Google Search to give it up.) But outsourced agency is particularly open to subterranean tinkering—and the more complex the trusted resource is, the more forms of invisible tinkering the trustor becomes open to. The basic functionality of Google Search might change without our knowing—and so part of our outsourced agency would also change without our knowing. The gullible person here, then, is a certain kind of early adopter. Their mistake is being willing to outsource their agency too readily—to let any old thing in.

It might be useful, then, to update our paradigm of gullibility. The traditionally gullible person is the person who believes anything that anybody tells them. In our age, there is a new form of gullibility. The technologically gullible person is the one that quickly and eagerly welds any new form of technology into their agency. They unreflectively integrate smartwatches that introduce metrics about exercise and sleeping, which can condition their values and motivations; they unreflectively integrate social media networks that transform their experience of discourse, argument, and interaction. They take up the unquestioning attitude too easily, without considering the vulnerabilities and changes they're bringing inside their agency.

7. Different Forms of Trust

I have suggested that there is a form of trust that involves taking up an unquestioning attitude, and that this form of trust has an important place alongside the agent-directed forms of trust. But why do we call these two very different attitudes "trust"? And why are our negative response to both grouped together under the notion of "betrayal"? Let me end by suggesting that these various attitudes and reactions are grouped together because of their relationship to our attempts to expand our agency.

It will help here to focus, for the moment, on one particular account of agent-directed trust. Recall Jones' responsiveness account of trust. According to her, to trust somebody is to depend on them because you take them to be trustworthy. And to be trustworthy is to be motivated to act to fulfill others' dependence on you. Trust and trustworthiness go hand in hand, says Jones; they let us coordinate our actions by permitting us to actively depend on others. When we trust somebody, we know they will be responsive to our needs, and so we can take their responsiveness into account when deciding what to do.

Jones suggests that we can get clearer on the particular value and normativity of trust by imagining a world without any trust in it at all. Imagine, she says, that people in this world follow all the other norms, like those of morality. Imagine that everybody in this world is fully rational and perfectly transparent to one another. But imagine that they simply do not engage in trust, and that nobody is trustworthy, in her sense. This world, she says, would be perfectly safe to live in, but there would be something very important missing. Because nobody would act out of the awareness that they were being depended on—and nobody would depend on others to so act—"agents would lack the capacity to directly enlist the agency of another in the service of their ends" (Jones 2017: 100). We could rely on each other and predict each other, but we could not formulate new plans for action that depended on each other's active cooperation. What trust, in Jones' sense, enables us to do is to "extend our agency"—to be able to recruit the agency of others into our own (101–2).

I think this is quite right—and plausibly right of any agent-directed theory of trust. And it points the way to a broader account of trust that encompasses both agent-directed trust and unquestioning trust. Both forms of trust are methods by which we attempt to extend our agency—to integrate the functionality of bits of the external world into our own efforts. We have at least two tools for this integration: we can coordinate with other people, who we can expect to be responsiveness to our needs; and we can turn off the questioning process. That is: we can cooperate with others, and we can plug things directly into our agency. We can use these tools separately. But we can, and often do, deploy these tools together—as I usually do with other drivers on the road. And betrayal is the characteristic response we have to failures of either form of integration.

Simpson suggests that we talk about various different forms of trust because talk of trust comes in response to the breach of trust—and there are so many different ways to breach trust. What unites the different forms is something very basic. Ur-trust, Simpson suggests, is simply the relationship we have towards other people we need to cooperate with. I suggest we borrow the structure of Simpson's account, but put an even more basic phenomenon at the center. The basic form of ur-trust, I'm suggesting, is agential integration. Trust—all trust—involves the attempt to bring other people and things into one's agency, or to join with other people and things into collective agencies. Interpersonal cooperation is one road to agential integration, but it is not the only one. There is also the unquestioning attitude. And we are betrayed when we are let down by something with which we had tried to agentially unite. Trust, in the broad sense, turns out to be a response to our essential cognitive and practical finitude. We need help, and we need to make the sources of that help things that we can rely on unquestioningly. Trust of both sorts involves various attempts to integrate other entities into our practical functioning—to bring them inside, or at least tightly knit them into, the boundaries of our selves.[17]

References

Alfano, Mark, Joseph Adam Carter, and Marc Cheong. 2018. "Technological Seduction and Self-Radicalization." *Journal of the American Philosophical Association* 4(3): 298–322.

Askwith, Richard. 2015. *Running Free: A Runner's Journey Back to Nature.* London: Yellow Jersey Press.

Baier, Annette. 1986. "Trust and Antitrust." *Ethics* 96(2): 231–60.

Baier, Annette. 1992. "Trusting People." *Philosophical Perspectives* 6: 137–53.

[17] I'd like to thank, for all their commentary, wisdom, and aid: Endre Begby, Julia Bursten, Anthony Cross, Sandy Goldberg, Kevin Lande, Neil Levy, Michaela McSweeney, Elijah Millgram, Geoff Pynn, Tim Sundell, Greta Thurnbull, Dennis Whitcomb, and Stephen White. I'd also like to thank the University of Kentucky Philosophy Department for a particularly exciting conversation that generated the entire discussion of agential gullibility and agential outsourcing.

Baker, Judith. 1987. "Trust and Rationality." *Pacific Philosophical Quarterly* 68(1): 1.

Berzon, Betty. 2002. *Surviving Madness: A Therapist's Own Story*. Madison, WI: University of Wisconsin Press.

Bratman, Michael. 1987. *Intention, Plans, and Practical Reason*. Stanford, CA: Center for the Study of Language and Information.

Buchak, Lara. 2017. "Faith and Steadfastness in the Face of Counter-Evidence." *International Journal for Philosophy of Religion* 81(1–2): 113–33.

Burge, Tyler. 1993. "Content Preservation." *Philosophical Review* 102(4): 457.

Carabantes, Manuel. 2019. "Black-Box Artificial Intelligence: An Epistemological and Critical Analysis." *AI and Society*, 1–9.

Carter, J. Adam, and Jesper Kallestrup. 2019. "Varieties of Cognitive Integration." *Noûs* 54(4): 867–90.

Clark, Andy. 2008. *Supersizing the Mind: Embodiment, Action, and Cognitive Extension*. Oxford: Oxford University Press.

Colombetti, Giovanna, and Joel Krueger. 2015. "Scaffoldings of the Affective Mind." *Philosophical Psychology* 28(8): 1157–76.

Faulkner, Paul. 2007a. "On Telling and Trusting." *Mind* 116(464): 875–902.

Faulkner, Paul. 2007b. "A Genealogy of Trust." *Episteme* 4(3): 305–21.

Faulkner, Paul. 2011. *Knowledge on Trust*. Oxford: Oxford University Press.

Frost-Arnold, Karen. 2014. "Trustworthiness and Truth: The Epistemic Pitfalls of Internet Accountability." *Episteme* 11(1): 63–81.

Frost-Arnold, Karen. 2016. "Social Media, Trust, and the Epistemology of Prejudice." *Social Epistemology* 30(5–6): 513–31.

Gibson, James J. [1974] 2014. *The Ecological Approach to Visual Perception: Classic Edition*. London: Psychology Press.

Gilbert, Margaret. 2015. *Joint Commitment: How We Make the Social World*. Reprint edition. New York: Oxford University Press.

Gillett, Alexander, and Richard Heersmink. 2019. "How Navigation Systems Transform Epistemic Virtues: Knowledge, Issues and Solutions." *Cognitive Systems Research* 56(56): 36–49.

Goldberg, Sanford C. 2017. "Epistemically Engineered Environments." *Synthese*, 1–20. https://doi.org/10.1007/s11229-017-1413-0.

Hardwig, John. 1985. "Epistemic Dependence." *Journal of Philosophy* 82(7): 335–49.

Hardwig, John. 1991. "The Role of Trust in Knowledge." *Journal of Philosophy* 88(12): 693–708.

Hawley, Katherine. 2014. "Trust, Distrust and Commitment." *Noûs* 48(1): 1–20.

Hawley, Katherine. 2017. "Trustworthy Groups and Organisations." In *The Philosophy of Trust*, edited by P. Faulkner and T. Simpson. Oxford: Oxford University Press.

Heersmink, Richard, and John Sutton. 2020. "Cognition and the Web: Extended, Transactive, or Scaffolded?" *Erkenntnis* 85(1): 139–64.

Hieronymi, Pamela. 2008. "The Reasons of Trust." *Australasian Journal of Philosophy* 86(2): 213–36.

Hinchman, Edward S. 2003. "Trust and Diachronic Agency." *Noûs* 37(1): 25–51.

Hinchman, Edward S. 2005. "Telling as Inviting to Trust." *Philosophy and Phenomenological Research* 70(3): 562–87.

Holton, Richard. 1994. "Deciding to Trust, Coming to Believe." *Australasian Journal of Philosophy* 72(1): 63–76.

Holton, Richard. 2009. *Willing, Wanting, Waiting*. Oxford: Oxford University Press.

Huebner, Bryce. 2014. *Macrocognition: A Theory of Distributed Minds and Collective Intentionality*. New York: Oxford University Press.

Hutchins, Edwin. 1996. *Cognition in the Wild*. Revised ed. Cambridge, MA: A Bradford Book.

Ilgner, Arno. 2006. *The Rock Warrior's Way: Mental Training for Climbers*. La Vergne, TN: Desiderata Institute.

Inness, Julie C. 1996. *Privacy, Intimacy, and Isolation*. New York: Oxford University Press.

Jaeggi, Rahel. 2014. *Alienation*. Translated by Frederick Neuhouser and Alan E. Smith. New York: Columbia University Press.

Jones, Karen. 1996. "Trust as an Affective Attitude." *Ethics* 107(1): 4–25.

Jones, Karen. 2004. "Trust and Terror." In *Moral Psychology: Feminist Ethics and Social Theory*, edited by Peggy DesAutels and Margaret Urban Walker, 3–18. Lanham: Rowman & Littlefield.

Jones, Karen. 2012. "Trustworthiness." *Ethics* 123(1): 61–85.

Jones, Karen. 2017. "But I Was Counting On You!" In *The Philosophy of Trust*, edited by Paul Faulkner and Thomas W. Simpson, 161–76. Oxford: Oxford University Press.

Kahn, Douglas. 2013. *Earth Sound Earth Signal: Energies and Earth Magnitude in the Arts*. Oakland, CA: University of California Press.

Kearl, Michael C. 1989. *Endings: A Sociology of Death and Dying*. New York: Oxford University Press.

Keren, Arnon. 2014. "Trust and Belief: A Preemptive Reasons Account." *Synthese* 191(12): 2593–615.

Krueger, Joel. 2013. "Affordances and the Musically Extended Mind." *Frontiers in Psychology* 4: 1–12.

Lackey, Jennifer. 2008. *Learning from Words: Testimony as a Source of Knowledge*. Oxford: Oxford University Press.

List, Christian, and Philip Pettit. 2011. *Group Agency: The Possibility, Design, and Status of Corporate Agents*. Oxford: Oxford University Press.

McLeod, Carolyn. 2002. *Self-Trust and Reproductive Autonomy*. Cambridge, MA: MIT Press.

McMyler, Benjamin. 2017. "Deciding to Trust." In *The Philosophy of Trust*, edited by Paul Faulkner and Thomas W. Simpson, 161–76. Oxford: Oxford University Press.

Merleau-Ponty, Maurice. 1962. *Phenomenology of Perception*. New York: Routledge.

Miller, Boaz, and Isaac Record. 2013. "Justified Belief in a Digital Age: On the Epistemic Implications of Secret Internet Technologies." *Episteme* 10(2): 117–34.

Millgram, Elijah. 2015. *The Great Endarkenment: Philosophy for an Age of Hyperspecialization*. Oxford: Oxford University Press.

Nguyen, C. Thi. 2018a. "Expertise and the Fragmentation of Intellectual Autonomy." *Philosophical Inquiries* 6(2): 107–24.

Nguyen, C. Thi. 2018b. "Echo Chambers and Epistemic Bubbles." *Episteme* 1–21. https://doi.org/10.1017/epi.2018.32.

Nguyen, C. Thi. 2020. *Games: Agency as Art*. New York: Oxford University Press.

Nguyen, C. Thi, and Matthew Strohl. 2019. "Cultural Appropriation and the Intimacy of Groups." *Philosophical Studies* 176(4): 981–1002.

Nickel, Philip J. 2012. "Trust and Testimony." *Pacific Philosophical Quarterly* 93(3): 301–16.

O'Neill, Onora. 2002a. *Autonomy and Trust in Bioethics*. Cambridge: Cambridge University Press.

O'Neill, Onora. 2002b. *A Question of Trust: The BBC Reith Lectures 2002*. Cambridge: Cambridge University Press.

Pariser, Eli. 2012. *The Filter Bubble: How the New Personalized Web Is Changing What We Read and How We Think*. Reprint edition. New York: Penguin Books.

Perrow, Charles. 1999. *Normal Accidents: Living with High-Risk Technologies*. Revised ed. Princeton, NJ: Princeton University Press.

Resch, Michael, and Andreas Kaminski. 2019. "The Epistemic Importance of Technology in Computer Simulation and Machine Learning." *Minds and Machines* 29(1): 9–17.

Rini, Regina. 2017. "Fake News and Partisan Epistemology." *Kennedy Institute of Ethics Journal* 27(S2): 43–64.

Rovane, Carol. 2019. *The Bounds of Agency: An Essay in Revisionary Metaphysics*. Princeton, NJ: Princeton University Press.

Simpson, Thomas W. 2012. "What Is Trust?" *Pacific Philosophical Quarterly* 93(4): 550–69.

Tufekci, Zeynep. 2017. *Twitter and Tear Gas: The Power and Fragility of Networked Protest*. New Haven, CT: Yale University Press.

Tufekci, Zeynep. 2018. "It's the (Democracy-Poisoning) Golden Age of Free Speech. *Wired*. January 10, 2018.

8
There's More to Transparency than Windows

Catherine Prueitt and Kateryna Samoilova

Introduction

One of the most fascinating and recurring anchors across different theories in philosophy of mind is the curious phenomenon of the transparency or diaphanousness of experience. Moore attempts to capture this observation here:

> Though philosophers have recognised that something distinct is meant by consciousness, they have never yet had a clear conception of what that something is. They have not been able to hold it and blue before their minds and to compare them, in the same way in which they can compare blue and green. And this for the reason I gave above: namely that the moment we try to fix our attention upon consciousness and to see what, distinctly, it is, it seems to vanish: it seems as if we had before us a mere emptiness. When we try to introspect the sensation of blue, all we can see is the blue: the other element is as if it were diaphanous. Yet it can be distinguished if we look attentively enough, and if we know that there is something to look for. My main object in this paragraph has been to try to make the reader see it: but I fear I shall have succeeded very ill. (Moore 1903: 450)

The tension in Moore's mind and his struggle with it are palpable. On the one hand, he is pointing to something we can all experience for ourselves—the elusive nature of experience, which we seemingly cannot focus on except by focusing on its objects. But on the other hand, what Moore is pointing to is so elusive—as he says, it "seems to vanish" upon closer inspection—that we can begin to doubt that anything is being successfully pointed out, making Moore "fear [he has] succeeded very ill."

This tension and the accompanying struggle to resolve it are the topics of this chapter. We hold that transparency is an important datum about natural human experience, but this datum has been interpreted in a number of different ways and has been used to scaffold different theories of mind. Appreciating what different

Catherine Prueitt and Kateryna Samoilova, *There's More to Transparency than Windows* In: *Oxford Studies in Epistemology, Volume 7.* Edited by: Tamar Szabó Gendler, John Hawthorne, and Julianne Chung, Oxford University Press.
 DOI: 10.1093/oso/9780192868978.003.0008

scaffolds bring to the fore sheds new light onto the elusive nature of experience and onto the nature of transparency as a datum, helping to resolve the Moorean tension.

To that end, this chapter is divided into three sections. In the first section, we sketch some major post-Moore contemporary attempts to capture the transparency datum in order to get clearer on some of the existing interpretative differences. In the second section, we consider two widespread frames or scaffolds (to borrow Bayne and Spener's 2010 term from a related context), the window scaffold and the mirror scaffold, that often structure those different interpretations. We note that these scaffolds have different strengths, but fail to fully capture certain salient features of the transparency datum. In the third section, we introduce a new scaffold for thinking about the transparency datum. This new scaffold, which we have developed through our cross-cultural engagement with Classical South Asian epistemology, suggests that the transparency of experience is like the polarization of purple into red and blue. We conclude by considering what the three scaffolds converge on, which we take to be the transparency datum itself.

1. Interpreting the Transparency Datum

One of the striking aspects of thinking about the transparency of experience is how many others have already done so, in great detail. The transparency observation in common seems to be roughly this: finding out your own thoughts on some subject matter sometimes seems to happen simply by considering that subject matter. There is no sense of additionally considering your thoughts, after having considered the subject matter, in order to know what you think about it. Let us term those who anchor some significant part of their overall view in the phenomenon of transparency "transparency theorists." Moore (1903), Wittgenstein (1958), Edgley (1969), Evans (1982), Harman (1986), Tye (2002), Peacocke (1996), Moran (2001), Boyle (2009), Hill (2009), and Byrne (2005, 2018), among others, all qualify as transparency theorists, even though they all capture this phenomenon in different ways.

Here is Edgley's way of capturing it, which is starkly different from Moore's:

> my own present thinking, in contrast to the thinking of others, is transparent in the sense that I cannot distinguish the question "Do I think that P?" from a question in which there is no essential reference to myself or my belief, namely "Is it the case that P?" This does not of course mean that the correct answers to these two questions must be the same; only I cannot distinguish them, for in giving my answer to the question "Do I think that P?" I also give my answer, more or less tentative, to the question "Is it the case that P?" (Edgley 1969: 90)

Edgley's observation is that the two questions are indistinguishable from the first-person perspective, even though one question is about some external subject matter while the other is about one's own thoughts or beliefs on that subject matter. As we can see, Edgley interprets this observation by describing his own present thinking as transparent, in this particular way. But as Moran points out, "[t]o claim one question is 'transparent' to another is not to claim that one question reduces to the other" (2001: 61).

Interestingly, Evans seems to disagree, suggesting that there is indeed something equivalent about the two questions—perhaps how we answer them:

> [I]n making a self-ascription of belief, one's eyes are, so to speak, or occasionally literally, directed outward—upon the world. If someone asks me "Do you think there is going to be a third world war?," I must attend, in answering him, to precisely the same outward phenomena as I would attend to if I were answering the question "Will there be a third world war?" (Evans 1982: 225)

Byrne follows Evans in emphasizing that experience is transparent because, when we turn our attention inward, all we get are objects. Byrne approvingly cites Tye's statement that, when we try to focus on experiences, we "see right through them to the world outside" (2009: 434). The "surely plausible" claim that Byrne sees here is the idea that "we do not know of our experiences by 'looking within'—by a quasi-perceptual faculty of introspection. How do we know of them, then? Tye's answer is that we know of them by looking without." Although both Tye and Byrne present their understanding of the outward direction of introspection as consistent with Moore's account of experience as diaphanous, the observations are starkly different. For Moore, the idea that we see right through experiences to the objects that they represent is merely the result of not attending carefully enough to our own awareness. However, if we do attend carefully, we can in fact focus on awareness itself.

The differences between what Moore, Edgley, Moran, Evans, and Byrne emphasize about transparency are so significant that a reasonable question arises: are they all trying to capture the same phenomenon, or are they pointing to different aspects of experience? This question presents a turning point: if there is no phenomenon in common that all transparency theorists are interested in, then there is much less common ground among them than the term "transparency theorist" suggests. In this chapter, we entertain and focus on a different possibility: that all transparency theorists indeed have something in common—an interest in the datum that transparency presents. What that datum is, why it is so differently captured by different transparency theorists, and why it has proven to be so elusive are all issues we address on our way to showing that entertaining this possibility—that there is a transparency datum in common among transparency theorists—leads to some valuable explanatory results.

One of those explanatory results is straight-forwardly accessible: if there is indeed a transparency datum in common, then the differences between the various transparency theorists could have more to do with how the transparency datum is interpreted, rather than their disagreement about the transparency datum itself. Just because transparency theorists agree on a datum does not mean that they all take the same thing away from it or put that datum to the same use. The interpretive scaffolding that transparency theorists bring to the datum matters.

One salient way in which interpretive scaffolding matters is that the framework a theorist brings to the datum will influence what, precisely, that theorist takes to be transparent. Already, we have put forward the observation in terms of (i) questions being transparent to each other (Edgley, Evans); (ii) one's own present thinking being transparent (Edgley); and (iii) perception or perceptual experiences being transparent (Byrne, Tye). And if we think of introspection as involving some mix of these three items—asking yourself some questions about what you believe, thinking about your own thinking, or as attending to your experiences, perceptual and otherwise—then, in addition to these three, transparency can also be cast as an observation about (iv) introspection, as Moore does:

> the moment we try to fix our attention upon consciousness and to see *what*, distinctly, it is, it seems to vanish: it seems as if we had before us a mere emptiness. When we try to introspect the sensation of blue, all we can see is the blue: the other element is as it if were diaphanous. (Moore 1903: 450)

Moore's descriptions of transparency—with which we began—are particularly telling of how difficult it is to capture the transparency datum neutrally, without interpreting it by hypothesizing or stipulating which metaphysical structures might be responsible for it. Transparency for him is experienced in the process of introspection—in his example, trying to focus on your current perceptual experience of blue—but he clearly has a very specific metaphysical explanation in mind. Indeed, for those fascinated by transparency, the value of transparency seems to come from its use as a guide to the underlying metaphysics—be it the metaphysics of perception, introspection, or something else. Even if transparency is just a phenomenological observation, it seems to be of the sort that can help us discover something important about the structure of our experiences and even our minds. It is for this reason that it is worth approaching transparency as a datum, open to interpretation, in the hopes of shedding light onto the nature of experience.

To better appreciate the existing differences in interpretation of the transparency datum and thereby get a better idea of what the transparency datum is as an agreed-upon phenomenon, let us now consider the interpretative scaffolding needed to turn the transparency datum into transparency-based theories, be those theories about thinking, perception, introspection, or something else.

While the transparency datum itself remains elusive as we try to converge on it, it is nonetheless possible to extract how different transparency theorists think we should approach interpreting that datum, whatever it happens to be. As we hope to show, it is the metaphysical expectations concerning the nature of awareness that each of the transparency theorists starts with that crucially constrain their interpretation of the transparency datum.

2. Interpretative Scaffolds for the Transparency Datum

If the transparency datum can be a guide to metaphysics, how the transparency datum is initially interpreted will be crucial to the metaphysical picture that will emerge as a result. Since the transparency datum emerges in awareness, our metaphysical expectations about the nature of awareness play a particularly significant role in our initial interpretations of the transparency datum. To demonstrate the significance of that initial metaphysically weighted interpretation of transparency, consider some of the mental scaffolds we could use to help us turn the transparency datum into a cornerstone of a theory. Since there is already some agreement that the transparency of experience could be understood in terms of certain questions being answerable in the same way, let us begin with that particular interpretative scaffold.

2.1 The Window Scaffold

To begin with, let us consider what sort of scaffolding could be made out of the suggestion that the question of what we think or believe is transparent to the question of how things are in the world. Evans presents this suggestion particularly clearly, hinting that he sees an important perceptual element in the transparency datum, insofar as our eyes are, "so to speak, or occasionally literally, directed outward" when answering a question about what we think (1982: 225). This way of putting the transparency datum is highly suggestive of an analogy with a transparent object such as a window: even though there is some object in our way (the glass of the window), this object is transparent and does not draw the focus away from what we are looking at or thinking about.

The window analogy presents the transparency datum in a particular light and in doing so, nudges us towards a particular view about the nature of awareness. What the window analogy suggests is that awareness is transparent in the sense of not requiring our attention to it in order to reap its benefits. Just as a window itself does not require our attention in order for us to see what's behind it, so does awareness itself not require any attention in order for us to know what we see or what we think.

This way of thinking about transparency nudges us towards representationalism or intentionalism (e.g. Tye 2002; Byrne 2001, 2018): the view on which, roughly, we do not (and on some versions, cannot) become aware of any of the intrinsic features of current and conscious experience. On this view, experience itself is rather like a window: it is the thing that grants us access to the world regardless of whether we can pay attention to it as an item in our minds. To that extent, experience is transparent because that's how awareness is thought to work on this view—we can be aware of all sorts of things without having to be aware of our awareness of them.

Thinking about the window scaffold can illuminate the starting point for observing the transparency datum. What the window scaffold brings out is the oddness of answering two radically different questions—one about your thoughts and the other about the world—in the same way. One would expect to have to investigate two different areas to answer them, the world and one's own mind, but it appears that investigating the world can (at least sometimes) suffice. Pressing questions arise immediately, motivating further investigation: Is this really what we do? And if so, is this another example of human epistemic shortcomings to overcome, or an unexpected insight into an epistemic shortcut we are still figuring out how to fully appreciate?

It is very difficult to tell at this stage how to answer these questions, in large part because the window scaffolding can only take us so far in illuminating the transparency datum. The issue is that the window analogy imports some details that also obscure, rather than only illuminate, the transparency datum. Some of those details have been brought out before:

> When we consider paradigmatic examples of transparent objects from everyday life, such as panes of glass, there is no question that the sense of transparency in question must be weak transparency (and thus, that weak transparency must be sufficient to capture the notion of transparency). The window next to my desk overlooks the roof of my neighbor's house. As I look out the window, it is difficult for me to avoid seeing right through it to my neighbor's roof, but it is by no means impossible for me to do so. If I angle my head just so, or if the light is right, I can undeniably focus on the pane of glass of the window itself. (And this is true even on those rare occasions when the window has been recently cleaned.)
>
> (Kind 2003: 233)

What Kind brings out is that the transparency of windows does not prevent them from being perceptually detected or becoming objects of awareness. If anything, it is rare for the window to go undetected, even when the window has been recently cleaned. So the window analogy has a built-in tension between the window being transparent and being detectable that prevents us from making more progress in capturing the transparency datum. This tension can unfortunately be inherited by some versions of representationalism, so the helpfulness of the window scaffolding in illuminating the transparency datum (and equally, clearly supporting a coherent view) is limited. To make further progress in converging on the transparency datum, it would be helpful to consider another interpretative scaffold that can help us see the transparency datum in a different light.

2.2 The Mirror Scaffold

Although the mirror scaffold and the window scaffold have been used interchangeably by some transparency theorists (see, for instance, Byrne's (2009: 434) discussion of Tye's understanding of Moore), the mirror provides a different frame for considering the transparency datum. To get from the window scaffold to the mirror scaffold, recall Moran's point from the introduction that just because two questions can be answered in the same way does not mean that they reduce to one another. But what if they did? Entertaining the possibility that the reason why the two questions can be answered in the same way is that they somehow reflect one another—presumably, because they both get at the very same item—brings us to the mirror scaffold. Here is Moore sketching the mirror scaffold:

> A mental image is conceived as if it were related to that of which it is the image (if there be any such thing) in exactly the same way as the image in a looking-glass is related to that of which it is the reflexion; in both cases there is identity of content, and the image in the looking-glass differs from that in the mind solely in respect of the fact that in the one case the other constituent of the image is 'glass' and in the other case it is consciousness. If the image is of blue, it is not conceived that this 'content' has any relation to the consciousness but what it has to the glass; it is conceived merely to be its content. (Moore 1903: 448–9)

Here, Moore is wondering whether there is any meaningful difference between an object that is being reflected/experienced and the object itself. The extent to which an experience vanishes, in Moore's sense, corresponds to the degree to which what is experienced just is the object. What the mirror analogy conveys is that, just as there is no difference between the blue reflected in the mirror and the blue causing the reflection, there is no difference between the object in experience and the object causing the experience.

The mirror scaffold does something similar to the window scaffold by suggesting the idea that it's possible for a representation (or on Moore's own view, a sense datum) to provide transparent access to an object: given a perfect mirror, when I see the reflection of the object in it, I just see the object. The central insight that the mirror scaffold brings is that the occasional similarity between what is out there in the world and what is in our minds is non-accidental. There is a metaphysical reason why when we ask certain questions or do certain things—perceive or introspect, as Moore is inviting us to do—not only the answer turns out to be the same, but also the method by which we get it can be the same (we gather this to be the basis for Byrne's 2018 view).

The insight of the mirror scaffold adds something to our understanding of the transparency datum that the window analogy obscures, namely, the pervasiveness of the transparency datum. The internal tension of the window scaffold, leaving it open whether and when the window is perfectly transparent or realistically detectable, makes it difficult to assess the nature and the significance of the transparency datum. Precisely because of that tension, the window scaffold is an excellent tool in motivating further investigation of the transparency datum, but the window scaffold itself does not offer much by way of guidance as to how to continue that investigation. That's where the mirror scaffold comes in: it offers us a way to continue that investigation of the transparency datum by introducing the hypothesis that there is some metaphysical regularity behind the transparency datum. Experience vanishes because the object in experience just is the object, perfectly reflected in a transparent medium.

Having said that, the mirror scaffold does have something important in common with the window scaffold: they both model transparency on transparent items such as glass, a component of both windows and mirrors. It is for this reason that both scaffolds ultimately hit a similar explanatory ceiling when it comes to the transparency datum. Neither is able to escape the tension inherent in postulating a transparent item that facilitates our awareness and having to explain how that item could do so while we are not aware of it (because it is transparent) while somehow being all we are aware of (because it is our current experience). This is one place where introducing descriptions under which we are and are not aware of the transparent item cannot help us, because the question of what we are aware of in this case is substantive: are we or are we not aware of any aspects of our experience under *any* description? Insofar as transparent items are being introduced by both the window and the mirror scaffolds, these scaffolds leave open both "yes" and "no" answers: there is an item we could become aware of, but since that item is transparent it can be left open as to whether we ever do become aware of it. This non-committal nature of both the window and the mirror scaffolds limits their ability to shed more light onto the transparency datum, so let us turn to a very different scaffold altogether: one on which transparency is understood not as a feature of items like windows or mirrors, but as a feature of processes, structures, or organizations. To construct this scaffold, we first need to introduce a framework that is quite different from the one we have been operating in thus far.

3. Transparency as Polarization

This section of the chapter will ask the reader to entertain, as a live possibility, an understanding of awareness in perception that is fundamentally different from the window and mirror scaffolds. The framework we consider now is derived from post-Dharmakīrtian Classical South Asian epistemology, and Pratyabhijñā Śaivism in particular.[1] Relying on this framework entails taking some aspects of these views outside of their historical purview, but in doing so, our aim is to draw out an approach that could provide an illuminating scaffold for unpacking the transparency datum.

3.1 A Primer in the Methods of Classical South Asian Epistemology

Setting up our alternative frame requires some background about how epistemology works in Classical South Asian traditions. The following presentation will necessarily over-simplify, but we endeavor to provide as accurate a basic orientation as possible. To begin with, South Asian logicians used linguistic analysis as the basic paradigm for examining reality. The starting point for South Asian philosophical analysis was the question of how the different factors of a sentence contribute to the realization of the action expressed by the verb. The verb itself defines the type of analysis under way; if we want to understand how awareness works, our analysis proceeds by analyzing the action of being aware. The rigorous precision of the Sanskrit language provided ample tools in this endeavor. Sanskrit, like Latin, is a case-based language: the role of various words in a sentence is denoted by their declensional endings. Six of the seven cases serve to show how various nominals relate to the action of the verb. Only the genitive relates nominals to each other. (An additional case, the vocative, calls to an outside entity and was treated separately.)

Philosophical attention fell, in particular, on how three cases express the action of the verb: the nominative (which names the subject of the sentence), the accusative (which names the object), and the instrumental (which names the instrument or the means of the action). To give a trivial example to clarify the analytical structure here, consider the sentence "The girl throws the ball with her arm." Here, "the girl" is the subject, "the ball" is the object, "her arm" is the instrument, and "throwing" is the action itself that is under consideration. The

[1] Dharmakīrti (seventh century) is a Buddhist philosopher whose works in logic, epistemology, metaphysics, and philosophy of language transformed subsequent debate in Classical South Asia. For an overview of Dharmakīrti's thought, see Dunne (2004). Pratyabhijñā is a Śaiva philosophical tradition that traces its works to Somānanda (ninth–tenth century), but was extensively developed by Utpaladeva (early tenth century) and Abhinavagupta (tenth–eleventh century). For an introduction to Pratyabhijñā Śaiva understandings of consciousness, see Ratié (2017). For a broader exploration into the non-Cartesian frame present in Classical Indian traditions, see Ram-Prasad (2018). For a more specific analysis of the relationship between exclusion and the formation of subject/object structured perceptions, see Prueitt (2017). To be clear on our methodology in this chapter: we are not claiming that any particular Classical South Asian tradition proposes or would support our view. Rather, we are acknowledging that our view emerges through dialogical engagement with these traditions.

overall aim of this analysis is to understand the action of throwing itself. The basic idea is that if we can understand what it is for the girl to be the subject of the action of throwing (that is, what the factors are that constitute being a thrower), and what it is for the ball to be the object (the factors that constitute being the thrown thing), and what it is for her arm to be the instrument (the factors that constitute being the means of throwing), then we can understand what it is for an action to be throwing. We can understand both what is invariant in the structure of the relationship between the action of throwing and the factors that express that action, and also what can change. For instance, the object of the action of throwing has to be a thing whose location is changed in a certain kind of way, but it doesn't have to be a ball. It could very well be a rock.

The basic consensus among various traditions, particularly from around the sixth century CE onward, was that if we can understand who is aware of something, what they are aware of, and how they are aware of it, then we can understand the action of being aware to which these factors all contribute. Subject, object, and instrument of awareness are relative terms that emerge only in relation to a particular moment of being aware. In line with this structure, we will use the following terminology. "Awareness" means the event under consideration that instantiates the action of being aware. "Awareness" is parallel with "throwing" in the above example; it is unfortunate that "aware-ing" is not an appropriately-signifying word in English. "Subject-side factors of awareness" means the factors that constitute being the subject of the action of being aware. These are parallel to the factors that constitute being the thrower in the above example. Likewise, "object-side factors of awareness" means the factors that constitute being the object of the action of being aware; they are parallel to the factors that constitute being thrown. We will sometimes speak of "subject" and "object" for brevity, but these terms should be understood as factors contributing to the expression of the action, not as independent entities.

The reader will notice that we will not talk explicitly about the factors that constitute the instrument of being aware in what follows. Readers familiar with post-Dharmakīrtian Classical South Asian epistemology will likely note that our presentation proceeds in line with the position that the instrument just is the awareness itself. Defending this position, however, is a complex matter that would take us far afield of the current discussion, and so we will set it aside for now.

Since knowing is a particular kind of being aware, in the sense that knowing is awareness of things as they actually are, an investigation of the nature of an act of awareness touches on both metaphysics and epistemology. This basic framework of *pramāṇa-vāda*, debate concerning the sources of knowledge, allowed different traditions to precisely and vociferously argue about the nature of reality in the context of how actions of knowing instantiate that reality. There were many traditions that argued that there is nothing faulty about our access to reality: our instruments of knowing allow us to have knowledge about all aspects of what they measure, and this knowledge generally accords with how things appear to us in the everyday world. There were other traditions that claimed that following through on what our instruments of knowing really reveal to us indicates that things are more complicated. On this line, it's true that the factors constituting an action appear to be distinct both from each other and from the action itself (the subject is not the object, and neither are the action itself), but an analysis of how the factors and the action relate to each other may indicate that the apparent transparency of a subject/object structured awareness depends on both the subject and the object being *nothing but* aspects of awareness itself. In this case, what an experience is transparent in relation to is not an external object, but only its own aspects. This line of thought allows us to construct a third interpretative scaffold for the transparency datum.

3.2 The Purple Scaffold

Let's try a new analogy or scaffold for interpreting the transparency datum. Say that awareness across time is like a purple stream coursing across a computer monitor. Pick out one moment in this stream and abstract it for analysis; think of this moment as a purple screenshot. Open the screenshot in a graphic design program and apply a filter that polarizes the purple into its constituent shades, red and blue. The screenshot is still there, but we no longer see the purple. We only see the red and the blue. The purple of the screenshotted moment contains within itself various factors that could be seen as blue if we exclude red from them, or red if we exclude blue. The red and the blue together are nothing but the purple, but if we try to analytically distinguish either red or blue, we automatically erase the purple as we polarize the moment as a whole. By its very nature, purple can be split into red and blue. Yet, once this split occurs, the purple itself vanishes. In this analogy, subject and object are like the red and blue into which the purple can be polarized. Awareness is like the purple that seems to vanish, and yet always remains as that which polarizes, when we split the purple into red and blue.

Following this analogy, awareness transparently expresses as a subject/object structured moment of perception just like how the exclusion of red from blue and blue from red just is the emergence of two apparently distinct entities that are actually particular ways of polarizing purple. Their appearance as distinct depends on their mutual exclusion from each other, and the creation of the exclusion just is the fact that purple no longer manifests as purple, but as polarized into red and blue. Neither the red nor the blue has any reality independent of the purple, and neither is more constitutive of purple than the other. In the same way, neither subject nor object have any reality independent of the moment of awareness within which they occur, and neither is more closely tied to awareness than the other. Even if we were to think of pure red, or pure blue—if we tried to analyze only the subject or only the object of an awareness—we necessarily form this thought by excluding the opposing color. This is why both the awareness and the subject seem to vanish when we focus intently on the object. Simply to focus on the object is to exclude the others.

Put the purple screenshot back into the stream out of which we abstracted it, and you have a flow of varyingly polarized moments of awareness, each moment shaped by previous moments and in turn shaping the possibilities for future expression. The purple stream itself represents the mix of all of the possible factors that could influence how a particular moment of awareness arises. This stream equally includes the factors that could polarize as blue and factors that could polarize as red. In the same way, awareness itself equally includes factors that can appear as objects and factors that can appear as subjects. So, awareness is not exhausted by the subject; the object is an equally significant aspect of awareness.

3.3 What the Purple Scaffold Shows

We are now in a position to consider the interpretation of the transparency datum that the polarization analogy brings with it. Any form of awareness, be it in perception or introspection, is like purple as described, which explains how it transparently reveals its object: both the subject and the object are undistorted by any mediators, such as glass or representations. The object just is an aspect of awareness, as is the subject, and directing our attention to that awareness (i.e. introspecting) polarizes it into particular constituent factors. It is precisely the absence of mediation between the subject and object that allows for this process to unfold transparently. In directing our attention to awareness, we are delimiting and excluding the subject-side factors from the object-side factors. If our eyes happen to be literally directed outward on the world, as Evans suggests, then our focus will be on the object-side factors at the expense of the subject-side factors, thereby creating the impression that all there is is the object. One thing that this analogy suggests is that something similar can happen with the subject: resonant with what Moore brought out, it is possible to focus on the subject-side factors at the expense of the object-side factors. As Moore also suggested, and as many South Asian contemplative traditions would affirm, focusing on the subject-side factors requires practice and skill. Yet, to echo Moore, these factors "can be distinguished if we look attentively enough, and if we know that there is something to look for" (Moore 1903: 450).

To make this more concrete, let's apply the analogy to a visual experience. First, we will see what it is for me to see my cat, then, what it is for me to think that I see my cat. Finally, we will consider what it means for me to have self-knowledge as I see my cat.

When I see my cat, the total awareness event (the purple) is co-constituted by (i) myself, where I am understood simply as the subset of subject-side factors that are active in shaping the awareness (the red), and (ii) the cat, where the cat is understood as the subset of the object-side factors that are active in shaping the awareness (the blue). In that moment of awareness the subject (myself) and the object (my cat) are excluded from each other by the polarizing effect of attention. The absence of mediation between the subject and object is experienced as the transparency of perceptual awareness, and revealed by the fact that I see nothing but my cat.

Now, what does it take for me to think that I see my cat? It's true that if I ask myself whether or not I'm seeing my cat, I direct my attention to the object-side factors that co-constitute my awareness, which are excluded from the subject-side factors. If my cat is present as an external object in my visual field, then I think that I'm seeing my cat. I'm able to think this precisely because I (the red) and my cat (the blue) are both just aspects of the underlying awareness (the purple), rather than because I am representing my cat. Adding a representation to mediate my awareness of my cat does not help, because the postulation of my cat as a representation obscures what it is for my cat to appear as an external object. The cat (the blue) transparently appearing as external (just as blue) depends on the exclusion of what is internal (the red), as well as on the fact that the external object and the internal subject are both just aspects of the underlying awareness (the purple). Although the direction of my attention is toward the aspect of my awareness delimited as external (my cat), the direction of attention is not in fact outward or inward. My attention never leaves the awareness event to turn to something else. It merely polarizes that awareness event to transparently reveal its co-constituting factors, including my cat. We could better describe the direction of my attention as depth-ward, towards the awareness itself.

Finally, let's consider what it would mean to have self-knowledge. To be precise on this point, we will follow Byrne in taking "self-knowledge" to mean "knowledge of one's mental states" (2018: 1). Byrne's own account indicates that self-knowledge is just first-personally acquired knowledge about particular facts about the world, such as the external p-facts that could indicate to me, via nociception, that I am in pain (2018: 149). In contrast, according to the purple scaffold, there are two distinct questions that I can ask about my awareness. I can question the object or I can question the subject. One's mental states as expressed in a particular moment of awareness are subject-side factors. Since subject-side factors equally co-constitute the awareness, subject-side factors are equally available for analysis precisely as the internal factors shaping the awareness. Self-knowledge, like vision, is founded on directly available perceptual data, but this data isn't some set of facts postulated to exist out in the world. There is no need to postulate something external to the awareness. Subject-side factors are available precisely to the extent that they are merely that: factors that co-constitute the particular way that the awareness happens. If one tries to get self-knowledge by interrogating the object in awareness—if one thinks that we need something like external p-facts out in the world to answer the question of whether or not we're in pain—one is simply focusing on the wrong set of factors constituting the awareness. It is as if one is asking questions about the red by focusing on the blue.

Consider how one might shift one's focus to the red instead. If I were to ask myself whether or not I'm happy as I see my cat, there's no particular object in my visual field that can answer this question. My happiness is not an external object. This does not mean that my happiness is not directly shaping the contents of my awareness, or that the object is something other than the awareness. Just as a particular shade of blue manifests only when purple is delimited in relation to a particular shade of red, the object (in this case, my cat) is delimited as it is only in relation to the subject (in this case, me). To see the affective aspects shaping the object, I need to attend to different aspects of the awareness: in this case, the happiness that is present not *as* an object, but *as that which co-constitutes the awareness alongside* the object. My awareness of my cat when I'm stressed, crabby, and trying to type is different than my awareness of my cat when I'm relaxed, happy, and want cuddles. This difference is not in the object, or even really in how the object appears, but rather of the presence or absence of particular subject-side factors that, together with the object, constitute my awareness as a whole.

Conclusion: The Transparency Datum

There are different ways of capturing and interpreting the transparency datum, and those different interpretations reflect the scaffolding of different theories of awareness. It has been our goal to show that despite those differences, there is something in common that transparency theorists share: the idea that there is an important datum about the nature of awareness that is worth theorizing, even though it may be difficult to capture. Entertaining the different scaffolds for interpreting that datum helps us do that, just as seeing something in different lights can help us converge on what that something is. What all three scaffolds converge on, then, is that the phenomenon of transparency is experienced during, and perhaps marks, normal human awareness—the experience of a living being trying to get by in the world they find themselves in.

What the purple scaffold brings is an illustration of what it could be to engage in the action of being aware such that we would experience the transparency that the window and the mirror scaffold highlight. This scaffold proposes that awareness is like purple and transparency is like polarization. Purple can polarize into two distinct things, red and blue, because red and blue together are nothing but purple. In the same way, a moment of awareness polarizes into two seemingly distinct things, subject and object, because the subject and the object are nothing but aspects of awareness. This analogy indicates that trying to direct your attention to your own experience polarizes the awareness into subject and object, thereby making the underlying awareness itself seem to vanish. But it also indicates that there is no buffer or mediator between the subject and the object. This is the sense in which experience is transparent: both subject and object are nothing but factors co-constituting an experience, which vanishes when we direct our attention to it, like purple vanishes when polarized into red and blue. In this framework, the direction of introspection is neither outward nor inward, but more depthward, into the details of the factors constituting a moment of awareness.

Reflecting back on Moore's struggle to put the transparency datum into words, that struggle is key to appreciating the transparency datum itself: the fact that awareness itself is elusive and can easily vanish without careful scrutiny.

References

Bayne, T., and M. Spener. 2010. Introspective Humility. *Philosophical Issues*, 20: 1–22.

Boyle, M. 2009. Two Kinds of Self-Knowledge. *Philosophy and Phenomenological Research*, 78(1): 133–64.

Byrne, A. 2001. Intentionalism Defended. *The Philosophical Review*, 110(2): 199–240.

Byrne, A. 2005. Introspection. *Philosophical Topics*, 3(1): 79–104.

Byrne, A. 2009. Experience and content. *The Philosophical Quarterly*, 59(236): 429–51.

Byrne, A. 2018. *Transparency and Self-knowledge*. Oxford: Oxford University Press.

Dunne, John. 2004. *Foundations of Dharmakīrti's Philosophy*. Boston, MA: Wisdom Publications.

Edgley, R. 1969. *Reason in Theory and Practice*. London: Hutchinson.

Evans, G. 1982. *The Varieties of Reference*. Oxford: Oxford University Press.

Harman, G. 1986. *Change in view*. Cambridge, MA: MIT Press.

Hill, C. 2009. *Consciousness*. Cambridge: Cambridge University Press.

Kind, A. 2003. What's so Transparent about Transparency. *Philosophical Studies*, 115(3): 225–44.

Moore, G. E. 1903. The Refutation of Idealism. *Mind*, 12(48): 433–53.

Moran, R. 2001. *Authority and Estrangement*. Princeton, NJ: Princeton University Press.

Peacocke, C. 1996. Entitlement, Self-Knowledge and Conceptual Redeployment. *Proceedings of the Aristotelian Society*, new series, 96: 117–58.

Prueitt, Catherine. 2017. Shifting Concepts: The Realignment of Dharmakīrti on Concepts and the Error of Subject/Object Duality in Pratyabhijñā Śaiva Thought. *Journal of Indian Philosophy*, 45(1): 21–47.

Ram-Prasad, Chakravarthi. 2018. *Human Being, Bodily Being: Phenomenology from Classical India*. Oxford: Oxford University Press.

Ratié, Isabelle. 2017. Utpaladeva and Abhinavagupta on the Freedom of Consciousness. *The Oxford Handbook of Indian Philosophy Online*. https://doi.org/10.1093/oxfordhb/9780199314621.013.27.

Tye, M. 2002. Representationalism and the Transparency of Experience. *Noûs*, 36(1): 137–51.

Wittgenstein, L. 1958. *Philosophical Investigations*. 2nd Ed. Oxford: Basil Blackwell.

9

Me-Knowledge and Effective Agency

Hagop Sarkissian

Consider the following predicament: a senior colleague (SC) of yours is planning to vote against a junior colleague's (JC) tenure case despite it being meritorious. SC's negative vote will be driven out of spite, in retaliation for a perceived slight by JC regarding the quality and importance of SC's research. Another senior colleague (SC2), closer to SC than you are and therefore well positioned to intervene, is disinclined to do so because SC2 believes that JC was not sufficiently apologetic about the relevant episode and did not do enough to make amends. JC thinks the situation is overblown and has no interest in talking to SC, which might (at any rate) simply inflame tensions. SC has started suggesting to other members of the tenure committee that JC should not be granted tenure, and that they should simply commit to a new search. Even if SC fails to persuade them and the tenure case is eventually successful, the negative vote(s) would lead to longstanding bitterness within the relatively small department, making it a less hospitable place for everyone concerned.

As a junior member of the department and a team player you would like to avoid this outcome as much as possible. You believe SC to be a good person who would come to regret the negative vote in due course, but you are not close to SC and are unsure how to proceed. You are friendly with SC2, and feel confident that SC2 sees JC's tenure case as otherwise meritorious, but your relationship is not close enough to permit any direct entreaties for SC2 to get involved. There is also the fact that you yourself are on the tenure-track and do not want to jeopardize your own case down the road.

It is clear to you that the best thing would be for SC to make amends with JC and vote in favor of tenure. What's more, it seems possible that a certain form of intervention could yield this result. You mull over the available courses of action, but they are numerous and it is not clear which route to take. Whom do you approach, and how? What tone should you take? When would be the best time? Do you make a personal visit, write an email, or invite them out to coffee or dinner?

Texts in the classical Chinese philosophical tradition are replete with discussions of cases such as these, where persons interact with one another in well-defined roles under what we might loosely refer to as normative hierarchical structures. These structures set parameters for appropriate interactions and therefore shape and

Hagop Sarkissian, *Me-Knowledge and Effective Agency* In: *Oxford Studies in Epistemology, Volume 7.* Edited by: Tamar Szabó Gendler, John Hawthorne, and Julianne Chung, Oxford University Press. © Hagop Sarkissian 2023. DOI: 10.1093/oso/9780192868978.003.0009

constrain the ways individuals interact. Several of these texts (stemming from the chaotic years spanning the Warring States period, ca. 475–221 BCE) maintain that seeing one's way through such situations and settling on a course of action can be facilitated by a particular kind of self-knowledge. It is not knowledge about one's beliefs or values, still less knowledge of one's own mental states. Instead, these texts emphasize that being an effective ethical agent—one who is able to foster cohesion and cooperation and make positive impacts on others—hinges on one's ability to make plausible first-pass predictions of how others are likely to react to one's interventions. One must know not simply the warrant of one's reasons but also how they will be received by others when issued forth in one's voice and from one's person. Such knowledge allows one to conscientiously modify one's presentation and manner to yield the ethically preferable result.[1] In short, effective agency is enhanced as one comes to know one's person in a particular way—knowing how one's person is experienced by others. This is the 'me' as seen from the perspective of a particular other, and so I'll use the term *perspectival self-knowledge* or more simply *me-knowledge* to refer to this sort of knowledge. Such knowledge can be acquired through observation, reflection, experimentation, and soliciting others' input. And, these texts argue, it is central to the project of leading an effective life.

In the first section, I characterize what I mean by effective agency and provide some context for why some early Confucian texts were especially concerned with it—namely, owing to their standing commitment to arbitrate disagreements and re-establish harmony within (often hierarchical) groups. Next, I explain why me-knowledge was vital in making good on this commitment, and then outline the central methods of cultivating it. In the final section, I show how other schools of thought during the same time period found the notion problematic, focusing on a probing and perspicacious critique found in the Inner Chapters of the *Zhuangzi*, a text in the Daoist tradition of thought.

1. Groups and the Problem of Effective Arbitration

The tenure case can be viewed as of a general type, where one is confident that outcome X is highly desirable given one's values and commitments, yet realizing X requires buy-in from others who are, to some degree or other, disinclined to realize X. It is important to note that in such cases X is not antithetical to generally recognized values, nor is X idiosyncratic in objectionable ways. In the current case, for example, the values that one wishes to promote are justice on the one hand (as JC merits tenure) and harmony on the other (as having well-functioning working relationships is preferable for all, other things being equal). Both values would be

[1] Throughout I will be referring to ethical or moral outcomes, as these were the focus of the Confucian texts. But everything I say will be applicable to any of one's projects more generally.

promoted if SC reverses course and votes in favor of JC's tenure case. As things stand, however, X will not be realized. One can, of course, blame the parties involved for being unwilling to take action and stand by while things unfold disastrously. Yet the very possibility of changing this course of events by nudging the group back toward more cooperative dynamics is, within Confucian ethics, a burden that can impel one to intervene in such cases.

Indeed, this aspect of Confucianism is broadly consequentialist, as it values the realization of harmonious states of affairs. Thus, even if one is not directly implicated in the current situation, this does not relieve one of the burden to try to intervene—if, that is, one can see a way to move the individuals toward the desired state of affairs. In short, if one can make an impact, one should. In a famous paper, Bernard Williams (1973) notes that these thoughts arise whenever one focuses on realizing valued states of affairs, or consequences.

> Consequentialism is basically indifferent to whether a state of affairs consists in what I do, or is produced by what I do, where that notion is itself wide enough to include, for instance, situations in which other people do things which I have made them do, or allowed them to do, or encouraged them to do, or given them a chance to do. All that consequentialism is interested in is the idea of these doings being *consequences* of what I do, and that is a relation broad enough to include the relations just mentioned, and many others...
>
> Correspondingly, there is no relevant difference which consists *just* in a state of affairs being brought about by me, without intervention of other agents, and another being brought about through the intervention of other agents... Granted that the states of affairs have been adequately described in causally and evaluatively relevant terms, it makes no further comprehensible difference who produces them. (Williams 1973: 93–5)[2]

Such considerations loom for the Confucian ethical agent, who seeks to achieve a level of optimal harmony amongst competing perspectives and diverging personalities (e.g. Angle 2008; Csikszentmihalyi 2004). Given this commitment, an ever-present question when confronted with hostility, ill will, or resentment is 'what can *I* do to help restore harmony in this group, considering that I am not at fault?' The question arises from the perspective of a group member who is positioned to possibly intervene, yet remains a number of causal links removed from what brought about the crisis.

[2] While there are real connections here, it is unclear whether the early Confucians would endorse the strong notion of 'negative responsibility' that Williams claims to be an entailment of consequentialism. One reason why is that Confucians thought certain actions and interventions were the prerogative of individuals occupying certain roles, such that it would simply be inappropriate in at least some cases for a person to get involved at all. In such cases, one would not be held responsible for inaction. In other words, one would not bear negative responsibility.

One might think: discovering an ethically desirable outcome backed with justifying reasons is the best way to gain others' assent or cooperation, allowing them to endorse the course of action themselves without requiring any further prompting or special intervention. While this is hard to deny in theory, gaining assent in practice will often require far more than presenting compelling reasons. After all, what may be an optimal result by one's own lights may involve disutility for others in the form of material or social costs, or the abnegation of some values or principles. Getting them to yield by dint of laying out the reasons favoring one's own preferred course of action may not counterbalance—from *their* perspective—the costs they would bear in doing so. In the face of such resistance, what is required is to get them to shift their perspectives, reassure them against doubt, or otherwise move them on a different tack. As David Wong notes, it may involve getting them to see that "a partial compensation for yielding is that a central part of that individual's good lies in the relationships with those others" (Wong, 2020). It may also involve approaching familiar people in unfamiliar ways, making inquiries about sensitive matters, or enlisting the help of those whose discretion, trustworthiness, or reasonableness are uncertain. Importantly, the particular ways that one does so may be crucial; it will matter what tone one takes, what time one chooses to intervene, or what precise language one adopts (Robertson 2019; Sarkissian 2010b). One's first moves, for example, will often play an oversized role.

Put another way, given diverging values (or even different weightings of shared values) persons may reasonably reject the normative force of the desired outcome X in favor of another state of affairs, Y, *even if* X is, *by their own lights*, something otherwise desirable. As Antonio Cua has written, in such cases the Confucian ethical agents work to shift perspectives and give salience to some value or good that is presumed to be already shared.

> In argumentative context, personal, ideal embedded principles may . . . be an articulation of the participant's understanding of the inherited core of common ethical knowledge, that is, the knowledge of those operative standards of conduct plausibly presumed to be a matter of conventional wisdom. Since such a presumption is defeasible, each participant carries a burden of reasonable persuasion in advocating her principles as "the" correct or sound interpretation of what is deemed implicit in common ethical knowledge. It is to be expected that there will be an absence of agreement or even disagreement among competent participants in their understanding of the import of ethical knowledge for a case at hand.
>
> (Cua 1989: 276)

Put another way, there are often multiple equally acceptable ways of resolving dilemmas, with no uniquely correct solution that recommends itself over and above all other ones, and so it would be unrealistic to view one's own solution as having uniquely effective normative force that will impel others' agreement. After all, *any* group of individuals with a protracted history will have some things on which they will not converge, some perspectives that will not align. As Kongzi (also known as Confucius, fl. ca. sixth century BCE) states:

> We may study together with some yet be ill suited to pursue a *dao* with them; we may be well suited to pursue a *dao* with some yet be unable to attain rank with them; we may attain rank with some yet be unable to agree on how to properly weigh conflicting ethical considerations. 可與共學，未可與適道；可與適道，未可與立；可與立，未可與權。 *Analects* 9.30[3]

Lack of agreement abounds even among those who share much in common, which is indeed *preferable* to full agreement or unity. "The Master said: The *junzi* harmonizes—he does not seek agreement; the petty person does precisely the opposite" 子曰：「君子和而不同，小人同而不和。」 (*Analects* 13.23). Here and in other early Confucian texts, the term *junzi* [pronounced joon-dz] refers to a person of integrity, ethical insight, and skill, esteemed by others and a model of wisdom and humaneness. Such a person does not seek to unify all perspectives, or to adjudicate among them to find out which are correct or false. Instead, the *junzi* seeks to accommodate and even foster the uniqueness of different perspectives to allow for individual expression and make use of the complementarity afforded by competing views. Antonio Cua (1989) has characterized this commitment in Confucian ethics as akin to a form of ethical arbitration.

> At issue in arbitration is an impartial resolution of disputes oriented toward the reconciliation of the contending parties in the light of the concern for harmonious human intercourse. The arbitrator, chosen by the parties in dispute, is concerned with repairing the rupture of human relationships rather than with deciding the rights or wrongs of the parties.[4] The task of an arbitrator is . . . to shape the expectations of the contending parties along the line of mutual concern, to get them to appreciate one another as interacting members in a community. (281)

[3] All translations are my own, following traditional numbering. 'Weighing conflicting ethical considerations' is my way of parsing a single character in the Chinese—*quan* 權 (pronounced 'chwhen'). It refers to an ability to appropriately accommodate conflicts in values, norms, or other ethically relevant considerations. More specifically, it refers to an ability to know when to deviate from ritually proper conduct (or *li* 禮) because the impropriety engendered thereby will be balanced out by some other more pressing moral need.

[4] Cua characterizes the arbitrator as *chosen* by the disputing parties, and this might suggest that the parties themselves agree to choose someone. In this case, it is better to think of a person being 'acceptable' to both parties (if the person offers to intervene).

How to do so? One must leverage what one knows about how one impacts others and thereby choose a course that moves them toward a stance of accommodation, which Wong sees as including

> an epistemic openness and preparedness to expand one's conception of the good and the right upon further understanding and appreciation of other ways of life; a willingness to act on one's own moral positions in ways that minimize or reduce potential damage to one's broader relationships to others who have opposing positions; and a willingness to compromise at least sometimes on what one might have achieved in realizing one's moral position for the sake of sustaining broader relationships with disagreeing others. (Wong 2006: 6; see also chapter 9)

The value of accommodation in the context of interpersonal (and especially protracted) relationships is obvious. So even while an accommodating attitude might not seem forthcoming, there may be ways to intervene to make it a live option.

As I argue in the next section, when confronted with such situations where one must nudge another toward a more accommodating stance, one must first consider and understand the numerous factors that might be working to shape their perspective and then see a way to have an impactful intervention with them. Me-knowledge, as I characterize it, follows from the conscientious adoption of another's perspective on oneself, seeing not only how another person experiences the current situation, but also how one might appear to them as a potential arbiter.

2. Me-Knowledge

In the tenure case, the problem can be resolved in many ways: by SC being moved directly by one's entreaties; by SC2 being swayed to intervene with SC; by JC resolving to make a gesture of reconciliation toward SC; or several other possibilities. Which person is more likely to be receptive? Where does one stand to make the most impact? Successful arbitration (or effective agency) in these types of cases requires *me-knowledge*—knowing, with some degree of confidence, how others will react to one's interventions in the relevant context.

But how can one be confident in such predictions? A first step, according to the Confucian view, is to consider what role the person is currently occupying, how that role may be shaping their relations to others, their history in that role, and other factors that might influence relations of power among the persons involved. These should be considered alongside any standing motivations, desires, and overall values one might take them to have in context. Beyond these, we are told to be attuned to more specific information that can only be gleaned when directly interacting with them, including the person's current mood and state of mind

(Sarkissian 2010a). These aspects are captured by the notion of *shu* 恕 or conscientious perspective taking.

As is often noted, the word *shu* 恕 consists of two components: *ru* 如 on top, meaning 'liken to' or 'resemble,' and *xin* 心 on the bottom, meaning 'mind' (sometimes translated as heart-mind)—the seat of affect, cognition, and volition. Likening oneself to others, putting oneself in their shoes and imagining how things would seem from their perspective is described as the method of 'humaneness' (*ren* 仁) (6.30). It helps one avoid offense and harm, and thereby close off the possibility of harmonizing. As Kwong-loi Shun writes, *shu* "has to do with potentially negative conditions of an individual in that the contemplated treatment from which I should refrain is either unwelcome to the individual or not in her interest" (Shun 2014: 269). A famous formulation along these lines occurs in *Analects* 15.24:

> "Zigong asked 'Is there a single word that might serve a guide for one's entire life?' The Master said, 'Wouldn't that be *shu* (恕)? What you do not desire do not impose on others." (15.24; see also 4.15, 5.12).

But this conscientious perspective taking is only half the picture. For in several passages *shu* appears alongside another term *zhong* (忠, pronounced roughly 'johng') which elsewhere means 'loyalty' yet here means something like thoughtful diligence or "being honest with oneself in dealing with others" (Goldin 2008). One cannot be *zhong* without first exercising *shu*, since one must first conscientiously consider the perspective of the other and only then will one know how to act oneself.[5] The 'Application of Centeredness' (*Zhongyong* 中庸) chapter of the *Record of Ritual* (*Liji* 禮記), an early anthology of Confucian writings, helps fill in this picture.

> The *junzi* governs persons taking them as they are, and stops [any involvement] once they've responded appropriately. *Zhong* and *shu* thus cannot be separate from *dao*: what you would not be willing to have done to you, do not impose it on others. The *junzi's dao* comprises four things, and I have yet to prove capable of even one: To serve my father as I would expect a son to serve me, I have proved incapable. To serve my prince as I would expect a minister to serve me, I have proved incapable. To serve my elder brother as I would expect a younger brother to serve me, I have proved incapable. To take the lead and favor friends as I would expect them to favor me, I have proved incapable.
>
> 子曰:「道不遠人。人之為道而遠人,不可以為道。。。故君子以人治人,改而止。忠恕違道不遠,施諸己而不願,亦勿施於人。君子之道四,丘未

[5] For more on the relationship between these concepts, see Chan (2000), Fingarette (1979), and Ivanhoe (1990).

能一焉：所求乎子以事父，未能也；所求乎臣以事君，未能也；所求乎弟以事兄，未能也；所求乎朋友先施之，未能也。

(Text from Johnston and Wang 2012: 250; translation my own)

Let us focus here on the first of the four relational pairings mentioned above—namely, father and son. What is demanded here is not simply that a *junzi*, having considered how he would like his own son to act toward him, then act in that very same way toward his own father (a common reading). Nor is it saying that a *junzi* must, more simply, conform to the general norms of comportment appropriate to the father-child relationship (as demanded by ritual propriety). Instead, in order to serve one's own father appropriately, one must take the perspective of one's own father and then see what is called for *from that perspective*. If one is unable to take one's own father's perspective—if one is unable to understand *how one appears to one's father in particular*—one will be ineffective in serving him and shaping one's relationship with him in one's preferred direction.

Me-knowledge is what results from this process of adopting others' perspectives on oneself. It may include broad generalizations or widely accepted norms governing one's relationship with the other in the relevant context (such as the father-son relationship above). Ritual propriety (*li* 禮, pronounced 'lee') provide these norms (Sarkissian 2014). However, these general norms require interpretation and discretion in practice, which includes imaginatively putting oneself in the other's (contextual) shoes.[6] This kind of know-how allows one to start seeing the perspectival 'me.'

What is *yi* 義 (pronounced 'ee') or appropriate for me to do is thus highly contextual. As Wong writes:

> The Confucian concept of *yi* 義 is often translated as 'rightness', but this requires the proviso that the connotation should be that of appropriateness or fittingness. The connotation builds context into the notion of rightness. Something is right in the sense that it fits the situation at hand, in the way that how one makes soup must be fitted to the particular ingredients one has . . . [H]armony among human beings is not static but an activity of harmonizing that requires continuous mutual adjustment of the interests of individuals to each other . . . What constitutes a satisfactory adjustment cannot be specified independently of the particular interests at stake and the present and future nature of the relationships of all the relevant parties. (Wong 2020)

[6] My thanks to Alec Sculley for helping me separate these two different kinds of knowledge (both of which are crucial to personal efficacy). The relative importance between them will vary from context to context. It should be noted that the kind of me-knowledge that is outlined in the chapter likely rests upon a notion of neurotypicality and requisite faculties that might not be as well developed in some persons as it is in others. My thanks again to Alec Scully for pointing this out.

3. Acquiring Me-Knowledge

It might be expected, then, that me-knowledge can only be gained through lived experience—gaining experience of others' perspectives and how one might figure in them. And this is indeed what we find in these sources. A range of previous observation points naturally disinclines one from undertaking steps that are unlikely to yield success while also pulling one in the direction of what is, based on lived experience, most likely to work. Many passages of the *Analects*, for example, note that becoming a better person means coming to know such facts about oneself and how one influences others. We are told of three things that a *junzi* values most: "By altering his own demeanor he avoids violence and arrogance [by others]; by rectifying his own countenance he welcomes trustworthiness [by others]; through his own words and tone of voice he avoids vulgarity and impropriety [by others]" (8.4).[7] This passage connects details of the *junzi's* observable behavior to that of others, suggesting that they are tightly correlated.

Peers, colleagues, and friends are particularly important sources of insight (e.g. 1.4, 1.7, 1.8, 9.25), and reflecting on them was something Kongzi obviously relished and found edifying (e.g. 1.15, 3.8).[8] They can, for example, observe how others react to oneself and therefore provide insights that might evade one's own awareness. Kongzi himself is often depicted as providing insight into his students' abilities—what they are capable of pulling off and where they will likely fall short (e.g. 11.22).[9]

Ultimately, though, one must be committed to understanding how one affects others through careful observation of one's own behavior—especially when one encounters difficulties. Consider *Mengzi 4B28*, which discusses this idea in some detail. The passage begins by making general claims about how to treat others and how such treatment is reciprocated in kind.

> A humane person loves others; a person with a sense of propriety respects others. One who loves others is loved in turn, one who respects others is respected in turn.
> 仁者愛人，有禮者敬人。愛人者人恆愛之，敬人者人恆敬之。

[7] I interpret 8.4 alongside other passages (such as 10.25, 12.1, 12.5, 13.4, 14.42, 16.10) that show the importance of modifying one's behavior in response to others and thereby putting them at ease. For discussion, see Sarkissian (2010b). An alternative reading of these lines maintains that altering one's demeanor is a way to avoid *being* violent and arrogant, that rectifying one's countenance is a way of *being* trustworthy, and that minding one's words and tone of voice is a way of *not* being vulgar and improper *to others*. My thanks to Myeong-seok Kim for asking how my interpretation relates to others in the literature.

[8] My thanks to Karyn Lai for emphasizing the importance of the peer relationship in acquiring accurate me-knowledge.

[9] However, since it is unlikely that any such knowledge gleaned ahead of time will be fully sufficient for dealing with how the other will react in the moment, a *junzi* must make spontaneous inductive inferences and attune one's behavior in the moment; acting on me-knowledge thus involves some improvisational skill (Lai 2012; Sarkissian 2010a).

This claim is both descriptive (about what tends to occur) as well as prescriptive (how one ought to act). (The enthymematic premise is something like a conditional: If you want to be a humane person, then . . .)

The passage then considers what one can reasonably infer if one is *not* in fact loved by others, or *not* treated with due consideration. The chain of reasoning is analogous to *modus tollens*: If I treat this person with respect, I will be respected in turn. But this person is not treating me respectfully. Might *I* have failed to initially convey respect?

> Suppose someone were to treat one in outrageous fashion. A *junzi* would, in such a case, surely examine his own person, thinking: "It must be that I wasn't benevolent; it must be that I lacked propriety. How else could such a thing have come about?" But if, after examining his person, he finds he had been humane, he had acted with propriety, and yet the person still treats him outrageously, then the *junzi* will again be certain to examine his own person, thinking "I must have failed to be diligent." But if he finds that he was, in fact, conscientious, and the person still treats him outrageously, only then would the *junzi* say, "I suppose he is the incorrigible one." (*Mengzi* 4B:28)
>
> 有人於此，其待我以橫逆，則君子必自反也：我必不仁也，必無禮也，此物奚宜至哉？其自反而仁矣，自反而有禮矣，其橫逆由是也，君子必自反也：我必不忠。自反而忠矣，其橫逆由是也，君子曰：『此亦妄人也已矣。』

The *junzi* sees how others treat him as a function of his own behavior—a kind of conditional prediction: A will do *x* if I do *y* (Morton 2002; Sarkissian 2010b). They examine and reflect on how they might have engendered the harsh treatment in question (Sarkissian 2015, 2017). There is a phrase—seeking its source from oneself (*qiu zhu ji* 求諸己)—that may be particularly relevant here.[10]

> Mengzi said, "If one cares for others and they do not respond with affection, one should revert and examine the humaneness [in one's care]; if one governs people and they are not well ordered, one should revert and examine the wisdom [in one's governing]; if one behaves with propriety yet others do not respond appropriately, one should revert and examine the reverence [in one's propriety]. In one's comportment whenever there are those who do not requite, in every case one must revert and seek the source of this in oneself— for when one's person is rectified the rest of the world follows it." (Mengzi 4A4)

[10] My thanks to Karyn Lai for pointing this out.

孟子曰：愛人不親反其仁，治人不治反其智，禮人不答反其敬。行有不得者，皆反求諸己，其身正而天下歸之。

Kongzi said, "A *junzi* seeks its source from himself; a petty person seeks its source in others." (*Analects* 15.21)

子曰：「君子求諸己，小人求諸人。」

Such passages enjoin readers to better understand how others may be experiencing and interpreting their behavior—how their demeanor, actions, and mere presence might be affecting others. Over time, this would help one avoid awkwardness, friction, hesitation, and doubt, paving the way toward accommodation, cooperation, and even trust. This is how one acquires me-knowledge.

Finally, perspectival me-knowledge is motivated by a desire to achieve congruence between one's ends and values on the one hand, and how these are conveyed through one's person on the other. Congruence facilitates interpretability; one should care about me-knowledge from the very drive one has to interact with others—namely, the desire to communicate and to be understood (Velleman 2015). Congruity here is not with a core, underlying, unchanging 'true' self, but rather with the 'me' in this context, with these persons and relationships—here and now. We aim for congruity generally by realizing it across several particulars.

4. Lacking Perspective, Lacking Me-Knowledge

Of course, there are downsides to becoming concerned about 'me.' For example, we find clues in the *Analects* suggesting that a *junzi*'s desire to seek harmony may go too far, leading them to accommodate persons who have no interest in being accommodating themselves (e.g. *Analects* 6.26). Moreover, excessive attention on oneself and how one might appear to others can lead one to become glib, aloof, or priggish in their eyes, thus undermining one's desire to be seen as trustworthy or upright instead (Sarkissian forthcoming).[11] In the pages of the *Mozi*, a text from a rival school of social reformers, we find Kongzi depicted as wholly consumed by his dazzling presence and impeccable decorum, while neglecting the project of actually reforming others' behavior and making changes for the good.[12]

In this section, though, I focus on a different kind of critique, one that highlights the dangers in failing to engage in *shu* (conscientious perspective taking), and instead focusing on the rightness of one's position and the attractiveness of one's preferred outcome—taking these to be so obvious as to only require stating them

[11] See Sarkissian (forthcoming) for further elaboration of this theme.

[12] See especially the 'Against the Confucians II' (Fei Ru Xia 非儒下) chapter in Johnston (2009).

aloud to have others yield. One might assume that one's values are widely shared and only require articulation or that one's judgment is sound and so will be taken as authoritative by persons who might, in fact, have no interest in hearing it. In such cases, one risks losing efficacy precisely because one imagines oneself as more persuasive or compelling than can be reasonably expected were one truly to adopt the other's perspective.

The most probing and damning critique along these lines can be found in the *Zhuangzi* (pronounced 'jwong-ds'), an anthology of early Daoist literature. In a fictitious dialogue that opens Chapter Four "In the World of Men" (*renjianshi* 人間世), Kongzi reproaches his exceptional student Yan Hui for asking a leave of absence in order to go and reform the callous ruler of the state of Wei. Yan Hui adverts to all the right reasons for undertaking this mission: the ruler is cruel, his people are dying in large numbers owing to his neglect, and someone needs to do something about it. Yan Hui resolves to be that someone. Nonetheless, Kongzi pushes back, questioning not only his motives but also his methods and his chances for success. He notes that 1) Yan Hui is not yet virtuous himself, so he should have no time to spare lecturing others and 2) Yan Hui is likely (perhaps even unconsciously) motivated by desires for fame and repute (which can be had by bravely attempting to reform such a heartless sovereign), even if his desire to ameliorate the plight of Wei's people is genuine.

A key theme throughout this dialogue is Yan Hui's continual focus on himself—his knowledge, his erudition, skills, and commitment—all while failing to appreciate how he, this person Yan Hui, would appear to the king from the king's own perspective—a powerful, complex, and dynamic individual on whose terms they will be meeting. In effect, the dialogue suggests that one's wholehearted commitment to realizing the good may, perversely, *undermine* one's ability to have efficacy 'in the world of [actual] persons' (as the chapter title states).[13] Kongzi concludes that Yan Hui will lack effective agency and accomplish nothing save annoying the ruler and dicing with death.

> Suppose your virtuosity (*de* 德) is ample, your sincerity firm, yet you fail to probe his mood; suppose you go in without reputation for being pugnacious, yet fail to earnestly search his mind; suppose you then go on to preach humaneness and rightness using artful speech right in the tyrant's face—well, you'd just be making yourself look good by making him look bad [by comparison]. That's what's called plaguing others—and he who plagues others will surely be plagued in return. It seems you're in danger of being plagued!

[13] For another interpretation of this famous passage that resonates with my own in many respects (while departing in others), see Chong (2016).

> 且德厚信矼，未達人氣；名聞不爭，未達人心。而彊以仁義繩墨之言術暴人之前者，是以人惡有其美也，命之曰菑人。菑人者，人必反菑之，若殆為人菑夫！ (4/9/4–6)[14]

('Probing his mood' and 'searching his mind' are the kinds of things one does when engaging in *shu*.) Kongzi then asks Yan Hui to share his plans for dealing with this eventuality, only to have Yan Hui once again affirm his fixation on himself. "Exacting and upright," he answers, "yet remaining empty and unassuming. Diligent in effort, with singular focus. Would that work?" 端而虛，勉而一，則可乎 (4/9/14)? Yan Hui's instincts are to pay attention to his commitments and bearing to see whether they measure up to his own ideals of conduct. Kongzi is unmoved.

> "No, no! How could that ever work? This man you are describing would stand out as overflowing with aggressive resolve (*yang* 陽), his complexion would be unsettled as he tries to constantly dwell in what others find acceptable, manipulating their feelings while seeking to ease their minds. Even a so-called 'gradually progressing charisma' cannot take hold, never mind anything grander than that. He will remain fixed in his ways and wholly unreformed. Outwardly he might play along yet remain unmoved within. How could that work?"
>
> 曰：「惡！惡可？夫以陽為充孔揚，采色不定，常人之所不違，因案人之所感，以求容與其心。名之曰日漸之德不成，而況大德乎！將執而不化，外合而內不訾，其庸詎可乎！」 (4/9/14–16)

Yan Hui tries once again to gain Kongzi's approval, but what he says is doubly disappointing. First, he claims that he will remain pure and committed within, though on the outside he will bow and kneel to signal his inferior social standing and avoid causing offense. Second, he claims that he will indeed criticize the tyrant, but his criticisms will be couched—and therefore cloaked—in stock sayings of antiquity and oral tradition. These boilerplate and rote examples will allow him to avoid triggering the ruler's ire as he will only be invoking what he takes to be commonly accepted truisms. "The words will really be criticisms and remonstrations, but they'll be those of the ancients, not mine!" 其言雖教，讁之實也。古之有也，非吾有也。(4/9/21–22) Kongzi's response is telling.

> "No, no! How could that ever work? You have a great multitude of policies, but your means are uninformed by reconnaissance. Although this might well allow you to get by without being faulted, that's about all you'll accomplish. How could

[14] Translations of the *Zhuangzi* are my own, though I've referred to Graham (2001), Kjellberg (2005), and Ziporyn (2009) to get through the tougher bits. Citations are to the standard ICS concordance, as quoted in Sturgeon (2011).

> it have any effect on the tyrant? You are still taking your made-up mind as your instructor."
>
> 惡！惡可？大多政，法而不諜，雖固，亦无罪。雖然，止是耳矣，夫胡可以及化！猶師心者也。 (4/9/25–26)

Let us take stock. Yan Hui is, on the one hand, doing what he thinks he should be doing: he is heeding his teacher's advice to adhere to the strictures of ritual propriety in all dealings (e.g. *Analects* 12.1) and is singularly focussed on promoting benevolence. His intentions are sincere. His reasons sound. However, precisely *because* he is overflowing with such thoughts, aims, and desires, he is guided by his made-up mind, making it his master (*you shi xin zhe ye* 猶師心者也) and is wholly (and tragically) lacking in perspectival *me-knowledge* that is facilitated through taking the ruler's perspective on his own person—seeing how he (Yan Hui) will appear *to him*.[15] Thus, according to Kongzi, he has no real prospect to find efficacy in his self-appointed (and precarious) mission.

Yan Hui is at his wit's end. "I have nothing left to put forward. Dare I ask what I should do?" Kongzi tells him that to find efficacy he must forget his plans, intentions, merits, and virtues—all of them. Yan Hui's first step must be to 'fast' (zhai 齋) his mind—that is, to empty himself from his mind and thus become responsive and present in the moment, unblinkered by previous thoughts.

> "This single-minded will of yours [to go and reform the ruler]—you have been fixated on it not with your ears but rather with your mind, indeed not simply with your mind but rather with your vital energy (qi) itself. Listening should remain at the [outward-facing] ears, and your mind should abide in recognition. As for the vital energy (qi)—it will then be empty, awaiting upon things (to stir it up). Your path forward (dao 道) will come together in this newfound emptiness. This is the fasting of the mind."[16]
>
> 若一志，无聽之以耳而聽之以心，无聽之以心而聽之以氣。聽止於耳，心止於符。氣也者，虛而待物者也。唯道集虛。虛者，心齋也。 (4/10/1–3)

[15] Moeller and D'Ambrosio (2017) offer a reading that complements my own: "Confucius here exposes a central aspect of the hypocrisy involved in the Confucian sincerity project: one's desire for the dual correspondence between one's actions and character and one's performance and (good) name implies a mutual confirmation of one's own persona and one's social recognition. One thereby not only defines oneself by socially constructed values but also presupposes that the goodness society will eventually ascribe to oneself reflects one's true personal goodness. By verifying social values, one thus intends to ultimately verify oneself. But this self-verification emerges paradoxically from an insincere desire to do and affirm that which is deemed good by society only in order to be acclaimed and considered—including by oneself—as sincerely good" (143).

[16] This is a difficult passage to translate. I follow Ziporyn's reading, which follows the original grammar in a more straightforward fashion. Nevertheless, all translators agree that the overall message here is to empty one's mind of preconceived plans and notions and instead turn one's attention to the present reality, to the here-and-now.

Yan Hui has a realization: "Before receiving this instruction—*that* Hui was full of Hui. Having now received it—there is yet to be a Hui. Is this what you mean by 'emptiness'?" 回之未始得使，實自回也；得使之也，未始有回也。可謂虛乎 "Precisely!", Kongzi exclaims. "I tell you: You can then go wander freely in his cage without letting his reputation get to you. If you can get inside him, sing your song. If not, let it be. No schooling; no prescriptions." 吾語若！若能入遊其樊而无感其名，入則鳴，不入則止。无門无毒。(4/10/3–5)[17]

It is difficult to pin down exactly what Kongzi means when he tells Yan Hui that he's been listening with his *qi* (vital energy). However, the general tenor of his remarks is undeniable: the more Yan Hui fixes his attention on himself the more he'll be blinded in his attempts to attend to others. The more he compares his conduct to ideals the more he will fail to see others for who they are and thereby see himself through their eyes. Without such perspective taking he will never attain me-knowledge. He will never realize that if the tyrant were the kind of person to be impressed by the erudition and moral entreaties of learned scholars he wouldn't need Yan Hui to begin with. Only a mental fast—a release of all of his preconceived plans—can allow him to see himself through the tyrant's eyes and therefore engage with the tyrant on his own terms. Even if he is ineffective, he might yet avoid plaguing the tyrant, and being plagued in return. That's no mean thing.

5. Conclusion

Me-knowledge promotes interpretability only when it is genuine—when one is able to conscientiously take the perspective of others and see oneself as one appears to them. This is difficult. Cringe-inducing audio recordings ("Did I really sound like that?") or video recordings ("Why was I slouching so much? Why did I look so distant?") are often potent reminders that how others experience us might escape our own attention. So while we may worry that others do not see us as we truly are—that the way they experience or interpret our behavior is laden with bias and misunderstanding—the reverse is also true.

Put another way, I may think that I know the perspectival 'me'—how I sound, how I appear, what the tone of my voice and the arch of my eyebrow convey to the person at hand. But whatever knowledge I have in these regards will be imperfect in some fairly obvious and non-obvious ways. All the more reason to get to know 'me' better.[18]

[17] I follow Kjellberg in my reading of the last line, which has proved vexing for many commentators. See, e.g., the long list of interpretations in Cui (2012: 139–41).

[18] My thanks to audiences at University of Vermont, University at Buffalo, California State, Fullerton for helpful discussion of this material. Special thanks as well to Nic Bommarito, Aram Kang, Ryan Nichols, and Alec Scully for helpful discussion, and to Julianne Chung, Myeong-seok Kim, Karyn Lai, David Santamaria Legarda, and David Wong for helpful comments on previous drafts.

References

Angle, S.C. 2008. No supreme principle: Confucianism's harmonization of multiple values. *Dao*, *7*(1): 35–40.

Chan, S. Y. 2000. Can Shu be the one word that serves as the guiding principle of caring actions? *Philosophy East & West*, *50*(4): 507–24.

Chong, K.-C. 2016. *Zhuangzi's Critique of the Confucians: Blinded by the Human*. SUNY Press.

Csikszentmihalyi, M. 2004. *Material Virtue*. Brill Academic Publishers.

Cua, A.S. 1989. The status of principles in Confucian ethics. *Journal of Chinese Philosophy*, *16*(3–4): 273–96.

Cui, D. 崔大華. 2012. 莊子岐解. 中华书局.

Fingarette, H. 1979. Following the "one thread" of the "Analects." *Journal of the American Academy of Religion. American Academy of Religion*, *47*(3, Thematic Issue S.): 373–405.

Goldin, P.R. 2008. When zhong 忠 does not mean "loyalty." *Dao*, *7*(2): 165–74.

Graham, A.C. 2001. *Chuang Tzu: The Inner Chapters*. Hackett Publishing.

Ivanhoe, P.J. 1990. Reweaving the "one thread" of the *Analects*. *Philosophy East & West*, *40*(1): 17–33.

Johnston, I. 2009. *The Mozi: A Complete Translation*. Chinese University Press.

Johnston, I. and Ping, W. 2012. *Daxue and Zhongyong (A Bilingual Edition)*. The Chinese University of Hong Kong Press.

Kjellberg, P. 2005. Zhuangzi. In P.J. Ivanhoe and B.W. Van Norden (Eds.), *Readings in Classical Chinese Philosophy* (2nd ed., pp. 207–54). Seven Bridges New York.

Lai, K.L. 2012. Knowing to act in the moment: Examples from Confucius' Analects. *Asian Philosophy*, *22*(4): 347–64.

Moeller, H.-G. and D'Ambrosio, P.J. 2017. *Genuine Pretending: On the Philosophy of the Zhuangzi*. Columbia University Press.

Morton, A. 2002. *The Importance of Being Understood: Folk Psychology as Ethics*. Routledge.

Robertson, S. 2019. Nunchi, Ritual, and Early Confucian Ethics. *Dao*, *18*(1): 23–40.

Sarkissian, H. 2010a. Confucius and the effortless life of virtue. *History of Philosophy Quarterly*, *27*(1): 1–16.

Sarkissian, H. 2010b. Minor Tweaks, Major Payoffs: The Problems and Promise of Situationism in Moral Philosophy. *Philosopher's Imprint*, *10*(9): 1–15.

Sarkissian, H. 2014. Ritual and rightness in the *Analects*. In A. Olberding (Ed.), *Dao Companion to the Analects* (pp. 95–116). Springer Netherlands.

Sarkissian, H. 2015. When you think it's bad, it's worse than you think: Psychological bias and the ethics of negative character assessments. In B. Bruya (Ed.), *The Philosophical Challenge from China* (pp. 3–22). MIT Press.

Sarkissian, H. 2017. Situationism, Manipulation, and Objective Self-Awareness. *Ethical Theory and Moral Practice*, *20*(3): 489–503.

Sarkissian, H. Forthcoming. Virtuous contempt (*wu* 惡) in the *Analects*. In J. Tiwald (Ed.), *The Oxford Handbook of Chinese Philosophy*. Oxford University Press.

Shun, K.-L. 2014. Early Confucian Moral Psychology. In V. Shen (Ed.), *Dao Companion to Classical Confucian Philosophy* (pp. 263–89). Springer Netherlands.

Sturgeon, D. (Ed.). 2011. Chinese Text Project. http://ctext.org.

Velleman, D.J. 2015. *Foundations for Moral Relativism: Second Expanded Edition*. Open Book Publishers.

Williams, B. 1973. A Critique of Utilitarianism. In J.J.C. Smart and B. Williams (Eds.), *Utilitarianism: For and Against* (pp. 77–150). Cambridge University Press.

Wong, D.B. 2006. *Natural Moralities: A Defense of Pluralistic Relativism*. Oxford University Press.

Wong, D.B. 2020. Soup, Harmony, and Disagreement. *Journal of the American Philosophical Association*, *6*(2): 139–55.

Ziporyn, B. 2009. *Zhuangzi: The Essential Writings with Selections from Traditional Commentaries*. Hackett Publishing.

10

Meditations on Beliefs Formed Arbitrarily

Miriam Schoenfield

> For to say under such circumstances, "Do not decide, but leave the question open," is itself a passional decision—just like deciding yes or no, and is attended with the same risk of losing the truth.
>
> William James, "The Will to Believe" (1896)

This chapter is about how to respond to the realization that many of our beliefs are formed, in a sense, arbitrarily. Especially when it comes to matters that play a fundamental role in structuring our lives (religion, morality, politics), people adopt remarkably similar beliefs to their parents and peer groups.[1] This suggests that social influences are largely responsible for the fact that we hold the beliefs that we do. Had we grown up in a different city, or attended a different school, or been raised with a different religious outlook, we would almost certainly see the world very differently. The question is: what to do about this?

I will be addressing the concern about beliefs formed arbitrarily in a somewhat untraditional way. Rather than providing arguments about which way of responding to such etiological information is *rational* or how you *should* respond to this information, or whether you can have *knowledge* in such cases, I am going to simply describe how I've come to think about the problem in my own case.[2] So, before I begin, I'd like to say a few words about what motivated this choice, and why I think a piece of this form can be philosophically illuminating.

There are two reasons that I have chosen to use the first personal form in addressing the problem of arbitrarily formed belief: First, many people who regard their beliefs as arbitrarily formed (more on exactly what that means later) find themselves in a state in which they are *doubting* their beliefs. There are various thoughts that have been appealed to in the literature on beliefs formed arbitrarily that won't be of much help for someone in such a state. One example is the

[1] Data from a Pew study on religious cross-generational retention rates as of 2007 can be found here: http://rationalwiki.org/wiki/Pew_Forum%27s_U.S._Religious_Landscape_Survey. See also Glass et al. (1986) and Argyle and Beit Hallahmi (1997: 98).

[2] The details, however, are not autobiographically accurate.

Miriam Schoenfield, *Meditations on Beliefs Formed Arbitrarily* In: *Oxford Studies in Epistemology, Volume 7.* Edited by: Tamar Szabó Gendler, John Hawthorne, and Julianne Chung, Oxford University Press.
DOI: 10.1093/oso/9780192868978.003.0010

thought that *if you actually got things right* (in some sense or another of 'right'), it can be rational for you to maintain your belief.[3] It is not my purpose in this chapter to argue against such views. My point is just that, for somebody engaged in a certain kind of doubt, these accounts won't be helpful. This is because, in these contexts of doubt, one is wondering precisely *about* whether one got things right. And so it is, at very least, also worth thinking about this predicament from the perspective of somebody who is, oneself, in the state of doubt. One reason, then, that I am writing this piece in the first person is that my aim is to *demonstrate* how someone experiencing what is sometimes called "genealogical anxiety,"[4] might navigate these concerns. (I take this to be at least part of what Descartes was doing in his *Meditations*: giving a demonstration of how someone who finds themselves beset with doubt might fish themselves out of the skeptical quicksand.)

The second reason for using the first personal form is that I think theorists with different background epistemological views might wish to draw different conclusions from the considerations I raise here. So rather than take a stand on such large issues as internalism versus externalism or coherentism versus foundationalism, I will simply demonstrate a way of thinking about arbitrarily formed belief and let the theorist choose her own adventure on the basis of her other philosophical commitments. Along the way I'll point out some of these choice points.

So now, without further ado:

1. First Meditation: Why Avoid Beliefs Formed Arbitrarily?

I'll begin with two preliminary remarks.

First, my interest in beliefs formed arbitrarily isn't primarily with on/off belief states. I'm interested in any doxastic state in which we're more confident in one of P or ~P, but we realize that this asymmetrical favoring of the proposition in question came about as a result of the sort of social influences described above. So in what follows I'll use the term "belief" in a very weak way so that an agent has a belief that P as long as she is more confident in P than in ~P. This is purely terminological: it will allow me to discuss under the heading of "beliefs formed arbitrarily" not only cases of certainty, or binary belief, but also cases in which one has, say, a 0.6 credence in P, or a state in which one regards P as more likely than not.

Second, it will be helpful to be a bit more precise about what it is to regard a belief as formed arbitrarily. Here's how I'll think of things: to regard a belief as formed arbitrarily is to regard which belief one ends up adopting with respect to

[3] For discussion of views in this spirit see Lasonen Aarnio (2010, 2014), White (2010), Srinivasan (2015, section 3.1), and Titelbaum (2015).

[4] Srinivasan (2015).

P as independent of whether P. (Formally, we can think of this as regarding Pr(I form the belief that P|P) = Pr(I form the belief that P|~P), and Pr(I form the belief that ~P|P) = Pr(I form the belief that ~P|~P).[5]

I'll illustrate this notion of arbitrarily formed belief by considering two toy cases inspired by White (2010). These cases are very artificial, but they'll be useful for getting some of the basic ideas on the table. (We'll get to the cases that initially concerned us—religious, moral, and political belief—in the Fourth Meditation, after some other warm-up cases.)

> Perceptual Coin Flip: One fair coin will determine whether the wall will be painted red or blue. Another fair coin will determine whether it will appear to me that the wall is red or it will appear to me that the wall is blue.[6]

If I thought that I'd find myself in Perceptual Coin Flip, and I expected to form a belief about the color of the wall on the basis of how things appear to me, then I'd regard my future belief as arbitrarily formed. This is because I'd think that the color of the wall, and my belief about its color, would be determined by two independent coin flips, and so I'd regard which belief I form as independent of the truth.

> Logic Coin Flip: One fair coin will determine whether I'll be given a logic problem whose premises entail H or a logic problem whose premises entail ~H. The flip of a second fair coin will determine whether I come up with a proof that seems to me to show that the premises entail H or I come up with a proof that seems to me to show that the premises entail ~H. (Whichever answer I come up with, checking and double-checking will yield the same answer.)

[5] A few notes about this definition: first, "Pr" refers to an agent's subjective probabilities. Second, the definition works most straightforwardly when thinking about cases in which I'm regarding some *future* belief of mine as one that will be arbitrarily formed (for instance, a case in which I know that I'll get some evidence later, but I don't know which belief I will form on the basis of the evidence, if I form one at all). Later, I'll talk about cases in which we're considering currently held beliefs and what's involved in regarding such beliefs as arbitrarily formed. Third, note that this is a definition of what it is *to regard* a belief as formed arbitrarily. At no point will I define what it *is* for a belief to be formed arbitrarily. One may be able to provide such a definition, but I'm primarily interested in what to think given an agent's perspective on things. So, for my purposes, it's enough to talk about what attitude the agent has that elicits the relevant concern. Finally, I'm using the term "regarding a belief as arbitrarily formed" stipulatively, to capture the sorts of cases that I'm interested in. There are many uses of the word "arbitrary" and one might think that some cases that meet my definition don't count, intuitively, as "arbitrarily" formed belief (for example, perhaps the beliefs are based on reasons and arguments). That's fine. My goal isn't to provide an analysis of our intuitive conception of arbitrariness, but rather to home in on cases in which we regard which opinion we form as independent of the truth as a result of learning about the belief's etiology.

[6] There are different ways to fill in the case, and the differences won't matter for my purposes. But note that it is perfectly consistent with the description of the case that if the color of the wall matches the color that it appears to me to be, then I have an ordinary veridical visual experience.

A similar line of reasoning applies to Logic Coin Flip. If I were to learn that I will find myself in such a situation in the future, and I expected to form beliefs on the basis of my reasoning, I would now regard my future belief state as arbitrarily formed. For I'll regard the facts about which belief I'll form as independent of whether I'm given an H-entailing problem or a ~H-entailing problem.

When I contemplate these toy cases I feel strongly that I'd much prefer maintaining a 0.5 credence in the relevant proposition to forming a belief arbitrarily. But why do I have this preference?

In trying to explain why I'm averse to forming beliefs arbitrarily in cases like the ones above, I started thinking about what it is, in general, that I'm after when I'm inquiring. And when I reflect on this question (things might go differently for you) the answer that comes to me is this: I'm trying to get at the truth. What I want out of my beliefs when I'm inquiring into some matter is that they provide me with an accurate representation of reality. There might be other goodies that would be nice to have: for example, it might be nice if my beliefs were not only true, but also couldn't have easily been false (and so could constitute knowledge),[7] or it might be nice if my beliefs contributed to my general well-being.[8] However, I want to set these other lovely features of belief aside for the moment. I'm interested, for now, in whether an aversion to arbitrarily formed beliefs can be made sense of given what I take my most immediate goal to be: the truth.[9]

So, can an aversion to arbitrarily formed belief be explained by a concern with truth? Answer: Yes, at least some of the time, but not in an obvious way. For note that, at first glance, it's not clear why, given a concern with truth, I'd be averse to forming a belief arbitrarily. It's true that if I expect to form a belief about the color of the wall in Perceptual Coin Flip, I'll think that I have a 50% chance of forming a false belief. That is, indeed, unfortunate. But, on the plus side, I'll also have a 50% shot at a true belief! If I adopt a 0.5 credence, on the other hand, I'm playing it safe—I'm not risking any falsehoods, but at the cost of not gaining any truths either. So why does 0.5 seem preferable? In the practical domain, I don't think that there's anything objectionable, given my concern with money, about taking a gamble that gives me a 50% shot at earning ten dollars and a 50% shot at losing ten dollars. I don't have a strong preference for maintaining my current monetary state. Given that I'm willing to take a monetary gamble, why am I so averse to a belief gamble?

[7] Friedman (2019) assumes (but "mostly for expository convenience") that the goal of inquiry is knowledge. This is also suggested in Srinivasan's (2015) discussion of arbitrarily formed belief.

[8] Rinard (2022) defends a view according to which all reasons for belief are practical.

[9] Despite the fact that my concern here is with truth, I think that what follows should still be interesting to those whose concern is, say, with knowledge, or rationality, rather than truth. For in many cases in which we're worried that our beliefs are not true, we're also worried that they don't constitute knowledge, or are not rational. So I'm going to stay focused on truth and accuracy, and you may draw your own connections between what I say and concerns about knowledge and rationality based on how you think concern with knowledge or rationality is related to concern with truth.

What these considerations illustrate is that not any way of caring about the truth will vindicate an aversion to belief gambles. However, some ways of caring about the truth do vindicate such an aversion. What are these "different ways of caring about truth?" As William James long ago pointed out, there are many ways of valuing accuracy—many ways of trading off the value of truth against the disvalue of falsehood. Different ways of valuing accuracy can be encoded by different accuracy measures, sometimes called "scoring rules." An accuracy measure gives a numerical accuracy score to a credence in a proposition, given the proposition's truth value. So, if a proposition is true, the higher the credence, the better the score, and, if a proposition is false, the lower the credence, the better the score. While all scoring rules will agree on that much, they will differ with respect to *how much* better or how much worse certain increases of decreases in credence will be. So, for example, if I'm more concerned about getting close to truths than I am at staying far from falsehood, a scoring rule that does good job at representing my concern with accuracy may assign a bigger accuracy boost to the move from 0.5 to 0.6 in a truth than to the move from 0.5 to 0.4 in a falsehood.

Now, our concern with the accuracy of our credences is not nearly precise enough to determine a unique scoring rule that represents the way we trade off the value of truth against the disvalue of falsehood. But I do think that there is good evidence for the claim that our concern with the accuracy of our credences has the feature that credences are *self-recommending*: for an agent with credence c in P and credence 1-c in ~P, her own credences will have higher *expected* accuracy than any alternative.[10] Accuracy measures according to which (probabilistic) credences are self-recommending in this way are sometimes called "strictly proper" or "immodest,"[11] and I will argue that immodest ways of caring about accuracy do vindicate an aversion to belief gambling in the cases discussed above.

But before presenting the argument, why think that we care about accuracy immodestly? Two points: First, I am sympathetic to Joyce's (ms.) claim that we discover the particular shape that our concern for accuracy takes in part by looking at the ways of forming belief we endorse. As it turns out, many of the fundamental ways of forming belief we endorse[12] are only licensed by the aim of getting at the truth on the assumption that our concern with truth is immodest. So one reason to think that we care about accuracy in immodest ways is that the claim that our concern for accuracy is immodest does an excellent job at explaining why, when we're aiming to get things right, we like to form beliefs in the particular ways that we do.

[10] The expected accuracy of c is just the average of the accuracy scores c might get in different worlds, weighted by the probability the agent assigns to those worlds obtaining.

[11] See, e.g. Oddie (1997), Greaves and Wallace (2006), Gibbard (2008), Joyce (2009), Horowitz (2013), and Pettigrew (2016) for discussion of immodesty.

[12] For example, being coherent, updating by conditionalization, conforming one's credences to the chances when they're known, and, as I will show in a moment, avoidance of certain belief gambles.

Here's the second point: There is a plausible story to be told about why we'd come to value accuracy immodestly: Results in Schervish (1989), which have been elaborated upon by Gibbard (2008) and Levinstein (2017), show that belief-forming methods aimed at accuracy, *when accuracy is valued immodestly*, are exactly what we'd hope for given the prominent role that our beliefs play in guiding action. The rough idea behind these results is this: because we don't know which choices our future selves will face, if we want our future selves to make good decisions, the best thing we can do in the absence of additional evidence is "give" our future selves our actual credences. So, for the purpose of guiding action, valuing accuracy in a way that makes credal states self-recommending (in other words: immodestly) is exactly what we'd want.

Here's an illustration (by no means a proof) of the main idea: Suppose I currently have a 0.5 credence that there's a post office half a mile away. (Perhaps I know that there was one there a month ago, but I think it may have closed.) There are many possible reasons it might matter practically to me whether this post office exists. One possibility is that I discover a job that I want to apply to at 4 p.m. this afternoon whose deadline is tomorrow. In that case, I'd need to get to a post office before 5 p.m., when the post offices close. (The job is at an old-fashioned institution that requires mail-in applications.) Given that now I'm only 0.5 confident that there's a post office half a mile away, I wouldn't want my future self in these circumstances to take a stroll to the possible post office on the assumption that it's still there. In such a case, I'd much prefer that my future self drive to some further post office that is definitely open, than take a chance on the one that might be half a mile away. On the other hand, if my future self wants to mail a wedding gift for a wedding that's three weeks away, and it's a beautiful afternoon, I wouldn't recommend against walking half a mile east and scoping things out. Worst-case scenario, I mail the gift on some later date. These are just two examples, but there are countless situations my future self might face, and which action I'd want my future self to take will depend on the details. Given that how I want my future self to act is a function of what my credences are, the best thing I can do for my future self so that she'll make good decisions (again, absent getting new evidence), is give her my actual credences. So, instead of gambling on what my credences will be, I'll want to keep the credences I have, and let my future self do the gambling on which *actions* to perform.

But wait—didn't I start out assuming that my goal was an accurate portrayal of the world and not an efficient arrival at the post office or a successful job application? I did. But as I mentioned earlier, there are many ways to care about accuracy: many ways to trade off the value of truth against the disvalue of falsehood. Given the role that our opinions play in governing action, it makes sense that the particular *way* in which we care about accuracy is immodest. This is not inconsistent with the idea that in an inquiry in which our sole concern is with accuracy, we are motivated to form beliefs in ways that are licensed by an immodest concern with accuracy. (Analogy: perhaps we came to find sweet things delicious because sugar is high in calories. Still, sometimes all we care about is a thing's deliciousness, and in those cases we can favor sweet things on purely deliciousness grounds.)

In sum: there are two reasons to think that our concern with the accuracy of our credences is of the immodest variety: first, the claim that we're concerned immodestly provides a good explanation of why we endorse the belief forming methods that we do when we're inquiring; and second, given the role that beliefs play in guiding action, it would make sense that we'd come to value accuracy immodestly.

Let me now explain why caring about accuracy immodestly can explain our aversion to belief gambles of the sort described above: if I assign a 0.5 credence to a proposition, and I value accuracy immodestly, then I'll prefer to be at 0.5 than to be anywhere else. So I'll prefer to be at 0.5 than to be at, say, 0.8 or 0.2. But if I don't want 0.8, and I don't want 0.2, I'm also not going to want to go through a procedure that gives me a 50% shot at arriving at 0.8 (one thing I don't want) and a 50% shot at arriving at 0.2 (another thing I don't want) in a way that I regard as independent of the truth.[13] If I expect to form a belief arbitrarily, say by forming a perceptual belief in Perceptual Coin Flip, then I'll regard the process of belief formation as involving a procedure which gives me a 50% shot at a higher credence, and a 50% shot at a lower credence in a way that I regard as independent of the actual color of the wall (this follows from the fact that I expect the belief to be arbitrarily formed). This is exactly the sort of procedure that an immodest way of caring about accuracy will recommend against. If I care about accuracy immodestly, I'll prefer sticking to 0.5 to undergoing a procedure of this sort. So if we care about the accuracy of our credences immodestly, we have an explanation as to why we don't like taking belief gambles.

In sum: my aversion to arbitrarily formed belief in the toy cases can be explained by my concern with accuracy, but *only* if my concern for accuracy is immodest. Non-immodest ways of caring about accuracy will license shifts from one credence to another (even in the absence of new evidence), and, as a result, they will also license certain belief gambles.[14] I gave some reasons for thinking that my concern with accuracy is, in fact, immodest and so there is indeed an accuracy-based vindication for my desire to avoid beliefs formed arbitrarily in such cases.[15]

[13] Immodesty is consistent with the idea that I'm happy to revise my credences if I think that the way in which I'll revise them is correlated with the truth. See Schoenfield (2018) for a more detailed argument explicating why immodesty prohibits belief gambles. See also Carter (2020) and Eder (2020) for a defense of the claim that the way in which we trade off the value of truth against the disvalue of falsehood favors the avoidance of falsehood over the gaining of truth.

[14] For example, on what's called the "absolute value score," a belief gamble which gives me a 50% shot at ending up at 0.8 and a 50% shot at ending up at 0.2 will look fine from the perspective in which I have a 0.5 credence.

[15] For those interested in thinking about rationality, the considerations in this section could have been presented as claims about the rationality of having certain belief-forming preferences. Although

Bottom Line: Assuming that my concern with accuracy is immodest, there is an accuracy-based vindication of my aversion to forming beliefs arbitrarily in cases like Perceptual and Logic Coin Flip.

2. Second Meditation: Graduate School

Big news: I've decided to pursue a PhD in neuroscience! I studied neuroscience when I was in college and I remember that around the time that I graduated there was a lively debate going on about whether olfactory information was encoded by the spatial arrangement of the neurons that fire, or in some other way (such as the temporal sequence of firing). In preparation for graduate school, I've been reading through some recent articles on the topic. But it's so complicated! I really have no idea what to think about the issue.

I had lunch with my neuroscience professor from college earlier today, Professor Katz, and I was asking him for advice about which school to attend. I've been considering two programs: Columbia and University of Arizona. He remembered my interest in the debate about olfactory coding and he said: "Well, I can tell you right now, if you go to Columbia, next time I see you you'll be favoring the spatial view, and if you end up at Arizona, you'll think that the spatial view is probably wrong. That's how things work in graduate school: everybody reads the same articles and journals but what you end up thinking about the matter depends on which social influences you are subject to."[16]

"Actually," I told Professor Katz, "I think that when I get to graduate school I won't form any opinion on the matter at all given what you've just told me. You see, I think that forming an opinion once I get to graduate school amounts to a belief gamble, and I don't like gambling on my beliefs." "Well, we'll see," he said, and chuckled in a way that seemed mildly condescending.

But this evening, as I've been pondering the matter further, I started rethinking my commitment to agnosticism. This thought occurred to me when I was reflecting on which of S (the spatial view) or ~S (its negation) I *currently* think is more likely to be true. When I was reading through these neuroscience papers over the past few days, I found myself moving back and forth between which I thought was

epistemologists rarely talk about the rationality of belief-forming preferences, here is how such an argument would go if one were to make one: the reason that it's rationally permitted/required to have a preference for maintaining a 0.5 credence over taking a belief gamble is that we are rationally permitted/required to care about accuracy in an immodest way and immodest ways of caring about accuracy recommend maintaining 0.5 over taking a belief gamble. Thus, at least in cases in which all that one wants out of one's future opinions is that they be accurate (and in which this is a rationally permissible/required attitude to take), it's rationally permissible/required to prefer a 0.5 credence to a belief-gamble. Later in the chapter I'll focus on beliefs themselves, rather than belief-forming preferences.

[16] This case is inspired by G.A. Cohen (2000), and by going to graduate school.

more likely, and when I sit back now and think through all of the evidence I've collected—well, I really have no idea. I wouldn't say that I regard S as more likely than ~S, and I also wouldn't say that I regard ~S as more likely than S. But I also don't have a 0.5 credence in S. One way to see that my attitude towards S is different from a precise 0.5 credence is to note that getting a teeny bit of evidence in favor of S (e.g. learning that one of the studies I read favoring S had a slightly larger sample size than I'd thought) wouldn't make me more confident in S than ~S. In contrast, when I have a precise 0.5 credence in a proposition, *any* evidence in favor of that proposition will break the tie (learning that the coin is weighted 0.5000001 towards Heads, rather than being fair, will make me more confident in Heads than Tails).

Why does it matter whether my credence is 0.5 or not? The reason it matters is that earlier I described some reasons for thinking that if I have a credence in a proposition, then I won't want to take a belief gamble. This followed from the fact that, given the way I care about accuracy, credences are self-recommending. But if my attitude towards S can't be represented by a credence, then the considerations I appealed to above don't, at least in a straightforward way, provide accuracy-based motivations for maintaining my current state over taking a belief gamble. So I started wondering: are there any accuracy-based grounds for avoiding a belief gamble of the sort I'd be subject to by going to graduate school given my actual attitude towards S? After some contemplation, I concluded that's it's very hard to see what sorts of accuracy-based grounds there might be for avoiding such a gamble. In fact, I'm not convinced that there are any.

To explain why it's difficult to provide an accuracy-based motivation for avoiding belief gambles in cases like the one above, it will be helpful to get clearer on the nature of my attitude towards olfactory coding in this case. I'm going to use the term "lacking an opinion about P" as follows:

> *S lacks an opinion about* P if it's not the case that *S* is more confident in P than in ~P, it's not the case that *S* is more confident in ~P than in P, and it's not the case that *S* has a precise 0.5 credence in P.[17]

An agent who lacks an opinion about P cannot be represented by a precise credence function. But some people think that such agents can be represented by a set of credence functions, called "a representor."[18] On this picture, if we want to describe an agent's level of confidence towards a particular proposition P that

[17] I intend the locution: "it's not the case that *S* is more confident in P than in ~P" to be consistent with it being indeterminate whether *S* is more confident in P than in ~P. So the sentence "it's not the case that *S* is more confident in P than in ~P" could be restated as: "it's not the case that, *determinately*, *S* is more confident in P than in ~P."

[18] For instance, Kyburg (1961) Levi (1974), Jeffrey (1983), van Fraassen (1990), and Joyce (2005, 2010).

she lacks an opinion about, rather than representing that attitude by a single number that represents the agent's confidence in the proposition, we can represent the agent's confidence level by an interval, like, for example, [0.1–0.9].

There are many unanswered questions about these "imprecise" or "mushy" credences and now is not the time to delve into the details. But since I think it's important to have in mind some psychological interpretation of this formalism, I'd like to offer what I take to be a promising way of thinking about what it is for an agent to be such that credence c is in an interval that represents her confidence-level towards P (I'll call such an interval a "P-representor"). It's worth noting, though, that nothing essential in what follows rests on this psychological interpretation of imprecise credences. If you have your own favorite interpretation you can use that one.

Here's how I'll understand the formalism. I'll say:

Credence c is a member of S's P-representor if both of the following conditions are met:

(a) It's not the case that *S* is more than c-confident that P.
(b) It's not the case *S* is less than c-confident that P.[19]

Since I'm reflecting on my own attitudes in this case, it's worth mentioning how I reflect on the question of whether some credence c is in my P-representor.[20] First, I note that I assign credence c to a c-weighted coin landing Heads. Next, I imagine someone presenting me with a c-weighted coin and asking: "what are you more confident in: that this coin will land Heads, or P?" Suppose it's not the case that I'd answer: "I'm more confident that the coin will land Heads than I am in P" and it's not the case that I'd answer: "I'm more confident in P than that the coin will land Heads." Perhaps I'd say: "I'm equally confident in both," or perhaps I'd shrug my shoulders, or say: "I don't know" or "I'm not sure" or maybe there is simply no fact of the matter about what I would say if asked this question. As long as I think that it's not the case that I'd answer: "P is more likely" and it's not the case that I'd answer: "Heads is more likely," I'll think that c is in my P-representor. If c is the only credence with this feature, then I'll think that I have a precise credence of c in P, since c will be the only element in the P-representor. But if there is more than one c with this feature, I'll judge my credence to be imprecise.[21]

[19] Note that there are plausibly cases in which it is indeterminate whether c is a member of *S*'s P-representor. Indeed, I am sympathetic with Rinard's (2017) claim that, in many cases, there is no maximally specific and fully accurate description of an agent's confidence level. Still, we can talk about some set of credences as being members of *S*'s P-representor so long as every member of the set in question, c, is such that it's not the case that (determinately) the agent is more than c-confident that P and it's not the case that (determinately) the agent is less than c-confident that P.

[20] This is not meant to imply that we're always able to tell, for every credence, whether or not it is in our representor.

[21] See Fishburn (1986) for a lovely representation theorem that delivers a unique set of credences on the basis of comparative confidence levels.

Back to my contemplations about graduate school: I find myself, prior to going to graduate school, in a state in which I lack an opinion about S: it's not the case that I'm more confident in S than in ~S, it's not the case that I'm more confident in ~S than in S, and it's not the case that I have a 0.5 credence in S (so there is more than one member in my S-representor). Let's call my state L (for "lacking an opinion"). The question is: are there accuracy-based motivations for maintaining L once I go to graduate school as opposed to letting my opinions be swayed by the influences around me?

If L were a self-recommending state, then we'd have an argument for trying to maintain L: if L is a state that recommends itself (from an accuracy perspective) over every other state, it will also recommend itself over a gamble between two states that it disprefers. But a combination of results in Seidenfeld et al. (2012), Mayo-Wilson and Wheeler (2016), Schoenfield (2017), and Berger and Das (2020) show that, given some plausible constraints on the way in which we value accuracy, there is no accuracy measure that has the feature that all imprecise credal states are self-recommending.[22] I won't summarize these results here. Instead, I want to argue for something more specific: that L doesn't recommend itself over every state in which I'm more confident in one of S or ~S. In other words: L doesn't recommend against every opinionated state. I'll argue for this by arguing for:

> (*) If I lack an opinion about P, and c is a number in my P-representor that is not equal to 0.5, then it's not the case that I'm in a state that recommends itself over having a credence of c in P.

If c is a number in my P-representor that is not equal to 0.5, adopting credence c in P amounts to becoming more confident in one of P or ~P. Thus, if I can show that my state L doesn't recommend itself over having credence c, I'll have shown that it doesn't recommend against every opinionated state.

The argument I'll provide for (*) is an argument by elimination: I'll consider a number of different ways one might try to motivate a preference for L over c when one is in L, on the basis of accuracy considerations, and show that none of them succeed. This strategy has the weakness that I can't claim to have exhausted all of the possible accuracy-based motivations for maintaining L. But I will have shown (a) that the accuracy-based motivations for avoiding belief gambles in the case of credences don't motivate avoiding belief gambles in cases in which I'm in a state of lacking an opinion, and (b) there is, at very least, no straightforward reason for preferring L to c on accuracy-based grounds. If there are accuracy-based reasons

[22] For related points see also Builes et al. (2022).

for preferring L to c, they are not the sorts of reasons that are based in a familiar decision theory.

There are three assumptions that I'll make in the course of arguing for (*) that are worth flagging. The first is that we value the accuracy of precise credal states in an immodest way. I make this assumption because, as I mentioned earlier, I think that our concern with the accuracy of credences does have this feature, and also because, if we weren't concerned about the accuracy of credences in an immodest way, there would be little hope of motivating an aversion to belief gambles even in cases in which we have precise credences, let alone cases of lacking an opinion.[23]

The second assumption I'll make for the purposes of this argument is that L isn't an accuracy self-undermining state: it doesn't, in every case, recommend against itself. One reason for this assumption is that if L were always self-undermining, an agent interested in accuracy would never enter state L to begin with, and so figuring out what L recommends becomes a much less interesting project.

The final assumption I'll make is that L is a state that it makes sense to evaluate for accuracy. The reason for this assumption is that if L is not evaluable for accuracy, then there is *definitely* no accuracy-based motivation for preferring L to c. Thus, if there is any hope of motivating a preference for L over c on the basis of accuracy considerations, L must be the kind of state whose accuracy it makes sense to evaluate.

Here's how I'll proceed with the argument for (*): first, I'll argue that one can't motivate a preference for L over c by claiming that L is more accurate than c no matter how the world is; second, I'll argue that L can't be favored over c on the basis of thinking that probably L is more accurate than c; third, I'll argue that one can't prefer L over c on the basis of expected accuracy, or on the basis of what I'll call "generalized expected accuracy"; and finally, I'll argue that one can't prefer L over c on the basis of other familiar decision rules like Minimax, Maximin or Hurwicz criteria more generally.

To start, note that L can't be more accurate than c in every world. For if L is more accurate than c no matter what, then accuracy considerations would tell us that, no matter what our current opinion is, we should never have credence c. But since we're assuming that credences are self-recommending (we're maintaining immodesty for credences), it must be the case that credence c doesn't accuracy-undermine itself.

Can an agent in L prefer L to c on the basis of thinking that *probably* L will be more accurate than c? No, for the accuracy of L and c depend only on the truth of the proposition in question: call it P. If you were in L and thought that L is probably more accurate than c, then you'd have to think that, in either the

[23] Konek (forthcoming)'s accuracy-based argument in favor of states like L violates this immodesty condition on credences. See Schoenfield (2017) note 14 for discussion.

P world, or the ~P world (but not both), L is more accurate than c. Without loss of generality, suppose you think that L is more accurate than c if P is true, but not if P is false. In that case, thinking that L is probably more accurate than c amounts to thinking that P is more likely than ~P (since L is more accurate than c if and only if P is true). However, by stipulation, it's not the case that you regard P as more likely than ~P.

But let's not give up too quickly. We know from decision theory that there are cases in which one doesn't think Option A is more likely to bring about a better outcome than Option B, but one still ought to choose Option A: these are cases in which Option A has greater *expected value* than Option B. Is it possible then, that, although it's not the case that an agent with L thinks L is likely to be more accurate than c, that she can assign L greater *expected* accuracy than c? Not straightforwardly. Since expected accuracy judgments are always relativized to a credence function, and our agent with L lacks a credence in P, the notion of "expected accuracy" is simply not defined for an agent with L.

Is there some way to generalize the notion of expected accuracy so that we can sensibly talk about the expected accuracy judgments of an agent in L? If we follow the kind of supervaluationist approach that has been prominent in the literature on imprecise credences[24] we can say something like this: if, for every credence function *c* in an agent's representor, *c* assigns greater expected accuracy to b_1 than to b_2, then the agent can be said to assign greater expected accuracy to b_1 than to b_2. Still, this way of proceeding won't motivate a preference for L over c. By stipulation, c is a credence in the agent's P-representor. This means that some credence function in the agent's representor, call it *c*, assigns c to P. Since credences are self-recommending, it won't be the case that every credence function in the representor assigns greater expected accuracy to L than to c, for this would require that *c* assigns greater expected accuracy to L than to c, and, if this were so, *c* wouldn't be self-recommending. Thus, this generalization of the notion of expected accuracy won't yield the result that an agent with L assigns greater expected accuracy to L than to c.

What about other decision rules? Since we want to maintain immodesty for credences, we need to consider whether any rules that make credences self-recommending yield a preference for L over c when one is in L. But it's not clear that there are plausible decision rules, other than expectation related ones, that can yield the result that credences are self-recommending. For note that other familiar decision rules like Maximin, Minimax, and Hurwicz rules don't take an agent's doxastic state into account when issuing a recommendation. But any rule that doesn't take the agent's doxastic state into account won't make credences self-recommending. This is because, for credences to be self-recommending, what's

[24] See, e.g. van Frassenn (1990, 2005, 2006), Hajek (2003), Joyce (2005, 2010), and Rinard (2015).

recommended for an agent with a 0.6 credence must be different from what's recommended for an agent with a 0.5 credence. If, however, what's recommended doesn't depend on the agent's credences, this won't be the case.[25]

In sum, it's hard to see what there is about the state of lacking an opinion which would privilege itself, from an accuracy perspective, over every state in which I have an opinion. Since I currently lack an opinion about how olfactory information is encoded, I don't think that I'm in a state that recommends itself over every state in which I am more confident in S than ~S. A similar argument would show that I'm not in a state that recommends itself over one in which I'm more confident in ~S than S. Having reflected on this, I find myself much less averse to taking a belief-gamble: letting myself become opinionated as a result of the school that I choose to attend.[26]

> *Bottom Line*: It's difficult to find an accuracy-based motivation for maintaining my state of lack of opinion over taking a belief gamble: allowing my opinions to be formed by whichever graduate school I choose to attend.

3. Third Meditation: Higher Order Evidence and the Perspective of Doubt

All of this meditating has been taxing, and yesterday my friend Jane suggested that we go out for a drink. "I really shouldn't," I said, "I have to finish an answer key for my logic class." But Jane can be very convincing, and before I knew it I was at the bar, sipping Merlot, as my concerns about beliefs formed arbitrarily melted away. When I arrived home, I was tired and inebriated, but I quickly got to work. I had just finished what seemed to me a very satisfying proof that the set of premises given by the problem entailed H when my spouse popped in and said: "Please

[25] Another type of decision rule for imprecise probabilities (more well known in the economics literature) is the ambiguity averse "GS decision theory" (Gilboa and Schmeidler 1989). Such a decision theory will also run into trouble maintaining immodesty for precise states. This is because, to apply the decision theory, we need a numerical score for the accuracy of L. Assigning such scores, however (given certain plausible constraints on accuracy measures) will have the result that precise states don't self-recommend (see e.g. Seidenfeld 2012 and Mayo Wilson and Wheeler 2016). Builes et al. (2022) offer an approach for thinking about the accuracy of imprecise states (based on the work of Horowitz 2019) on which precise states do self-recommend, but their approach doesn't offer a score that can be plugged into an ambiguity averse decision theory.

[26] Once again, these arguments could be reformulated as claims about the rationality of belief-forming preferences. Here's how such an argument would go: it's not the case that if one's aim is accuracy, and one is in L, there is a rational requirement to prefer maintaining L over becoming opinionated in the graduate school case. Why? Because it is rationally permissible for one's belief forming preferences to be determined by accuracy considerations, it is rationally permissible to be in L, and it's not the case that, for an agent in L, there are accuracy-based reasons for preferring L to every opinionated state. (I'm not defending these claims about rationality here. I'm merely describing which premises concerning rationality would need to be accepted for the considerations here to be turned into such an argument).

don't tell me you're doing logic problems. You know what happens when you do logic problems in this state. Your answers are complete nonsense! Remember last time? You checked in the morning and only half of your answers were correct!"[27]

I started to get worried. Did those premises actually entail H? At first I cheered myself with the thought that I could just double or triple check my answers, but then I remembered that, last time, when I was doing logic problems while tired and drunk, I did just that and *still* only half of the problems were correctly answered.

It occurred to me that I am currently in a state that is in some respects similar to that of the hypothetical subject I had imagined in Logic Coin Flip. When I'm drunk and am reasoning about these logic problems in a way that's no better than chance, my answers are correct only 50% of the time. Looking back through my notes, I remembered that I had concluded that it's better to adopt a 0.5 credence than to form a belief that's only 50% likely to be true. Indeed, I planned that if I ever find myself in a situation like this one I'll adopt a 0.5 credence. But now I find myself with the belief that the premises entail H, and it is only after having formed this belief, that I realized what kind of situation I'm in. If the accuracy-based motivations for *avoiding* forming a belief are to motivate *abandoning* a belief that I already formed I must *now* think that the belief is only 50% likely to be true. But is that what I think? It's not so clear. If I were thinking about this matter from a perspective that includes all of the beliefs that I formed, then I don't think the belief is only 50% likely to be correct. For I formed the belief that the premises entail H. In fact, I was certain or nearly certain that the premises entail H. This means that the perspective that includes the belief that I formed is one in which it's certain, or nearly certain, that the belief I formed is correct (since the belief is correct if and only if the premises entail H). If I think it's certain or nearly certain that the belief I formed is correct, then I *don't* think the belief is only 50% likely to be correct. So how do the considerations I raised prior to being in such a situation carry over to the case in which I now am in that situation?

Here's what I realized: it's true that, from the perspective in which I am certain or nearly certain that the premises entail H (let's call this proposition "EH"), I'll think that my belief is highly likely to be true. But when I started wondering: "should I give up my belief that EH?" upon being reminded of my track record, I wasn't asking this question from a perspective that takes my belief that EH for granted.[28] Why? In general, if I have some belief, and I start wondering whether

[27] This case is inspired by Christensen's (2010: 187) "Drugs" case.

[28] When I say that I take some proposition P for granted I mean that I'm willing to deliberate on the basis of my belief that P. Because I'm including credal states favoring P as beliefs in P, it's worth pointing out that when I say that an agent is taking P for granted, this should not be taken to mean that the agent is ignoring all possibilities in which P is false. It merely means that whatever her asymmetrical attitude favoring P is, she is willing to reason with it.

to give it up, then I'm engaged in *doubt*.[29] When I doubt a belief that I currently have, I am considering whether to give up that belief, but I am considering whether to give it up from a perspective that doesn't take the belief in question for granted. After all, if I were taking it for granted, then it would be obvious, assuming my goal is accuracy, that I wouldn't want to give it up. Why would I want to give up a true belief? (In credal talk: if I have a high credence, I will regard it as more expectedly accurate than a middling credence, so why would I want to give it up?)[30]

The perspective of doubt that I occupy in this case is also one in which I'm not willing to take for granted that the inferences I made in deriving H from the premises are good ones. After all, if I took the inferences I made in deriving H from the premises for granted, then it would also be clear that I wouldn't want to give up my belief: for if all of the inferences are good ones, then EH must be true! So the fact that I'm wondering whether to give up my belief and wondering whether to rely on these inferences tells me that the perspective from which I want to deliberate isn't one that takes the belief and associated inferences for granted.

There are many interesting questions about what's going on when we doubt beliefs or inferences and I won't delve into a discussion of the psychology of doubt here. But I do want to address two questions that might arise about what sort of perspective I have in mind when I talk about "the perspective of doubt."

First question: if we believe P, and then subject this belief to doubt, is P the *only* belief that we aren't taking for granted in the deliberation? What about beliefs like "P or 2 + 2 = 5"? Answer: there is no univocal answer to the question "what are we setting aside when we doubt our belief that P?" A perspective of doubt is one in which we're not willing to rely on certain kinds of reasoning that we are willing to rely on when we're not engaged in doubt. For example, if we're doubting P, we're not willing to engage in a pattern of reasoning like this: "Since P is true, and P entails Q, Q is true." Almost always, when we're doubting P, we're also not willing to engage in a pattern of reasoning like this: "Since P or 2 + 2 =5 is true and

[29] For an extended discussion of doubt and its relation to higher order evidence cases see Schoenfield (forthcoming).

[30] The dogmatism paradox raises the question of why we don't dismiss or avoid evidence that disconfirms our beliefs. Why not think: P is true, so any disconfirming evidence must be misleading? This is an interesting puzzle, but not the one that I'm concerned with here. First, the dogmatist reasoning doesn't apply straightforwardly in cases in which we're less than certain that P (if I'm 0.6 in P, I can't reasonably assert "any evidence against P must be misleading"), but it is compatible with the cases I'm focusing on here that the agent is less than certain in the proposition in question. Second, the dogmatism paradox concerns cases in which one gets evidence that disconfirms P, but the cases I'll be focusing on are cases in which we subject a belief to doubt either in the absence of new evidence, or, if there is new evidence, it's such that the prior probability of P conditional on that evidence is the same as the prior probability of P. The reason for this focus is that reduction of confidence in higher order evidence cases, of the sort described here, can't be accommodated by ordinary conditionalization (Christensen 2010: 200; Schoenfield 2018). However, as I'll argue, we can explain a reduction of confidence in such cases by appealing to the fact that the beliefs become subject to doubt. See Schoenfield (forthcoming) for more on this point.

2 + 2 doesn't equal five, then P is true." It's not that it's impossible engage in a deliberation that doesn't take it for granted that P, but does take it for granted that either P or 2 + 2 = 5. It's just that, generally, when we doubt our belief that P, the perspective we wish to be deliberating from is one that *also* won't rely on a number of other closely related beliefs. Which beliefs exactly are the ones that we don't take for granted when we doubt that P? It depends. Doubting that P doesn't *entail* some particular set of beliefs that one is not willing to take for granted. In any given case in which an agent is doubting, there *just are* the beliefs that she's willing to rely on and the ones that she isn't.

Second question: How confident is one in P in the perspective of doubt? The perspectives of doubt that I'm particularly interested in are ones in which, relative to the perspective of doubt, it's not the case that one is more confident in P than in ~P and it's not the case that one is more confident in ~P than in P. This is because I'm interested in doubt that's elicited when we worry about what caused us to asymmetrically favor P over ~P or ~P over P, so the perspective of doubt is one that removes this asymmetric favoring. But, as I mentioned earlier, there are many doxastic attitudes one might take towards P that are consistent with it not being the case that one is more confident in P than in ~P and it's not being the case that one is more confident in ~P than in P. So, here too, there is no univocal answer to the question "what attitude does one take towards P once one sets aside one's belief that P?" It might be that when we set aside our asymmetrical favoring of P over ~P we find ourselves in a perspective in which our credence in P is 0.5. Or it might be that when we set aside our asymmetrical favoring of P over ~P we find ourselves in a perspective that is represented by some wide interval of credences.

With these preliminaries about doubt on the table, I now want to think about how things look from the perspective in which I doubt my belief that the premises entail H. In this case, my degree of confidence in EH once I start doubting EH is 0.5. (This is because, in the book that I'm working with, half of the answers have premises that entail H and half have premises that entail ~H.) So I'm now interested in thinking about how to proceed from the perspective in which I'm doubting EH, and in which my degree of confidence in EH, in the perspective of doubt, is 0.5. Can I recover my belief that EH from the perspective in which I doubt it?

There are two primary ways that we recover beliefs that we doubt. The most straightforward way involves engaging in first order reasoning. For example, suppose, having left my apartment, I begin to doubt my belief that I turned off the stove. I may be able to recover that belief by engaging in reasoning like this: "I remember cleaning the stovetop before leaving the apartment, I would have noticed if the stove were on when I was cleaning it, at which point I would have turned it off. So I must have turned off the stove." But this way of recovering a belief from doubt doesn't always work: sometimes, once we set aside what is in doubt, we don't have the resources left to recover the belief in this way. In these cases, we can sometimes appeal to higher order considerations. For example, consider my belief that my grandmother grew up in Massachusetts. Suppose that I subject this belief to doubt. I don't have many other beliefs about my grandmother's upbringing and so I can't find any biographical information in my stock of remaining beliefs from which I could infer that she grew up in Massachusetts. I also don't remember an occasion on which I was told that she grew up in Massachusetts. I just find myself believing it. Still, I can recover my belief that my grandmother grew up in Massachusetts in the perspective of doubt by thinking: "I find myself with the belief that my grandmother grew up in Massachusetts. The best explanation for why I have this belief is that a family member told me that she grew up in Massachusetts, and if a family member told me that she grew up in Massachusetts, she probably did grow up in Massachusetts." In this way of recovering a belief from doubt, I use the very fact that I formed a certain belief as evidence for its truth.

Unfortunately, however, when I doubt my belief that EH, I can't recover my belief in either of these ways. I can't recover the belief using first order reasoning because the perspective I'm occupying when I doubt my belief that EH in this case doesn't license the very reasoning that I would need to derive the answer—my reasoning about this logic problem is *itself* part of what I am doubting. I also can't recover the belief in the higher order way because, given what I know about the circumstances, I don't take the fact that I formed the belief that EH as evidence for its truth.

Given that I can't inferentially recover my belief that EH in this perspective of doubt, and that, in this perspective, my credence in EH is 0.5, if I deliberate about whether to give up my belief that EH from the perspective of doubt, the answer will be yes. This is because, from this perspective, maintaining the belief that I formed will look like a belief gamble: it will involve a 50% chance of having a true belief and a 50% chance of having a false belief.[31] Since, when I'm at 0.5, I prefer a 0.5 credence to a belief gamble, the perspective of doubt will recommend that I abandon the belief that I formed and adopt a 0.5 credence instead.[32]

[31] Returning to the probabilistic interpretation I gave of "regarding a belief as arbitrarily formed": the sense in which we can regard a currently held belief as independent of the truth is that *from the perspective in which we subject the belief in question to doubt* we regard the fact that we believe P as probabilistically independent of the truth of P. One might worry about talk of independence in such cases given that, once I've formed the belief, I may already be certain about which belief I formed. This is just the problem of old evidence, so I will not address this issue here. It's worth noting, however, that since, as I mentioned, there are different ways of subjecting a belief to doubt, there won't be a univocal answer to the question of whether some subject *S* regards a currently held belief as arbitrarily formed: the answer will be relativized to some particular way of doubting that belief.

[32] In the literature, it has been common to explain judgments about the rationality of abandoning belief in such cases by appealing to a rational requirement along the following lines: if, *independently of one's reasoning about P*, one has good reason to think that one is unreliable with respect to P, one is required to abandon one's belief that P. (See, e.g. Elga 2007; Christensen 2007, 2010; Horowitz and

I set my alarm for 6:00 a.m. I'll finish the answer key tomorrow morning.

Bottom Line: When I doubt a belief P, and the reasoning that I would need to infer P, the perspective of doubt will recommend that I abandon my belief if, from the perspective of doubt, I have a 0.5 credence in P, and I regard which belief I formed as independent of the truth.[33]

4. Fourth Meditation: Religious Belief

It is time to turn to the cases that initially worried me: the cases of religious, moral, and political beliefs. I'm going to focus on a particular religious belief that I have: my belief that individuals don't come back to earth after they die as other life forms. Call this proposition "NR" (for "no reincarnation"). I think that I believe NR because I was subject to certain social influences rather than others. Upon realizing this, I begin subjecting my belief that NR to doubt. As I mentioned in the previous section, there are many different ways to subject a belief to doubt, and right now I'll consider two:

Way 1: I subject NR to doubt, but I don't subject various related beliefs to doubt. For example, I maintain my beliefs about the reliability of various religious texts, my beliefs about what it takes for me to persist, and my beliefs about what happens to my body and mind when I die.

If I doubt in Way 1, then I can easily recover NR from the perspective of doubt using the various related beliefs that I haven't subjected to doubt.

Way 2: I subject NR doubt, and also my beliefs about the reliability of religious texts, my persistence conditions, and my beliefs about what happens to my body and mind after I die. In other words, I subject to doubt *a cluster* of beliefs surrounding my belief in NR. I hope you have a feel for the cluster of beliefs

Sliwa 2015; and Vavova 2018.) This requirement is sometimes described as a requirement to "bracket" part of one's evidence or to not "give all of one's evidence its' due" (Christensen 2010). But this raises two questions: First, *why* is one rationally required to bracket part of one's evidence or not give all of one's evidence its due? Second, exactly what does one need to bracket in order to satisfy this requirement? Note that on the approach I'm taking in this chapter, these questions don't arise. For I'm not claiming that one is rationally required to deliberate from some perspective that doesn't take all of one's evidence into account. Rather, so far, all I'm claiming is that when we engage in doubt, we *just do* take up a perspective in which we're not willing to rely on certain beliefs or inferences that normally we're inclined to rely on. And indeed, there are many different perspectives one could take up that are compatible with doubting, and, in any given instance of doubt, we *just do* take up one of them. Recall, my primary aim is to illustrate a way of navigating one's doubts—not to comment on the merits or demerits of taking up the perspective of doubt to begin with. I'll say more at the end of the chapter about what implications these considerations have concerning the rationality of taking up a doubtful perspective, and thereby the rationality of maintaining belief in cases like this one.

[33] Here and in what follows I'm considering worst-case scenarios: complete independence. My claims can be generalized to cases in which we expect to be compromised in some way, but still do better than chance. See Schoenfield 2018.

I have in mind. Unfortunately, I can't write them all down on a list, (in part because the cluster includes an infinite number of beliefs such as NR, NR or 2 + 2 = 5, NR or 2 + 2 = 6 . . .). The perspective I have in mind can be very roughly described as one that doesn't take for granted the beliefs that I have but that I wouldn't have had if I were raised in a reincarnation-believing community. But even if I can't fully articulate the perspective, *I* have a sense of the perspective that I want to be deliberating from when I subject my belief that NR to doubt in Way 2 (and I have dispositions concerning which deliberative moves I'm willing to make when engaged in this kind of doubt and which I'm not).

And indeed, when I find myself doubting NR upon realizing that I believe NR because of the environment I grew up in, the kind of doubt I'm engaged in is of this latter variety. I suspect that the reason that, not just NR, but a cluster of related beliefs is being subject to doubt is that what elicited the doubt to begin with was a realization about the causal origins of this belief, and the causal origins of my belief that NR are the same as the causal origins of the cluster of beliefs from which NR could be inferred.

So the question is: when I engage in doubt in Way 2, can my belief in NR be recovered? It cannot be recovered using either of the two strategies I mentioned previously. I can't recover the belief using first order reasoning because all of the beliefs from which I could infer that I won't be reincarnated are being subject to doubt in Way 2. What about higher order considerations appealing to the fact that I formed the belief that NR? To determine whether this will work, I need to consider the following question: When I occupy the perspective of doubt, do I think that the fact that I formed the belief that NR makes it likely that NR is true? Answer: I do not. This is because I think that what determined whether I'd believe NR or R are facts about which community I grew up in, and I don't take the fact that I grew up amongst NR-believers as any evidence for NR.

But perhaps this is too quick: for in the perspective of doubt, I don't know *just* that I grew up amongst NR-believers. I know all sorts of things about the people I grew up with and I regard these people as a reliable source of information. So perhaps I can appeal to the fact that my belief was caused by growing up in *this* community of reliable people to recover my belief that NR. I don't think this will work. It is true that the people I was raised by are generally reliable about a host of mundane issues, but so are the people who believe in reincarnation. So the question is, in this perspective of doubt, do I think that the people I was raised by are more likely to be right than those I would have been raised by if I were raised, say, Hindu, *about reincarnation*? The problem is that the considerations I would ordinarily appeal to in defending the claim that the people I was raised by are particularly likely to be right about reincarnation rely on the various beliefs that I'm subjecting to doubt. For in this perspective of doubt, I can't appeal to considerations like "the people who I was raised by have true beliefs about a number of related issues concerning the persistence conditions of human beings, the reliability of religious texts, and so on. Thus, being raised by these particular people made it very likely that I'd end up with a true belief about reincarnation."

Here's one final attempt to use higher order considerations to recover my belief that NR in the perspective of doubt: Perhaps I can think: "my community's beliefs are better aligned with a naturalistic or scientific world view than religious communities, and views that are better aligned with a naturalistic or scientific world view are more likely to be correct." Whether this strategy will work will depend on whether part of what I'm subjecting to doubt are the very beliefs that this chain of reasoning relies on. Am I subjecting to doubt my belief that my community's views are better aligned with science than the views of certain Hindu communities? Am I subjecting to doubt my belief that views that are better aligned with science are more likely to be true? If I am subjecting either of these to doubt, then I won't be able to use this sort of reasoning as a basis for thinking that I was more likely to arrive at the truth if I was raised in my community than in an alternative community. So I now face the question of whether, in the deliberation that I'm engaged in, I'm willing to rely on these beliefs. I find that I am not. This may be because I think that these beliefs are socially influenced in much the same way that my belief that NR was. So when worries about the social influences on belief lead me to take up the perspective of doubt, they lead me to doubt these beliefs as well.[34]

I've argued that the two primary ways we recover beliefs in the perspective of doubt won't help me in this case: first order reasoning won't help because the beliefs from which I can infer NR are subject to doubt, and higher order reasoning won't help because of what I know about the way in which my belief was brought about. But it occurs to me that there is third way to recover a belief in the perspective of doubt, at least in one sense of the word "recover." This involves thinking about whether the perspective of doubt recommends that I abandon the belief that I formed, given that my aim is truth.

To figure out whether the perspective of doubt recommends abandoning my belief in NR, I need to think about how confident I am that NR when I adopt the perspective of doubt. As with other features of the perspective of doubt, I don't think that there is one unique attitude towards NR that anyone subjecting NR to doubt will take. But in my own case, I don't find that, setting aside my belief in NR, I have a sharp credence, say, of 0.5 in NR. Rather, I find myself in a state in which I lack an opinion about NR—a state represented by quite a wide interval of credences.

I already established that the state in which I lack an opinion doesn't recommend itself over all states in which I'm more confident in NR than not. So, while in

[34] You may find that things go differently for you: perhaps, if you are an NR believer like me, beliefs along these lines are not ones that you are subjecting to doubt when you subject NR to doubt. In this case, congratulations! Your belief can be recovered.

the case of certain beliefs formed arbitrarily, I can't recover my beliefs from the perspective of doubt inferentially, I can recognize that the perspective I'm occupying when I doubt isn't one that favors itself over a more opinionated state. Having realized this, I feel disinclined to abandon my belief that NR.[35]

Let me end with a cautionary note: the fact that the perspective of doubt in which I lack an opinion doesn't recommend against *every* state in which I have a belief, doesn't mean that it doesn't recommend against *some* such states. For example, it might be true that in the perspective of doubt I am (determinately) less than 0.99 confident in the proposition that I won't be reincarnated. In this case, 0.99 won't be in my perspective-of-doubt NR-representor. If 0.99 is not in my NR-representor, then the arguments I've given do not support the claim that my state of lacking an opinion in the perspective of doubt permits being more than 0.99 confident that I won't be reincarnated. The arguments only show that the perspective doesn't recommend against degrees of confidence that are in my representor.[36] So if, in the non-doubting perspective (my ordinary one), I am more than 0.99 confident that I won't be reincarnated, then the perspective of doubt may recommend a significant reduction of confidence.

> *Bottom Line:* Many of the beliefs that we're concerned are arbitrarily formed can be recovered from the perspective of doubt. This is because the attitude we take towards these propositions when we doubt them is the state of lacking an opinion. However, sometimes the perspective of doubt will recommend that we be less confident in these beliefs than we were previously.

5. Fifth Meditation: Disagreement

Jane and I went out for dinner tonight and at the end of the meal we each calculated our share of the restaurant bill.[37] We shared our answers: I concluded that we each owed 48.30 and Jane concluded that we each owed 46.50. As Jane started counting out her change, blatantly ignoring my opinion, I said to her: "Jane, don't you think you should reconsider, perhaps redo your math, or use a calculator? After all, we've been keeping track of our arithmetical successes and

[35] An interesting feature of this way of recovering a belief from doubt is that the perspective of doubt not only permits believing that I won't be reincarnated; it also permits believing I *will* be reincarnated. It's just that, in my own case, believing NR comes much more naturally to me than believing R or lacking an opinion about NR. This explains why, having subject my belief that NR to doubt, I return to a state in which I believe NR, rather than adopt one of the many other attitudes that are left open by the perspective of doubt.

[36] For example, according to the generalized expected accuracy rule, if every credence in my representor is below 0.99, then the state I'm in will recommend against being more than 0.99 confident.

[37] This case is from Christensen 2007.

failures during our nights out together, and when we've disagreed, I've been right 50% of the time." "True," Jane said, "but I must be right this time. After all, 1.2% of the total divided by two is 46.50, you say it's not 46.50, so this must be one of the times in which I'm right and you're wrong."[38]

I started wondering: is there anything I could say to Jane that would lead her to abandon her opinion? If Jane were to doubt her belief, then I could show her that, given the circumstances, the perspective of doubt recommends abandoning it. But so long as she isn't inclined to doubt her belief, I don't think there is any accuracy-based *argument* I could give her that would sway her. For as long as Jane is taking it for granted that 1.2% of the total is 46.50, abandoning this belief will look like a bad idea.

This frustrating experience with Jane led me to think that there isn't much in the way of accuracy-aimed deliberation that we can engage in about whether to take up the perspective of doubt. For any such deliberation must take place from some perspective, and every perspective takes certain things for granted. Since a coherent perspective that takes P for granted will recommend continuing to take P for granted,[39] no amount of accuracy-aimed deliberation from such a perspective will motivate a shift to a perspective that doesn't take P for granted. It follows that deliberating about which perspective to adopt can't be done in a non-trivial way on the basis of accuracy considerations.[40]

So what determines what we take for granted and what we subject to doubt? I suspect that it is largely arational processes: we try on different perspectives, some of them stick, and some of them don't. Doubt, in my view, is something that happens *to* us, not the outcome of a reasoning process that originates in our non-doubtful stance. Perhaps, in an epistemology class, I'm led to take up the perspective of doubt concerning all external world propositions. But this perspective doesn't stick. Once I leave the seminar, I find myself once again occupying a perspective that takes all sorts of external world propositions for granted. In contrast, in cases like Logic Coin Flip, once I realize that I can't recover my belief from the perspective in which I doubt it, I'm inclined to give it up. The doubtful perspective sticks. Those are clear cases in which I expect that there is a great deal of agreement. But some cases are murkier. When Jane and I disagreed, I was led to occupy a perspective in which I doubted my belief about the bill. But Jane wasn't.

[38] This is the sort of reasoning that would be encouraged by, e.g., Kelly 2005; White 2010; and Titelbaum 2015.

[39] For recall that taking P for granted means that one is willing to reason on the basis of one's belief that P. And if one is more than 0.5 confident that P, and willing to reason on the basis of this attitude, then one will think that maintaining a greater than 0.5 credence in P is advisable. (This will hold if one has a sharp credence in P, because credences are self-recommending, but also if one has a representor all of whose members are above 0.5, and one appeals to the notion of "generalized expected accuracy" discussed earlier). Since a belief that P will be recommended, reasoning on the basis of this attitude (in accuracy-approved ways, like conditionalization) will also be recommended. Thus, a perspective in one which one takes P for granted will recommend that one continue to take P for granted.

[40] I present this argument in detail in Schoenfield (forthcoming).

There are likely a variety of factors that contribute to whether we take up the perspective of doubt in any given case and whether it sticks once it's taken up. They might include the degree to which the belief is embedded in our overall web of beliefs, the degree to which error is made salient, the practical costs of abandoning the belief, our personality, which beliefs our friends and families are inclined to doubt, and so forth.

> *Bottom Line*: Accuracy-based considerations don't privilege the perspective of doubt. Doubt is something that happens to us—not the output of accuracy-aimed deliberation.

6. Interlude: Normative Upshots

So far, I've simply noted that sometimes we're bothered when we can't recover a belief or inference from doubt, and other times we're not. But if you're someone that theorizes about rationality, this may be the juncture at which you wish to intercede. You may claim that there are substantive constraints along the following lines: If a belief of sort *B*, or an inference of sort *I*, can't be recovered from a perspective of doubt of sort *D*, then it is irrational to hold the belief that *B*. For instance, some internalists, like Descartes, may think that any belief other than a belief about one's mental states must be recoverable from a perspective in which all of one's external world beliefs are subject to doubt. Other internalists may claim that perceptual beliefs needn't be recoverable from a perspective of doubt unless there are special circumstances (e.g. "defeaters," or "positive reasons to think one is unreliable"). Externalists may claim that so long as the belief or inference is reliably produced, it doesn't matter whether it can be recovered from a perspective in which it's doubted. Coherentists might claim that beliefs at the periphery of our web need to be recoverable from doubt, but not beliefs at the center. I won't take a stand on these issues here. I will, however, register that I'm somewhat skeptical of the possibility of providing a well-motivated account that explains why in some cases it's irrational to maintain a belief that is not recoverable from a perspective of doubt and in other cases it isn't.[41] My reasons for skepticism are similar to the reasons provided by Greco (2017), who is skeptical of the possibility of providing a well-motivated account of which propositions are "foundational."[42]

[41] See Schoenfield (forthcoming) for more on this point.

[42] A belief is foundational in this sense if it justified without the support of other beliefs. The questions of whether a belief is foundational, and of whether it's rational to maintain a belief that can't be recovered from a certain perspective of doubt are related but not identical.

However, if you do have a theory on hand that tells you when a particular doubtful stance is required, then you can add the arguments I've given here to your theory, and derive verdicts about what's rationally required in any given case, so long as you think that there is a reasonably tight connection between thinking rationally and thinking in a way that's aimed at being accurate.[43] It's worth noting two points though: the first is that, depending on your theory, these verdicts may not be ones that can be arrived at from a first personal deliberative stance. The second is that, depending on your theory, the parts that tell you when you're rationally required to take up the doubtful stance may go beyond what would be licensed by an interest in accuracy alone. These are not criticisms: just points to be aware of in thinking about the relationship between the rationality theorist's project and my primary project: demonstrating ways of navigating the doubt that arises when one regards one's belief as arbitrarily formed, from an accuracy-aimed, first-person point of view.

7. Sixth Meditation: Conclusion

What's disturbing about beliefs that have been heavily socially influenced is that these beliefs aren't easily recoverable from a perspective in which we subject those beliefs to doubt. The beliefs aren't recoverable in the first order manner because, in these cases, we're not usually doubting just one particular belief, but a cluster of beliefs, a certain "picture" of how the world is. We can't recover the belief in a higher order way either because, from the perspective of doubt, we regard the belief as arbitrarily formed: we regard which belief we ended up with as independent of the truth. This blocks off two of the primary ways we can recover a belief from doubt. What I've suggested here, however, is that there is a third way to recover belief: so long as the state we're in when we doubt is the state of lacking an opinion, we can recognize that the perspective of doubt isn't one that recommends abandoning belief if our aim is to be accurate.[44] This consideration may not compel us to maintain belief, but it allows us to realize that, if we are inclined to maintain an opinionated state, there is nothing accuracy-wise to be said against doing so.[45]

[43] Thanks to Will Fleisher for discussion on this point.

[44] If we have some other aim, there may well be considerations that tell against arbitrarily formed belief in such cases. For example, we might regard it as desirable that we have a sort of epistemic agency over our beliefs, and think that if our beliefs are not going to be brought about in the appropriately agential sort of way, it's better not to have them at all (see Callahan forthcoming). I won't, in this chapter, take a stand on whether there are good non accuracy-based motivations for preferring L to an arbitrarily formed opinion, but I certainly don't want to rule out such a possibility.

[45] For helpful discussion, and for reading and commenting on earlier drafts, I am thankful to Brian Cutter, Tom Donaldson, Jane Friedman, Daniel Greco, Sophie Horowitz, Sarah Moss, Will Fleisher, and especially Susanna Rinard. Thanks also to audiences at the PeRFECt Conference at University of

References

Argyle, M., and B. Beit Hallahmi. 1997. *The Psychology of Religious Belief, Behavior and Experience*. Routledge.

Berger, D., and N. Das 2020. Accuracy and Credal Imprecision. *Noûs*, 54(3): 666–703.

Builes, D., S. Horowitz, M. and Schoenfield. 2022. Dilating and Contracting Arbitrarily. *Noûs* 56(1): 3–20.

Callahan, L. Forthcoming. Epistemic Existentialism. *Episteme*.

Carter, J.A. 2020. Sosa on Knowledge, Judgment and Guessing. *Synthese*, 197: 5117–36.

Christensen, D. 2007. Epistemology of Disagreement: The Good News. *Philosophical Review*, 116(2): 187–217.

Christensen, D. 2010. Higher Order Evidence. *Philosophy and Phenomenological Research*, 81(1): 185–215.

Cohen, G.A. 2000. *If You're an Egalitarian, How Come You're so Rich?* Harvard University Press.

Descartes, Rene. 2008. *Meditations on First Philosophy*. Translated by M. Moriarty. Oxford University Press.

Eder, A.M. 2020. No Commitment to the Truth. *Synthese* 8: 1–24.

Elga, A. 2007. Reflection and Disagreement. *Noûs* 41(3): 478–502.

Fishburn, P.C. 1986. The Axioms of Subjective Probability. *Statistical Science* 1(3): 335–45.

Friedman, J. 2019. Inquiry and Belief. *Noûs*, 53(2): 296–315.

Gibbard, A. 2008. Rational Credence and the Value of Truth. In T. Gendler and J. Hawthorne (Eds.), *Oxford Studies in Epistemology Volume 2*. Oxford University Press.

Gilboa, I., and D. Schmeidler. 1989. Maxmin Expected Utility with Non-Unique Prior. *Journal of Mathematical Economics*, 18(2): 141–53.

Glass, J., V.L. Bengston, and C.C. Dunham. 1986. Attitude Similarity in Three Generation Families: Socialization, Status Inheritance, or Reciprocal Influence? *American Sociological Review*, 51(1): 685–98.

Greaves, H., and D. Wallace. 2006. Justifying Conditionalisation: Conditionalization Maximizes Expected Epistemic Utility. *Mind*, 115(459): 607–32.

Greco, D. 2017. Cognitive Mobile Homes. *Mind*, 126(501): 93–121.

Hájek, A. 2003. What Conditional Probabilities Could Not Be. *Synthese* 137(3): 273–323.

Horowitz, S. 2013. Immoderately Rational. *Philosophical Studies*, 167(1): 1–16.

Pennsylvania, the Ranch Metaphysics Workshop, the University of Pittsburgh conference on Formal Representations of Ignorance, Tel-Hai University, Australian National University, The University of Sydney and the "Epistemic Rationality: Conceptions and Challenges Conference" in Barcelona.

Horowitz, S. 2019. Accuracy and Educated Guesses. In T. Gendler and J. Hawthorne (Eds.). *Oxford Studies in Epistemology Volume 6*, (pp. 85–113). Oxford University Press.

Horowitz, S., and P. Sliwa. 2015. Respecting *All* the Evidence. *Philosophical Studies*, 172(11): 2835–58.

James, W. 1896. The Will to Believe. *The New World*, 5: 327–47.

Jeffrey, R. 1983. Bayesianism with a Human Face. In John Earman (Ed.), *Testing Scientific Theories* (pp. 133—56). University of Minnesota Press.

Joyce, J. 2005. How Probabilities Reflect Evidence. *Philosophical Perspectives*, 19(1): 153–78.

Joyce, J. 2009. Accuracy and Coherence: Prospects for an Alethic Epistemology of Partial Belief. In F. Huber and C. Schmidt-Petri (Eds.), *Degrees of Belief*. Synthese Library.

Joyce, J. 2010. A Defense of Imprecise Credences in Inference and Decision Making. *Philosophical Perspectives*, 24(1): 281–323.

Joyce, J. ms. Evidence and the Accuracy of Credences.

Kelly, T. 2005. The Epistemic Significance of Disagreement. In J. Hawthorne and T. Gendler (Eds.), *Oxford Studies in Epistemology, Volume 1*. Oxford University Press.

Konek, J. Forthcoming. Epistemic Conservativity and Imprecise Credence. *Philosophy and Phenomenological Research*.

Kyburg Jr, H.E. 1961. *Probability and the Logic of Rational Belief*. Wesleyan University Press.

Lasonen Aarnio, M. 2010. Unreasonable Knowledge. *Philosophical Perspectives*, 24(1): 1–21.

Lasonen Aarnio, M. 2014. Higher Order Evidence and the Limits of Defeat. *Philosophy and Phenomenological Research*, 88(2): 314–45.

Levi, I. 1974. On Indeterminate Probabilities. *Journal of Philosophy*, 71(13): 391–418.

Levinstein, B. 2017. A Pragmatist's Guide to Epistemic Utility. *Philosophy of Science* 84(4): 613–38.

Mayo-Wilson, C. and G. Wheeler. 2016. Scoring Imprecise Credences: A Mildly Immodest Proposal. *Philosophy and Phenomenological Research*, 93(1): 55–78.

Oddie, J. 1997. Conditionalization, Cogency and Cognitive Value. *British Journal of the Philosophy of Science*, 48: 533–41.

Pettigrew, R. 2016. *Accuracy and the Laws of Credence*. Oxford University Press.

Rinard, S. 2015. A Decision Theory for Imprecise Probabilities. *Philosophers' Imprint*, 15(7): 1–16.

Rinard, S. 2017. Imprecise Probability and Higher Order Vagueness. *Res Philosophica*, 94(2): 257–73.

Rinard, S. 2022. Pragmatic Skepticism. *Philosophy and Phenomenical Research*, 104(2): 434–53.

Schervish, M. 1989. A General Method for Comparing Probability Assessors. *Annals of Statistics*, 17(4): 1856–79.

Schoenfield, M. 2017. The Accuracy and Rationality of Imprecise Credences. *Noûs*, 51(4): 667–85.

Schoenfield, M. 2018. An Accuracy Based Approach to Higher Order Evidence. *Philosophy and Phenomenological Research*, 96(3): 690–715.

Schoenfield, M. Forthcoming. Deferring to Doubt. *Proceedings of the Aristotelian Society*.

Seidenfeld, T., M.L. Schervish, and J.B. Kadane. 2012. Forecasting with Imprecise Probabilities. *International Journal of Approximate Reasoning*, 53: 1248–61.

Srinivasan, A. 2015. The Archimedean Urge. *Philosophical Perspectives*, 29(1): 325–62.

Titelbaum, M. 2015. Rationality's Fixed Point. *Oxford Studies in Epistemology*, 5(2015): 253–94.

van Fraassen, B. 1990. Figures in a Probability Landscape. In J. Dunn and A. Gupta (Eds.), *Truth or Consequences* (pp. 345–56). Kluwer Academic Publishers.

van Fraassen, B. 2005. Conditionalizing on Violated Bell's Inequalities. *Analysis*, 65(1): 27–32.

van Fraassen, B. 2006. Vague Expectation Value Loss. *Philosophical Studies*, 127(3): 483–91.

Vavova, K. 2018. Irrelevant Influences. *Philosophy and Phenomenological Research*, 96(1): 134–52.

White, R. 2010. You Just Believe That Because... *Philosophical Perspectives*, 24(1): 573–615.

11

"Getting It Oneself" as an Alternative to Testimonial Knowledge and Deference to Tradition

Justin Tiwald

1. Introduction

Generally speaking, this chapter is about the moral epistemology of three giants of post-classical Chinese philosophy. The three giants are Zhu Xi 朱熹 (1130–1200) and the Cheng brothers, the latter being Cheng Hao 程顥 (1032–1085) and his younger but longer-lived brother Cheng Yi 程頤 (1033–1107). The Cheng brothers were by most accounts the founding figures in a revolution in Chinese philosophy that anglophones now call Neo-Confucianism (the brothers called their movement *Daoxue* 道學, "The Study of the Way"). To simplify somewhat, the iterations of Confucianism before their time (the Confucianism of Confucius and Mencius, among others) had well-developed views on issues in ethics, political thought, and moral psychology, but hadn't yet developed much metaphysics, epistemology, systematicity, or technical terminology. The Cheng brothers gave Confucianism a metaphysics, an epistemology, a systematic philosophical framework, and numerous philosophical terms of art, and this helped Confucianism to compete more favorably with Chinese Buddhism, which had metaphysics, systematicity, and technical terminology in abundance. The last of these philosophers, Zhu Xi, saw himself as continuing the legacy of the Cheng brothers, but eclipsed them in importance and influence. He is now known as the great synthesizer of Neo-Confucianism, the one whose views became orthodoxy for at least six centuries and whose interpretation of the Confucian tradition is arguably still regarded as orthodoxy by many Confucians today, not just in China but in much of East Asia. His interpretations of the classical Confucian texts became the basis for the civil service exam in 1313–15, a position they held almost without interruption until 1905. Because of his widely accepted authority and the need to master his thought in order to get China's most coveted jobs, nearly every adult male who aspired to government service memorized his commentaries and interpretations, and even those who did not so aspire had to be conversant with

Justin Tiwald, *"Getting It Oneself" as an Alternative to Testimonial Knowledge and Deference to Tradition* In: *Oxford Studies in Epistemology, Volume 7.* Edited by: Tamar Szabó Gendler, John Hawthorne, and Julianne Chung, Oxford University Press. © Justin Tiwald 2023. DOI: 10.1093/oso/9780192868978.003.0011

a philosophical worldview that was thoroughly suffused with his ideas. Few philosophers have had so much direct influence on so many.

My specific focus is Zhu and the Cheng brothers' account of a technical term translated as "getting it oneself." The term in Chinese is *zide* 自得. By most accounts, the most salient feature of "getting it oneself" is that the epistemic agent knows something of direct ethical significance on her own authority, and not (for example) on the authority of an expert or a well-tested and proven ethical tradition. Roughly, in cases of *zide*, what warrants the knowledge claim (the claim that one "knows it") is that it is the proper result of one's own reliable faculties and processes of good judgment. This is to be contrasted with other familiar ways of arriving at a correct ethical view, which are to rely on the credible testimony of an expert or on the credibility of a tradition that has been tested and proven over generations. Philosophical accounts of getting it oneself thus have implications for broader philosophical issues of autonomy, moral expertise, and testimonial knowledge in ethics.

For the thinkers under discussion, "getting it oneself" was a second-tier term of art. It wasn't the focus of so much controversy as to warrant entire treatises, but just about everyone who was interested in Confucianism after the Cheng brothers was interested in the term and the phenomenon to which it referred. You find the most elucidation of it in commentaries on some Confucian classics and in dialogues with students (the students of Zhu Xi and the Cheng brothers recorded and circulated summaries of those dialogues), and it is clear that the philosophers and students were concerned with developing a consistent and coherent account of both *zide* itself and its roles and functions in ethics and epistemology more generally. Cheng Yi famously claimed that nothing in ethical learning was more important than getting it oneself.[1] Although Zhu sometimes disagreed with the Cheng brothers on some issues, he took himself to be right on the same page as them with respect to *zide* and its moral and epistemic functions, usually presenting his own views as clarifications of or elaborations upon those of the Chengs.[2] (Although there may have been a difference of emphasis between Zhu and the Chengs, as I will explain in section 3.4.) Given its importance, you would think that there would be at least much sustained discussion of it in secondary literature on Confucianism or Neo-Confucianism. In fact, only one scholar, the late

[1] *Henan Chengshi yishu* ("*The Surviving Works of the Chengs of Henan*") 25.7. In this chapter, all citations of the *Henan Chengshi yishu* will refer to the version found in Cheng and Cheng 1981, and will cite text by *juan* ("fascicle") number and passage or paragraph numbers. For example, the text cited above is identified as "25.7," indicating that it appears in the 7th passage in *juan* 25. The demarcation of passages is relatively consistent across editions, so readers of Chinese should be able to find the intended text in various sources.

[2] *Mengzi jizhu* 4B14. *Mengzi jizhu* ("*Collected Commentaries on the* Mencius") is Zhu Xi's highly influential commentary on the *Mencius* or *Mengzi,* one of the canonical Confucian classics. All citations of Zhu's commentaries refer to Zhu 1987 and identify the relevant passages in the primary text by the primary text's traditional citation conventions.

historian and sinologist Wm. Theodore de Bary (1919–2017), has written more than passing comments about it. He devoted a chapter to it in his *Learning for One's Self* (1991) and offered some sustained discussion of it in his *The Liberal Tradition in China* (1983). Given his disciplinary priorities, his analysis is understandably somewhat loose about the precise philosophical features and implications. The dearth of scholarship may be due to the fact that very few of the relevant texts have been translated into modern languages, and even for regular readers of Song dynasty literary Chinese the passages can be difficult to decipher.

With this in mind, I would like to make a first attempt at offering a more careful, philosophical analysis of "getting it oneself" as characterized by the three giants of post-classical Chinese philosophy. Since there is so little other work on this topic, it might be safe to say that this chapter is, in the first instance, an excuse to translate some of the more interesting comments and offer a defensible account of the primary features of getting it oneself. But I do want to advance what I take to be some subtler (and probably more controversial) theses. The first of these will have to do with the norms of "individualism" underlying some of their remarks about getting it oneself. One of the most notable features of *zide* as Zhu and the Chengs describe it, is that it seems to require that some of the deliberative work be unforced or come easily and naturally. It is tempting to read this feature as arising from an independent ethical commitment to independence of thought or free and uncoerced expression, and that seems to be the strong suggestion of the aforementioned historian, who took *zide* to reflect an independent commitment to what he called "individualism" and a "liberal tradition" in Neo-Confucianism (de Bary 1991: 68–97). Against this view, I will argue that what seems to have motivated them (and helped to justify their account of *zide*) was in fact a cognitive requirement of the mode of knowledge acquisition that Zhu and the Cheng brothers had in mind. If there was an independent commitment to individualism and liberal education, this could help to explain the naturalness or ease of getting it oneself. But if so, it was overdetermined, as the conditions necessary for the particular sort of knowledge acquisition that Zhu and the Chengs were concerned with are quite enough to explain why they were adamant that "getting it oneself" come naturally and easily. And this brings me to my second notable thesis, which is that some of the most important features of getting it oneself are meant to point to an epistemic requirement that I will call the *unbiased appreciation of the inferential force of one's reasons*. I will say more about what this means later, but to give a rough idea, it's the attitude and capacity we exhibit when we can detect how certain conclusions follow from certain reasons, and thus feel inclined to draw the relevant conclusions. I read them as holding that this is an indispensable requirement of *zide* that cannot be explained away. My claim is somewhat controversial because Zhu and the Chengs do not explicitly talk about "appreciation of the inferential force of reasons" in the passages in question. I think that's just because they struggled to find the language to describe this thing (just as we do), and found it easier to talk about the necessary conditions for such appreciation than to characterize the appreciation itself.

Zhu and the Cheng brothers also make subtle and astute observations about other notions and phenomena related to this ability to appreciate inferential force. For example, they proposed a new metric that is useful in explaining how someone might succeed or fail to achieve unbiased appreciation of inferential force, which I will call *auto-epistemic proximity*. I also read them as claiming that one cannot adequately characterize a particular instance of inferential force in words, so that there is necessarily a component of getting it for oneself that we cannot account for linguistically, except to define it ostensively by pointing to personal experiences of appreciating it.

My plan of action is as follows. In the next section (section 2), I will provide just enough historical background to help readers situate discussions of *zide* in the broader discourse of the time, and better understand what motivated them to pin so much of their account of moral virtue and moral knowledge on it. In section 3, I will give what I am calling a "general account" of getting it oneself, highlighting what I take to be some of the more obvious features and providing some informed speculation as to their ethical or epistemological significance. In section 4, I will provide textual evidence for my several observations about the need for unbiased appreciation of inferential force. Finally, in section 5, I draw out some of the broader implications of this study, not just for scholarship on East Asian philosophy but also for current debates about moral deference and testimonial moral knowledge.

2. Some Historical Background: Moral Deference and the Confucian Tradition

On an influential and plausible reading of the Confucian philosophical discourse, one of the issues at the center of its moral epistemology and theories of virtue—arguably the beating heart of much Confucian and Neo-Confucian debate—had to do with moral deference. That is, it had to do with the practice of deferring to the authoritative tradition and its reliable interpreters in determining which ethical views to adopt and enact. This is because Confucianism broadly construed was pulled in two directions. On the one hand, what supposedly united all Confucians was a belief in the great ethical tradition—a tradition whose salient parts included rituals, canonical texts, and views about the importance of family and virtue, and one that came down to them from supposed golden ages in the distant past, where the tradition had demonstrated its credibility by bringing peace, just rulership, and strong community bonds, among other goods. This would seem to suggest that it's constitutive of being a Confucian that one defers to the time-tested tradition, even if that means adopting views against one's own better judgment.

On the other hand, Confucians were also drawn to the idea that there was something fundamentally problematic about adopting an ethical view without understanding its right-making features for oneself.[3] Virtuous people generally understand why the ethical practices that they adopt are good ones, and ethical sensibilities are best acquired by coming to see for oneself what makes one's practices the correct ones (and other practices the wrong ones).[4]

The most forceful defense of pervasive moral deference came from a classical Confucian philosopher named Xunzi 荀子 (third century BCE). In separate papers, I have reconstructed some of Xunzi's main arguments for pervasive moral deference and some Neo-Confucian responses to it (Tiwald 2012 and Tiwald ms). For purposes of understanding the Neo-Confucians' interest in *zide*, it helps to know some of their principal objections to pervasive moral deference as I understand them. The first argument is largely implicit. As I read them, many Confucians share an intuition with many philosophers today that acting on views acquired through moral deference lacks full moral worth (Hills 2009). The underlying thought, I suspect, is that in order to for an act to count as morally worthy for a person, that person must at least bear some responsibility or credit for doing the morally worthy thing, and in order to get credit for doing the morally worthy thing, she must have knowingly done it under some thick description that discloses what's morally worthy about it. So, for example, it would be odd to give credit to Meihua for doing something compassionate or loyal if she isn't aware of or responding to the features of her situation that make her behavior compassionate or loyal, as when she's just following someone else's instructions (just as Meihua wouldn't get credit for winning a card game if she just put cards down at random without knowing what made them winning hands). Second, and more explicitly, knowledge acquired through moral deference fails to give rise to a feature of complete virtue that I call wholeheartedness, which is my expedient translation (for some purposes) of the Chinese term *cheng* 誠 (also translated as integrity or sincerity).[5] Wholeheartedness is the quality of having well-integrated feelings, desires, beliefs, and commitments, such that the agent experiences no significant internal opposition or resistance to virtuous behavior. For example, someone who can quit a deeply corrupt employer without regret is more wholeheartedly righteous than someone who stalls or looks for excuses to stay on, and someone who wants to visit a sick friend in the hospital is more wholeheartedly benevolent or compassionate than someone who is committed

[3] A study by James Andow (2020) suggests that this discomfort with moral testimony and moral deference is widely shared today, at least among the demographic groups that he tested.

[4] For an influential study of Confucianism that illuminates the tensions between ethical self-reliance and ethical deference among various philosophers, see Ivanhoe 2000.

[5] Cheng Hao and Cheng Yi, *Henan Chengshi yishu* 1.5, 11.116 (in Cheng and Cheng 1981). Zhu Xi, *Daxue zhangju* (*Commentary on the* Greater Learning), commentary section 6. All citations of Zhu's commentaries refer to Zhu 1987 and identify the relevant passages in the primary text by the primary text's traditional citation conventions.

to visiting the friend but does so grudgingly. The Neo-Confucians propose (plausibly) that when one acquires ethical knowledge by deference rather than by getting it oneself, the resultant ethical views and commitments won't be well integrated into one's other ethical convictions, desires, feelings, etc. Finally, the Neo-Confucians seem to believe that if pervasive moral deference were really the correct practice, then following the correct practice would make it impossible to cultivate the virtues. There must be at least some domains of life in which we can trust our own capacities of autonomous ethical knowledge, or else there would be no root or foundation from which autonomous ethical knowledge of any kind could grow.[6]

It is easy to overstate the differences between the parties in this debate. Both Xunzi (the great defender of deference to the Confucian tradition) and his Neo-Confucian critics believed that, all other things being equal, it is more virtuous for people to understand what makes their practices the right ones. Accordingly, all sides would agree that when one can be confident about one's own ethical judgments, it is better to endorse and act on ethical views that one believes to be correct by one's own lights. Sages rightly rely on their own deliberative processes to assess ethical affairs (Tiwald 2012: 286–7).

Nevertheless, these concessions still leave a great number of questions of deference and autonomy open. For example, they don't tell us whether ethical novices—people who don't have reason to trust their own ethical judgments—should adopt and act on ethical views that they endorse on their own authority. For Xunzi, the answer is clear: the ethical views that the novice adopts (that is, the novice's ethical beliefs) should be those recommended by the Confucian tradition and its authoritative interpreters, and the views that the novice acts on (the novice's ethical behavior) should also be those that come from the tradition. For Neo-Confucians like the Cheng brothers and Zhu Xi, the expectations of novices are more complicated. First, while they acknowledge that there are many domains of life in which we are better off deferring to experts and tradition, they also believe that, if virtue is to be possible for novices, the novices must assume that there are some domains of life in which their naïve or inexpert judgments are reliable. Oft-mentioned evidence of reliable ethical knowledge in novices are children's tendency to love and obey their parents, the natural human inclination to save a child from falling into a well, and the natural human aversion to certain shameless displays of self-debasement such as accepting food given with open contempt (I will have much more to say about this last example in section 4). Second, it is arguable that Zhu and the Cheng brothers also thought that *sometimes* it is better to let people follow their own ethical compasses, however flawed, than to adopt and follow a traditional practice that they do not entirely

[6] See Tiwald ms and Dai Zhen 2009: sections 21 and 26.

understand. This second claim is somewhat more controversial. At least one interpreter of Neo-Confucianism has proposed that sages alone can act on their own ethical judgment and that everyone else must follow good instructions (Munro 1988: 155–91). But I find places where Zhu and the Chengs think the instructional value of "getting it oneself" is sufficiently high and the costs of defying the tradition are sufficiently low to allow people some discretion. For example, there is a famous case in the *Analects*, traditionally attributed to Confucius (Kongzi), in which a student declares that he doesn't see the point in the traditional practice of mourning the death of a parent for three years—given all of the opportunity costs, he suggests, one year should be enough. After determining that the student really would be comfortable with the abbreviated mourning ritual, Confucius countenances the practice for that student, but laments that the student is so callous and ungrateful.[7] In Zhu Xi's commentary, he suggests that it was more important to get the student to seek in himself the considerations that should have made him uncomfortable with the shorter mourning period, so that he could "get them himself."[8] I read this as suggesting that the pedagogical and long-run ethical advantages of "getting it oneself" sometimes provide pro tanto reasons to give novices some leeway to do wrong, provided that the wrong isn't too severe or the harm too great.[9] Presumably Zhu would allow that there are other situations in which the advantages of getting it oneself can justify allowing novices some leeway to make mistakes.

One more bit of historical context. In most (but not all) cases, Zhu Xi and the Cheng brothers are able to find some classical source for their major philosophical claims, some passage in their canon that helps to prove that ancient Confucian sages affirm the position that they propound. Ultimately, they think, we won't need to rely on the ancient sources to believe in the veracity of their teachings (we'll know it for ourselves, of course). Still, they often weave some of the language of classical sources into their remarks, or artfully allude to phrases or ideas that come from those sources. With this in mind, it will be useful to have in view what I take to be the *locus classicus* of Confucian accounts of *zide*, which is from the *Mencius* or *Mengzi* 孟子, a text traditionally attributed to a Confucian philosopher of the same name. In that passage, Mencius himself offers a stirring account of the advantages of grasping the Confucian Way by *zide*, suggesting that the knowledge so acquired imparts numerous advantages to the knower:

[7] *Analects* 17.21 (see Slingerland 2003).

[8] *Lunyu jizhu* ("*Collected Commentaries on the* Analects") 17.21. All citations of Zhu's commentaries refer to Zhu 1987 and identify the relevant passages in the primary text by the primary text's traditional citation conventions.

[9] I also suspect that, for both Confucius and for Zhu Xi, insincere mourning is of little value when the mourning child has so little love and gratitude for the parents in the first place. For children who are more loving and grateful it would be a mistake to skimp on the ritual grieving process.

> Mencius said, "The superior person steeps himself in it deeply, following the Way, desiring to get it himself. Getting it himself, he dwells in it securely. Dwelling in it securely, he deeply relies on it. Deeply relying on it, he draws upon it left and right, encountering its source. Hence, the superior person desires to get it himself."[10]

As we will see, later Confucians came to understand the phrase translated as "steep in it deeply" (*shenzao* 深造) to refer to an intermediate stage where one is still immersed in and gathering thoughts about a matter (a sense that still occasionally appears in modern Chinese). And many later Confucians make artful reference to the sense of "security" (*an* 安) afforded by getting it oneself.

3. A General Account of Getting It Oneself

3.1 Knowing It on One's Own Authority

In this section, I will discuss what I take to be some of the most important distinguishing features of *zide*, and engage in some textually informed conjecture about what justifies or motivates the emphasis on each feature. As I mentioned in the introduction, probably the most important feature of getting it oneself is that the knowledge that one acquires is known on one's own authority. My working account of knowledge on one's own authority is that in those cases, what warrants the claim that the agent knows something is that it is the proper result of her own processes and faculties of good judgment.[11] I find many passages that call attention to this feature. One that is particularly interesting is the following, which uses this feature of *zide* to draw a favorable contrast between Confucian knowledge and Chan (Zen) Buddhist "enlightenment." By their own account, many Chan Buddhists claim that enlightenment is also grasped in a personal way, such that they can know some profound truth for themselves without depending on the authority of others. But Chan Buddhists also have a custom of reassuring their disciples by having a Chan Buddhist master give them a seal to verify that their

[10] *Mengzi* 4B14. My translation follows Zhu Xi's interpretation in his *Mengzi jizhu* (*Collected Commentaries on the* Mencius) 4B14 (in Zhu 1987).

[11] For present purposes, I prefer an account of "knowledge on one's own authority" that is neutral with respect to a wide range of theories of knowledge. If your theory says that knowing that p requires that someone have a good justification for p, then it counts as knowledge on my own authority only if *my* justification of p warrants the claim that I know that p. If your theory says that knowledge that p depends on someone having truth-conducive epistemic virtues, then it counts as knowledge on my authority only if it's the truth-conduciveness of *my* epistemic virtues that warrants the claim that I know that p. If it turns out that "I know that p" is warranted in part by the justificatory process or epistemic virtues of my trusted advisor or friend, then it isn't knowledge on my own authority.

enlightenment is authentic. As Cheng Hao points out, this seems to suggest that the disciples aren't "getting it themselves."

> Buddhists speak of having their insights confirmed by their master,[12] but how can this qualify as *zide* ("getting it oneself")? When people have "gotten it themselves" then their minds should remain unaffected no matter who might comment on their views. How can the views that one "gets oneself" depend on anyone else's say-so?[13]

There are things we could say in defense of Chan Buddhism here. Maybe the Chan *disciples* don't get it themselves, but the practice of confirming enlightenment is consistent with the view that the *masters*, at least, do get it themselves. Also, one might point out that there are really two different sorts of achievements here: there's knowing something, and then there's being confident that one knows something. Just because the disciples lack confidence that they really do know the doctrine of emptiness or Buddha-nature, it doesn't necessarily follow that they don't know the doctrine of emptiness or Buddha-nature. Maybe confidence would require higher-order knowledge (they would need to *know that they know*), which is precisely what the practice of getting a master's confirmation is supposed to provide.

However, even if Cheng Hao is uncharitable, my point is that he seems to be presupposing that when one gets it oneself, one will know it on one's own authority and thus won't need the further confirmation of an external authority to count as knowing it, and this is evidence that knowing something on one's own authority is an important feature of getting it oneself. As Cheng says, one's "getting it" shouldn't depend on another person's say-so.

3.2 Enhancement of Joy and Epistemic Confidence

Two other oft-mentioned features of *zide* have to do with the quality of wholeheartedness that I mentioned in section 2, understood as having well-integrated feelings, desires, beliefs, and commitments, such that they robustly and consistently support a virtuous course of action. For Zhu and the Chengs, two good indicators of wholeheartedness are (1) a distinctive sort of joy that comes from understanding, and (2) epistemic self-confidence. To give just one representative

[12] "Confirmed" is my approximate translation of *yinzheng* 印證 (*lit.* 'confirming by seal'). This refers to the verification part of a process called "confirmation by seal of approval" (*yinke zhengming* 印可證明) in Chan Buddhism, whereby Chan Buddhist authorities verify that a person's enlightenment experience is authentic and then confer public recognition on them, often as members of a particular Chan lineage or tradition.

[13] Cheng Hao, *Henan Chengshi yishu* 11.67 (in Cheng and Cheng 1981).

passage that makes this connection, I offer an intriguing recorded lesson attributed to Cheng Hao. Alluding to a memorable passage in the *Analects* of Confucius (*Analects* 6.20), he starts from the assumption that there is a significant ethical difference between merely loving the Way (the ethical order) and taking joy in it. Taking joy, on my reading, suggests greater psychological integration and wholeheartedness than mere loving. Cheng proposes that truly taking joy in the Way requires "getting it oneself," and proposes (I think) that this is because at the stage of loving the Way, one still regards it as something external, whereas at the stage of taking joy in the Way, it becomes a thing of one's own.

> Learning isn't complete until it reaches the point of joy. One can "be sincere and love learning" something and yet not know the joy of getting it oneself.[14] Such is the person who is still steeping himself in the Way [i.e., still in the process of learning].[15] When someone merely loves the Way [without deriving joy from getting it himself] it's as if he were touring someone else's garden. *When someone takes joy in the Way [from getting it oneself] it's a thing of his own.*[16] Only then can a person trust in the Way, which is indeed difficult for people to be able to do.[17]

So merely loving the Way is like touring someone else's garden, which is a pleasant thing but doesn't elicit the distinctive sort of joy that Cheng believes getting the Way oneself will elicit, and doesn't impart trust or confidence in what one may know. That's because the Way stands to the mere lover as the beautiful plants and objects in another person's garden stand to a person who is merely touring it. In contrast, when one gets it oneself, it's a thing of one's own. Speculatively, what Cheng means to suggest is that, once a person has acquired knowledge in this way then the knowledge is like an earned possession in which one can take justifiable pride. Even more speculatively, Cheng may also be suggesting that once one gets (something important about) the Way oneself, one's knowledge has a kind of personal immediacy that imparts trust and confidence, trust and confidence that is, just as matter of deep-seated psychological disposition, hard to achieve when our beliefs are derived from someone else's testimony (no matter how reliable we may sincerely believe them to be). It might help to think about the difference it makes to cross a busy street whilst seeing for oneself that there are no oncoming cars, rather than relying on someone else's say-so that it's safe to cross. Even if that other person is a most trusted friend or a parent, most of us will feel some trepidation stepping into the street.

[14] "Be sincere and love learning" 篤信好學 quotes from *Analects* 8.13.

[15] A reference to *Mencius* 4B14.

[16] This rank ordering of those who "take joy in [the Way]" (*le zhi* 樂之) above those who merely "love [the Way]" (*hao zhi* 好之) references *Analects* 6.20.

[17] Cheng Hao, *Henan Chengshi yishu* 11.116 (in Cheng and Cheng 1981); my emphasis.

3.3 Self-Discovery Aspects

There are some grander and seemingly more theoretically ambitious claims for *zide* that I should mention in the interest of giving a well-rounded sense of the phenomenon. On many descriptions of the experience of getting some profound ethical insight in this distinctive way, it seems as though one finds or discovers the insight *in* oneself.[18] Often they also suggest that getting it oneself consists in part in discovering innate ethical knowledge or activating an innate and fully-formed capacity to know based entirely on one's own cognitive resources (I think the latter of these two descriptions is more precise). Some twentieth- and twenty-first-century scholars of Chinese thought have described this mode of knowledge acquisition as "maieutic" and illustrated it by invoking a famous moment in Plato's *Meno* where Socrates demonstrates that even an uneducated boy or slave already knows some axioms of geometry.[19] For ease of reference, we can call these the "self-discovery aspects" of *zide.*

I find the self-discovery aspects fascinating and useful for understanding *zide* phenomenologically. It does seem to me that some of our most notable moments of personal insight are experienced as something akin to discoveries of our own implicit or dormant ideas or beliefs. Sometimes it seems like the insight is one that we had previously but hadn't fully recognized or articulated, or that it's just a short inferential step beyond beliefs that we already endorse and deeply understand. Still, if we take the Chengs and Zhu Xi literally then they would appear to hold that we already have a well-formed capacity to know a wide range of ethical views based entirely on our own internal cognitive resources. And I'm with later Confucian critics of Zhu and the Chengs, who say that this strong position has some absurd implications.[20] Since this isn't the main concern of the present chapter, however, I will leave it be for now. It is worth noting that the later Confucian tradition has at least one major advocate for getting it oneself—Dai Zhen 戴震 (1724–1777)—who emphatically rejected the view that we have well-formed faculties of ethical knowledge innately, and it's a sure bet that he'd tell us not to take the appearance of self-discovery too literally (Dai 2009: 267–86).

[18] For example, see Cheng and Cheng, *Henan Chengshi yishu* 17.2 (in Cheng and Cheng 1981), and Zhu Xi, *Sishu huowen* (*Some Questions on the Four Books*) 33.10. All citations of the *Sishu huowen* refer to Zhu 2001 and reference the text by *juan* ("fascicle") number and passage or paragraph number within that *juan*. For example, the text cited here is identified as "33.10," indicating that it appears in the 10th passage in *juan* 33.

[19] Ivanhoe 2000: 57n25; Slingerland 2003: 66; Plato 1961: 82d–84b.

[20] One of the earliest scholars and translators of Confucian classics, James Legge, found the self-discovery aspects of *zide* too "misty" to take seriously, and tried to downplay them (Legge 1892: 2:22). Theodore de Bary takes Legge to task for this and cites them as evidence of a more religious or "mystical" view (de Bary 1991: 46–7). On my reading, Zhu and the Cheng brothers could have interesting reasons for thinking that these capacities must necessarily be fully formed and innate. Among other things, if they weren't fully formed and innate then it wouldn't be possible for us to "get for oneself" the objective implications of one's reasons. I will say more about this in the next section.

3.4 Unforced Deliberation

Finally, another intriguing feature of "getting it oneself" has to do with effort expended on the deliberative process itself. Zhu Xi and the Cheng brothers stress that this particular type of knowledge acquisition is incompatible with certain kinds of forcing or artificial striving in seeking ethical knowledge. We can call their preferred alternative quality the "unforced" or "spontaneous and natural" quality of deliberation. There are numerous passages that make mention of this quality. Here is the most widely quoted remark by Cheng Hao, reproduced in a popular primer or introduction to Neo-Confucianism that was read by many millions of aspiring scholars in East Asia:

> Generally speaking, only when you get it naturally through unspoken learning does it truly count as 'getting it yourself.' If there is any element of deliberate planning or contrivance then it won't at all qualify as 'getting it yourself.'[21]

At this broad level, it is not obvious what specific kinds of deliberation, or which stages in the deliberative process, are supposed to be unforced. Neo-Confucians like Zhu and the Cheng brothers don't hide the fact that their regimen of ethical education requires perseverance and work, that students have to develop a sense of commitment and discipline in order to succeed, and that the insights gained are, in many respects, hard-won. But presumably they think that some parts of the deliberative process should come more spontaneously and naturally. In the next section, I will argue that the expectation that the deliberation be spontaneous and natural applies more narrowly to the process of drawing conclusions about specific ethical norms or principles (*daoli* 道理). This allows that there can be other parts of the deliberative process that require forcing or artifice, such as reading philosophical or ethical texts, gathering information about probable consequences, entertaining conceptual possibilities, or pushing oneself to consider a wider range of ethical reasons or considerations than one may currently recognize.

Before looking at the evidence for my reading, however, I should note that some of the features mentioned so far are more central or peripheral—more or less part of the "core meaning" of *zide*—than others. Zhu and the Cheng brothers would surely be reluctant to give up the proposal that *zide* enhances joy and epistemic confidence, but if it turned out that this weren't typically the case, that wouldn't make it pointless or completely non-sensical to characterize the relevant sort of knowledge acquisition as *zide*. By contrast, there are two other features mentioned

[21] *Jinsi lu* 近思錄 (*Reflections on Things at Hand*) 2.41. All citations of the *Jinsi lu* reference Zhu and Lü 2008 and are identified by *juan* ("fascicle") number and the paragraph or passage number within that *juan*. For example, the text cited above is cited as "2.41," indicating that it is the 41st passage in *juan* 2.

which, if they were absent, really would make the Chinese phrase *zide* nonsensical for participants in this discourse. These are the features that the critical parts of deliberative process should be *unforced* and, to put it crudely for now, that the *self* figures prominently in "getting" it. In the two-character phrase *zide* 自得, the Chinese character *zi* 自 can plausibly be read as an adverbial modifier meaning "naturally" or "spontaneously" or a reflexive adverb roughly equivalent to "of the self" or "of one's own accord." If we wanted to emphasize the former sense of *zi* we could translate the phrase "getting it naturally" to suggest that one gets it without artificial compulsion or forcing.

While the textual evidence strongly suggests that the Cheng brothers and Zhu Xi saw *both* senses of *zi* as critical for understanding the whole phrase, there may be a slight difference of emphasis between Zhu and the Chengs. As the twentieth-century scholar Wing-tsit Chan 陳榮捷 has observed, Zhu Xi's students were aware of a debate between Zhu and his contemporary Zhang Shi 張栻 (1133–1181) about the relative importance of the naturalness and self in *zide* (Chan 1989: 301). Zhang apparently thought it most important that the object that one "gets" is one's own virtuous nature, and thus emphasized the role of the self in *zide*. Zhu taught that this explanation was defective, perhaps because it neglected to mention the critical quality of spontaneity or naturalness (*ziran* 自然) in deliberation, or maybe because it focused too much on what I have called the "self-discovery aspects" of *zide*. For much of Zhu's life, he took issue with Confucians who suggested that people could directly access or intuit the good ethical ideas and inclinations of their own virtuous natures without engaging in much reading or investigation of the larger world (Angle and Tiwald 2017: 135–55). Zhu may have wanted to downplay self-discovery more than the Cheng brothers themselves. Unfortunately, there is little surviving record of the dispute. A brief mention of it is attributed to Zhu's student Chen Chun 陳淳 (1159–1223) in a Ming dynasty edition and commentary on the *Mencius*, but the original text from which the Ming edition quotes appears to be lost (Chan 1989: 317n64).

Because Zhu Xi was so adamant that people shouldn't neglect the natural or spontaneous quality of *zide*, Chan concludes that when the phrase is used in Zhu Xi's sense it is best translated as "getting it in the natural way" (Chan 1989: 302). My own view is that *zide*'s most essential feature is, roughly put, reliance on the self's own epistemic processes and aptitudes. That is why it seemed absurd that Buddhist enlightenment could count as acquired through *zide* only if it is confirmed by a master, as we saw in section 3.1. It also explains why Zhu is so adamant that epistemic agents must take certain steps themselves in order to count as "getting it" in the right way, as we will see in section 5. It might be that Zhu Xi sought to downplay the self-discovery aspects of *zide*, but he still sought to underscore the self's pivotal part in acquiring the relevant knowledge and found *zide* a felicitous phrase for that reason.

4. Inferential Force

The view that deliberation in *zide* must be unforced is a little surprising at first pass. If we think about other areas of inquiry where knowledge based on one's own authority is preferred, it doesn't seem to matter all that much whether the relevant deliberations were forced or free and spontaneous. It seems odd to suggest that someone's novel mathematical proof or penetrating insight into the beauty of a piece of music is any less autonomous just because she had to push herself to find a solution or explanation. So why should autonomous ethical knowledge be any different?

In de Bary's discussions of *zide*, he seems to understand the unforced or spontaneous quality of getting it oneself as evidence for what he calls "individualism" in Neo-Confucian thought. What he appears to have in mind by "individualism" are a cluster of overlapping commitments to social and individual behavioral norms such as independence of thought, individual expression, and epistemic self-reliance, provided that one is entitled to these things in virtue of one's status as an individual self or individual person and not, say, one's social position or class (de Bary 1991: 2–7, 68–97). If Neo-Confucian individualism didn't permeate into the general culture, he suggests, that's primarily because imperial China never realized the institutional structures that help nurture and protect such norms on a large scale, but the ideological commitment to individualism was present in China's leading thinkers at the time (de Bary 1991: 265–7). In another work he suggests that *zide* is evidence of a "liberal tradition" in Neo-Confucian-era China, understood as a commitment to free and open inquiry and individual creativity in thought (de Bary 1983: 58–66). He finds individualism evident in the writings of Zhu and the Cheng brothers, especially in their remarks on *zide*, but he takes them to be on the more moderate end of what seems to be an individualist-holist spectrum ("holism" is his word for the opposite of individualism). His most compelling example of individualism (and liberalism) is the radical Ming-dynasty Neo-Confucian Li Zhi 李贄 (1527–1602). Famously, Li Zhi prized a certain sort of authenticity (*zhen* 真) in one's art, literature, and ethical behavior, which in a famous essay he described as the spontaneous expressions of one's own highly particularistic "child-mind" (*tongxin* 童心).[22]

I admit to being a little unclear about what, precisely, de Bary means by "individualism" and "liberalism." My sense, however, is that whatever he may mean by these terms, we would do well to pay attention to two different ways of accounting for the unforced and spontaneous quality in one's process of learning. The first proposes that the unforced or spontaneous quality of *zide* is justified by a

[22] See de Bary 1991, 203–70. For Li Zhi's essay on the child-mind see Li 1961: 98–9. For English translations see Tiwald and Van Norden 2014: 304–7 or Li 2016: 106–10. For a scholarly overview of Li Zhi's ethics of authenticity see Lee 2013.

cognitive requirement, made necessary by the nature of *zide* itself or the type of knowledge or understanding that it is supposed to produce. The other tempting way is to see the unforced and spontaneous quality of *zide* as justified by some cognition-independent social value, such as the value of free and open inquiry as fundamental features of a just society, or the value of autonomy as such, or the value of being an authentic individual, true to one's child-mind and heedless of social pressures. My sense is that de Bary thinks the unforced and spontaneous quality of *zide* is justified by cognition-independent values of the latter sort, which suggests commitments to individualism and liberalism that go deep and have relatively broad implications.

But I am skeptical. I happily concede that there are some Neo-Confucians who do treat independence of thought and authenticity as independent values, and of these, Li Zhi is probably the most outstanding example. But in the Cheng-Zhu account of *zide*, I think there's a very different concern at work. They think getting it oneself is unforced and spontaneous because that is generally a necessary condition for judgments free of certain biases—namely, biases that interfere with our ability to appreciate how certain conclusions follow from certain reasons, which I am calling appreciation of the inferential force of one's reasons. Perhaps they would have appealed to an independent commitment to individualism to justify ease and spontaneity in ethical deliberation and judgment, but if so, their promotion of ease and spontaneity was overdetermined. Their devotion to forms of inquiry necessary for unbiased appreciation of inferential force gave them reason enough to endorse the particular sort of ease and spontaneity that they did.

I will start to make my reading more plausible by providing more context for the widely-read quotation on *zide*'s unforced quality given in section 3.4. Here are Cheng Hao's full remarks, with the additional material (material omitted from the Neo-Confucian primer's version) in italics:

> Only when you get it naturally through unspoken learning does it truly count as "getting it yourself." If there is any element of deliberate planning or contrivance then it won't at all qualify as "getting it yourself." *You must concentrate your mind and accumulate your thoughts and then wander among them in a carefree manner, having your fill of them. Only then can you "get it." If you seek it in haste or under pressure then it becomes a mere selfish pursuit, so that in the end it will be insufficient to "get it."*[23]

In the longer passage, there is a strong suggestion that the unforced and spontaneous quality is meant to forestall a certain kind of selfishness, one that prevents us from having the right relation to or grasp of the knowledge in question (from

[23] Cheng Hao, as quoted in Zhu Xi, *Mengzi jizhu* (*Collected Commentaries on the* Mencius) 4B14 (in Zhu 1987); my emphasis.

"getting it"). This is consistent with a pervasive feature of Neo-Confucian moral psychology, which is its thoroughgoing concern with self-serving biases and motivated reasoning. In one memorable passage, for example, Zhu says that people must guard against the habit of seeking fault only with rival views, which he likens to the frame of mind of people engaged in litigation.[24] Like numerous other philosophers in the Neo-Confucian era, many of the virtues and habits of thought that Zhu and the Chengs were interested in were meant to undercut incipient "selfish thoughts" or "selfish inclinations" (*siyi* 私意), which they took to be responsible for so much self-serving rationalization and moral failure (Angle and Tiwald 2017: 145–51). I suggest that we add a linked pair to the long list of techniques that combat or blunt the effects of self-serving cognitive biases, a pair that Cheng here describes as "wandering among [one's thoughts] in a carefree manner" and "having your fill of them" (*youyou yanyu yu qijian* 優游饜飫於其間). The idea seems to be that by gathering ideas and considering them in a relatively carefree frame of mind, one can come to see for oneself without self-serving bias what conclusions should be drawn from those ideas—or, as I will argue shortly, the reasons implicit in those ideas.

Further evidence for this interpretation is that the unforced or spontaneous quality of getting it oneself is stage-specific and content-specific. That is, it is not the entire process of getting it oneself that is supposed to be unforced, but rather the process at just those times when we need to figure out what inferences or conclusions to draw about some important matter of inherent or direct ethical significance, typically described by Zhu and the Cheng brothers as matters of the human Way (or "the Way" for short). There can be other work that is very much forced and doesn't come so naturally. The most obvious candidate is the "thought-gathering" work, when we read widely or listen carefully to gather ideas and competing views. In the passage above, Cheng Hao seems to suggest that there's a stage in which we "concentrate the mind" and "gather thoughts." Wandering in a carefree manner comes after that, seemingly when it is time to decide what conclusions to draw from the thoughts presented. Zhu Xi replicates some of Cheng's stage-sensitive language in one of his descriptions of the process. His account also makes it clear that the conclusions drawn in this unforced manner are ethical in content, conclusions that disclose something important about "moral principles" or "moral patterns" (*daoli* 道理) or the Way (*Dao* 道):

> The moral principles [*daoli*] are inherently broad in scope. You just need to concentrate your mind and accumulate thoughts, then proceed to nourish them

[24] *Zhuzi yulei* (*The Classified Sayings of Master Zhu*), 11.73 and 11.80. All citations of the *Zhuzi yulei* refer to Zhu 1986 and identify text by *juan* ("fascicle") number and by passage number within that *juan*. For example, the passages cited here are identified as "11.73 and 11.80," indicating that they are the 73rd and 80th passages in *juan* 11. For an English translation of these passages see Chu 1990: 150–1.

> oh-so-gradually so that naturally they will ripen until you are intimately familiar with them. If you seek the principles in haste or under pressure then this will arouse an inclination to rush the pursuit of them, so that you end up with nothing but selfish thoughts, and how could that suffice to enter the Way?[25]

In another passage, Zhu indicates that getting it oneself does in fact require a great deal of effort and exertion, but stipulates that the effort shouldn't be motivated by a push to get to the conclusion of one's deliberations. The conclusion should come naturally and unbidden:

> What's required is that you apply more of your effort to the task without becoming anxious about the result, and that you attend fully to the procedure without skipping over any steps. Then, even though you won't have any predetermined expectation of getting it you will naturally get it yourself.[26]

I think the evidence is clear that Zhu Xi and the Cheng brothers were adamant about "not forcing" the *zide* process because they were concerned that forcing would give rise to inclinations to rush the conclusion, which in turn cause or perhaps manifest as self-serving cognitive biases and motivated reasoning. What is perhaps less clear is the nature of the thing that they thought our unforced and spontaneous cognition was supposed to track. I propose that we understand this thing as "inferential force of reasons." Roughly, this is that relational or intrinsic property of reasons—whatever it consists in—that makes it appropriate to draw certain conclusions from them. The attitude that we're supposed to adopt toward that inferential force I call "appreciation," which I take to combine understanding and motivation. When we appreciate something, we both understand what makes it valuable or worth promoting and we have some inclination (even if a very weak one) to promote or protect it.

Another bit of textual evidence for this interpretation is more impressionistic but more vivid, and it has to do with a popular metaphor used to illustrate the sort of thing that the later Confucians have in mind by "getting it oneself." According to a famous passage in the *Analects* of Confucius (a canonical source text for the Neo-Confucians), Confucius says that he is only interested in teaching students who are proactive learners, such that when Confucius "holds up one corner" they will "come back to him with the other three."[27] Figuratively speaking, the passage implies that teacher and students are engaged in the process of specifying the shape or angle of three corners of a quadrilateral, with the teacher providing dimensions for just one corner and the students filling in the rest. The Neo-Confucians take this image to capture succinctly the work of getting it oneself,

[25] Zhu Xi, *Zhuzi yulei* 95.150 (in Zhu 1986). [26] Zhu Xi, *Sishu huowen* 33.10 (in Zhu 2001).
[27] *Analects* 7.8; Slingerland translation (2003), slightly modified.

which consists in showing how certain conclusions (the angles of the other three corners) follow from ideas taken as sound or given (the angle of one corner). And it is critical that the answers be generated by students themselves and not provided by the teacher. As Cheng Hao explains in his own elucidation of the "three corners" metaphor, sage teachers of ancient times "taught by pointing out what wasn't the case" rather than giving their students answers outright.[28] This strongly suggests that it is not enough for the teacher to tell students that certain views or ideas should lead them to certain conclusions; the students have to figure out for themselves that the views or ideas can be seen as reasons to reach ethically significant conclusions, and which specific conclusions they are reasons for.

Zhu and the Cheng brothers don't talk about the inferential force of reasons by name, but they had a great deal of interest in reasons, and were keenly interested in the role and function of inference-making in the acquisition of epistemic goods. In a recent book on Neo-Confucianism, Stephen Angle and I highlight some long-neglected text in the work of Zhu Xi that makes his views relatively explicit. There, Zhu distinguishes between three types of ethical knowledge (or perhaps three types of knowledge-ascription). The first is when one knows a particular rule of behavior but knows it because the tradition and wise individuals affirm it. The second is when one knows a particular rule of behavior and can't resist the power of that rule, but don't have any explicit understanding of the reasons for the rule (think of someone who suddenly sees a child teetering at the edge of a well and about to fall in—Zhu suggests that we can know that we ought to save the child without really knowing why). The third and most important sort of ethical knowledge Zhu calls "knowing the reasons why it is so" (*zhi qi suoyiran zhi gu* 知其所以然之故). I take the "reasons" in question to be those that disclose the grounds for an ethical norm, and not just any reasons to believe an ethical norm to be right. "Easily preventing an innocent, sentient being and those who love her from suffering unnecessary harm" could be a "reason why it is so" for the rule that we should save an endangered child. "Wise sages say that you should save endangered children" or "the only people I know who wouldn't save endangered children are shiftless characters" are not "reasons why it is so" for the rule. Angle and I also observed that when Zhu uses the Chinese character *tui* 推 in the sense of "inference," he tends to use it in one of two ways. First, he thinks we infer reason A from claims B, C, and D, when we see that A best harmonizes with or coheres with B, C, and D. Zhu models this kind of inference when, for example, he shows how the work of certain virtues is analogous to the different behavior of living things in different seasons of the year, all of which work in concert to sustain and reproduce life. Second, there is a special and critical sort of inference that Zhu sometimes calls "inference based on similarity in kind" (*leitui* 類推). Very

[28] *Henan Chengshi yishu* 11.67 (in Cheng and Cheng 1981).

roughly, this is the sort of inference one makes when one sees two ethical scenarios as relevantly similar to one another, so that one sees how a conclusion that applies to one should apply to the other as well.[29] This latter sort provides a particularly powerful example of inferential force, so let me illustrate it by using an example that Zhu and the Cheng brothers would have been well acquainted with.

In the canonical Confucian text known in the West as the *Mencius* (also as the *Mengzi* 孟子), Mencius himself makes an interesting observation about public corruption. He notes that many public officials accept bribes for political favors, which is shameful and self-debasing, but don't seem to appreciate or fully recognize it as shameful and self-debasing. In contrast, he observes, there are other scenarios where the shamefulness and self-debasingness of similar behavior is plain to see. He gives the example of receiving and eating food given in a way that is meant to humiliate the receiver. Imagine that you are a beggar, he says, so deprived of food that you are on the verge of starvation. And imagine that someone offers you food but stomps or spits on it, and then presumably stands back and waits for you to eat it nonetheless, thereby making a spectacle of yourself to the delight of the giver and passers-by. Most people, Mencius suggests, would refuse to eat food offered to them in this manner, and that's because the shamefulness and self-debasement is plain to see. And yet state officials debase themselves for a great deal less. After all, how much do a larger house and more chariots really add to one's life compared to the value of preserving one's own life itself?[30]

Not everyone shares Mencius' view (which must have been ubiquitous in his time and place) that accepting food given with open contempt is so self-debasing that one would sooner starve. Even so, I think most of us can at least appreciate a beggar's reluctance to make a spectacle of himself for the entertainment of some higher-status bully, so there is a sense in which we can appreciate more readily and intuitively the self-debasing quality of accepting food given with contempt than we can the self-debasing quality of accepting a bribe. Furthermore, it is quite plausible that accepting a bribe in return for giving a special political favor is self-debasing in a relevantly similar way. It makes oneself the instrument of someone else's vicious scheme, and makes one complicit in one's own instrumentalization.[31] Framed in that way, it seems hard to resist the conclusion that accepting a bribe is similarly shameful. Insofar as someone finds it hard to resist drawing that conclusion merely for the reasons given, one appreciates the inferential force of the reasons for not taking bribes.

[29] Angle and Tiwald 2017: 39–40, 127–9.

[30] *Mencius* 6A10.

[31] For more on this thought experiment in the *Mencius*, see Van Norden 2007: 218–23. My analysis closely follows his. For another vivid example of the use of analogy to elicit autonomous moral knowledge (or moral understanding), see Hills 2020: 6–7.

5. Implications of the Inferential Force Reading

5.1 Auto-Epistemic Proximity

If this reading of Zhu and the Chengs on "getting it oneself" (*zide*) is correct, then it points the way to a rich array of new interpretations and lines of inquiry, not just in the history of East Asian thought but in twenty-first-century global philosophy as well. The first concerns a certain metric or dimension of measurement in Neo-Confucian epistemology. My reading so far has pointed to one factor that can account for failure to appreciate the inferential force of reasons: a person might have self-serving cognitive biases that interfere with her ability to do so. But that is not the only factor that Zhu and the Chengs theorize about. More generally, both Zhu and the Cheng brothers are known for emphasizing a certain dimension or factor that also accounts for successes and failures to know, one that is hinted at in their famous imperative to "reflect on things nearby" (*jinsi* 近思, sometimes translated as "reflect on things at hand"). Preliminarily, we could call this dimension "epistemic proximity." The idea is that for purposes of gaining knowledge, some objects of knowledge are "closer" and others are "further away" to one's pre-existing knowledge, so that if you want to come to have the right epistemic grasp of some difficult (distant) object of knowledge, you would do well to approach it in a stepwise manner from objects that are nearer to things that you already know. Both Cheng Yi and Zhu Xi took epistemic proximity to be a factor in knowing by inference based on similarity in kind (*leitui*). Zhu Xi illustrates the relation between the two in his answer to a student's question:

> [A student] asked: "Cheng [Yi] said that to reflect on things nearby is to take what's similar in kind and draw inferences from that.[32] What is meant by 'inferring from what's similar kind [*leitui*]'"?
> Zhu Xi replied: . . . You shouldn't skip over steps while gazing too far ahead. Nor should you wander off in this or that direction or come to abrupt stops. You should begin nearby at a place you know and then go on from there. If you thoroughly understand *this* one thing and you go on to make inferences about *that* thing on the basis of this one, then your knowledge of the latter will be a certain way. If you see how *this* lamp emits a certain amount of light and make inferences from this lamp, then you will know how *that* candle emits light like that. It's like ascending a flight of stairs. Having climbed onto the first step one can then on the basis of that first step advance to the second step, and also on the basis of the third step advance to the fourth step. Only attend to whatever is adjacent and proceed from there. Only concern yourself with looking to what's

[32] *Henan Chengshi yishu* 22A.30 (in Cheng and Cheng 1981).

> easy and not to what's difficult. When you face a distant objective just concern yourself with grasping what is near. If you want to skip from the first step to the third, then your stride will be too broad and the effort you exert will only be wasted on looking to what's difficult and far away.... For example, when you truly understand love of your family you then can, by inferring from what's similar in kind, go on to understand humane love of people in general, for humane love of people in general is of the same kind as love of family. And when you truly understand humane love of people in general you can, by inferring from what's similar in kind, come to understand care for animals, for care for animals and humane love of people in general are similar in kind.[33]

In short, there is something in virtue of which one cannot know (the value and ethical import of) care for animals unless one first knows (the value and ethical import of) humane love of people in general, and for similar reasons one must know love of family before either of the other two. This is due to the fact that love of family is epistemically closer than the other two to our natural or inborn knowledge, and that humane love of people in general is epistemically closer to love of family than care for animals. This much, I think, is relatively clear and already of some significance for Neo-Confucian epistemology. What is easy to overlook is that the real concern is not knowledge of all kinds, but what we might call autonomous knowledge—knowledge that one "gets oneself"—in particular. Two considerations should make this relatively clear. First, it is hard to see why there should be a fixed, stepwise manner by which to approach knowledge of any kind, and it is hard to see why the relative ease or difficulty of knowing it should correlate with those steps. There are many facts that can be very difficult to know but are nevertheless knowable so long as one has access to reliable sources, such as the numerical value of *pi* or obscure facts about ancient history. So epistemic proximity must be a factor in acquiring a certain subset of knowledge, not knowledge of all types. Second, Zhu Xi is never more adamant about following a stepwise process of knowledge acquisition than when discussing "getting it oneself." We saw in section 5 a passage in which Zhu states that one can't naturally or spontaneously get the conclusion for oneself if one "skips steps" or fails to attend closely to the proper procedure.[34] The language there echoes the language about skipping steps that we see in this passage. It seems a relatively safe assumption that when Zhu Xi speaks about the necessary stepwise manner in which one makes inferences based on similarity in kind, that stepwise manner is necessary in part because of the cognitive requirements for getting it oneself.

[33] Zhu Xi, *Zhuzi yulei* 49.27 (in Zhu 1986); emphasis added. "Love of family," "humane love of people in general," and "care for animals" are presented as three different kinds and degrees of care in *Mencius* 7A45.

[34] See p. 322 of this article and Zhu Xi, *Sishu huowen* 33.10 (in Zhu 2001).

Epistemic agents need to be able to reach their own, unforced conclusions about moral principles or the Way, and that can't happen unless they already grasp other objects of knowledge that resemble them closely enough to appreciate their similar implications. With this in mind, I suggest that it would be better to characterize epistemic proximity as a factor not in knowledge-acquisition more generally but in acquiring autonomous ethical knowledge (the knowledge that properly comes from *getting* the Way or moral principles *oneself*) in particular. Accordingly, it would be more precise to call the relevant factor *auto*-epistemic proximity, and to say that it applies paradigmatically or most clearly to the acquisition of ethical knowledge.

5.2 A Non-Mystical Interpretation of "Unspoken Learning"

Zhu Xi and the Cheng brothers frequently allude to the fact that "getting it oneself" depends on elements of the learning process that cannot be fully articulated in language.[35] As Cheng Hao says in that quotable line from the Neo-Confucian primer, "Only when you get it naturally through unspoken learning does it truly count as 'getting it yourself.'"[36] Many scholars have read this as an indication of mysticism in Neo-Confucian philosophy. De Bary's brief discussion of the issue is representative. He notes that for both the Cheng brothers and for Zhu Xi, the ultimate aim or goal in getting it oneself is to merge or unite one's self with a greater whole, and that describing the process in language effectively trivializes it, reducing it to a normal course of study (de Bary 1991: 46–7).

For my part, I certainly don't want to deny that some post-classical Confucians characterize the ultimate goal in terms of forming a unity with a greater whole, and that there are parts or aspects of this experience that are ineffable. But it is worth noting that some Neo-Confucians actively resisted mystical interpretations of the ultimate goal. Zhu Xi, for example, complained that rival scholars who treated the experience of "forming one body with Heaven, Earth, and the myriad things" as fundamentally mysterious were, for that very reason, unable to articulate what one must do in order to achieve this goal.[37] In any case, we don't need to presuppose mysticism in order to make sense of the "unspoken" (*buyan* 不言) aspect of getting it oneself. Given the context in which it is mentioned, the more plausible explanation is just that there are epistemic conditions required for *zide* that ordinary speakers of a language cannot meet merely by knowing more linguistic propositions.

A good example of such an achievement is what I call appreciation of the inferential force of reasons. On my reading of Zhu and the Cheng brothers on

[35] Zhu Xi, *Mengzi jizhu* 4B14 (in Zhu 1987) and *Sishu huowen* 33.10 (in Zhu 2001).
[36] *Jinsi lu* 2.41 (in Zhu and Lü 2008), translated in section 3.4 of this chapter.
[37] Zhu Xi, *Renshou* 仁說 ("Treatise on Benevolence"), in Zhu 1996: 3542–4 (*juan* 67).

inference based on similarity in kind, there will be cases where some people have the right pre-existing knowledge and frame of mind to see relevant similarities and others lack them. In these cases, there is nothing more that one can say to help the latter group recognize the inferential force of the relevant reasons. Imagine two people—Persuadable Pam and Intransigent Isaac—both of whom fail to fully grasp the shamefulness of accepting a bribe for a special political favor. And further imagine that when their teacher compares accepting bribes to accepting food given with contempt, Pam realizes that accepting a bribe would be very shameful and Isaac does not. What might make the difference between Pam's persuadability and Isaac's intransigence (or ignorance)? Admittedly, there might be some propositions that would tip Isaac over to Pam's side. For example, it might help to point out all the ways in which accepting bribes contributes to a culture of corruption, one that tends to reward people for morally arbitrary advantages like having more wealth or being born into the right family. However, my sense of Zhu and the Cheng brothers is that they still think there will be many cases where moral novices like Isaac will remain unmoved (unreceptive to the inferential force of the relevant reasons) no matter what a skillful teacher might say at the moment. Some will fully appreciate how accepting a bribe for special political favors is self-debasing and others will not. If my reading is correct, one likely explanation for the difference between the Pams and Isaacs in this scenario is that the Pams have more auto-epistemically proximate knowledge—that is, they have already gotten for themselves how situations similar to the bribery scenario are self-debasing and shameful, probably from some combination of ethical reflection and life experience. Many of the Isaacs, by contrast, won't have gotten enough of the relevantly similar scenarios to fully appreciate the reasons not to accept a bribe. In Zhu Xi's terms, they will be like someone who is trying to acquire autonomous knowledge of care for animals without yet having the right grasp of humane love of people in general. For such people, words will not make a meaningful difference, and yet no more words are needed for the Pams to appreciate the various ways in which accepting a bribe is wrong.[38] Getting it for oneself depends on "learning without words" in these respects.

[38] On my reading, in fact, Pam's appreciation of the inferential force of the relevant reasons doesn't even require that she represent the reasons as propositions. For example, it should be enough that she can see the relevant similarities between accepting a bribe and accepting food given with contempt. That will often be enough to get her see why accepting a bribe would be wrong, even if she never represents it as "self-debasing" or "shameful" in her mind. Philip J. Ivanhoe writes about a similar sort of ethical insight in his accounts of "extension" (*tui* or *da*) in the *Mencius*. Just as one can hear a major 7th chord in one key and thereby learn to recognize it in other keys without knowing much of anything about the nature of the major 7th chord, one can recognize the shamefulness in accepting a bribe by seeing the similarity to accepting food given with contempt without knowing much about the nature of that shamefulness (see Ivanhoe 2002). So long as Pam's recognition of the shamefulness is appropriately responsive to the shameful-making features of accepting a bribe, that will provide her with the reasons to consider it shameful (and thus wrong) in the relevant sense.

It might be tempting to understand the role of inference-making in *zide* somewhat differently. The textual evidence seems to suggest that when a person gets some important ethical insight for herself, she is making her own inferences from the relevant reasons to the proper conclusion. Some might think the activity of making one's own inferences is the crucial feature of getting it oneself and that it is otiose to speculate about some further requirement—"appreciation of inferential force." I am sympathetic with the aversion to positing too many extraneous entities, but the achievement of making correct inferences on one's own doesn't suffice to account for the value and function of getting it oneself. Imagine a slightly different version of Intransigent Isaac, someone who doesn't really see how accepting a bribe for a special favor is self-debasing in the same way that accepting food given with contempt is self-debasing. Still, he suspects that others will see some similarity between the two scenarios and recognizes that something important is supposed to follow from this similarity. Accordingly, he makes an informed guess and decides that accepting a bribe must also be wrong. Isaac has made his own inferences, but it seems like something quite important is lacking. I suggest that we can best account for what's missing by talking about his failure to appreciate the inferential force of the relevant reasons, using language ("reasons" and "inference") that closely tracks the language that Zhu Xi uses in talking about ideal ethical knowledge and getting it oneself.

5.3 The Metaphysics of Objective Inferential Force

My reading of Zhu and the Chengs on *zide* likely has significant implications for their metaphysics. For people of a certain anti-metaphysical temperament, it might be tempting to say that what I have been calling "the inferential force of reasons" can be explained away by reference to subjective psychological dispositions. Maybe, when self-serving biases have been cleared away and agents continue to feel the pull of the idea that accepting bribes is wrong, all they are feeling is a contingent, subjective attraction to the view that accepting bribes is wrong, or perhaps they are expressing a contingent, subjective preference that political officials should not accept bribes. Similarly, when Zhu and the Chengs talk about care for animals being more proximate to humane love of people than to love of family, perhaps all they mean is that human beings, given the psychology that we happen to have, are more inclined to "get" care for animals for themselves if they already "get" humane love of people in general for themselves. But this is just an accident of human cognition and emotion, not accountable to any objective fact of the matter.

To be sure, there are some Neo-Confucians that arguably come close to flirting with subjective metaethical positions that could be consistent with these views. However, Zhu Xi and the Cheng brothers are emphatically not Neo-Confucians of that strong, subjectivist kind. As I and other have tried to show in our work on the debates between them and their Buddhist counterparts, one of their great preoccupations was specifying theories and methods of moral knowledge acquisition such that our moral convictions and behavior aren't just expressing subjective whims or contingent features of human psychology. If someone did propose that inferential force could be fully explained by contingent inclinations or predispositions to accept that a certain ethical conclusion follows from a certain ethical reason, they would have been quick to call attention to this as a dangerous theoretical seed of Buddhist subjectivism, just as they did other worrisome concessions to subjectivism in less orthodox Neo-Confucian rivals (Angle and Tiwald 2017: 71-88; Zhu 2019: 148–60). Inferential force thus requires that we posit some entity to account for the existence and objectivity of inferential force. Zhu Xi illustrates auto-epistemic proximity by comparing objects of knowledge to steps in a staircase. Just as objective facts about the physical arrangement of a staircase help account for the fact that we must get from step one to step three by way of step two, so too do objective facts about reasons and their inferential force help explain why we must get from love of family to care for animals by way of humane love for people in general.

Moreover, it seems reasonable to assume that part of what so concerned them about selfish inclinations in reasoning—part of what motivated them to insist that the appreciation of inferential force should be without self-serving bias—is that they feared motivated reasoning would interfere with our ability to track the objective force of the reasons. In fact, my reading of *zide* raises an interesting question which I take to be in the background of some of Zhu's and the Cheng's metaphysics—namely, what guarantees that we even have the capacity to appreciate objective inferential force in the first place?

The short answer, I think, is their famous metaphysical view that ethical norms are grounded in Heavenly (and thus objective) patterns or principles of good order (*Tianli* 天理) and, at the same time, that these Heavenly patterns are manifest in our own nature, so that we will feel some natural inclination to endorse and follow them once selfish thoughts and desires are cleared away. Heavenly patterns are thus both objective and an essential constituent of our natural psychology (Angle and Tiwald 2017: 50–69). One way to explain why they arrived at this provocative and challenging metaphysical thesis is to suggest that they needed Heavenly patterns to account both for the objectivity and for the natural psychological pull of the inferential force of reasons. But this is an ambitious and somewhat speculative line of argument that I don't have the space to pursue here.

5.4 Moral Deference and Moral Understanding

In twenty-first-century anglophone philosophy, there is a burgeoning literature on the use of testimonial moral knowledge, moral deference, and moral expertise.

Very roughly, philosophers that are sometimes called "testimony pessimists" argue that there is something objectionable about claims to have moral knowledge on the authority of others, as when a novice claims to know that she should adopt a vegetarian diet simply because she trusts (even if for good reasons) a reliable expert on animal and environmental ethics. Moreover, what's objectionable about this sort of deference is peculiar to moral knowledge and not so problematic for non-moral knowledge.[39] On most accounts, "testimony optimists" deny that this sort of deference is problematic or, more often, that the problem is peculiar to moral knowledge (what's objectionable about this sort of deference in the context of moral knowledge is objectionable about deference in the context of non-moral knowledge as well).[40] In certain respects, the contemporary debate between testimony pessimists and testimony optimists overlaps with the historical debate between proponents of pervasive moral deference like Xunzi and defenders of getting it oneself like Zhu Xi and the Cheng brothers.[41] Most notably, Alison Hills has argued against moral deference by proposing that testimony-based knowledge cannot by itself give a moral agent enough insight for her to have good character and moral worth. Good character and moral worth require something more robust than moral knowledge, something Hills calls moral *understanding* (Hills 2009). In several respects, her account of moral understanding resembles what I have been calling autonomous knowledge, the sort of knowledge that we acquire through getting it oneself. For example, there are a variety of abilities that someone with understanding of a moral proposition will necessarily have but which someone with mere knowledge of a moral proposition is not guaranteed to have. Agents with understanding of a moral proposition can follow explanations of it and draw their own conclusions about the proposition in various ways (Hills 2009: 98–104). Furthermore, Hills says that understanding a moral proposition requires what she calls a "grasp" of the reasons for that proposition, and her account of grasping reasons seems compatible with my account of appreciating the inferential force of reasons (Hills 2009: 100–1).

This points to a wealth of interesting areas of cross-cultural inquiry. To start, one notable difference between Neo-Confucian *zide* and Hills' "moral understanding" is that the former phrase was used specifically to distinguish autonomous from deference-based forms of knowledge acquisition, and then discussed and refined over several centuries of Neo-Confucian discourse. By contrast,

[39] Hills 2009, 2010; McGrath 2011. [40] Enoch 2014, Sliwa 2012.

[41] One major difference is that in the Confucian debate, even the staunchest defenders of moral deference will admit that deference is problematic—it's just that its problems are outweighed or canceled by the greater hazards of letting moral novices decide for themselves (as explained in section 2 of this chapter). Another major difference is that there aren't testimony pessimists who argue, as Sarah McGrath does, that our discomfort with moral deference reveals our deep commitment to antirealist or non-realist metaethics (McGrath 2011). In fact, some of the Confucian tradition's strongest would-be proponents of testimony pessimism qualify as the tradition's most adamant metaethical realists.

"moral understanding," at least as the phrase is used in natural language, does not track this distinction so neatly. Ordinary speakers of English are comfortable saying that they "understand" veganism or vegetarianism even if they don't actually know veganism or vegetarianism to be true or correct. So long as they have some grasp of the reasons for these dietary practices and, perhaps, can appreciate the normative appeal of them in some counterfactual sense, most will count themselves as having the right sort of understanding. This does not prevent philosophers from stipulating that "moral understanding" in the relevant sense should describe a narrower range of epistemic states or abilities, as Hills does (2009: 99). But it does suggest that the Neo-Confucians had a much longer time to think about and refine their use of the relevant term of art, a term that they sometimes used in ordinary discourse and not just in philosophical letters, commentaries, and treatises. Accordingly, it is reasonable to expect that *zide* will take account of a wider range of human experience and will be used more adroitly (and perhaps more organically—that is, without always adhering to one account or definition) in their writings.

I take "getting it oneself" to describe a type of knowledge acquisition, not, strictly speaking, a form of knowledge or understanding itself. However, it is worth asking what the Neo-Confucian philosophers would make of the distinction between moral knowledge and moral understanding in Hills' sense. In one intriguing passage, Zhu Xi proposes that there is a difference between "getting" (*de* 得) some normative pattern or principle (*li*) and "getting it oneself" (*zide* 自得). He spells out that difference in terms of an analogy to making some room or building one's home. When one merely "gets" the normative pattern, that is like having a place to dwell. But when one gets it oneself, he says, that is like being comfortable and feeling secure (*an* 安) in one's dwelling, as when living in a home that is well suited to one's domestic habits and daily life.[42] On one reading of this suggestive metaphor, this implies that grasping reasons for a moral view helps to ensure that one stably affirms or endorses the view, but that something further is needed—something available only to autonomous epistemic agents—in order to make one truly comfortable with it.

Finally, I find no twenty-first-century philosopher who takes as much interest in some of the features of *zide* that I have explicated in this study. There is little discussion of what I have called the self-discovery aspects of autonomous knowledge acquisition, or of a possible requirement that certain sorts of moral conclusions should come from the relevant reasons spontaneously or naturally. There is no discussion at all of what I am calling auto-epistemic proximity as a factor in the acquisition of moral understanding. And there are, I am sure, many more questions raised by the Neo-Confucians that present-day testimony pessimists and optimists would do well to entertain. In these respects among many others,

[42] Zhu Xi, *Sishu huowen* 33.10 (in Zhu 2001).

there is still much that is rich in epistemic, ethical, and psychological significance and texture that could be revealed through cross-cultural work. An important step in this direction will be to translate more of the relevant Chinese materials and conduct historically and philosophically sensitive studies of both moral deference and getting it oneself in Confucian thought.

6. Conclusion

In this chapter, I have introduced an important term from the moral epistemology of Zhu Xi and the Cheng brothers, "getting it oneself" or *zide.* At first pass, the most notable feature of getting it oneself appears to be that it is Zhu's and the Chengs' alternative to problematic moral deference. This suggests that what matters most about it is that what we know by getting it ourselves is something that we know on our own authority. But as I have shown, there is a great deal more to getting it oneself than that. There is also a general predisposition to elicit greater joy in knowledge acquisition and greater confidence in one's knowledge. There is a distinctive phenomenology: when we get it ourselves, it seems to us as though we've discovered something about ourselves. More controversially, I have argued that an indispensable feature of getting it oneself is what I call the unbiased appreciation of the inferential force of reasons. Although they don't talk about this feature in precisely those terms, I have argued that my interpretation makes better sense of the evidence than other candidates. I have also noted some of the wider implications of this interpretation for contemporary work on moral deference and moral testimony, and for reading Zhu Xi, the Cheng brothers, and Neo-Confucianism more generally. It suggests that there is some interesting notion of proximity at work in explaining why some people can and others cannot appreciate the particular inferential force of particular reasons, and it suggests that there is a distinctive sort of philosophical problem—the problem of ensuring or guaranteeing the objectivity of our "appreciation"—that helps to justify some of their more ambitious metaphysical claims. Most importantly, we have in these later Confucian philosophers a rich, philosophical account of a phenomenon which plays a critical role in the acquisition of good ethical insight, a phenomenon that we all know by acquaintance but which few other philosophical traditions have explored in as much depth.[43]

[43] I thank Princeton's University Center for Human Values for supporting this research through a Laurance S. Rockefeller Fellowship. I have benefitted from comments by thoughtful audiences at the University of Toronto, Johns Hopkins University, Yale NUS College, Princeton University, San Francisco State University, and the University of Hong Kong, all in response to presentations given in 2020 and 2021. I am particularly indebted to Ari Borrell, Randolph Clarke, Eric L. Hutton, Philip J. Ivanhoe, Harvey Lederman, Dorota Mokrosinska, and Hwa Yeong Wang for generous and perceptive feedback on earlier drafts.

References

Andow, James. 2020. "Why Don't We Trust Moral Testimony?" *Mind and Language*, 35(4): 465–74.

Angle, Stephen C., and Justin Tiwald. 2017. *Neo-Confucianism: A Philosophical Introduction*. Cambridge Polity Press.

Chan, Wing-tsit. 1989. *Chu Hsi: New Studies*. Honolulu: University of Hawaii Press.

Cheng, Hao 程顥 and Cheng Yi 程頤. 1981. "*Henan Chengshi yishu* 河南程氏遺書" ("*The Surviving Works of the Chengs of Henan*"). In Wang Xiaoyu 王孝魚 (Ed.), *Ercheng ji* 二程集 (*The Collected Works of the Two Chengs*), vol. 1 (pp. 1–349). Beijing: Zhonghua shuju.

Chu, Hsi (Zhu, Xi). 1990. *Learning to Be a Sage: Selections from the* Conversations of Master Chu, Arranged Topically, Daniel K. Gardner, trans. and comm. Berkeley, CA: University of California Press.

Dai, Zhen 戴震. 2009. 孟子字義疏證 ("Evidential Analysis of the Meanings of Terms in the *Mengzi*"). In 戴震集 (*The Collected Works of Dai Zhen*) (pp. 263–329). Shanghai: Shanghai guji chuban she.

de Bary, Wm. Theodore. 1983. *The Liberal Tradition in China*. New York: Columbia University Press.

de Bary, Wm. Theodore. 1991. *Learning for One's Self: Essays on the Individual in Neo-Confucian Thought*. New York: Columbia University Press.

Enoch, David. 2014. "A Defense of Moral Deference." *Journal of Philosophy*, 111(5): 229–58.

Hills, Alison. 2009. "Moral Testimony and Moral Epistemology." *Ethics*, 120(1): 94–127.

Hills, Alison. 2020. "Moral Testimony: Transmission Versus Propagation." *Philosophy and Phenomenological Research*, 101(2): 399–414.

Ivanhoe, Philip J. 2000. *Confucian Moral Self Cultivation*. Cambridge, MA: Hackett.

Ivanhoe, Philip J. 2002. "Confucian Self Cultivation and Mengzi's Notion of Extension." In Xiusheng Liu and Philip J. Ivanhoe (Eds.), *Essays on the Moral Philosophy of Mengzi* (pp. 221–41). Indianapolis, IN: Hackett.

Lee, Pauline C. 2013. *Li Zhi, Confucianism, and the Virtue of Desire*. Albany, NY: SUNY Press.

Legge, James, tr. and comm. 1892. "Mencius." In *The Chinese Classics*, vol. 2, 2nd edition, revised. Oxford: Clarendon Press.

Li, Zhi 李贄. 1961. *Fenshu* 焚書 (*A Book to Burn*). Beijing: Zhonghua shuju.

Li, Zhi. 2016. *A Book to Burn and a Book to Keep (Hidden): Selected Writings*. Rivi Handler-Spitz, Pauline C. Lee, and Haun Saussy, trans. New York: Columbia University Press.

McGrath, Sarah. 2011. "Skepticism about Moral Expertise as a Puzzle for Moral Realism." *Journal of Philosophy*, 108(3): 111–37.

Munro, Donald J. 1988. *Images of Human Nature: A Sung Portrait*. Princeton, NJ: Princeton University Press.

Plato. 1961. "Meno." *The Collected Dialogues of Plato, Including the Letters*, Edith Hamilton and Huntington Cairns, eds. Princeton: Princeton University Press. Pp. 353–84.

Mengzi 孟子 (Mencius). 1987. *Mengzi zhengyi* 孟子正義 (*The Correct Meaning of the Mengzi [Mencius]*), Jiao Xun 焦循, comm. and ed. Beijing: Zhonghua shuju.

Mengzi (Mencius). 2008. *Mengzi: With Selections from Traditional Commentaries*. Bryan W. Van Norden, trans. Cambridge: Hackett.

Slingerland, Edward, trans. 2003. *Analects: With Selections from Traditional Commentaries*. Indianapolis, IN: Hackett.

Sliwa, Paulina. 2012. "In Defense of Moral Testimony." *Philosophical Studies*, 158: 175–95.

Tiwald, Justin. MS. "Confucian Arguments for and against Pervasive Moral Deference."

Tiwald, Justin. 2012. "Xunzi on Moral Expertise." *Dao*, 11(3): 275–93.

Tiwald, Justin, and Bryan W. Van Norden. 2014. *Readings in Later Chinese Philosophy: Han Dynasty to the 20th Century*. Cambridge, MA: Hackett.

Van Norden, Bryan W. 2007. *Virtue Ethics and Consequentialism in Early Chinese Philosophy*. Cambridge: Cambridge University Press.

Xunzi 荀子. 1996. *Xunzi zhuzi suoyin* 荀子逐字索引 (*A Concordance to the* Xunzi). D.C. Lau 劉殿爵 and F.C. Chen 陳方正, eds. Hong Kong: Shangwu yinshu guan.

Xunzi. 2014. *Xunzi: The Complete Text*. Eric L. Hutton, trans. Princeton, NJ: Princeton University Press.

Zhu Xi 朱熹. 1986. *Zhuzi yulei* 朱子語類 (*The Classified Sayings of Master Zhu*). Beijing: Zhonghua shuju.

Zhu, Xi 朱熹. 1987. *Sishu zhangju jizhu* 四书章句集注 (*The Collected Commentaries on the Four Books*). Shanghai: Shanghai shudian.

Zhu, Xi 朱熹. 1996. *Zhu Xi ji* 朱熹集 (*The Collected Works of Zhu Xi*), Guo Qi 郭齊 and Yin Bo 尹波, eds. Chengdu: Sichuan jiaoyu chubanshe.

Zhu, Xi 朱熹. 2001. *Sishu huowen* 四書或問 (*Some Questions on the Four Books*). Shanghai and Hefei: Shanghai guji chubanshe and Anhui jiaoyu chubanshe.

Zhu, Xi. 2019. *Zhu Xi: Selected Writings*. Philip J. Ivanhoe, ed. New York: Oxford University Press.

Zhu, Xi 朱熹 and Lü Zuqian 呂祖謙, eds. 2008. *Jinsi lu* 近思錄 (*Reflections on Things at Hand*). Zhengzhou: Zhongzhou guji chuban she.

12

Elements of Knowledge-First Epistemology in Gaṅgeśa and Nyāya

Anand Vaidya

1. Preface

Gaṅgeśa Upādhyāya was a fourteenth-century philosopher in the Nyāya tradition of Hindu Philosophy. *Nyāya* is both a proper name for a tradition, and a term that means *rule or method.* It is commonly associated with logical and epistemological analysis. The tradition begins with the work of its founder, the second-century philosopher, Gautama Akṣapāda, who wrote the *Nyāya-Sūtras*. The long commentarial tradition on the *Nyāya-Sūtra*s begins with the key exponent of the *Sūtra*s, Vātsyāyana (5th), who is followed by Uddyotakara (6th), Vācaspati (10th), and Udayana (11th–12th). Arguably, Gaṅgeśa is the founder of the New School of Nyāya (*Navya-Nyāya*). His key work, *Jewel of Reflection on the Truth about Epistemology* (*Tattva-Cintā-Maṇi*), focuses on the nature and sources of knowledge: *perception, inference, analogy, and testimony.*[1] Gaṅgeśa made Nyāya more precise, systematic, and consistent, as he defended it against opponents.

In the latter half of the twentieth century several important works on Nyāya epistemology were written.[2] It was common to find Nyāya epistemology presented and interpreted through the lens of belief-first epistemology, which takes belief to be central, or process reliabilism, which takes reliable processes to be central. In the twenty-first century, this trend continued.[3,4] For example, both Stephen Phillips (2012) and Jay Shaw (2016a, b, c) explored how Nyāya epistemology could provide solutions to the problems of epistemic luck articulated by Gettier

[1] Some argue that Udayana is the actual founder of the New School of Nyāya.

[2] See Mukhopadhyay (1984, 1991) and Chakrabarti (2020).

[3] Part of the reason for this is that the Gettier problem has cast a long shadow over twentieth-century epistemology after the 1960s, see Shope (1983) for contributions to the post-Gettier analysis of knowledge research program.

[4] See Sukharanjan (2003) for discussion of Nyāya and Gaṅgeśa. Because I have not studied his work, I am not attributing to him the lens of approaching Nyāya through the belief-first paradigm or reliabilist paradigm.

Anand Vaidya, *Elements of Knowledge-First Epistemology in Gaṅgeśa and Nyāya* In: *Oxford Studies in Epistemology, Volume 7.* Edited by: Tamar Szabó Gendler, John Hawthorne, and Julianne Chung, Oxford University Press.
 DOI: 10.1093/oso/9780192868978.003.0012

(1966) and Goldman (1986).[5] More recently, Turri (2017)[6] has argued that Nyāya epistemology fits abilism, which holds that knowledge is an accurate representation produced by cognitive ability. A view that is close to the one I will defend here.

I will use "Nyāya" to stand for *extracted-Nyāya epistemology* according to a specific interpretation. For example, "Phillips' Nyāya" refers to Phillips' translation and interpretation of Nyāya thinkers found in his (2012, 2020), and "Shaw's Nyāya" refers to Shaw's translation and interpretation found in his (2016a, b, c). "Nyāya" without qualification refers to my own claims. Although there are many translations of portions of Gaṅgeśa's *Jewel*[7], it is Stephen Phillips' (and N.S. Ramanuja Tatacharya) (2020) three-volume, 1850-page translation of *Jewel* that I turn to.

In what follows, I will explore the extent to which Gaṅgeśa can be situated within Timothy Williamson's (2000) knowledge-first program. While Gaṅgeśa is not reacting to a tradition in the manner that Williamson is, there are aspects of knowledge-first epistemology that fit Gaṅgeśa better than belief-first, agent-first, or reliabilist epistemology. Two questions drive my exploration. The *composition* question: *is knowledge composed of parts*, such as justification, truth, belief, and some condition *x*, which is strong enough to block internal and external luck? And: The *entailment* question: *does seeing that A entail knowing that A*? I proceed as follows:

I. I begin with a presentation of Williamson's knowledge-first program, which provides a framework for exploring Gaṅgeśa's epistemology. Williamson holds that knowledge is non-compositional and that entailment holds. The question going forward is where does Gaṅgeśa stand with respect to non-composition and entailment.

II. I argue that there is a reading of *Gaṅgeśa's definition of knowledge* on which he holds a non-compositional account of it. On this account, neither belief nor justification are components of knowledge. While Gaṅgeśa does hold that the self, awareness, and truth are components of knowledge, I will argue that he can still be credited with holding a non-compositional account of knowledge on a *narrow*, as opposed to a *wide*, reading of what composition is.

III. I move on to show that there is a reading of *Gaṅgeśa's definition of perception* on which he holds a version of the *entailment* thesis: *seeing that A is a way of knowing that A*. That is, Gaṅgeśa doesn't hold that we base knowledge of the world on perception. Rather, we come to know the

[5] See Phillips (2012), especially Ch. 7. The generality problem within Nyāya is also discussed by Phillips.

[6] Amita Chatterjee has informed me that my reading of Gaṅgeśa is consistent with Turri (2017).

[7] See Mohanty (1966) for *jñapti-vāda* and Matilal (1968, 1992) for *abhāva-vāda* and of Gaṅgeśa's *Jewel*.

world directly through perception. To clarify one version of the view, I present *Multi-Factor Causal-Disjunctivism*, (MFCD), an account of Nyāya perceptual theory articulated in Vaidya (2021), and apply it to three cases.

IV. I then present Phillip's account of Gaṅgeśa's theory of knowledge, where Gaṅgeśa draws a distinction between perceptual knowledge and certified knowledge. I show that on this theory, perceptual knowledge, which is direct, is a basis for certified knowledge, where each is a distinct kind of epistemic success. I close with a discussion of the question: did Gaṅgeśa hold the KK-principle, *that when one knows, they know that they know*, with respect to a specific kind of case? I argue that Gaṅgeśa need not be read as having held the KK-principle.

Phillips provides alternative translations of some key Sanskrit epistemological terms from what one finds in prior translations.[8] Unless stated otherwise, I will use Phillips' (2020) translation of Gaṅgeśa for the following terms: (i) *pratyakṣa* means *perception*, (ii) *pramāṇa* means *knowledge source* or *knowledge generator*, (iii) *pramā* means *knowledge episode*;[9,10] (iv) *pramātva* means *being knowledge*; (v) *jñāna* means *cognition*; (vi) *anubhava* means *prima facie awareness of fresh news* (or: *appearance of new information*).[11]

2. Williamson on Non-Composition and Directness

In his (2000), *Knowledge and its Limits*, Timothy Williamson argues for (1) and (2).

(1) Knowing is a state of mind.
(2) Seeing that A is a way of knowing that A.

Williamson is arguing against theories of knowledge that hold (3), if not at least some of (4)–(6).

(3) Knowledge is a composite state made out of parts.
(4) Belief is a mental component of knowledge.

[8] See Phillips (2020: 11) for discussion of the mistakes made by other translators of Gaṅgeśa, for example G. Bhattacharya (1976). Shaw disagrees with some of Phillips' translations, such as *pramā* as *knowledge episode*. See Ganeri (2007) for a critical discussion of Phillips and Tatacharya's (2004) translation of the *perception* chapter of *Jewel*. And Dasti and Phillips (2010) for a response to Ganeri.

[9] Bhattacharya (1996) disagrees that *pramā* means *knowledge episode* within the Nyāya tradition.

[10] Ganeri (2018) agrees that *jñāna* is not a good translation of *knowledge*, he argues that *pramā* more closely captures English uses of *knowledge*, but is not an exact match.

[11] Shaw holds that another translation of *anubhava* is *apprehension excluding memory*. Phillips' main point about the term is that it applies properly to *new information*.

(5) Justification is a mental component of knowledge.
(6) Truth is a non-mental component of knowledge.

Within Anglo-analytic epistemology, Gettier is taken to have shown that (4)–(6) are not jointly sufficient for knowledge because they allow for epistemic luck.[12] However, in the wake of Gettier's examples, Anglo-analytic epistemologists did not immediately abandon (3).[13] Rather, Armstrong (1973) held (3) and added a condition to (4)–(6), the no-false lemmas condition, to try and rule out certain kinds of epistemic luck.[14] Sartwell (1992) also held (3), and sought an analysis of knowledge that holds (4) and (6), but drops (5). Forty years after Gettier, Williamson's knowledge-first program challenges (3), and thus the whole program of trying to analyze knowledge into parts.

Williamson argues against (3), and for (1), via *the primeness argument.*

> [W]e can show that C is prime simply by exhibiting three cases α, β, and γ, where γ is internally like α and externally like β, and C obtains in α and β but not in γ. So, consider a subject S and input into their left eye and right eye in α and β, which are then swapped to create γ with respect to both an internal and external condition. (Williamson 2000: 68–9)

Williamson argues that from two cases, α and β, where water is seen, we arrive at a case γ through recombination where water is not seen. In other words, since we cannot recombine elements in an act of seeing and preserve the seeing, seeing is *prime* and not composite.

To understand (2), we ought to draw a distinction between two uses of 'seeing that.' One use of 'seeing that' is for vision-related knowledge. Another use is for vison in a metaphorical sense, such as when one says, "I see your point." For the purposes of the discussion to follow, the focus is only on the vision-related use of 'seeing that.'[15] In the

[12] See Stoltz (2007) for a presentation of *Dharmottara*, the Buddhist philosopher, and Gettier. See Parikh and Renero (2017) for a presentation of *Praśatapāda*, the Vaiśeṣika philosopher, and Gettier. Gaṅgeśa also offers an example, see Phillips (2020). A rough version of the example is the following. Suppose Maya appears to see smoke on the hill (but does not see smoke, since it is actually dust, and she cannot distinguish between the two). Now suppose she reasons that because there is fire where there is smoke, like in a kitchen, there must be fire on the hill as well. Now suppose that there is actually fire on the hill below the smoke. Does Maya know there is fire on the hill? Gaṅgeśa would argue that she does not, at least in part because the awareness was not of smoke, but instead of dust, which is not the appropriate mark for fire. Gaṅgeśa doesn't take knowledge to be consistent with epistemic luck. Whether or not his example counts as a "Gettier" examples depends in part on whether Gettier examples require that epistemic luck be produced by a fallible conception of justification.

[13] See Shope (1983) for presentation of the analysis of knowledge program after Gettier. See Ichikawa and Steup (2018) for discussion of the analysis of knowledge beyond Shope.

[14] See (Armstrong 1973: 152).

[15] I would like to thank both Williamson and Littlejohn for pointing out this distinction. Littlejohn also points out that there is an important distinction drawn by Dretske between *simple seeing* and *epistemic seeing* where the former is extensional and the latter is non-extensional, which is relevant to

primeness argument above object-seeing, as opposed to seeing-that, is explicitly in play. This is important because of two cases. First, it is possible to see water without seeing that it is water, such as when one believes that they are looking at Gin, and there is cognitive penetration from belief into perception. Second, it is possible to see that there is water without seeing the water, such as when one sees an opaque waterbed that is inflated. Although the argument is offered in the frame of object-seeing, it works for seeing-that as well, when one takes the appropriate trio of cases.[16] Williamson's (1) and (2) make available the following argument: *if seeing is a way of knowing, and seeing is prime, then knowing is also prime.*

Williamson's (1) is connected to the composition question. He is arguing that knowledge is not composite. Williamson's (2) is connected to the directness question. He is arguing that perception, in the case of vision-related seeing, is a direct way of knowing the world.

3. The Question of Compositionality in Nyāya and Gaṅgeśa

With respect to (1), Williamson holds (a), while, Naiyāyikas hold (b).[17]

(a) Knowing is a state of mind.
(b) Knowing, in the occurrent sense, is a mental event.[18]

Given the technical difference between (a) and (b), could Naiyāyikas hold (a)? Phillips says, "[o]ntologically, a cognition is a short lived, episodic quality of an individual self. Strictly speaking, it is a mental event and *a short-lived state* rather than an act (Phillips 2020: 6, *emphasis added*)." Thus, on Phillips' account of mental ontology in Nyāya, (a) and (b) are *not that* far apart. What about (3)–(6)? There are two readings.

On the *compositional* reading, one accepts (3), and argues that Gaṅgeśa either accepts (4)–(6), denies some of (4)–(6), or articulates completely different

how (2) can be understood. See Littlejohn (2017) and (2019) for discussion of Williamson's account of perceptual knowledge, and the difference between McDowell (1996) and Williamson (2000) on perceptual knowledge.

[16] I would like to thank Williamson for pointing out the importance of these distinctions to the proper understanding of his argument and position, as well as how the argument can be restructured for seeing that.

[17] In conversation, Prabal Kumar Sen has told me that it is not precise to say that Nyāya holds that knowledge is a mental event, since it holds that knowledge is a property of the self as a knower, and the notion of 'mental event' in English does not properly locate what exactly knowledge is a property of. However, Phillips uses this locution.

[18] Many scholars of Indian epistemology have pointed out that one major difference between Western approaches to knowledge and Indian approaches centers around whether or not the discussion is focused on occurrent knowledge or standing knowledge. Bilimoria (1985) discusses the fact that classical Indian epistemology is concerned with episodes of knowing as mental events. Stoltz (2007) also makes this claim in his investigation of Dharmottara in relation to Gettier. Here I discuss Phillips because of his translation of Gaṅgeśa.

components for knowledge. For example, one could hold (6), that truth is a component of knowledge, but that neither (4), belief, nor (5), justification, are components. Rather, some mental event, such as awareness or apprehension, serves as a component of an episode of knowledge, while the self and facts out in the world are the other components.

On the *non-compositional* reading, one denies (3), and argues that Gaṅgeśa holds that there are *no* components to knowledge. For example, neither justification nor belief are components of knowledge. And any other factors, such as the self, awareness, and facts out in the world are not metaphysical components. Rather, they are simply the relata of an episode of knowledge as a relational mental event. The non-compositional reading makes contact with Williamson's (1).[19]

I will defend the non-compositional reading of Gaṅgeśa based on three theses. First, (KVA): Knowledge is veridical awareness.[20]

> Knowledge is (D^{25}) "awareness of something there where it is." Or, D^{26} awareness with *F* as predication content about an object that it is *F*." Non-knowledge (conversely) is (D^{25e}) "cognition with *F* as predication content about an object that is not *F*." (Phillips 2020: 227)

Second, (GTB): True beliefs come from occurrent knowledge.[21]

> [T]rue beliefs are formed by episodes of occurrent knowledge defined as veridical awareness—embedding a true proposition, *savikalpaka-jñāna*—that is produced by a veritable knowledge source, *pramāṇa*. (Phillips 2020: 12–13)

Third, (NSB): Knowledge is not a species of belief.[22]

> [K]knowledge... is a species of mental event, *not of belief*, although a certain range of mental states—thoughts, testimonial comprehensions, inferences, perceptions—have belief—i.e., propositional—content.[23,24] (Phillips 2012: 6, *emphasis added*) (KVA) and (GTB), support (NSB).[25]

[19] Neither Phillips nor Shaw explore the relation between Williamson's knowledge-first program and either Nyāya or Gaṅgeśa.

[20] Based on Phillips' (2020) translation.

[21] Based on Phillips' (2020) interpretation of Gaṅgeśa.

[22] Based on Phillip's Nyāya (2012).

[23] It is important to note that although Phillips uses the term 'propositional' here, there is a debate about whether the Nyāya tradition accepts propositions. For an excellent investigation into the question of whether Nyāya accepts propositions see Krishna et al. (1991). By 'propositional' Phillips only claims that cognition minimally has a qualifier/qualificand structure that purports to capture reality, not that there are Fregean propositions in Nyāya.

[24] Shaw notes that Phillips' use of 'propositional content' is problematic, since there are only relations to objects and qualities, which is related to the issue of whether we *see facts* or *objects* and *qualities*.

[25] Phillips (2020: 6) appears to hedge on (NSB). He says, "Although cognitions are moments of consciousness, not species of belief, we may say that cognitions form beliefs in forming dispositions and that properly produced cognitions –instances of occurrent knowledge—form true beliefs, *ipso facto*

Neither of these theses, alone, or in combination, are sufficient for a non-compositional account of knowledge. First, with respect to (GTB), even if true beliefs are generated from knowledge episodes, it doesn't follow that belief isn't a component of a knowledge episode. For example, one might hold that true beliefs are generated from knowledge episodes only because knowledge episodes contain them in some implicit form. Second, with respect to (NSB), even if knowledge is *not* a species of belief, it doesn't follow that belief is not a component of knowledge. For example, one might hold that belief is a component of knowledge, even if knowledge is not a species of it, because *belief* isn't the main category that is used to classify knowledge. Knowledge can be a species of mental event, and still have belief as a component. Third, (KVA) uses awareness and truth. So, it appears to have parts. It is instructive to try and use (NSB) to create an argument for the view that knowledge is not composite by adding in additional premises. The result is a two-stage argument.[26]

To move from (NSB) to the position that belief is not a component of knowledge, one also needs the *non-species-non-component* thesis, (NSC): *if x is not a species of W, W is not a component of x.* One can defend (NSC) through examples. Given that humans are a species of mammal, they have mammality as a component, and are differentiated from other mammals in virtue of a difference maker (for Aristotle that difference maker was rationality). Given that spiders are not a species of mammal, they don't have mammality as a component. Thus, by analogy, if knowledge is *not* a species of belief, but of *cognition*, knowledge does not have belief as a component.

Stage 1: absence of belief

1. If *x* is not a species of *W*, then *W* is not a component of *x*. (NSC)
2. Knowledge is not a species of belief. (NSB)
3. So, belief is not a component of knowledge.

Given (3), one can also argue that justification is not a component of knowledge, as long as one accepts the additional *non-component non-property* thesis, (NPT): If *E* is only a property of *G*, and *G* is not a component of *H*, then *E* is not a component of *H*.

Stage 2: absence of justification

4. Justification is only a property of belief.
5. If *E* is only a property of *G*, and *G* is not a component of *H*, then *E* is not a component of *H*. (NPT)
6. So, justification is not a component of knowledge.

warranted true beliefs. Unlike Western epistemology from Aristotle through Russell, Gettier, and even Goldman, Nyāya focuses not on beliefs but on cognitions that are identified by their objects or 'objecthood' (*viṣayatā*), their 'intentionality,'...."

[26] The argument I offer here is inspired by an argument given by Pranab Kumar Sen (2000).

The argument is problematic.

First, is (NSB) true of Nyāya? On Shaw's Nyāya it is false. The textual historical argument over whether (NSB) is in Nyāya depends on how we understand *belief* in English. Suppose one takes *belief* in a colloquial sense, where one can believe something while still having some doubt about its truth, such as when Karina says, "I believe the café is around the corner," and Karina is slightly doubtful about it. On such an understanding of *belief*, Shaw holds we could not take Naiyāyikas, as Phillips points out, to hold that occurrent knowledge is a species of occurrent episodic belief. However, if we were to take the special class of *beliefs*, where to believe *p* is to simultaneously have a *doubt free cognition* of *p*, Shaw argues, it would be fair to say that Naiyāyikas hold that occurrent knowledge is a species of occurrent episodic belief. That is, episodic knowledge (*pramā*) is only a species of episodic true belief when the belief arises *free* of *doubt*. In Shaw's (2016a) Nyāya, knowledge is compositional. And belief is a component of it when it is understood in the sense of being an apprehension that is doubt free and a quality of the self who is the knower. Justification is also a component of knowledge when it is understood as a qualifier of a true-belief that guarantees the truth of the belief. On Shaw's Nyāya, to know is to have a true-belief which is infallibly justified.

Second, one can argue that justification is not *only* a property of belief. For example, one could argue that justification is also a property of propositions, independently of occurrent belief.[27,28] If Naiyāyikas accepted propositions, it could be argued that justification is a component of knowledge, but not in virtue of attaching to belief primarily.[29,30]

Third, even if the argument is successful in showing that a certain kind of belief and justification are not components of knowledge, it won't follow that Gaṅgeśa's account is not compositional. For he explicitly uses *awareness* and *truth* in his definition of knowledge. As a consequence, one could think he endorses the view that awareness and truth are components of knowledge. And if he does hold that truth is a component of knowledge, that would stand against Williamson's view that truth is not a non-mental component of knowledge. So, where does Gaṅgeśa stand with respect to the claim that truth is a non-mental component of knowledge?

[27] Notice in (NSB) Phillips' claim acknowledges the possibility of propositional content independently of the presence of belief.

[28] See Turri (2010) for discussion of the distinction between propositional and doxastic justification.

[29] Shaw (2016a, b, c) holds that justification in Nyāya is a property of true-belief. But not belief alone.

[30] See fn. 13. Krishna et al. (1991) has an investigation into whether or not propositions, as understood by Frege and Russell, is part of the Indian philosophical tradition. My understanding is that they are not, and so, the distinction between doxastic and propositional justification might not be sufficient to allow for justification to be a component of knowledge. Nevertheless, there might be another way to argue for how justification can be a component of knowledge, which doesn't depend on it being a property of belief, such as in Shaw (2016a, b, c).

To answer this, I will distinguish between a *wide* and *narrow* reading of composition. On the *narrow* reading of composition, a mental state is composite when it is a relation between a subject and something else, such as a fact, and the structure is: *aRb*, where *R* has no parts itself, and is a mental state. On the *wide* reading of composition, a mental state is composite when it is a relational state that is non-basic. And its parts are other basic mental states and non-mental states. Williamson is arguing against the *wide* reading of composition, not the *narrow* reading, since he is not arguing that knowledge is not a relational mental state. Gaṅgeśa's definition of knowledge is only compositional on the *narrow* reading, since it relates the self, as a knower, via awareness (as a vehicle), to facts out in the world.

On my view, Gaṅgeśa holds that the knower, the vehicle of awareness, and the fact out in the world, are *non-separable metaphysical constituents* of the token *aRb*, and *epistemically separable components* of the type *aRb*. That is, we can separate them conceptually via the questions: Who is *the knower*? And: What *fact out in the world* is the knower related to? For example, *seeing that there is water in the pond* has a different knower in the case of Karina than it does in the case of Lazarre. And the knowing relation has a different fact out in the world when Lazarre sees salt water in the distance *vs.* when she sees fresh water in the distance.

To further illustrate my view of Gaṅgeśa's theory of knowledge, let me distinguish between two models of knowledge acquisition. On the *assembly model*, to know that *p* is to assemble the composite kind *knowledge* out of parts, such as belief, truth, and an ability to justify one's belief against defeaters. On the *positional model*, one kind of knowing requires either that one *be* or *put oneself* in a position, relative to objects and qualities, where certain relations obtain. Gaṅgeśa holds the *positional model*, and not the *assembly model*, with respect to perceptual knowledge.[31]

In this section I have explored two readings of Gaṅgeśa, on the metaphysics of knowledge. The goal was to present arguments as to where Gaṅgeśa stands with respect to (1) and (3)–(6). These readings offer two options with respect to Williamson's program.

On the one hand, there is *constructive engagement*. Suppose Gaṅgeśa's *narrow* compositional account of knowledge, where the self, awareness, and truth are the components, is still problematic from the perspective of the primeness of knowledge that Williamson defends. Do the arguments that Williamson offers against compositional accounts, which use belief, justification, and truth carry over to Gaṅgeśa, where awareness and truth are central? Moreover, is Gaṅgeśa's view a competitor to the primeness of knowledge in a way that is distinct from belief-first and agent-first approaches to knowledge? On the other hand, there is *cross-traditional similarity*. If Gaṅgeśa's *narrow* compositional account is not

[31] On my understanding, Williamson and Gaṅgeśa share a resistance to the *assembly model*.

problematic from the perspective of the primeness of knowledge that Williamson defends, then perhaps Gaṅgeśa can be credited with having a non-compositional view, different from Williamson's, but nevertheless sufficiently similar to it, so that it can be seen as a contribution to the paradigm, and studied alongside it to assess its merits. Note that Williamson's defense of the non-compositionality of knowledge is focused on establishing the view that knowledge is its own unique mind to world relation, on a par with other states of mind or mental events, which are not composed out of other more basic mental states. In holding that one kind of knowledge is an awareness that relates the self to facts in the world, Gaṅgeśa has a similar view.

However, one clarification needs to be made. Williamson not only argues for the primeness of knowledge, but also that knowledge is first in the order of epistemic explanation.[32] (GTB) can be used to support the claim that Gaṅgeśa's account is consistent with knowledge-first epistemology, since knowledge episodes are the formation base for true beliefs. However, because of the difference between the generation of a state and the explanation of it, there is a gap between knowledge being first in the order of epistemic explanation and knowledge being the source of belief.[33]

Historically, Śrīharṣa, a twelfth-century CE Indian philosopher and poet, also challenged the idea that knowledge can be analyzed or defined. However, neither Śrīharṣa nor Gaṅgeśa, who is responding to Śrīharṣa's work, explicitly hold that knowledge is first. Rather, Gaṅgeśa and Śrīharṣa differ as to whether defining knowledge is a worthy project. Arguably, Śrīharṣa thinks it is a mistake to try and define knowledge because he is skeptical about the project of epistemology. He gives several examples that challenge the idea that knowledge can be defined. By contrast, Gaṅgeśa examines many definitions before settling on his own.[34] Thus, with respect to the debate over whether knowledge can be defined, Gaṅgeśa and Śrīharṣa have contributions that fit within Williamson's knowledge-first program. Even if they don't adhere to every part of it.

4. Multi-Factor Causal Disjunctivism about Perception and the Entailment Thesis

In this section, I argue that Gaṅgeśa holds Williamson's (2)—*seeing that A is a way of knowing that A*.[35] The argument begins with an examination of Gautama's

[32] For a critical discussion of the knowledge-first part of Williamson's project see Gerken (2017).

[33] Phillips et al. (2020) argue that there is evidence for holding that knowledge is more basic than belief. This evidence could be used to help close the gap.

[34] See Mills (2018), Ganeri (2018), and Das (2018) for discussion of Śrīharṣa.

[35] One important background assumption concerning (2) is that we *see facts*. Fish (2009) argues that we do. Vernazzani (2020) provides a critical treatment of Fish's arguments. The opposition between whether we see facts or objects and relations is a dispute that should be carried over into debates on the plausibility and proper interpretation of Gaṅgeśa on perception.

definition of perception and Gaṅgeśa's definition, then to the details of multi-factor causal-disjunctivism, (MFCD). I close with an analysis of three cases of perceptual knowledge.

The original definition of perception in Nyāya comes from Gautama's *Nyāya-Sūtras* at 1.1.4. On one translation, it holds that *perception is a cognition which arises from the contact of the sense organ and object and is not impregnated with words, is unerring, and well-ascertained* (*definite* or *non-dubious*).[36] I would like to note that *avyabhicārī*, which is translated here as *unerring*, has also been translated as *inerrant* and *non-erroneous*. These different renderings can shade how one understands the definition of perception. Is it that perception is a reliable process, which is captured by *non-erroneous* or is perception infallible, which is captured by *inerrant*.[37] These translation issues pertain to Gautama's definition. Perception is discussed in Nyāya long after Gautama. Discussions of it are found in Vātsyāyana, Uddyotakara, Vācaspati, and Udayana all the way to Gaṅgeśa and beyond.

Perhaps the key innovator of the definition is Vācaspati. He innovates on the definition by reading *non-verbal* and *definite* as indicating two distinct types of perception. Thus, he draws the important distinction between determinate (*savikalpaka*) and indeterminate (*nirvikalpaka*) perception. The former has conceptual content, is central to epistemology, and the kind of perception where we can talk about truth and falsity. The latter lacks conceptual content, but is a necessary condition for the construction of the former.[38] It plays a crucial role in explaining how we can be subject to illusions through the *misplacement theory of illusion*,[39] a theory which holds that a foul up in perceptual processing between the non-conceptual and the conceptual stage is one source for illusions (see the rope-snake case below, for further discussion).

Gautama's definition doesn't show why any Naiyāyika would or could accept (2)—*seeing that A is a way of knowing that A*, since no matter how it is read, it does not claim that perception is a way of knowing simply in virtue of what perception is. The fact that perceptual states might be interpreted as being the output of a reliable process, or that individual perceptions hit facts, and thus are never false, does not show that perception is a direct source of knowledge. In order for that to hold, a link must be made between perception and knowledge, on a par

[36] See Dasti and Phillips (2017) and Chadha (2021) for an account of 1.1.4. Stephen Phillips adds that *definite* works better than *well-ascertained*. Shaw argues that *non-dubious* is better than *well-ascertained*. In general, well-ascertained appears to be wider than either *non-dubious* or *definite*. In addition, what Phillips' means by *definite* is that the perception is non-vacillating between distinct things, and what Shaw means by *non-dubious* is that the perception is non-vacillating between distinct things. I use Chadha's definition because it is wider, although I prefer *non-dubious*.

[37] See Turri (2017) for a discussion of these points in his defense of abilism in Nyāya.

[38] See Chaturvedi (2020) for a discussion of whether or not indeterminate perception is necessary for Nyāya epistemology.

[39] See Matilal (1968) for discussion of the misplacement theory of illusion. Another account of it is in Vaidya (2013, 2015).

with Williamson's (2), which can be read as an entailment between *seeing that A* and *knowing that A*.

Gaṅgeśa rejects Gautama's definition because it is too broad. Too many things that are not cases of perception satisfy the definition, such as introspection.[40] Whether Gaṅgeśa is correct about Gautama's definition being too broad is not of importance here. Rather, in rejecting the definition, he advocates two points. First, *perception* has the essential mark of *cognitive immediacy*. Second, following Udayana, that *a perception is an instance of a sense-organ-produced knowledge whose chief instrumental cause*[41] *is not a cognition*.[42] Gaṅgeśa's definition hits Williamson's (2)—*seeing that A is a way of knowing that A*. Gaṅgeśa makes the link to knowledge in the definition of perception directly.[43] In effect he is claiming that *perception* is *a* kind of *knowledge*. To bring texture to this view it will be useful to see more details and a version of a broader account of perceptual theory in Nyāya that can illuminate it.

Phillips (2012, 2020) and Dasti (2012) argue that Vātsyāyana and Gaṅgeśa embrace some form of disjunctivism about perception. Dasti maintains that it is a form of McDowell's epistemic disjunctivism.[44] Vaidya (2021), building off of Shaw (2016a, b, c) argues that it is a kind of metaphysical disjunctivism, called *multi-factor causal-disjunctivism*, (MFCD).[45] It is not clear that Gaṅgeśa subscribes to every detail of (MFCD). However, his account of perception does follow the general lines of (MFCD). I will point out some central features of Gaṅgeśa's view that are consistent with (MFCD) prior to illustrating the view in detail.

(MFCD) is a causal account of perception. However, the account is distinct from Grice's (1961) account on which: *x* being a cause of *S*'s perception of *x* is a necessary condition on *S* perceiving *x*. In contrast to Grice, Shaw (2016a, b, c) articulates Nyāya perceptual theory as a complex causal theory on which the satisfaction of both *positive* and *negative* causal conditions is required. The

[40] See Phillips (2020: 306) for discussion.

[41] The notion of *chief instrumental cause* is to be understood within the context of how Gaṅgeśa, and prior Naiyāyikas, theoretically present and articulate causal processes. It is not on strict analogy with, for example, Aristotle on the four causes.

[42] See Phillips (2020: 311–13) for discussion of Gaṅgeśa in relation to Udayana.

[43] Gaṅgeśa's definition of perception can fruitfully be brought into contact with Papineau's (2019) critique of knowledge. Perhaps Papineau is correct when we think in terms of the debate over knowledge that has occurred in Western philosophy. But what if we consider the Nyāya tradition, and in particular Gaṅgeśa's two-tier theory of knowledge: does Papineau's claim that knowledge is crude apply to Gaṅgeśa's account?

[44] Vaidya (2013) argues that the evidence Dasti bases his claims on do not show that the view isn't a version of Burge's *perceptual anti-individualism*, as opposed to McDowell's (1996) *epistemic-metaphysical disjunctivism*. In addition, Dasti is not claiming that it is a version of Pritchard's (2012) *epistemological disjunctivism*.

[45] See Haddock and Macpherson (2008) for presentation of the distinction between epistemological and metaphysical disjunctivism. See Vaidya (2015) for a discussion of it in relation to Nyāya.

approaches of Grice and Shaw yield the distinction between single-factor and multi-factor causal analysis.[46]

In *single-factor* causal analysis we pay attention to one factor concerning the role of causation in perception: the causal chain moving from the object of perception to the subject of perception. In *multi-factor* causal analysis we pay attention to additional causal factors that play a role in a person having a perception as a way of knowing. It is only when all factors, both positive and negative are satisfied, that one has an episode of perception, which is an instance of knowledge.

(MFCD) is not only a theory of perception, but one of illusion as well. As long as one of the positive or negative conditions fails, we are in a situation where there is a failure to perceive. Typically, although not always, an illusion (in the broad sense) has occurred. Illusions can either be anchor-dependent or anchor-independent. Anchor-dependent illusions involve a ground *x* that is *F*, which is perceived otherwise as *G* due to some malfunction in the perceptual system. A common example is the rope that appears as a snake. Typically a perceiver at some distance from the rope, who fears snakes, has a snake appearance because of the objective similarity between snakes and ropes triggering a mis-placement of a snake concept for a rope concept at the determinate level of perception. In contrast, anchor-independent illusions lack a ground *x* that is perceived otherwise as *G*, when in fact it is *F*. Illusions of this kind are often called *hallucinations*.[47]

For Gaṅgeśa, and for Gautama, a sensory connection between the knower and the objects and qualities in the world is a central component of perception. Gaṅgeśa devotes a whole section of *Jewel* to the discussion of various types of sensory connection. Gaṅgeśa says the following.

> For different types of perception, different sensory connections are indeed required as uniform causal conditions. (1) Substances are grasped through a contact (between a sense organ and the object perceived). (2) Through inherence-in-what-is-in-contact, colors (and other qualities) and motions are grasped. (3) Through inherence-in-what-is-inhering-in-what-is-in-contact, col-orhood (the universal of color) and the like are grasped. (4) Through inherence,

[46] I do not intend to draw the conclusion that Grice would have denied that there are other causally relevant factors or that contemporary perceptual science would not take these factors into account as well. Rather, I mean to draw attention to the fact that the Nyāya do offer a multi-factor causal analysis, which may or may not line up with various accounts of causation in the perceptual science literature.

[47] Prabal Kumar Sen, in conversation, has expressed skepticism as to whether Nyāya has an account of hallucinations—illusions with no object as support, since he holds that hallucinations are generally reduced to illusions in Nyāya. Nilanjan Das, however, has presented work at the 2018 Pacific APA, that suggests that Jayanta Bhaṭṭa, a ninth-century thinker in the Nyāya tradition, has an account of hallucination, which does not reduce to illusion. Phillips points out that Matilal (1992) also has a discussion of the status of hallucinations. Shaw points out that Pandit Dinesh Chandra Shastri also holds that there are accounts of hallucination in Nyāya.

> sound is grasped. (5) Through inherence-in-what-is-inhering, soundhood (the universal of sound) and the like are grasped. (6a) Through being-a-qualifier, absence of sound is grasped. (6b) Through being-a-qualifier-of-what-is-in-relation-to-a-sense-organ, inherence and such absences as of a pot are grasped. The grasping in each case results from the *appropriate* sensory connection, not from sensory connection in general. (Phillips 2020: 319)

For many contemporary researchers of perception, especially vision scientists, this will be a difficult, if not impossible, part of the story to accept for two reasons. First, representationalism is the dominant paradigm in the scientific study of perception.[48] Second, the idea that sense organs make *literal* contact with objects and qualities is, at present, scientifically implausible. Thus: how might we make sense of Gaṅgeśa's view for the purposes of contemporary epistemology?

With respect to the issue of *contact*, one can try to explain away the seeming implausibility. One can let go of the literal interpretation of *contact*, and interpret Gautama and Gaṅgeśa as merely holding that *contact* means *there is a causal chain between the object and the sense organ* through the *medium* the sense organ operates in, for example, light, in the case of vision.[49] Or *contact* could be interpreted in a way that is consistent with the phenomenon of *quantum entanglement* and *spooky action at a distance*, where there is coordination between particles, but no literal contact.[50] My preferred stance on the issue is to simply leave in place the core of Nyāya perceptual theory and what Gaṅgeśa says. Instead of interpreting away the claims of various Naiyāyikas, one can simply emphasize what was important to them. *We engage the world external to us when we perceive it. That is, we don't merely construct everything we see.* As I see it, the metaphysical contrast with *contact* is *construction*. To hold that we make *contact* in an epistemologically relevant sense is to emphasizes that we don't construct everything. We are in fact tracking some features of the world.

Central to Nyāya perceptual theory is the view that perceptual error is asymmetrically dependent on truth. It is because we have seen snakes and ropes out in the world and not as pure constructions, that we can have illusions of snakes based on interacting with ropes. While it is true that we can have illusions based on concepts that don't track anything in reality, such as when we see a cloud as a witch. It doesn't follow that every element of the non-tracking concept, witch, is foreign to our engagement with the world. After all, witches are like things that are real and that we have seen. As Burge (2005: 1) points out: vision science depends on *perceptual anti-individualism*, which is the view that a constitutively

[48] See Burge (2005) for arguments against a variety of forms of naïve realism.

[49] See Chadha (2021) for discussion of this interpretation.

[50] See Berkovitz (2007) for discussion of quantum entanglement and spooky action at a distance.

necessary condition on perceptual representation by an individual is that any such representation should be associated with a background of some veridical perceptual representations. Perception depends on veridical experience. The commitment in Nyāya is to a form of contact that grounds asymmetric dependence.

Two questions for vision science are: how exactly, and in what sense, does contact happen? And: how much construction is at work when we see the "world"? However, vision science, doesn't settle all questions in the epistemology of perception. We need prior conceptual analysis in epistemology and metaphysics to guide the epistemology of perception. Gaṅgeśa is obviously not giving a scientific account of how information at the indeterminate stage of perception gets translated to produce conscious perception. Gaṅgeśa does offer an account of the metaphysics of indeterminate perception and determinate perception. However, his goal is to give an account of perception for the purposes of epistemology, and in particular to vindicate the claim that *knowledge is for action*, a position his predecessor Vātsyāyana, holds as well.

Nyāya perceptual theory does not fall into the representationalist paradigm *at all*. Thus, while the account I have offered of Nyāya perceptual theory through MFCD is similar to Turri's (2017) abilism view, one should note that there is a difference. Abilism uses *representation* in its definition of knowledge, and on my view no Naiyāyika offers a representationalist view of perception. Matilal (1992), for example, presents Nyāya as a naïve realist school of philosophy, where he half-jokingly claims that the "naïve" part of the view is actually not so naive. If Nyāya perceptual theory, from Gautama to Gaṅgeśa, falls into a specific classification of theories within Anglo-analytic epistemology, it would be the relationalist paradigm. However, one might wonder whether the taxonomy of classical Indian theories of perception offers an alternative map for thinking about how perception can work than what is found in analytic philosophy.[51]

Sensory connection is only one kind of causal property that is important to Naiyāyikas. In (MFCD) one will see a complex set of causal conditions whose satisfaction constitute a factive episode of perception that is an instance of knowledge. There are two kinds of causal conditions: positive and negative. While some of these conditions might not be scientifically serviceable, some of the elements and the structure of the theory as a whole are.

On (MFCD) a factive episode of perception is a consequence of the joint satisfaction of both positive and negative causal conditions in concert. These conditions work together, and must be satisfied for an episode of perception to occur.

[51] Nanay (2014) also challenges the representationalist-relationalist distinction. His resultant view is important to consider when trying to understand Nyāya perceptual theory. In future work I plan to do this.

Positive Conditions:
(i) The presence of a self or locus of awareness.
(ii) The presence of a properly directed faculty of attention.
(iii) The presence of properly functioning sense organ.
(iv) Connection between the sense organ and the object.
(v) Connection between the sense organ and the faculty of attention.
(vi) Connection between the faculty of attention and the self.

Negative Conditions:
(vii) The perceptual object must not be beyond the proper range of the sense faculties.
(viii) The perceptual object must not be too close to be apprehended by the sense faculties.
(ix) The perceptual object must not be overshadowed or covered by a more perceptually salient object.
(x) The perceptual object must not be mixed up with similar objects.

(MFCD) is also a theory of perceptual error. Whenever there is an error due to a weakness on a positive condition, we have *an inappropriate causal condition* (*kāraṇavaiguṇya*). Whenever there is an error due to a negative condition, we have a defect (*doṣa*). For example, a perceptual error can be due either to distance or weakness of the eye. When it is due to distance, it is a failure on the negative branch. When it is due to weakness of the eye, it is a failure on the positive branch. As noted before, the epistemologically relevant seeing that involves truth occurs at the determinate stage of perception (*savikalpaka*) where there is conceptual content, and not the indeterminate stage of perception (*nirvikalpaka*) where there is no conceptual content. Central to the determinate stage of perception are two claims. First, that there are *limiters* or *modes of presentation* in perception (how something is presented in conscious perception).[52] These *limiters* or *modes of presentation* facilitate our ability to discriminate objects and qualities. For example, when *x* is presented as *F*, we are able to distinguish it from *G*. However, when *x* is presented as *H*, we might lack the ability to discriminate it from *F*. Second, *limiters* or *modes of presentation* come from prior experience. The first time, or several times thereafter, that we experience *F*s and *G*s, provides us with the capacity to have *F* and *G* as modes of presentation at the determinate level of perception, which also plays a role in how we can mistake *G*s for *F*s. Often, it is

[52] One of the important questions about modes of presentation in perception, from a cross-traditional perspective, concerns the role of the object in perception. Roughly, are the modes of perception *Fregean* or *Russellian*? My hypothesis is that they are Russellian, but this is a complex issue that requires more investigation.

because a foul up has occurred between the indeterminate stage of perception and the determinate stage of perception, that we end up experiencing an illusion of some kind.

To illustrate (MFCD), it will be useful to examine three cases, and show how *multi-factor* differs from *single-factor* causal analysis. I will examine these cases by also looking at what happens when (MFCD) is joined to (2)—*seeing that A is a way of knowing that A*.

> *Distance*: rope-snake
> You are walking toward an object in the distance. As you move toward it, it appears strikingly as a snake, you move closer, and it appears strikingly as a rope. In fact, it is a rope. Did you know it was a snake, and later know it is a rope because you had two distinct perceptual episodes, and perception is a way of knowing?

According to both single-factor and a multi-factor causal analysis, one has a causal connection to the object in the distance, which is a rope, and if we assume that there are no deviant causal chains, the causal connection is good. If we add disjunctivism about perception to both the single-factor and the multi-factor analysis, one can be said to *see* the rope, but not the snake (it is only an appearance). Nevertheless, it is only because one has seen snakes and ropes, that one can make the mistake of seeing a rope as a snake. On both single-factor and multi-factor causal analysis there would be no answer to the question of whether one knows there is a rope in the distance until (2)—*seeing that A is a way of knowing that A*—is added. Once (2) is added, one knows there is a rope, but not that there is a snake. In the rope-snake case, single-factor and multi-factor allow for the same analysis when disjunctivism and (2) are added.

> *Distance*: rock-person
> You are walking toward an object in the distance. As you move toward it, it non-vividly appears to you as a person sitting, but not as anything else either non-vividly or vividly. You move closer, and it vividly appears to you as a large rock, and it is a rock. Did you know it was a person sitting, and later come to know that it was a large rock, because you had two distinct perceptual episodes, and perception is a way of knowing?

According to the single-factor analysis one has a causal connection to the object in the distance, and if we assume there are no deviant causal chains, the causal connection is good. Adding in disjunctivism about perception allows for us to say that one sees the large rock, but not the person sitting. Rather, one has an illusion of a person sitting, since the large rock is presented otherwise. On the multi-factor causal analysis with disjunctivism we get the same result. However, one is also entitled to argue for a distinct view based on the structure of multi-factor analysis. Namely, that one doesn't even see the person sitting, since the visual state where one seems to see the person is a case of *non-vivid perceptual seeming*. Because of the distance, a visual appearance due to causal contact with the object is not sufficient. Rather, using condition (vii) and (viii), it must objectively be the case that the object has *come into view* by being *within the proper range of the sense faculties* for the purpose of seeing.[53] Objects *can* be in a subject's visual and attentional field, without being well-ascertained, definite, or non-dubious, because not in view; and thus, consciously sub-optimal with respect to viewing. As a consequence, although Naiyāyikas would typically classify the appearance of the person sitting in the distance as a case of an illusion, it can be argued that it is neither an illusion nor a perception, but rather a non-perception. Although there is visual consciousness of an object, and engagement of the perceptual mechanism increasing in clarity as one approaches the large rock, there is no *seeing* the object until (vii) and (viii) are satisfied with respect to the particular in the field of vision. In addition, we don't know illusory contents, since they are false, so we don't know that there is a person sitting in the distance. But one can also say in this case that we don't know there is a person sitting in the distance because we don't even see a person sitting in the distance, since nothing is objectively in *optimal view*.

> *Similarity*: red ball-red lighting
> You walk into a room which, unbeknownst to you, has red lighting, and you are looking at a ball which is in fact red, but also illuminated by the red lighting in the room. Do you know that the ball is red, since seeing is a way of knowing and you see a ball that is red even though it is overlaid with red lighting?

On the single-factor view with disjunctivism one has causal contact with the object of perception and thus sees the ball. However, single-factor analysis does not give us any additional resources for thinking about whether one sees the target property: *redness*. On (MFCD) there are two positions we can take.

On the one hand, we see the ball, but the mode of presentation under which the redness of the ball is presented isn't good. Why? Because we cannot discriminate the color from the lighting. The mode of presentation doesn't allow us to

[53] The distinction found in conditions (vii) and (viii) in the Nyāya theory of perception can be brought into contact with Merleau-Ponty's (1962) discussion of optimal grip in perception, see *Phenomenology of Perception* (pg. 302).

> For each object, as for each picture in an art gallery, there is an optimum distance from which it requires to be seen, a direction viewed from which it vouchsafes most of itself: at a shorter or greater distance we have merely a perception blurred through excess or deficiency. We therefore tend towards the maximum of visibility, and seek a better focus as with a microscope.

discriminate it from the light. So, we have a mode of presentation that fails to provide us with a way of discriminating the property in question.

On the other hand, we see the ball, but cannot see the color because two of the negative conditions fail to be satisfied. Arguably, one cannot see the redness of the ball, because the lighting is *too similar* to the color of the ball, violating condition (xi)–(x). While you have an appearance of seeing a red ball, you don't see the redness of the ball. Rather, you see a ball, and cannot discriminate the color of the ball from the lighting. Trying to see an object colored red in red lighting puts determination of the color of the object outside of *the proper range of the visual system*. As a consequence, while you see and know that there is a ball, you don't see or know that the ball is red. Given that the objective conditions on perception set by (MFCD) have not been satisfied, you in fact don't see the redness of the ball. This is consistent with the view that you *seem to see a red ball*. But because (MFCD) is a disjunctivist view, the seeming to see doesn't count as seeing.

To summarize, I have argued that Gaṅgeśa's account of perception captures a version of Williamson's (2)—*seeing that A is a way of knowing that A*. Using (MFCD) as an account of an elaborated version of Gaṅgeśa's definition of perception, I have presented a view of how perception can be a direct source of knowledge. To explain this account I have also analyzed three cases to show how (MFCD) is different from single-factor causal analysis. The position advocated here is *not* that other theories cannot do what (MFCD) can do, *only* that (MFCD) can effectively analyze some cases. Furthermore, while components of (MFCD) can be scientifically criticized, it does not follow that the structure of the theory cannot make a valuable contribution to the philosophy of perception in relation to metaphysics, epistemology, and philosophy of mind.

5. Perceptual Knowledge versus Certified Knowledge

Gaṅgeśa's theory of perceptual knowledge is coupled to a two-tier theory of the structure of knowledge. On this structure, *perceptual knowledge* is an animal way through which minds are related to the world, and *certified knowledge* is a reflective way in which minds relate to each other in collective reasoning and debate.[54] These are two distinct kinds of *epistemic success*, which have

[54] See Sosa (2007, 2009) for comparison. Phillips uses the language of animal *vs*. reflective levels, which bears a striking resemblance to the work of Sosa.

similarities in common. Gaṅgeśa holds the following with respect to certification. *S possesses certified knowledge*[55] that *p* if and only if

a. *p is true.*
b. *S believes p.*
c. *S's belief* that *p* has been produced by a genuine knowledge source.

Gaṅgeśa holds (a) because both perceptual knowledge and certified knowledge are factive. One cannot know something that is false. He holds (b), because while perceptual knowledge is *not* a species of belief, *certified knowledge* either has belief as a component or as a consequence of knowing. He holds (c) partly because of (GTB).[56] Recall, that on Phillips' Nyāya knowledge sources generate true beliefs. The general idea is that perceptual knowledge (episodes of occurrent knowledge) generate true beliefs. Those true beliefs can be certified or uncertified.

One of Phillips' goals with respect to comparative epistemology is to show where Gaṅgeśa's two-tier theory might sit with respect to the Anglo-analytic distinction between internalism and externalism about justification.[57]

> [D]espite the externalism, conscious justification is not just important but thematic for Gaṅgeśa and Nyāya. When a doubt, dispute, or desire to know arises, then turning to knowledge sources as best we can is our method of resolving it. Thus, the knowledge sources are for Gaṅgeśa not only generators of so-to-say unreflective knowledge (some of which we share with animals) but in the context of debate and dispute [....] certifiers and methods of inquiry. Certification with respect to a recognized knowledge source elevates, moreover, a subject's level of confidence, and presents a higher barrier to doubt and dispute than there would be otherwise. Bits of inferential knowledge—just as perceptual awareness and knowledge from testimony—become more secure through checking to make sure they are true. But though knowledge can be coupled with degrees of certainty, a bottom level of, so-to-say, sense certainty (without being actually certified) naturally accompanies our cognitions purporting to present the world (called by Gaṅgeśa "awareness," *anubhava*). Otherwise, there would not be what Western philosophers call belief, or, as Gaṅgeśa would say, trust in cognition as shown in action. (Phillips 2020: 10)

55 See Phillips (2020: 13). It is important to note that here Phillips should be talking about certified knowledge, thus I have added the parenthetical to make it clear. Were he to be talking about perceptual knowledge he would contradict (NSB)—that knowledge is not a species of belief.

56 Since Gaṅgeśa holds that there are other sources of knowledge, such as inference, analogy, and testimony, he likely would not hold (iii) only because of (GTB) which has been discussed here only with respect to perceptual knowledge. Nevertheless, one would suspect that (GTB) is consistent with knowledge arising from other sources of knowledge.

57 See Pappas (2017) for a presentation of the internalist *vs.* externalist distinction in Anglo-analytic philosophy.

Phillips' view appears to be that Gaṅgeśa is neither an internalist, externalist, nor a combination of them.[58,59] The internalism *vs.* externalism debate is not part of classical Indian epistemology. Rather, the debate over intrinsic validity (*svataḥ-prāmāṇya*) *vs.* extrinsic validity (*paratha-prāmāṇya*) is. Those debates are not the same. Nevertheless, Gaṅgeśa has commitments that fall in line with various parts of internalism and externalism. Consider Gaṅgeśa on occurrent knowledge.

> Occurrent knowledge is not only known but produced, too, from something extrinsic, not "of itself," i.e., not from a collection of causes sufficient to produce just any cognition. (Phillips 2020: vol 1: 145)

For Gaṅgeśa the source of an episode of knowledge, both the *seeing that A*, and *that something is known*, are produced from something extrinsic to the subject that has the episode of knowing. The episode as an instance of perceptual knowledge relationally ties the subject to the world. Thus, justification, on an internalist model, where it is taken to be an ability tied to the subject, could not be a component of perceptual knowledge. This is *an* externalist commitment of Gaṅgeśa.

However, as Phillips points out, Gaṅgeśa also holds that perceptual knowledge can either be certified or uncertified, and that conscious justification is important. For Gaṅgeśa some instances of perceptual knowledge do not require certification. Instances of perceptual knowledge that are not certified, or don't need to be certified, are still instances of epistemic success. As long as a given perception satisfies constraints set by (MFCD) the subject can be credited with perceptual knowledge, certification is not required. As noted before, central to both Gaṅgeśa, and Vātsyāyana before him, is the view that knowledge is for action's sake, and it is through action in the world that our knowledge is revealed.[60] As a consequence, when we are in the right position with respect to objects and qualities in our environment we are subject to episodes of knowing that are relational states of mind. And it is in virtue of those episodes arising in us through the satisfaction of a complex causal network that we are able to effectively act and cope in the world.

[58] I read Phillips this way because of his (2012). The reason why is that the traditional way of understanding the debate between internalism and externalism in epistemology is with respect to a single tier theory of knowledge, where justification is a component of it either on an internalist or an externalist theory of justification. But Gaṅgeśa is offering a two-tier theory. As a consequence, it would seem that one cannot strictly apply the distinction to Gaṅgeśa because the architecture is different. Thus, it seems more appropriate to read Phillips as trying to sort out where Gaṅgeśa's commitments are with respect to the distinction found in Anglo-analytic epistemology.

[59] Phillips (2012: 14–15, *emphasis added*) says: Nyāya agrees [with internalism] but with the important *addendum* that by attending to the nature of perception, inference, and testimony, which at the first level operate with us unselfconsciously, we at the second level self-consciously certify what we know and believe. *The internalism flows out of the externalism.* It is useful to consider Phillips' remarks in light of the work of Das and Salow (2018).

[60] See Dasti (2017) for discussion of Vātsyāyana on knowledge for action.

Often enough we act in ways that are beneficial to us, and these actions are made possible by episodes of knowing.

Moreover, it doesn't follow from the fact that perceptual knowledge does not *always* require certification that it never needs to be certified. For Gaṅgeśa, philosophical debate is one place where certification is crucially required. His philosophical methodology requires that we use knowledge sources, such as inference and perception, as well as counterfactual reasoning (*tarka*) to resolve philosophical disputes.

A feature of Gaṅgeśa's model of certification is that it is disjunctive in nature.[61] Not only did Gaṅgeśa hold a disjunctivist account of perception, he also thought of certification as being disjunctive. Just as one can distinguish between perception and pseudo-perception via the causal profile of each, one can also distinguish between certification and pseudo-certification. Certification is objective and requires that certain objective constraints are satisfied. Pseudo-certification is subjective. Pseudo-certification looks right from the first-person point of view, but is objectively misleading. Pseudo-certification is subject to correction.

If *S* is pseudo-certified in holding *p*, then there is some information that *S* could learn such that they would no longer be certified in holding that *p*. By contrast, *genuine certification* is such that if *S* is certified, then there is nothing that *S* could **non-mistakenly** learn that would undermine or override the holding of *p*.[62] The relation between certification and perceptual knowledge is such that two conditions hold.

(i) *S* can know that *p* and not be certified with respect to *p* at a time *t*.
(ii) If *S* knows that *p*, then for *S*, *p* is *certifiable* in principle, but perhaps not at *t*.

Gaṅgeśa's view of certification, for Anglo-analytic epistemologists, invites the question: is there a conception of justification in Gaṅgeśa that matches the view that *S* can be justified via reasons that turn out to be false? If certification is the place where conscious justification is to be found in Gaṅgeśa, one might look there for a fallibilist conception of justification? Phillips holds that *appearance of certification* is a good translation of *prāmāṇya-ābhāsa* and a suitable rendering of a fallibilist conception of justification. Given that certification is disjunctive, taking *appearance of certification* for a fallibilist conception of justification is appropriate.[63]

[61] See Phillips (2012) for discussion of certification. [62] See Phillips (2012: 21).

[63] In addition, if what it takes for something to be a "Gettier Counterexample" to the JTB analysis of knowledge is that epistemic luck is a consequence of a fallibilist conception of knowledge, then while there might be a suitable term in Sanskrit for a fallibilist conception of justification that is amenable to Gaṅgeśa's epistemology, it might, nevertheless, not be central to his epistemology. While he has an example that can be used to undermine the JTB analysis in the way that Gettier does. It is, arguably, not an example that is put forward under a fallibilist conception of justification. See Das (2021) on Gaṅgeśa and Epistemic Luck.

One should consider Gaṅgeśa's view of (iii) and how it relates to the KK-principle, that when one knows they know that they know. Consider (iii) and the following case.

(iii) If S knows that p via perception at t_1, but S cannot certify that p in a context C, at t_2, then S no longer knows that p.

Suppose early in the day Maya sees water in a pond in the center of a desert in *proper* viewing conditions. Assume that Maya knows that there is water in the pond because the causal requirements for seeing as a way of knowing on (MFCD) are satisfied. Suppose later that Simone asks Maya, "is there any water nearby?" Simone notes to Maya that heat in the air is causing mirages in their area. Because Maya knows she cannot discriminate between a mirage and water from a distance, doubt arises in her mind as to what she saw. Maya's says to Simone, "I don't know, but I might have seen water over there (pointing to the pond)."[64]

According to Phillips, Gaṅgeśa holds that one's knowledge can be *shaken off* through the introduction of defeaters.[65] As a consequence, one might conclude that Maya doesn't know that there is water in the desert pond, since she says she doesn't know on the basis of the fact that she cannot respond to Simone's introduction of a defeater. However, how exactly her knowledge is *shaken off* can be interpreted in different ways. Importantly, Maya no longer has an occurrent episode of knowledge, for that was *shaken off* as soon as she looked away from the pond. So, what is it for Maya's knowledge, in the context of the conversation with Simone, to be *shaken off*? Is Maya's knowledge simply gone in virtue of Simone's defeater?

First, we need to take note of the *priority thesis*, (PT), of Phillips' Nyāya: *all standing knowledge requires a first moment of episodic knowledge*. Given (PT) and the fact that Maya's seeing event has passed, we should ask: what is the status of the standing knowledge that was generated from the episodic knowledge event. Is it still a piece of knowledge for Maya?

Second, we need to distinguish between the context of assertion in which a knowledge claim could be made and the metaphysical realizer of an instance of standing knowledge. The core distinction between them is that one can possess the metaphysical complex that realizes a piece of knowledge, yet fail to be able to assert the knowledge in a context because they have lost warrant for doing so. That is, Maya has standing knowledge that there is water in the pond because she has it as

[64] This example has been constructed out of a conversation between Phillips and I. It captures one question about Gaṅgeśa's two-tier epistemology that needs to be addressed: what exactly is the epistemic status of the knowledge that remains after both the knowledge episode has transpired and defeaters, which can shake off the knowledge, have been introduced?

[65] See Phillips (2020: 10–11) for discussion of the two-tier view and the KK-principle. I am offering an analysis of it that deviates from his own view of it.

a trace of the knowledge episode by which she saw it. Once she learns from Simone the prevailing conditions, and recognizes that it could be a mirage that she saw, she simply loses the warrant to assert her knowledge, since assertion is governed by knowledge, and she is aware of a defeater to her knowledge. Were it a mirage she would not be warranted in asserting that there is water in the pond.

Arguably, *shaken off* only means that a person has lost their warrant to assert what they know. It need not mean that they no longer possess the knowledge. It is important to bring this insight about Gaṅgeśa's theory of certification into connection with the KK-principle to show that they are distinct. In examining Phillips' example, we should at least conclude that Gaṅgeśa holds, *Failure to Rebut, then Impermissible to Assert: If S cannot appropriately respond to defeaters concerning p in context C, then S loses their warrant to assert p in C.*

The KK-principle, however, holds, *If S knows that p, then S knows that S knows that p*. There are stronger and weaker versions of it. On one weakening, when *S* knows that *p*, it is in principle possible for *S* to know that they know that *p*. On one strengthening, when *S* knows that *p*, merely in virtue of knowing that *p*, S knows that they know that *p*. Because these versions of the KK-principle are different from what Gaṅgeśa is concerned with in picking out certification as a kind of epistemic success, we need not attribute the KK-principle to Gaṅgeśa in virtue of the phenomenon that Phillips' example draws our attention to. The distinction between *the context of assertion* and *the metaphysical realizer* of knowledge is sufficient to explain Maya's standing. The upshot is that Maya can still have knowledge, but fail to be able to assert it because of the norms governing certification. One need not argue that because Maya cannot prove that she knows that she knows, that Maya loses her knowledge. The possession of knowledge is independent from the ability to assert it.

In this section I have presented Gaṅgeśa's two-tier theory of knowledge with the aim of showing how some of its features make contact with an example that leads to the KK-principle. It is unclear whether Gaṅgeśa's distinction between perceptual knowledge and certified knowledge is amenable to Williamson's knowledge-first program, since it is not clear whether Williamson holds a single-tier or a multi-tier theory of knowledge.

Williamson also argues for the claim that *E* = *K*, which means that *S*'s evidence consists of all and only the propositions *S* knows.[66]

> Suppose that knowledge, and only knowledge, justifies belief. That is, in any possible situation in which one believes a proposition *p*, that belief is justified, if at all, by propositions $q_1, \ldots, q_n$ (usually other than *p*) which one knows. On that supposition, if justified belief is central to epistemological-skeptical inquiry and

[66] See Williamson (1997) and (2000).

> the philosophy of science, then so too is knowledge. Now assume further that what justifies belief is *evidence*... Then the supposition just made is equivalent to the principle that knowledge, and only knowledge, constitutes evidence.... [This principle] equates *S*'s evidence with *S*'s knowledge, for every individual or community *S* in any possible situation. Call this equation $E = K$.[67]
>
> (Williamson 2000: 185)

Williamson's $E = K$ thesis has at least two parts: (L) If *e* is evidence for *S*, then *S* knows *e*, and (R) if *S* knows *e*, then *e* is evidence for *S*. Where might Gaṅgeśa stand with respect to (L) and (R)?

Gaṅgeśa holds that knowledge sources feed certification, since he holds that certified knowledge involves (c): *S's belief* that *p* has been produced by a genuine *knowledge source*. Knowledge sources are what we base certified knowledge on. Thus, it can be argued that Gaṅgeśa would agree with (L), even if the items by which *S* knows *e* do not properly qualify as propositions for him. Gaṅgeśa can also be credited with holding (R), since in a context of certification, where one is required to defend a claim, what they are supposed to appeal to are knowledge sources: perception, testimony, analogy, and inference.[68, 69]

References

Armstrong, D. 1973. *Belief, Truth, and Knowledge*. Cambridge: Cambridge University Press.

Berkovitz, J. 2007. Action at a Distance in Quantum Mechanics. In Edward N. Zalta (Ed.), *The Stanford Encyclopedia of Philosophy* (Spring 2016 Edition). https://plato.stanford.edu/archives/spr2016/entries/qm-action-distance/.

Bhattacharya, G. 1976. Tarkasaṃgraha-dīpikā on Tarkasaṃgraha. Kolkata: Progressive Publishers.

[67] Following Williamson (2000) and Gerken (2017) the equation $E = K$ should be understood to be about the extension of the concepts of *evidence* and *knowledge* and not about the concepts being equivalent.

[68] Since counterfactual reasoning (*tarka*) is not a *pramāṇa*, but part of debate, I use the qualification here. In addition, just because Gaṅgeśa holds (L) and (R), it won't follow that knowledge is first for him.

[69] This chapter grew out of a conversation between Tim Williamson and I in 2014. I would like to thank Julianne Chung for inviting me to contribute to *Oxford Studies in Epistemology*, which has allowed me to explore Gaṅgeśa and Nyāya in the context of Williamson's knowledge-first paradigm. This chapter has benefited from many discussions. Thanks, first and foremost, to Stephen Phillips, Jay Shaw, and Tim Williamson. I would also like to thank Manjula Rajan, Swami Medhananda, Jennifer Nagel, Ajay Rao, Parimal Patil, Jonardon Ganeri, Amit Chaturvedi, Jack Beaulieu, Nilanjan Das, Mark Siderits, Arindam Chakrabarti, Prabal Kumar Sen, Chakravarthi Ram-Prasad, Purushottama Bilimoria, Agnieszka Rostalska, Krupa Patel, and participants at the November 2019 *Gaṅgeśa* conference at Toronto, Ontario, Canada; and the January 2020—*Logic, Language, and Epistemology in Nyāya*—conference at the Ramakrishna Mission Institute of Culture, Gol-Park, Kolkata, India.

Bhattacharya, S. 1996. *Gaṅgeśa's Theory of Indeterminate Perception Nirvikalpakavāda: Part 1*. Delhi: Indian Council of Philosophical Research.

Bilimoria, P. 1985. *Jñāna* and *Pramā*: The Logic of Knowing—A Critical Appraisal. *Journal of Indian Philosophy*, 13(1): 73–102.

Burge, T. 2005. Disjunctivism and Perceptual Psychology. *Philosophical Topics*, 33(1): 1–78.

Chadha, M. 2021. Perceptual Experience and Concepts in Classical Indian Philosophy. In Edward N. Zalta (Ed.), *The Stanford Encyclopedia of Philosophy* (Spring 2016 Edition). http://plato.stanford.edu/archives/spr2016/entries/perception-india/.

Chakrabarti, A. 2020. Seeing Daffodils, Seeing as Daffodils, and Seeing Things called Daffodils. In his *Realisms Interlinked: Objects, Subjects, and Other Subjects*. London: Bloomsbury.

Chaturvedi, A. 2020. There is Something Wrong with Raw Perception, After All: Vyāsatīrtha's Refutation of *Nirvikalpaka-Pratyakṣa*.

Das, N. 2018. Śrīharṣa. In Edward N. Zalta (Ed.), *The Stanford Encyclopedia of Philosophy* (Spring 2018 Edition). https://plato.stanford.edu/archives/spr2018/entries/sriharsa/.

Das, N. 2021. Gaṅgeśa on Epistemic Luck. *Journal of Indian Philosophy*, 49(2): 153-202.

Das, N., and Salow, B. (2018). Transparency and the KK Principle. *Nous*, 52(1): 3–23.

Dasti, M. 2012. Parasitism and Disjunctivism in Nyāya Epistemology. *Philosophy East & West*, 62(1):1–15.

Dasti, M. 2017. Vātsyāyana: Cognition as a Guide to Action. In J. Ganeri (Ed.), *Oxford Handbook of Indian Philosophy* (pp. 209–31). Oxford: Oxford University Press.

Dasti, M., and Phillips, S. 2010. *Pramāṇa* Are Factive-A Response to Jonardon Ganeri. *Philosophy East & West*, 60(4): 535–40.

Dasti, M., and Phillips, S. 2017. *Nyāya-Sūtra: Selections with Early Commentary*. Indianapolis, IN: Hackett Publishing.

Fish, W. 2009. *Perception, Hallucination, and Illusion*. New York: Oxford University Press.

Ganeri, J. 2007. Review of *Epistemology of Perception: Gaṅgeśa's Tattvacintāmaṇi, Jewel of Reflection on the Truth (about Epistemology): The perception chapter (pratyakṣa-khaṇḍa)*, by Stephen Phillips and N.S. Ramanuja Tatacharya. *Journal of the American Orientale Society*, 127(3): 349–54.

Ganeri, J. 2018. Epistemology from a Sanskritic Point of View. In M. Mizumoto, S. Stich, and E. McCready (Eds.), *Epistemology for the Rest of the World* (pp. 12–21). Oxford: Oxford University Press.

Gerken, M. 2017. Against Knowledge-First. In J. Adam Carter, Emma C. Gordon, and Benjamin W. Jarvis (Eds.) *Knowledge-First: Approaches in Episetmology and Mind* (pp. 46–72). Oxford: Oxford University Press.

Gettier, E. 1966. Is Justified True Belief Knowledge? *Analysis* 23(6): 121–23.

Goldman, A. 1986. *Epistemology and Cognition*. Cambridge, MA: Harvard University Press.

Grice, P. 1961. The Causal Theory of Perception. *Proceedings of the Aristotelian Society*, 121: 121–52.

Haddock, A., and Macpherson, F. 2008. *Disjunctivism: Perception, Action, Knowledge*. Oxford: Oxford University Press.

Ichikawa, J.J., and Steup, M. 2018. The Analysis of Knowledge. In Edward N. Zalta (Ed.), *The Stanford Encyclopedia of Philosophy*. https://plato.stanford.edu/archives/sum2018/entries/knowledge-analysis/.

Krishna, D. Rege, M.P., Dwivedi, R.C., Lath, M. 1991. *Saṃvāda: A Dialogue Between Two Philosophical Traditions*. Delhi: Indian Council of Philosophical Research in Association with Motilal Banarsidass Publishers.

Littlejohn, C. 2017. How and Why Knowledge Is First. In A. Carter, E. Gordon, and B. Jarvis (Eds.), *Knowledge First* (pp. 19–45). Oxford: Oxford University Press.

Littlejohn, C. 2019. Neither/Nor. In C. Doyle, J. Milburn, and D. Pritchard (Eds.), *New Issues in Epistemological Disjunctivism*. London: Routledge.

Matilal, B. K. 1968. *The Navya-Nyāya Doctrine of Negation*. Cambridge, MA: Harvard University Press.

Matilal, B. K. 1992. *Perception: An Essay on Classical Indian Theories of Knowledge*. Oxford: Oxford University Press.

McDowell, J. 1996. *Mind and World*. Cambridge, MA: Harvard University Press.

Merleau-Ponty, M. 1962. *Phenomenology of Perception*. tr. Colin Smith. New York: Routledge and Kegan Paul.

Mills, E. 2018. *Three Pillars of Skepticism in Classical Indian Philosophy, Nāgārjuna, Jayarāśi, Śrīharṣa*. Lanham, MD: Lexington Books, a division of Rowman and Littlefield.

Mohanty, J. 1966. *Gaṅgeśa's Theory of Truth*. Delhi: Motilal Banarsidass.

Mukhopadhyay, P. K. 1984. *Indian Realism A Rigorous Descriptive Metaphysics*. Kolkata: K.P. Bagchi & Company.

Mukhopadhyay, P.K. 1991. *The Nyāya Theory of Linguistic Performance*. Kolkata: K. P. Bagchi & Company.

Nanay, B. 2014. The Representationalism vs. Relationalism Debate: Explanatory Contextualism about Perception. *European Journal of Philosophy* 23(2): 321–36.

Papineau, D. 2019. Knowledge is Crude. In https://aeon.co/essays/knowledge-is-a-stone-age-concept-were-better-off-without-it.

Pappas, G. 2017. Internalist vs. Externalist Conceptions of Epistemic Justification. In Edward N. Zalta (Ed.), *The Stanford Encyclopedia of Philosophy*, https://plato.stanford.edu/archives/fall2017/entries/justep-intext/.

Parikh, R., and Renero, A. 2017. Justified True Belief: Plato, Gettier, and Turing. In J. Floyd and A. Bokulich (Eds.), *Philosophical Explorations of the Legacy of Alan Turing*: Turing at 100 (pp. 93–102). Dordrecht: Springer.

Phillips, J., Buckwalter, W., Cushman, F., Friedman, O., Martin, A., Turri, J., Santos, L., and Knobe, J. 2020. Knowledge Before Belief. *Behavioral and Brain Sciences*. https://doi.org/10.1017/S0140525X20000618

Phillips, S. 2012. *Epistemology in Classical India: The Knowledge Sources of the Nyāya School*. New York: Routledge Publishing.

Phillips, S. 2020. *Jewel of Reflection on the Truth about Epistemology: A Complete and Annotated Translation of the Tattva-cintā-mani—Volume 1: Perception—Volume 2: Inference*. London: Bloomsbury.

Phillips, S. and Tatacharya, R. 2004. *Epistemology of Perception: Gaṅgeśa's Tattvacintāmaṇi Jewel of Reflection on the Truth (About Epistemology): The Perception Chapter (Pratyakṣa-Khaṇḍa), Transliterated Text, Translation, And Philosophical Commentary*, Treasury of the Indic Sciences. New York: American Institute of Buddhist Studies.

Pritchard, D. 2012. *Epistemological Disjunctivism*. Oxford: Oxford University Press.

Sartwell, K. 1992. Why Knowledge is Merely True Belief. *Journal of Philosophy*, 89(4): 167–80.

Sen, P.K. 2000. Knowledge, Truth, and Skepticism. In Jay Shaw (Ed.), *Concepts of Knowledge East and West* (pp. 234–43). Kolkata: The Ramakrishna Mission Institute of Culture Publishing.

Shaw, J.L. 2016a. Nyāya on the Sources of Knowledge. In J.L. Shaw (Ed.), *The Collected Writings of Jaysankar Lal Shaw: Indian Analytic and Anglophone Philosophy*. London: Bloomsbury Publishing.

Shaw, J.L. 2016b. Knowledge, Doubt, and Belief: Some Contemporary Problems and their Solutions from the Nyāya Perspective. In J.L. Shaw (Ed.), *The Collected Writings of Jaysankar Lal Shaw: Indian Analytic and Anglophone Philosophy*. London: Bloomsbury Publishing: 121–50.

Shaw, J.L. 2016c. The Nature of Nyāya Realism. In J.L. Shaw (Ed.), *The Collected Writings of Jaysankar Lal Shaw: Indian Analytic and Anglophone Philosophy* (pp. 66–72). London: Bloomsbury Publishing.

Shope, R.K. 1983. *The Analysis of Knowing: A Decade of Research*. Princeton, NJ: Princeton University Press.

Sosa, E. 2007. *A Virtue Epistemology: Apt Belief and Reflective Knowledge Volume I*. Oxford: Oxford University Press.

Sosa, E. 2009. *Reflective Knowledge: Apt Belief and Reflective Knowledge Volume II*. Oxford: Oxford University Press.

Stoltz, J. 2007. Gettier and Factivity in Indo-Tibetan Epistemology. *Philosophical Quarterly* 57(228): 394–415.

Sukharanjan, S. 2003. Episetmology in Pracina Navya-Nyāya. Kolkata: Jadavpur University Publishing.

Turri, J. 2010. On the Relationship Between Propositional and Doxastic Justification. *Philosophy and Phenomenological Research*, 80(2): 312–26.

Turri, J. 2017. Experimental, Cross-Cultural, and Classical Indian Epistemology. *Journal of Indian Council of Philosophical Research*, 34(3): 501–16.

Vaidya, A. 2013. Nyāya Perceptual Theory: Disjunctivism or Anti-Individualism. *Philosophy East & West*, 63(4): 562–85.

Vaidya, A. 2015. The Nyāya Misplacement Theory of Illusion and the Metaphysical Problem of Perception. In P. Bilimoria and M. Hemmingsen (Eds.), *Comparative Philosophy and J. L. Shaw*. Dordrecht: Springer Publishing.

Vaidya, A. 2021. Multi-Factor Causal Disjunctivism: A Nyāya Informed Account. *Sophia* 60(4): 917–914.

Vernazzani, A. 2020. Do We See Facts? *Mind and Language*. https://doi.org/10.1111/mila.12336.

Williamson, T. 1997. *Knowledge as Evidence. Mind*, 106(424): 717–41.

Williamson, T. 2000. *Knowledge and Its Limits*. Oxford: Oxford University Press.

13

Vaidya on Nyāya and Knowledge-First Epistemology

Timothy Williamson

1. Preamble

I welcome precedents for my epistemology in classical Indian and other traditions.[1] In part, I do so because they confirm the naturalness of the knowledge-first approach I favour: it is no blip peculiar to one moment of Western philosophy. Rather, it is arguably rooted in basic human ways of understanding the cognitive states of ourselves and others. Those ways are so basic, one may speculate, because they have survived the test of evolution: they *work*. Although the specific forms they take even in pre-theoretical thought and talk will always be to some extent culturally and linguistically inflected, the underlying template may turn out to be a universal of the human cognitive system. If so, the knowledge-first approach is likely to do better than its rivals as a starting-point for comparative epistemology. Here as elsewhere, different philosophical traditions are often much less alien to each other than their stereotypes may suggest, and their commonalities facilitate mutual learning—at least in principle.

In 'Elements of Knowledge-First Epistemology in Gaṅgeśa and Nyāya', Anand Vaidya discusses the epistemology of the fourteenth-century Indian philosopher Gaṅgeśa Upādhyāya, a key figure in the Nyāya tradition, focussing on aspects comparable to features of my own work. One of the shared features is a view of *seeing* as a way of *knowing*, a connection which gives a hint of the practical utility of thinking in terms of knowing, since it is often easy to observe what others can see and what they cannot (sightlines, direction of gaze, occluding obstacles). By contrast, it is typically much harder to observe what others *believe* and what they do not. If one wonders what classifying a case as *knowing* adds in practice to classifying it as *seeing*, the natural response is that, thanks to memory, agents tend to continue *knowing* something long after they have ceased to *see* it. For practical

[1] I speak loosely of traditions, for instance classical Indian philosophy and Western analytic philosophy. Such phrases are vague and potentially invidious. Nevertheless, for 'big picture' purposes, they are more helpful than elaborate attempts at precision. Few traditions are bounded by discontinuities.

Timothy Williamson, *Vaidya on Nyāya and Knowledge-First Epistemology* In: *Oxford Studies in Epistemology, Volume 7.* Edited by: Tamar Szabó Gendler, John Hawthorne, and Julianne Chung, Oxford University Press.
 DOI: 10.1093/oso/9780192868978.003.0013

purposes, we need to track what others currently know, not just what they currently see. Indeed, the value of sight itself is vastly enhanced by our ability to preserve what it gives us in memory. I will say more about the relation between seeing and knowing in the next section.

A warning is needed. When we consider past philosophers, there is a danger of injustice if we insist on judging them by how their ideas support specific interventions in current technical debates, or threaten to undermine those debates. By that criterion, the long-dead giants of both Western and non-Western philosophical tradition may come out badly, much worse than historians of philosophy have a professional interest in imagining. Indeed, such a measure of value is anachronistic and deeply unhistorical, since it ignores the context in which past philosophers wrote, on which depends the difficulty, the novelty, and the fruitfulness of what they did. Of course, their works *may* supply the material for new moves in contemporary philosophy, and such uses are quite legitimate, but we should not feel obliged to find such applications in order to defend either the reputations of past philosophers or the study of their works. Such study has value for its own sake. Moreover, ignorance of the history of our discipline makes us naïve in various ways, which can harm present practice, though we should not expect to read off its lessons pat from the texts.[2]

Like the history of science, the history of philosophy is more useful as a source of inspiration than as a reason for nostalgia. One can certainly draw inspiration from classical Indian philosophy. But for that to happen, the work must be philosophically *available*, which involves far more than just a published translation of the text into one's native language, if (like me) one does not know Sanskrit. Translations of philosophical texts by scholarly philologists or historians tend to lie dead on the page, because the translator has no feel for what philosophy is like when alive, no first-hand experience of deep, active engagement in fresh philosophical thought or dialectic. Medieval scholastic philosophy had to be rescued from such deadening translations into obsolescent jargon. Analytically oriented philosophers such as Vaidya are doing the world a great service by helping bring the classical Indian tradition philosophically alive, making it intellectually available to those educated primarily in contemporary philosophy. Thereby they undermine an old-fashioned stereotype of Indian philosophy as religious, mystical, or irrational, which may have discouraged many philosophers from trying to engage with it—though the same stereotype may have encouraged others! Recent work by Vaidya and others also helps combat another stereotype, perhaps equally damaging, of classical Indian philosophy as intelligible only through the lens of minute philological and textual scholarship, an attitude always hostile in effect to the growth of interest in the philosophy at issue.

[2] For a more extensive broad-brush discussion of the philosophical use of the history of philosophy, see Williamson 2018b: 98–110.

Life is short. No one has time to find out about everything worth finding out about. Including one thing often means excluding another. My own knowledge of classical Indian philosophy will surely remain bitty and superficial; I am no historian of philosophy, East or West. Still, I value intellectual links to brilliant philosophers so distant in time and space, but—in some crucial respects—so close in outlook.

In this response to Vaidya's piece, I will briefly comment from the standpoint of knowledge-first epistemology as developed in *Knowledge and its Limits* (Williamson 2000) and my subsequent publications on some of the issues he raises.

2. Seeing and Knowing

In section III of his paper, Vaidya argues that Gaṅgeśa holds a version of the principle that *seeing that p is a way of knowing that p*, which I also endorse (Williamson 2000: 37–8). For instance, in his example, if Karina sees that the ball is red, she thereby knows that the ball is red. As usual, the red ball against a red wall is illuminated by red lighting, making it impossible to discriminate colours. Thus Karina is in no position to *know* that the ball is red, even though she has the true belief that it is red; she is of course unaware of the red lighting. Correspondingly, she is in no position to *see* that the ball is red, even though she sees the ball and it is red. We might compare her to a juror who is erroneously confident that he can tell whether someone is guilty by looking into their eyes. He looks into the accused's eyes and judges that the accused is guilty, which happens to be true. Still, he is in no position to *know* that the accused is guilty; equally, he is in no position to *see* that the accused is guilty. By contrast, if lighting conditions were as Karina thinks they are, she would know that the ball was red by seeing that the ball was red, and if the juror had the powers he thinks he has, he would know that the accused was guilty by seeing that the accused was guilty.

The italicized connection between seeing and knowing links fact-seeing and fact-knowing, *seeing that p* and *knowing that p*, neither of which one can do if not *p*. As Vaidya's discussion of his examples brings out, fact-seeing must not be confused with object-seeing. Karina sees the red ball (object-seeing) without seeing that the ball is red (fact-seeing). As a partial converse, you might see that there is water in a waterbed (fact-seeing) without seeing the water in the waterbed (object-seeing), because the waterbed is taut but opaque, though you do see the waterbed itself (object-seeing). As Vaidya makes clear by quotation, Gaṅgeśa was alert to such variations in type amongst the objects of perception.[3]

There is a temptation to regard fact-seeing and fact-knowing as the special cases of object-seeing and object-knowing respectively where the object is a fact. The connection between fact-seeing and fact-knowing might then be a special case of a more

[3] The *locus classicus* for the distinction between object-seeing and fact-seeing is Dretske 1969.

general connection between object-seeing and object-knowing, conceived as knowledge by acquaintance: if you see an object, you thereby know it, at least minimally. Similarly, the factiveness of fact-seeing and fact-knowing would be a special case of the object-dependence of object-seeing and object-knowing. In Vaidya's rope-snake example, Karina fails to see a snake, because there is no snake for her to see, just as she fails to see that the object is a snake, because it is not a snake. Likewise, she fails to have knowledge by acquaintance with a snake, because there is no snake for her to be acquainted with, just as she fails to know that the object is a snake, because it is not a snake. One might also attempt to derive the causal conditions on fact-seeing as a special case from the causal conditions on object-seeing.

However, the complete assimilation of fact-seeing and fact-knowing to object-seeing and object-knowing would be a mistake. One can see an object despite being radically mistaken about its nature. Karina sees the rope, despite seeing it *as* a snake. If the analogy between fact-seeing and object-seeing went all the way, she should be able to see the fact that the object is a rope, despite seeing it *as* the fact that the object is a snake. But if she simply sees it as the fact that the object is a snake, she does not see that the object is a rope. To assimilate fact-seeing fully to object-seeing, one must interpret 'seeing' in 'object-seeing' metaphorically with respect to the visual sense of 'see'. Thus fact-seeing is not a special case of specifically *visual* object-seeing. Nevertheless, the cognitive system may in some sense *model* fact-seeing on object-seeing, without eliminating the role of judgment in fact-seeing, which object-seeing lacks. For similar reasons, fact-knowing is not just the special case of object-knowing where the object is a fact (see also Williamson 2000: 43).

In addition to object-seeing and fact-seeing, Vaidya sometimes seems to contemplate *property*-seeing, as when he says 'Karina doesn't see the redness of the ball' and 'she doesn't really see the color'. However, if seeing redness is not simply seeing *that* something is red, the intended difference is obscure, leaving the explanatory gain from invoking property-seeing unclear, so I will not discuss this third category further.

3. Disjunctivism and Knowledge-First Epistemology

Vaidya attributes to Gaṅgeśa a theory he calls 'multi-factor causal-disjunctivism' (MFCD). Unfortunately, he does not clarify what is supposed to be disjunctivist about MFCD. When he invokes disjunctivism as such, it is mainly to insist that Gaṅgeśa distinguishes genuine perception from illusion or hallucination. If there is no snake, you do not genuinely see a snake or see that there is a snake, even if you seem to yourself to be doing so. But any reasonable account of perception will draw some distinction between appearance and reality. Much more than that is needed for disjunctivism in any useful sense.

Let *No Illusion* be the conjunction of the principles that fact-seeing is fact-dependent (if you see that p, then p) and that object-seeing is object-dependent (if you see an *F*, then there is an *F*).[4] No Illusion falls far short of the highly distinctive views standardly associated with the term 'disjunctivism' and with philosophers of perception such as J.M. Hinton, John McDowell, Paul Snowdon, and Michael Martin.[5] For example, a philosopher could validate No Illusion by first postulating a fundamental mental state of being appeared to in a specific way, which one can be in irrespective of whether the appearance is veridical or non-veridical, and then define object-seeing and fact-seeing in terms of suitable causal relations between the neutral appearance state and the object or fact at issue. That is exactly the sort of view disjunctivists mean to reject. For it treats the difference between good and bad cases as external to the subject's mental state, and just a matter of good or bad causal relations to the environment. By contrast, disjunctivists insist that the subject's mental states in a good case of genuine perception and a bad case of mere illusion are profoundly different in nature, even though the states are in some sense indiscriminable from the inside. That is why it is called 'disjunctivism': it analyses being appeared to in a given way as a disjunction of two quite disparate states, one's mental state in the good case and one's mental state in the bad case. Those remarks generalize from mental states to mental processes.

It is not for me to say how close Nyāya came to such full-blooded disjunctivism. A large step towards it would be to treat object-dependent object-seeing and fact-dependent fact-seeing as genuine, naturally individuated mental states or processes in their own right, which one is in only in the relevant good cases. By itself, however, that is consistent with treating the corresponding neutral state or process of being appeared to in the relevant way as an equally genuine, naturally individuated mental state or process in its own right, which is not in the spirit of disjunctivism as standardly understood.

At one point in section III, following other scholars, Vaidya identifies a Nyāya view closer to full-blooded disjunctivism: that 'perceptual error is asymmetrically dependent on truth'. In his example, 'It is because we have seen snakes and ropes out in the world that we can have illusions of snakes based on interacting with ropes'. This suggests the usual disjunctivist conception of the bad case as a sort of fake good case. Malfunctioning is to be understood by its contrast with proper functioning, not the other way round; nor are they to be understood as simply two states or processes of the system on a par with each other. This asymmetry is built into the content of perceptual appearances, which already 'prefers' the good case to the bad. When things are not as they appear to be, you are in the bad case. Usually, when things are as they appear to be, you are in the good case—though there are lucky exceptions (Lewis 1980). Even when your perceptual system is malfunctioning, things may nevertheless happen to be as they appear to be: such cases resemble cases of true belief without knowledge. Anyway, the asymmetric

[4] Some adjustment of the tense may be needed, since you can see a star which is no longer there, because it exploded millions of years ago.

[5] For an introductory survey of the varieties of disjunctivism about perception, see Soteriou 2016.

dependence of the bad case on the good case also supports an asymmetric dependence of the generic neutral appearance case (which subsumes both good and bad subcases) on the good case, for what unifies the subcases of the generic neutral case is their relation to the good case, some sort of indiscriminability or local similarity. The bad case has such a relation to the good case, and of course the good case has it to itself: everything is indiscriminable from, and locally similar to, itself.

However, on further reflection, such asymmetric dependence does not support the letter of disjunctivism. The strict disjunctivist analyses the generic neutral appearance case as a disjunction of the good case and the bad case, understood as two disparate disjuncts. Given asymmetric dependence, by contrast, to be in the bad case is to be in a case which is indiscriminable from (or locally similar to) the good case but is not itself good. Thus to be in the generic neutral appearance case is to be in a case which is *either* good *or* indiscriminable from (or locally similar to) the good case but not itself good. But the disjunctive form of that analysis is an artefact of gerrymandering. It is like claiming that the property of being less than a metre from a point is disjunctive because it is equivalent to the disjunction of the property of being at the point with the property of being less than a metre from it but not at it. The second disjunct is artificial, because it is just the analysandum with the first disjunct arbitrarily excluded. What unifies the subcases of the second disjunct also subsumes the first disjunct. Given asymmetric dependence, the natural analysis of the generic neutral appearance case is simply that to be in it is to be in a case indiscriminable from (or locally similar to) the good case, without further subdivision of cases.

Since I accept the asymmetric dependence of the bad case on the good case, I reject the letter of disjunctivism (Williamson 2000: 44–8). However, what matters is the spirit of disjunctivism, not the letter, and the spirit of disjunctivism is consistent with asymmetric dependence. A key insight underlying disjunctivism is that we should not treat the generic neutral appearance case as prior to the good case by analysing the good case as a combination of the generic neutral appearance case with further conditions, for example concerning its causal relations to the environment. Rather, the generic neutral appearance case is to be understood as unified by its relation to the good case. That insight does not require a strictly disjunctive understanding of the generic neutral appearance case, and it chimes with asymmetric dependence.

The asymmetric dependence of the bad case on the good case is not confined to perception. On a unified approach to cognition along such lines, just as mere appearance asymmetrically depends on genuine perception, so mere belief asymmetrically depends on genuine knowledge. Just as the generic neutral appearance case is unified by its relation to perception, so the generic neutral belief case is unified by its relation to knowledge. Just as non-defective cases of appearance attain the status of perception, so non-defective cases of belief attain the status of knowledge (Williamson 2000: 41–8). The principle that seeing that *p* is a way of knowing that *p* tightens the connection between the two species of asymmetric dependence, though it does not entail the objectionable idea that visual appearances *are* beliefs.[6] The two species are analogous, but neither subsumes the other.

Clearly, such asymmetric dependence principles together already constitute something like a knowledge-first approach to epistemology, although the approach can of course be taken much further.[7] I cannot say how far Nyāya went or would have been willing to go down this road. If they accepted the general asymmetric dependence of falsity on truth in a full-blooded sense, they went quite far down the road.

Vaidya refrains from characterizing Nyāya epistemology as knowledge-first. He grants that they were not belief-first epistemologists, since belief did not play a major role in their epistemology, but, as he rightly notes, knowledge-first and belief-first approaches are not the only approaches. A philosopher might give priority to something that is neither knowledge nor belief, or deny that any one thing has priority. However, the postulated asymmetric dependence of falsity on truth implies some sort of priority of truth over falsity, whose epistemological upshot is presumably some sort of priority of truth-entailing cognitive states and processes over those which are not truth-entailing. The entailment from seeing that *p* to knowing that *p*, attributed by Vaidya to Nyāya, implies that the truth-entailing attitude of seeing-that is also knowledge-entailing. I have provided evidence elsewhere that this is a special case of a far more general pattern (Williamson 2000: 33–41). Thus, if Nyāya give priority to truth-entailing cognitive attitudes, they may in effect be giving priority to knowledge-entailing cognitive attitudes, and so by implication to knowledge itself.

Of course, that line of thought rests on the hypothesis that Nyāya do treat falsity as asymmetrically dependent on truth, or at least non-truth-entailing cognitive states and processes as asymmetrically dependent on truth-entailing ones. That hypothesis is for qualified interpreters of Nyāya to assess.

Naturally, whether Nyāya gave priority to knowledge is not the same question as whether Nyāya *said* that knowledge had priority. It is in the nature of traditions to take the priority of their most basic concerns for granted. In my work, I have explicitly emphasized the priority of knowledge because I was consciously opposing a tradition which had taken the opposite for granted. In a different philosophical context, absent the internalist burdens of post-Cartesian Western epistemology, one might start from the distinction between knowledge and ignorance without feeling the need to justify not starting somewhere else. Unsurprisingly,

[6] The standard example is the Müller-Lyer illusion: even once you know that the two lines are the same length, one of them still *looks* longer than the other to you, but your background knowledge inhibits the temptation to *believe* that it is longer. Such examples are consistent with the claim that perceptual appearances involve *dispositions* to believe.

[7] See, for example, the accounts of evidence, evidential probability, and assertion in Williamson 2000, and the accounts of action in Williamson 2017 and Hawthorne and Stanley 2008. In section IV of his paper, Vaidya argues that something like the equation of one's total evidence with one's total knowledge would be in the spirit of Gaṅgeśa's epistemology.

how close Nyāya came to knowledge-first epistemology is a matter more of how they did epistemology than of how they said it ought to be done.

4. Primeness

Suppose that some conditions on a subject are *purely internal*, some are *purely external*, and others are neither. For instance, the condition of *feeling thirsty* may be purely internal, the condition of *being within a mile of an oasis* purely external, and the condition of *being within a mile of someone else who feels the same way* neither purely internal nor purely external. For present purposes we need not get more precise than that. On a straightforward internalist view of the mind, the condition of being in a given mental state is purely internal. Thus, whenever the proposition that *p* non-trivially constrains the external environment, knowing that *p* is not a mental state because the condition of *knowing that p* is not purely internal, for the condition obtains only when *p*, and so only when the external environment complies. But the condition of *knowing that p* is also not purely external, for it entails the condition of *believing that p*, which non-trivially constrains how things are internally for the subject. On the internalist view, knowing that *p* is a sort of hybrid of the mental and the non-mental, and of the internal and the external.

A simple view of such hybrid conditions is that they can be analysed into conjunctions of purely internal conditions and purely external conditions. Since any conjunction of purely internal conditions is itself a purely internal condition, and any conjunction of purely external conditions is itself a purely external condition, it follows that any such hybrid condition is the conjunction of one purely internal condition with one purely external condition. Call any condition equivalent to such a conjunction *composite*. For instance, the condition of *feeling thirsty and being within a mile of an oasis* is composite. Thus the condition of *knowing that p* is composite, if it can be analysed in the envisaged way.

A *prime* condition is one which is not composite. There is a simple recipe for showing a condition to be prime. Using it, one can show that conditions such as *seeing that p* and *knowing that p* are prime on many substitutions for '*p*' (Williamson 2000: 65–72). Thus seeing-that and knowing-that cannot in principle be analysed along the envisaged lines: the simple internalist view does not work. The internal and the external cannot so easily be disentangled.

Vaidya treats primeness as pivotal to *Knowledge and its Limits*. For example, in section I, he takes it as central to my argument that knowing is a state of mind. That puts more weight on it than I intended it to carry. Before turning to primeness, I had already argued that the default presumption should be that knowing is a mental state, and that standard attempts to defeat that assumption all fail, because the constraints on mental states they invoke are either satisfied by knowing or violated by internalist paradigms of mental states (Williamson 2000: 21–64). Those considerations in favour of classifying knowing as a mental state have since been powerfully extended by the work of Jennifer Nagel (2013) and others. Nor was the primeness argument intended by itself to show that knowing cannot be analysed into any combination of purely internal and purely external conditions, for it only concerns *conjunctive* analyses. As I acknowledged, disjunctions of composite conditions need not themselves be composite (Williamson 2000: 89–92). The strongest evidence for the general unanalysability of knowing comes from the lamentable track record of attempts to analyse it.

Instead, the main point of considering primeness was to defeat an internalist strategy for showing hybrid conditions such as *knowing that p* to be explanatorily redundant, in particular, for the explanation of action: the strategy works only for composite conditions, and so does not work in general for knowing. This argument that knowing is not redundant for the explanation of action deepens the case for the conclusion that knowing is a genuine mental state in its own right, although primeness by itself is quite insufficient for mental statehood.

For purposes of historical comparison, the primeness considerations are by no means the most natural aspect of my epistemology to focus on. Not only are they distinctively technical, they are so in a way contoured to engage with the internalist mindset against which they are directed. As I emphasized in the book, it is *internalists* who needs a clear distinction between the internal and the external in order to articulate their theoretical perspective (Williamson 2000: 74–5). Externalists do not need the distinction in their positive theorizing. They use it dialectically, when they engage with internalists, for purposes of argument, but if it starts crumbling, that is the internalists' problem, not the externalists'. Without the distinction between internal and external, there is no distinction between prime and composite. Thus one would not expect those distinctions to have been drawn or emphasized in a philosophical context where internalism was absent or marginal.

5. Conclusion

The justified true belief conception of knowledge is sometimes assumed to have been central to Western philosophy from Plato's *Meno* and *Theaetetus* through to Ayer, Chisholm, Gettier, and beyond. That is a myth (Dutant 2015). Arguably, the twentieth-century recurrence of the tripartite view was a product of characteristically modern anxiety, as paradigms of certainty were overturned—for instance, the belief that physical space is Euclidean. After all, the justified true belief analysis presupposes some sort of fallibilism, for if justification entailed truth, the truth component would be redundant.

Belief-first epistemology is not a feature of the whole Western philosophical tradition, but a much more specific phenomenon. In my case, one predecessor was John Cook Wilson, the dominant Oxford realist before the First World War, who advocated a knowledge-first view of mind. His epistemology was taken on by his pupil Harold Prichard, who in turn taught J.L. Austin and Wilfrid Sellars. Both disjunctivism (see section 3) and my own epistemology show the indirect influence of Cook Wilson (Marion 2000; Williamson 2018a).

These considerations suggest a much wider scope for comparisons and mutual interaction between the Western and Indian epistemological traditions. Of course, my particular concern is knowledge-first epistemology; I hope to learn much more in the future about its similarities and differences with various forms of Indian epistemology. In the longer run, such communication gives hope for a single (though not uniform) ongoing enterprise of global *epistemology* (*tout court*), drawing from all such more local traditions, to which people from all cultures can contribute.[8]

References

Dretske, Fred. 1969. *Seeing and Knowing*. London: Routledge and Kegan Paul.

Dutant, Julien. 2015. The Legend of the Justified True Belief Analysis. *Philosophical Perspectives*, 1: 95–145.

Hawthorne, John, and Jason Stanley. 2008. Knowledge and Action. *Journal of Philosophy*, 105: 571–90.

Lewis, David. 1980. Veridical Hallucination and Prosthetic Vision. *Australasin Journal of Philosophy*, 58: 239–49.

Marion, Mathieu. 2000. Oxford Realism: Knowledge and Perception, parts I and II. *British Journal for the History of Philosophy*, 8: 299–338 and 485–519.

Nagel, Jennifer. 2013. Knowledge as a Mental State. *Oxford Studies in Epistemology*, 4: 275–310.

Soteriou, Matthew. 2016. The Disjunctive Theory of Perception. *Stanford Encyclopedia of Perception*. https://plato.stanford.edu/cgi-bin/encyclopedia/archinfo.cgi?entry=perception-disjunctive

Vaidya, Anand. 2021. Elements of Knowledge-First Epistemology in Gaṅgeśa and Nyāya, this volume.

Williamson, Timothy. 2017. Acting on Knowledge. In J. Adam Carter, Emma C. Gordon, and Benjamin W. Jarvis (Eds.), *Knowledge First: Approaches in Epistemology and Mind* (pp. 163–81). Oxford: Oxford University Press.

Williamson, Timothy. 2018a. Knowledge, Action, and the Factive Turn. In Veli Mitova (Ed.), *The Factive Turn in Epistemology* (pp. 125–41). Cambridge: Cambridge University Press.

Williamson, Timothy. 2018b. *Doing Philosophy: From Common Curiosity to Logical Reasoning*. Oxford: Oxford University Press.

Williamson, Timothy. 2000. *Knowledge and its Limits*. Oxford: Oxford University Press.

[8] I owe many thanks to Anand Vaidya, not least for first alerting me in 2014 to the analogies between my work on knowledge and classical Indian epistemology, and then to him and Julianne Chung for setting up this exchange. As Anand's contribution developed, it increasingly emphasized the scholarly interpretation of Nyāya texts, which I am not competent to comment on in detail.